NNING taste of home WINNING RECIPE
RECIPES VOL. 2

taste of home WINNING taste

NNING taste of home WINNING
RECIPES VOL. 2 RECIPE

aste of home WINNING taste

NNING taste of home WINNING
RECIPES VOL. 2 RECIPE

aste of home WINNING taste
RECIPES VOL. 2

NNING taste of home WINNING
RECIPES VOL. 2 RECIPE

aste of home WINNING taste
RECIPES VOL. 2

NNING taste of home WINNING
RECIPES VOL. 2 RECIPE

aste of home WINNING taste
RECIPES VOL. 2

NNING taste of home WINNING
RECIPES VOL. 2 RECIPE

aste of home WINNING taste
RECIPES VOL. 2

NNING taste of home WINNING
RECIPES VOL. 2 RECIPE

D0516443

taste of home WINNING RECIPES VOL. 2

taste of home

B O O K S

REIMAN MEDIA GROUP, INC. • GREENDALE, WISCONSIN

taste of home   Reader's Digest

A TASTE OF HOME/READER'S DIGEST BOOK

© 2009 Reiman Media Group, Inc.
  5400 S. 60th St., Greendale WI 53129
  All rights reserved.

Taste of Home and Reader's Digest are registered trademarks of The Reader's Digest Association, Inc.

Editor in Chief: **Catherine Cassidy**
Vice President, Executive Editor/Books:
Heidi Reuter Lloyd
Creative Director: **Ardyth Cope**
Chief Marketing Officer: **Lisa Karpinski**
Food Director: **Diane Werner RD**
Senior Editor/Books: **Mark Hagen**
Editor: **Janet Briggs**
Art Director: **Edwin Robles, Jr.**
Content Production Supervisor: **Julie Wagner**
Design Layout Artists: **Catherine Fletcher,**
Emma Acevedo
Proofreaders: **Linne Bruskewitz, Amy Glander**
Recipe Asset System: **Coleen Martin, Sue A. Jurack**
Premedia Supervisor: **Scott Berger**
Recipe Testing & Editing: **Taste of Home Test Kitchen**
Food Photography: **Taste of Home Photo Studio**
Administrative Assistant: **Barb Czysz**

The Reader's Digest Association, Inc.
President and Chief Executive Officer: **Mary G. Berner**
President, U.S. Affinities: **Suzanne M. Grimes**
SVP, Chief Marketing Officer: **Amy J. Radin**
President, Global Consumer Marketing: **Dawn M. Zier**
President/Publisher Trade Publishing: **Harold Clarke**
Asssociate Publisher: **Rosanne McManus**
Vice President, Sales & Marketing: **Stacey Ashton**

"Timeless Recipes from Trusted Home Cooks"
is a registered trademark of Reiman Media Group, Inc.

America's Best Loved Recipe Contest is a trademark of Reiman Media Group, Inc.

For other Taste of Home books and products,
visit **tasteofhome.com.**

For more Reader's Digest products and information,
visit **rd.com** (in the United States)
or see **rd.ca** (in Canada).

International Standard Book Number (10): 0-89821-777-6
International Standard Book Number (13): 978-0-89821-777-3
Library of Congress Control Number: 2009926640

Cover Photography
Photographers: James Wieland, Rob Hagen
Food Stylists: Jennifer Janz, Kaitlyn Besasie
Set Stylists: Melissa Haberman, Grace Natoli Sheldon

Pictured on front cover (clockwise from top left):
Chocolate Velvet Dessert (p. 456), Chicken Tortilla Soup (p. 110), Raspberry Greek Salad (p. 73), Two-Season Squash Medley (p. 297) and Stuffed Iowa Chops (p. 210).

Printed in China
1 3 5 7 9 10 8 6 4 2

CONTENTS

You'll be a Winner
When You Serve These
Top-Rated Recipes!

With this unbeatable collection of 654 recipes from *Taste of Home,* you can cook like a blue-ribbon champion and spoil your family with sensational dishes. In this all new edition of **WINNING RECIPES**, you will find foods ideal for weeknight, weekend and even holiday meals. You'll discover savory appetizers, main dishes, sides, sandwiches and breads, both yeast and quick as well as 168 delectable prize-winning desserts!

Home cooks from coast to coast sent their best recipes to one of many cooking contests conducted by *Taste of Home,* the world's #1 cooking magazine. Our Test Kitchen professionals reviewed those submissions, seeking recipes that were sure to please. They looked for recipes that had tasty flavor combinations, gave new twists to old standbys or had unique and interesting presentations.

Once the recipes were selected for a contest, they were prepared and evaluated by our taste-test panel of food editors and magazine editors. Recipes were judged by taste, appearance, quality and mass appeal. After much review and discussion, the grand-prize winner and the runners-up were selected!

In this remarkable collection, you'll find winners from **200 national contests**, including America's Best Loved Recipes, Express Entrees, Blue-Ribbon Winners, Mmm Chocolate, Pick of the Pork, Slow Cooker Favorites, Fuss-Free Holiday Fare, Chicken Delight, Southwestern Specialties, Holiday Baking Bonanza, Big on Beef and Pie Potpourri.

You'll be able to quickly find the magazine editors' top picks by looking for the First Place Winner ribbon (at right). In addition, quick reference icons are included for lighter dishes, time-saver recipes and items that serve two.

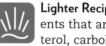

Lighter Recipes start with ingredients that are lower in fat, cholesterol, carbohydrates and sodium, and they take advantage of heart-smart cooking methods.

Time-Saver Recipes require less effort to make, less time to cook or both! Most of these delicious dishes are ready to eat in 30 minutes or less. Other time-saver recipes rely on the convenience and simplicity of a bread machine or slow cooker.

Serves 2 Recipes have been scaled down to make the perfect amount for two. You won't have to deal with leftovers when serving these handy dishes. Many of the desserts and breads make enough to allow for a second delightful serving.

Each recipe includes a beautiful full-color photo. You'll find the directions are easy to follow, and all the ingredients are readily available in most supermarkets.

Best of all, with this book you can enjoy the home-style goodness for which *Taste of Home* is trusted and loved. With **WINNING RECIPES**, it has never been easier to become a champion cook in your own home.

Chedder-Veggie Appetizer Torte, PAGE 33

"A line forms quickly behind this quiche-like torte at family gatherings. The wedges are easy to eat as finger food—plus, it's delicious hot or cold."

Barbara Estabrook
Rhinelander, Wisconsin

APPETIZERS & BEVERAGES

DO YOU HAVE A WINNING RECIPE?
Enter your most prized recipes in the *Taste of Home* recipe contests, and you may win some money and the chance to have your recipe published. Log onto **tasteofhome.com/RecipeContests** for a list of our current contests and submission deadlines. Good luck...we'll be looking for your recipe.

Visit us @
tasteofhome
.com

appetizers & beverages

Orange and Jicama Salsa

🕐 Orange and Jicama Salsa

PREP/TOTAL TIME: 25 MIN.

Tiny cubes of crunchy jicama and ripe juicy oranges make for a change-of-pace salsa. Adjust the amount of jalapeno pepper to best suit your taste.

Cheryl Perry ✳ Hertford, North Carolina

- 6 medium oranges, peeled, sectioned and chopped
- 1-1/2 cups cubed peeled jicama
- 1/4 cup chopped red onion
- 1/4 cup chopped sweet red pepper
- 2 green onions, thinly sliced
- 1/4 cup minced fresh cilantro
- 1 tablespoon lime juice
- 2 teaspoons chopped seeded jalapeno pepper
- 1/2 teaspoon sugar
- 1/8 teaspoon salt
- Baked tortilla chips *or* scoops

In a large bowl, combine oranges, vegetables, cilantro, lime juice, jalapeno, sugar and salt. Serve with chips. Refrigerate leftovers. **YIELD: 4 CUPS.**

EDITOR'S NOTE: When cutting hot peppers, disposable gloves are recommended. Avoid touching your face.

NUTRITION FACTS: 1/4 cup (calculated without chips) equals 22 calories, trace fat (trace saturated fat), 0 cholesterol, 20 mg sodium, 5 g carbohydrate, 1 g fiber, trace protein. DIABETIC EXCHANGE: Free food.

Mini Bagelizzas

🕐 Mini Bagelizzas

PREP/TOTAL TIME: 25 MIN.

Garlic powder gives these speedy mini pizzas extra pizzazz. Not only are they a snap to put together, but best of all, the ingredient list is easy on your pocketbook.

Stephanie Klos-Kohr ✳ Moline, Illinois

- 8 miniature bagels, split
- 1 cup spaghetti sauce with miniature meatballs
- 32 slices pepperoni
- 3/4 teaspoon garlic powder
- 2 cups (8 ounces) shredded part-skim mozzarella cheese

Spread the cut sides of bagels with spaghetti sauce. Top each with two slices of pepperoni; sprinkle with garlic powder and cheese.

Place on ungreased baking sheets. Bake at 350° for 15-20 minutes or until cheese is melted and bubbly. **YIELD: 8 SERVINGS.**

Sweet 'n' Crunchy Mix

Sweet 'n' Crunchy Mix

PREP/TOTAL TIME: **30 MIN.**

My kids like snacks with a lot of crunch. So I combined a few of their favorite ingredients for this recipe, and it was an instant success. In fact, I've become famous in our neighborhood for this simply delicious mix.

Amy Briggs ✳ Zimmerman, Minnesota

2-1/2 cups Rice Chex
2-1/2 cups Honey-Nut Cheerios
  1 package (10 ounces) honey-flavored bear-shaped graham crackers
  2 cups miniature pretzels
1/2 cup butter, melted
1/3 cup packed brown sugar
4-1/2 teaspoons ground cinnamon

In a large bowl, combine the cereals, graham crackers and pretzels. In a small bowl, combine the butter, brown sugar and cinnamon. Pour over cereal mixture; toss to coat. Spread into two ungreased 15-in. x 10-in. x 1-in. baking pans.

Bake at 275° for 10 minutes. Stir; bake 10 minutes longer. Store in an airtight container.

YIELD: **ABOUT 1-1/2 QUARTS.**

Goat Cheese 'n' Veggie Quesadillas

PREP: **55 MIN.** BAKE: **5 MIN.**

The roasted veggies and goat cheese make this an elegant party food. We love to top them with our favorite salsa for an extra kick!

Sara Longworth ✳ Bristol, Connecticut

  1 small eggplant, peeled, quartered and cut into 1/2-inch slices
  1 medium zucchini, cut into 1/4-inch slices
  1 medium sweet red pepper, chopped
  1 medium onion, chopped
1/4 cup chopped ripe olives
  2 garlic cloves, minced
  2 tablespoons olive oil
  1 tablespoon lemon juice
1/2 teaspoon chili powder
1/2 teaspoon cayenne pepper
  1 tablespoon minced fresh cilantro
1/2 cup semisoft goat cheese
  8 whole wheat tortillas (8 inches)

Place the vegetables, olives and garlic in an ungreased 15-in. x 10-in. x 1-in. baking pan. Combine the oil, lemon juice, chili powder and cayenne; drizzle over vegetables and toss to coat. Bake, uncovered, at 400° for 35-40 minutes or until tender, stirring once. Stir in cilantro.

Spread 1 tablespoon goat cheese over one side of each tortilla. Place two tortillas, plain side down, on an ungreased baking sheet; spread each with 2/3 cup vegetable mixture. Top each with another tortilla. Repeat. Bake at 400° for 5-10 minutes or until golden brown. Cut each quesadilla into six wedges. Serve warm.

YIELD: **2 DOZEN APPETIZERS.**

NUTRITION FACTS: 1 wedge equals 171 calories, 8 g fat (2 g saturated fat), 7 mg cholesterol, 191 mg sodium, 20 g carbohydrate, 3 g fiber, 6 g protein.

Savory Ham Cheesecake

PREP: **35 MIN.** BAKE: **1 HOUR + CHILLING**

My mom was the best cook—everything she made was special. She served this fancy cheesecake on Sunday following a Saturday ham dinner. Now my family loves it.

Shannon Soper ✳ West Bend, Wisconsin

- 3 cups oyster crackers, crushed
- 1 cup grated Parmesan cheese
- 1/3 cup butter, melted

FILLING:

- 4 packages (8 ounces *each*) cream cheese, softened
- 4 eggs, lightly beaten
- 2 cups finely chopped fully cooked ham
- 2 cups (8 ounces) shredded Swiss cheese
- 1/3 cup snipped chives
- 1/4 cup minced fresh basil
- 1/4 teaspoon salt
- 1/4 teaspoon white pepper

Assorted crackers

In a large bowl, combine the cracker crumbs, Parmesan cheese and butter. Set aside 1/4 cup for topping. Press remaining crumb mixture onto the bottom and 2 in. up the sides of a greased 9-in. springform pan. Cover and chill for at least 30 minutes.

In a large bowl, beat cream cheese until smooth. Add eggs; beat on low speed just until combined (mixture will be thick). Add the ham, Swiss cheese, chives, basil, salt and pepper; beat just until combined. Pour into crust. Sprinkle with reserved crumb mixture.

Place pan on a baking sheet. Bake at 325° for 60-70 minutes or until filling is almost set. Turn oven off. Leave cheesecake in oven with door ajar for 30 minutes.

Cool on a wire rack for 10 minutes. Carefully run a knife around edge of the pan to loosen; cool for 1 hour. Refrigerate overnight. Remove sides of the pan. Serve chilled or at room temperature with crackers. **YIELD: 24-30 SERVINGS.**

Goat Cheese 'n' Veggie Quesadillas

Savory Ham Cheesecake

So-Healthy Smoothies

PREP/TOTAL TIME: **15 MIN.**

This tastes like a milk shake, but it doesn't have all the guilt or fat. My husband and I look forward to it every day for breakfast. It's so good for you, and it will keep you energized for hours.

Jessica Gerschitz * Jericho, New York

  1 cup fat-free milk
1/4 cup orange juice
  2 tablespoons vanilla yogurt
  1 tablespoon honey
  1 small banana, sliced and frozen
2/3 cup frozen blueberries
1/2 cup chopped peeled mango, frozen
1/4 cup frozen unsweetened peach slices

In a blender, combine all the ingredients; cover and process until smooth. Pour into chilled glasses; serve immediately. **YIELD: 4 SERVINGS.**

NUTRITION FACTS: 1 serving (3/4 cup) equals 107 calories, 1 g fat (trace saturated fat), 2 mg cholesterol, 38 mg sodium, 24 g carbohydrate, 2 g fiber, 3 g protein. DIABETIC EXCHANGES: 1 fruit, 1/2 starch.

So-Healthy Smoothies

Warm Bacon Cheese Spread

PREP: **15 MIN.** BAKE: **1 HOUR**

My friends threaten not to come by unless this dip is on the menu! The rich spread bakes right in the bread bowl and goes well with almost any dipper.

Nicole Marcotte * Smithers, British Columbia

    1 round loaf (1 pound) sourdough bread
    1 package (8 ounces) cream cheese, softened
1-1/2 cups (12 ounces) sour cream
    2 cups (8 ounces) shredded cheddar cheese
1-1/2 teaspoons Worcestershire sauce
  3/4 pound sliced bacon, cooked and crumbled
  1/2 cup chopped green onions
Assorted crackers

Cut the top fourth off the loaf of bread; carefully hollow out the bottom, leaving a 1-in. shell. Cut the removed bread and top of loaf into cubes; set aside. In a large bowl, beat the cream cheese until fluffy. Add the sour cream, cheddar cheese and Worcestershire sauce until blended; stir in bacon and onions.

Warm Bacon Cheese Spread

Roasted Carrot Dip

Spoon into bread shell. Wrap in a piece of heavy-duty foil (about 24 in. x 17 in.). Bake at 325° for 1 hour or until heated through. Serve with crackers and reserved bread cubes. **YIELD: 4 CUPS.**

Roasted Carrot Dip

PREP: 15 MIN. BAKE: 45 MIN.

Once you start eating this delicious dip, it's difficult to stop. The smooth texture and sweet carrot flavor go great with the crisp pita wedges.

Alana Rowley ✳ Calgary, Alberta

- 10 medium carrots
- 5 garlic cloves, peeled
- 2 tablespoons olive oil
- 6 to 8 tablespoons water
- 2 teaspoons white wine vinegar
- 1/2 cup mayonnaise
- 1/4 cup sour cream
- 1/8 teaspoon sugar
- 1/8 teaspoon salt
- 1/8 teaspoon pepper
- 4 to 6 pita breads (6 inches)
- 2 to 3 tablespoons butter, melted

Cut carrots in half widthwise; cut lengthwise into 1/2-in.-thick slices. In a bowl, combine the carrots, garlic and oil; toss to coat. Transfer to a greased 15-in. x 10-in. x 1-in. baking pan. Bake, uncovered, at 425° for 20 minutes. Stir; bake 15-20 minutes longer or until carrots are tender. Cool slightly.

In a blender, combine 6 tablespoons water, vinegar, mayonnaise, sour cream, sugar, salt, pepper and carrot mixture; cover and process until smooth. Add additional water if needed to achieve desired consistency. Transfer to a bowl; refrigerate until serving.

Brush both sides of pita breads with butter. Cut in half; cut each half into six wedges. Place on ungreased baking sheets. Bake at 350° for 4 minutes on each side or until lightly browned. Serve with carrot dip. **YIELD: 8-10 SERVINGS.**

Chocolate Fruit Dip

Chocolate Fruit Dip

PREP/TOTAL TIME: **10 MIN.**

I've been told I'm not allowed to come to neighborhood parties unless I bring this dip! It's always a big hit. I usually serve it with strawberries and pineapple, but it's good with other fruit, such as apples and melon.

Sarah Maury Swan ✳ Granite, Maryland

- 1 package (8 ounces) cream cheese, softened
- 1/3 cup sugar
- 1/3 cup baking cocoa
- 1 teaspoon vanilla extract
- 2 cups whipped topping

Assorted fruit for dipping

In a large bowl, beat cream cheese and sugar until smooth. Beat in cocoa and vanilla. Beat in whipped topping until smooth. Serve with fruit.
YIELD: 2 CUPS.

Meatballs in Plum Sauce

PREP: **50 MIN. + STANDING BAKE: 30 MIN.**

A tasty sauce made of plum jam and chili sauce coats these moist meatballs beautifully. Make sure these delightful appetizers are on your holiday menus.

Mary Poninski ✳ Whittington, Illinois

- 1/2 cup milk
- 1 cup soft bread crumbs
- 1 egg, lightly beaten
- 1 tablespoon Worcestershire sauce
- 1 medium onion, finely chopped
- 1/4 teaspoon salt
- 1/4 teaspoon pepper
- 1/8 teaspoon ground cloves
- 1/2 pound lean ground beef
- 1/2 pound ground pork
- 1/2 pound ground veal
- 2 tablespoons canola oil
- 1/2 teaspoon beef bouillon granules
- 1/2 cup boiling water
- 3 tablespoons all-purpose flour
- 1 cup plum jam
- 1/2 cup chili sauce

In a large bowl, pour the milk over the bread crumbs; let stand for 10 minutes. Add the egg, Worcestershire sauce, onion, salt, pepper and cloves. Crumble the beef, pork and veal over mixture and mix well (mixture will be soft). Shape into 1-in. balls.

In a large skillet, brown meatballs in oil in batches. Drain on paper towels. Place in a greased 13-in. x 9-in. baking dish.

In a small bowl, dissolve bouillon in water. Stir flour into pan drippings until blended; add the bouillon mixture, jam and chili sauce. Bring to a boil; cook and stir for 1-2 minutes or until thickened. Pour over meatballs.

Cover and bake at 350° for 30-45 minutes or until meat is no longer pink and sauce is bubbly.
YIELD: 10-12 SERVINGS.

Party Cheese Balls

PREP: 20 MIN. + CHILLING

These tangy cheese balls are guaranteed to spread cheer at your next gathering. The ingredients create a colorful presentation and a savory combination of flavors.

Shirley Hoerman ✳ Nekoosa, Wisconsin

- 1 package (8 ounces) cream cheese, softened
- 2 cups (8 ounces) shredded cheddar cheese
- 1 jar (5 ounces) sharp American cheese spread
- 1 jar (5 ounces) pimiento cheese spread
- 3 tablespoons finely chopped onion
- 1 tablespoon lemon juice
- 1 teaspoon Worcestershire sauce

Dash garlic salt

- 1/2 cup chopped pecans, toasted
- 1/2 cup minced fresh parsley

Assorted crackers

Meatballs in Plum Sauce

In a large bowl, beat the cream cheese, cheddar cheese, cheese spreads, onion, lemon juice, Worcestershire sauce and garlic salt until blended. Cover and refrigerate for 15 minutes or until easy to handle.

Shape into two balls; roll one ball in pecans and one in the parsley. Cover and refrigerate. Remove from the refrigerator 15 minutes before serving with the crackers. **YIELD: 2 CHEESE BALLS (1-3/4 CUPS EACH).**

Party Cheese Balls

Whole Wheat Pepperoni Pizzas

🌾 Whole Wheat Pepperoni Pizzas

PREP: **15 MIN.** + **STANDING** BAKE: **15 MIN.**

People say that the crispy whole wheat crust of this pizza recipe is the best they've tasted. Plus, it's so easy to prepare in the bread machine...and it makes enough for two pizzas.

Beth Zaring ✳ Wellston, Ohio

1-2/3   cups water
    2   tablespoons olive oil
    2   tablespoons sugar
    2   tablespoons nonfat dry milk powder
    1   teaspoon salt
    1   teaspoon lemon juice
2-1/2   cups bread flour
    2   cups whole wheat flour
    2   teaspoons active dry yeast

TOPPINGS:
    4   teaspoons olive oil
    1   can (15 ounces) pizza sauce
    2   teaspoons dried oregano
    4   cups (16 ounces) shredded part-skim mozzarella cheese
    2   ounces turkey pepperoni, diced
 1/4   cup grated Parmesan cheese
 2/3   cup chopped onion
 2/3   cup chopped green pepper

In bread machine pan, place the first nine ingredients in order suggested by manufacturer. Select dough setting (check dough after 5 minutes of mixing; add 1 to 2 tablespoons of water or flour if needed). When cycle is completed, turn dough onto a lightly floured surface. Divide dough in half. Cover and let stand for 10 minutes.

Roll into two 14-in. circles. Transfer to two 14-in. pizza pans coated with cooking spray. Spread oil over each crust. Top with the pizza sauce, oregano, mozzarella cheese, pepperoni, Parmesan cheese, onion and green pepper. Bake at 450° for 15-20 minutes or until crust is golden brown. YIELD: **2 PIZZAS (6 SLICES EACH).**

NUTRITION FACTS: 1 slice equals 343 calories, 11 g fat (5 g saturated fat), 29 mg cholesterol, 611 mg sodium, 43 g carbohydrate, 4 g fiber, 19 g protein. DIABETIC EXCHANGES: 2-1/2 starch, 2 lean meat, 1 vegetable, 1/2 fat.

Buffalo Wing Poppers

PREP: **20 MIN.** BAKE: **20 MIN.**

The taste of buffalo wings and pepper poppers pairs up in this appealing appetizer. It will disappear fast...so make a double batch, and have copies of the recipe handy to pass out.

Barbara Nowakowski ✳ Mesa, Arizona

- 20 jalapeno peppers
- 1 package (8 ounces) cream cheese, softened
- 1-1/2 cups (6 ounces) shredded part-skim mozzarella cheese
- 1 cup diced cooked chicken
- 1/2 cup blue cheese salad dressing
- 1/2 cup buffalo wing sauce

Cut peppers in half lengthwise, leaving stems intact; discard seeds. In a small bowl, combine the remaining ingredients. Pipe or stuff into pepper halves.

Place in a greased 15-in. x 10-in. x 1-in. baking pan. Bake, uncovered, at 325° for 20 minutes for spicy flavor, 30 minutes for medium and 40 minutes for mild. YIELD: **40 APPETIZERS.**

EDITOR'S NOTE: When cutting hot peppers, disposable gloves are recommended. Avoid touching your face.

1st place

Buffalo Wing Poppers

Banana Shakes

PREP/TOTAL TIME: **10 MIN.**

I love bananas, and these shakes are the best. Though we're stationed overseas, I've fed my two young kids these made-in-moments drinks since they were babies. Pop them into the freezer for a few minutes if you like them thicker.

Martha Miller ✳ Camp Zama, Japan

- 1 cup half-and-half cream
- 4 cups vanilla ice cream, softened
- 1 medium banana, sliced
- 1/4 teaspoon banana extract

In a blender, combine all ingredients; cover and process until smooth. Pour into chilled glasses; serve immediately. YIELD: **4 SERVINGS.**

Banana Shakes

Taco Crackers

Taco Crackers

PREP/TOTAL TIME: **30 MIN.**

One handful of these crispy oyster crackers is never enough. Taco seasoning and chili powder give the munchies a fun Southwestern flavor. Partygoers always come back for more.

Diane Earnest ✳ Newton, Illinois

- 3 packages (10 ounces *each*) oyster crackers
- 3/4 cup canola oil
- 1 envelope taco seasoning
- 1/2 teaspoon garlic powder
- 1/2 teaspoon dried oregano
- 1/2 teaspoon chili powder

Place the crackers in a large roasting pan; drizzle with oil. Combine the seasonings; sprinkle over crackers and toss to coat.

Bake at 350° for 15-20 minutes or until golden brown, stirring once. YIELD: **16 CUPS.**

Honey-Glazed Wings

PREP: **20 MIN. + MARINATING** BAKE: **50 MIN.**

My family favors chicken wings that are mildly flavored with honey, ginger, soy sauce and chili sauce. Tasty and tender, they are sure to be a hit at your next get-together. They're a crowd-pleaser!

Marlene Wahl ✳ Baldwin, Wisconsin

- 15 whole chicken wings (about 3 pounds)
- 1/2 cup honey
- 1/3 cup soy sauce
- 2 tablespoons canola oil
- 2 tablespoons chili sauce
- 2 teaspoons salt
- 1 teaspoon garlic powder
- 1 teaspoon Worcestershire sauce
- 1/2 teaspoon ground ginger

Cut chicken wings into three sections; discard wing tip section. Set wings aside. In a small saucepan, combine the honey, soy sauce, oil, chili sauce, salt, garlic powder, Worcestershire sauce and ginger. Cook and stir until blended and heated through. Cool to room temperature.

Place the chicken wings in a large resealable plastic bag; add honey mixture. Seal bag and turn to coat. Refrigerate for at least 8 hours or overnight.

Honey-Glazed Wings

Hearty Rye Melts

Drain and discard marinade. Place wings in a well-greased 15-in. x 10-in. x 1-in. baking pan. Bake, uncovered, at 375° for 30 minutes. Drain; turn wings. Bake 20-25 minutes longer or until chicken juices run clear and glaze is set. **YIELD: 2-1/2 DOZEN.**

EDITOR'S NOTE: Uncooked chicken wing sections (wingettes) may be substituted for whole chicken wings.

🕐 Hearty Rye Melts

PREP/TOTAL TIME: **30 MIN.**

When we moved from the Midwest to Kentucky, we were invited to a neighborhood gathering, where this appetizer was served. "Hanky panky"—as it's often called around here—is traditionally served at Derby Day parties, but at our home it's become a year-round favorite.

Melanie Schlaf ✴ Edgewood, Kentucky

1/2 **pound lean ground beef**
1/2 **pound bulk pork sausage**
1-1/2 **teaspoons chili powder**
8 **ounces process cheese (Velveeta), shredded**
24 **slices snack rye bread**
Fresh parsley sprigs, stems removed

In a large skillet, cook the beef and sausage over medium heat until no longer pink; drain. Add chili powder and cheese; cook and stir until cheese is melted. Spread a heaping tablespoonful onto each slice of bread. Place on a baking sheet.

Bake at 350° for 12-15 minutes or until edges of bread begin to crisp. Garnish with parsley. Serve warm. **YIELD: 2 DOZEN.**

Apple 'n' Prosciutto Sandwiches

Beef 'n' Cheese Dip

PREP: **10 MIN.** BAKE: **1 HOUR**

I combined two favorite recipes and trimmed them down to create this yummy fondue-type dip. It's great for receptions, parties and get-togethers. It was a hit with the guys at our house last Christmas!

Heather Melnic ✳ Macedon, New York

- 1 package (8 ounces) reduced-fat cream cheese
- 1-1/2 cups (6 ounces) shredded reduced-fat cheddar cheese
- 1/2 cup fat-free sour cream
- 2 packages (2-1/2 ounces *each*) thinly sliced dried beef
- 1/2 cup chopped green onions
- 1/2 cup mild pepper rings, drained and chopped
- 2 teaspoons Worcestershire sauce
- 1 loaf (1 pound) unsliced round rye bread

Assorted fresh vegetables

In a large bowl, combine the cream cheese, cheddar cheese and sour cream. Stir in the beef, onions, peppers and Worcestershire sauce.

Cut the top fourth off the loaf of bread; carefully hollow out bottom, leaving a 1-in. shell. Cube the removed bread and top of loaf; set aside.

Fill bread shell with beef mixture. Wrap in foil; place on baking sheet. Bake at 350° for 60-70 minutes or until heated through. Serve with vegetables and reserved bread cubes. **YIELD: 3 CUPS.**

EDITOR'S NOTE: Mild pepper rings come in jars and can be found in the pickle and olive aisle of most grocery stores.

NUTRITION FACTS: 3 tablespoons dip (calculated without vegetables) equals 159 calories, 6 g fat (4 g saturated fat), 22 mg cholesterol, 386 mg sodium, 16 g carbohydrate, 2 g fiber, 9 g protein. DIABETIC EXCHANGES: 1 starch, 1 lean meat, 1/2 fat.

Apple 'n' Prosciutto Sandwiches

PREP/TOTAL TIME: **20 MIN.**

Prepared on an indoor grill, these Italian-style sandwiches are spread with homemade rosemary pesto. They're wonderful on a cool day with a bowl of butternut squash soup.

Elizabeth Bennett ✳ Mill Creek, Washington

- 1/4 cup olive oil
- 1/2 cup chopped walnuts
- 2 tablespoons grated Parmesan cheese
- 2 tablespoons minced fresh rosemary
- 1 loaf (12 ounces) focaccia bread
- 8 thin slices prosciutto
- 1 medium apple, sliced
- 6 ounces Brie cheese, rind removed and sliced

In a blender, combine oil, walnuts, Parmesan cheese and rosemary; cover and process until blended and nuts are finely chopped. With a bread knife, split focaccia into two horizontal layers. Spread rosemary mixture over cut sides of bread. On the bottom of the bread, layer prosciutto, apple and Brie; replace bread top. Cut into quarters.

Cook on an indoor grill for 2-3 minutes or until bread is browned and cheese is melted. To serve, cut each wedge in half. **YIELD: 8 SERVINGS.**

Chicken Lettuce Wraps

PREP/TOTAL TIME: 25 MIN.

Filled with chicken, mushrooms, water chestnuts and carrots, these wraps are both healthy and yummy. The gingerroot, rice wine vinegar and teriyaki sauce give them delicious Asian flair.

Kendra Doss ✳ Smithville, Missouri

Beef 'n' Cheese Dip

1-1/2 **pounds boneless skinless chicken breasts, cubed**

1 **tablespoon plus 1-1/2 teaspoons peanut oil,** *divided*

3/4 **cup chopped fresh mushrooms**

1 **can (8 ounces) water chestnuts, drained and diced**

1 **tablespoon minced fresh gingerroot**

2 **tablespoons rice vinegar**

2 **tablespoons reduced-sodium teriyaki sauce**

1 **tablespoon reduced-sodium soy sauce**

1/2 **teaspoon garlic powder**

1/4 **teaspoon crushed red pepper flakes**

1-1/2 **cups shredded carrots**

1/2 **cup julienned green onions**

12 **Bibb** *or* **Boston lettuce leaves**

1/3 **cup sliced almonds, toasted**

In a large nonstick skillet coated with cooking spray, cook chicken in 1 tablespoon oil for 3 minutes; drain. Add the mushrooms, water chestnuts and ginger; cook 4-6 minutes longer or until the chicken juices run clear. Drain and set aside.

In a small bowl, whisk the vinegar, teriyaki sauce, soy sauce, garlic powder, red pepper flakes and remaining oil. Stir in the carrots, onions and chicken mixture. Spoon onto lettuce leaves; sprinkle with almonds. If desired, fold sides of lettuce over filling and roll up. **YIELD: 6 SERVINGS.**

NUTRITION FACTS: 2 wraps equals 230 calories, 9 g fat (2 g saturated fat), 63 mg cholesterol, 278 mg sodium, 12 g carbohydrate, 3 g fiber, 26 g protein. DIABETIC EXCHANGES: 3 very lean meat, 2 vegetable, 1 fat.

Chicken Lettuce Wraps

⬤ Olive Bruschetta

PREP/TOTAL TIME: **30 MIN.**

This convenient and colorful party classic can be made several days in advance. In fact, it actually tastes better if prepared ahead so all the fresh flavors can blend together. It's best served at room temperature with a crusty loaf of toasted French bread or your favorite crackers.

Linda Austin ✳ Lake Hopatcong, New Jersey

- 2 cups grape tomatoes, quartered
- 2 celery ribs, chopped
- 1/2 cup shredded carrot
- 1/4 cup chopped red onion
- 1/4 cup sliced ripe olives
- 1/4 cup sliced pimiento-stuffed olives
- 1/4 cup minced fresh flat-leaf parsley
- 1 teaspoon minced garlic
- 3 tablespoons olive oil
- 2 tablespoons balsamic vinegar
- 1/4 teaspoon salt
- 1/8 teaspoon pepper
- 1 loaf (1 pound) French bread baguette, sliced and toasted

In a large bowl, combine the vegetables, olives, parsley and garlic. In a small bowl, combine the oil, vinegar, salt and pepper; pour over vegetables and toss to coat. Serve on toasted baguette slices. **YIELD: 2-1/2 DOZEN.**

Olive Bruschetta

Prosciutto Chicken Kabobs

PREP: **30 MIN.** + MARINATING GRILL: **10 MIN.**

Everyone will think you spent hours preparing these simple, clever grilled wraps, which are served with a guacamole-like dip. Basil gives the chicken a lovely fresh herb flavor.

Elaine Sweet ✳ Dallas, Texas

- 3/4 cup five-cheese Italian salad dressing
- 1/4 cup lime juice
- 2 teaspoons white Worcestershire sauce for chicken
- 1/2 pound boneless skinless chicken breasts, cut into 3-inch x 1/2-inch strips
- 12 thin slices prosciutto
- 24 fresh basil leaves

Prosciutto Chicken Kabobs

Crimson Cranberry Punch

AVOCADO DIP:

- 2 medium ripe avocados, peeled
- 1/4 cup minced fresh cilantro
- 2 green onions, chopped
- 2 tablespoons lime juice
- 2 tablespoons mayonnaise
- 1-1/2 teaspoons prepared horseradish
- 1 garlic clove, minced
- 1/4 teaspoon salt

In a large resealable plastic bag, combine the salad dressing, lime juice and Worcestershire sauce; add chicken. Seal bag and turn to coat; refrigerate for 1 hour.

Drain and discard marinade. Fold prosciutto slices in half; top each with two basil leaves and a chicken strip. Roll up jelly-roll style, starting with a short side. Thread onto metal or soaked wooden skewers.

Grill, covered, over medium heat for 5 minutes on each side or until chicken is no longer pink.

Meanwhile, in a small bowl, mash the avocados. Stir in the cilantro, onions, lime juice, mayonnaise, horseradish, garlic and salt. Serve with kabobs. **YIELD: 12 APPETIZERS.**

Crimson Cranberry Punch

PREP: 20 MIN. + FREEZING

You can stir up this punch quickly because it calls for only a few ingredients. The pretty ice ring keeps it nicely chilled.

Judie White ✳ Florien, Louisiana

- 1/2 cup frozen cranberries
- 3-1/2 cups cold water
- 1 bottle (48 ounces) white grape juice, chilled
- 2 cans (12 ounces *each*) frozen cranberry juice concentrate, thawed
- 4 cans (12 ounces *each*) diet lemon-lime soda, chilled
- 3 orange slices
- 3 lemon slices

Place the cranberries in a 4-1/2-cup ring mold coated with cooking spray. Slowly pour a small amount of cold water into the mold to barely cover berries; freeze until solid. Add remaining water; freeze until solid.

Just before serving, combine the grape juice and cranberry juice concentrate in a large punch bowl; stir in soda. Unmold ice ring; place fruit side up in punch bowl. Add orange and lemon slices. **YIELD: 5 QUARTS.**

NUTRITION FACTS: 1 cup equals 113 calories, trace fat (trace saturated fat), 0 cholesterol, 13 mg sodium, 28 g carbohydrate, trace fiber, trace protein. **DIABETIC EXCHANGE:** 1 starch, 1 fruit.

Chicken Enchilada Dip

Chicken Enchilada Dip

PREP/TOTAL TIME: **20 MIN.**

A friend brought this appetizer to our house for a dinner party. Everyone loved the zesty chicken and cheese dip so much that no one was hungry for supper. My friend graciously shared the recipe, and I've served it many times, always with rave reviews.

Leah Davis ✳ Morrow, Ohio

- 2 cups shredded cooked chicken
- 1 can (10-3/4 ounces) condensed cream of chicken soup, undiluted
- 1 cup (4 ounces) shredded cheddar cheese
- 1 can (5 ounces) evaporated milk
- 1/2 cup chopped celery
- 1/3 cup finely chopped onion
- 1 can (4 ounces) chopped green chilies
- 1 envelope taco seasoning
Tortilla chips

In a 2-qt. microwave-safe dish, combine the first eight ingredients. Microwave, uncovered, on high for 4-5 minutes; stir the dip. Microwave, uncovered, 3-4 minutes longer or until heated through. Serve with tortilla chips. **YIELD: 3 CUPS.**

EDITOR'S NOTE: This recipe was tested in a 1,100-watt microwave.

Baked Egg Rolls

PREP/TOTAL TIME: **30 MIN.**

Chinese take-out can be high in sodium, fat and calories, so these crispy appetizers are a nice alternative. Whenever my husband craves a take-out egg roll, I make these instead.

Barbra Annino ✳ Galena, Illinois

- 1-1/3 cups chopped fresh broccoli stir-fry vegetable blend
- 1 cup shredded cooked chicken breast
- 4-1/2 teaspoons reduced-sodium soy sauce
- 2 teaspoons sesame oil
- 2 garlic cloves, minced
- 1/2 teaspoon ground ginger
- 8 egg roll wrappers

In a small bowl, combine the vegetable blend, chicken, soy sauce, sesame oil, garlic and ginger. Place 1/4 cup chicken mixture in the center of one egg roll wrapper. (Keep remaining wrappers covered with a damp paper towel until ready to use.) Fold bottom corner over filling; fold sides toward center. Moisten remaining corner with water; roll up tightly to seal. Repeat with remaining wrappers and filling.

Place seam side down on a baking sheet coated with cooking spray. Spray tops of egg rolls with cooking spray. Bake at 425° for 10-15 minutes or until lightly browned. Serve warm. Refrigerate leftovers. **YIELD: 8 EGG ROLLS.**

NUTRITION FACTS: 1 egg roll equals 140 calories, 2 g fat (trace saturated fat), 16 mg cholesterol, 315 mg sodium, 21 g carbohydrate, 1 g fiber, 9 g protein. DIABETIC EXCHANGES: 1 starch, 1 lean meat, 1 vegetable.

Flavorful Tomato Juice

PREP: **20 MIN.** COOK: **45 MIN. + CHILLING**

Jalapenos, spicy pepper sauce and horseradish are some of my favorite cooking ingredients. I knew they were the perfect way to spice up this thick, homemade tomato juice.

Jeannie Linsavage
Albuquerque, New Mexico

- 8 medium tomatoes, chopped
- 1-1/2 cups water
- 1 small onion, chopped
- 3 garlic cloves, minced
- 1 jalapeno pepper, seeded and chopped
- 3 tablespoons sugar
- 3 tablespoons lime juice
- 2 teaspoons celery seed
- 1 teaspoon salt
- 1 teaspoon ground mustard
- 1 teaspoon prepared horseradish
- 1/8 teaspoon dried basil
- 1/8 teaspoon dried parsley flakes

Dash hot pepper sauce

In a large saucepan, combine all ingredients. Bring to a boil. Reduce heat; simmer, uncovered, for 30 minutes or until tomatoes are tender. Cool to room temperature.

Transfer mixture to a blender; cover and process until blended. Strain and discard seeds. Return tomato juice to saucepan. Bring to a boil. Reduce heat; simmer, uncovered, for 12-18 minutes or until juice measures 3 cups. Cool. Transfer to a pitcher; cover and refrigerate until chilled. **YIELD: 4 SERVINGS.**

EDITOR'S NOTE: When cutting hot peppers, disposable gloves are recommended. Avoid touching your face.

NUTRITION FACTS: 3/4 cup equals 121 calories, 2 g fat (trace saturated fat), 0 cholesterol, 624 mg sodium, 27 g carbohydrate, 4 g fiber, 3 g protein. DIABETIC EXCHANGES: 2 vegetable, 1 starch.

Baked Egg Rolls

Flavorful Tomato Juice

Chunky Blue Cheese Dip

Chunky Blue Cheese Dip

PREP/TOTAL TIME: **10 MIN.**

Every time I make this quick dip, someone asks for the recipe. It requires only a few items, so it's a snap to put together. I often prepare the spread with Gorgonzola cheese.

Sandy Schneider ✳ Naperville, Illinois

1 package (8 ounces) cream cheese, softened
1/3 cup sour cream
1/2 teaspoon white pepper
1/4 to 1/2 teaspoon salt
1 cup (4 ounces) crumbled blue cheese
1/3 cup minced chives
Apple and pear slices *and/or* toasted pecan halves

In a small bowl, beat the cream cheese, sour cream, pepper and salt until blended. Fold in the blue cheese and chives. Serve with apple and pear slices and/or pecans. YIELD: **1-3/4 CUPS.**

1st place

Berry Fruit Punch

Berry Fruity Punch

PREP/TOTAL TIME: **15 MIN.**

I created this fun punch for a summer boat trip last year...and it was a big hit. Melons and pineapple are a lovely complement to raspberries and strawberries in this refreshing thirst quencher.

Phyllis Shaughnessy ✳ Livonia, New York

2 cups unsweetened pineapple juice
2 cups fresh *or* frozen unsweetened raspberries
2 cups fresh strawberries
2 cups cubed honeydew
1 cup cubed seedless watermelon
3/4 cup sugar
1/2 teaspoon ground ginger
4 cups diet ginger ale, chilled
1 cup lime juice, chilled
1/2 cup lemon juice, chilled
Crushed ice

In a blender, process the pineapple juice, berries and melons in batches.

Strain and transfer fruit mixture to a punch bowl or large pitcher. Stir in sugar and ginger. Add the ginger ale, lime and lemon juices. Pour into chilled glasses over crushed ice; serve immediately. **YIELD: 11 CUPS.**

NUTRITION FACTS: 1 cup equals 121 calories, trace fat (trace saturated fat), 0 cholesterol, 27 mg sodium, 31 g carbohydrate, 3 g fiber, 1 g protein. DIABETIC EXCHANGE: 2 fruit.

Walnut Balls

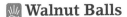 Walnut Balls

PREP: **30 MIN.** BAKE: **25 MIN.**

Most of my family members don't eat meat, so I've made these appetizers for special occasions ever since a friend shared them with me. The moist bites and tangy sauce are always well received.

Bonnie Young ✳ Desert Hot Springs, California

- 2 eggs, lightly beaten
- 3 egg whites, lightly beaten
- 1 small onion, finely chopped
- 3 tablespoons minced fresh parsley
- 1-1/2 teaspoons poultry seasoning
- 2 garlic cloves, minced
- 1/2 teaspoon salt
- 1-1/4 cups finely crushed reduced-sodium saltine crackers
- 3/4 cup ground walnuts
- 3/4 cup shredded reduced-fat cheddar cheese

APRICOT BARBECUE SAUCE:
- 3/4 cup apricot spreadable fruit
- 1/2 cup ketchup
- 1/4 cup lemon juice
- 2 tablespoons brown sugar
- 2 tablespoons finely chopped onion
- 1 tablespoon canola oil
- 1/2 teaspoon salt
- 1/2 teaspoon dried oregano

In a large bowl, combine the first seven ingredients. Stir in the crackers, walnuts and cheese. Coat hands with cooking spray; shape mixture into 1-in. balls. Place in a 13-in. x 9-in. baking dish coated with cooking spray.

In a small saucepan, combine the sauce ingredients. Bring to a boil. Pour over walnuts balls. Bake, uncovered, at 350° for 25 minutes or until a meat thermometer reads 160°. **YIELD: 8 SERVINGS.**

NUTRITION FACTS: 4 balls with sauce equals 265 calories, 12 g fat (3 g saturated fat), 61 mg cholesterol, 585 mg sodium, 34 g carbohydrate, 1 g fiber, 8 g protein. DIABETIC EXCHANGES: 1-1/2 fat, 1 lean meat, 1 starch, 1 fruit.

Rosemary Cheese Patties

⏱ Rosemary Cheese Patties

PREP/TOTAL TIME: 25 MIN.

We're a family that loves snacks, and I combined some of our favorite ingredients in this fast, easy and delicious recipe. Great for entertaining, it can be prepared ahead of time and browned just before guests arrive. It's quickly doubled for a crowd and extra special with marinara sauce.

Judy Armstrong ✳ Prairieville, Louisiana

- 1 package (8 ounces) cream cheese, softened
- 1 cup grated Parmesan cheese
- 3/4 cup seasoned bread crumbs, *divided*
- 2 eggs
- 1-1/2 to 2 teaspoons minced fresh rosemary
- 1-1/2 teaspoons minced garlic
- 1/8 to 1/4 teaspoon cayenne pepper
- 2 tablespoons olive oil

Marinara sauce, warmed, optional

In a large bowl, beat the cream cheese, Parmesan cheese, 1/4 cup bread crumbs, eggs, rosemary, garlic and cayenne until blended.

Place the remaining crumbs in a shallow bowl. Shape heaping tablespoonfuls of cheese mixture into 1-1/2-in. balls; flatten to 1/2-in. thickness. Coat with remaining bread crumbs.

In a large skillet, brown the patties in oil in batches over medium heat until golden brown. Drain on paper towels. Serve warm with marinara sauce if desired. **YIELD: 12 SERVINGS.**

Marinated Mozzarella

PREP: 15 MIN. + MARINATING

I always come home with an empty container when I bring this dish to a party and I've used the recipe for years. It can be made ahead to free up time later. I serve it with pretty party picks for a festive, holiday look.

Peggy Cairo ✳ Kenosha, Wisconsin

- 1/3 cup olive oil
- 1 tablespoon chopped oil-packed sun-dried tomatoes
- 1 tablespoon minced fresh parsley

- 1 teaspoon crushed red pepper flakes
- 1 teaspoon dried basil
- 1 teaspoon minced chives
- 1/4 teaspoon garlic powder
- 1 pound cubed part-skim mozzarella cheese

In a large resealable plastic bag, combine the oil, tomatoes, parsley and seasonings; add cheese cubes. Seal bag and turn to coat; refrigerate for at least 30 minutes. Transfer to a serving dish; serve with toothpicks. **YIELD: 8-10 SERVINGS.**

Marinated Mozzarella

Honey Banana Punch

PREP: 15 MIN. + FREEZING

Here's a great punch recipe I got from a beekeeper's association. The mix of banana, pineapple and citrus gives it a light sunny flavor. With its pretty honey color, it makes an elegant beverage for weddings and other special events.

Patricia Stephens ✳ Monticello, Kentucky

- 2 cups frozen orange juice concentrate
- 5 ripe bananas, cut into chunks
- 1 can (46 ounces) pineapple juice
- 2 cups water
- 3/4 cup honey
- 1/2 cup sugar
- 1/3 cup sugar sweetened lemonade soft drink mix
- 4 liters lemon-lime soda, chilled

In a blender, combine orange juice concentrate and bananas; cover and process until smooth.

Pour into a large bowl; add the pineapple juice, water, honey, sugar and soft drink mix. Stir until sugar is dissolved. Pour into two 2-qt. freezer containers. Cover and freeze until mixture is slushy.

To serve, transfer each portion of the fruit slush to a large pitcher. Add 2 liters of soda to each pitcher; stir to blend. **YIELD: 7-1/2 GALLONS (THIRTY 1-CUP SERVINGS).**

Honey Banana Punch

Wontons with Sweet-Sour Sauce

Wontons with Sweet-Sour Sauce

PREP: **40 MIN.** COOK: **30 MIN.**

This super-simple finger food makes an awesome appetizer and is perfect for potlucks. I serve these crispy pork rolls with sweet-and-sour sauce, and they disappear in a hurry—folks can't seem to get enough of them.

Korrin Grigg ✴ Neenah, Wisconsin

- 1 can (14 ounces) pineapple tidbits
- 1/2 cup packed brown sugar
- 1 tablespoon cornstarch
- 1/3 cup cider vinegar
- 1 tablespoon soy sauce
- 1/2 cup chopped green pepper
- 1/2 pound ground pork
- 2 cups finely shredded cabbage
- 3/4 cup finely chopped canned bean sprouts
- 1 small onion, finely chopped
- 2 eggs, lightly beaten
- 1/2 teaspoon salt
- 1/4 teaspoon pepper
- 2 packages (12 ounces *each*) wonton wrappers

Oil for deep-fat frying

Drain pineapple, reserving juice. Set pineapple aside. In a large saucepan, combine brown sugar and cornstarch; gradually stir in the pineapple juice, vinegar and soy sauce until smooth. Bring to a boil; cook and stir for 2 minutes or until thickened. Reduce heat; stir in green pepper and reserved pineapple. Cover and simmer for 5 minutes; set aside and keep warm.

In a large bowl, combine the pork, cabbage, sprouts, onion, eggs, salt and pepper. Place about 1 tablespoonful in the center of a wrapper. (Keep remaining wrappers covered with a damp paper towel until ready to use.) Moisten edges with water; fold opposite corners together over filling and press to seal. Repeat.

In an electric skillet, heat 1 in. of oil to 375°. Fry wontons for 2-1/2 minutes or until golden brown, turning once. Drain on paper towels. Serve with sauce. **YIELD: ABOUT 8-1/2 DOZEN (2-1/2 CUPS SAUCE).**

Rhubarb Cheesecake Smoothies

Rhubarb Cheesecake Smoothies

PREP: **20 MIN. + COOLING**

We love smoothies, so there isn't much we don't use to make unusual combinations. Cream cheese adds an extra-special touch to this yummy concoction that our friends and family just love.

Kathy Specht * Cambria, California

- 2 cups diced fresh *or* frozen rhubarb
- 1/4 cup water
- 4 tablespoons honey, *divided*
- 1-1/2 cups vanilla ice cream
- 1 cup milk
- 1 cup frozen sweetened sliced strawberries
- 2 packages (3 ounces *each*) cream cheese, cubed
- 1/2 cup vanilla yogurt
- 1/4 cup confectioners' sugar
- 5 ice cubes

In a large saucepan, bring the rhubarb, water and 2 tablespoons honey to a boil. Reduce heat; cover and simmer for 5-10 minutes or until rhubarb is tender. Remove from the heat; cool to room temperature.

In a blender, combine the ice cream, milk, rhubarb mixture, strawberries, cream cheese, yogurt, confectioners' sugar, ice cubes and the remaining honey; cover and process for 1 minute or until smooth. Pour into chilled glasses; serve immediately. **YIELD: 6 SERVINGS.**

Asparagus Salsa

Asparagus Salsa

PREP: **20 MIN. + CHILLING**

Jalapeno pepper and cilantro spice up this refreshing salsa that's made with tomatoes, onion and fresh asparagus. Served chilled with tortilla chips, this chunky sauce won't last long.

Emma Thomas * Rome, Georgia

- 1 pound fresh asparagus, trimmed and cut into 1/2-inch pieces
- 1 cup chopped seeded tomatoes
- 1/2 cup finely chopped onion
- 1 small jalapeno pepper, seeded and finely chopped
- 1 tablespoon minced fresh cilantro
- 1 garlic clove, minced
- 1 teaspoon cider vinegar
- 1/4 teaspoon salt

Tortilla chips

Place asparagus in a large saucepan; add 1/2 in. of water. Bring to a boil. Reduce heat; cover and simmer for 2 minutes. Drain asparagus and rinse in cold water.

In a large bowl, combine the asparagus, tomatoes, onion, jalapeno, cilantro, garlic, vinegar and salt. Cover and refrigerate for at least 4 hours, stirring several times. Serve with tortilla chips. **YIELD: 3 CUPS.**

EDITOR'S NOTE: When cutting hot peppers, disposable gloves are recommended. Avoid touching your face.

Cheese Puffs

Cheese Puffs

PREP: **15 MIN.** BAKE: **15 MIN./BATCH**

I found this recipe in one of my mother's old cookbooks and updated the flavor by adding cayenne and mustard. Tasty and quick, these tender, golden puffs go together in minutes and simply disappear at parties!

Jamie Wetter ✳ Boscobel, Wisconsin

- 1 cup water
- 2 tablespoons butter
- 1/2 teaspoon salt
- 1/8 teaspoon cayenne pepper
- 1 cup all-purpose flour
- 4 eggs
- 1-1/4 cups shredded Gruyere *or* Swiss cheese
- 1 tablespoon Dijon mustard
- 1/4 cup grated Parmesan cheese

In a large saucepan, bring the water, butter, salt and cayenne to a boil. Add flour all at once and stir until a smooth ball forms. Remove from the heat; let stand for 5 minutes. Add eggs, one at a time, beating well after each addition. Continue beating until mixture is smooth and shiny. Stir in Gruyere and mustard.

Drop by rounded teaspoonfuls 2 in. apart onto greased baking sheets. Sprinkle with Parmesan cheese. Bake at 425° for 15-20 minutes or until golden brown. Serve warm or cold. **YIELD: 4 DOZEN.**

Greek Salsa

PREP/TOTAL TIME: **30 MIN.**

Color, texture and a fantastic blend of flavors—this salsa has it all. It's easy to adapt to the taste preferences of your family or guests. I've made it dozens of times, and it's foolproof!

Heidi Mitchell ✳ Cornwall, Prince Edward Island

- 1 tablespoon white balsamic vinegar
- 2 tablespoons olive oil, *divided*
- 2-1/2 teaspoons Greek seasoning, *divided*
- 1 garlic clove, minced

1 cup grape tomatoes, quartered
3/4 cup chopped cucumber
1/2 cup crumbled feta cheese
1/2 cup chopped red onion
1 can (2-1/4 ounces) sliced ripe olives, drained
1 package (12 ounces) whole wheat pita breads

In a small bowl, combine the vinegar, 1 tablespoon oil, 1-1/2 teaspoons Greek seasoning and garlic; set aside.

In a large bowl, combine the tomatoes, cucumber, feta cheese, onion and olives. Drizzle with vinegar mixture and toss to coat. Chill until serving.

Cut each pita bread into eight wedges. Place on an ungreased baking sheet. Brush with remaining oil; sprinkle with remaining Greek seasoning. Bake at 400° for 6-8 minutes or until crisp. Serve with salsa. **YIELD: 2-3/4 CUPS SALSA AND 40 PITA CHIPS.**

Greek Salsa

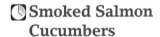 Smoked Salmon Cucumbers

PREP/TOTAL TIME: **20 MIN.**

This super-easy appetizer has pleased many guests at our house and is sure to be a hit at yours, too! The four-ingredient bites offer a light and refreshing taste any time of the year.

Cheryl Lama ✳ Royal Oak, Michigan

1 large English cucumber
1 carton (8 ounces) spreadable chive and onion cream cheese
7 to 8 ounces smoked salmon *or* lox, chopped

Minced chives

With a fork, score cucumber peel lengthwise; cut into 1/4-in. slices. Pipe or spread cream cheese onto each slice; top with salmon. Sprinkle with chives. Refrigerate until serving. **YIELD: ABOUT 3 DOZEN.**

Smoked Salmon Cucumbers

Deep-Fried Chicken Wings

Deep-Fried Chicken Wings

PREP: 15 MIN. + MARINATING COOK: 20 MIN.

A soy sauce mixture with sesame seeds and green onion adds flavor to these deep-fried wings. My mom got the recipe from a friend and passed it on to me. My husband just loves chicken wings, and these are by far his favorite.

Tami McLean ✳ Brampton, Ontario

- 15 chicken wings (about 3 pounds)
- 1/2 cup cornstarch
- 1/4 cup all-purpose flour
- 1/4 cup sugar
- 2 teaspoons sesame seeds
- 1-1/2 teaspoons salt
- 2 eggs
- 1/4 cup canola oil
- 5 teaspoons soy sauce
- 2 green onions, finely chopped

Oil for deep-fat frying

Cut chicken wings into three sections; discard wing tip section.

In a large bowl, combine the cornstarch, flour, sugar, sesame seeds and salt. Combine the eggs, oil and soy sauce; gradually whisk into dry ingredients until blended. Stir in onions. Add chicken wings and stir to coat. Cover and refrigerate for at least 3 hours.

Remove wings and discard the batter. In an electric skillet or deep-fat fryer, heat 1-1/2 in. of oil to 375°. Fry wings, 8-10 at a time, for 5-6 minutes on each side or until juices run clear. Drain on paper towels. **YIELD: 2-1/2 DOZEN.**

EDITOR'S NOTE: Uncooked chicken wing sections (wingettes) may be substituted for whole chicken wings.

Frosty Mocha Drink

Frosty Mocha Drink

PREP/TOTAL TIME: 15 MIN.

I like to make this chilly chocolate-flavored coffee drink when friends stop by for a visit. I always double the recipe, because I know they'll come back for seconds. For a richer and creamier version, replace the milk with half-and-half cream.

Lauren Nance ✳ San Diego, California

- 1 cup milk
- 3 tablespoons instant chocolate drink mix

Cheddar-Veggie Appetizer Torte

2 tablespoons instant coffee granules

2 tablespoons honey

1 teaspoon vanilla extract

14 to 16 ice cubes

In a blender, combine all ingredients; cover and process until smooth. Pour into chilled glasses; serve immediately. **YIELD: 4 SERVINGS.**

Cheddar-Veggie Appetizer Torte

PREP: 25 MIN. BAKE: 30 MIN. + COOLING

A line forms quickly behind this quiche-like torte at family gatherings. The wedges are easy to eat as finger food—plus, it's delicious hot or cold.

Barbara Estabrook ✳ Rhinelander, Wisconsin

1-1/3 cups finely crushed multigrain crackers

1/4 cup butter, melted

2 cups (8 ounces) shredded sharp cheddar cheese

1 small zucchini, finely chopped

5 small fresh mushrooms, sliced

1/3 cup finely chopped red onion

1/4 cup finely chopped sweet red pepper

1 tablespoon olive oil

1 carton (8 ounces) spreadable garlic and herb cream cheese

4 eggs, lightly beaten

2 tablespoons crumbled cooked bacon

2 tablespoons grated Parmesan cheese

In a small bowl, combine cracker crumbs and butter. Press onto the bottom of a greased 9-in. springform pan. Sprinkle with cheddar cheese. In a large skillet, saute the zucchini, mushrooms, onion and red pepper in oil until tender. Spoon over cheese.

In a large bowl, beat cream cheese until smooth. Add eggs; beat on low speed just until combined. Stir in bacon. Pour over vegetable mixture. Sprinkle with Parmesan cheese.

Place pan on a baking sheet. Bake at 375° for 30-35 minutes or until center is almost set. Cool on a wire rack for 10 minutes. Carefully run a knife around edge of pan to loosen; remove sides of pan. Serve warm or chilled. Refrigerate leftovers. **YIELD: 16 SERVINGS.**

Cheddar Ham Cups

⬤Cheddar Ham Cups

PREP/TOTAL TIME: **30 MIN.**

When a college classmate and I threw a party for our professor, a friend contributed these savory appetizers. Everyone in the class requested the recipe before the party was done. Try the cups with chicken instead of ham if you'd like.

Brandi Ladner ✳ Gulfport, Mississippi

- 2 cups (8 ounces) finely shredded cheddar cheese
- 2 packages (2-1/2 ounces *each*) thinly sliced deli ham, chopped
- 3/4 cup mayonnaise
- 1/3 cup real bacon bits
- 2 to 3 teaspoons Dijon mustard
- 1 tube (10.2 ounces) large refrigerated flaky biscuits

In a large bowl, combine the cheese, ham, mayonnaise, bacon and mustard. Split the biscuits into thirds. Press onto the bottom and up the sides of ungreased miniature muffin cups. Fill each with about 1 tablespoon of cheese mixture.

Bake at 450° for 9-11 minutes or until golden brown and the cheese is melted. Let stand for 2 minutes before removing from the pans. Serve warm. **YIELD: 2-1/2 DOZEN.**

Caramel Crunch

PREP: **15 MIN.** BAKE: **45 MIN.**

Our whole family has a sweet tooth, so this caramel-drizzled mix of popcorn, almonds and cereal goes quickly. My off-limits batches are divided into plastic bags, tied with ribbon and shared with all the snackers on my Christmas list.

Mary Koogler ✳ Mitchellville, Iowa

- 9 cups popped popcorn
- 9 cups Crispix cereal
- 1 cup slivered almonds
- 1 cup butter, cubed
- 1/2 cup light corn syrup
- 2 cups packed brown sugar
- 1/2 teaspoon baking soda

Caramel Crunch

In a very large, heat-proof bowl, combine the popcorn, cereal and almonds; set aside. In a large, heavy saucepan, melt butter; stir in corn syrup and brown sugar. Cook and stir over medium heat until mixture comes to a boil. Reduce heat to medium-low. Cook 5 minutes longer, stirring occasionally.

Remove from the heat. Stir in baking soda. (Mixture will foam up and get lighter in color.) Carefully pour over popcorn mixture; stir to coat evenly.

Transfer to two 15-in. x 10-in. x 1-in. baking pans coated with cooking spray. Bake at 250° for 45 minutes, stirring every 15 minutes. Spread on waxed paper to cool. Store in airtight containers. **YIELD: ABOUT 4-1/2 QUARTS.**

Chocolate Chip Cheese Ball

Chocolate Chip Cheese Ball

PREP: **10 MIN. + CHILLING**

Your guests are in for a sweet surprise when they try this unusual cheese ball...it tastes just like cookie dough! Rolled in chopped pecans, the chip-studded spread is wonderful on regular or chocolate graham crackers. I especially like it because it can be assembled in a wink.

Kelly Glascock ✳ Syracuse, Missouri

- 1 package (8 ounces) cream cheese, softened
- 1/2 cup butter, softened
- 1/4 teaspoon vanilla extract
- 3/4 cup confectioners' sugar
- 2 tablespoons brown sugar
- 3/4 cup miniature semisweet chocolate chips
- 3/4 cup finely chopped pecans

Graham crackers

In a large bowl, beat the cream cheese, butter and vanilla until fluffy. Gradually add sugars; beat just until combined. Stir in chocolate chips. Cover and refrigerate for 2 hours.

Place cream cheese mixture on a large piece of plastic wrap; shape into a ball. Refrigerate for at least 1 hour.

Just before serving, roll cheese ball in pecans. Serve with graham crackers. **YIELD: 1 CHEESE BALL (ABOUT 2 CUPS).**

Cornmeal Onion Rings

Cornmeal Onion Rings

PREP/TOTAL TIME: 30 MIN.

My husband says these onion rings are the best he's ever eaten. The cornmeal and pecans give them a special crunch that we both really enjoy.

Mila Bryning ✳ Alexandria, Virginia

- 2 **pounds onions**
- 2 **eggs**
- 1 **cup buttermilk**
- 2 **cups all-purpose flour**
- 1 **cup cornmeal**
- 1/2 **cup chopped pecans**
- 1 **to 1-1/2 teaspoons salt**
- 1/2 **teaspoon pepper**

Oil for deep-fat frying

Cut onions into 1/2-in. slices; separate into rings. In a shallow bowl, whisk the egg and buttermilk until blended. In another shallow bowl, combine the flour, cornmeal, pecans, salt and pepper. Dip onion rings in the egg mixture, then coat with flour mixture.

In an electric skillet or deep-fat fryer, heat 1 in. of oil to 375°. Fry onion rings, a few at a time, for 1 to 1-1/2 minutes on each side or until golden brown. Drain on paper towels. **YIELD: 8 SERVINGS.**

Festive Baked Brie

PREP/TOTAL TIME: **30 MIN.**

Rich, smooth Brie cheese accented with caramelized onions is reminiscent of fondue. With a red and green tomato and herb topping, it's quite a showpiece on a holiday table.

Genny Derer ✳ Madison, Wisconsin

- 1 large onion, halved and thinly sliced
- 2 tablespoons butter
- 2 tablespoons olive oil
- 1/2 cup oil-packed sun-dried tomatoes, drained and chopped
- 1/4 cup minced fresh parsley
- 2 tablespoons minced fresh basil

Dash pepper

- 1 round (8 ounces) Brie *or* Camembert cheese

Assorted crackers

In a large skillet, cook onion in butter and oil over medium heat for 15-20 minutes or until golden brown, stirring frequently; set aside.

In a small bowl, combine the tomatoes, parsley, basil and pepper. Remove rind from the top of the Brie; place Brie in an ungreased ovenproof serving dish. Top with tomato mixture and onion mixture.

Bake, uncovered, at 400° for 10-12 minutes or until cheese is softened. Serve warm with crackers. **YIELD: 6-8 SERVINGS.**

Festive Baked Brie

Cranberry Spritzer

PREP/TOTAL TIME: **10 MIN.**

Lemon-lime soda puts the fizz in this fresh-tasting juice blend. This is my version of a cranberry drink I've had many times at a local restaurant. I like the mix of flavors, and it's easy to increase the amount.

LaVonne Hegland ✳ St. Michael, Minnesota

- 1 can (12 ounces) lemon-lime soda, chilled
- 1 cup cranberry juice, chilled
- 1/2 cup unsweetened pineapple juice, chilled
- 1/4 cup orange juice, chilled

Ice cubes

In a pitcher, combine the soda and juices. Serve over ice. **YIELD: 2 SERVINGS.**

Cranberry Spritzer

Garlic Pizza Wedges

⏱ Garlic Pizza Wedges

PREP/TOTAL TIME: **25 MIN.**

Our pastor made this for a get-together, and my husband and I just couldn't stay away from this treat. The cheesy slices taste great served warm, but they're still wonderful when they've cooled slightly.

Krysten Johnson ✳ Simi Valley, California

1	prebaked Italian bread shell crust (14 ounces)
1	cup grated Parmesan cheese
1	cup mayonnaise
1	small red onion, chopped
3-1/2	teaspoons minced garlic
1	tablespoon dried oregano

Place the crust on an ungreased 14-in. pizza pan. In a small bowl, combine the Parmesan cheese, mayonnaise, onion, garlic and oregano; spread over crust. Bake at 450° for 8-10 minutes or until edges are lightly browned. Cut into wedges. **YIELD: 2 DOZEN.**

EDITOR'S NOTE: Reduced-fat or fat-free mayonnaise is not recommended for this recipe.

Roasted Cumin Cashews

PREP: **15 MIN.** BAKE: **50 MIN. + COOLING**

Kick up parties and get-togethers with these well-seasoned snacks. They're sweet, salty, crunchy...and oh, so munchable.

Martha Fehl ✳ Brookville, Indiana

1	egg white
1	tablespoon water
2	cans (9-3/4 ounces *each*) salted whole cashews
1/3	cup sugar
3	teaspoons chili powder
2	teaspoons salt
2	teaspoons ground cumin
1/2	teaspoon cayenne pepper

Roasted Cumin Cashews

Wassail Bowl Punch

In a large bowl, whisk egg white and water. Add cashews and toss to coat. Transfer to a colander; drain for 2 minutes. In another bowl, combine the remaining ingredients; add cashews and toss to coat.

Arrange in a single layer in a greased 15-in. x 10-in. x 1-in. baking pan. Bake, uncovered, at 250° for 50-55 minutes, stirring once. Cool on a wire rack. Store in an airtight container. **YIELD: 3-1/2 CUPS.**

Wassail Bowl Punch

PREP: 10 MIN. COOK: 1 HOUR

All ages will enjoy this warming punch. The blend of spice, fruit and citrus flavors is scrumptious. You can assemble it before heading out for a winter activity and sip away the chill when you return. It's ready whenever you are.

Margaret Harms ✳ Jenkins, Kentucky

- 4 cups hot brewed tea
- 4 cups cranberry juice
- 4 cups unsweetened apple juice
- 2 cups orange juice
- 1 cup sugar
- 3/4 cup lemon juice
- 3 cinnamon sticks (3 inches)
- 12 whole cloves

In a 5-qt. slow cooker, combine the first six ingredients. Place the cinnamon sticks and cloves on a double thickness of cheesecloth; bring up corners of cloth and tie with string to form a bag. Add to slow cooker.

Cover and cook on high for 1 hour or until punch begins to boil. Discard spice bag. Serve warm. **YIELD: 3-1/2 QUARTS.**

Swiss Walnut Cracker Snack

Swiss Walnut Cracker Snack

PREP: **10 MIN. + CHILLING**

This spread is simple to prepare and makes an excellent snack for holiday and family gatherings. It has a nice crunch from the walnuts.

Geraldine Muth ✳ Black River Falls, Wisconsin

  1   package (8 ounces) cream cheese, softened
1-1/2 cups (6 ounces) shredded Swiss cheese
  1/2 cup sour cream
    2   tablespoons Dijon mustard
  1/3 cup chopped walnuts
  1/3 cup minced fresh parsley
  1/4 cup chopped green onions
Crackers *and/or* bagel chips

In a large bowl, beat cream cheese until smooth. Add the Swiss cheese, sour cream and mustard. Stir in the walnuts, parsley and onions.

Refrigerate for at least 1 hour before serving. Serve with crackers and/or bagel chips. **YIELD: 2 CUPS.**

Marmalade Soy Wings

PREP: **15 MIN. + MARINATING** BAKE: **40 MIN.**

Whether I use drumettes or chicken wings, these savory bites are always popular. I keep the pretty glazed appetizers warm during parties by serving them in my slow cooker.

Carole Nelson ✳ Parkville, Missouri

  15   whole chicken wings (about 3 pounds)
    1   cup soy sauce
    1   cup orange marmalade
    3   garlic cloves, minced
    1   teaspoon ground ginger
  1/4 teaspoon pepper

Cut chicken wings into three sections; discard wing tip sections. In a bowl, combine the soy sauce, marmalade, garlic, ginger and pepper. Cover and refrigerate 1/2 cup marinade for basting.

Place the remaining marinade in a large resealable plastic bag. Add wing sections; seal the bag and toss to coat evenly. Refrigerate for 8 hours or overnight.

Drain and discard marinade. Place chicken wings in a greased 15-in. x 10-in. x 1-in. baking pan. Bake, uncovered, at 350° for 15 minutes.

Baste with a third of the reserved marinade; bake 15 minutes longer. Baste with remaining marinade. Bake 10-20 minutes more or until chicken juices run clear. **YIELD: 8 SERVINGS.**

EDITOR'S NOTE: Uncooked chicken wing sections (wingettes) may be substituted for whole chicken wings.

Marmalade Soy Wings

Black Forest Ham Pinwheels

PREP: **20 MIN. + CHILLING**

My popular pinwheels wow guests at holiday parties I attend. People like the smokiness of the ham and the sweet surprise of the cherries. I appreciate the make-ahead convenience.

Kate Dampier ✳ Quail Valley, California

- 1 package (8 ounces) cream cheese, softened
- 4 teaspoons minced fresh dill
- 1 tablespoon lemon juice
- 2 teaspoons Dijon mustard

Dash salt and pepper

- 1/2 cup dried cherries, chopped
- 1/4 cup chopped green onions
- 5 flour tortillas (10 inches), room temperature
- 1/2 pound sliced deli Black Forest ham
- 1/2 pound sliced Swiss cheese

In a small bowl, beat the cream cheese, dill, lemon juice, mustard, salt and pepper until blended. Stir in the cherries and onions. Spread over each tortilla; layer with ham and cheese.

Roll up tightly; wrap in plastic wrap. Refrigerate for at least 2 hours. Cut into 1/2-in. slices. **YIELD: ABOUT 3-1/2 DOZEN.**

Black Forest Ham Pinwheels

Salmon Mousse Cups

Salmon Mousse Cups

PREP: **25 MIN. + CHILLING** BAKE: **10 MIN. + COOLING**

I make these tempting little tarts frequently for parties. They disappear at an astonishing speed, so I usually double or triple the recipe. The salmon-cream cheese filling and flaky crust will melt in your mouth.

Fran Rowland ✳ Phoenix, Arizona

- 1 package (3 ounces) cream cheese, softened
- 1/2 cup butter, softened
- 1 cup all-purpose flour

FILLING:

- 1 package (8 ounces) cream cheese, softened
- 1 cup fully cooked salmon chunks *or* 1 can (7-1/2 ounces) salmon, drained, bones and skin removed
- 2 tablespoons chicken broth
- 2 tablespoons sour cream
- 1 tablespoon finely chopped onion
- 1 teaspoon lemon juice
- 1/2 teaspoon salt
- 2 tablespoons minced fresh dill

In a small bowl, beat the cream cheese and butter until smooth. Add flour and mix well. Shape into 24 balls; press onto the bottom and up the sides of greased miniature muffin cups.

Bake at 350° for 10-15 minutes or until golden brown. Cool the cups for 5 minutes before removing from the pans to wire racks to cool.

For filling, in a large bowl, beat cream cheese until smooth. Add the salmon, broth, sour cream, onion, lemon juice and salt until blended. Spoon into the shells. Refrigerate for at least 2 hours before serving. Sprinkle with the dill. YIELD: **2 DOZEN.**

Cheese Fries

Horseradish Crab Dip

⏱ Cheese Fries

PREP/TOTAL TIME: **20 MIN.**

I came up with this recipe after my daughter had cheese fries at a restaurant and couldn't stop talking about them.

Melissa Tatum ✳ Greensboro, North Carolina

- 1 package (28 ounces) frozen steak fries
- 1 can (10-3/4 ounces) condensed cheddar cheese soup, undiluted
- 1/4 cup milk
- 1/2 teaspoon garlic powder
- 1/4 teaspoon onion powder

Paprika

Arrange the steak fries in a single layer in two greased 15-in. x 10-in. x 1-in. baking pans. Bake at 450° for 15-18 minutes or until tender and golden brown.

Meanwhile, in a small saucepan, combine the soup, milk, garlic powder and onion powder; heat through. Drizzle over fries; sprinkle with paprika. YIELD: **8-10 SERVINGS.**

⏱ Horseradish Crab Dip

PREP/TOTAL TIME: **10 MIN.**

I depend on this mildly seasoned crab dip when hosting parties. It's a terrific time-saver when accompanied by celery sticks or your favorite raw veggies. It's so simple to prepare that it gives me time to get other appetizers ready or mingle with my guests.

Kathleen Snead ✳ Lynchburg, Virginia

- 1 package (8 ounces) cream cheese, softened
- 2 to 3 tablespoons picante sauce
- 1 to 2 tablespoons prepared horseradish
- 1 can (6 ounces) crabmeat, drained, flaked and cartilage removed

Celery sticks

In a large bowl, beat the cream cheese, picante sauce and horseradish until blended. Stir in crab. Serve with celery. YIELD: **ABOUT 1-1/2 CUPS.**

Hawaiian Cheese Bread

Hawaiian Cheese Bread

PREP: **15 MIN.** BAKE: **25 MIN.**

This bread is absolutely delicious. My mother's friend brought it to a party at work, and after one bite, Mom knew she had to have the recipe. With constant nagging, she eventually got it! Simple and fast, this mouthwatering loaf is a hit with everybody and at every kind of function.

Amy McIlvain * Wilmington, Delaware

- 1 loaf (1 pound) Hawaiian sweet bread
- 1 block (8 ounces) Swiss cheese
- 3 slices red onion, chopped
- 1/2 cup butter, melted
- 1 tablespoon minced garlic
- 1 teaspoon salt

Cut bread diagonally into 1-in. slices to within 1 in. of bottom. Repeat cuts in opposite direction. Cut cheese into 1/4-in. slices; cut slices into small pieces. Insert into bread. Combine the onion, butter, garlic and salt; spoon over bread.

Wrap loaf in foil. Bake at 350° for 25-30 minutes or until cheese is melted. Serve warm. **YIELD: 12-16 SERVINGS.**

Cappuccino Punch

Cappuccino Punch

PREP: **10 MIN. + CHILLING**

When I tried this punch at a friend's wedding shower, I had to have the recipe. Guests will eagerly gather around the punch bowl when you ladle out this frothy mocha ice cream drink.

Rose Reich * Nampa, Idaho

- 1/2 cup sugar
- 1/4 cup instant coffee granules
- 1 cup boiling water
- 8 cups milk
- 1 quart vanilla ice cream, softened
- 1 quart chocolate ice cream, softened

In a small bowl, combine the sugar and coffee; stir in boiling water until dissolved. Cover and refrigerate until chilled.

Just before serving, pour the coffee mixture into a 1-gal. punch bowl. Stir in the milk. Add scoops of ice cream; stir until melted. **YIELD: ABOUT 1 GALLON.**

Raspberry Greek Salad, PAGE 72

" *An interesting combination of sweet and salty flavors gives this Greek salad a delicious twist. And the tart chewiness of the dried cranberries makes a wonderful complement to the salty feta cheese. I often take this to work for lunch.* "

Carine Nadel
Laguna Hills, California

SALADS

DO YOU HAVE A WINNING RECIPE?

Enter your most prized recipes in the *Taste of Home* recipe contests, and you may win some money and the chance to have your recipe published. Log onto **tasteofhome.com/RecipeContests** for a list of our current contests and submission deadlines. Good luck...we'll be looking for your recipe.

salads

Rainbow Pasta Salad

PREP: 1 HOUR + CHILLING

This colorful salad is hearty enough to be a light meal in itself. It's a great make-ahead dish, since the full flavors of the herbs and veggies need a little time to blend.

Benjamin & Sue Ellen Clark ✳ Warsaw, New York

- 2 packages (12 ounces *each*) tricolor spiral pasta
- 2 packages (16 ounces *each*) frozen California-blend vegetables, thawed
- 2 pints grape tomatoes
- 1 large zucchini, halved and thinly sliced
- 1 large yellow summer squash, quartered and thinly sliced
- 1 large red onion, finely chopped
- 1 block (8 ounces) cheddar cheese, cubed
- 1 block (8 ounces) Monterey Jack cheese, cubed
- 2 packages (4 ounces *each*) crumbled tomato and basil feta cheese
- 1 bottle (16 ounces) Italian salad dressing
- 3 tablespoons minced fresh parsley
- 1 tablespoon minced fresh basil
- 1 teaspoon Italian seasoning
- 1 teaspoon seasoned salt
- 1/2 teaspoon pepper
- 1 can (3.8 ounces) sliced ripe olives, drained

Grated Romano cheese, optional

Cook pasta according to package directions. Rinse with cold water; drain well. In two large bowls, combine the California vegetables, tomatoes, zucchini, yellow squash, onion, cheeses and pasta.

Rainbow Pasta Salad

In a small bowl, combine the salad dressing, parsley, basil, Italian seasoning, seasoned salt and pepper. Pour over pasta mixture; toss to coat. Stir in olives. Cover and refrigerate for 8 hours or overnight.

Toss before serving. Serve with Romano cheese if desired. **YIELD: 36 SERVINGS.**

Special Summer Berry Medley

1st place

Special Summer Berry Medley

PREP/TOTAL TIME: 30 MIN.

No matter how big the meal, folks always find room for this delightfully "special" dessert. With its hint of citrus and mint, this medley makes a light, pretty side dish at casual cookouts or potlucks. Best of all, it's as fast and easy to make as it is to clean up!

Nancy Whitford ✳ Edwards, New York

- 1 cup sparkling wine *or* white grape juice
- 1/2 cup sugar
- 1 tablespoon lemon juice
- 1-1/2 teaspoons grated lemon peel
- 1/2 teaspoon vanilla extract
- 1/8 teaspoon salt
- 3 cups sliced fresh strawberries
- 2 cups fresh blueberries
- 1 cup fresh raspberries
- 1 cup fresh blackberries
- 1 tablespoon minced fresh mint

In a small heavy saucepan, bring wine and sugar to a boil. Cook, uncovered, for about 15 minutes or until reduced to 1/2 cup, stirring occasionally. Cool slightly. Stir in the lemon juice and peel, vanilla and salt.

In a large bowl, combine berries and mint. Add syrup and toss gently to coat. Cover and refrigerate until serving. **YIELD: 12 SERVINGS.**

Harvest Green Salad

PREP: **25 MIN.** BAKE: **1 HOUR + COOLING**

This salad always gets praised for its great flavor. Guests say that it fills them up without weighing them down.

Beth Royals ✳ Richmond, Virginia

- 3 whole medium fresh beets
- 1 large sweet potato, peeled and cubed
- 2 tablespoons water
- 1/2 cup reduced-fat balsamic vinaigrette
- 2 tablespoons jellied cranberry sauce
- 1 package (5 ounces) spring mix salad greens
- 1/2 cup dried cranberries
- 4 ounces crumbled Gorgonzola cheese

Wash beets; trim stem and leave root intact. Wrap beets in aluminum foil. Place on a baking sheet. Bake at 400° for 1 hour or until tender. Remove foil and cool.

In a microwave-safe bowl, combine the sweet potato and water. Cover and microwave on high for 4-5 minutes or until tender. Cool.

In a blender, combine the vinaigrette and cranberry sauce; cover and process until smooth. Peel the beets and cut into slices.

On six salad plates, arrange greens, beets and sweet potatoes. Sprinkle with cranberries and cheese. Drizzle with dressing. **YIELD: 6 SERVINGS.**

EDITOR'S NOTE: Use plastic gloves when peeling beets to avoid stains. This recipe was tested in a 1,100-watt microwave.

NUTRITION FACTS: 1-1/8 cups equals 187 calories, 9 g fat (4 g saturated fat), 17 mg cholesterol, 438 mg sodium, 23 g carbohydrate, 3 g fiber, 6 g protein. DIABETIC EXCHANGES: 1 starch, 1 vegetable, 1 fat, 1/2 fruit.

Peanut Chicken Salad

PREP: **15 MIN. + MARINATING** GRILL: **15 MIN.**

Our former neighbor, a native of Indonesia, made this peanut chicken salad, which she called "sate." My family liked it so much that after she moved away, I had to learn to make it.

Della Byers * Rosamond, California

Harvest Green Salad

- 1/3 cup soy sauce
- 3 tablespoons minced garlic
- 3 tablespoons peanut butter
- 1/4 cup minced fresh cilantro
- 1/2 teaspoon hot pepper sauce
- 4 boneless skinless chicken breast halves (4 ounces *each*)
- 4 cups torn mixed salad greens
- 4 small tomatoes, seeded and chopped
- 4 green onions, chopped
- 1 cup shredded cabbage
- 1 medium cucumber, sliced
- 1 cup honey-roasted peanuts
- 1 cup ranch salad dressing
- 2 to 4 drops hot pepper sauce

In a large saucepan, combine the soy sauce, garlic, peanut butter, cilantro and hot pepper sauce; cook and stir until heated through and blended. Cool to room temperature.

Pour the soy sauce mixture into a large resealable plastic bag; add chicken. Seal bag and turn to coat; refrigerate for 1 hour.

Drain and discard marinade. Grill chicken, uncovered, over medium heat for 3 minutes on each side. Grill 6-8 minutes longer or until a meat thermometer reads 170°.

Place the salad greens, tomatoes, onions, cabbage, cucumber and peanuts on a serving platter. Slice chicken; arrange over salad.

In a small bowl, combine the salad dressing and hot pepper sauce. Serve with the salad.

YIELD: **6 SERVINGS.**

Peanut Chicken Salad

Shrimp Salad-Stuffed Avocados

Shrimp Salad-Stuffed Avocados

PREP/TOTAL TIME: **15 MIN.**

This is one of my husband's favorites, even though it's pretty enough to serve at a ladies luncheon. When I needed a quick main-dish salad for my book club, I just tripled the recipe and the group just loved it! Try it with imitation crabmeat, too.

Suzanne VanAlstyne ✳ Petoskey, Michigan

- 1/2 **pound deveined peeled cooked medium shrimp, coarsely chopped**
- 1/2 **cup chopped celery**
- 1/4 **cup chopped onion**
- 3 **tablespoons mayonnaise**
- 4-1/2 **teaspoons capers, drained**
- 1 **tablespoon minced fresh parsley**
- 2 **teaspoons Dijon mustard**
- 1-1/2 **teaspoons lemon juice**
- 3/4 **teaspoon dried tarragon**
- 1/4 **teaspoon seasoned salt**
- 1/8 **teaspoon pepper**
- 2 **medium ripe avocados, halved and pitted**

In a small bowl, combine the shrimp, celery, onion, mayonnaise, capers, parsley, mustard, lemon juice and seasonings. Spoon into the avocado halves. Serve immediately. **YIELD: 4 SERVINGS.**

Heirloom Tomato Salad

PREP: **20 MIN. + CHILLING**

This is a simple yet elegant dish that always pleases my guests. Not only is it tasty, but it is healthy, too. The more varied the colors of the tomatoes you choose, the prettier the salad will be.

Jessie Apfel ✳ Berkeley, California

- 2 **cups torn fresh spinach**
- 2 **cups sliced multicolored heirloom tomatoes**
- 1 **cup red and yellow cherry tomatoes, halved**
- 1 **cup sliced red onion**

DRESSING:
- 3 **tablespoons olive oil**
- 2 **tablespoons white balsamic vinegar**
- 1 **garlic clove, minced**
- 1/2 **teaspoon salt**
- 1/4 **teaspoon** *each* **dried basil, oregano, thyme and sage**
- 1/4 **teaspoon dried rosemary, crushed**
- 1/4 **teaspoon pepper**
- 1/8 **teaspoon dried parsley flakes**

In a large bowl, combine the spinach, tomatoes and onion.

In a small bowl, whisk together the dressing ingredients. Pour over salad and toss to coat.

Cover and refrigerate for at least 2 hours. Serve with a slotted spoon. **YIELD: 6 SERVINGS.**

NUTRITION FACTS: 2/3 cup equals 79 calories, 5 g fat (1 g saturated fat), 0 cholesterol, 165 mg sodium, 8 g carbohydrate, 2 g fiber, 1 g protein. **DIABETIC EXCHANGES:** 1 vegetable, 1 fat.

Heirloom Tomato Salad

Frosted Orange Salad

PREP: **35 MIN. + CHILLING**

Pineapple, bananas and marshmallows are folded into orange Jell-O in this refreshing salad. Frosted with a creamy topping, pecans and coconut, this yummy dish is a real crowd-pleaser. I have been making it for years.

Anna Jean Key * Muskogee, Oklahoma

      3 packages (3 ounces *each*) orange gelatin
      3 cups boiling water
      1 can (20 ounces) crushed pineapple
      3 cups cold water
      4 medium firm bananas, sliced
  2-1/2 cups miniature marshmallows
    1/2 cup sugar
      1 tablespoon all-purpose flour
      1 egg, lightly beaten
      1 package (8 ounces) cream cheese, softened
      1 cup heavy whipping cream, whipped
    3/4 cup chopped pecans, toasted
    1/2 cup flaked coconut, toasted

In a large bowl, dissolve gelatin in boiling water. Drain pineapple, reserving juice. Stir cold water, bananas, marshmallows and pineapple into gelatin.

Pour into a 13-in. x 9-in. dish coated with cooking spray; refrigerate until firm.

Meanwhile, in a large saucepan, combine sugar and flour. Stir in reserved pineapple juice until smooth. Bring to a boil over medium heat; cook and stir for 2 minutes or until thickened and bubbly. Reduce the heat; cook and stir 2 minutes longer.

Remove from the heat. Stir a small amount of hot filling into the egg; return all to the pan, stirring constantly. Bring to a gentle boil, cook and stir 2 minutes longer. Cool.

In a large bowl, beat the cream cheese until smooth. Beat in cooled filling. Fold in whipped cream. Spread over the gelatin (dish will be full). Sprinkle with the nuts and coconut. **YIELD: 12 SERVINGS.**

Frosted Orange Salad

Cashew-Pear Tossed Salad

Cashew-Pear Tossed Salad

PREP/TOTAL TIME: **15 MIN.**

A friend who does a lot of catering fixed this salad for our staff Christmas party several years ago, and we all asked for the recipe. The unexpected sweet-salty mix and lovely dressing make it a hit with everyone who tastes it.

Arlene Muller ✳ Kingwood, Texas

- 1 bunch romaine, torn
- 1 cup (4 ounces) shredded Swiss cheese
- 1 cup salted cashews
- 1 medium pear, thinly sliced
- 1/2 cup dried cranberries

POPPY SEED VINAIGRETTE:

- 2/3 cup olive oil
- 1/2 cup sugar
- 1/3 cup lemon juice
- 2 to 3 teaspoons poppy seeds
- 2 teaspoons finely chopped red onion
- 1 teaspoon prepared mustard
- 1/2 teaspoon salt

In a large salad bowl, combine the romaine, Swiss cheese, cashews, pear and cranberries.

In a bowl, whisk together the vinaigrette ingredients. Drizzle over salad and toss to coat. Serve immediately. **YIELD: 15 SERVINGS.**

Greens 'n' Fruit Salad

PREP/TOTAL TIME: **10 MIN.**

I concocted this recipe in my kitchen, and I've received a lot of compliments on it. I make it often for my husband and me, and I've also served it to guests at brunches and dinner gatherings.

Jean Martin ✳ Raleigh, North Carolina

- 6 cups torn mixed salad greens
- 2 medium navel oranges, peeled and sectioned

Greens 'n' Fruit Salad

Pina Colada Molded Salad

1 cup halved red seedless grapes
1/2 cup golden raisins
1/4 cup chopped red onion
1/4 cup sliced almonds
4 bacon strips, cooked and crumbled

DRESSING:

1/2 cup mayonnaise
1/2 cup honey
1/4 cup orange juice
2 tablespoons grated orange peel

In a large salad bowl, combine the greens, oranges, grapes, raisins, onion, almonds and bacon.

In a small bowl, combine the mayonnaise, honey, orange juice and peel. Pour over salad; toss to coat. Refrigerate leftover dressing. **YIELD: 6 SERVINGS (1 CUP DRESSING).**

Pina Colada Molded Salad

PREP: **25 MIN. + CHILLING**

An original recipe, my molded gelatin gets a tropical twist from coconut, pineapple and macadamia nuts. It's a wonderful anytime treat. Now that I'm retired from teaching, I have more time for kitchen experiments.

Carol Gillespie ✳ Chambersburg, Pennsylvania

1 can (20 ounces) unsweetened crushed pineapple
2 envelopes unflavored gelatin
1/2 cup cold water
1 cup cream of coconut
1 cup (8 ounces) sour cream
3/4 cup lemon-lime soda
3/4 cup flaked coconut
1/2 cup chopped macadamia nuts
Pineapple chunks and freshly shredded coconut, optional

Drain pineapple, reserving juice; set the pineapple aside. In a large saucepan, sprinkle gelatin over cold water; let stand for 1 minute. Cook and stir over low heat until gelatin is completely dissolved, about 2 minutes.

Remove from the heat; stir in the cream of coconut, sour cream, soda and reserved pineapple juice. Transfer to a large bowl. Cover and refrigerate for 30 minutes or until thickened, stirring occasionally.

Fold in the flaked coconut, nuts and reserved pineapple. Pour into a 6-cup ring mold coated with cooking spray. Cover and refrigerate for 3 hours or until firm.

To serve, unmold salad onto a platter. Fill the center with pineapple chunks and shredded coconut if desired. **YIELD: 8 SERVINGS.**

EDITOR'S NOTE: This recipe was tested with Coco Lopez cream of coconut.

Black Bean Bow Tie Salad

Cook pasta according to package directions. Rinse with cold water and drain; set aside. In a small saucepan, bring broth and garlic to a boil. Reduce heat; simmer, uncovered, for 5 minutes or until garlic is tender. Cool slightly.

Transfer to a food processor, add 1/4 cup black beans, cilantro, lime juice, oil, tomato paste, oregano and salt; cover and process until mixture is smooth.

Transfer to a large serving bowl. Stir in the pasta, zucchini, peppers, onion and remaining beans; toss gently to coat. Refrigerate until serving. **YIELD: 10 SERVINGS.**

NUTRITION FACTS: 1 cup equals 159 calories, 4 g fat (1 g saturated fat), 0 cholesterol, 352 mg sodium, 26 g carbohydrate, 4 g fiber, 6 g protein. DIABETIC EXCHANGES: 1-1/2 starch, 1 vegetable, 1/2 fat.

Herbed Raspberry-Hazelnut Salad

PREP/TOTAL TIME: **20 MIN.**

I receive great comments whenever I serve this salad at parties. It's refreshing and tasty.

Wendy Matejek ✳ Corpus Christi, Texas

- 9 cups torn iceberg lettuce
- 1 medium red onion, sliced and separated into rings
- 1 cup chopped fresh parsley
- 1/2 cup chopped fresh cilantro
- 1/4 cup chopped fresh tarragon
- 1 cup raspberry vinaigrette
- 1/2 cup fresh raspberries
- 1/2 cup chopped hazelnuts

In a large salad bowl, combine the lettuce, onion, parsley, cilantro and tarragon. Add the vinaigrette and toss to coat. Top with the raspberries and hazelnuts. **YIELD: 9 SERVINGS.**

Black Bean Bow Tie Salad

PREP/TOTAL TIME: **25 MIN.**

Even people who don't like beans compliment me on this delicious salad! It's a favorite at family get-togethers and potlucks. The slimmed-down dressing gets a little kick from cilantro and lime.

Teresa Smith ✳ Huron, South Dakota

- 8 ounces uncooked bow tie pasta
- 2/3 cup reduced-sodium chicken broth *or* vegetable broth
- 3 garlic cloves, sliced
- 1 can (15 ounces) black beans, rinsed and drained, *divided*
- 1/2 cup fresh cilantro
- 3 tablespoons lime juice
- 2 tablespoons olive oil
- 1 tablespoon tomato paste
- 1-1/2 teaspoons dried oregano
- 3/4 teaspoon salt
- 1 medium zucchini, cut in half lengthwise and sliced
- 1 medium sweet red pepper, chopped
- 1 medium green pepper, chopped
- 1/3 cup chopped red onion

Grilled Steak Caesar Salad

PREP/TOTAL TIME: **30 MIN.**

A tangy anchovy dressing coats this hearty Caesar salad. It's my version of a scrumptious dish offered at one of our finer restaurants. My quilting group really enjoys this salad, which I serve with hard rolls and a fruit dessert.

Eleanor Froehlich ✳ Rochester Hills, Michigan

- 4 hard-cooked egg yolks
- 4 anchovy fillets *or* 2 tablespoons anchovy paste
- 4 garlic cloves, minced
- 3 tablespoons Dijon mustard
- 2 tablespoons lemon juice
- 2 tablespoons red wine vinegar
- 1 tablespoon Worcestershire sauce
- 2 teaspoons coarsely ground pepper
- 1 teaspoon sugar
- 1 cup olive oil
- 1 boneless beef sirloin steak (about 1-1/4 pounds)
- 1 large bunch romaine, torn
- 2/3 cup shredded Parmesan cheese, *divided*
- 2 medium tomatoes, cut into wedges
- 2 cups Caesar salad croutons

In a blender, combine yolks, anchovies, garlic, mustard, lemon juice, vinegar, Worcestershire sauce, pepper and sugar; cover and process until blended. While processing, gradually add oil in a steady stream. Cover and refrigerate.

Grill steak, covered, over medium heat for 5-7 minutes on each side or until meat reaches desired doneness (for medium-rare, a meat thermometer should read 145°; medium, 160°; well-done, 170°).

In a large bowl, toss the romaine, 1/3 cup Parmesan cheese and salad dressing. Divide among salad plates. Slice the steak; arrange steak and tomatoes on salads. Top with the croutons and the remaining Parmesan cheese.

YIELD: 6 SERVINGS.

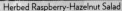
Herbed Raspberry-Hazelnut Salad

Grilled Steak Caesar Salad

Fiery Chicken Spinach Salad

Fiery Chicken Spinach Salad

PREP/TOTAL TIME: 20 MIN.

This hearty and colorful main-course salad is easy to throw together when I get home from work because it uses canned black beans and Mexicorn and packaged chicken breast strips. I sometimes add a can of ripe olives and cherry tomatoes from our garden.

Kati Spencer ✳ Taylorsville, Utah

- 6 frozen breaded spicy chicken breast strips, thawed
- 1 package (6 ounces) fresh baby spinach
- 1 medium tomato, cut into 12 wedges
- 1/2 cup chopped green pepper
- 1/2 cup fresh baby carrots
- 1 can (15 ounces) black beans, rinsed and drained
- 1 can (11 ounces) Mexicorn, drained
- 3 tablespoons salsa
- 3 tablespoons barbecue sauce
- 3 tablespoons prepared ranch salad dressing
- 2 tablespoons shredded Mexican cheese blend

Heat chicken strips in a microwave according to package directions. Meanwhile, arrange the spinach on individual plates; top with tomato, green pepper, carrots, beans and corn.

In a small bowl, combine the salsa, barbecue sauce and ranch dressing. Place chicken over salads. Drizzle with dressing; sprinkle with cheese. YIELD: 6 SERVINGS.

EDITOR'S NOTE: This recipe was tested in a 1,100-watt microwave.

Grilled Three-Potato Salad

PREP: 25 MIN. GRILL: 10 MIN.

Everyone in our extended family loves to cook, so I put together all of our favorite recipes in a cookbook to be handed down from generation to generation. This recipe comes from that cookbook. It's a delicious twist on traditional potato salad.

Suzette Jury ✳ Keene, California

- 3/4 pound Yukon Gold potatoes (about 3 medium)
- 3/4 pound red potatoes (about 3 medium)
- 1 medium sweet potato, peeled
- 1/2 cup thinly sliced green onions
- 1/4 cup canola oil
- 2 to 3 tablespoons white wine vinegar
- 1 tablespoon Dijon mustard

1 teaspoon salt
1/2 teaspoon celery seed
1/4 teaspoon pepper

Place all of the potatoes in a Dutch oven; cover with water. Bring to a boil. Reduce heat; cover and simmer for 15-20 minutes or until tender. Drain and rinse in cold water. Cut potatoes into 1-in. chunks.

Place the potatoes in a grill wok or basket. Grill, uncovered, over medium heat for 8-12 minutes or browned, stirring frequently. Transfer to a large salad bowl; add onions.

In a small bowl, whisk together the oil, vinegar, mustard, salt, celery seed and pepper. Drizzle over the potato mixture and toss to coat. Serve the potato salad warm or at room temperature. **YIELD: 6 SERVINGS.**

EDITOR'S NOTE: If you do not have a grill wok or basket, use a disposable foil pan. Poke holes in the bottom of the pan with a meat fork to allow liquid to drain.

Grilled Three-Potato Salad

Raspberry Poppy Seed Dressing

PREP/TOTAL TIME: **10 MIN.**

I simply love this creamy, fresh-tasting dressing! It's so quick to assemble and adds a summery gourmet touch when drizzled over a salad. I often serve it with lettuce or fresh spinach tossed with sliced strawberries and sugared almonds.

Kendra Stoller ✳ Kouts, Indiana

6 tablespoons red wine vinegar
1/2 cup plus 2 tablespoons sugar
1 teaspoon salt
1 teaspoon ground mustard
1 cup canola oil
1 cup fresh *or* frozen raspberries, thawed
1 teaspoon poppy seeds

In a blender, combine the vinegar, sugar, salt and mustard. While processing, gradually add oil in a steady stream. Add raspberries; cover and process until blended. Stir in poppy seeds. Serve immediately. Refrigerate the leftovers. **YIELD: 2 CUPS.**

Raspberry Poppy Seed Dressing

Grilled Apple Tossed Salad

Grilled Apple Tossed Salad

PREP: **15 MIN.** + **MARINATING** GRILL: **15 MIN.**

The grilled apples in this salad combine so well with the blue cheese, walnuts and balsamic dressing. I like to serve it on pink Depression glass dessert plates, which were passed down to me from my great-grandmother.

Paul Soska ✳ Toledo, Ohio

- 6 tablespoons olive oil
- 1/4 cup orange juice
- 1/4 cup white balsamic vinegar
- 1/4 cup minced fresh cilantro
- 2 tablespoons honey
- 1/2 teaspoon salt
- 1/2 teaspoon chili sauce
- 1 garlic clove, minced
- 2 large apples, cut into wedges
- 1 package (5 ounces) spring mix salad greens
- 1 cup walnut halves
- 1/2 cup crumbled blue cheese

For dressing, in a small bowl, combine the oil, juice, vinegar, cilantro, honey, salt, chili sauce and garlic. Pour 1/4 cup into a large resealable plastic bag; add apples. Seal bag and turn to coat; refrigerate for at least 10 minutes. Cover and chill remaining dressing until serving.

Drain the apples, reserving marinade for basting. Thread onto six metal or soaked wooden skewers. Grill apples, covered, over medium heat for 6-8 minutes or until golden brown, basting frequently. Turn and grill 6-8 minutes longer or until golden and tender.

In a large salad bowl, combine the greens, walnuts and blue cheese. Add the apples. Drizzle with reserved dressing and toss to coat. **YIELD: 4 SERVINGS.**

Asian Bulgur Rice Salad

🌿 Asian Bulgur Rice Salad

PREP: 15 MIN. + STANDING

Some people call me the "Queen of Wheat" because I'm always telling them how to use it in creative ways. This tasty salad is a hit with my family. I often add cooked chicken or seafood to turn it into a main dish.

Brenda Tew ✳ Shelley, Idaho

- 1/2 cup uncooked bulgur
- 1-1/2 cups boiling water
- 1-1/2 cups cooked long grain rice
- 1/2 cup thinly sliced celery
- 1/2 cup coarsely grated carrot
- 1/2 cup sliced green pepper
- 1/4 cup dried cranberries

SALAD DRESSING:

- 1/4 cup minced fresh parsley
- 1/4 cup rice vinegar
- 2 tablespoons olive oil
- 1 tablespoon finely chopped onion
- 1 tablespoon water
- 1 teaspoon sesame oil
- 1 teaspoon honey
- 1 garlic clove, minced
- 1/2 teaspoon *each* salt, ground mustard and Chinese five-spice powder
- 1/4 teaspoon pepper
- 9 cups torn mixed salad greens
- 1/4 cup sliced almonds, toasted

Place bulgur in a small bowl. Stir in boiling water. Cover and let stand for 30 minutes or until most of the liquid is absorbed. Drain and squeeze dry.

In a bowl, combine rice, celery, carrot, green pepper, cranberries and bulgur. In a bowl, whisk together parsley, vinegar, olive oil, onion, water, sesame oil, honey, garlic and seasonings.

Pour over rice mixture; toss gently to coat. Arrange greens on salad plates. Top with the rice mixture; sprinkle with the almonds. **YIELD: 6 SERVINGS.**

NUTRITION FACTS: 2/3 cup equals 203 calories, 8 g fat (1 g saturated fat), 0 cholesterol, 227 mg sodium, 30 g carbohydrate, 5 g fiber, 5 g protein. **DIABETIC EXCHANGES:** 1-1/2 starch, 1-1/2 fat, 1 vegetable.

Misty Melon Salad

Misty Melon Salad

PREP: 20 MIN. + CHILLING

The pleasant poppy seed dressing complements the mixture of cantaloupe, honeydew, strawberries and pineapple. This salad adds color to any meal.

Rita Reifenstein ✳ Evans City, Pennsylvania

- 1 medium cantaloupe, cut into cubes
- 1 medium honeydew, cut into cubes
- 2 cups fresh strawberries, halved
- 1 can (20 ounces) pineapple chunks
- 1/2 cup sugar
- 1 tablespoon chopped onion
- 1 teaspoon salt
- 1 teaspoon ground mustard
- 1/2 cup canola oil
- 2 to 3 teaspoons poppy seeds

In a large bowl, combine the cantaloupe, honeydew and strawberries. Drain pineapple, reserving 1/3 cup juice; set juice aside. Add pineapple to fruit mixture; cover and refrigerate until chilled.

For the dressing, in a blender, combine the sugar, onion, salt, mustard and reserved pineapple juice; cover and process until blended. While processing, gradually add the oil in a steady stream. Stir in the poppy seeds. Cover and refrigerate until chilled. Serve with the fruit salad. **YIELD: 10-12 SERVINGS.**

Mandarin Couscous Salad

🌿 Mandarin Couscous Salad

PREP: 25 MIN. + CHILLING

I help teach a healthy lifestyles program and often share this recipe. Instead of mandarin oranges, you can add fresh chopped oranges...or replace the peas with diced cucumber or green pepper.

Debbie Anderson ✳ Hillsdale, Michigan

1-1/3 cups water
   1 cup uncooked couscous
   1 can (11 ounces) mandarin oranges, drained
   1 cup frozen peas, thawed
 1/2 cup slivered almonds, toasted
 1/3 cup chopped red onion
   3 tablespoons cider vinegar
   2 tablespoons olive oil
   1 tablespoon sugar
 1/4 teaspoon salt
 1/4 teaspoon hot pepper sauce

Place water in a saucepan; bring to a boil. Stir in couscous. Cover and remove from the heat; let stand for 5 minutes. Fluff with a fork. Cover and refrigerate for at least 1 hour.

In a large bowl, combine the oranges, peas, almonds, onion and couscous. In a bowl, whisk together the vinegar, oil, sugar, salt and pepper sauce. Pour dressing over couscous mixture; toss to coat. **YIELD: 7 SERVINGS.**

NUTRITION FACTS: 3/4 cup equals 221 calories, 8 g fat (1 g saturated fat), 0 cholesterol, 108 mg sodium, 31 g carbohydrate, 4 g fiber, 6 g protein. **DIABETIC EXCHANGES:** 1-1/2 starch, 1-1/2 fat, 1/2 fruit.

🌙 Spicy Chicken Salad with Mango Salsa

PREP/TOTAL TIME: 30 MIN.

When I need a different weeknight meal, I pull out this salad. To make it in record time, I use fully cooked chicken strips, jarred mango, bottled vinaigrette and packaged, shredded cheese.

Jan Warren-Rucker
Clemmons, North Carolina

   2 cups chopped peeled mangoes
   1 medium red onion, chopped
 1/2 cup chopped sweet red pepper
 1/4 cup minced fresh cilantro
   1 jalapeno pepper, seeded and chopped
   2 tablespoons lime juice
   2 packages (9 ounces *each*) ready-to-use grilled chicken breast strips
   2 garlic cloves, minced
   2 teaspoons ground cumin
   1 teaspoon onion powder
   1 teaspoon chili powder
 1/4 teaspoon cayenne pepper
Dash salt
   2 tablespoons olive oil
   2 packages (8 ounces *each*) ready-to-serve European blend salad greens
 1/3 cup oil and vinegar salad dressing
   2 cups (8 ounces) shredded pepper Jack cheese
Tortilla chips

For salsa, in a large bowl, combine the mangoes, onion, red pepper, cilantro, jalapeno and lime juice; chill until serving.

In a large skillet, saute the chicken, garlic, cumin, onion powder, chili powder, cayenne and salt in oil until heated through.

Toss greens with dressing; divide among seven serving plates. Top with chicken mixture, mango salsa and cheese. Serve immediately with tortilla chips. **YIELD: 7 SERVINGS.**

EDITOR'S NOTE: When cutting hot peppers, disposable gloves are recommended. Avoid touching your face.

Apple Cider Gelatin Salad

PREP: 20 MIN. + CHILLING

Apple cider and crisp apples lend a hint of fall to this refreshing salad that's perfect for autumn and holiday gatherings. A neighbor lady shared the dish with me.

Cyndi Brinkhaus ✳ South Coast Metro, California

- 2 envelopes unflavored gelatin
- 1/2 cup cold water
- 2 cups apple cider *or* juice
- 1/2 cup sugar
- 1/3 cup lemon juice
- 1/4 teaspoon ground cloves

Dash salt

- 1 cup diced unpeeled apples
- 1/2 cup chopped walnuts
- 1/2 cup chopped celery

TOPPING:

- 3/4 cup sour cream
- 1/4 cup mayonnaise
- 1 tablespoon sugar

Ground cinnamon

Cinnamon sticks, optional

In a small bowl, sprinkle gelatin over cold water; let stand for 1 minute.

In a large saucepan, bring cider to a boil; stir in the gelatin mixture and sugar until dissolved. Stir in the lemon juice, cloves and salt. Pour into a large bowl. Refrigerate until slightly thickened, about 1 hour.

Fold in the apples, walnuts and celery. Pour into a 1-qt. dish or individual dishes. Refrigerate until firm, about 2 hours.

For topping, in a small bowl, combine the sour cream, mayonnaise and sugar until blended. Dollop over salad; sprinkle with cinnamon. Serve with cinnamon sticks if desired. **YIELD: 6 SERVINGS.**

Spicy Chicken Salad with Mango Salsa

Apple Cider Gelatin Salad

Hearty Pasta Salad

Hearty Pasta Salad

PREP: **20 MIN. + CHILLING**

When made with tricolor pasta, this is a colorful—and tasty—dish to take to any summer gathering.

Marcia Buchanan ✳ Philadelphia, Pennsylvania

> 2 cups uncooked spiral pasta
> 1 cup cubed pastrami, cooked turkey or roast beef
> 1/4 cup *each* chopped carrot, celery and onion
> 3/4 cup mayonnaise
> 1/4 cup grated Parmesan cheese
> 1/4 teaspoon salt
> 1/4 teaspoon pepper
> 1/4 teaspoon lemon juice

Cook pasta according to package directions; drain and rinse in cold water.

In a large bowl, combine the pasta, pastrami, carrot, celery and onion. Combine mayonnaise, Parmesan cheese, salt, pepper and lemon juice. Add to the pasta mixture; toss to coat. Cover and refrigerate for 1 hour or until serving. **YIELD: 4 SERVINGS.**

Warm Asparagus Spinach Salad

PREP/TOTAL TIME: **30 MIN.**

Spinach, cashews and pasta are mixed with roasted asparagus in this delightful spring salad. The mixture is topped with a light vinaigrette, seasoned with soy sauce and sprinkled with Parmesan cheese. I've used this recipe many times.

Kathleen Lucas ✳ Trumbull, Connecticut

> 1-1/2 pounds fresh asparagus, trimmed and cut into 1-inch pieces
> 2 tablespoons plus 1/2 cup olive oil, *divided*
> 1/4 teaspoon salt
> 1-1/2 pounds uncooked penne pasta
> 3/4 cup chopped green onions
> 6 tablespoons white wine vinegar
> 2 tablespoons soy sauce
> 1 package (6 ounces) fresh baby spinach

Warm Asparagus Spinach Salad

1 cup coarsely chopped cashews

1/2 cup shredded Parmesan cheese

Place asparagus in a 13-in. x 9-in. baking dish. Drizzle with 2 tablespoons oil; sprinkle with salt. Bake, uncovered, at 400° for 20-25 minutes or until crisp-tender, stirring every 10 minutes. Meanwhile, cook pasta according to package directions; drain.

In a blender, combine the onions, vinegar and soy sauce; cover and process until smooth. While processing, gradually add the remaining oil in a steady steam.

In a large salad bowl, combine pasta, spinach and asparagus. Drizzle with dressing; toss to coat. Sprinkle with cashews and Parmesan cheese. **YIELD: 14-16 SERVINGS.**

Spicy Pork Tenderloin Salad

Spicy Pork Tenderloin Salad

PREP: **20 MIN.** COOK: **35 MIN.**

A friend served this curry-flavored recipe at a luncheon, and I tweaked it to fit our tastes. Since it's a meal in one, it's perfect for weeknights and is also great for entertaining.

Pat Sellon ✳ Monticello, Wisconsin

4-1/2 teaspoons lime juice

1-1/2 teaspoons orange juice

1-1/2 teaspoons Dijon mustard

1/2 teaspoon curry powder

1/4 teaspoon salt

1/8 teaspoon pepper

2 tablespoons olive oil

SPICE RUB:

1/2 teaspoon salt

1/2 teaspoon ground cumin

1/2 teaspoon ground cinnamon

1/2 teaspoon chili powder

1/4 teaspoon pepper

1 pork tenderloin (1 pound)

2 teaspoons olive oil

1/3 cup packed brown sugar

6 garlic cloves, minced

1-1/2 teaspoons hot pepper sauce

1 package (6 ounces) fresh baby spinach

In a small bowl, whisk the juices, mustard and seasonings; gradually whisk in oil. Cover and refrigerate vinaigrette. Combine the salt, cumin, cinnamon, chili powder and pepper; rub over the meat.

In a ovenproof skillet, brown the meat on all sides in the oil, about 8 minutes. Combine the brown sugar, garlic and the hot pepper sauce; spread over meat.

Bake at 350° for 25-35 minutes or until a meat thermometer reads 160°. Let stand for 5 minutes before slicing.

Toss spinach with vinaigrette. Arrange the spinach on four salad plates; top with sliced pork. Drizzle with pan juices. **YIELD: 4 SERVINGS.**

NUTRITION FACTS: 3 ounces cooked pork with 1-3/4 cups spinach equals 301 calories, 13 g fat (3 g saturated fat), 63 mg cholesterol, 591 mg sodium, 22 g carbohydrate, 2 g fiber, 24 g protein. DIABETIC EXCHANGES: 3 lean meat, 1 starch, 1 vegetable, 1/2 fat.

Corn Medley Salad

1st place

Corn Medley Salad

PREP: **15 MIN.** COOK: **10 MIN. + CHILLING**

Whenever I need a dish to pass that's guaranteed to please, I put together this easy corn salad. Whether you serve it from a crystal dish, a ceramic crock or a plastic bowl, it will stand out as a mealtime highlight.

Judy Meckstroth ✴ New Bremen, Ohio

- 2/3 cup sugar
- 2/3 cup cider vinegar
- 2/3 cup canola oil
- 1 can (15-1/4 ounces) whole kernel corn, drained
- 1 can (15 ounces) whole baby corn, rinsed and drained, halved
- 1 can (11 ounces) yellow and white whole kernel corn, drained
- 1 can (11 ounces) white *or* shoepeg corn, drained
- 1 large sweet red pepper, chopped
- 1 medium red onion, chopped
- 4 to 5 celery ribs, sliced

Leaf lettuce, optional

In a small saucepan, combine the sugar, vinegar and oil. Cook over medium heat for 5 minutes, stirring until the sugar is completely dissolved. Cool completely.

In a bowl, combine the corn, red pepper, onion and celery. Add dressing and toss to coat. Cover and refrigerate overnight.

Stir well. Serve with a slotted spoon in a lettuce-lined bowl if desired. **YIELD: 10-12 SERVINGS.**

🍽 Holiday Gelatin Mold

PREP: **25 MIN. + CHILLING**

Because I care for a teenager with diabetes, I decided to change my annual Thanksgiving salad so she could have some.

Mareen Robinson ✴ Spanish Fork, Utah

- 1 package (.3 ounce) sugar-free lemon gelatin
- 1 package (.3 ounce) sugar-free strawberry gelatin
- 1 package (.3 ounce) sugar-free cherry gelatin
- 1-3/4 cups boiling water
- 1 can (20 ounces) unsweetened crushed pineapple
- 1 can (16 ounces) whole-berry cranberry sauce
- 1 medium navel orange, peeled and sectioned
- 3/4 cup reduced-fat whipped topping
- 1/4 cup fat-free sour cream

In a large bowl, dissolve the gelatins in boiling water. Drain the pineapple, reserving juice in a 2-cup measuring cup; add enough cold water to measure 2 cups. Stir into gelatin mixture.

Place the pineapple, cranberry sauce and orange in a food processor; cover and pulse until blended. Stir into gelatin mixture. Transfer to an 8-cup ring mold coated with cooking spray. Refrigerate until firm.

In a small bowl, combine whipped topping and sour cream. Unmold gelatin; serve with topping. **YIELD: 12 SERVINGS (3/4 CUP TOPPING).**

NUTRITION FACTS: 2/3 cup gelatin with 1 tablespoon topping equals 105 calories, 1 g fat (1 g saturated fat), 1 mg cholesterol, 62 mg sodium, 24 g carbohydrate, 2 g fiber, 3 g protein. **DIABETIC EXCHANGES:** 1 fruit, 1/2 starch.

Summary Chicken Salad

PREP: 10 MIN. COOK: 25 MIN. + CHILLING

I found this recipe many years ago in a church cookbook. It's special enough for a fancy dinner but simple enough to fix for a light lunch. There's a kick to the tangy citrus dressing, which even my picky son enjoys.

Nancy Whitford * Edwards, New York

- 4 boneless skinless chicken breast halves (4 ounces *each*)
- 1 can (14-1/2 ounces) chicken broth
- 6 cups torn mixed salad greens
- 2 cups halved fresh strawberries

CITRUS DRESSING:

- 1/2 cup fresh strawberries, hulled
- 1/3 cup orange juice
- 2 tablespoons canola oil
- 1 tablespoon lemon juice
- 2 teaspoons grated lemon peel
- 1 teaspoon sugar
- 1/2 teaspoon chili powder
- 1/4 teaspoon salt
- 1/4 teaspoon pepper
- 1/4 cup chopped walnuts, toasted

Place the chicken in a large skillet; add the broth. Bring to a boil. Reduce heat; cover and simmer for 20-25 minutes or until a meat thermometer reads 170°. Drain chicken; cover and refrigerate. In a large bowl, combine greens and sliced strawberries; refrigerate.

In a blender, combine hulled strawberries, orange juice, oil, lemon juice and lemon peel, sugar, chili powder, salt and pepper. Cover and process until mixture is smooth. Pour into a small saucepan. Bring to a boil. Reduce heat; simmer for 5-6 minutes until slightly thickened. Cool slightly.

Drizzle half of the dressing over greens and berries; toss to coat. Divide among four plates. Cut chicken into 1/8-in. slices; arrange over salads. Drizzle remaining dressing over chicken; sprinkle with walnuts. **YIELD: 4 SERVINGS.**

Holiday Gelatin Mold

Summer Chicken Salad

Smoked Turkey Pasta Salad

Smoked Turkey Pasta Salad

PREP: **30 MIN. + CHILLING**

I made a large version of this colorful pasta salad for a Super Bowl party, and all my guests loved it. They wanted to know what I put in it to make it taste so good.

Ana Colon ✳ Wisconsin Rapids, Wisconsin

- 1 cup uncooked tricolor spiral pasta
- 1/4 pound cubed deli smoked turkey
- 1 cup (4 ounces) cubed Monterey Jack cheese
- 1/2 small cucumber, thinly sliced and halved
- 1/3 cup chopped sweet red pepper
- 1 green onion, thinly sliced
- 3 tablespoons sour cream
- 2 tablespoons mayonnaise
- 1-1/2 teaspoons 2% milk
- 1 teaspoon honey
- 1 teaspoon Dijon mustard

Dash pepper

Cook pasta according to package directions; drain and rinse in cold water. In a serving bowl, combine the pasta, turkey, cheese, cucumber, red pepper and onion.

In a small bowl, whisk together the sour cream, mayonnaise, milk, honey, mustard and pepper. Pour over salad and toss to coat. Cover and refrigerate for at least 2 hours before serving. **YIELD: 2 SERVINGS.**

1st place

Confetti Broccoli Slaw

Confetti Broccoli Slaw

PREP: **15 MIN. + CHILLING**

With its flavorful dressing and flecks of tomato and green pepper, this pretty coleslaw is great for a variety of summertime meals. Instead of purchasing the broccoli coleslaw mix, you can use broccoli stalks—just peel them, then shred in a food processor. You'll want about 3 cups for this recipe.

Kathy Murphy ✳ Fort Thomas, Arizona

- 1 package (12 ounces) broccoli coleslaw mix
- 1 medium green pepper, chopped
- 1 medium tomato, seeded and chopped
- 1 small onion, finely chopped
- 1/2 teaspoon salt
- 1/4 teaspoon pepper

DRESSING:

- 1/2 cup mayonnaise
- 1/3 cup sugar
- 2 tablespoons cider vinegar
- 2 tablespoons ketchup
- 1 tablespoon canola oil
- 1-1/2 teaspoons prepared mustard
- 1 teaspoon lemon juice
- 1/8 teaspoon paprika
- 1/8 teaspoon pepper
- 1/8 teaspoon salt
- Dash garlic powder
- Dash hot pepper sauce

In a large bowl, combine the coleslaw mix, green pepper, tomato, onion, salt and pepper.

In a blender or food processor, combine the dressing ingredients; cover and process until blended. Pour over coleslaw and toss to coat. Cover and refrigerate for at least 2 hours before serving. **YIELD: 6 SERVINGS.**

Barley Corn Salad

Barley Corn Salad

PREP: **15 MIN. + CHILLING**

A great alternative to pasta salads, this decorative side dish adds refreshing herb flavor to corn, barley, and red and green peppers. Bring it to your next get-together and see how fast it disappears!

Mary Ann Kieffer ✳ Lawrence, Kansas

- 2 cups cooked medium pearl barley
- 2 cups frozen corn, thawed
- 1/2 cup chopped sweet red pepper
- 1/2 cup chopped green pepper
- 3 green onions, chopped
- 1 tablespoon minced fresh cilantro
- 2 tablespoons lemon juice
- 2 tablespoons canola oil
- 1/2 teaspoon salt
- 1/2 teaspoon dried thyme
- 1/8 teaspoon pepper

In a large bowl, combine barley, corn, peppers, onions and cilantro.

In a bowl, whisk together the lemon juice, oil, salt, thyme and pepper. Drizzle over salad and toss to coat. Cover and refrigerate for at least 2 hours before serving. **YIELD: 6 SERVINGS.**

NUTRITION FACTS: 2/3 cup equals 163 calories, 5 g fat (trace saturated fat), 0 cholesterol, 201 mg sodium, 29 g carbohydrate, 4 g fiber, 3 g protein. DIABETIC EXCHANGES: 1-1/2 starch, 1 vegetable, 1 fat.

Blue Cheese Pear Salad

🥗 Blue Cheese Pear Salad

PREP/TOTAL TIME: 20 MIN.

Serve this refreshing salad as a main course on hot days or as a side with grilled meat. It only takes a few minutes to prepare while the grill is warming. I first tried it at a restaurant and adopted it to our tastes.

Tina Green ✳ Albany, Oregon

- 3 tablespoons sugar
- 2 tablespoons chopped walnuts
- 1-1/2 cups torn Bibb *or* Boston lettuce
- 1/2 cup cubed cheddar cheese
- 1 medium pear, thinly sliced
- 1 slice sweet onion, separated into rings
- 2 tablespoons crumbled blue cheese
- 3 tablespoons poppy seed salad dressing

In a small heavy skillet, melt sugar over low heat. Add walnuts and stir to coat. Remove from the heat.

Divide lettuce between two serving plates; top with the cheddar cheese, pear and onion.

Sprinkle with blue cheese and sugared walnuts. Drizzle with dressing. **YIELD: 2 SERVINGS.**

🥗 Spring Greens With Berries

PREP/TOTAL TIME: 15 MIN.

My busy sister-in-law gave me this delightful salad recipe years ago, and it quickly became a favorite with my family—just as it is with hers. It's crisp, colorful, goes together in a snap and complements a variety of entrees.

Vikki Peck ✳ Poland, Ohio

- 2 packages (5 ounces *each*) spring mix salad greens
- 1 can (11 ounces) mandarin oranges, drained
- 3/4 cup sliced fresh strawberries
- 3/4 cup fresh raspberries
- 1/2 cup slivered almonds, toasted

ORANGE VINAIGRETTE:

1/4 cup canola oil
1 tablespoon red wine vinegar
1 tablespoon orange juice
1 tablespoon honey
1 teaspoon grated orange peel
1 teaspoon Dijon mustard
1/4 teaspoon salt
1/8 teaspoon pepper

In a large bowl, combine the greens, oranges, berries and almonds.

In a bowl, whisk together the vinaigrette ingredients. Drizzle over salad and toss to coat.
YIELD: 7 SERVINGS.

Spring Greens with Berries

Albacore Tuna Salad

PREP/TOTAL TIME: **15 MIN.**

There are so many great things about this recipe... sweet apples, golden raisins, celery, nuts, tuna and a tropical taste of pineapple that add up to a simply wonderful salad. And leftovers are as delicious as the first bite.

Barbara Moravek ✳ Jay, Florida

2 cans (8 ounces *each*) unsweetened crushed pineapple, drained
2 cans (5 ounces *each*) solid white tuna, drained
1 large apple, chopped
1 cup sliced celery
1 cup golden raisins
1/2 cup sliced almonds, toasted
1 cup mayonnaise
1 tablespoon lemon juice
Bread slices *or* lettuce leaves

In a large bowl, combine the pineapple, tuna, apple, celery, raisins and almonds. Combine mayonnaise and lemon juice; stir into tuna mixture. Spread on bread or serve on lettuce-lined plates. **YIELD: 5 SERVINGS.**

Albacore Tuna Salad

Special Sesame Chicken Salad

Special Sesame Chicken Salad

PREP: **30 MIN. + CHILLING**

With its delicious mix of crunchy peanuts, tangy dried cranberries and mandarin oranges, this colorful pasta salad is a definite crowd-pleaser. Water chestnuts and a teriyaki dressing give this main dish its Asian flair.

Carolee Ewell ✳ Santaquin, Utah

- 1 package (16 ounces) bow tie pasta
- 1 cup canola oil
- 2/3 cup white wine vinegar
- 2/3 cup teriyaki sauce
- 1/3 cup sugar
- 1/2 teaspoon pepper
- 3 cans (11 ounces *each*) mandarin oranges, drained
- 2 cans (8 ounces *each*) sliced water chestnuts, drained
- 2 cups cubed cooked chicken
- 1-1/3 cups honey roasted peanuts
- 1 package (9 ounces) fresh spinach, torn
- 1 package (6 ounces) dried cranberries
- 6 green onions, chopped
- 1/2 cup minced fresh parsley
- 1/4 cup sesame seeds, toasted

Cook the pasta according to package directions; drain and place in a very large bowl.

In a small bowl, combine the oil, vinegar, teriyaki sauce, sugar and pepper. Pour over the pasta and toss to coat. Cover and refrigerate for 2 hours.

Just before serving, add the remaining ingredients; gently toss to coat. YIELD: **22 SERVINGS (1 CUP EACH).**

Beef Fajita Salad

Beef Fajita Salad

PREP/TOTAL TIME: 30 MIN.

This easy salad features colorful peppers, beans, tomato and tender strips of beef. The beef marinates for only 10 minutes, but it gets great flavor from the lime juice, cilantro and chili powder.

Ardeena Harris ✳ Roanoke, Alabama

- 1/4 cup lime juice
- 2 tablespoons minced fresh cilantro
- 1 garlic clove, minced
- 1 teaspoon chili powder
- 3/4 pound boneless beef sirloin steak, cut into thin strips
- 1 medium green pepper, julienned
- 1 medium sweet red pepper, julienned
- 1 medium onion, sliced and halved
- 1 teaspoon olive oil
- 1 can (16 ounces) kidney beans, rinsed and drained
- 4 cups torn mixed salad greens
- 1 medium tomato, chopped
- 4 tablespoons fat-free sour cream
- 2 tablespoons salsa

In a large resealable plastic bag, combine the lime juice, cilantro, garlic and chili powder; add beef. Seal bag and turn to coat; refrigerate for 10 minutes, turning once.

Meanwhile, in a nonstick skillet, cook the peppers and onion in oil over medium-high heat for 5 minutes or until tender. Remove and keep warm. Add beef with marinade to the skillet; cook and stir for 4-5 minutes or until meat is tender and mixture comes to a boil. Add beans and pepper mixture; heat through.

Divide the salad greens and tomato among four bowls; top each with 1-1/4 cups of the beef mixture, 1 tablespoon sour cream and 1-1/2 teaspoons salsa. **YIELD: 4 SERVINGS.**

NUTRITION FACTS: 1 serving equals 291 calories, 6 g fat (2 g saturated fat), 50 mg cholesterol, 291 mg sodium, 34 g carbohydrate, 9 g fiber, 27 g protein. DIABETIC EXCHANGES: 2 lean meat, 2 vegetable, 1-1/2 starch.

Colorful Coleslaw

Colorful Coleslaw

PREP: 25 MIN. + CHILLING

Every time I prepare this salad, I adjust the ingredients a bit. This version tastes the best and has the fewest calories.

Jeanette Jones ✳ Muncie, Indiana

- 5 cups shredded cabbage
- 1 *each* medium green, sweet red and yellow pepper, julienned
- 2 cups julienned carrots
- 6 green onions, thinly sliced

DRESSING:

- 2/3 cup rice vinegar
- 1/4 cup olive oil

Sugar substitute equivalent to 1/3 cup sugar

- 1/4 cup reduced-fat creamy peanut butter
- 1 teaspoon salt
- 1 teaspoon minced fresh gingerroot
- 1/2 teaspoon pepper

In a large bowl, combine the cabbage, peppers, carrots and onions.

In a blender, combine dressing ingredients; cover and process until smooth. Drizzle over the vegetables and toss to coat. Cover; refrigerate for at least 1 hour. Toss; serve with a slotted spoon. **YIELD: 8 SERVINGS.**

EDITOR'S NOTE: This recipe was tested with Splenda no-calorie sweetener.

NUTRITION FACTS: 2/3 cup equals 153 calories, 10 g fat (1 g saturated fat), 0 cholesterol, 362 mg sodium, 15 g carbohydrate, 3 g fiber, 4 g protein. DIABETIC EXCHANGES: 2 vegetable, 2 fat.

In a large bowl, combine rice, chicken, apples, pepper, celery, onions, pecans and parsley.

In a bowl, whisk together the vinegar, oil, lemon juice, salt and pepper. Pour over the rice mixture and toss to coat. Serve immediately or refrigerate. Serve in a lettuce-lined bowl if desired. **YIELD: 9 SERVINGS.**

NUTRITION FACTS: 1 cup equals 236 calories, 11 g fat (1 g saturated fat), 26 mg cholesterol, 295 mg sodium, 23 g carbohydrate, 3 g fiber, 12 g protein. DIABETIC EXCHANGES: 1-1/2 fat, 1 starch, 1 lean meat, 1/2 fruit.

Raspberry Greek Salad

PREP/TOTAL TIME: **20 MIN.**

An interesting combination of sweet and salty flavors gives this Greek salad a delicious twist. And the tart chewiness of the dried cranberries makes a wonderful complement to the salty feta cheese. I often take this to work for lunch.

Carine Nadel ✳ Laguna Hills, California

- 2 packages (6 ounces *each*) ready-to-use grilled chicken breast strips
- 1 package (6 ounces) fresh baby spinach
- 1/2 pound sliced fresh mushrooms
- 1 medium cucumber, peeled and sliced
- 4 plum tomatoes, seeded and sliced
- 1/2 cup crumbled feta cheese
- 1/4 cup chopped Greek olives
- 1/4 cup dried cranberries
- 1/4 cup chopped red onion
- 1/3 cup raspberry vinaigrette
- 4 whole wheat pita breads (6 inches), cut into quarters and warmed, optional

In a large salad bowl, toss chicken, vegetables, cheese, olives, cranberries and onion. Just before serving, drizzle with vinaigrette; toss to coat. Serve with the pita bread if desired. **YIELD: 8 SERVINGS.**

Brown Rice Salad with Grilled Chicken

1st place

Brown Rice Salad with Grilled Chicken

PREP/TOTAL TIME: **20 MIN.**

This delightful dish is nutritious and simple to fix. It brightens up a buffet table, and I think it's a terrific way to use leftover chicken.

Glenda Harper ✳ Cable, Ohio

- 3 cups cooked brown rice
- 2 cups cubed grilled chicken breast
- 2 medium tart apples, diced
- 1 medium sweet red pepper, diced
- 2 celery ribs, finely chopped
- 2/3 cup chopped green onions
- 1/2 cup chopped pecans
- 3 tablespoons minced fresh parsley
- 1/4 cup cider vinegar
- 3 tablespoons canola oil
- 1 tablespoon lemon juice
- 1 teaspoon salt
- 1/4 teaspoon pepper
Lettuce leaves, optional

✿ Honey-Dijon Potato Salad

PREP: **10 MIN. + CHILLING** COOK: **15 MIN. + COOLING**

No matter which recipe I tried, my potato salad always turned out bland. So I came up with this creamy version that has plenty of pizzazz. It's so tangy and flavorful, you wouldn't realize it calls for fat-free honey-Dijon salad dressing. It's a favorite at picnics.

Kristie Kline Jones ✳ Douglas, Wyoming

Raspberry Greek Salad

2-1/4 **pounds red potatoes (about 14 small)**
   3 **tablespoons vinegar**
 3/4 **cup chopped green pepper**
 1/2 **cup chopped onion**
   5 **tablespoons chopped dill pickles**
   1 **teaspoon salt-free seasoning blend**
 1/4 **teaspoon pepper**
   1 **cup fat-free mayonnaise**
 1/3 **cup fat-free honey-Dijon salad dressing**
   2 **tablespoons Dijon mustard**
   2 **hard-cooked egg whites, chopped**

Place potatoes in a large saucepan and cover with water. Bring to a boil. Reduce heat; cover and cook for 15-20 minutes or until tender. Drain and cool.

Cube the potatoes and place in a large bowl. Sprinkle with vinegar. Add green pepper, onion, pickles, seasoning blend and pepper.

In a small bowl, combine the mayonnaise, salad dressing, mustard and egg whites. Pour over potato mixture; toss to coat. Cover and refrigerate for at least 1 hour. **YIELD: 8 SERVINGS.**

NUTRITION FACTS: 3/4 cup equals 147 calories, 1 g fat (trace saturated fat), 3 mg cholesterol, 439 mg sodium, 30 g carbohydrate, 4 g fiber, 4 g protein. DIABETIC EXCHANGES: 2 starch, 1 vegetable.

Honey-Dijon Potato Salad

Black-Eyed Pea Salad

Black-Eyed Pea Salad

PREP: **15 MIN. + CHILLING**

This is a wonderful recipe to serve any time of the year, but it's especially good with ripe cherry tomatoes picked fresh from the garden.

Ruth Hunter ✳ Newton, Pennsylvania

- 1 package (16 ounces) frozen black-eyed peas
- 1 package (10 ounces) frozen peas, thawed
- 4 green onions, sliced
- 2 celery ribs, chopped
- 1 medium sweet yellow pepper, diced
- 2 medium carrots, coarsely chopped
- 1/3 cup chopped fresh mint
- 1/2 cup olive oil
- 1/3 cup white wine vinegar
- 2 garlic cloves, minced
- 1 teaspoon salt
- 1/4 teaspoon pepper
- 1 cup halved cherry tomatoes
- 1/4 pound sliced bacon, cooked and crumbled

Cook the black-eyed peas according to package directions; drain and place in a large bowl. Stir in peas, onions, celery, yellow pepper, carrots and mint.

In a bowl, whisk together the oil, vinegar, garlic, salt and pepper. Drizzle over salad; toss to coat. Cover and refrigerate overnight. Top with tomatoes and bacon. **YIELD: 10-12 SERVINGS.**

Broccoli Waldorf Salad

Broccoli Waldorf Salad

PREP/TOTAL TIME: **15 MIN.**

This combination of apples, raisins and pecans jazzes up broccoli florets in this summery side dish.

Vicki Roehrick ✳ Chubbuck, Idaho

- 6 cups fresh broccoli florets
- 1 large red apple, chopped
- 1/2 cup raisins
- 1/4 cup chopped pecans
- 1/2 cup coleslaw dressing

In a large serving bowl, combine the broccoli, apple, raisins and pecans. Drizzle with dressing; toss to coat. Refrigerate leftovers. **YIELD: 10 SERVINGS.**

Strawberry Salad Dressing

🕐 Strawberry Salad Dressing

PREP/TOTAL TIME: **10 MIN.**

A bit of honey perfectly balances puckery raspberry vinegar with sweet strawberries in this homemade dressing. Drizzle it over mixed greens of your choice and enjoy!

Rebekah Hubbard ✳ Las Vegas, Nevada

- 1 package (20 ounces) frozen unsweetened strawberries, thawed
- 1/2 cup water
- 3 tablespoons raspberry vinegar
- 2 tablespoons honey
- 2 teaspoons canola oil
- 1 teaspoon reduced-sodium soy sauce
- 1/4 teaspoon salt
- 1/4 teaspoon dried thyme
- 1/4 teaspoon pepper

Torn mixed salad greens and sliced onion

In a blender, combine the strawberries, water, vinegar, honey, oil, soy sauce and seasonings. Cover and process until smooth. Serve over greens and onion. Store in the refrigerator. **YIELD: 3 CUPS.**

NUTRITION FACTS: 2 tablespoons dressing equals 17 calories, trace fat (trace saturated fat), 0 cholesterol, 33 mg sodium, 4 g carbohydrate, 1 g fiber, trace protein. **DIABETIC EXCHANGE:** Free food.

Tangerine Tossed Salad

Tangerine Tossed Salad

PREP/TOTAL TIME: **40 MIN.**

I learned to cook from my mother when I was a young girl. I like the combination of sweet tangerines and crunchy, caramelized almonds in this recipe.

Helen Musenbrock ✳ O'Fallon, Missouri

- 1/2 cup sliced almonds
- 3 tablespoons sugar, *divided*
- 2 medium tangerines *or* navel oranges
- 6 cups torn lettuce
- 3 green onions, chopped
- 2 tablespoons cider vinegar
- 2 tablespoons olive oil
- 1/4 teaspoon salt
- 1/4 teaspoon pepper

In a small skillet, cook and stir the almonds and 2 tablespoons sugar over medium-low heat for 25-30 minutes or until the sugar is melted and the almonds are toasted. Remove from the heat. Peel and section the tangerines, reserving 1 tablespoon juice.

In a large bowl, combine the lettuce, onions, tangerines and almonds. In a small bowl, whisk together the vinegar, oil, salt, pepper, reserved juice and remaining sugar. Drizzle over salad and toss to coat. **YIELD: 6 SERVINGS.**

Summer Avocado Salad

PREP/TOTAL TIME: **30 MIN.**

Garden-fresh veggies, creamy avocado and a sprinkling of feta cheese make this chunky salad a healthy summer standout!

Deborah Williams ✳ Peoria, Arizona

1-1/2 teaspoons lemon juice

1-1/2 teaspoons olive oil

Dash garlic powder

- 1/2 cup chopped seeded peeled cucumber
- 1/3 cup chopped sweet yellow pepper
- 6 cherry tomatoes, seeded and quartered
- 2 tablespoons finely chopped sweet onion
- 1 tablespoon minced fresh basil
  or 1 teaspoon dried basil

1 medium ripe avocado, peeled and chopped

2 tablespoons crumbled feta cheese

Bibb lettuce leaves, optional

In a small bowl, combine the lemon juice, oil and garlic powder. Add the cucumber, pepper, tomatoes, onion and basil; toss to coat. Cover and refrigerate for 15-20 minutes.

Add the avocado; toss gently. Sprinkle with feta cheese. Serve immediately on lettuce-lined plates if desired. **YIELD: 2 SERVINGS.**

Summer Avocado Salad

Curried Rice Salad

PREP: 10 MIN. + CHILLING

Rice is truly one of the world's most versatile foods. This flavorful salad makes a nice dish for lunch.

Lula Young ✳ Newport, Arkansas

1 can (20 ounces) pineapple tidbits

2 cups cooked rice, cooled

2 cups cubed cooked chicken

1/2 cup chopped celery

1/3 cup slivered almonds, toasted

1/3 cup raisins

1/4 cup chopped green onions

2/3 cup mayonnaise

1 tablespoon Dijon mustard

3/4 teaspoon curry powder

1/4 teaspoon salt

Lettuce leaves, optional

Drain pineapple, reserving juice; set aside 1 cup pineapple and 3 tablespoons juice (refrigerate remaining pineapple for another use).

In a large bowl, combine the rice, chicken, celery, almonds, raisins, green onions and the reserved pineapple.

In a small bowl, combine the mayonnaise, mustard, curry powder, salt and reserved juice. Gently stir into the rice mixture. Cover and refrigerate for at least 1 hour. Serve in a lettuce-lined bowl if desired. **YIELD: 8 SERVINGS.**

Curried Rice Salad

Polynesian Shrimp Salad

PREP: 20 MIN. + CHILLING

Pineapple is one of our state's best-known products. It's delicious paired with shrimp and pasta in this crowd-pleasing salad, which is great for luncheons.

Elaine Carncross ✳ Hilo, Hawaii

- 1 can (20 ounces) pineapple chunks
- 2 teaspoons cornstarch
- 1/2 to 1 teaspoon curry powder
- 1/8 teaspoon salt
- 1/8 teaspoon pepper
- 1/3 cup mayonnaise
- 1/3 cup sour cream
- 1 pound cooked medium shrimp, peeled and deveined
- 2 cups cooked medium pasta shells
- 1 can (8 ounces) sliced water chestnuts, drained
- 1/4 cup chopped sweet red pepper

Drain pineapple, reserving 3/4 cup juice; set pineapple aside. In a small saucepan, combine the cornstarch, curry powder, salt, pepper and reserved pineapple juice until smooth. Bring to a boil; cook and stir for 1 minute or until thickened. Remove from the heat; cool to room temperature. Stir in the mayonnaise and sour cream.

In a large bowl, combine the shrimp, pasta, water chestnuts, red pepper and reserved pineapple. Add dressing and toss to coat. Cover and refrigerate for at least 2 hours before serving.
YIELD: 6-8 SERVINGS.

Creamy Chicken Salad

Creamy Chicken Salad

PREP/TOTAL TIME: 15 MIN.

I modified the original recipe for this chicken salad to make it healthier. The ingredients are so flavorful that my changes didn't take away from the taste. This refreshing salad never lasts long at our house. Even if I double the recipe, my husband asks, "Why didn't you make more?"

Kristi Abernathy ✳ Lewistown, Montana

- 2 cups cubed cooked chicken breast
- 1 cup cooked small ring pasta
- 1 cup halved seedless red grapes
- 1 can (11 ounces) mandarin oranges, drained
- 3 celery ribs, chopped

Polynesian Shrimp Salad

Hawaiian Ham Salad

1/2 cup sliced almonds
1 tablespoon grated onion
1 cup reduced-fat mayonnaise
1 cup reduced-fat whipped topping
1/4 teaspoon salt
Lettuce leaves, optional

In a large bowl, combine the chicken, pasta, grapes, oranges, celery, almonds and onion.

In a small bowl, combine the mayonnaise, whipped topping and salt. Add to the chicken mixture; stir to coat. Serve in a lettuce-lined bowl if desired. **YIELD: 6 SERVINGS.**

NUTRITION FACTS: 1 cup equals 261 calories, 13 g fat (0 saturated fat), 38 mg cholesterol, 307 mg sodium, 25 g carbohydrate, 2 g fiber, 11 g protein. DIABETIC EXCHANGES: 1-1/2 fat, 1 starch, 1 meat, 1/2 fruit.

Hawaiian Ham Salad

PREP: **15 MIN. + CHILLING**

There's plenty of flavor and crunch in this tasty salad. I like to use both red and green apples, and sometimes I substitute celery for the water chestnuts.

Vickie Lowrey ✳ Fallon, Nevada

1 can (8 ounces) unsweetened pineapple chunks
3 cups cooked brown rice
2 cups cubed fully cooked ham
1 can (8 ounces) sliced water chestnuts, drained and halved
1/4 cup finely chopped red onion
1/2 cup plain yogurt
1/2 teaspoon salt
1 medium apple, chopped
Lettuce leaves
1/3 cup chopped macadamia nuts, toasted
1/4 cup flaked coconut, toasted

Drain pineapple, reserving 1 tablespoon juice. In a large bowl, combine the pineapple, rice, ham, water chestnuts and onion. Cover and refrigerate for at least 2 hours.

In a small bowl, combine the yogurt, salt and reserved pineapple juice. Pour over the ham mixture and toss to coat. Stir in apple.

Serve on lettuce-lined plates; sprinkle with macadamia nuts and coconut. **YIELD: 4 SERVINGS.**

Cranberry-Chutney Turkey Salad

🕐 🖐 Cranberry-Chutney Turkey Salad

PREP/TOTAL TIME: 15 MIN.

Dried cranberries give this refreshing salad sweetness while chopped pecans add a pleasant crunch. Whether served on a lettuce leaf or stuffed inside a pita, it makes a perfect lunch or midday snack.

Andrea Yacyk ✳ Brigantine, New Jersey

- 3 cups diced cooked turkey breast
- 1/2 cup dried cranberries
- 1/3 cup chopped pecans
- 1/3 cup finely chopped onion
- 1/3 cup finely chopped green pepper
- 1/2 cup fat-free mayonnaise
- 1/2 cup reduced-fat sour cream
- 1 tablespoon lemon juice
- 1/2 teaspoon ground ginger
- 1/8 teaspoon cayenne pepper

In a large bowl, combine the turkey, cranberries, pecans, onion and green pepper.

In a small bowl, combine the mayonnaise, sour cream, lemon juice, ginger and cayenne. Pour over turkey mixture; stir gently to coat. Cover and refrigerate until serving. **YIELD: 6 SERVINGS.**

NUTRITION FACTS: 2/3 cup equals 226 calories, 8 g fat (2 g saturated fat), 69 mg cholesterol, 214 mg sodium, 15 g carbohydrate, 2 g fiber, 23 g protein. **DIABETIC EXCHANGES:** 3 very lean meat, 1 fat, 1/2 starch, 1/2 fruit.

Red, White and Bleu Slaw

🕐 Red, White and Bleu Slaw

PREP/TOTAL TIME: 10 MIN.

One of my favorite all-time recipes is this refreshing salad perfect for Fourth of July celebrations—or any time at all. The blend of flavors is wonderful. I use this recipe as often as I can...it's just simply the best!

Bonnie Hawkins ✳ Elkhorn, Wisconsin

- 6 cups angel hair coleslaw
- 12 cherry tomatoes, halved
- 3/4 cup coleslaw salad dressing
- 3/4 cup crumbled blue cheese, *divided*
- 1/2 cup real bacon bits

In a large bowl, combine the coleslaw, tomatoes, salad dressing and 1/2 cup blue cheese. Cover and refrigerate until serving. Just before serving, sprinkle with bacon bits and remaining cheese. **YIELD: 6 SERVINGS.**

Chicken Tortilla Soup, PAGE 110

> " *Chock-full of veggies and autumn color, this soup is ideal for using up fresh garden bounty. Broiling the chicken and vegetables adds richness and wonderful flavor.* "
>
>
>
> **Kathy Averbeck**
> Dousman, Wisconsin
>
>

SOUPS & CHILI

DO YOU HAVE A WINNING RECIPE?

Visit us @
tasteofhome
.com

soups & chili

Hearty Beef Vegetable Soup

PREP: 20 MIN. COOK: 2-1/4 HOURS

My husband's stew-like soup is loaded with nutritious ingredients but is easy to prepare. It gets its kick from green chilies. He makes wonderful bread and breadsticks to serve with it.

Mrs. Sherman Snowball ✳ Salt Lake City, Utah

- 3 tablespoons all-purpose flour
- 1/2 teaspoon salt
- 1/4 teaspoon pepper
- 1 pound beef stew meat, cut into 1/2-inch cubes
- 2 tablespoons olive oil
- 1 can (14-1/2 ounces) Italian diced tomatoes
- 1 can (8 ounces) tomato sauce
- 2 tablespoons red wine vinegar
- 2 tablespoons Worcestershire sauce
- 3 garlic cloves, minced
- 1 teaspoon dried oregano
- 3 cups hot water
- 4 medium potatoes, peeled and cubed
- 6 medium carrots, sliced
- 2 medium turnips, peeled and cubed
- 1 medium zucchini, halved lengthwise and sliced
- 1 medium green pepper, julienned
- 1 cup sliced fresh mushrooms
- 1 medium onion, chopped
- 1 can (4 ounces) chopped green chilies
- 2 tablespoons sugar

Hearty Beef Vegetable Soup

In a large resealable plastic bag, combine the flour, salt and pepper. Add beef, a few pieces at a time, and shake to coat.

In a Dutch oven, brown the beef in oil over medium-high heat. Stir in the tomatoes, tomato sauce, vinegar, Worcestershire sauce, garlic and oregano. Bring to a boil. Reduce heat; cover and simmer for 1 hour.

Stir in the remaining ingredients. Bring to a boil. Reduce heat; cover and simmer for 1 hour or until meat and vegetables are tender. **YIELD: 8 SERVINGS (ABOUT 2-1/2 QUARTS).**

Rocky Ford Chili

Rocky Ford Chili

PREP/TOTAL TIME: **10 MIN.**

When my brother and sister were in grade school in little Rocky Ford, Colorado, this comforting chili dish was served in the school cafeteria. My siblings described it to my mother so she could duplicate it at home. We all enjoy preparing it for our own families now.

Karen Golden * Phoenix, Arizona

- 2 cans (14.3 ounces *each*) chili with beans
- 1 package (10 ounces) frozen corn
- 4 cups corn chips
- 1 cup shredded lettuce
- 1 cup (4 ounces) shredded Mexican cheese blend
- 1 can (2-1/4 ounces) sliced ripe olives, drained
- 1/4 cup sour cream
- 1/4 cup salsa

In a large microwave-safe bowl, microwave chili and corn on high for 2-4 minutes or until heated through. Place corn chips in four large soup bowls; top with chili mixture, lettuce, cheese, olives, sour cream and salsa. **YIELD: 4 SERVINGS.**

EDITOR'S NOTE: This recipe was tested in a 1,100-watt microwave.

Hearty Turkey Vegetable Soup

PREP: **20 MIN.** COOK: **50 MIN.**

I found this recipe on the Internet, but it was too high in fat. After experimenting, I created a more nutritious version. I often double this chili-like soup to freeze or to share with friends.

Julie Anderson * Bloomington, Illinois

- 1 pound lean ground turkey
- 1 medium onion, chopped
- 2 small zucchini, quartered lengthwise and sliced
- 1 large carrot, cut into 1-inch julienne strips
- 3 cans (14 ounces *each*) reduced-sodium beef broth
- 1 jar (26 ounces) garden-style pasta sauce *or* meatless spaghetti sauce
- 1 can (16 ounces) kidney beans, rinsed and drained
- 1 can (15-1/2 ounces) great northern beans, rinsed and drained
- 1 can (14-1/2 ounces) Italian diced tomatoes, undrained
- 1 tablespoon dried parsley flakes
- 2 teaspoons dried oregano
- 1 teaspoon pepper
- 1 teaspoon hot pepper sauce
- 1 cup uncooked small shell pasta

In a Dutch oven coated with cooking spray, cook turkey and onion over medium heat until meat is no longer pink; drain. Add zucchini and carrot; cook and stir 1 minute longer. Stir in the broth, pasta sauce, beans, tomatoes, parsley, oregano, pepper and hot pepper sauce.

Bring to a boil. Reduce heat; cover and simmer for 45 minutes. Meanwhile, cook pasta according to package directions; drain. Just before serving, stir in the pasta. **YIELD: 10 SERVINGS (3-3/4 QUARTS).**

NUTRITION FACTS: 1-1/2 cups equals 242 calories, 4 g fat (1 g saturated fat), 38 mg cholesterol, 888 mg sodium, 34 g carbohydrate, 7 g fiber, 17 g protein. DIABETIC EXCHANGES: 2 lean meat, 2 vegetable, 1-1/2 starch.

Bacon Clam Chowder

PREP: 15 MIN. COOK: 25 MIN.

Chopping the clams into tiny pieces adds big flavor to this full-bodied chowder. Everyone says it's the best they've ever tasted. I like to serve it with garlic bread or a side salad.

Betty Lineaweaver ✴ Paradise, California

- 1 can (6-1/2 ounces) minced clams
- 1 cup reduced-sodium chicken broth
- 1 medium potato, peeled and cubed
- 1/2 cup chopped celery
- 1/4 cup chopped onion
- 1/2 teaspoon chicken bouillon granules
- 1/4 teaspoon dried thyme
- 1 tablespoon cornstarch
- 1/2 cup half-and-half cream
- 1-1/2 teaspoons butter
- Dash cayenne pepper
- 2 bacon strips, cooked and crumbled

Hearty Turkey Vegetable Soup

Drain clams, reserving juice; set aside. Place the clams in a food processor; cover and process until finely chopped. Set aside.

In a large saucepan, combine the broth, potato, celery, onion, bouillon and thyme. Bring to a boil. Reduce heat; simmer, uncovered, for 10-12 minutes or until vegetables are tender. Stir in the reserved clam juice.

Combine the cornstarch and cream until smooth; gradually stir into soup. Bring to a boil; cook and stir for 2 minutes or until thickened. Stir in the butter, cayenne and clams. Cook and stir over medium heat for 3-4 minutes or until heated through. Garnish with the bacon. **YIELD: 2 SERVINGS.**

Bacon Clam Chowder

Refried Bean Soup

⊘ Refried Bean Soup

PREP/TOTAL TIME: **25 MIN.**

This fast and simple dish combines the ease of soup with the heartiness of chili. It's a perfect filler-upper on nippy afternoons and a great last-minute lunch. If you like it spicier, use medium or hot green chilies instead of mild.

Darlene Brenden ✳ Salem, Oregon

1 can (16 ounces) spicy fat-free refried beans
1 can (15-1/4 ounces) whole kernel corn, drained
1 can (15 ounces) black beans, rinsed and drained
1 can (14-1/2 ounces) chicken broth
1 can (14-1/2 ounces) stewed tomatoes, cut up
1/2 cup water
1 can (4 ounces) chopped green chilies
1/4 cup salsa
Tortilla chips

In a large saucepan, combine the refried beans, corn, black beans, broth, tomatoes, water, chilies and salsa. Bring to a boil. Reduce heat; simmer, uncovered, for 8-10 minutes or until heated through. Serve with tortilla chips. **YIELD: 8 SERVINGS (2 QUARTS).**

Chilled Berry Soup

PREP: **10 MIN. + CHILLING**

I sampled a cool strawberry soup while visiting Walt Disney World. I enjoyed it so much that the restaurant gave me the recipe, but I eventually found this combination, which I like even better. The ginger ale adds a special zing.

Lisa Watson ✳ Sparta, Michigan

1 quart fresh strawberries, hulled
1/3 cup ginger ale
1/4 cup milk
1/3 cup sugar
1 tablespoon lemon juice
1 teaspoon vanilla extract
1 cup (8 ounces) sour cream

Place strawberries in a food processor; cover and process until pureed. Add the ginger ale, milk, sugar, lemon juice and vanilla; cover and process until blended.

Pour into a large bowl; whisk in the sour cream until smooth. Cover and refrigerate until soup is thoroughly chilled, about 2 hours. **YIELD: 4 SERVINGS.**

Garlic Butternut Bisque

PREP: **40 MIN.** COOK: **30 MIN.**

With its pleasant squash and garlic flavor and golden-orange color, this rich and creamy soup is sure to be a hit whether you serve it for an everyday meal or a special holiday dinner.

Della Clarke ✳ Vista, California

Chilled Berry Soup

- 2 whole garlic bulbs
- 1 teaspoon olive oil
- 3 large onions, chopped
- 3/4 cup chopped carrots
- 1/2 cup chopped celery
- 3/4 cup butter, *divided*
- 4 pounds butternut squash, peeled, seeded and cubed (about 8 cups)
- 6 cups chicken broth
- 3 tablespoons chopped fresh sage, *divided*
- 1/2 cup plus 1 tablespoon heavy whipping cream, *divided*
- 1-1/2 teaspoons salt
- 1/4 teaspoon pepper

Remove papery outer skin from garlic (do not peel or separate cloves). Cut tops off bulbs; brush with oil. Wrap each in heavy-duty foil. Bake at 425° for 30-35 minutes or until softened. Cool 10-15 minutes.

Meanwhile, in a Dutch oven or stockpot, saute the onions, carrots and celery in 1/2 cup butter until tender. Add the squash, broth and 2 tablespoons sage. Bring to a boil. Reduce heat; simmer, uncovered, for 25-30 minutes or until squash is tender.

Squeeze softened garlic into a small bowl; mash with a fork. Stir into squash mixture. Cool slightly. Puree squash mixture in batches in a blender; return to pan. Stir in 1/2 cup cream, salt and pepper and remaining butter; heat through. Garnish with remaining cream and sage. **YIELD: 9 SERVINGS (3 QUARTS).**

Garlic Butternut Bisque

Black Bean Soup with Fruit Salsa

🍴 Black Bean Soup with Fruit Salsa

PREP: 20 MIN. COOK: 20 MIN.

Flavorful and filling, this hearty soup is laced with a hint of lime and has a zesty Southwestern flair. It's really a meal in itself. Fresh fruit salsa makes an unusual but perfect topping!

Michaela Rosenthal
Woodland Hills, California

SALSA:
- 1/4 cup diced seeded peeled cucumber
- 1/4 cup diced peeled mango
- 1/4 cup diced fresh pineapple
- 2 tablespoons chopped sweet onion
- 4-1/2 teaspoons lime juice
- 1-1/2 teaspoons grated lime peel
- 1-1/2 teaspoons minced fresh cilantro
- 1/4 teaspoon chopped seeded jalapeno pepper

SOUP:
- 3 bacon strips, diced
- 3/4 cup chopped red onion
- 1 Anaheim pepper, seeded and chopped
- 2 garlic cloves, minced
- 2 cups reduced-sodium chicken broth
- 1 can (15 ounces) black beans, rinsed and drained
- 4 teaspoons lime juice
- 1 teaspoon ground cumin
- 1/2 teaspoon lemon-pepper seasoning
- 1/2 teaspoon ground coriander

For salsa, combine the salsa ingredients in a small bowl; set aside. In a saucepan, saute bacon and onion until bacon is crisp and onion is tender. Add Anaheim pepper and garlic; saute for 2 minutes. Stir in the remaining ingredients. Bring to a boil. Reduce heat; simmer, uncovered, for 10 minutes. Cool slightly.

Puree half of the soup in a blender; return all to the pan. Bring to a boil. Reduce heat; simmer for 5 minutes. Serve with the fruit salsa.
YIELD: 2 SERVINGS.

EDITOR'S NOTE: When cutting hot peppers, disposable gloves are recommended. Avoid touching your face.

Kielbasa Cabbage Soup

◐ Kielbasa Cabbage Soup

PREP/TOTAL TIME: **30 MIN.**

A friend brought samples of this delicious dish to a soup-tasting class sponsored by our extension homemakers club. It was a great hit with my family. The mix of sausage, apples and vegetables makes a different and tasty combination.

Marcia Wolff ✳ Rolling Prairie, Indiana

- 3 cups coleslaw mix
- 2 medium carrots, chopped
- 1/2 cup chopped onion
- 1/2 cup chopped celery
- 1/2 teaspoon caraway seeds
- 2 tablespoons butter
- 1 carton (32 ounces) chicken broth
- 3/4 to 1 pound smoked kielbasa *or* Polish sausage, cut into 1/2-inch pieces
- 2 medium unpeeled Golden Delicious apples, chopped
- 1/4 teaspoon pepper
- 1/8 teaspoon salt

In a large saucepan, saute the coleslaw mix, carrots, onion, celery and caraway seeds in butter for 5-8 minutes or until vegetables are crisp-tender. Stir in the remaining ingredients.

Bring soup to a boil. Reduce the heat; simmer, uncovered, for 20-30 minutes; stir occasionally. **YIELD: 6 SERVINGS (2 QUARTS).**

Minestrone with Italian Sausage

PREP: **25 MIN.** COOK: **1 HOUR**

I make this zippy, satisfying soup all the time, and it's my dad's favorite. The recipe makes a lot, and I have found that it freezes well and is just as great reheated.

Linda Reis ✳ Salem, Oregon

- 1 pound bulk Italian sausage
- 1 large onion, chopped
- 2 large carrots, chopped
- 2 celery ribs, chopped
- 1 medium leek (white portion only), chopped
- 3 garlic cloves, minced

Minestrone with Italian Sausage

- 1 medium zucchini, cut into 1/2-inch pieces
- 1/4 pound fresh green beans, trimmed and cut into 1/2-inch pieces
- 6 cups beef broth
- 2 cans (14-1/2 ounces *each*) diced tomatoes with basil, oregano and garlic
- 3 cups shredded cabbage
- 1 teaspoon dried basil
- 1 teaspoon dried oregano
- 1/4 teaspoon pepper
- 1 can (15 ounces) garbanzo beans *or* chickpeas, rinsed and drained
- 1/2 cup uncooked small pasta shells
- 3 tablespoons minced fresh parsley
- 1/3 cup grated Parmesan cheese

In a Dutch oven, cook sausage and onion over medium heat until meat is no longer pink; drain. Stir in the carrots, celery, leek and garlic; cook for 3 minutes. Add zucchini and green beans; cook 2 minutes longer.

Stir in the broth, tomatoes, cabbage, basil, oregano and pepper. Bring to a boil. Reduce heat; cover and simmer for 45 minutes.

Return to a boil. Stir in the garbanzo beans, pasta and parsley. Cook for 6-9 minutes or until pasta is tender. Serve with cheese. **YIELD: 11 SERVINGS (ABOUT 3 QUARTS).**

Florentine Chicken Soup

2 tablespoons pine nuts, toasted
1 tablespoon shredded Parmesan cheese

Cook the pasta according to package directions. Meanwhile, in a large saucepan, saute the chicken, spinach, red peppers, rosemary, garlic powder and pepper in butter until spinach is wilted. Stir in broth, Alfredo sauce and pesto; cook for 4-5 minutes or until heated through.

Drain pasta and add to the soup. Sprinkle with pine nuts and Parmesan cheese. YIELD: 5 SERVINGS.

Florentine Chicken Soup

PREP/TOTAL TIME: **30 MIN.**

My husband loves Alfredo sauce, so I'm always looking for new ways to use it. This easy-to-make soup is wonderful with crusty Italian bread and a tomato-mozzarella-basil salad. Best of all, it's the perfect amount for two of us...with a little left over for lunch the next day.

Cindie Henf ✳ Sebastian, Florida

1 cup uncooked penne pasta
1 package (6 ounces) ready-to-use chicken breast cuts
4 cups chopped fresh spinach
1 jar (7 ounces) roasted sweet red peppers, drained and sliced
3 fresh rosemary sprigs, chopped
1/2 teaspoon garlic powder
1/4 teaspoon pepper
1 tablespoon butter
1-1/2 cups reduced-sodium chicken broth
3/4 cup Alfredo sauce
3 tablespoons prepared pesto

Mexican Shrimp Bisque

PREP/TOTAL TIME: **30 MIN.**

I enjoy both Cajun and Mexican cuisine, and this rich, elegant soup combines the best of both. I serve it with a crispy green salad and glass of white wine for a simple but very special meal.

Karen Harris ✳ Castle Rock, Colorado

1/2 cup chopped onion
2 garlic cloves, minced
1 tablespoon olive oil
1 tablespoon all-purpose flour
1 cup water
1/2 cup heavy whipping cream
1 tablespoon chili powder
2 teaspoons chicken bouillon granules
1/2 teaspoon ground cumin
1/2 teaspoon ground coriander
1/2 pound uncooked medium shrimp, peeled and deveined
1/2 cup sour cream
Fresh cilantro and cubed avocado, optional

In a large saucepan, saute onion and garlic in oil until tender. Stir in flour until blended. Stir in the water, cream, chili powder, bouillon, cumin and coriander; bring to a boil. Reduce heat; cover and simmer for 5 minutes.

Cut shrimp into bite-size pieces; add to soup. Simmer 5 minutes longer or until shrimp turn pink. Gradually stir 1/2 cup hot soup into sour cream; return all to the pan, stirring constantly. Heat through (do not boil). Garnish with cilantro and avocado if desired. YIELD: **2 SERVINGS.**

Southwestern Chicken Black Bean Soup

PREP: 25 MIN. COOK: 35 MIN.

This recipe was given to me by a good friend a couple of years ago, and I've been making it ever since. We love Southwestern food, and bowls of this pack enough flavor to please even my husband.

Emily Fast ✳ Leavenworth, Kansas

- 1 pound boneless skinless chicken breast, cubed
- 1 tablespoon canola oil
- 1 tablespoon chopped onion
- 1 jalapeno pepper, seeded and finely chopped
- 3 garlic cloves, minced
- 2 cans (14-1/2 ounces *each*) reduced-sodium chicken broth
- 3 cups corn
- 1 can (15-1/2 ounces) black beans, rinsed and drained
- 2 tablespoons lime juice
- 1/2 teaspoon salt
- 1/2 teaspoon hot pepper sauce
- 1/4 teaspoon pepper
- 1/2 cup minced fresh cilantro
- 16 baked tortilla chip scoops, crumbled
- 1/2 cup shredded reduced-fat cheddar cheese

In a Dutch oven, saute chicken in oil until no longer pink. Remove with a slotted spoon and set aside. In the same pan, saute onion and jalapeno pepper until tender; add garlic and saute for 1 minute.

Stir in the broth, corn, beans, lime juice, salt, hot pepper sauce, pepper and reserved chicken; bring to a boil. Reduce heat; simmer, uncovered, for 30 minutes. Stir in cilantro. Top each serving with crumbled tortilla chips and cheese. **YIELD: 8 SERVINGS (2 QUARTS).**

EDITOR'S NOTE: When cutting hot peppers, disposable gloves are recommended. Avoid touching your face.

NUTRITION FACTS: 1 cup soup with 1 tablespoon cheese and two crumbled tortilla chips equals 227 calories, 4 g fat (1 g saturated fat), 37 mg cholesterol, 647 mg sodium, 27 g carbohydrate, 4 g fiber, 21 g protein. DIABETIC EXCHANGES: 2 lean meat, 1-1/2 starch, 1 vegetable.

Mexican Shrimp Bisque

Southwestern Chicken Black Bean Soup

Turkey Pasta Soup

Turkey Pasta Soup

PREP/TOTAL TIME: 30 MIN.

This quick soup has such great flavor that everyone I've shared this recipe with has added it to their recipe collection.

Marie Ewert ✳ Richmond, Michigan

- 1 cup uncooked small pasta shells
- 1 pound lean ground turkey
- 2 medium onions, chopped
- 2 garlic cloves, minced
- 3 cans (14-1/2 ounces *each*) reduced-sodium chicken broth
- 2 cans (15 ounces *each*) white kidney *or* cannellini beans, rinsed and drained
- 2 cans (14-1/2 ounces *each*) Italian stewed tomatoes
- 2 teaspoons dried oregano
- 2 teaspoons dried basil
- 1 teaspoon fennel seed, crushed
- 1 teaspoon pepper
- 1/2 teaspoon salt
- 1/4 teaspoon crushed red pepper flakes

Cook pasta according to package directions. In a Dutch oven, cook the turkey, onions and garlic over medium heat until meat is no longer pink; drain. Stir in the broth, beans, tomatoes and seasonings. Bring to a boil. Reduce heat; simmer, uncovered, for 10 minutes.

Drain pasta and add to the soup. Cook 5 minutes longer or until heated through. **YIELD: 10 SERVINGS.**

NUTRITION FACTS: 1-1/3 cups equals 211 calories, 4 g fat (1 g saturated fat), 36 mg cholesterol, 868 mg sodium, 28 g carbohydrate, 6 g fiber, 15 g protein. DIABETIC EXCHANGES: 2 very lean meat, 2 vegetable, 1 starch.

Mushroom Potato Soup

Mushroom Potato Soup

PREP: 15 MIN. COOK: 25 MIN.

A buttery mushroom flavor blends with potatoes, leeks and carrots to make this soup hearty and warming. A big steaming bowl hits the spot on a cold fall day. Waxy red potatoes and all-purpose Yukon Golds hold together well in boiling water.

Clare Wallace ✳ Lynchburg, Virginia

- 2 medium leeks, sliced
- 2 large carrots, sliced
- 6 tablespoons butter, *divided*
- 6 cups chicken broth
- 5 cups diced peeled potatoes
- 1 tablespoon minced fresh dill
- 1 teaspoon salt
- 1/8 teaspoon pepper
- 1 bay leaf
- 1 pound sliced fresh mushrooms
- 1/4 cup all-purpose flour
- 1 cup heavy whipping cream

In a Dutch oven, saute leeks and carrots in 3 tablespoons butter for 5 minutes or until tender. Stir in the broth, potatoes, dill, salt, pepper and bay leaf. Bring to a boil. Reduce the heat; cover and simmer for 15-20 minutes or until potatoes are tender.

Meanwhile, in a large skillet, saute the mushrooms in remaining butter for 4-6 minutes or until tender. Discard bay leaf from soup. Stir in mushroom mixture.

In a small bowl, combine flour and cream until smooth; gradually stir into soup. Bring to a boil; cook and stir for 2 minutes or until thickened. **YIELD: 12 SERVINGS (3 QUARTS).**

Chipotle Butternut Squash Soup

PREP: 25 MIN. COOK: 30 MIN.

Using herbs and vegetables from the garden along with convenient pantry items makes this robust soup easy and fast to fix. Your family will devour it.

Roxanne Chan ✳ Albany, California

- 2 cups diced peeled butternut squash
- 1 small carrot, finely chopped

Chipotle Butternut Squash Soup

- 1 green onion, sliced
- 2 garlic cloves, minced
- 1/2 teaspoon ground cumin
- 1 tablespoon olive oil
- 2 cups vegetable broth, *divided*
- 1 can (14-1/2 ounces) diced tomatoes, undrained
- 1 package (3 ounces) cream cheese, cubed
- 1/4 cup minced fresh basil
- 1 chipotle pepper in adobo sauce, chopped
- 1 can (15 ounces) black beans, rinsed and drained
- 1 can (11 ounces) Mexicorn, drained
- 2 cups fresh baby spinach

In a large saucepan, saute the squash, carrot, onion, garlic and cumin in oil for 10 minutes. Add 1-1/2 cups broth; bring to a boil. Reduce heat. Cover and simmer for 10-12 minutes or until vegetables are tender; cool slightly.

Transfer mixture to a blender; add the tomatoes, cream cheese, basil, chipotle pepper and remaining broth. Cover and process for 1-2 minutes or until smooth.

Return to the saucepan; stir in beans, corn and spinach. Cook and stir until spinach is wilted and soup is heated through. **YIELD: 5 SERVINGS.**

EDITOR'S NOTE: If garnish is desired, sprinkle butternut squash seeds with 1/8 teaspoon salt. Place on a baking sheet. Bake at 350° for 10-13 minutes or until golden brown.

Lime Chicken Chili

Lime Chicken Chili

PREP: **25 MIN.** COOK: **40 MIN.**

Lime juice gives this chili a zesty twist, while canned tomatoes and beans make preparation a snap. Try serving bowls with toasted tortilla strips.

Diane Randazzo ✳ Sinking Spring, Pennsylvania

- 1 medium onion, chopped
- 1 *each* medium sweet yellow, red and green pepper, chopped
- 3 garlic cloves, minced
- 2 tablespoons olive oil
- 1 pound ground chicken
- 1 tablespoon all-purpose flour
- 1 tablespoon baking cocoa
- 1 tablespoon ground cumin
- 1 tablespoon chili powder
- 2 teaspoons ground coriander
- 1/2 teaspoon salt
- 1/2 teaspoon garlic pepper blend
- 1/4 teaspoon pepper
- 2 cans (14-1/2 ounces *each*) diced tomatoes, undrained
- 1/4 cup lime juice
- 1 teaspoon grated lime peel
- 1 can (15 ounces) white kidney *or* cannellini beans, rinsed and drained
- 2 flour tortillas (8 inches), cut into 1/4-inch strips
- 6 tablespoons reduced-fat sour cream

In a large saucepan, saute the onion, peppers and garlic in oil for 7-8 minutes or until crisp-tender. Add chicken; cook and stir over medium heat for 8-9 minutes or until no longer pink.

Stir in the flour, cocoa and seasonings until blended. Add the tomatoes, lime juice and lime peel. Bring to a boil. Reduce heat; simmer, uncovered, for 20-25 minutes or until thickened, stirring frequently. Stir in beans; heat through.

Meanwhile, place tortilla strips on a baking sheet coated with cooking spray. Bake at 400° for 8-10 minutes or until crisp. Serve chili with sour cream and tortilla strips. **YIELD: 6 SERVINGS.**

NUTRITION FACTS: 1 cup with 5 tortilla strips and 1 tablespoon sour cream equals 357 calories, 14 g fat (4 g saturated fat), 55 mg cholesterol, 643 mg sodium, 40 g carbohydrate, 8 g fiber, 21 g protein. **DIABETIC EXCHANGES:** 3 vegetable, 2 lean meat, 1-1/2 starch, 1 fat.

Sausage Chicken Soup

Sausage Chicken Soup

PREP/TOTAL TIME: **30 MIN.**

I've been making this satisfying soup for years, but my husband still is thrilled whenever I put it on the table. It's loaded with slices of smoked sausage, chunks of chicken, fresh peppers and hearty potatoes. Spice it up or tone it down with your family's favorite picante sauce.

Helen MacDonald ✳ Lazo, British Columbia

3/4 **pound boneless skinless chicken breasts**
2 **medium potatoes, peeled and cut into 1/4-inch cubes**
1 **can (14-1/2 ounces) chicken broth**
1 **medium onion, diced**
1 **medium sweet red pepper, diced**
1 **medium green pepper, diced**
1 **garlic clove, minced**
3/4 **cup picante sauce**
3 **tablespoons all-purpose flour**
3 **tablespoons water**
1/2 **pound smoked sausage, diced**
Sliced habanero peppers, optional

Place chicken in a greased microwave-safe dish. Cover and microwave on high for 3-6 minutes or until a meat thermometer reads 170°, turning every 2 minutes. Cut into cubes; set aside.

Place the potatoes and broth in a 2-1/2-qt. microwave-safe bowl. Cover and microwave on high for 3-1/2 minutes. Add the onion, peppers and garlic; cook 3-1/2 minutes longer or until potatoes are tender. Stir in the picante sauce.

In a small bowl, combine flour and water until smooth. Gradually add to potato mixture. Cover and cook on high for 2-3 minutes or until thickened. Add the chicken and sausage; cook 1-2 minutes longer or until heated through. Sprinkle with the habanero peppers if desired. YIELD: **6 SERVINGS.**

EDITOR'S NOTE: This recipe was tested in a 1,100-watt microwave.

Kielbasa Split Pea Soup

Kielbasa Split Pea Soup

PREP: **15 MIN.** COOK: **55 MIN.**

Turkey kielbasa brings great flavor to this simple split pea soup. It's been a hit with my entire family—even our picky toddler enjoys it.

Sandra Bonde ✳ Brainerd, Minnesota

2 **celery ribs, thinly sliced**
1 **medium onion, chopped**
1 **package (16 ounces) dried green split peas**
9 **cups water, *divided***
1 **pound smoked turkey kielbasa, halved and sliced**
4 **medium carrots, halved and thinly sliced**
2 **medium potatoes, peeled and cubed**
1 **tablespoon minced fresh parsley**
1 **teaspoon dried basil**
1-1/2 **teaspoons salt**
1/2 **teaspoon pepper**

In a Dutch oven coated with cooking spray, cook celery and onion until tender. Stir in split peas and 6 cups water. Bring to a boil. Reduce heat; cover and simmer for 25 minutes.

Stir in the kielbasa, carrots, potatoes, parsley, basil, salt, pepper and remaining water. Return to a boil. Reduce heat; cover and simmer for 20-25 minutes or until peas and vegetables are tender. YIELD: **12 SERVINGS (3 QUARTS).**

NUTRITION FACTS: 1 cup equals 208 calories, 2 g fat (trace saturated fat), 13 mg cholesterol, 635 mg sodium, 34 g carbohydrate, 11 g fiber, 15 g protein. DIABETIC EXCHANGES: 2 starch, 2 very lean meat.

Golden Seafood Chowder

Golden Seafood Chowder

PREP: **25 MIN.** COOK: **25 MIN.**

Flavored with crab, shrimp and cheddar cheese, this chowder is so good that I make it weekly. Sometimes I substitute chicken or ham for the seafood and leave out the juice. Either way, this pretty soup is a winner.

Ami Paton ✳ Waconia, Minnesota

- 1/2 cup finely chopped onion
- 1/4 cup butter, cubed
-   1 can (14-1/2 ounces) chicken broth
-   1 cup cubed peeled potato
-   2 celery ribs, chopped
-   2 medium carrots, chopped
- 1/4 cup Clamato juice
- 1/4 teaspoon lemon-pepper seasoning
- 1/4 cup all-purpose flour
-   2 cups milk
-   2 cups (8 ounces) shredded sharp cheddar cheese
-   1 can (6 ounces) crabmeat, drained, flaked and cartilage removed
-   1 cup cooked medium shrimp, peeled and deveined

In a large saucepan, saute onion in butter until tender. Stir in the broth, potato, celery, carrots, Clamato juice and lemon-pepper. Bring to a boil. Reduce heat; cover and simmer for 15-20 minutes or until vegetables are tender.

In a small bowl, whisk flour and milk until smooth; add to soup. Bring to a boil; cook and stir for 2 minutes or until thickened. Reduce heat. Add the cheese, crab and shrimp; cook and stir until cheese is melted. YIELD: **4 SERVINGS.**

Lemony Chicken Soup

PREP/TOTAL TIME: **25 MIN.**

While living in California, I enjoyed a delicious chicken-lemon soup at a local restaurant. When I returned to Texas, I longed for it but never came across a recipe. I experimented with many versions before creating this one.

Brenda Tollett ✳ San Antonio, Texas

- 1/3 cup butter, cubed
- 3/4 cup all-purpose flour
-   6 cups chicken broth
-   1 cup milk

1 cup half-and-half cream
1-1/2 cups cubed cooked chicken
1 tablespoon lemon juice
1/2 teaspoon salt
1/8 teaspoon pepper
Dash ground nutmeg
8 lemon slices

In a Dutch oven, melt butter. Stir in flour until smooth; gradually add the broth, milk and cream. Bring to a boil; cook and stir for 2 minutes or until thickened.

Stir in the chicken, lemon juice, salt, pepper and nutmeg. Cook over medium heat until heated through, stirring occasionally. Garnish each serving with a lemon slice. **YIELD: 8 SERVINGS (2 QUARTS).**

Lemony Chicken Soup

Tomato-Basil Orzo Soup

PREP/TOTAL TIME: 30 MIN.

Tender pasta, sauteed vegetables and lots of flavor...this tasty soup comes really close to the Tomato Rosamarina Soup they serve in the best Greek establishments in Chicago. I like it with a small Greek salad and pita chips. Enjoy!

Mary Lu Wasniewski ✳ Orland Park, Illinois

1/2 cup *each* chopped carrot, celery and onion
1/8 teaspoon *each* dried basil, oregano and thyme
2 tablespoons olive oil
1 can (19 ounces) ready-to-serve tomato basil *or* hearty tomato soup
1 cup chicken broth
1/3 cup uncooked orzo pasta

In a small saucepan, saute the carrot, celery, onion, basil, oregano and thyme in oil for 8-10 minutes or until vegetables are crisp-tender.

Add soup and broth. Bring to a boil. Stir in orzo. Reduce heat; simmer, uncovered, for 10-12 minutes or until orzo and vegetables are tender. **YIELD: 2 SERVINGS.**

EDITOR'S NOTE: This recipe was tested with ready-to-serve Progresso Tomato Basil soup.

Tomato-Basil Orzo Soup

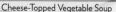
Cheese-Topped Vegetable Soup

Cheese-Topped Vegetable Soup

PREP: **15 MIN.** COOK: **25 MIN.**

Just-picked garden flavor makes this hearty vegetable soup a summer staple. It warms the soul.

Anna Minegar ✳ Zolfo Springs, Florida

- 1-1/2 cups water
- 1 can (28 ounces) Italian stewed tomatoes
- 1 can (8-3/4 ounces) whole kernel corn, drained
- 3/4 cup chopped sweet red pepper
- 2/3 cup chopped red onion
- 2/3 cup chopped green pepper
- 1/4 cup minced fresh basil
- 1 garlic clove, minced
- 1/2 teaspoon salt
- 1/4 teaspoon pepper
- 1/2 cup salad croutons
- 1/4 cup shredded part-skim mozzarella cheese

In a large saucepan, combine water, vegetables, basil, garlic, salt and pepper. Bring to a boil. Reduce heat; simmer, uncovered, for 20-25 minutes or until heated through and vegetables are tender.

Ladle the soup into ovenproof bowls. Top each with croutons and cheese. Broil 6 in. from the heat until cheese is melted. YIELD: **4 SERVINGS.**

Rich Broccoli Cream Soup

Rich Broccoli Cream Soup

PREP: **10 MIN.** COOK: **65 MIN.**

Go ahead and indulge in a bowl of this rich and creamy soup...it's deliciously thick, flavorful and full of broccoli. Homemade soup never tasted so good!

Carol Macagno ✳ Fresno, California

- 4 celery ribs, chopped
- 1 large onion, chopped
- 3 tablespoons butter
- 2 bunches broccoli, trimmed and coarsely chopped (about 8 cups)
- 1-1/2 cups chicken broth
- 2 teaspoons garlic salt
- 1/2 teaspoon pepper
- 2 tablespoons cornstarch

Roasted Yellow Pepper Soup

1/4 cup water
1 pint heavy whipping cream

In a large saucepan, saute celery and onion in butter until tender. Add the broccoli, broth, garlic salt and pepper; bring to a boil. Reduce heat; cover and simmer for 45 minutes or until broccoli is tender.

In a small bowl, combine cornstarch and water until smooth. Stir into soup. Bring to a boil; cook and stir for 2 minutes or until thickened. Reduce heat to low. Stir in cream; cook 10 minutes longer or until heated through. **YIELD: 6-8 SERVINGS.**

Roasted Yellow Pepper Soup

PREP: 25 MIN. COOK: 40 MIN.

We got this recipe from a good friend and Merchant Marine in New Hampshire. My husband and our two children liked it so much that I started raising yellow peppers. We enjoy it in the middle of summer or on a cool fall day.

Amy Spurrier ✳ Wellsburg, West Virginia

6 large sweet yellow peppers
1 large onion, chopped
1 cup chopped leeks (white portion only)
1/4 cup butter, cubed
3 small potatoes, peeled and cubed
5 cups chicken broth
1/2 teaspoon salt
1/2 teaspoon pepper
Shredded Parmesan cheese, optional

Halve peppers; remove and discard tops and seeds. Broil peppers 4 in. from the heat until skins blister, about 4 minutes. Immediately place peppers in a bowl; cover and let stand for 15-20 minutes.

Meanwhile, in a large saucepan, saute onion and leeks in butter until tender. Add the potatoes, broth, salt and pepper. Bring to a boil. Reduce heat; cover and simmer for 30 minutes or until potatoes are tender.

Peel off and discard charred skin from peppers. Finely chop peppers; add to potato mixture. Cool slightly.

In a blender, cover and process soup in batches until smooth. Return to the pan; heat through (do not boil). Serve with Parmesan cheese if desired. **YIELD: 8 CUPS (2 QUARTS).**

Hearty Beef Barley Soup

Hearty Beef Barley Soup

PREP: **10 MIN.** COOK: **30 MIN.**

My entire family just loves this delicious and comforting soup. Loaded with chunks of tender beef, the rich broth also includes plenty of fresh mushrooms, sliced carrots and quick-cooking barley.

Barbara Beattie ∗ Glen Allen, Virginia

- 2 tablespoons all-purpose flour
- 1/2 teaspoon salt
- 1/4 teaspoon pepper, *divided*
- 1 pound lean boneless beef sirloin steak, cut into 1/2-inch cubes
- 1 tablespoon canola oil
- 2 cups sliced fresh mushrooms
- 2 cans (14-1/2 ounces *each*) reduced-sodium beef broth
- 2 medium carrots, sliced
- 1/4 teaspoon garlic powder
- 1/4 teaspoon dried thyme
- 1/2 cup quick-cooking barley

In a large resealable plastic bag, combine the flour, salt and 1/8 teaspoon pepper. Add beef and shake to coat. In a Dutch oven, brown beef in oil over medium heat or until the meat is no longer pink. Remove beef and set aside.

In the same pan, saute mushrooms. Add the broth, carrots, garlic powder, thyme and remaining pepper; bring to a boil. Add barley and beef. Reduce heat; cover and simmer for 20-25 minutes until the meat, vegetables and barley are tender. **YIELD: 4 SERVINGS.**

NUTRITION FACTS: 1-1/4 cups equals 300 calories, 9 g fat (2 g saturated fat), 68 mg cholesterol, 782 mg sodium, 26 g carbohydrate, 5 g fiber, 28 g protein.

Asparagus Leek Chowder

PREP/TOTAL TIME: **20 MIN.**

To us, asparagus is the taste of spring, so we enjoy it in as many meals as we can. When this thick, creamy, and tasty chowder is on the table, we know spring has arrived.

Elisabeth Harders ∗ West Allis, Wisconsin

- 1 pound fresh asparagus, trimmed and cut into 1-inch pieces
- 3 cups sliced fresh mushrooms
- 3 large leeks (white portion only), sliced
- 6 tablespoons butter
- 1/4 cup all-purpose flour
- 1/2 teaspoon salt

Dash pepper

2 cups chicken broth

2 cups half-and-half cream

1 can (11 ounces) whole kernel corn, drained

1 tablespoon chopped pimientos

In a large saucepan, saute the asparagus, mushrooms and leeks in butter for 10 minutes or until tender.

Stir in the flour, salt and pepper until blended. Gradually stir in broth and cream. Bring to a boil. Reduce heat; cook and stir for 2 minutes or until thickened. Stir in corn and pimientos; heat through. **YIELD: 7 SERVINGS.**

Asparagus Leek Chowder

Onion Cream Soup

PREP/TOTAL TIME: **30 MIN.**

My whole family loves this hearty soup, especially on cool autumn evenings. It's so satisfying with a mild onion-cheese flavor. When I need an easy dinner, I stir up this soup and serve it with warm, crusty bread and a crisp salad.

Janice Hemond ✳ Lincoln, Rhode Island

2 cups thinly sliced sweet onions

6 tablespoons butter, *divided*

1 can (14-1/2 ounces) chicken broth

2 teaspoons chicken bouillon granules

1/4 teaspoon pepper

3 tablespoons all-purpose flour

1-1/2 cups milk

1/4 cup diced process cheese (Velveeta)

Shredded cheddar cheese and minced fresh parsley

In a large skillet, cook onions in 3 tablespoons butter over medium-low heat until tender. Add the broth, bouillon and pepper; bring to a boil. Remove from the heat.

In a large saucepan, melt the remaining butter. Stir in flour until smooth; gradually add milk. Bring to a boil; cook and stir for 1-2 minutes or until thickened. Reduce heat; add process cheese and onion mixture. Cook and stir until heated through and cheese is melted. Sprinkle with cheddar cheese and parsley. **YIELD: 4 SERVINGS.**

Onion Cream Soup

Garlic Tomato Soup

Garlic Tomato Soup

PREP: 30 MIN. COOK: 30 MIN.

Roasted garlic adds a mellow background flavor to this rich, creamy tomato soup. Canned tomatoes and puree make it a year-round favorite.

Marilyn Coomer ✳ Louisville, Kentucky

- 12 garlic cloves, peeled and sliced
- 1-1/2 teaspoons olive oil
- 1 can (14-1/2 ounces) diced tomatoes, undrained
- 1 cup tomato puree
- 1 pint heavy whipping cream
- 1/4 teaspoon dried oregano
- 1/4 teaspoon minced fresh basil
- 1/4 teaspoon salt
- 1/8 teaspoon pepper

In a 3-cup baking dish, combine the garlic and oil. Cover and bake at 300° for 25-30 minutes or until lightly browned.

In a large saucepan, bring the garlic, tomatoes and tomato puree to a boil. Reduce heat; cover and simmer for 30 minutes.

Add the cream, oregano, basil, salt and pepper. Cool slightly. Place half of the soup at a time in a blender; cover and process until pureed. Return to the pan; heat through. **YIELD: 3 SERVINGS.**

🂠 Black Bean Soup

PREP: 15 MIN. COOK: 70 MIN.

I cooked for two people for the first seven years of my marriage. Today, I'm a stay-at-home mom, but I still appreciate small-scale recipes. I like to serve this zesty soup with tortillas topped with melted cheese.

Wendy Anderson ✳ Santa Rosa, California

- 1/4 cup chopped onion
- 2 garlic cloves, minced
- 1 tablespoon olive oil
- 1 teaspoon ground cumin
- 1 teaspoon dried oregano
- 1/2 teaspoon chili powder
- 1 can (15 ounces) tomato sauce

Black Bean Soup

Winter Squash Soup

1 can (15 ounces) black beans, rinsed and drained
1 can (14 ounces) vegetable *or* beef broth
1 bay leaf
1 to 2 tablespoons lime juice
1/8 teaspoon hot pepper sauce
Pepper to taste

In a large saucepan, saute onion and garlic in oil until tender. Stir in the cumin, oregano and chili powder; saute 2 minutes longer. Add the tomato sauce, beans, broth and bay leaf.

Bring to a boil. Reduce heat; cover and simmer for 45 minutes. Stir in lime juice; simmer 10-15 minutes longer. Discard bay leaf. Add pepper sauce and pepper. **YIELD: 2 SERVINGS.**

Winter Squash Soup

PREP: 15 MIN. COOK: 30 MIN.

I enjoy trying all sorts of new recipes and adding different seasonings to enhance the flavor. This is a tasty way to serve squash.

Angela Liette ✳ Sidney, Ohio

2 celery ribs, chopped
1 medium onion, chopped
1 garlic clove, minced
3 tablespoons butter
3 tablespoons all-purpose flour
3 cups chicken broth
2 cups mashed cooked butternut, acorn *or* Hubbard squash
2 tablespoons minced fresh parsley
1/2 teaspoon salt
1/4 teaspoon dried savory
1/4 teaspoon dried rosemary, crushed
1/8 to 1/4 teaspoon ground nutmeg
1/8 teaspoon pepper
1 cup half-and-half cream

In a large saucepan, saute the celery, onion and garlic in butter until tender. Stir in flour until blended. Gradually add the broth. Bring to a boil; cook and stir for 2 minutes or until thickened. Reduce heat; stir in the squash, parsley, salt, savory, rosemary, nutmeg and pepper. Simmer, uncovered, for 10 minutes or until heated through. Cool slightly.

In a blender, process soup in batches until smooth. Return to the pan and heat through. Gradually stir in cream. Cook 5 minutes longer, stirring occasionally. **YIELD: 6 SERVINGS.**

Creamy Corn Crab Soup

🕐 Creamy Corn Crab Soup

PREP/TOTAL TIME: **30 MIN.**

This creamy soup is fast, easy and very tasty. Corn really stars in this delectable recipe, and crabmeat makes it a little more special. It will get high marks from both busy cooks and lovers of flavorful, homemade food.

Carol Ropchan ✳ Willingdon, Alberta

1 medium onion, chopped
2 tablespoons butter
3 cups chicken broth
3 cups frozen corn
3 medium potatoes, peeled and diced
1 can (6 ounces) crabmeat, drained, flaked and cartilage removed *or* 1 cup flaked imitation crabmeat
1 cup milk
1/2 teaspoon salt
1/4 teaspoon pepper

In a large saucepan, saute onion in butter until tender. Add the broth, corn and potatoes; bring to a boil. Reduce heat; cover and simmer for 15 minutes. Remove from the heat; cool slightly.

In a blender, puree half of the corn mixture. Return to pan. Stir in the crab, milk, salt and pepper; cook over low heat until heated through (do not boil). **YIELD: 7 SERVINGS.**

🕐 Spicy Two-Bean Chili

PREP: **20 MIN.** COOK: **8 HOURS**

Chili fans will get a kick out of this untraditional recipe. Tomatoes with green chilies, lime juice and kidney and black beans give it an original twist. It's wonderful over rice.

Lesley Pew ✳ Lynn, Massachusetts

2 pounds ground beef
3 large onions, chopped
6 garlic cloves, minced
2 cans (16 ounces *each*) kidney beans, rinsed and drained
2 cans (15 ounces *each*) black beans, rinsed and drained
2 cans (10 ounces *each*) diced tomatoes and green chilies, undrained
1 can (14-1/2 ounces) chicken broth
1/2 cup lime juice
6 tablespoons cornmeal
1/4 cup chili powder
4 teaspoons dried oregano
3 teaspoons ground cumin
2 teaspoons salt
2 teaspoons rubbed sage
1/2 teaspoon white pepper
1/2 teaspoon paprika
1/2 teaspoon pepper
Hot cooked rice
Shredded cheddar cheese

In a Dutch oven, cook the beef, onions and garlic over medium heat until meat is no longer pink; drain. Transfer to a 5-qt. slow cooker. Stir in the beans, tomatoes, broth, lime juice, cornmeal and seasonings.

Cover and cook on low for 8 hours or until heated through. Serve with rice; sprinkle with cheese. **YIELD: 11 SERVINGS.**

Land of Enchantment Posole

PREP: **30 MIN.** COOK: **1 HOUR**

My family named this spicy soup after our state moniker, "New Mexico, Land of Enchantment." We usually make it around Christmas when we have lots of family over...and we never have leftovers.

Suzanne Caldwell ✳ Artesia, New Mexico

- 1-1/2 pounds pork stew meat, cut into 3/4-inch cubes
- 1 large onion, chopped
- 2 garlic cloves, minced
- 2 tablespoons canola oil
- 3 cups beef broth
- 2 cans (15-1/2 ounces *each*) hominy, rinsed and drained
- 2 cans (4 ounces *each*) chopped green chilies
- 1 to 2 jalapeno peppers, seeded and chopped, optional
- 1/2 teaspoon salt
- 1/2 teaspoon ground cumin
- 1/2 teaspoon dried oregano
- 1/4 teaspoon pepper
- 1/4 teaspoon cayenne pepper
- 1/2 cup minced fresh cilantro

Tortilla strips, optional

In a Dutch oven, cook the pork, onion and garlic in oil over medium heat until meat is no longer pink; drain. Stir in the broth, hominy, chilies, jalapeno if desired, salt, cumin, oregano, pepper and cayenne.

Bring to a boil. Reduce heat; cover and simmer for 45-60 minutes or until meat is tender. Stir in cilantro. Serve with tortilla strips if desired. **YIELD: 5 SERVINGS.**

EDITOR'S NOTE: When cutting hot peppers, disposable gloves are recommended. Avoid touching your face.

Spicy Two-Bean Chili

Land of Enchantment Posole

Beefy Mushroom Soup

Beefy Mushroom Soup

PREP/TOTAL TIME: **30 MIN.**

This is a tasty way to use leftover roast or steak and get a delicious supper on the table in about a half hour. The warm, rich taste of this mushroom soup is sure to please.

Ginger Ellsworth ✳ Caldwell, Idaho

- 1 medium onion, chopped
- 1/2 cup sliced fresh mushrooms
- 2 tablespoons butter
- 2 tablespoons all-purpose flour
- 2 cups reduced-sodium beef broth
- 2/3 cup cubed cooked lean roast beef
- 1/2 teaspoon garlic powder
- 1/4 teaspoon paprika
- 1/4 teaspoon pepper
- 1/8 teaspoon salt
- Dash hot pepper sauce
- 1/4 cup shredded part-skim mozzarella cheese, optional

In a large saucepan, saute the onion and mushrooms in butter until onion is tender; remove with a slotted spoon and set aside. In a small bowl, whisk flour and broth until smooth; gradually add to the pan. Bring to a boil; cook and stir for 1-2 minutes or until thickened.

Add the roast beef, garlic powder, paprika, pepper, salt, pepper sauce and onion mixture; cook and stir until heated through. Garnish with cheese if desired. YIELD: **2 SERVINGS.**

Hearty Chili Mac

PREP: **20 MIN.** COOK: **1-1/4 HOURS**

Luckily, this recipe makes a lot, since everyone is apt to want another bowl. It freezes well and makes excellent leftovers...if there is any left.

Fannie Wehmas ✳ Saxon, Wisconsin

- 2 pounds ground beef
- 1 medium onion, chopped
- 1 can (46 ounces) tomato juice
- 1 can (28 ounces) diced tomatoes, undrained
- 2 celery ribs without leaves, chopped
- 3 tablespoons brown sugar
- 2 tablespoons chili powder

Hearty Chili Mac

Chunky Taco Soup

1 teaspoon salt

1 teaspoon prepared mustard

1/4 teaspoon pepper

2 cans (16 ounces *each*) kidney beans, rinsed and drained

1/2 cup uncooked elbow macaroni

In a Dutch oven, cook beef and onion over medium heat until meat is no longer pink; drain. Stir in the tomato juice, tomatoes, celery, brown sugar, chili powder, salt, mustard and pepper. Bring to a boil. Reduce heat; simmer, uncovered, for 1 hour, stirring occasionally.

Add the beans and macaroni; simmer 15-20 minutes longer or until macaroni is tender. **YIELD: 10-12 SERVINGS.**

Chunky Taco Soup

PREP: 20 MIN. COOK: 20 MIN.

I've gotten great response at our church dinners and senior groups whenever I bring this thick, easy-to-fix soup. I usually take home an empty pot and often get requests for the recipe. The flavor seems to improve on the second day.

Evelyn Buford ✳ Belton, Missouri

1-1/2 pounds boneless beef sirloin *or* round steak, cut into 3/4-inch cubes

1 medium onion, chopped

1 tablespoon olive oil

2 cans (15 ounces *each*) pinto beans, rinsed and drained

2 cans (14-1/2 ounces *each*) diced tomatoes and green chilies, undrained

2 cups water

1 can (15 ounces) black beans, rinsed and drained

1 can (14-3/4 ounces) cream-style corn

1 envelope ranch salad dressing mix

1 envelope taco seasoning

1/4 cup minced fresh cilantro

In a stockpot or Dutch oven, brown beef and onion in oil. Add the pinto beans, tomatoes, water, black beans, corn, salad dressing mix and taco seasoning. Bring to a boil. Reduce heat; cover and simmer for 20-30 minutes or until the meat is tender. Sprinkle with cilantro. **YIELD: 12 SERVINGS (ABOUT 3 QUARTS).**

Cheeseburger Paradise Soup

Cheeseburger Paradise Soup

PREP: **30 MIN.** COOK: **25 MIN.**

I've never met a person who didn't enjoy this creamy soup, and it's hearty enough to serve as a main course with your favorite bread or rolls.

Nadina Ladimarco * Burton, Ohio

- 6 medium potatoes, peeled and cubed
- 1 small carrot, grated
- 1 small onion, chopped
- 1/2 cup chopped green pepper
- 2 tablespoons chopped seeded jalapeno pepper
- 3 cups water
- 2 tablespoons plus 2 teaspoons beef bouillon granules
- 2 garlic cloves, minced
- 1/8 teaspoon pepper
- 2 pounds ground beef
- 1/2 pound sliced fresh mushrooms
- 2 tablespoons butter
- 5 cups milk, *divided*
- 6 tablespoons all-purpose flour
- 1 package (16 ounces) process cheese (Velveeta), cubed

Crumbled cooked bacon

In a stockpot, combine the vegetables, jalapeno, water, bouillon, garlic and pepper; bring to a boil. Reduce heat; cover and simmer for 15-20 minutes or until potatoes are tender.

Meanwhile, in a large skillet, cook beef and mushrooms in butter over medium heat until meat is no longer pink; drain. Add to soup. Stir in 4 cups milk; heat through.

Combine flour and remaining milk until smooth; gradually stir into soup. Bring to a boil; cook and stir for 2 minutes or until thickened. Reduce heat; stir in cheese until melted. Garnish with the bacon. YIELD: **14 SERVINGS (ABOUT 3-1/2 QUARTS).**

EDITOR'S NOTE: When cutting hot peppers, disposable gloves are recommended. Avoid touching your face.

Anytime Turkey Chili

PREP: **15 MIN.** COOK: **1-1/4 HOURS**

I created this dish to grab the voters' attention at a chili contest we held in our backyard. With pumpkin, brown sugar and cooked turkey, it's like an entire Thanksgiving dinner in one bowl.

Brad Bailey * Cary, North Carolina

- 2/3 cup chopped sweet onion
- 1/2 cup chopped green pepper
- 1-1/2 teaspoons dried oregano
- 2 garlic cloves, minced
- 1 teaspoon ground cumin
- 1 teaspoon olive oil
- 1 can (16 ounces) kidney beans, rinsed and drained
- 1 can (15-1/2 ounces) great northern beans, rinsed and drained
- 1 can (15 ounces) solid-pack pumpkin
- 1 can (15 ounces) crushed tomatoes
- 1 can (14-1/2 ounces) reduced-sodium chicken broth
- 1/2 cup water
- 2 tablespoons brown sugar
- 2 tablespoons chili powder
- 1/2 teaspoon pepper
- 3 cups cubed cooked turkey breast

In a large saucepan, saute the onion, green pepper, oregano, garlic and cumin in oil until vegetables are tender. Stir in beans, pumpkin, tomatoes, broth, water, brown sugar, chili powder and pepper; bring to a boil. Reduce heat; cover and simmer for 1 hour. Add turkey; heat through. YIELD: **8 SERVINGS (2 QUARTS).**

NUTRITION FACTS: 1 cup equals 241 calories, 2 g fat (trace saturated fat), 45 mg cholesterol, 478 mg sodium, 32 g carbohydrate, 10 g fiber, 25 g protein. DIABETIC EXCHANGES: 3 very lean meat, 1-1/2 starch, 1 vegetable.

Two-Potato Soup

PREP/TOTAL TIME: **30 MIN.**

Potato chunks, Swiss cheese and onions fill this smooth soup that's a comfort on crisp autumn afternoons. My mother passed this recipe along to me. For variety, I sometimes add chopped celery and a dash of green hot sauce.

Pamela Reiling-Kemp ✳ Roselle, Illinois

- 1/2 **pound small unpeeled red potatoes, cut into chunks**
- 1/2 **pound medium russet potatoes, peeled and cut into chunks**
- 1 **can (14-1/2 ounces) reduced-sodium chicken broth**
- 1 **cup water**
- 1/4 **cup chopped onion**
- 2 **teaspoons canola oil**
- 1 **tablespoon all-purpose flour**
- 1/4 **cup 2% milk**
- 2 **tablespoons evaporated milk**
- 3 **tablespoons cream cheese, cubed**
- 1 **tablespoon minced fresh parsley**
- 1/4 **teaspoon salt**
- 1/8 **teaspoon white pepper**
- 1/3 **cup shredded Swiss cheese**

Place the potatoes in a large saucepan; add broth and water. Bring to a boil. Reduce heat; cover and cook for 10-15 minutes or until almost tender. Meanwhile, in a small skillet, saute onion in oil until tender; add to potatoes.

In a small bowl, combine the flour, milk and evaporated milk until smooth; add to potato mixture. Bring to a boil; cook and stir for 2 minutes or until thickened. Reduce heat; stir in the cream cheese, parsley, salt and pepper. Cover and simmer for 5-10 minutes or until cream cheese is melted and potatoes are tender, stirring occasionally. Garnish with Swiss cheese.
YIELD: 2 SERVINGS.

Anytime Turkey Chili

Two-Potato Soup

Chicken Tortilla Soup

Chicken Tortilla Soup

PREP: 30 MIN. COOK: 25 MIN.

Chock-full of veggies and autumn color, this soup is ideal for using up fresh garden bounty. Broiling the chicken and vegetables adds richness and wonderful flavor.

Kathy Averbeck ✷ Dousman, Wisconsin

- 2 medium tomatoes
- 1 small onion, cut into wedges
- 1 garlic clove, peeled
- 4 teaspoons canola oil, *divided*
- 1 boneless skinless chicken breast half (6 ounces)
- 1/4 teaspoon lemon-pepper seasoning
- 1/8 teaspoon salt
- 2 corn tortillas (6 inches)
- 1/2 cup diced zucchini
- 2 tablespoons chopped carrot
- 1 tablespoon minced fresh cilantro
- 3/4 teaspoon ground cumin
- 1/2 teaspoon chili powder
- 1 cup reduced-sodium chicken broth
- 1/2 cup spicy hot V8 juice
- 1/3 cup frozen corn
- 2 tablespoons tomato puree
- 1-1/2 teaspoons chopped seeded jalapeno pepper
- 1 bay leaf
- 1/4 cup cubed *or* sliced avocado
- 1/4 cup shredded Mexican cheese blend

Brush the tomatoes, onion and garlic with 1 teaspoon oil. Broil 4 in. from the heat for 3-4 minutes on each side or until tender. Peel and discard charred skin from tomatoes; place in a blender. Add the onion and garlic; cover and process for 1-2 minutes or until smooth.

Sprinkle chicken with lemon-pepper and salt; broil for 5-6 minutes on each side or until a meat thermometer reads 170°. Cut one tortilla into 1/4-in. strips; coarsely chop remaining tortilla.

In a large saucepan, heat remaining oil. Fry tortilla strips until crisp and browned; remove with a slotted spoon.

Bratwurst Potato Soup

In same pan, cook zucchini, carrot, cilantro, cumin, chili powder and chopped tortilla over medium heat for 4 minutes. Stir in the tomato mixture, broth, V8 juice, corn, tomato puree, jalapeno and bay leaf. Bring to a boil. Reduce heat; simmer, uncovered, for 20 minutes.

Cut the chicken into strips and add to the soup; simmer 5 minutes longer or until chicken is no longer pink. Discard the bay leaf. Garnish with the avocado, cheese and tortilla strips. YIELD: 3 SERVINGS.

EDITOR'S NOTE: When cutting hot peppers, disposable gloves are recommended. Avoid touching your face.

Ham and Corn Chowder

Bratwurst Potato Soup

PREP/TOTAL TIME: 30 MIN.

My husband, Frank, a former Army cook, adapted this nourishing creation from my mother's homemade potato soup. We've created recipes as a team for over 50 years. Our motto is, "The couple who cooks together, stays together."

JoAnn Hilliard * East Liverpool, Ohio

1 pound fully cooked bratwurst links, cut into 1/2-inch slices
2 medium potatoes, peeled and chopped
2 cups water
1 medium onion, chopped
1/2 teaspoon salt
Dash pepper
4 cups shredded cabbage
3 cups milk, *divided*
2 tablespoons all-purpose flour
1 cup (4 ounces) shredded Swiss cheese

In a Dutch oven or stockpot, combine the bratwurst, potatoes, water, onion, salt and pepper. Bring to a boil. Reduce heat; cover and simmer for 10 minutes. Add cabbage. Cover and simmer for 10-15 minutes or until vegetables are tender.

Stir in 2-1/2 cups milk. Combine flour and remaining milk until smooth. Gradually stir into soup. Bring to a boil; cook and stir for 2 minutes or until thickened. Remove from the heat. Stir in cheese until melted. YIELD: 8-10 SERVINGS.

Ham and Corn Chowder

PREP/TOTAL TIME: 25 MIN.

I'm always on the lookout for easy soups because my husband and I love them, particularly in the winter months. This cream chowder gets a little kick from cayenne and chopped jalapeno pepper. Extra servings freeze very well.

Sharon Price * Caldwell, Idaho

2 celery ribs, chopped
1/4 cup chopped onion
1 jalapeno pepper, seeded and chopped
2 tablespoons butter
2 tablespoons all-purpose flour
3 cups milk
2 cups cubed fully cooked ham
2 cups cubed cooked potatoes
1-1/2 cups fresh *or* frozen corn
1 can (14-3/4 ounces) cream-style corn
3/4 teaspoon minced fresh thyme or 1/4 teaspoon dried thyme
1/8 to 1/4 teaspoon cayenne pepper
1/8 teaspoon salt

In a large saucepan, saute the celery, onion and jalapeno in butter until vegetables are tender. Stir in flour until blended. Gradually add milk. Bring to a boil; cook and stir for 2 minutes or until thickened. Stir in remaining ingredients. Bring to a boil. Reduce heat; cover and simmer for 10 minutes or until heated through. YIELD: 8 SERVINGS (2 QUARTS).

EDITOR'S NOTE: When cutting hot peppers, disposable gloves are recommended. Avoid touching your face.

Creamy Bacon Mushroom Soup

Creamy Bacon Mushroom Soup

PREP/TOTAL TIME: **30 MIN.**

I've always enjoyed cooking and recently created this rich soup. It's always a hit. You can also garnish it with chopped green onion tops or shredded Swiss cheese. For a creamier, smoother consistency, try pouring the soup through a strainer.

Nathan Mercer ✳ Inman, South Carolina

- 10 bacon strips, diced
- 1 pound sliced fresh mushrooms
- 1 medium onion, chopped
- 3 garlic cloves, minced
- 1 quart heavy whipping cream
- 1 can (14-1/2 ounces) chicken broth
- 1-1/4 cups shredded Swiss cheese
- 3 tablespoons cornstarch
- 1/2 teaspoon salt
- 1/2 teaspoon pepper
- 3 tablespoons water

In a large saucepan, cook bacon over medium heat until crisp. Using a slotted spoon, remove to paper towels; drain, reserving 2 tablespoons drippings. In the drippings, saute mushrooms, onion and garlic. Stir in the cream and broth. Gradually stir in cheese until melted.

In a small bowl, combine the cornstarch, salt, pepper and water until smooth. Stir into soup. Bring to a boil; cook and stir for 2 minutes or until thickened. Garnish with bacon. YIELD: **8 SERVINGS (2 QUARTS).**

Ginger Chicken Burgers with Sesame Slaw, PAGE 116

" This chicken burger gets an Asian-flavor twist with ginger and garlic. It's topped off with a fabulous coleslaw. If you like, serve the coleslaw as a side for grilled items, like chicken breasts, fish fillets or chops. "

Deborah Biggs
Omaha, Nebraska

SANDWICHES

DO YOU HAVE A WINNING RECIPE?
Enter your most prized recipes in the *Taste of Home* recipe contests, and you may win some money and the chance to have your recipe published. Log onto **tasteofhome.com/RecipeContests** for a list of our current contests and submission deadlines. Good luck...we'll be looking for your recipe.

sandwiches

Hearty Muffuletta

PREP: 55 MIN. + CHILLING

Famous in Louisiana, muffulettas are cold cuts, cheese and olive salad layered into an Italian bread shell. I was happy when a friend and co-worker gave me this recipe so I could make them myself. More than a meal, it's a dining experience!

Ruth Hayward ✳ Lake Charles, Louisiana

- 1/2 cup finely chopped celery
- 1/2 cup sliced pimiento-stuffed olives, drained
- 1/2 cup sliced ripe olives, drained
- 1/2 cup giardiniera
- 1/3 cup finely chopped onion
- 1/3 cup olive oil
- 1/4 cup finely chopped green onions
- 1/4 cup minced fresh parsley
- 3 tablespoons lemon juice
- 1 teaspoon dried oregano
- 1 garlic clove, minced
- 1/8 teaspoon pepper
- 1 round loaf (24 ounces) unsliced Italian bread
- 1/4 pound thinly sliced hard salami
- 1/4 pound provolone cheese
- 1/4 pound thinly sliced deli ham

In a large bowl, combine the first 12 ingredients. Cover and refrigerate for at least 8 hours. Drain, reserving 2 tablespoons liquid.

Cut loaf of bread in half; hollow out top and bottom, leaving a 1-in. shell (discard removed bread or save for another use). Brush cut sides of bread with reserved liquid. Layer bottom of bread shell with salami, half of the olive mixture, cheese, remaining olive mixture and ham. Replace bread top. Cut into wedges. **YIELD: 8-10 SERVINGS.**

EDITOR'S NOTE: Giardiniera is a vegetable mixture available in mild and hot varieties. Look for it in the Italian or pickle section of your local grocery store.

Hearty Muffuletta

Ginger Chicken Burgers with Sesame Slaw

Ginger Chicken Burgers with Sesame Slaw

AMERICA'S
**BEST
LOVED**
•RECIPE CONTEST•

PREP/TOTAL TIME: **25 MIN.**

This chicken burger gets an Asian-flavor twist with ginger and garlic. It's topped off with a fabulous coleslaw. If you like, serve the coleslaw as a side for grilled items, like chicken breasts, fish fillets or chops.

Deborah Biggs ✳ Omaha, Nebraska

- 1 teaspoon minced fresh gingerroot
- 3/4 teaspoon minced garlic
- 1/2 teaspoon kosher salt
- 1/2 pound ground chicken
- 1-1/4 cups coleslaw mix
- 2 tablespoons thinly sliced green onion
- 2 tablespoons Asian toasted sesame salad dressing
- 1 tablespoon mayonnaise
- 1-1/4 teaspoons black sesame seeds
  or sesame seeds
- 2 sesame seed hamburger buns, split

In a small bowl, combine the ginger, garlic and salt. Crumble the chicken over the mixture and mix well. Shape into two patties. Broil 4-6 in. from the heat for 4-6 minutes on each side or until a meat thermometer reads 165° and juices run clear.

In a large bowl, combine the coleslaw mix, onion, salad dressing, mayonnaise and sesame seeds. Serve burgers on buns with coleslaw. **YIELD: 2 SERVINGS.**

Mushroom Crab Melts

PREP/TOTAL TIME: **30 MIN.**

I received this recipe from my grandmother. The rich, open-faced treats are wonderful with a green salad, but I have also cut them into quarters to serve as hors d'oeuvres. To save time, make the crab topping early in the day and store it in the refrigerator.

Jean Bevilacqua ✳ Rohdodendron, Oregon

- 3 bacon strips, diced
- 1 cup sliced fresh mushrooms
- 1/4 cup chopped onion
- 1 can (6 ounces) crabmeat, drained, flaked and cartilage removed *or* 1 cup chopped imitation crabmeat
- 1 cup (4 ounces) shredded Swiss cheese
- 1/2 cup mayonnaise

1/3 cup grated Parmesan cheese

2 tablespoons butter, softened

6 English muffins, split

Dash *each* cayenne pepper and paprika

In a large skillet, cook the bacon over medium heat until crisp; remove to paper towels. Drain, reserving 2 tablespoons drippings. Saute the mushrooms and onion in drippings until tender.

In a large bowl, combine crab, Swiss cheese, mayonnaise, the mushroom mixture, Parmesan cheese and bacon.

Spread butter over muffin halves. Top with the crab mixture; sprinkle with cayenne and paprika. Place on an ungreased baking sheet. Bake at 400° for 10-15 minutes or until lightly browned. **YIELD: 6 SERVINGS.**

Mushroom Crab Melts

Tortilla Turkey Sandwiches

PREP/TOTAL TIME: **20 MIN.**

As my kids learned how to cook, this was always one of their favorite lunches to fix. We all love the creamy blend of flavors. The original recipe came from my husband, but I tweaked it a bit to make it even easier.

Leslie Heath ✳ Salt Lake City, Utah

4 ounces cream cheese, softened

2 tablespoons mayonnaise

1-1/2 teaspoons prepared pesto

4 flour tortillas (8 inches), room temperature

1 cup shredded lettuce

1/2 pound sliced deli smoked turkey

3/4 cup chopped tomato

1 can (2-1/4 ounces) sliced ripe olives, drained

1 cup (4 ounces) shredded Colby-Monterey Jack cheese

In a small bowl, beat the cream cheese, mayonnaise and pesto until blended. Spread about 2 tablespoons over each tortilla. Layer with the lettuce, turkey, tomato, olives and cheese; roll up. Secure with toothpicks. **YIELD: 4 SERVINGS.**

Tortilla Turkey Sandwiches

Grilled Roast Beef Sandwiches

PREP/TOTAL TIME: 30 MIN.

This fast favorite hits the spot when we're short on time. Roast beef, cheese, and sauteed onion, green pepper and mushrooms are sandwiched between slices of sourdough bread, then toasted on a griddle to buttery perfection.

Jolie Goddard ✶ Elko, Nevada

 1 medium onion, sliced
 1 medium green pepper, sliced
1/2 pound fresh mushrooms, sliced
 2 to 3 garlic cloves, minced
 2 tablespoons canola oil
1/4 teaspoon salt
1/8 teaspoon pepper
 8 slices sourdough bread
16 slices Colby-Monterey Jack *or* Swiss cheese, *divided*
 8 slices deli roast beef
1/2 cup butter, softened
Garlic salt, optional

In a large skillet, saute the onion, green pepper, mushrooms and garlic in oil until tender; sprinkle with salt and pepper. On four slices of bread, layer two slices of cheese, two slices of beef and a fourth of the vegetable mixture. Top with the remaining cheese and bread.

    Butter outside of bread; sprinkle with garlic salt if desired. On a hot griddle or large skillet, toast sandwiches for 3-4 minutes on each side or until golden brown. **YIELD: 4 SERVINGS.**

Cinnamon-Apple Grilled Cheese

PREP/TOTAL TIME: 25 MIN.

These sandwiches are great for breakfast or lunch, or even as a snack. To intensify the cinnamon flavor, try using cinnamon raisin bread instead of raisin bread.

Deborah Puette ✶ Lilburn, Georgia

 1 cup sliced peeled tart apple
 3 teaspoons butter, softened, *divided*

Grilled Roast Beef Sandwiches

Cinnamon-Apple Grilled Cheese

1/3   cup chopped walnuts
  1   tablespoon honey
  3   tablespoons cream cheese, softened
  2   tablespoons confectioners' sugar
1/4   teaspoon ground cinnamon
  4   slices raisin bread
  2   slices Muenster cheese (3/4 ounce *each*)

In a large skillet, saute apple slices in 1 teaspoon butter until tender. Meanwhile, in a small skillet, cook and stir the walnuts and honey over medium heat for 2-3 minutes or until lightly toasted.

In a small bowl, beat the cream cheese, confectioners' sugar and cinnamon until smooth. Stir in walnut mixture. Spread over two slices of bread; layer with Muenster cheese, apple slices and remaining bread. Spread remaining butter over the outsides of each sandwich.

In a large nonstick skillet coated with cooking spray, toast sandwiches for 1-2 minutes on each side or until golden brown and cheese is melted. **YIELD: 2 SERVINGS.**

Pizza Hoagies

Pizza Hoagies

PREP: 30 MIN. BAKE: 15 MIN.

My husband and three sons love these crispy sandwiches filled with a moist, pizza-flavored mixture. They're so popular, I often make them on a weekend and double the recipe.

Barbara Mery ✳ Bothell, Washington

  1   pound ground beef
1/2   cup chopped onion
  1   can (15 ounces) pizza sauce
1/4   cup chopped ripe olives
  2   teaspoons dried basil
  1   teaspoon dried oregano
  8   hoagie *or* submarine sandwich buns
      or French rolls
  2   cups (8 ounces) shredded part-skim
      mozzarella cheese

In a large skillet, cook the beef and onion over medium heat until meat is no longer pink; drain. Stir in the pizza sauce, olives, basil and oregano. Cook for 10 minutes or until heated through.

Cut 1/4 in. off the top of each roll; set aside. Carefully hollow out bottom of roll, leaving a 1/4-in. shell. Sprinkle 2 tablespoons cheese inside each shell. Fill each with about 1/2 cup meat mixture. Sprinkle with remaining cheese, gently pressing down to flatten. Replace the bread tops.

Individually wrap four sandwiches tightly in foil; freeze for up to 3 months. Place remaining sandwiches on a baking sheet. Bake at 375° for 15 minutes or until heated through.

TO USE FROZEN: Place the foil wrapped sandwiches on the baking sheets. Bake at 375° for 60-70 minutes or until heated through. **YIELD: 8 SERVINGS.**

Colorful Beef Wraps

Colorful Beef Wraps

PREP/TOTAL TIME: **30 MIN.**

I stir-fry a combination of sirloin steak, onions and peppers for these hearty wraps. Spreading a little fat-free ranch salad dressing inside the tortillas really jazzes up the taste.

Robyn Cavallaro * Easton, Pennsylvania

- 1 boneless beef sirloin steak (1 pound), cut into thin strips
- 3 garlic cloves, minced
- 1/4 teaspoon pepper
- 3 tablespoons reduced-sodium soy sauce, *divided*
- 3 teaspoons olive oil, *divided*
- 1 medium red onion, cut into wedges
- 1 jar (7 ounces) roasted sweet red peppers, drained and cut into strips
- 1/4 cup dry red wine *or* reduced-sodium beef broth
- 6 tablespoons fat-free ranch salad dressing
- 6 flour tortillas (8 inches)
- 1-1/2 cups torn iceberg lettuce
- 1 medium tomato, chopped
- 1/4 cup chopped green onions

In a large nonstick skillet coated with cooking spray, saute the beef, garlic, pepper and 2 tablespoons soy sauce in 2 teaspoons oil until meat is no longer pink. Remove and keep warm.

Saute onion in remaining oil for 2 minutes. Stir in the red peppers, wine and remaining soy sauce; bring to a boil. Return beef to pan; simmer for 5 minutes or until heated through.

Spread the ranch dressing over one side of each tortilla; sprinkle with the lettuce, tomato and green onions. Spoon about 3/4 cup beef mixture down the center of each tortilla; roll up. **YIELD: 6 SERVINGS.**

NUTRITION FACTS: 1 wrap equals 325 calories, 9 g fat (2 g saturated fat), 43 mg cholesterol, 830 mg sodium, 39 g carbohydrate, 1 g fiber, 20 g protein. DIABETIC EXCHANGES: 2 starch, 2 lean meat, 1 vegetable, 1 fat.

Zesty Turkey Burgers

PREP/TOTAL TIME: **25 MIN.**

My husband and I were watching our weight last summer and we found that this recipe was really easy to make. Plus, it's delicious!

Louise Gilbert * Quesnel, British Columbia

- 1/2 cup ketchup
- 1 tablespoon cider vinegar
- 1 tablespoon Worcestershire sauce
- 2 garlic cloves, minced
- 1/4 teaspoon pepper
- 1/4 teaspoon crushed red pepper flakes
- 1/4 teaspoon hot pepper sauce
- 1/3 cup quick-cooking oats
- 1 pound lean ground turkey
- 4 lettuce leaves
- 4 hamburger buns, split

In a small bowl, combine the ketchup, vinegar, Worcestershire sauce, garlic, pepper, red pepper flakes and hot pepper sauce. Transfer half of the mixture to a large bowl; stir in the oats. Set remaining ketchup mixture aside for basting. Crumble turkey over oat mixture and mix well. Shape into four patties.

Coat grill rack with cooking spray before starting the grill. Grill the patties, covered, over medium heat for 5-7 minutes on each side or until a meat thermometer reads 165° and meat juices run clear, basting occasionally with the ketchup mixture. Serve on lettuce-lined buns. **YIELD: 4 SERVINGS.**

NUTRITION FACTS: 1 burger equals 355 calories, 12 g fat (3 g saturated fat), 90 mg cholesterol, 746 mg sodium, 36 g carbohydrate, 2 g fiber, 25 g protein. DIABETIC EXCHANGES: 3 lean meat, 2 starch.

Zesty Turkey Burgers

Italian Sausage Calzone

PREP: **20 MIN.** BAKE: **30 MIN. + STANDING**

My teenage daughter and I have been experimenting in the kitchen to re-create some old-time family dishes. This calzone with spinach and sausage is definitely a favorite. Using a refrigerated pizza crust, it's a cinch to prepare one for us or several for a crowd.

Terri Gallagher ✳ King George, Virginia

- 1 tube (13.8 ounces) refrigerated pizza crust
- 1 can (8 ounces) pizza sauce
- 1 package (10 ounces) frozen chopped spinach, thawed and squeezed dry
- 1 pound bulk Italian sausage, cooked and drained
- 1 jar (4-1/2 ounces) sliced mushrooms, drained
- 2 cups (8 ounces) shredded part-skim mozzarella cheese

Unroll pizza dough onto an ungreased baking sheet; pat into a 14-in. x 11-in. rectangle. Spread the pizza sauce over one long side of dough to within 1/2 in. of edges.

Layer the spinach, sausage, mushrooms and cheese over sauce. Fold dough over filling; pinch seams to seal.

Bake at 400° for 30-35 minutes or until golden brown. Let stand for 10-15 minutes before slicing. **YIELD: 6 SERVINGS.**

Italian Sausage Calzone

Beef Gyros

PREP/TOTAL TIME: **30 MIN.**

Going out to restaurants for gyros got to be expensive for our family, so I came up with this homemade version. Usually, I set out the fixings so everyone can assemble their own. My husband and our kids request them often.

Sheri Scheerhorn ✳ Hills, Minnesota

- 1 cup ranch salad dressing
- 1/2 cup chopped seeded peeled cucumber
- 1 pound boneless beef sirloin steak, cut into thin strips
- 2 tablespoons olive oil
- 5 whole gyro-style pitas (6 inches)
- 1 medium tomato, chopped
- 1 can (2-1/4 ounces) sliced ripe olives, drained
- 1/2 small onion, thinly sliced
- 1 carton (4 ounces) crumbled feta cheese
- 2-1/2 cups shredded lettuce

In a small bowl, combine the salad dressing and cucumber; set aside. In a large skillet, brown beef in oil over medium heat.

Layer half of each pita with steak, tomato, olives, onion, feta cheese, lettuce and dressing mixture. Bring edges of each pita over filling and secure with a toothpick. **YIELD: 5 SERVINGS.**

Beef Gyros

Hearty Veggie Sandwiches

PREP/TOTAL TIME: **20 MIN.**

This vegetarian delight is not only healthy, it tastes great, too. Any way you slice it, this is one refreshing, flavor-filled sandwich!

Micki Sannar ✳ Highland, Utah

- 2 teaspoons mayonnaise
- 2 teaspoons prepared mustard
- 4 slices whole wheat bread
- 4 slices cheddar cheese (3/4 ounce *each*)
- 2 slices red onion
- 1/4 cup sliced ripe olives, drained
- 1 small tomato, sliced
- 1 medium ripe avocado, peeled and sliced
- 1/8 teaspoon pepper
- 4 tablespoons Italian salad dressing
- 2 lettuce leaves

Hearty Veggie Sandwiches

Fresh Mozzarella Sandwiches

Spread the mayonnaise and mustard over two slices of bread; layer with cheese, onion, olives, tomato and avocado. Sprinkle with the pepper.

Drizzle each sandwich with 1 tablespoon of dressing. Top with lettuce. Drizzle remaining dressing over remaining bread; place over the sandwiches dressing side down. **YIELD: 2 SERVINGS.**

Fresh Mozzarella Sandwiches

PREP: 25 MIN. COOK: 35 MIN.

As girls, my sisters and I always helped our mother make these melted cheese sandwiches. Served with a robust tomato sauce for dipping, they made a quick lunch or dinner.

Kristine Chayes ✳ Smithtown, New York

1/4 cup chopped onion
  1 garlic clove, minced
  2 tablespoons olive oil
  1 can (28 ounces) crushed tomatoes in puree
  1 teaspoon grape jelly
1/2 teaspoon dried oregano
1/2 teaspoon dried basil
1/2 teaspoon salt
1/8 teaspoon pepper

SANDWICHES:
  1 pound fresh mozzarella cheese, cut into 1/2-inch slices
  8 slices sourdough bread (3/4 inch thick)
  2 eggs, lightly beaten
3/4 cup milk
1/2 teaspoon salt
1/4 teaspoon pepper
  2 tablespoons butter

In a large saucepan, saute the onion and garlic in oil until tender. Stir in the tomatoes, jelly, oregano, basil, salt and pepper. Bring to a boil. Reduce the heat; simmer, uncovered, for 20 minutes, stirring several times.

Meanwhile, for sandwiches, arrange cheese on four slices of bread to within 1/2 in. of edges. Top with remaining bread. In a shallow bowl, combine the eggs, milk, salt and pepper. Dip the sandwiches in egg mixture.

Melt 1 tablespoon butter in a large skillet over medium heat. Add two sandwiches; toast over medium heat for 4-5 minutes on each side or until golden brown and the cheese is melted. Repeat with remaining sandwiches and butter. Serve with the tomato sauce for dipping. **YIELD: 4 SERVINGS.**

Genoa Sandwich Loaf

Genoa Sandwich Loaf

PREP: **20 MIN.** BAKE: **15 MIN. + STANDING**

Being an Italian American, I love this open-faced meat and cheese sandwich because it tastes like home. My Irish husband enjoys it as much as my relatives do when I fix it for family gatherings. Homemade pesto adds that something special.

Melita Doyle ✳ Milton-Freewater, Oregon

- 1/3 cup olive oil
- 1-1/4 cups packed minced fresh parsley
- 1 cup minced fresh basil
- 1/2 cup shredded Parmesan cheese, *divided*
- 4 garlic cloves, peeled
- 1/4 teaspoon ground nutmeg
- 1 package (8 ounces) cream cheese, softened
- 1 loaf (1 pound) French bread, halved lengthwise
- 1 pound thinly sliced hard salami
- 2 large tomatoes, thinly sliced

For pesto, in a blender, combine the oil, parsley, basil, 1/4 cup Parmesan cheese, garlic and nutmeg. Cover and process on high until blended.

Spread the cream cheese over cut sides of bread; spread with pesto. Layer the salami and tomatoes over the pesto; sprinkle with the remaining Parmesan cheese. Place on an ungreased baking sheet. Bake at 350° for 15-20 minutes or until cheese is melted. Let stand for 10 minutes before cutting. **YIELD: 8-10 SERVINGS.**

Curried Chicken Salad Sandwiches

PREP/TOTAL TIME: **20 MIN.**

This sandwich is perfect to serve when you want to show off a little. It features an interesting blend of chicken, nuts, cranberries and curry. I mix it up the night before so the flavors meld.

Carole Martin ✳ Coffeeville, Mississippi

- 2 cups cubed cooked chicken breast
- 3/4 cup chopped apple
- 3/4 cup dried cranberries
- 3/4 cup mayonnaise
- 1/2 cup chopped walnuts
- 1/2 cup chopped celery

2 teaspoons lemon juice

1 tablespoon chopped green onion

1 teaspoon curry powder

6 lettuce leaves

6 croissants, split

In a large bowl, combine the chicken, apple, cranberries, mayonnaise, walnuts, celery, lemon juice, onion and curry powder. Place lettuce on croissants. Top with chicken salad mixture. **YIELD: 6 SERVINGS.**

Curried Chicken Salad Sandwiches

Bavarian Meatball Sandwiches

PREP: **15 MIN.** COOK: **3-1/2 HOURS**

I use my slow cooker so much, and these mouth-watering meatballs are just one reason why. They're a guaranteed crowd-pleaser. You can also serve them as yummy party appetizers.

Peggy Rios ✳ Mechanicsville, Virginia

1 package (38 ounces) frozen cooked Italian meatballs

1/2 cup chopped onion

1/4 cup packed brown sugar

1 envelope onion soup mix

1 can (12 ounces) beer *or* nonalcoholic beer

12 hoagie buns, split

3 cups (12 ounces) shredded Swiss cheese

In a 3-qt. slow cooker, combine the meatballs, onion, brown sugar, soup mix and beer. Cover and cook on low for 3-1/2 to 4-1/2 hours or until heated through.

Place the six meatballs on each bun bottom. Sprinkle each sandwich with 1/4 cup cheese. Place on baking sheets. Broil 4-6 in. from the heat for 2-3 minutes or until cheese is melted. Replace bun tops. **YIELD: 12 SERVINGS.**

EDITOR'S NOTE: To serve as an appetizer, keep the meatballs warm in the slow cooker on a buffet and serve with a slotted spoon. Or plate the meatballs and serve with toothpicks.

Bavarian Meatball Sandwiches

Special Turkey Sandwiches

Special Turkey Sandwiches

PREP/TOTAL TIME: **25 MIN.**

Every Saturday night, my family loves to have sandwiches for dinner. With their rich cream cheese spread, these have become a favorite. They don't taste at all light.

Maria Bertram ✳ Waltham, Massachusetts

- 4 ounces reduced-fat cream cheese
- 1/2 cup finely chopped fresh spinach
- 1/2 cup minced fresh basil
- 1/3 cup shredded Parmesan cheese
- 1 garlic clove, minced
- 1/2 large red onion, sliced
- 2 tablespoons dry red wine *or* reduced-sodium beef broth
- 8 slices whole wheat bread, toasted
- 3/4 pound sliced deli turkey
- 8 slices tomato
- 8 lettuce leaves

In a small bowl, beat the cream cheese, spinach, basil, Parmesan cheese and garlic until blended; set aside. In a small skillet, cook onion in wine until tender; set aside.

Place four slices of toast on a broiler pan; top with turkey. Place remaining toast on broiler pan; spread with cream cheese mixture.

Broil 3-4 in. from the heat for 2-3 minutes or until heated through. Layer the onion, tomato and lettuce over turkey. Top with remaining toast. **YIELD: 4 SERVINGS.**

NUTRITION FACTS: 1 sandwich equals 348 calories, 11 g fat (6 g saturated fat), 63 mg cholesterol, 1,426 mg sodium, 36 g carbohydrate, 5 g fiber, 29 g protein. DIABETIC EXCHANGES: 3 very lean meat, 2 starch, 1-1/2 fat.

Buffalo Chicken Wraps

Buffalo Chicken Wraps

PREP/TOTAL TIME: **25 MIN.**

Blue cheese dressing and hot pepper sauce enhance these yummy tortilla wraps. Filled with chicken, cheese, lettuce and tomatoes, they're colorful, fun to eat...and totable, too!

Athena Russell ✳ Florence, South Carolina

- 1 cup all-purpose flour
- 1 teaspoon salt

1/4 teaspoon pepper

1/2 cup buttermilk

4 boneless skinless chicken breast halves
   (4 ounces *each*)

1 cup canola oil

1/2 cup hot pepper sauce

1/4 cup butter, melted

4 spinach tortillas (10 inches)

1 cup shredded lettuce

1 cup (4 ounces) shredded cheddar cheese

2/3 cup chopped tomatoes

1/2 cup blue cheese salad dressing

In a shallow bowl, combine the flour, salt and pepper. Place buttermilk in another shallow bowl. Dip chicken in buttermilk, then roll in flour mixture.

In a large skillet, cook the chicken in oil for 4-5 minutes on each side or until a meat thermometer reads 170°. Drain on paper towels; cut into strips.

In a small bowl, combine hot pepper sauce and butter. Dip chicken strips into mixture, coating both sides. Place chicken in the center of each tortilla. Layer with the lettuce, cheese and tomatoes; drizzle with salad dressing. Bring up sides of tortillas; secure with toothpicks if desired. **YIELD: 4 SERVINGS.**

Greek Turkey Burgers

PREP/TOTAL TIME: **30 MIN.**

I pared down the recipe for these mouthwatering burgers after it was given to me by a dear friend. Cumin and cayenne pepper add to the turkey's wonderful taste.

Marianne Shira ∗ Osceola, Wisconsin

SAUCE:

1/3 cup fat-free plain yogurt

1/3 cup reduced-fat mayonnaise

1/4 cup chopped seeded peeled cucumber

1/4 teaspoon Worcestershire sauce

1/4 teaspoon garlic powder

1/8 teaspoon salt

1/8 teaspoon pepper

Dash dried thyme

Greek Turkey Burgers

BURGERS:

1/2 cup finely chopped sweet onion

1/2 cup finely chopped green pepper

1 teaspoon ground cumin

1/4 teaspoon salt

1/4 teaspoon pepper

1/4 teaspoon cayenne pepper

1-1/2 pounds extra-lean ground turkey

1/2 cup thinly sliced cucumber

6 slices tomato

6 hamburger buns, split

For cucumber sauce, in a small bowl, combine the sauce ingredients. Cover and refrigerate until serving.

In a large bowl, combine the onion, green pepper, cumin, salt, pepper and cayenne. Crumble turkey over mixture and mix well. Shape into six patties.

If grilling the burgers, coat grill rack with cooking spray before starting the grill. Grill, covered, over medium heat or broil 4 in. from the heat for 5-7 minutes on each side or until a meat thermometer reads 165° and the juices run clear.

Place the cucumber and tomato slices on buns; top each bun with a burger and about 2 tablespoons cucumber sauce. **YIELD: 6 SERVINGS.**

NUTRITION FACTS: 1 burger equals 316 calories, 9 g fat (1 g saturated fat), 51 mg cholesterol, 586 mg sodium, 28 g carbohydrate, 2 g fiber, 33 g protein. DIABETIC EXCHANGES: 4 very lean meat, 1-1/2 starch, 1 vegetable, 1 fat.

Roast Beef Barbecue

Pizza Loaf

PREP: **20 MIN.** BAKE: **35 MIN.**

This savory stromboli relies on frozen bread dough, so it comes together in no time. The golden loaf is stuffed with cheese, pepperoni, mushrooms, peppers and olives. I often add a few this slices of ham, too. It's tasty served with warm pizza sauce for dipping.

Jenny Brown ✳ West Lafayette, Indiana

- 1 loaf (1 pound) frozen bread dough, thawed
- 2 eggs, *separated*
- 1 tablespoon grated Parmesan cheese
- 1 tablespoon olive oil
- 1 teaspoon minced fresh parsley
- 1 teaspoon dried oregano
- 1/2 teaspoon garlic powder
- 1/4 teaspoon pepper
- 8 ounces sliced pepperoni
- 2 cups (8 ounces) shredded part-skim mozzarella cheese
- 1 can (4 ounces) mushroom stems and pieces, drained
- 1/4 to 1/2 cup pickled pepper rings
- 1 medium green pepper, diced
- 1 can (2-1/4 ounces) sliced ripe olives
- 1 can (15 ounces) pizza sauce

On a greased baking sheet, roll out dough into a 15-in. x 10-in. rectangle. In a small bowl, combine the egg yolks, Parmesan cheese, oil, parsley, oregano, garlic powder and pepper. Brush over the dough.

Sprinkle with the pepperoni, mozzarella cheese, mushrooms, pepper rings, green pepper and olives. Roll up jelly-roll style, starting with a long side; pinch seam to seal and tuck ends under.

Place seam side down; brush with the egg whites. Do not let rise. Bake at 350° for 35-40 minutes or until golden brown. Warm the pizza sauce; serve with sliced loaf. YIELD: **10-12 SLICES.**

🍲 Roast Beef Barbecue

PREP/TOTAL TIME: **10 MIN.**

When I'm in a hurry and want something good, this sandwich fills the bill. It tastes great with a salad and pork and beans on the side. Instead of using ketchup, I occasionally use barbecue sauce with a little Tabasco for extra zip.

Agnes Ward ✳ Stratford, Ontario

- 2/3 pound thinly sliced deli roast beef
- 1/2 cup water
- 1/4 cup ketchup
- 1 tablespoon brown sugar
- 1/2 teaspoon prepared mustard
- 1/4 teaspoon hot pepper sauce
- 1/8 teaspoon salt
- 1/8 teaspoon pepper
- 1/8 teaspoon chili powder
- 4 hamburger buns, split

In a small saucepan, combine the beef, water, ketchup, sugar, mustard, hot pepper sauce, salt, pepper and chili powder. Cook over medium-high heat for 4-6 minutes or until heated through. Serve on buns, using a slotted spoon. YIELD: **4 SERVINGS.**

Reunion Steak Sandwiches

PREP: **20 MIN.** GRILL: **20 MIN.**

Every year, my grandma hosts a family reunion where these flank steak subs steal the show. They're topped with a "special sauce" that requires only three ingredients. For a quick dinner, serve them with coleslaw and macaroni salad from the deli.

Jan Clark ✳ Ridgewood, New Jersey

- 1 beef flank steak (1-1/2 pounds)
- 1/4 teaspoon salt
- 1/4 teaspoon pepper
- 2 tablespoons butter, softened
- 6 sesame submarine sandwich buns, split
- 2 medium tomatoes, thinly sliced
- 1 medium onion, thinly sliced
- 6 slices process American cheese

MUSTARD SAUCE:

- 1/2 cup mayonnaise
- 2 tablespoons Dijon mustard
- 4-1/2 teaspoons Worcestershire sauce

Pizza Loaf

Sprinkle the steak with salt and pepper. Grill, covered, over medium-hot heat for 6-10 minutes on each side or until the meat reaches desired doneness (for medium-rare, a meat thermometer should read 145°; medium, 160°; well-done, 170°). Let stand for 5 minutes before thinly slicing.

Spread butter over inside of buns. Place the tomatoes, onion, sliced steak and cheese on the bun bottoms. Broil 5-6 in. from the heat for 2-3 minutes or until cheese is melted. In a small bowl, whisk the mayonnaise, mustard and Worcestershire sauce until blended; spoon over cheese. Replace bun tops. **YIELD: 6 SERVINGS.**

Reunion Steak Sandwiches

Pineapple-Stuffed Burgers

Pineapple-Stuffed Burgers

PREP/TOTAL TIME: **30 MIN.**

I really enjoy making these special burgers with a surprise inside. The homemade sauce, with brown sugar, mustard and ketchup, makes these tropical grilled sandwiches even better.

Ann Couch ✳ Halifax, North Carolina

- 1/4 cup packed brown sugar
- 1/4 cup ketchup
- 1 tablespoon prepared mustard
- 1/2 pound lean ground beef
- 2 slices unsweetened pineapple
- 1/8 teaspoon salt
- 1/8 teaspoon pepper
- 2 hamburger buns, split
- 2 lettuce leaves

In a small saucepan, combine the brown sugar, ketchup and mustard. Cook over medium heat for 2-3 minutes, stirring occasionally.

Meanwhile, shape beef into four patties. Place pineapple slices on two patties; top with remaining patties. Seal edges; sprinkle with salt and pepper.

Coat grill rack with cooking spray before starting the grill. Grill burgers, covered, over medium-hot heat for 7-9 minutes on each side or until a meat thermometer reads 160° and juices run clear. Serve on buns with the sauce and lettuce. **YIELD: 2 SERVINGS.**

Bacon 'n' Egg Salad Sandwiches

PREP: **25 MIN. + CHILLING**

On days I don't have much time to cook, egg salad on croissants hits the spot. It's also nice made with toasted bread or English muffins. Our family loves egg dishes of any kind. Luckily, my mom owns 30 chickens and keeps me supplied with farm-fresh ingredients.

Jane Ozment ✳ Purcell, Oklahoma

- 10 hard-cooked eggs, chopped
- 4 bacon strips, cooked and crumbled
- 1/2 cup shredded cheddar cheese

Bacon 'n' Egg Salad Sandwiches

Italian Sausage Subs

1/2 cup sour cream
1/3 cup mayonnaise
2 tablespoons snipped chives
1/4 teaspoon salt
1/4 teaspoon pepper
8 lettuce leaves
8 croissants, split

In a large bowl, combine the eggs, bacon, cheese, sour cream, mayonnaise, chives, salt and pepper. Cover and refrigerate for at least 2 hours. Serve on lettuce-lined croissants. **YIELD: 8 SERVINGS.**

Italian Sausage Subs

PREP/TOTAL TIME: **30 MIN.**
This sausage sub is dressed up with onion, sweet red pepper and pizza sauce. It's sure to fill you up!

Sue Hoyt ✳ Portland, Oregon

2 Italian sausage links (4 ounces *each*)
1/4 cup reduced-sodium chicken broth
1/3 cup thinly sliced onion
2 teaspoons olive oil
1/3 cup julienned sweet red pepper
1 garlic clove, minced
Dash pepper
2 teaspoons balsamic vinegar
2 Italian rolls *or* submarine buns, split
1/4 cup pizza sauce
1 slice provolone cheese, halved (3/4 ounce)

In a small nonstick skillet, brown sausages on all sides over medium heat. Add broth; cover and simmer for 10 minutes. Remove sausages and keep warm; discard broth.

In the same pan, saute onion in oil until crisp-tender. Add the red pepper, garlic and pepper; cook until red pepper is crisp-tender. Add vinegar and sausages; heat through.

Spread rolls with pizza sauce; top with the sausage, cheese and onion mixture. Broil 4-6 in. from the heat for 2-3 minutes or until cheese is melted. **YIELD: 2 SERVINGS.**

Southwestern Burgers

🍳 Southwestern Burgers

PREP/TOTAL TIME: **15 MIN.**

We love burgers and have them every Saturday in summer. We also have a favorite burrito recipe. One day, we got the bright idea to combine two of our favorite recipes. Voila! Our Southwestern Burgers were created.

Tammy Fortney ✳ Deer Park, Washington

- 1 can (4 ounces) chopped green chilies
- 4 teaspoons ground cumin
- 1 teaspoon chili powder
- 3/4 teaspoon garlic powder
- 3/4 teaspoon salt
- 1/2 teaspoon pepper
- 2 pounds lean ground beef
- 3/4 pound bulk pork sausage
- 8 slices Monterey Jack cheese
- 8 hamburger buns, split, toasted
- 8 lettuce leaves
- 1 large tomato, sliced
- 1 to 2 ripe avocados, peeled and sliced

Mayonnaise *or* mustard, optional

In a large bowl, combine the green chilies and seasonings. Crumble beef and sausage over mixture; mix well. Shape into eight patties.

Grill, covered, over medium heat for 5 minutes on each side or until a meat thermometer reads 160° and juices run clear. Top each burger with a cheese slice.

Grill 1-2 minutes longer or until cheese begins to melt. Serve on buns with the lettuce, tomato, avocado and mayonnaise or mustard if desired. **YIELD: 8 SERVINGS.**

🥪 Chicken Salad Panini

PREP/TOTAL TIME: **25 MIN.**

Grilled indoors, this delightful sandwich can be enjoyed any time of the year. The honey-mustard dressing gives the chicken plenty of pizzazz, and the apple and pecans lend a lively crunch.

Lisa Huff ✳ Birmingham, Alabama

- 1/4 cup mayonnaise
- 1-1/2 teaspoons honey
- 3/4 teaspoon snipped fresh dill
- 3/4 teaspoon Dijon mustard

Dash salt

Dash pepper

- 1 cup cubed cooked chicken breast
- 3/4 cup shredded cheddar cheese
- 1/2 cup chopped peeled apple
- 1/4 cup chopped pecans, toasted
- 6 slices white bread
- 4 teaspoons butter, softened

In a bowl, combine the first six ingredients. In another bowl, combine the chicken, cheese, apple and pecans; add the dressing and toss to coat.

Spread half of the chicken salad on two slices of bread. Top each with another slice of bread, remaining chicken salad and remaining bread. Spread the butter on both sides of the sandwiches. Cook on a panini maker or indoor grill until bread is toasted and cheese is melted. **YIELD: 2 SERVINGS.**

Chicken Salad Panini

Cobb Salad Wraps

PREP/TOTAL TIME: 15 MIN.

A homemade dressing lightens up these refreshing tortilla wraps. The avocado, bacon, blue cheese and tomato deliver the flavors I enjoy most while keeping me on my healthy eating plan.

Lynne Van Wagenen * Salt Lake City, Utah

- 1/2 pound boneless skinless chicken breasts, cooked and shredded
- 1/2 cup chopped avocado
- 4 bacon strips, cooked and crumbled
- 1 celery rib, thinly sliced
- 1 green onion, sliced
- 2 tablespoons chopped ripe olives
- 2 tablespoons crumbled blue cheese
- 2 tablespoons lemon juice
- 1 tablespoon honey
- 1-1/2 teaspoons Dijon mustard
- 1 garlic clove, minced
- 1/4 teaspoon dill weed
- 1/4 teaspoon salt
- 1/8 teaspoon pepper
- 1 tablespoon olive oil
- 4 romaine leaves, torn
- 4 whole wheat tortillas (8 inches), warmed
- 1 medium tomato, chopped

In a small bowl, combine the chicken, avocado, bacon, celery, onion, olives and cheese.

In another small bowl, combine the lemon juice, honey, mustard, garlic, dill weed, salt and pepper. Whisk in the oil. Pour over the chicken mixture; toss to coat. Place romaine on each tortilla; top with 2/3 cup chicken mixture. Sprinkle with tomato; roll up. **YIELD: 4 SERVINGS.**

NUTRITION FACTS: 1 wrap equals 324 calories, 14 g fat (4 g saturated fat), 57 mg cholesterol, 608 mg sodium, 30 g carbohydrate, 4 g fiber, 24 g protein. DIABETIC EXCHANGES: 3 lean meat, 2 starch.

Cobb Salad Wraps

Italian Chicken Wraps

PREP/TOTAL TIME: **25 MIN.**

After enjoying a chicken wrap at a restaurant, I experimented at home to create something similar. This delicious version is as fast as it is delicious.

Cathy Hofflander ✳ Adrian, Michigan

- 1 package (16 ounces) frozen stir-fry vegetable blend
- 2 packages (6 ounces *each*) ready-to-use grilled chicken breast strips
- 1/2 cup fat-free Italian salad dressing
- 3 tablespoons shredded Parmesan cheese
- 6 flour tortillas (8 inches), room temperature

In a large saucepan, cook vegetables according to package directions; drain. Stir in the chicken, salad dressing and cheese. Simmer, uncovered, for 3-4 minutes or until heated through. Spoon about 3/4 cup down the center of each tortilla; roll up tightly. YIELD: **6 SERVINGS.**

NUTRITIONAL FACTS: 1 wrap equals 290 calories, 6 g fat (2 g saturated fat), 40 mg cholesterol, 1,129 mg sodium, 38 g carbohydrate, 3 g fiber, 20 g protein. DIABETIC EXCHANGES: 2 lean meat, 2 vegetable, 1-1/2 starch.

Italian Chicken Wraps

Raspberry Grilled Cheese

Raspberry Grilled Cheese

PREP/TOTAL TIME: **15 MIN.**

My favorite appetizer is a raspberry-glazed cheese ball, so I used similar ingredients to dress up a plain grilled cheese sandwich. The quick combination was unique but tasty, and it became a popular request in my house.

Jane Beers ✳ Siloam Springs, Arkansas

- 2 tablespoons seedless red raspberry preserves
- 4 slices sourdough bread
- 2 tablespoons chopped pecans
- 1 to 2 tablespoons sliced green onion
- 4 slices Muenster *or* baby Swiss cheese
- 3 tablespoons butter, softened

Spread preserves on two slices of bread; top with the pecans, onion and cheese. Top with remaining bread; butter outsides of bread. Toast on a hot griddle for 3-4 minutes on each side or until golden brown. YIELD: **2 SERVINGS.**

Waffles with Peach-Berry Compote, PAGE 144

"This recipe was created one summer on a Sunday morning when I was looking for a more healthful alternative to butter and maple syrup to top my waffles. I was amazed at the results!"

Brandi Waters
Fayetteville, Arkansas

BREAKFAST & BRUNCH

DO YOU HAVE A WINNING RECIPE?

Enter your most prized recipes in the *Taste of Home* recipe contests, and you may win some money and the chance to have your recipe published. Log onto **tasteofhome.com/RecipeContests** for a list of our current contests and submission deadlines. Good luck...we'll be looking for your recipe.

breakfast & brunch

🍎 Apple Pancakes with 🍎 Cider Syrup

PREP/TOTAL TIME: **30 MIN.**

These tender pancakes are filled with minced apple and raisins and then drizzled with apple cider syrup. They are a wonderful treat in the summer or on a cool fall morning.

April Harmon ✳ Greeneville, Tennessee

1/2 cup all-purpose flour

1/4 cup whole wheat flour

2 teaspoons sugar

1/4 teaspoon baking soda

1/4 teaspoon salt

1/4 teaspoon ground cinnamon

2/3 cup minced peeled apple

1/4 cup raisins

2/3 cup buttermilk

1 egg, *separated*

2 teaspoons butter, melted

1/4 teaspoon vanilla extract

SYRUP:

1/4 cup sugar

2 teaspoons cornstarch

2/3 cup apple cider *or* juice

1 cinnamon stick (1-1/2 inches)

Dash ground nutmeg

Additional butter, optional

In a small bowl, combine the flours, sugar, baking soda, salt and cinnamon; stir in apple and raisins. Combine the buttermilk, egg yolk, butter and vanilla; stir into dry ingredients. In a small bowl, beat egg white until soft peaks form; fold into batter.

Pour batter by heaping 1/4 cupfuls onto a hot griddle coated with cooking spray; turn when bubbles form on top. Cook until the second side is lightly browned.

Apple Pancakes with Cider Syrup

Meanwhile, in a small saucepan, combine the sugar, cornstarch and cider until smooth; add the cinnamon stick. Bring to a boil over medium heat; cook and stir for 2 minutes or until thickened. Discard cinnamon stick. Stir nutmeg into syrup. Serve pancakes with warm syrup and additional butter if desired. YIELD: **6 PANCAKES (2/3 CUP SYRUP).**

Toasty Pumpkin Waffles

⏲ Toasty Pumpkin Waffles

PREP/TOTAL TIME: **30 MIN.**

When I really want to impress folks, I serve these waffles. They're beautiful with a fresh sprig of mint atop the sweet butter. It was my most requested recipe when I owned a bed and breakfast.

Brenda Ryan ✳ Marshall, Missouri

- 1 cup all-purpose flour
- 1 tablespoon brown sugar
- 1 teaspoon baking powder
- 1/4 teaspoon salt
- 1 egg, lightly beaten
- 1-1/4 cups milk
- 2/3 cup canned pumpkin
- 4-1/2 teaspoons butter, melted
- 1/3 cup chopped pecans

MAPLE CRANBERRY BUTTER:

- 1/2 cup fresh *or* frozen cranberries
- 1/4 cup maple syrup
- 1 cup butter, softened

Additional maple syrup, optional

In a large bowl, combine the flour, brown sugar, baking powder and salt. Whisk the egg, milk, pumpkin and butter; stir into dry ingredients until blended. Fold in pecans.

Bake in a preheated waffle iron according to manufacturer's directions until golden brown.

Meanwhile, in a small saucepan, combine cranberries and syrup. Cook over medium heat until the berries pop, about 10 minutes. Transfer to a small bowl; cool slightly. Beat in the butter until blended.

Serve waffles with maple cranberry butter and syrup if desired. Refrigerate or freeze the leftover butter. **YIELD: 4 SERVINGS (1 CUP BUTTER).**

Warm 'n' Fruity Breakfast Cereal

◐ Warm 'n' Fruity
Breakfast Cereal

PREP: **10 MIN.** COOK: **6 HOURS**

We love the heartiness of this nutritious cooked cereal seasoned with cinnamon and loaded with chopped fruit and nuts. We like it served with plain yogurt and sliced bananas or blueberries. It will start your day right!

John Vale ✳ Hardin, Montana

- 5   cups water
- 2   cups seven-grain cereal
- 1   medium apple, peeled and chopped
- 1   cup unsweetened apple juice
- 1/4 cup dried apricots, chopped
- 1/4 cup dried cranberries
- 1/4 cup raisins
- 1/4 cup chopped dates
- 1/4 cup maple syrup
- 1   teaspoon ground cinnamon
- 1/2 teaspoon salt

Chopped walnuts, optional

In a 5-qt. slow cooker, combine the first 11 ingredients. Cover and cook on low for 6-7 hours or until fruits are softened. Sprinkle individual servings with walnuts if desired. **YIELD: 10 CUPS.**

NUTRITION FACTS: 1 cup (calculated without walnuts) equals 185 calories, 3 g fat (trace saturated fat), 0 cholesterol, 120 mg sodium, 37 g carbohydrate, 5 g fiber, 5 g protein. **DIABETIC EXCHANGES:** 1 starch, 1 fruit, 1/2 fat.

◐ Caramelized Onion
Broccoli Quiche

PREP: **55 MIN. + RISING** BAKE: **50 MIN. + STANDING**

This is a wonderful dish for brunch or for supper, paired with a green salad. The combination of broccoli, sweet onions and feta cheese is delicious.

Kim Pettipas ✳ Oromocto, New Brunswick

- 3   cups sliced sweet onions
- 1   teaspoon sugar
- 1/2 teaspoon salt
- 2   teaspoons olive oil
- 2   cups frozen shredded hash brown potatoes, thawed

Caramelized Onion Broccoli Quiche

- 1   tube (11 ounces) refrigerated breadsticks
- 3   cups frozen chopped broccoli, thawed and drained
- 1   cup (4 ounces) crumbled feta cheese
- 2   eggs
- 2   egg whites
- 3/4 cup fat-free milk

In a large nonstick skillet, cook the onions, sugar and salt in oil over low heat for 40 minutes or until onions are softened and liquid has evaporated. Reduce heat to medium-low; add hash browns. Cook 8-10 minutes longer or until potatoes are golden brown. Remove from the heat and set aside.

To make crust, unroll breadstick dough onto a lightly floured surface and separate into strips. Pinch several breadsticks together, end to end, forming a rope. Holding one end of rope, loosely coil dough to form a circle. Add the remaining breadsticks to coil, one at a time, pinching ends together. Tuck end under; pinch to seal. Cover and let rest for 10 minutes.

Roll into a 10-1/2-in. to 11-in. circle. Transfer to an ungreased 9-in. pie plate. Spoon onion mixture into crust. Top with broccoli and cheese.

In a large bowl, whisk the eggs, egg whites and milk; pour over cheese (pie plate will be full). Bake 350° for 40 minutes. Cover the edges with foil. Bake 10-12 minutes longer or until a knife inserted near the center comes out clean. Let stand for 10 minutes before cutting. **YIELD: 6 SERVINGS.**

EDITOR'S NOTE: This recipe was tested with Pillsbury refrigerated breadsticks.

NUTRITION FACTS: 1 piece equals 365 calories, 12 g fat (5 g saturated fat), 94 mg cholesterol, 928 mg sodium, 50 g carbohydrate, 5 g fiber, 14 g protein. **DIABETIC EXCHANGES:** 2-1/2 starch, 2 vegetable, 1-1/2 fat, 1 lean meat.

Italian Garden Frittata

⏱ Italian Garden Frittata

PREP/TOTAL TIME: **30 MIN.**

I like to serve this pretty frittata with melon wedges for a delicious breakfast or brunch.

Sally Maloney ✳ Dallas, Georgia

- 6 egg whites
- 4 eggs
- 1/2 cup grated Romano cheese, *divided*
- 1 tablespoon minced fresh sage
- 1/2 teaspoon salt
- 1/4 teaspoon pepper
- 1 small zucchini, sliced
- 2 green onions, sliced
- 1 teaspoon olive oil
- 2 plum tomatoes, thinly sliced

In a large bowl, whisk egg whites, eggs, 1/4 cup Romano cheese, sage, salt and pepper; set aside.

In a 10-in. ovenproof skillet coated with cooking spray, saute zucchini and onions in oil for 2 minutes. Add egg mixture; cover and cook for 4-6 minutes or until eggs are nearly set.

Uncover; top with the tomato slices and remaining cheese. Broil 3-4 in. from heat for 2-3 minutes or until the eggs are completely set. Let stand for 5 minutes. Cut into wedges. **YIELD: 4 SERVINGS.**

NUTRITION FACTS: 1 wedge equals 183 calories, 11 g fat (5 g saturated fat), 228 mg cholesterol, 655 mg sodium, 4 g carbohydrate, 1 g fiber, 18 g protein.

Hot Fruit Compote

PREP: **15 MIN.** BAKE: **40 MIN.**

This sweet and colorful fruit compote is perfect with an egg casserole at a holiday brunch. It can bake right alongside the eggs, so everything is conveniently done at the same time.

Joyce Moynihan ✳ Lakeville, Minnesota

- 2 cans (15-1/4 ounces *each*) sliced pears, drained
- 1 can (29 ounces) sliced peaches, drained
- 1 can (20 ounces) unsweetened pineapple chunks, drained
- 1 package (20 ounces) pitted dried plums
- 1 jar (16 ounces) unsweetened applesauce
- 1 can (21 ounces) cherry pie filling
- 1/4 cup packed brown sugar

In a bowl, combine fruit and applesauce. Pour into a 13-in. x 9-in. baking dish coated with cooking spray. Spread pie filling over fruit mixture; sprinkle with brown sugar.

Cover and bake at 350° for 40-45 minutes or until bubbly. Serve warm. **YIELD: 20 SERVINGS.**

Garden Vegetable Quiche

PREP: 20 MIN. BAKE: 40 MIN. + STANDING

Make your next brunch special with this fluffy, deep-dish quiche. Fresh rosemary enhances this delightful egg dish that's chock-full of savory garden ingredients. It cuts nicely, too.

Kristina Ledford ✳ Indianapolis, Indiana

       1 unbaked deep-dish pastry shell (9 inches)
       1 small red onion, sliced
     1/2 cup sliced fresh mushrooms
     1/4 cup diced yellow summer squash
       3 garlic cloves, minced
       1 tablespoon butter
     1/2 cup fresh baby spinach
       1 cup (4 ounces) shredded Swiss cheese
       4 eggs
   1-2/3 cups heavy whipping cream
     1/2 teaspoon salt
     1/2 teaspoon minced fresh rosemary
     1/4 teaspoon pepper

Let pastry shell stand at room temperature for 10 minutes. Line unpricked pastry shell with a double thickness of heavy-duty foil. Bake at 400° for 4 minutes. Remove foil; bake 4 minutes longer. Cool on a wire rack. Reduce heat to 350°.

In a skillet, saute onion, mushrooms, squash and garlic in butter until tender. Add spinach; saute 1 minute longer. Spoon into crust; top with cheese.

In a large bowl, whisk the eggs, cream, salt, rosemary and pepper until blended; pour over the cheese.

Cover edges of crust loosely with foil. Bake for 40-45 minutes or until a knife inserted near the center comes out clean. Let stand for 10 minutes before cutting. **YIELD: 6-8 SERVINGS.**

Hot Fruit Compote

Garden Vegetable Quiche

Blue Cheese Spinach Frittata

✿ Blue Cheese Spinach Frittata

PREP: **30 MIN.** BAKE: **30 MIN.**

When my husband and I decided to lose weight, I turned to my cookbook collection and lightened up several recipes. With its fresh spinach salad, this hearty frittata quickly became a favorite.

Joyce Fairchild ✳ Marina Del Rey, California

- 1/2 cup chopped onion
- 4 garlic cloves, minced
- 1 package (10 ounces) fresh spinach, coarsely chopped
- 2 cups egg substitute
- 1-1/2 cups (6 ounces) shredded part-skim mozzarella cheese
- 1 cup (4 ounces) crumbled blue cheese
- 2 plum tomatoes, diced
- 1/4 cup chopped walnuts

SALAD:

- 2 cups coarsely chopped fresh spinach
- 2 plum tomatoes, diced
- 1 teaspoon rice vinegar
- 1/2 teaspoon olive oil
- 1/4 teaspoon garlic salt

In a large nonstick skillet coated with cooking spray, cook onion and garlic over medium heat for 3 minutes or until tender. Remove from the skillet. Add spinach to skillet in batches, cooking for 1 minute or until wilted. Remove from the heat.

In a large bowl, beat the egg substitute until frothy. Stir in the onion mixture, spinach, mozzarella, blue cheese, tomatoes and nuts. Place in a 10-in. ovenproof skillet coated with cooking spray.

Bake, uncovered, at 400° for 30-35 minutes or until a knife inserted near the center comes out clean. Combine the salad ingredients; serve with frittata. YIELD: **6 SERVINGS.**

NUTRITION FACTS: 1 piece with 1/3 cup salad equals 244 calories, 14 g fat (7 g saturated fat), 33 mg cholesterol, 689 mg sodium, 9 g carbohydrate, 3 g fiber, 22 g protein. DIABETIC EXCHANGES: 3 lean meat, 1 vegetable, 1 fat.

Jelly Doughnuts

Jelly Doughnuts

PREP: **30 MIN.** COOK: **10 MIN.**

There's no need to run to the bakery for delicious jelly doughnuts! These sweet treats are lighter than air. I've been fixing them for more than 25 years for my husband, our two daughters and their families. They disappear almost as fast as I make them.

Kathy Westendorf ✳ Westgate, Iowa

- 2 packages (1/4 ounce *each*) active dry yeast
- 1/2 cup warm water (110° to 115°)
- 1/2 cup warm milk (110° to 115°)
- 1/3 cup butter, softened
- 1-1/3 cups sugar, *divided*
- 3 egg yolks
- 1 teaspoon salt
- 3-3/4 cups all-purpose flour
- 3 tablespoons jelly *or* jam
- 1 egg white, lightly beaten

Oil for deep-fat frying

In a large bowl, dissolve yeast in warm water. Add the milk, butter, 1/3 cup sugar, egg yolks and salt; mix well. Stir in enough flour to form a soft dough (do not knead). Place in a greased bowl, turning once to grease top. Cover and let rise in a warm place until doubled, about 1-1/2 hours.

Punch the dough down. Turn onto a lightly floured surface; knead about 10 times. Divide dough in half.

Roll each portion to 1/4-in. thickness; cut with a floured 2-1/2-in. round cutter. Place about 1/2 teaspoon jelly in the center of half of the circles; brush edges with egg white. Top with remaining circles; press edges to seal tightly. Place on greased baking sheet. Cover and let rise until doubled, about 1 hour.

In an electric skillet or deep-fat fryer, heat oil to 375°. Fry doughnuts, a few at a time, for 1-2 minutes on each side or until golden brown. Drain the doughnuts on paper towels. Roll the doughnuts in the remaining sugar while warm. YIELD: **16 DOUGHNUTS.**

Onion Pie

Onion Pie

PREP: **15 MIN.** BAKE: **40 MIN.**

My mother got this recipe over 30 years ago and said it originated in a Pennsylvania Dutch kitchen.

Marian Benthin ✳ Apalachin, New York

- 1-1/3 cups biscuit/baking mix
- 1 teaspoon rubbed sage
- 1/2 teaspoon salt
- 4 to 5 tablespoons milk

FILLING:

- 5 cups thinly sliced onions (about 5 medium)
- 2 tablespoons canola oil
- 1/2 teaspoon salt
- 1 egg
- 1 cup half-and-half cream

In a large bowl, combine the biscuit mix, sage and salt. Add enough milk until mixture hold together. Press onto the bottom and up the sides of a 9-in. pie plate; set aside.

In a large skillet, saute onions in oil until tender. Sprinkle with salt. Spoon into crust. In a bowl, beat egg and cream; pour over onions.

Bake, uncovered, at 375° for 15 minutes. Reduce heat to 325°. Bake 25-30 minutes longer or until a knife inserted near the center comes out clean. YIELD: **6-8 SERVINGS.**

Waffles with Peach-Berry Compote

In a small saucepan, combine the peaches, orange juice, brown sugar and cinnamon; bring to a boil over medium heat. Add berries; cook and stir for 8-10 minutes or until thickened.

In a bowl, combine flours, flaxseed, baking powder, baking soda and cinnamon. Combine the buttermilk, orange juice, oil and vanilla; stir into dry ingredients just until moistened.

Bake in a preheated waffle iron according to the manufacturer's directions until golden brown. Serve with the compote. **YIELD: 12 WAFFLES (1-1/2 CUPS COMPOTE).**

NUTRITION FACTS: 2 waffles with 1/4 cup compote equals 251 calories, 4 g fat (1 g saturated fat), 2 mg cholesterol, 324 mg sodium, 47 g carbohydrate, 4 g fiber, 7 g protein. **DIABETIC EXCHANGES:** 2-1/2 starch, 1/2 fruit, 1/2 fat.

Waffles with Peach-Berry Compote

PREP: **25 MIN.** COOK: **5 MIN./BATCH**

This recipe was created one summer on a Sunday morning when I was looking for a more healthful alternative to butter and maple syrup to top my waffles. I was amazed at the results!

Brandi Waters ✳ Fayetteville, Arkansas

- 1 cup fresh *or* frozen peeled peach slices, chopped
- 1/2 cup orange juice
- 2 tablespoons brown sugar
- 1/4 teaspoon ground cinnamon
- 1 cup fresh *or* frozen blueberries
- 1/2 cup sliced fresh *or* frozen strawberries

BATTER:

- 1-1/4 cups all-purpose flour
- 1/2 cup whole wheat flour
- 2 tablespoons flaxseed
- 1 teaspoon baking powder
- 1 teaspoon baking soda
- 1/2 teaspoon ground cinnamon
- 1 cup buttermilk
- 3/4 cup orange juice
- 1 tablespoon canola oil
- 1 teaspoon vanilla extract

Egg and Broccoli Casserole

PREP: **10 MIN.** COOK: **3-1/2 HOURS**

For years, I've prepared this filling egg casserole—which is delicious for brunch—in my slow cooker. It's an unusual recipe for this appliance but is welcomed wherever I serve it. Folks always go back for seconds.

Janet Sliter ✳ Kennewick, Washington

- 3 cups (24 ounces) 4% cottage cheese
- 3 cups frozen chopped broccoli, thawed and drained
- 2 cups (8 ounces) shredded cheddar cheese
- 6 eggs, lightly beaten
- 1/3 cup all-purpose flour
- 1/4 cup butter, melted
- 3 tablespoons finely chopped onion
- 1/2 teaspoon salt

Additional shredded cheddar cheese, optional

In a large bowl, combine first eight ingredients. Pour into a greased 3-qt. slow cooker. Cover and cook on high for 1 hour. Stir.

Reduce heat to low; cover and cook 2-1/2 to 3 hours longer or until a thermometer placed in the center reads 160° and the eggs are set. Sprinkle with cheese if desired. **YIELD: 6 SERVINGS.**

Gran's Granola Parfaits

PREP: **15 MIN.** BAKE: **30 MIN. + COOLING**

When my mother-in-law (Gran to our kids) has us over for brunch, I especially enjoy her yogurt parfaits. They are refreshing, light and wholesome. I made a few changes to her recipe and came up with this sweet, crunchy and nutty variation. Yum!

Angela Keller ✳ Newburgh, Indiana

- 2 cups old-fashioned oats
- 1 cup Wheaties
- 1 cup whole almonds
- 1 cup pecan halves
- 1 cup flaked coconut
- 4-1/2 teaspoons toasted wheat germ
- 1 tablespoon sesame seeds, toasted
- 1 teaspoon ground cinnamon
- 1/4 cup butter, melted
- 2 tablespoons maple syrup
- 2 tablespoons honey
- 1 can (20 ounces) pineapple tidbits, drained
- 1 can (15 ounces) mandarin oranges, drained
- 1 cup halved green grapes
- 2 to 3 medium firm bananas, sliced
- 1 cup sliced fresh strawberries
- 1 carton (32 ounces) vanilla yogurt

In a large bowl, combine the oats, cereal, nuts, coconut, wheat germ, sesame seeds and cinnamon. Combine butter, syrup and honey; drizzle over the oat mixture and stir until well coated. Pour into a greased 13-in. x 9-in. baking pan. Bake, uncovered, at 350° for 30 minutes, stirring every 10 minutes. Cool on a wire rack; crumble into pieces.

    Combine fruits in a bowl. For each parfait, layer 2 tablespoons yogurt, 2 tablespoons of granola and 3 round tablespoons fruit in a parfait glass or dessert bowl. Repeat the layers. Sprinkle with the remaining granola. Serve immediately. **YIELD: 16 SERVINGS.**

Egg and Broccoli Casserole

Gran's Granola Parfaits

Crustless Four-Cheese Quiche

Crustless Four-Cheese Quiche

PREP: 30 MIN. BAKE: 35 MIN.

My husband is a real meat fan—but this luscious quiche is one meatless recipe he loves. In fact, he'll even go to the store and bring home Jarlsberg cheese as a hint that it's time for me to make it.

Susan Anderson ✳ Park City, Utah

- 1/4 cup butter
- 1/4 cup all-purpose flour
- 3/4 cup milk
- 1-1/4 cups 4% cottage cheese
- 1/2 teaspoon baking powder
- 1/2 teaspoon ground mustard
- 1/4 teaspoon salt
- 5 eggs
- 2 packages (3 ounces *each*) cream cheese, cubed
- 1/2 pound Jarlsberg *or* Swiss cheese, shredded
- 1/4 cup grated Parmesan cheese

In a small saucepan, melt butter. Stir in the flour until smooth; gradually add milk. Bring to a boil; cook and stir for 2 minutes or until thickened and bubbly. Remove from the heat; cool for 15 minutes.

Meanwhile, in a small bowl, combine the cottage cheese, baking powder, mustard and salt. In a large bowl, beat eggs. Slowly beat in the cream cheese, cottage cheese mixture and white sauce until smooth. Fold in the Jarlsberg and Parmesan.

Pour into a greased 9-in. pie plate. Bake at 350° for 35-40 minutes or until a knife inserted near the center comes out clean. Let stand for 5 minutes before cutting. Serve warm. Refrigerate leftovers. **YIELD: 6 SERVINGS.**

Meaty Apple Skillet

PREP/TOTAL TIME: 30 MIN.

I love having family over for breakfast, and they all look forward to this down-home, hearty specialty. Cinnamon, nutmeg and apple slices help combine the flavors of the four different meats in this robust dish. I slice and cook the meat the day before to beat the clock in the morning!

Sharon Berry ✳ Henderson, Nevada

Meaty Apple Skillet

1 large tart apple, peeled and thinly sliced

2 tablespoons butter

1 teaspoon ground cinnamon

1/8 teaspoon ground nutmeg

2 teaspoons cornstarch

2/3 cup cranberry-apple juice

1 pound smoked kielbasa *or* Polish sausage

3/4 pound bulk pork sausage, cooked and drained

3/4 pound pork sausage links, cooked and sliced

1-1/2 cups cubed fully cooked ham

In a large skillet, saute apple slices in butter; sprinkle with cinnamon and nutmeg. Cover and cook for 5 minutes or until apples are tender.

Combine cornstarch and juice until smooth; stir into the apple mixture. Bring to a boil; cook and stir for 2 minutes or until thickened. Add the sausage and ham and heat through. **YIELD: 12-16 SERVINGS.**

Sunshine Crepes

Sunshine Crepes

PREP: **15 MIN. + CHILLING** COOK: **15 MIN.**

My family wanted just a light brunch and coffee this year for Christmas morning, so I whipped up these sweet and fruity crepes that were a big hit with everyone! To save even more time, use premade crepes.

Mary Hobbs * Campbell, Missouri

2/3 cup milk

2 eggs

1 tablespoon canola oil

1/2 cup all-purpose flour

1 teaspoon sugar

1/4 teaspoon salt

FILLING:

1 can (20 ounces) crushed pineapple, drained

1 can (11 ounces) mandarin oranges, drained

1 teaspoon vanilla extract

1 carton (8 ounces) frozen whipped topping, thawed

Confectioners' sugar

In a large bowl, beat the milk, eggs and oil. Combine the flour, sugar and salt; add to milk mixture and mix well. Cover and refrigerate for 1 hour.

Coat an 8-in. nonstick skillet with cooking spray; heat over medium heat. Stir crepe batter; pour 2 tablespoons into center of skillet. Lift and tilt pan to coat bottom evenly. Cook until top appears dry; turn and cook 15-20 seconds longer. Remove to a wire rack. Repeat with remaining batter, coating skillet as needed. When cool, stack crepes with waxed paper or paper towels in between.

For filling, in a large bowl, combine the pineapple, oranges and vanilla; fold in whipped topping. Spoon 1/3 cup down the center of each crepe; roll up. Dust with confectioners' sugar. **YIELD: 6 SERVINGS.**

Apple-Stuffed French Toast

Apple-Stuffed French Toast

PREP: **20 MIN. + CHILLING** BAKE: **35 MIN.**

This is a great breakfast dish to make ahead for holidays or Sunday brunch. I run a bed and breakfast and tea room cafe, and this recipe is often requested by customers.

Kay Clark * Lawrenceburg, Kentucky

       1 **cup packed brown sugar**
     1/2 **cup butter, cubed**
       2 **tablespoons light corn syrup**
       1 **cup chopped pecans**
      12 **slices Italian bread (1/2 inch thick)**
       2 **large tart apples, peeled and thinly sliced**
       6 **eggs**
   1-1/2 **cups milk**
   1-1/2 **teaspoons ground cinnamon**
       1 **teaspoon vanilla extract**
     1/4 **teaspoon salt**
     1/4 **teaspoon ground nutmeg**
CARAMEL SAUCE:
     1/2 **cup packed brown sugar**
     1/4 **cup butter, cubed**
       1 **tablespoon light corn syrup**

In a small saucepan, combine the brown sugar, butter and corn syrup; cook and stir over medium heat until thickened. Pour into a greased 13-in. x 9-in. baking dish; top with half of the pecans, a single layer of bread and remaining pecans. Arrange the apples and the remaining bread over the top.

In a large bowl, whisk the eggs, milk, cinnamon, vanilla, salt and nutmeg. Pour over bread. Cover and refrigerate overnight.

Remove from the refrigerator 30 minutes before baking. Bake, uncovered, at 350° for 35-40 minutes or until lightly browned.

In a small saucepan, combine the sauce ingredients. Cook and stir over medium heat until thickened. Serve with French toast. **YIELD: 6 SERVINGS.**

Italian Meatball Tortes, PAGE 168

> " With classic Italian flavor, this hearty pie—filled with tomatoes, mozzarella and moist homemade meatballs—will be a hit with your family. Preparation takes some time, but it's well worth it. "
>
> **Sandy Blessing**
> Ocean Shores, Washington

BEEF

DO YOU HAVE A WINNING RECIPE?
Enter your most prized recipes in the *Taste of Home* recipe contests, and you may win some money and the chance to have your recipe published. Log onto **tasteofhome.com/RecipeContests** for a list of our current contests and submission deadlines. Good luck...we'll be looking for your recipe.

beef

Meat Loaf Potato Surprise

PREP: **20 MIN.** BAKE: **50 MIN.**

Although I'm retired after years of teaching school, my days continue to be full. So easy dishes like this are still a blessing to me.

Lois Gallup Edwards ✳ Woodland, California

- 1 cup soft bread crumbs
- 1/2 cup beef broth
- 1 egg, lightly beaten
- 4 teaspoons dried minced onion
- 1 teaspoon salt
- 1/4 teaspoon Italian seasoning
- 1/4 teaspoon pepper
- 1-1/2 pounds ground beef
- 4 cups frozen shredded hash brown potatoes, thawed
- 1/3 cup grated Parmesan cheese
- 1/4 cup minced fresh parsley
- 1 teaspoon onion salt

SAUCE:
- 1 can (8 ounces) tomato sauce
- 1/4 cup beef broth
- 2 teaspoons prepared mustard

Additional Parmesan cheese, optional

In a large bowl, combine crumbs, broth, egg and seasonings; let stand for 2 minutes. Crumble beef over mixture and mix well.

On a piece of waxed paper, pat meat mixture into a 10-in. square. Combine the hash browns, cheese, parsley and onion salt; spoon over meat.

Roll up, jelly-roll style, removing waxed paper as you roll. Pinch edges and ends to seal; place with seam side down in an ungreased shallow baking pan.

Bake at 375° for 40 minutes longer. Combine the first three sauce ingredients; spoon over loaf. Bake 10 minutes longer. Sprinkle with Parmesan if desired. **YIELD: 8 SERVINGS.**

Meat Loaf Potato Surprise

Southern Barbecued Brisket

Carefully open foil to allow steam to escape. Remove brisket from foil; let stand for 20 minutes. Thinly slice meat across the grain. Place in an ungreased 13-in. x 9-in. baking dish. Spoon sauce over meat. Cover and bake for 1 hour or until heated through. **YIELD: 12 SERVINGS.**

EDITOR'S NOTE: This is a fresh beef brisket, not corned beef.

Sweet 'n' Sour Meatballs

PREP: **15 MIN.** BAKE: **25 MIN.**

This Asian-flavored dinner served over rice is a welcome change of pace from our routine menus. My husband isn't normally a big fan of stir-fries, and our children can be picky eaters, but I never have leftovers when I serve this sensational dish.

Andrea Busch ✻ Brackenridge, Pennsylvania

- 1 egg
- 1/4 cup seasoned bread crumbs
- 1/2 teaspoon salt
- 1/4 teaspoon ground ginger
- Dash pepper
- 1 pound ground beef
- 1 can (20 ounces) pineapple chunks
- 1/4 cup cider vinegar
- 1/4 cup packed brown sugar
- 2 tablespoons soy sauce
- 1 cup sliced carrots
- 1 medium green pepper, julienned
- 1 tablespoon cornstarch
- 2 tablespoons cold water
- Hot cooked rice

Southern Barbecued Brisket

PREP: **10 MIN.** BAKE: **3 HOURS + STANDING**

Ever since a former neighbor shared this recipe with me, it has been a family favorite. Since it makes a lot, it's good for a company dinner or buffet. The meat gets nice and tender from baking slowly for several hours.

Lorraine Hodge ✻ McLean, Virginia

- 1 fresh beef brisket (5 pounds)
- 1 large onion, chopped
- 1 cup ketchup
- 1/4 cup water
- 3 tablespoons brown sugar
- 1 tablespoon Liquid Smoke, optional
- 2 teaspoons celery seed
- 1 teaspoon salt
- 1 teaspoon ground mustard
- 1/8 teaspoon cayenne pepper

Place brisket on a large sheet of heavy-duty foil; seal tightly. Place in a greased shallow roasting pan. Bake at 325° for 2 to 2-1/2 hours or until meat is tender.

Meanwhile, in a small saucepan, combine the remaining ingredients. Bring to a boil. Reduce heat; cover and simmer for 20 minutes, stirring occasionally. Remove from the heat.

In a large bowl, combine the egg, bread crumbs, salt, ginger and pepper. Crumble the beef over mixture and mix well. Shape into 1-in. balls. In a large skillet, cook meatballs over medium heat until no longer pink; drain.

Drain the pineapple, reserving juice; set the pineapple aside. Add water to juice to measure 1 cup. Stir in the vinegar, brown sugar and soy sauce; pour over meatballs. Add carrots. Bring to a boil. Reduce heat; cover and simmer for 5-8 minutes or until carrots are crisp-tender. Stir in green pepper and reserved pineapple; cover and simmer 5 minutes longer or until pepper is crisp-tender.

Combine the cornstarch and water until smooth; stir into meatball mixture. Bring to a boil; cook and stir for 2 minutes or until thickened. Serve over rice. **YIELD: 4-6 SERVINGS.**

Indiana Swiss Steak

PREP: 20 MIN. COOK: 1 HOUR

I entered the Indiana State Beef Contest and won first place with this recipe. A mixture of picante sauce, ketchup, cider vinegar and veggies enhances the tender slices of steak that are served over pasta. I use bow tie pasta, but you could substitute rice.

Ann Dixon ✳ North Vernon, Indiana

- 1/4 cup all-purpose flour
- 1 teaspoon salt
- 1/2 teaspoon pepper
- 1-1/2 pounds boneless beef top round steak, cut into serving-size pieces
- 1 tablespoon canola oil
- 1 medium onion, chopped
- 3/4 cup grated carrot
- 3/4 cup water
- 1/2 cup chopped celery
- 1/2 cup chopped green pepper
- 1/2 cup ketchup
- 1/4 cup picante sauce
- 1 tablespoon cider vinegar

Hot cooked pasta

In a large resealable plastic bag, combine the flour, salt and pepper. Add the beef, a few pieces at a time, and shake to coat. In a large skillet, brown beef in oil.

Combine onion, carrot, water, celery, green pepper, ketchup, picante sauce and vinegar; pour over the beef. Bring to a boil. Reduce heat; cover and simmer for 60-75 minutes or until beef is tender. Serve with pasta. **YIELD: 6 SERVINGS.**

Sweet 'n' Sour Meatballs

Indiana Swiss Steak

Taco Skillet

Taco Skillet

PREP/TOTAL TIME: 30 MIN.

I like preparing one-dish dinners, and this is one of my favorites. Served with tortilla chips or taco shells, it's a fun meal for everyone.

Tina Schaubroeck
Greencastle, Pennsylvania

- 1 pound ground beef
- 1 medium onion, chopped
- 1 can (16 ounces) refried beans
- 1 can (4 ounces) chopped green chilies
- 1/4 to 1/2 teaspoon garlic powder
- 3/4 cup sour cream
- 1/2 to 1 teaspoon ground cumin
- 1/2 to 1 teaspoon chili powder
- 1 medium tomato, seeded and chopped
- 1 can (2-1/4 ounces) sliced ripe olives, drained
- 1 small green pepper, chopped
- 1 cup (4 ounces) shredded Mexican cheese blend

Tortilla chips *or* taco shells, shredded lettuce and salsa

In a large skillet, cook beef and onion over medium heat until meat is no longer pink; drain. Stir in the beans, chilies and garlic powder; cook until heated through.

In a small bowl, combine the sour cream, cumin and chili powder; spread over beef mixture. Top with the tomato, olives and green pepper. Sprinkle with the cheese. Serve with the tortilla chips or taco shells, lettuce and salsa.
YIELD: 4-6 SERVINGS.

Pizza Rice Casserole

PREP: 25 MIN. BAKE: 30 MIN.

Anyone who enjoys pizza and lasagna will like this Italian-style rice. It sure has a broad appeal with my family and friends. Usually, I make two or three of these casseroles at one time and freeze some for future enjoyment.

Christine Reimer ✳ Niverville, Manitoba

- 3/4 pound ground beef
- 1 medium onion, chopped

Pizza Rice Casserole

2 cans (8 ounces *each*) tomato sauce

1 teaspoon sugar

1 teaspoon salt

1 teaspoon dried parsley flakes

1/4 teaspoon garlic powder

1/4 teaspoon oregano

Dash pepper

2 cups cooked rice

1/2 cup 4% cottage cheese

1/2 cup shredded part-skim mozzarella cheese

In a skillet, cook beef and onion over medium heat until meat is no longer pink; drain. Add the tomato sauce, sugar, salt, parsley, garlic powder, oregano and pepper. Bring to a boil. Reduce heat; cover and simmer for 15 minutes.

Combine the rice and cottage cheese; spoon half into a greased 11-in. x 7-in. baking dish. Top with half of the meat mixture. Repeat layers. Sprinkle with mozzarella cheese.

Bake, uncovered, at 325° for 30-35 minutes or until heated through and bubbly. **YIELD: 4 SERVINGS.**

French Canadian Meat Pie

French Canadian Meat Pie

PREP: **40 MIN. + COOLING** BAKE: **45 MIN.**

I'm a seventh-generation French Canadian, and my ancestors started the tradition of serving this meat pie on Christmas Eve. One year I didn't make it, and my daughter and I felt something was missing. The savory pie goes well with salad and fresh rolls for a lighter meal, and it's good served in small portions with turkey and all the trimmings, too.

Angie Moline * Calgary, Alberta

1-1/4 pounds ground pork

1/2 pound ground beef

1/4 pound ground veal

1 cup grated peeled potatoes

1/2 cup grated onion

3 garlic cloves, minced

1-1/2 teaspoons salt

1/2 teaspoon pepper

1/4 teaspoon dried savory

1/4 teaspoon rubbed sage

1/8 teaspoon ground cloves

1/4 cup plus 2 tablespoons water, *divided*

1/4 cup dry bread crumbs

1 egg

Pastry for double-crust pie (9 inches)

In a large skillet over medium heat, cook the pork, beef, veal, potatoes and onion until meat is no longer pink; drain. Stir in the garlic, seasonings and 1/4 cup water. Bring to a boil. Reduce heat; cover and simmer for 15 minutes, stirring frequently.

Remove from the heat; cool to room temperature. Stir in bread crumbs. Combine egg and remaining water; stir into meat mixture.

Line a 9-in. pie plate with bottom pastry; trim even with edge. Fill with meat mixture. Roll out remaining pastry to fit top of pie; place over filling. Trim, seal and flute edges. Cut slits in pastry. Cover edges loosely with foil.

Bake at 400° for 15 minutes. Remove foil. Reduce heat to 375°; bake 30-35 minutes longer or until crust is golden brown and filling is heated through. **YIELD: 6-8 SERVINGS.**

Beef Cabbage Roll-Ups

Beef Cabbage Roll-Ups

PREP: **30 MIN.** BAKE: **30 MIN.**

Cooking up original recipes is a hobby of mine. My version of classic cabbage rolls is delicious served with rice or noodles.

Irma Finely * Lockwood, Missouri

- 1 head cabbage
- 1 large potato, peeled and shredded
- 1 large carrot, shredded
- 1/2 cup finely chopped celery
- 1/2 cup finely chopped green pepper
- 1/2 cup finely chopped onion
- 2 eggs, beaten
- 2 garlic cloves, minced
- 3/4 teaspoon salt
- 1/2 teaspoon pepper
- 1 pound lean ground beef
- 2 cans (8 ounces *each*) tomato sauce
- 1/2 teaspoon dried basil
- 1/2 teaspoon dried parsley flakes

Cook cabbage in boiling water just until the leaves fall off head. Cut out the thick vein from the bottom of 12 large leaves, making a V-shaped cut; set aside. (Refrigerate remaining cabbage for another use.)

In a bowl, combine the potato, carrot, celery, green pepper, onion, eggs, garlic, salt and pepper. Crumble beef over mixture; mix well. Shape into 12 logs; place one on each cabbage leaf. Overlap cut ends of leaf, fold in sides, beginning from the cut end. Roll up completely to enclose filling. Secure with a toothpick.

Place in a greased 13-in. x 9-in. baking dish. Pour tomato sauce over roll-ups. Sprinkle with basil and parsley. Cover and bake at 350° for 30-35 minutes or until a meat thermometer reads 160° and cabbage is tender. YIELD: **6 SERVINGS.**

Round Steak with Dumplings

PREP: **30 MIN.** BAKE: **1 HOUR 50 MIN.**

My grandma taught me how to make this old-fashioned dish. I like to serve it for special occasions.

Sherri Odom * Plant City, Florida

- 3/4 cup all-purpose flour
- 1 tablespoon paprika
- 3 pounds boneless beef top round steak, cut into serving-size pieces
- 2 tablespoons canola oil
- 1 medium onion, chopped
- 2-2/3 cups water
- 2 cans (10-3/4 ounces *each*) condensed cream of chicken soup, undiluted
- 1/2 teaspoon pepper

DUMPLINGS:
- 3 cups all-purpose flour
- 1/4 cup dried minced onion
- 2 tablespoons baking powder
- 1 tablespoon poppy seeds
- 1-1/2 teaspoons celery salt
- 1-1/2 teaspoons poultry seasoning
- 3/4 teaspoon salt
- 1-1/2 cups milk
- 6 tablespoons canola oil
- 1 cup dry bread crumbs
- 1/4 cup butter, melted

In a large resealable plastic bag, combine flour and paprika. Add beef, a few pieces at a time, and shake to coat.

In a Dutch oven over medium-high heat, brown steak in oil on both sides in batches; add more oil if necessary. Remove and keep warm.

In the drippings, saute onion until tender. Stir in the water, soup and pepper. Bring to a boil. Return the meat to pan. Cover and bake at 325° for 1-1/2 hours.

Meanwhile, for the dumplings, combine the flour, minced onion, baking powder, poppy seeds, celery salt, poultry seasoning and salt in a bowl. Combine the milk and oil; stir into dry ingredients just until moistened.

Increase oven temperature to 425°. In a large bowl, combine bread crumbs and butter. Drop dumpling batter by rounded tablespoonfuls into crumb mixture; roll to form dumplings. Place on top of simmering beef mixture.

Cover and bake 20-25 minutes longer or until a toothpick inserted in a dumpling comes out clean (do not lift the cover while baking). **YIELD: 10-12 SERVINGS.**

Round Steak with Dumplings

Beef Stir-Fry on a Stick

PREP: **20 MIN.** GRILL: **15 MIN.**

A thick Asian-style sauce coats these tender beef and veggie kabobs. They're loaded with flavor and always a hit when they're on the menu.

Gwendolyn Lambert ✳ Frisco City, Alabama

- 1/2 cup hoisin sauce
- 3 tablespoons water
- 2 tablespoons canola oil
- 1 tablespoon soy sauce
- 1 garlic clove, minced
- 1/4 to 1/2 teaspoon crushed red pepper flakes
- 3 cups large fresh broccoli florets
- 2 medium yellow summer squash, cut into 3/4-inch slices
- 1 large sweet red pepper, cut into 1-inch pieces
- 1 pound beef tenderloin, cut into 1-inch cubes

Hot cooked rice

For glaze, in a bowl, combine the hoisin sauce, water, oil, soy sauce, garlic and pepper flakes.

On four metal or soaked wooden skewers, alternately thread the broccoli, squash, red pepper and beef. Brush with 1/3 cup of glaze.

Grill, covered, over medium heat for 6-7 minutes on each side or until meat reaches desired doneness and vegetables are tender, basting once with remaining glaze. Serve with rice. **YIELD: 4 SERVINGS.**

Beef Stir-Fry on a Stick

Beef 'n' Bean Enchiladas

Beef 'n' Bean Enchiladas

PREP/TOTAL TIME: **30 MIN.**

After cooking ground beef in the microwave, I combine it with canned bean dip and chilies to fill flour tortillas. Cheese and olives easily jazz up the prepared enchilada sauce.

Linda Lundmark * Martinton, Illinois

- 3 tablespoons all-purpose flour
- 1 teaspoon salt, *divided*
- 1/4 teaspoon paprika
- 1-1/2 cups milk
- 1 can (10 ounces) enchilada sauce
- 1 cup (4 ounces) shredded cheddar cheese
- 1 can (2-1/4 ounces) sliced ripe olives, drained
- 3/4 pound ground beef
- 1 medium onion, chopped
- 1 can (9 ounces) bean dip
- 1 can (4 ounces) chopped green chilies
- 1/8 teaspoon pepper
- 1 large tomato, seeded and diced
- 9 white *or* yellow corn tortillas (6 inches), warmed

In a 1-qt. microwave-safe bowl, combine flour, 1/2 teaspoon salt, paprika, milk and enchilada sauce until smooth. Microwave, uncovered, on high for 1-1/2 minutes; stir. Cook 3-4 minutes longer or until thickened, stirring every minute. Stir in cheese and olives; set aside.

Place the beef and onion in a microwave-safe dish. Cover and microwave on high for 3-4 minutes or until the meat is no longer pink; drain. Stir in the bean dip, chilies, pepper and remaining salt.

Spoon about 1/3 cup meat mixture and 1 tablespoon of diced tomato down the center of each tortilla; roll up tightly.

Place the enchiladas seam side down in an ungreased 11-in. x 7-in. microwave-safe dish. Top with sauce. Microwave, uncovered, on high for 7-8 minutes or until bubbly around the edges, rotating dish twice. YIELD: **4 SERVINGS.**

EDITOR'S NOTE: This recipe was tested in a 1,100-watt microwave.

Italian Swiss Steak

Italian Swiss Steak

PREP: **20 MIN.** COOK: **1 HOUR 25 MIN.**

The Swiss steak supper combines tender beef and vegetables in tangy sauce that melds tomato basil under a cheesy topping. It's quick to put together. Add a salad and warm bread, and you have a complete meal.

Janice Lyhane ✳ Marysville, Kansas

- 3 tablespoons all-purpose flour
- 2 pounds boneless beef top round steak, cut into serving-size pieces
- 1/4 cup butter, cubed
- 1 can (14-1/2 ounces) diced tomatoes, undrained
- 1-1/2 teaspoons salt
- 1/4 teaspoon dried basil
- 1/8 teaspoon pepper
- 1/2 cup chopped green pepper
- 1/2 cup chopped onion
- 1 cup (4 ounces) shredded part-skim mozzarella cheese

Tangy Meat Sauce

Place flour in a large resealable plastic bag. Add beef, a few pieces at a time, and shake to coat. Remove meat from bag; pound to flatten.

In a large skillet over medium-high heat, brown steak on both sides in butter. Add the tomatoes, salt, basil and pepper; bring to a boil. Reduce heat; cover and simmer for 1 hour or until meat is tender.

Add the green pepper and onion. Cover and simmer for 25-30 minutes or until vegetables are tender. Sprinkle with the cheese; cook 2 minutes longer or until the cheese is melted.
YIELD: **6-8 SERVINGS.**

🕐 Tangy Meat Sauce

PREP/TOTAL TIME: **25 MIN.**

This is the best meat sauce I've ever tried. It's economical, timely and absolutely delicious. I often prepare batches for new moms because it can be kept in the freezer for future meals. Try it with ground chicken instead of beef, if you prefer.

Adalia Schweitzer ✳ Hamilton, Ontario

- 1/2 pound lean ground beef
- 1/2 cup chopped onion
- 1/2 cup chopped green pepper
- 1/2 teaspoon minced garlic
- 1 can (15 ounces) tomato sauce
- 1 can (6 ounces) tomato paste
- 1 tablespoon sugar
- 1 tablespoon red wine vinegar
- 1/2 teaspoon salt
- 1/2 teaspoon dried basil
- 1/4 teaspoon dried oregano
Hot cooked spaghetti

Crumble beef into a 2-qt. microwave-safe dish. Add the onion, green pepper and garlic. Cover and microwave on high for 5-6 minutes or until meat is no longer pink and vegetables are tender, stirring frequently; drain.

Stir in the tomato sauce, tomato paste, sugar, vinegar, salt, basil and oregano. Cover and microwave at 70% power for 6-8 minutes or until heated through, stirring once. Serve with spaghetti. YIELD: **3 CUPS.**

EDITOR'S NOTE: This recipe was tested in a 1,100-watt microwave.

Vegetable Beef Potpie

In a large skillet, cook beef over medium heat until no longer pink; drain. Stir in pepper and salt; remove and set aside. In the same skillet, saute the onions, carrots and parsnip in butter for 7 minutes. Add garlic; cook 2 minutes longer or until vegetables are crisp-tender. Stir in flour.

Combine the broth, vinegar and mustard; gradually stir into vegetable mixture. Bring to a boil; cook and stir for 2-3 minutes or until thickened. Stir in beef mixture and 2 teaspoons rosemary; heat through. Transfer to a greased 8-in. square baking dish.

On a lightly floured surface, roll the pastry into a 10-in. square. Sprinkle with the remaining rosemary; press into pastry. Place over filling; flute edges and cut slits in top. Brush with egg. Bake, uncovered, at 400° for 25-30 minutes or until crust is golden brown. **YIELD: 6 SERVINGS.**

Herbed Pot Roast

PREP: **25 MIN.** BAKE: **3 HOURS**

I prepare this delicious entree several times a month. The herbs give the beef an excellent taste. Adding the onion, carrots and potatoes makes this a meal-in-one. My husband, Jack, a real meat-and-potatoes man, even enjoys the leftovers, which isn't always the case.

Christel McKinley ✳ East Liverpool, Ohio

- 1 boneless beef rump *or* chuck roast (3 to 3-1/2 pounds)
- 1 tablespoon canola oil
- 1 teaspoon salt
- 1 teaspoon dried marjoram
- 1 teaspoon dried thyme
- 1/2 teaspoon dried oregano
- 1/2 teaspoon garlic powder
- 1/2 teaspoon pepper
- 1 can (10-1/2 ounces) condensed beef broth, undiluted
- 8 medium carrots, cut into thirds
- 8 medium potatoes, peeled and quartered
- 1 large onion, quartered
- 1 cup water

Vegetable Beef Potpie

PREP: **40 MIN.** BAKE: **25 MIN.**

This old-fashioned main dish is tried-and-true comfort food. The golden crust and savory filling make such a pretty presentation.

Trudy Williams ✳ Shannonville, Ontario

- 1 pound ground beef
- 1/2 teaspoon pepper
- 1/4 teaspoon salt
- 2 cups frozen pearl onions, thawed
- 1-1/2 cups baby carrots, halved
- 1 medium parsnip, peeled, halved lengthwise and sliced
- 2 tablespoons butter
- 3 garlic cloves, minced
- 1/4 cup all-purpose flour
- 1-1/3 cups beef broth
- 4-1/2 teaspoons red wine vinegar
- 4-1/2 teaspoons Dijon mustard
- 3 teaspoons minced fresh rosemary, *divided*
- 1 sheet frozen puff pastry, thawed
- 1 egg, lightly beaten

In a Dutch oven, brown roast in oil over medium heat. Combine the seasonings; sprinkle over meat. Add broth and bring to a boil.

Cover and bake at 325° for 2 hours, basting occasionally. Add the carrots, potatoes, onion and water.

Cover and bake for 1 hour or until vegetables are tender. Thicken pan juices for the gravy if desired. **YIELD: 8 SERVINGS.**

Herbed Pot Roast

Taco Casserole

PREP: 15 MIN. BAKE: 30 MIN.

My preschooler doesn't eat ground beef unless it's taco flavored, so I came up with this casserole we all like. To make assembly easy, I prepare the taco meat and freeze several bags at a time.

Kathy Wilson ✳ Romeoville, Illinois

- 3 cups uncooked bow tie pasta
- 1 pound ground beef
- 1/4 cup chopped onion
- 2 cups (8 ounces) shredded cheddar cheese
- 1 jar (16 ounces) salsa
- 1 can (14-1/2 ounces) diced tomatoes, undrained
- 1 envelope taco seasoning
- 2 cups nacho tortilla chips, crushed

Cook pasta according to package directions. In a large skillet, cook beef and onion over medium heat until meat is no longer pink; drain. Add the cheese, salsa, tomatoes and taco seasoning. Drain pasta; stir into beef mixture.

Transfer to a greased 11-in. x 7-in. baking dish. Cover and bake at 350° for 20 minutes. Uncover and sprinkle with tortilla chips. Bake 10 minutes longer or until heated through. **YIELD: 7 SERVINGS.**

Taco Casserole

Braised Short Ribs

Braised Short Ribs

PREP: **25 MIN.** COOK: **1-1/2 HOURS**

These delicious ribs are often on the menu when my husband and I have company for dinner. The allspice and bay leaf come through nicely, and the meat is very tender.

Mary Gill ✳ Florence, Oregon

- 3 pounds beef short ribs
- 1-1/2 teaspoons butter
- 1-1/2 teaspoons canola oil
- 1 large onion, thinly sliced
- 1 cup water
- 1-1/4 teaspoons salt
- 1 teaspoon sugar
- 1/4 teaspoon coarsely ground pepper
- 2 bay leaves
- 1 teaspoon whole allspice
- 1 tablespoon all-purpose flour
- 1/4 cup cold water

In a Dutch oven, brown ribs in butter and oil for 3 minutes on each side; drain. Remove and keep warm. In the same pan, cook and stir onion for 2 minutes. Add water, salt, sugar and pepper, stirring to loosen browned bits from pan.

Place bay leaves and allspice on a double thickness of cheesecloth; bring up corners of cloth and tie with kitchen string to form a bag. Place in pan. Return ribs to pan. Bring to a boil. Reduce the heat; cover and simmer for 1-1/2 to 1-3/4 hours or until meat is tender.

Remove ribs and keep warm. Discard spice bag. Skim fat from pan drippings. Combine flour and cold water until smooth; gradually stir into drippings. Bring to a boil; cook and stir for 2 minutes or until thickened. Serve with ribs.
YIELD: **4 SERVINGS.**

🌿 Spinach-Stuffed Beef Tenderloin

PREP: **20 MIN.** BAKE: **30 MIN.**

This makes a fabulous entree for guests. Filled with a combination of spinach, blue cheese and mushrooms, it gets rave reviews whenever I serve it.

Deborah DeMers ✳ Lakewood, Washington

- 1/2 pound sliced fresh mushrooms
- 4 garlic cloves, minced

Spinach-Stuffed Beef Tenderloin

- 1 package (6 ounces) fresh baby spinach, chopped
- 1 cup (4 ounces) crumbled blue cheese
- 1 beef tenderloin (2 pounds)
- 1/2 teaspoon salt, *divided*
- 1/2 teaspoon pepper, *divided*

In a small nonstick skillet coated with cooking spray, saute the mushrooms until tender. Add the garlic; cook and stir for 1 minute. In a small bowl, combine the mushroom mixture, spinach and cheese; set aside.

Cut a lengthwise slit down the center of the tenderloin to within 1/2 in. of bottom. Open tenderloin so it lies flat; cover with plastic wrap. Flatten to 3/4-in. thickness. Remove the plastic wrap; sprinkle with 1/4 teaspoon salt and 1/4 teaspoon pepper. Spread stuffing over meat to within 1 in. of edges. Close tenderloin; tie at 2-in. intervals with kitchen string. Place on a rack in a shallow roasting pan. Sprinkle with remaining salt and pepper.

Bake, uncovered, at 425° for 30 minutes or until the meat reaches desired doneness (for medium-rare, a meat thermometer should read 145°; medium, 160°; well-done, 170°). Let stand for 5-10 minutes before slicing. **YIELD: 8 SERVINGS.**

NUTRITION FACTS: 5 ounces stuffed cooked beef equals 238 calories, 12 g fat (6 g saturated fat), 82 mg cholesterol, 417 mg sodium, 3 g carbohydrate, 1 g fiber, 28 g protein. DIABETIC EXCHANGES: 3 lean meat, 1-1/2 fat.

Cheesy Veal Pie

PREP: **45 MIN.** BAKE: **35 MIN.**

This pie tastes just like veal Parmesan in a savory pastry crust. My daughter often asked me to make it for her birthday dinner. I've also made it with chicken.

Grace Epperson ✳ Richmond, Michigan

- 1/2 cup all-purpose flour
- 1 pound veal *or* boneless skinless chicken breasts, cubed
- 1/4 cup butter
- 1 can (14-1/2 ounces) diced tomatoes, undrained
- 1 can (8 ounces) tomato sauce
- 1/4 cup chopped onion

Cheesy Veal Pie

- 1 teaspoon dried basil
- 1/2 teaspoon garlic salt
- 1/2 teaspoon dried oregano
- 1/8 teaspoon pepper
- 3 tablespoons grated Parmesan cheese

HERB-CHEESE CRUST:
- 1-1/2 cups all-purpose flour
- 1/4 cup grated Parmesan cheese
- 1 teaspoon garlic salt
- 1 teaspoon dried oregano
- 1/2 cup cold butter
- 4 to 6 tablespoons cold water
- 1/2 cup shredded cheddar cheese

Place flour in a large resealable bag; add veal in batches and shake to coat. In a skillet, cook veal in butter until no longer pink. Add tomatoes, tomato sauce, onion and seasonings. Bring to a boil. Reduce the heat; cover and simmer for 30 minutes or until the meat is tender. Stir in Parmesan cheese.

In a small bowl, combine the first four crust ingredients. Cut in the butter until crumbly. Gradually add water, tossing with a fork until dough forms a ball. Divide in half. Roll out one portion to fit a 9-in. pie plate; place in plate. Trim pastry to 1/2 in. beyond edge of plate; fluted edges. Add filling. Top with cheddar cheese.

Roll out the remaining pastry to 1/8-in. thickness. With a 2-in. biscuit cutter, cut out circles; place over cheese, overlapping slightly. Bake at 400° for 35-40 minutes or until golden brown. **YIELD: 6-8 SERVINGS.**

Grilled Beef Burgers

Grilled Beef Burgers

PREP/TOTAL TIME: **20 MIN.**

I rely on a few common ingredients to put a new twist on a backyard barbecue staple. To make handling the patties even easier, let them firm up in the freezer a bit before grilling.

Lynda Ferguson ✳ Sarnia, Ontario

- 2 **egg whites**
- 2/3 **cup fat-free evaporated milk**
- 1 **cup (4 ounces) shredded reduced-fat cheddar cheese**
- 1/2 **cup dry bread crumbs**
- 1/4 **cup chopped onion**
- 1 **teaspoon prepared mustard**
- 1/4 **teaspoon salt**
- 1/8 **teaspoon pepper**
- 1-1/2 **pounds lean ground beef**
- 8 **mulitgrain hamburger buns, split**
- 8 **lettuce leaves**
- 8 **tomato slices**

In a large bowl, combine the egg whites, milk, cheese, bread crumbs, onion, mustard, salt and pepper. Crumble the beef over mixture and mix well. Shape into eight patties.

Coat the grill rack with cooking spray before starting the grill. Grill burgers, uncovered, over medium heat for 5-6 minutes on each side or until juices run clear and a meat thermometer reads 160°. Serve on buns with lettuce and tomato. YIELD: **8 SERVINGS.**

NUTRITION FACTS: 1 burger equals 351 calories, 13 g fat (5 g saturated fat), 40 mg cholesterol, 530 mg sodium, 30 g carbohydrate, 2 g fiber, 29 g protein. DIABETIC EXCHANGES: 4 lean meat, 2 starch.

Spicy Spaghetti Sauce

PREP: **30 MIN.** COOK: **2-1/2 HOURS**

I appreciate that this hearty pasta sauce is quick to assemble and cooks in just a few hours. My husband and I have our hands full raising two children and 25,000 game birds on our farm.

Jennifer Mai ✳ Pierceville, Kansas

- 1 **pound ground beef**
- 1 **large onion, chopped**
- 1 **can (46 ounces) tomato juice**

1 can (12 ounces) tomato paste
1 can (4 ounces) mushroom stems and
  pieces, drained
2 tablespoons minced fresh parsley
1 tablespoon garlic salt
1 tablespoon dried basil
2 teaspoons sugar
2 teaspoons dried oregano
1/4 to 1/2 teaspoon crushed red pepper flakes
3 bay leaves
Hot cooked spaghetti

In a Dutch oven, cook the beef and onion over medium heat until meat is no longer pink; drain. Stir in the tomato juice, tomato paste, mushrooms and seasonings; bring to a boil.

Reduce heat; simmer, uncovered, for 2-1/2 hours, stirring occasionally. Discard bay leaves. Serve over spaghetti. **YIELD: 6-1/2 CUPS.**

Spicy Spaghetti Sauce

Favorite Meat Loaf Cups

PREP/TOTAL TIME: **30 MIN.**

My family enjoys meat loaf, but sometimes I can't spare the hour or more it takes to bake in the traditional shape. A quick alternative is to divide the meat mixture into muffin cups for individual servings that are ready in less than 30 minutes.

Sue Gronholz ✳ Beaver Dam, Wisconsin

2 eggs, lightly beaten
1/4 cup milk
1/4 cup ketchup
1/2 cup crushed cornflakes
4 tablespoons dried minced onion
1 teaspoon prepared mustard
1 teaspoon salt
1/4 teaspoon pepper
2 pounds lean ground beef
Additional ketchup, optional

In a large bowl, combine the egg, milk, ketchup, cornflakes, onion, mustard, salt and pepper. Crumble beef over mixture and mix well.

Press into 12 foil-lined or greased muffin cups. Bake at 350° for 25 minutes or until a meat thermometer reaches 160°. Drain before serving. Drizzle with ketchup if desired. **YIELD: 6 SERVINGS.**

Favorite Meat Loaf Cups

Spicy Beef Brisket

Spicy Beef Brisket

PREP: **30 MIN.** COOK: **2-1/2 HOURS**

This fork-tender brisket is just as good when cooked a day ahead, refrigerated and reheated. I like to serve it with mashed potatoes, rice or noodles to take advantage of the flavorful sauce.

Wendy Kiehn ✶ Sebring, Florida

- 1 fresh beef brisket (3 pounds)
- 1/2 teaspoon seasoned salt
- 1/4 teaspoon pepper
- 2 tablespoons olive oil
- 2 large onions, sliced
- 3 garlic cloves, minced
- 1 cup beef broth
- 1 cup chili sauce
- 1/3 cup packed brown sugar
- 1/3 cup cider vinegar
- 2 to 3 tablespoons chili powder
- 2 bay leaves
- 3 tablespoons all-purpose flour
- 1/4 cup cold water

Sprinkle beef with seasoned salt and pepper. In a Dutch oven, brown beef in oil on both sides. Remove and set aside. In the drippings, saute onions and garlic until tender. Return the beef to the pan.

Combine the broth, chili sauce, brown sugar, vinegar, chili powder and bay leaves; pour over beef. Bring to a boil. Reduce heat; cover and simmer for 2-1/2 to 3 hours or until the meat is tender.

Discard bay leaves. Remove beef to a cutting board; slice across the grain. Combine flour and cold water until smooth; stir into cooking juices. Bring to a boil; cook and stir for 2 minutes or until thickened. Serve gravy with sliced beef. YIELD: **10-12 SERVINGS.**

EDITOR'S NOTE: This is a fresh beef brisket, not corned beef.

German-Style Short Ribs

German-Style Short Ribs

PREP: **15 MIN.** COOK: **8 HOURS**

Our whole family is excited when I plug in the slow cooker to make these fall-off-the-bone tender ribs. We like them served over rice or egg noodles.

Bregitte Rugman ✳ Shanty Bay, Ontario

3/4 cup dry red wine *or* beef broth
1/2 cup mango chutney
  3 tablespoons quick-cooking tapioca
1/4 cup water
  3 tablespoons brown sugar
  3 tablespoons cider vinegar
  1 tablespoon Worcestershire sauce
1/2 teaspoon salt
1/2 teaspoon ground mustard
1/2 teaspoon chili powder
1/2 teaspoon pepper
  4 pounds bone-in beef short ribs
  2 medium onions, sliced
Hot cooked egg noodles

In a 5-qt. slow cooker, combine wine, chutney, tapioca, water, sugar, vinegar, Worcestershire sauce and seasonings. Add the ribs and turn to coat. Top with onions. Cover and cook on low for 8-10 hours or until the meat is tender. Remove the ribs from the slow cooker. Skim the fat from cooking juices; serve with the ribs and noodles. **YIELD: 8 SERVINGS.**

NUTRITION FACTS: 1 serving (calculated without noodles) equals 302 calories, 11 g fat (5 g saturated fat), 55 mg cholesterol, 378 mg sodium, 28 g carbohydrate, 1 g fiber, 19 g protein.

Spicy Bean and Beef Pie

1st place

Spicy Bean and Beef Pie

PREP: **20 MIN.** BAKE: **30 MIN.**

My daughter helped me create this recipe one day when we wanted a one-dish meal that was something other than a casserole. This pie slices nicely and is a fun dinner.

Debra Dohy ✳ Massillon, Ohio

  1 pound ground beef
  2 to 3 garlic cloves, minced
1/4 cup cornstarch
  1 can (11-1/2 ounces) condensed bean with bacon soup, undiluted
  1 jar (16 ounces) thick and chunky picante sauce, *divided*
  1 tablespoon chopped fresh parsley
  1 teaspoon paprika
  1 teaspoon salt
1/4 teaspoon pepper
  1 can (16 ounces) kidney beans, rinsed and drained
  1 can (15 ounces) black beans, rinsed and drained
  2 cups (8 ounces) shredded cheddar cheese, *divided*
3/4 cup sliced green onions, *divided*
Pastry for double-crust pie (10 inches)
  1 cup (8 ounces) sour cream
  1 can (2-1/4 ounces) sliced ripe olives, drained

In a skillet, cook beef and garlic over medium heat until beef is no longer pink; drain. In a large bowl, combine the cornstarch, soup, 1 cup picante sauce, parsley, paprika, salt and pepper; mix well. Fold in the beans, 1-1/2 cups cheese, 1/2 cup onions and the beef mixture.

Line pie plate with bottom pastry; fill with bean mixture. Top with remaining pastry; seal and flute edges. Cut slits in the top crust.

Bake at 425° for 30-35 minutes or until the crust is lightly browned. Let stand for 5 minutes before cutting. Garnish with the sour cream, olives and remaining picante sauce, cheddar cheese and onions. **YIELD: 8 SERVINGS.**

Italian Meatball Tortes

Italian Meatball Tortes

PREP: **1-1/4 HOURS** + **RISING** BAKE: **30 MIN.**

With classic Italian flavor, this hearty pie—filled with tomatoes, mozzarella and moist homemade meatballs—will be a hit with your family. Preparation takes some time, but it's well worth it.

Sandy Blessing ∗ Ocean Shores, Washington

- 1 package (1/4 ounce) active dry yeast
- 1/4 cup warm water (110° to 115°)
- 3/4 cup warm milk (110° to 115°)
- 1/4 cup sugar
- 1/4 cup shortening
- 1 egg
- 1 teaspoon salt
- 3-1/2 to 3-3/4 cups all-purpose flour

MEATBALLS:

- 1 can (5 ounces) evaporated milk
- 2 eggs, beaten
- 1 cup quick-cooking oats
- 1 cup crushed saltines
- 1/2 cup chopped onion
- 1/2 cup chopped celery
- 2 teaspoons salt
- 2 teaspoons chili powder
- 1/2 teaspoon garlic powder
- 1/2 teaspoon pepper
- 3 pounds ground beef

FILLING:

- 1 can (15 ounces) crushed tomatoes
- 1/2 cup chopped onion
- 1/3 cup grated Parmesan cheese
- 1 teaspoon minced fresh parsley
- 1-1/2 teaspoons dried basil
- 1-1/2 teaspoons dried oregano
- 1 teaspoon salt
- 1-1/2 cups (6 ounces) shredded part-skim mozzarella cheese

In a large bowl, dissolve yeast in warm water. Add the milk, sugar, shortening, egg, salt and 2 cups flour. Beat until smooth. Stir in enough remaining flour to form a soft dough.

Turn onto a floured surface; knead until smooth and elastic, about 6-8 minutes. Place in a greased bowl, turning once to grease the top. Cover and let rise in a warm place until doubled, 1 to 1-1/2 hours.

In a large bowl, combine the milk, eggs, oats, saltines, onion, celery and seasonings. Crumble the beef over mixture; mix well. Shape into 1-1/2-in. balls. In a skillet over medium heat, cook meatballs in batches until no longer pink.

Meanwhile, place tomatoes and onion in a small saucepan. Bring to a boil. Reduce the heat; simmer, uncovered, for 10 minutes or until slightly thickened. Stir in the Parmesan cheese, herbs and salt.

Punch the dough down. Divide into three portions. Roll two portions into 11-in. circles; line the bottoms and press partially up the sides of two greased 9-in. springform pans. Roll third portion into a 12-in. x 10-in. rectangle; cut into twelve 10-in. x 1-in. strips.

Place meatballs in prepared crusts; top with tomato mixture and mozzarella cheese. Make a lattice crust with strips of dough; trim and seal edges. Cover and let rise for 30 minutes. Bake at 350° for 30-35 minutes or until golden brown. Cut into wedges. **YIELD: 2 TORTES (6 SERVINGS EACH).**

Thai Beef Stir-Fry

Thai Beef Stir-Fry

PREP: 20 MIN. COOK: 25 MIN.

A distinctive peanut sauce complements this colorful combination of tender sirloin strips, cauliflower, carrots, broccoli and mushrooms. I like to serve it over spaghetti, but you could also use fried noodles.

Janice Fehr ✳ Austin, Manitoba

- 1/2 cup packed brown sugar
- 2 tablespoons cornstarch
- 2 cups beef broth
- 1/3 cup soy sauce
- 1 teaspoon onion powder
- 1 teaspoon garlic powder
- 1 teaspoon ground ginger
- 1/4 teaspoon hot pepper sauce
- 2 pounds boneless beef sirloin steak, cut into thin strips
- 6 tablespoons olive oil, *divided*
- 2 cups fresh cauliflowerets
- 1-1/2 cups julienned carrots
- 4 cups fresh broccoli florets
- 2 cups sliced fresh mushrooms
- 1/4 cup peanut butter
- Hot cooked spaghetti
- 1/2 cup chopped peanuts

In a small bowl, combine the sugar, cornstarch, broth, soy sauce and seasonings until smooth; set aside. In a large skillet or wok, stir-fry beef in 3 tablespoons oil until meat is no longer pink. Remove and keep warm.

In the same skillet, stir-fry cauliflower and carrots in the remaining oil for 5 minutes. Add broccoli; stir-fry for 7 minutes. Add mushrooms; stir-fry 6-8 minutes longer or until vegetables are crisp-tender.

Stir broth mixture and add to the pan. Bring to a boil; cook and stir for 2 minutes or until thickened. Reduce heat; add beef and peanut butter. Cook and stir over medium heat until peanut butter is blended. Serve over spaghetti. Sprinkle with peanuts. **YIELD: 6 SERVINGS.**

Blue Cheese Stroganoff

⏱ Blue Cheese Stroganoff

PREP/TOTAL TIME: 30 MIN.

This out-of-the-ordinary Stroganoff is made with snap peas and a mild blue cheese sauce. You can serve it with any kind of pasta.

Doris Heath ✳ Franklin, North Carolina

- 1 bacon strip, diced
- 1/2 pound boneless beef sirloin steak, cut into thin strips
- 1/4 teaspoon beef bouillon granules
- 1/4 cup hot water
- 3/4 cup frozen sugar snap peas
- 4 ounces cream cheese, softened
- 1/3 cup crumbled blue cheese
- 1 tablespoon all-purpose flour
- 1/8 teaspoon salt
- 1/8 teaspoon pepper
- 1/3 cup 2% milk

Hot cooked egg noodles

In a small skillet, cook bacon over medium heat until crisp. Using a slotted spoon, remove to paper towel. In the same skillet, cook beef in drippings over medium heat until no longer pink. Combine the bouillon and water; stir into skillet. Add peas. Bring to a boil. Reduce heat; cover and simmer for 10 minutes or until peas are tender.

Meanwhile, in a small bowl, beat the cream cheese, blue cheese, flour, salt and pepper until smooth. Stir in the milk. Gradually stir into beef mixture. Cook and stir for 2-3 minutes or until heated through. Serve over noodles; sprinkle with bacon. **YIELD: 2 SERVINGS.**

⏱ Zesty Onion Burgers

PREP/TOTAL TIME: 30 MIN.

My mother found this simple recipe on a soup can over 40 years ago. The oniony sandwiches starred many of our Sunday suppers. I carry on the tradition today, making them for my husband and our two grown sons.

Mary Welle ✳ Lake Elmo, Minnesota

- 1 pound ground beef
- 1 cup chopped celery

Zesty Onion Burgers

Oven Beef Stew

1 can (10-1/2 ounces) condensed onion
   soup, undiluted
1/2 cup water
1/4 cup ketchup
1 teaspoon Worcestershire sauce
1 teaspoon prepared mustard
Dash pepper
6 hamburger buns, split
3 tablespoons butter, softened

In a skillet, cook beef and celery over medium heat until meat is no longer pink; drain. Add soup, water, ketchup, Worcestershire sauce, mustard and pepper. Bring to a boil. Reduce heat; simmer, uncovered, for 20-25 minutes or until thickened, stirring occasionally.

Spread cut sides of buns with butter and toast. Top with beef mixture. **YIELD: 4 SERVINGS.**

Oven Beef Stew

PREP: **15 MIN.** ✦ STANDING COOK: **2 -1/2 HOURS**

No one guesses that this traditional combination is low in fat. A thick flavorful sauce makes this hearty dish one that will be requested time and again.

Debbie Patton ✳ Westchester, Illinois

2 pounds boneless beef top round roast,
   cut into 1-1/2-inch cubes

2 medium potatoes, peeled and cut into
   1/2-inch cubes
2 medium onions, cut into eighths
3 celery ribs, cut into 1-inch pieces
4 medium carrots, cut into 1-inch slices
1 can (11-1/2 ounces) tomato juice
1/3 cup dry sherry *or* water
1/3 cup quick-cooking tapioca
1 tablespoon sugar
1 teaspoon salt
1/2 teaspoon dried basil
1/4 teaspoon pepper
2 cups fresh green beans, cut into
   1-inch pieces

In a Dutch oven, combine the beef, potatoes, onions, celery and carrots; set aside.

In a large bowl, combine the tomato juice, sherry, tapioca, sugar, salt, basil and pepper. Let stand for 15 minutes.

Pour over beef mixture. Cover and bake at 325° for 2 to 2-1/2 hours or until the meat is almost tender. Add the beans; cook 30 minutes longer or until the beans and meat are tender. **YIELD: 8 SERVINGS.**

NUTRITION FACTS: 1 cup equals 268 calories, 7 g fat (2 g saturated fat), 70 mg cholesterol, 519 mg sodium, 25 g carbohydrate, 4 g fiber, 25 g protein. DIABETIC EXCHANGES: 3 lean meat, 2 vegetable, 1 starch.

Mexican Beef and Mushrooms

Mexican Beef and Mushrooms

PREP: **15 MIN.** COOK: **1-1/2 HOURS**

This main dish made an impression on our children. Now grown, every one of them has requested the recipe. Often, I stir my home-canned salsa into the mix.

Sharon De Motts ✳ Waupun, Wisconsin

- 2-1/2 pounds boneless beef top round steak, cut into 1-inch cubes
- 1 large onion, chopped
- 1 garlic clove, minced
- 2 tablespoons butter
- 2 jars (6 ounces *each*) sliced mushrooms, drained
- 1 jar (16 ounces) salsa
- 1 cup water
- 1/2 teaspoon salt
- 1/4 teaspoon chili powder
- 3 cups hot cooked rice
- 1 cup (8 ounces) sour cream
- 1 cup (4 ounces) shredded cheddar cheese

In a Dutch oven, cook beef, onion and garlic in butter over medium-high heat for 4-6 minutes or until meat is no longer pink; drain. Stir in the mushrooms, salsa, water, salt and chili powder. Reduce the heat; cover and simmer for 1-1/2 to 2 hours or until the meat is tender.

Serve over rice and top with sour cream and cheese. **YIELD: 6-8 SERVINGS.**

Herbed Cornish Pasties

PREP: **1-1/4 HOURS + CHILLING** BAKE: **25 MIN.**

These hand-held golden packets are packed with the irresistible combination of beef and potatoes.

Maribeth Edwards ✳ Follansbee, West Virginia

- 2 cups all-purpose flour
- 1 teaspoon salt
- 1/2 teaspoon dried basil
- 1/2 teaspoon dried thyme
- 1/2 cup shortening
- 1/4 cup cold butter
- 5 to 6 tablespoons ice water

FILLING:

- 1 pound boneless beef chuck, cut into 1/2-inch cubes
- 2 tablespoons canola oil, *divided*
- 1 teaspoon salt
- 1/8 teaspoon pepper
- 2 tablespoons all-purpose flour
- 1 cup water
- 2 medium potatoes, peeled and diced
- 1/2 cup diced carrot
- 1/2 cup diced onion
- 1 egg, lightly beaten

In a large bowl, combine the flour, salt, basil and thyme; cut in the shortening and butter until crumbly. Add the water, 1 tablespoon at a time, tossing lightly with a fork until mixture forms a ball. Cover and chill for at least 30 minutes.

Meanwhile, in a skillet, brown the beef in 1 tablespoon oil until no longer pink; sprinkle with salt and pepper. Remove with a slotted spoon; set aside. Add remaining oil to skillet; gradually stir in flour until smooth. Cook and stir over medium heat for about 2-3 minutes or until lightly browned. Gradually add the water; whisk until smooth.

Return beef to skillet. Reduce heat; cover and simmer for 20 minutes. Add the potatoes, carrot and onion. Cover and simmer for 25 minutes or until tender. Remove from the heat; cool.

Divide pastry into four equal portions. On a lightly floured surface, roll out one portion into a 9-in. circle. Mound 3/4 cup filling on half of circle. Moisten the edges with water; fold dough over filling and press edges with a fork to seal.

Place on an ungreased baking sheet. Repeat with the remaining pastry and filling. Cut three slits in the top of each; brush with egg. Bake at 400° for 25-30 minutes or until golden brown. **YIELD: 4 SERVINGS.**

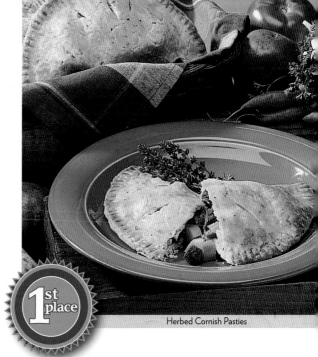

Herbed Cornish Pasties

⏱ Zippy Spaghetti Sauce

PREP: **20 MIN.** COOK: **6 HOURS**

This thick and hearty sauce goes a long way to fill a hungry family! Any leftovers are enjoyed another day ladled over thick grilled slices of garlic bread. To make sure I have the ingredients on hand, I keep a bag of chopped green pepper in my freezer and minced garlic in my fridge.

Elaine Priest ✶ Dover, Pennsylvania

- 2 pounds ground beef
- 1 cup chopped onion
- 1/2 cup chopped green pepper
- 2 cans (15 ounces *each*) tomato sauce
- 1 can (28 ounces) diced tomatoes, undrained
- 1 can (12 ounces) tomato paste
- 1/2 pound sliced fresh mushrooms
- 1 cup grated Parmesan cheese
- 1/2 to 3/4 cup dry red wine *or* beef broth
- 1/2 cup sliced pimiento-stuffed olives
- 1/4 cup dried parsley flakes
- 1 to 2 tablespoons dried oregano
- 2 teaspoons Italian seasoning
- 2 teaspoons minced garlic
- 1 teaspoon salt
- 1 teaspoon pepper

Hot cooked spaghetti

In a skillet, cook beef, onion and green pepper over medium heat until meat is no longer pink; drain. Transfer to a 5-qt. slow cooker.

Stir in the tomato sauce, tomatoes, tomato paste, mushrooms, Parmesan cheese, wine, olives, parsley, oregano, Italian seasoning, garlic, salt and pepper.

Cover and cook on low for 6-8 hours. Serve with spaghetti. **YIELD: ABOUT 3 QUARTS.**

Zippy Spaghetti Sauce

Stuffed Burgers on Portobellos

Stuffed Burgers On Portobellos

PREP/TOTAL TIME: **30 MIN.**

Here's a low-carb treat that allows my husband and me to still enjoy burgers without compromising any of the taste. It's actually a combination of several recipes pulled together into one...and no one misses the bun.

Debbie Driggers ✳ Greenville, Texas

- 1 teaspoon Worcestershire sauce
- 1/2 teaspoon salt
- 1/2 teaspoon pepper
- 1-1/3 pounds ground beef
- 1/2 cup shredded cheddar cheese
- 5 bacon strips, cooked and crumbled
- 4 portobello mushroom caps (about 4-inch diameter)
- 1 tablespoon olive oil
- 4 lettuce leaves
- 4 tomato slices

In a large bowl, combine the Worcestershire sauce, salt and pepper. Crumble beef over the mixture; mix well. Shape into eight thin patties. Combine cheese and bacon. Spoon into center of four patties. Top with remaining patties; press edges firmly to seal. Grill the burgers, covered, over medium heat for 6 minutes on each side or until a meat thermometer reads 160°.

Meanwhile, remove the mushroom stems if necessary; brush with oil. Grill, covered, over medium heat for 3-4 minutes on each side or until tender. Place mushrooms, rounded side down, on serving plates. Top each with tomato, lettuce and a burger. **YIELD: 4 SERVINGS.**

Ginger Sirloin Strips

PREP/TOTAL TIME: **20 MIN.**

A wonderful blend of fruity flavors with just the right touch of ginger makes this fabulous stir-fry dish a winner with our family.

Jill Cox ✳ Lincoln, Nebraska

- 1 can (14 ounces) pineapple tidbits
- 1 can (11 ounces) mandarin oranges

Ginger Sirloin Strips

2 tablespoons cornstarch

1-1/2 pounds boneless beef sirloin steak, cut into strips

4-1/2 teaspoons minced fresh gingerroot

1 tablespoon olive oil

1 can (16 ounces) whole-berry cranberry sauce

1 cup thinly sliced green onions

Hot cooked rice

Drain pineapple and oranges, reserving juice; set fruit aside. In a small bowl, combine the cornstarch and juices until smooth; set aside.

In a large skillet or wok, stir-fry the beef and ginger in oil until meat is no longer pink. Add the cranberry sauce, onions and reserved pineapple. Stir the cornstarch mixture and gradually add to skillet; cook and stir until slightly thickened. Gently stir in the reserved oranges. Serve with rice. **YIELD: 7 SERVINGS.**

Beef Fillets with Grilled Vegetables

Beef Fillets with Grilled Vegetables

PREP/TOTAL TIME: **30 MIN.**

Here's a special, quick and easy, end-of-summer grilled entree...with no pots or pans to clean! Romaine lettuce leaves are a must for this recipe because they stand up to grilling. And basting with butter seals in the meat's juices and adds extra flavor.

Cindie Haras ✳ Boca Raton, Florida

4 beef tenderloin fillets (1-1/2 inches thick and 4 ounces *each*)

3 teaspoons pepper, *divided*

1/2 cup creamy Caesar salad dressing

8 to 12 romaine leaves

2 medium tomatoes, cut into 1-inch slices

1 medium onion, sliced

3 tablespoons olive oil

2 tablespoons butter, melted

1/2 teaspoon salt

Rub fillets with 2 teaspoons pepper; place in a large resealable plastic bag. Add salad dressing; seal bag and turn to coat. Chill for 10 minutes.

Meanwhile, brush romaine, tomatoes and onion with the oil. Grill tomatoes and onion, uncovered, over medium heat for 4-5 minutes on each side or until onion is crisp-tender. Grill romaine for 30 seconds on each side or until heated through. Wrap the vegetables in foil; set aside.

Drain and discard marinade. Grill, covered, over medium heat for 7-8 minutes on each side or until meat reaches desired doneness (for medium-rare, a meat thermometer should read 145°; medium, 160°; well-done, 170°), basting occasionally with butter.

Serve with grilled vegetables. Sprinkle with salt and remaining pepper. **YIELD: 4 SERVINGS.**

Santa Fe Supper

🥄 Santa Fe Supper

PREP/TOTAL TIME: 30 MIN.

This zesty skillet meal is a great way to bring a little variety to your dinnertime lineup. Green chilies spice up the rice, while salsa, zucchini and onion and cheddar cheese dress up the ground beef mixture.

Valerie Collier ✳ Charleston, South Carolina

- 1 cup uncooked long grain rice
- 1 pound ground beef
- 2 small zucchini, cut into 1/4-inch slices
- 1 large onion, halved and sliced
- 1-1/2 cups chunky salsa, *divided*
- 1/4 teaspoon salt
- 1/4 teaspoon pepper
- 1 cup (4 ounces) shredded pepper Jack cheese
- 1 can (4 ounces) chopped green chilies, drained
- 1 cup (4 ounces) shredded cheddar cheese

Cook the rice according to package directions. Meanwhile, in a large skillet, cook beef over medium heat until no longer pink; drain. Stir in the zucchini, onion, 1 cup salsa, salt and pepper; cook until vegetables are crisp-tender.

Add pepper Jack cheese and chilies to the rice. Sprinkle cheddar cheese over beef mixture; serve with the rice and remaining salsa. **YIELD: 4 SERVINGS.**

Marinated Chuck Roast

PREP: 10 MIN. + MARINATING BAKE: 3 HOURS + STANDING

It's the simple marinade of orange juice, soy sauce, brown sugar and Worcestershire sauce that makes this beef roast so tasty and tender.

Mary Lee Baker ✳ Enon, Ohio

- 1/2 cup orange juice
- 3 tablespoons soy sauce
- 3 tablespoons brown sugar
- 1 teaspoon Worcestershire sauce
- 1 boneless beef chuck roast (3 to 4 pounds)

In a large resealable plastic bag, combine the orange juice, soy sauce, brown sugar and Worcestershire sauce; add the roast. Seal the bag and turn to coat; refrigerate for 8 hours or overnight.

Pour the marinade into a Dutch oven. Bring to a boil; boil for 2 minutes. Add roast to the pan. Cover and bake at 325° for 3 to 3-1/2 hours or until the meat is tender. Let stand for 10 minutes before slicing. Thicken juices for gravy if desired. **YIELD: 8-10 SERVINGS.**

Marinated Chuck Roast

Spiral Pepperoni Pizza Bake

PREP: 30 MIN. BAKE: 40 MIN.

My grandmother used to fix this yummy dish for my Girl Scout troop when I was growing up. Now, I make it for my stepdaughters' scout troop. It's easy to prepare, and the girls always beg me to make it.

Kimberly Howland ✳ Fremont, Michigan

- 1 package (16 ounces) spiral pasta
- 2 pounds ground beef
- 1 large onion, chopped
- 1 teaspoon salt
- 1/2 teaspoon pepper
- 2 cans (15 ounces *each*) pizza sauce
- 1/2 teaspoon garlic salt
- 1/2 teaspoon Italian seasoning
- 2 eggs
- 2 cups milk
- 1/2 cup shredded Parmesan cheese
- 4 cups (16 ounces) shredded part-skim mozzarella cheese
- 1 package (3-1/2 ounces) sliced pepperoni

Cook pasta according to package directions. Meanwhile, in a Dutch oven, cook the beef, onion, salt and pepper over medium heat until meat is no longer pink; drain. Stir in the pizza sauce, garlic salt and Italian seasoning; remove from the heat and set aside.

In a small bowl, combine the eggs, milk and Parmesan cheese. Drain pasta; toss with egg mixture. Transfer to a greased 3-qt. baking dish. Top with the beef mixture, mozzarella cheese and pepperoni.

Cover and bake at 350° for 20 minutes. Uncover; bake 20-25 minutes longer or until golden brown. **YIELD: 12 SERVINGS.**

Spiral Pepperoni Pizza Bake

Picante Cranberry Meatballs

PREP: 20 MIN. BAKE: 30 MIN.

These zippy ground beef meatballs are my favorite, and the recipe is so easy. Cranberry, chili and picante sauce sound like an unusual combination, but it's delicious!

Marge Wyse ✳ Winfield, British Columbia

- 2 eggs, lightly beaten
- 1/3 cup ketchup
- 1/3 cup minced fresh parsley
- 2 tablespoons soy sauce
- 2 tablespoons dried minced onion
- 1/2 teaspoon garlic powder
- 1/4 teaspoon pepper
- 1 cup crushed saltines (about 30 crackers)
- 2 pounds lean ground beef

SAUCE:

- 1 can (16 ounces) jellied cranberry sauce
- 1 cup chili sauce
- 1/4 cup picante sauce
- 2 tablespoons brown sugar
- 1 tablespoon lemon juice

Hot cooked noodles, optional

In a large bowl, combine the eggs, ketchup, parsley, soy sauce, onion, garlic powder and pepper. Add cracker crumbs. Crumble beef over mixture and mix well. Shape into 1-1/2-in. balls.

In a medium skillet, brown the meatballs over medium heat. Transfer to a greased 13-in. x 9-in. baking dish.

In a large saucepan, combine the cranberry sauce, chili sauce, picante sauce, brown sugar and lemon juice. Cook and stir until cranberry sauce is melted and mixture is heated through. Pour over meatballs.

Cover and bake at 350° for 30-35 minutes or until meat is no longer pink. Serve with noodles if desired. **YIELD: 8 SERVINGS.**

Picante Cranberry Meatballs

Asian Pot Roast

Asian Pot Roast

PREP: **30 MIN.** COOK: **2 HOURS 40 MIN.**

I love Asian food, so this pot roast satisfies my cravings. The original recipe called for spinach, but I use sugar snap peas and carrots instead. Sometimes I serve the roast, vegetables and pineapple over rice or egg noodles.

Donna Staley ✳ Randleman, North Carolina

- 1 boneless beef rump roast (3 pounds)
- 1 tablespoon canola oil
- 1 large onion, chopped
- 1 can (20 ounces) pineapple chunks
- 3 tablespoons soy sauce
- 1 garlic clove, minced
- 1 teaspoon ground ginger
- 3 celery ribs, sliced
- 2 medium carrots, sliced
- 1 cup fresh sugar snap peas
- 1 cup sliced fresh mushrooms
- 1 to 2 tablespoons cornstarch
- 1/4 cup cold water

In a Dutch oven over medium heat, brown roast in oil on all sides; drain. Add the onion. Drain pineapple, reserving juice; set pineapple aside. In a small bowl, combine the pineapple juice, soy sauce, garlic and ginger.

Pour over roast. Bring to a boil. Reduce heat; cover and simmer for 2 hours or until meat is almost tender.

Add celery and carrots. Cover and simmer for 20 minutes or until vegetables are crisp-tender. Add the peas, mushrooms and reserved pineapple. Cover and simmer 15 minutes longer or until the vegetables and meat are tender.

Remove the roast, vegetables and pineapple; keep warm. Skim fat from the pan drippings. Combine the cornstarch and cold water until smooth; gradually stir into the drippings. Bring to a boil; cook and stir for 2 minutes or until thickened. Slice roast across the grain. Serve the meat, vegetables and pineapple with gravy. **YIELD: 6 SERVINGS.**

Meat Sauce for Spaghetti

🕐 Meat Sauce for Spaghetti

PREP: **30 MIN.** COOK: **8 HOURS**

Here's a thick, hearty sauce that turns ordinary spaghetti and garlic bread into a filling feast. When I'm in a hurry, I make this slow cooker recipe in an electric frying pan instead.

Mary Tallman ✳ Arbor Vitae, Wisconsin

- 1 pound ground beef
- 1 pound bulk Italian sausage
- 1 can (28 ounces) crushed tomatoes, undrained
- 1 medium green pepper, chopped
- 1 medium onion, chopped
- 1 cup finely chopped carrots
- 1 cup water
- 1 can (8 ounces) tomato sauce
- 1 can (6 ounces) tomato paste
- 1 tablespoon brown sugar
- 1 tablespoon Italian seasoning
- 2 garlic cloves, minced
- 1/2 teaspoon salt
- 1/4 teaspoon pepper

Hot cooked spaghetti

In a large skillet, cook beef and sausage over medium heat until no longer pink; drain. Transfer meat to a 5-qt. slow cooker. Stir in the tomatoes, green pepper, onion, carrots, water, tomato sauce, tomato paste, brown sugar, Italian seasoning, garlic, salt and pepper. Cover and cook on low for 8-10 hours or until bubbly. Serve with spaghetti. **YIELD: 9 SERVINGS.**

Taco Lasagna

Taco Lasagna

PREP: **20 MIN.** BAKE: **25 MIN.**

If you like foods with Southwestern flair, this just might become a new favorite. Loaded with cheese, meat and beans, the layered casserole comes together in a snap.

Terri Keenan ✴ Tuscaloosa, Alabama

- 1 pound ground beef
- 1/2 cup chopped green pepper
- 1/2 cup chopped onion
- 2/3 cup water
- 1 envelope taco seasoning
- 1 can (15 ounces) black beans, rinsed and drained
- 1 can (14-1/2 ounces) Mexican diced tomatoes, undrained
- 6 flour tortillas (8 inches)
- 1 can (16 ounces) refried beans
- 3 cups (12 ounces) shredded Mexican cheese blend

In a large skillet, cook the beef, green pepper and onion over medium heat until meat is no longer pink; drain. Add water and taco seasoning; bring to a boil. Reduce heat; simmer, uncovered, for 2 minutes. Stir in the black beans and tomatoes. Simmer, uncovered, for 10 minutes.

Place two tortillas in a greased 13-in. x 9-in. baking dish. Spread with half of the refried beans and beef mixture; sprinkle with 1 cup cheese. Repeat the layers. Top with remaining tortillas and cheese.

Cover and bake at 350° for 25-30 minutes or until heated through and cheese is melted. **YIELD: 9 SERVINGS.**

Garlic Chuck Roast

PREP: **15 MIN.** BAKE: **2-1/4 HOURS + STANDING**

Having never made a roast before, I experimented with a few ingredients to come up with this hearty all-in-one meal. Not only is it easy, but the tender entree gets terrific flavor from garlic, onion and bay leaves.

Janet Boyer ✴ Nemacolin, Pennsylvania

- 1 boneless beef chuck roast (3 pounds)
- 15 garlic cloves, peeled
- 1 teaspoon salt
- 1/4 teaspoon pepper
- 2 tablespoons canola oil
- 5 bay leaves
- 1 large onion, thinly sliced
- 2 tablespoons butter, melted
- 1-1/2 cups water
- 1 pound baby carrots

With a sharp knife, cut 15 slits in roast; insert garlic into slits. Sprinkle the meat with salt and pepper.

In a Dutch oven, brown meat in oil; drain. Place bay leaves on top of roast; top with onion slices. Drizzle with butter. Add water to pan. Cover and bake at 325° for 1-1/2 hours.

Baste roast with pan juices; add carrots. Cover and bake 45-60 minutes longer or until meat and carrots are tender. Discard bay leaves. Let roast stand for 10 minutes before slicing. Thicken pan juices if desired. **YIELD: 6-8 SERVINGS.**

Garlic Chuck Roast

Cheese-Topped Meat Loaves

PREP/TOTAL TIME: **20 MIN.**

This is one of my favorite entrees for two. I found this tender meat loaf recipe in a supermarket's cookbook almost 20 years ago and have enjoyed it ever since. Sometimes I substitute ground turkey or chicken for the ground beef or make extra loaves to freeze for later meals.

Lois Kinneberg ✳ Phoenix, Arizona

- 1 egg
- 2 tablespoons plus 1/3 cup picante sauce, *divided*
- 1/4 cup old-fashioned oats
- 1 teaspoon dried minced onion
- 1/4 teaspoon chili powder
- 1/8 teaspoon salt
- 1/2 pound ground beef
- 1/4 cup shredded cheddar cheese

In a small bowl, combine the egg, 2 tablespoons picante sauce, oats, onion, chili powder and salt. Crumble beef over mixture and mix well. Shape into two 4-in. x 2-in. loaves.

Place in a microwave-safe dish. Cover and microwave on high for 5-6 minutes or until a meat thermometer reads 160°.

Place the remaining picante sauce in a small microwave-safe bowl; cover and microwave on high for 30 seconds. Pour over meat loaves. Sprinkle with cheese. Cover and microwave on high for 45 seconds or until cheese is melted. **YIELD: 2 SERVINGS.**

EDITOR'S NOTE: This recipe was tested in a 1,100-watt microwave.

Cheese-Topped Meat Loaves

Pizza Burgers

Pizza Burgers

PREP: 20 MIN. GRILL: 20 MIN.

Kids usually love anything with the word "pizza" attached to it, so I came up with this top-your-own pizza burger recipe.

Robin Kornegay * Seffner, Florida

- 1 package (11-1/4 ounces) frozen garlic Texas toast
- 1-3/4 pounds ground beef
- 1 cup pizza sauce, *divided*
- 18 slices pepperoni
- 12 sliced part-skim mozzarella cheese, *divided*
- 1 cup sliced fresh mushrooms
- 2 teaspoons butter
- 6 teaspoons grated Parmesan cheese

Sliced green pepper and ripe olives, optional

Prepare six Texas toast slices according to package directions. Save remaining Texas toast for another use. Shape beef into 12 thin patties.

Top six patties with 1 tablespoon pizza sauce, three slices of pepperoni and one slice of mozzarella cheese. Top with remaining patties; press edges firmly to seal.

Grill, covered, over medium heat for 8 minutes on each side or until a meat thermometer reads 160°. Meanwhile, in a small skillet, saute mushrooms in butter.

Place a rounded tablespoonful of pizza sauce and one mozzarella cheese slice on each burger. Serve burger on prepared Texas toast with sauteed mushrooms, Parmesan cheese and green peppers and olives, if desired. **YIELD: 6 SERVINGS.**

Beefy Vegetable Soup

PREP: 20 MIN. COOK: 1 HOUR 50 MIN.

This chunky soup is loaded with tender beef stew meat, carrots, potatoes and green beans—and it sure is tasty! A little steak sauce and garlic powder season the broth perfectly.

Jimmy Osmon * Upper Darby, Pennsylvania

- 1-1/2 pounds lean beef stew meat
- 1 tablespoon canola oil

Beefy Vegetable Soup

        2 cans (14-1/2 ounces *each*) reduced-sodium
            beef broth
1-1/2 cups water
        2 tablespoons reduced-sodium soy sauce
        3 medium potatoes, cubed (about 1 pound)
        3 medium carrots, cubed
        3 celery ribs, chopped
        2 tablespoons Worcestershire sauce
        2 tablespoons steak sauce
        1 tablespoon garlic powder
    1/2 teaspoon salt
    1/4 teaspoon dried oregano
    1/8 teaspoon ground nutmeg
    1/8 teaspoon pepper
        2 cups fresh corn *or* frozen corn
1-3/4 cups frozen cut green beans

In a Dutch oven, cook beef in oil over medium
heat until no longer pink; drain. Add the broth,
water and soy sauce. Bring to a boil. Reduce
heat; cover and simmer for 1 hour.

Add potatoes, carrots, celery, Worcestershire
sauce, steak sauce and seasonings. Bring to a
boil. Reduce heat; cover and simmer for 30-40
minutes or until the vegetables are just tender.

Add corn and beans. Bring to a boil. Reduce
heat; cover and simmer for 5-10 minutes or
until vegetables are tender. **YIELD: 9 SERVINGS
(ABOUT 3-1/4 QUARTS).**

NUTRITION FACTS: 1-1/2 cups equals 227 calories, 7 g fat (2 g
saturated fat), 49 mg cholesterol, 584 mg sodium, 24 g carbohydrate,
4 g fiber, 19 g protein. **DIABETIC EXCHANGES:** 2 lean meat, 2
vegetable, 1 starch.

Macaroni 'n' Cheese Pizza

PREP: **35 MIN.** BAKE: **15 MIN. + STANDING**

Here's a fun and flavorful dish that will please those who
like pizza and macaroni and cheese. It will likely top the
popularity poll for most-requested recipes.

Edna Havens ✳ Bartlesville, Oklahoma

        8 ounces uncooked elbow macaroni
        3 eggs
        1 cup (4 ounces) shredded cheddar cheese

Macaroni 'n' Cheese Pizza

        1 pound ground beef
    3/4 cup chopped onion
        1 can (15 ounces) pizza sauce
        1 can (4 ounces) mushroom stems and
            pieces, drained
      28 pepperoni slices
        1 cup (4 ounces) shredded Mexican
            cheese blend

Cook macaroni according to package directions;
drain. Meanwhile, in a large bowl, beat the eggs;
stir in cheddar cheese and macaroni.

Spread onto a greased 14-in. pizza pan. Bake
at 375° for 15 minutes. Meanwhile, in a large
skillet, cook beef and onion over medium heat
until the meat is no longer pink; drain. Stir in
the pizza sauce.

Spread over macaroni crust. Sprinkle with
mushrooms, pepperoni and Mexican cheese.
Bake for 15-20 minutes or until the cheese is
melted. Let stand for 5-10 minutes before
slicing. **YIELD: 6-8 SERVINGS.**

Garden-Style Beef Lasagna

Crumble the beef into a microwave-safe dish. Add the onion and garlic; mix well. Cover and microwave on high for 3 minutes; stir. Cook 2-3 minutes longer or until meat is no longer pink. Stir in pasta sauce, tomato sauce, 1 tablespoon parsley and oregano; cover and microwave for 2 minutes or until heated through. Set aside.

In a small bowl, combine the cottage cheese, 1/4 cup Parmesan cheese, egg, basil and the remaining parsley. Spread 1-1/3 cups meat sauce in a greased microwave-safe 11-in. x 7-in. baking dish.

Layer with three noodles, 1 cup cheese mixture and 1/2 cup mozzarella cheese. Repeat layers. Top with remaining meat sauce.

Cover loosely and microwave at 50% power for 15-18 minutes or until noodles are tender. Sprinkle with the remaining mozzarella and Parmesan. Microwave, uncovered, 5 minutes longer or until cheese is melted. Let stand for 15 minutes before serving. **YIELD: 6-8 SERVINGS.**

EDITOR'S NOTE: This recipe was tested in a 1,100-watt microwave.

Garden-Style Beef Lasagna

PREP: **25 MIN.** COOK: **30 MIN. + STANDING**

Everyone who has tried this fabulous lasagna dish absolutely loves it and asks me for the recipe. People are always surprised that it can be prepared entirely in the microwave. For a change of pace, I like to add a layer of sliced zucchinis.

Micaela Miller ✳ Corinth, Texas

- 1-1/2 pounds lean ground beef
-   3/4 cup chopped onion
-     1 teaspoon minced garlic
- 1-1/2 cups garden-style pasta sauce
-     1 can (15 ounces) tomato sauce
-     2 tablespoons dried parsley flakes, *divided*
-     1 teaspoon dried oregano
-     2 cups (16 ounces) 4% cottage cheese
-   1/2 cup grated Parmesan cheese, *divided*
-     1 egg
-     1 teaspoon dried basil
-     6 no-cook lasagna noodles
-     2 cups (8 ounces) shredded part-skim mozzarella cheese, *divided*

🌵 Southwest Beef Stew

PREP: **20 MIN.** COOK: **20 MIN.**

Add your family's favorite picante sauce to this tasty stew, then watch how quickly they empty their bowls! I like to make an extra batch and freeze it for another day.

Janet Brannan ✳ Sidney, Montana

-     2 pounds lean ground beef
- 1-1/2 cups chopped onions
-     1 can (28 ounces) diced tomatoes, undrained
-     1 package (16 ounces) frozen corn, thawed
-     1 can (15 ounces) black beans, rinsed and drained
-     1 cup picante sauce
-   3/4 cup water
-     1 teaspoon ground cumin
-   3/4 teaspoon salt
-   1/2 teaspoon garlic powder
-   1/2 teaspoon pepper
-   1/2 cup shredded reduced-fat cheddar cheese

In a Dutch oven, cook the beef and onions over medium heat until meat is no longer pink; drain. Stir in the tomatoes, corn, beans, picante sauce, water, cumin, salt, garlic powder and pepper. Bring to a boil. Reduce heat; cover and simmer for 15 minutes or until corn is tender. Sprinkle with cheese. YIELD: 8 SERVINGS.

NUTRITION FACTS: 1-1/3 cups equals 344 calories, 12 g fat (5 g saturated fat), 45 mg cholesterol, 847 mg sodium, 28 g carbohydrate, 7 g fiber, 31 g protein. DIABETIC EXCHANGES: 4 lean meat, 1-1/2 starch, 1 vegetable.

Southwest Beef Stew

Tender Beef and Noodles

PREP: **20 MIN.** COOK: **1-3/4 HOURS**

Because I often work outside with my husband on our cattle ranch, I appreciate convenient recipes like this. The main dish cooks by itself and is ready for us when we come in the house. If you like, substitute stew meat for the roast. Either way, it's a hearty every day meal with a special tasty twist.

Nancy Peterson ✳ Farmington, British Columbia

- 1 boneless beef chuck roast (2 to 2-1/2 pounds), cut into 1-inch cubes
- 2 large onions, chopped
- 3 tablespoons butter
- 1 can (8 ounces) tomato sauce
- 2 teaspoons sugar
- 2 teaspoons paprika
- 1 to 2 teaspoons salt
- 1-1/2 teaspoons caraway seeds
- 1 teaspoon dill weed
- 1/4 teaspoon pepper
- 1/8 teaspoon garlic powder
- 2 teaspoons Worcestershire sauce
- 1 cup (8 ounces) sour cream

Hot cooked noodles

In a large saucepan or Dutch oven, cook beef and onions in butter until the meat is browned. Add the tomato sauce, sugar, seasonings and Worcestershire sauce; bring to a boil. Reduce heat; cover and simmer for 1-3/4 to 2 hours or until meat is tender.

Remove from the heat; stir in sour cream. Serve with noodles. YIELD: **4-6 SERVINGS.**

Tender Beef and Noodles

Cube Steaks Parmigiana

Cube Steaks Parmigiana

PREP: **20 MIN.** BAKE: **40 MIN.**

Are you tired of chicken fried steak? This recipe dresses up cube steaks Italian-style with cheese, tomato sauce, basil and oregano. My husband and I like this main dish with a side of fettuccine Alfredo.

Sarah Befort ✳ Hays, Kansas

- 3 tablespoons all-purpose flour
- 1/2 teaspoon salt
- 1/4 teaspoon pepper
- 2 eggs
- 3 tablespoons water
- 1/3 cup finely crushed saltines
- 1/3 cup grated Parmesan cheese
- 1/2 teaspoon dried basil
- 4 beef cube steaks (1 pound)
- 3 tablespoons canola oil
- 1-1/4 cups tomato sauce
- 2-1/4 teaspoons sugar
- 1/2 teaspoon dried oregano, *divided*
- 1/4 teaspoon garlic powder
- 4 slices part-skim mozzarella cheese
- 1/3 cup shredded Parmesan cheese

In a shallow bowl, combine the flour, salt and pepper. In another bowl, beat eggs and water. Place the cracker crumbs, grated Parmesan cheese and basil in a third bowl.

Coat steaks with flour mixture, then dip in egg mixture and coat with crumb mixture. In a large skillet, brown steaks in oil for 2-3 minutes on each side.

Arrange steaks in a greased 13-in. x 9-in. baking dish. Bake, uncovered, at 375° for 25 minutes or until meat thermometer reads 160°. Combine the tomato sauce, sugar, 1/4 teaspoon oregano and garlic powder; spoon over steaks. Bake 10 minutes longer.

Top each steak with mozzarella cheese; sprinkle with shredded Parmesan cheese and remaining oregano. Bake 2-3 minutes longer or until cheese is melted. **YIELD: 4 SERVINGS.**

Pomegranate Pork Tenderloin, PAGE 208

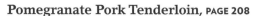

" *Tender cubes of pork are paired with a flavorful sweet-tart pomegranate juice sauce. Add a salad or some steamed veggies to complete the meal. If you are making this during the week, try using a long grain and wild rice mix, which cooks more quickly than wild rice.* " Elizabeth Dumont
Boulder, Colorado

PORK

DO YOU HAVE A WINNING RECIPE?
Enter your most prized recipes in the *Taste of Home* recipe contests, and you may win some money and the chance to have your recipe published. Log onto **tasteofhome.com/RecipeContests** for a list of our current contests and submission deadlines. Good luck...we'll be looking for your recipe.

pork

Asian-Style Baby Back Ribs

PREP: **1-1/4 HOURS** GRILL: **10 MIN.**

AMERICA'S **BEST** *LOVED* •RECIPE CONTEST•

The combination of tender grilled pork and an irresistible sauce will have you licking your fingers. Be ready to add this dish to your list of all-time summer favorites!

Esther Danielson ✳ San Marcos, California

- 1-1/2 pounds pork baby back ribs
- 4-1/2 teaspoons molasses
- 1 tablespoon garlic salt
- 1 teaspoon onion powder
- 1 teaspoon Worcestershire sauce

GLAZE:
- 1/2 cup reduced-sodium soy sauce
- 3 tablespoons thawed pineapple juice concentrate
- 2 tablespoons rice vinegar
- 2 tablespoons hoisin sauce
- 2 tablespoons ketchup
- 1 teaspoon lemon juice
- 1 teaspoon whole grain mustard
- 1 teaspoon Worcestershire sauce
- 1 teaspoon minced fresh gingerroot
- 1/2 teaspoon minced garlic

Chopped green onion

Pat ribs dry. Combine the molasses, garlic salt, onion powder and Worcestershire sauce; brush over meat. Place the ribs on a rack in a small shallow roasting pan. Cover and bake at 300° for 1 hour or until tender.

In a small saucepan, combine the first 10 glaze ingredients. Bring to a boil. Reduce the heat; simmer, uncovered, for 10 minutes or until slightly thickened, stirring occasionally.

Asian-Style Baby Back Ribs

Coat the grill rack with cooking spray before starting grill. Brush the ribs with some of the glaze; grill over medium heat for 8-12 minutes or until browned, turning frequently and brushing with additional glaze. Serve remaining glaze on the side. Garnish with the onion. **YIELD: 2 SERVINGS.**

Pork 'n' Pepper Tacos

Pork 'n' Pepper Tacos

PREP: 25 MIN. COOK: 25 MIN.

As a Texas native, I prefer spicy food. But since my husband and I both work nights, I also need quick entrees like this. I've taken it to parties at work, too, and most tasters enjoy it—with an icy cold soda in most cases!

Jacquie Baldwin * Raleigh, North Carolina

- 1 medium onion, chopped
- 2 medium jalapeno peppers, diced
- 3 tablespoons canola oil
- 2 pounds boneless pork, cut into bite-size pieces
- 1 tablespoon chili powder
- 1/2 teaspoon salt
- 1/4 teaspoon pepper
- 8 taco shells, warmed

Shredded lettuce and cheddar cheese, chopped tomato and salsa

In a large skillet, saute onion and jalapenos in oil for 3-4 minutes or until tender. Add the pork; cook and stir over medium heat for about 8 minutes or until meat is no longer pink.

Stir in chili powder, salt and pepper. Reduce heat; cover and simmer for 25-30 minutes or until the meat is tender, stirring occasionally.

Serve in taco shells with the lettuce, cheese, tomato and salsa. **YIELD: 8 TACOS.**

EDITOR'S NOTE: When cutting hot peppers, disposable gloves are recommended. Avoid touching your face.

Ham and Vegetable Linguine

PREP/TOTAL TIME: 20 MIN.

I've been pleasing dinner guests with this delicious pasta combo for years. The delicate cream sauce blends well with the colorful and hearty mix of vegetables. I chop the vegetables ahead and later prepare this meal in a snap.

Kerry Kerr McAvoy * Rockford, Michigan

- 1 package (8 ounces) linguine
- 1/2 pound fresh asparagus, trimmed and cut into 1-inch pieces
- 1/2 pound fresh mushrooms, sliced
- 1 medium carrot, thinly sliced
- 1 medium zucchini, diced
- 2 cups julienned fully cooked ham
- 1/4 cup butter
- 1 cup heavy whipping cream
- 1/2 cup frozen peas
- 3 green onions, sliced
- 1/4 cup grated Parmesan cheese
- 1 teaspoon dried basil
- 3/4 teaspoon salt

Dash ground nutmeg

Dash pepper

Additional Parmesan cheese, optional

Cook linguine according to package directions. Meanwhile, in a large skillet, saute asparagus, mushrooms, carrot, zucchini and ham in butter until the vegetables are tender.

Add the cream, peas, onions, Parmesan, basil, salt, nutmeg and pepper; bring to a boil. Reduce heat; simmer for 3 minutes, stirring frequently.

Rinse and drain linguine; add to vegetable mixture and toss to coat. Sprinkle with additional Parmesan cheese if desired. **YIELD: 4 SERVINGS.**

Pear-Stuffed Pork Loin

PREP: **30 MIN.** BAKE: **1-1/4 HOURS + STANDING**

From just two trees, we get an abundance of pears. So I'm always looking for new ideas on how to use them. This elegant roast offers a delectable way to incorporate pears into a main dish.

Mary Shivers * Ada, Oklahoma

- 1 boneless whole pork loin roast (3 to 4 pounds)
- 1/2 cup chopped peeled ripe pears
- 1/2 cup chopped dried pears
- 1/2 cup chopped walnuts
- 1/4 cup minced fresh cilantro
- 3 tablespoons honey
- 2 garlic cloves, minced
- 1/4 teaspoon crushed red pepper flakes

GLAZE:

- 1 cup finely chopped peeled ripe pears
- 1/2 cup finely chopped onion
- 1/4 cup maple syrup
- 2 tablespoons Worcestershire sauce
- 2 tablespoons chili sauce
- 1 jalapeno pepper, seeded and finely chopped
- 1/8 teaspoon cayenne pepper

Cut a lengthwise slit down the center of roast to within 1/2 in. of bottom. Open roast so it lies flat. On each half, make another lengthwise slit down the center to within 1/2 in. of bottom; open roast and cover with plastic wrap. Flatten to 3/4-in. thickness. Remove plastic wrap.

In a small bowl, combine the ripe pears, dried pears, walnuts, cilantro, honey, garlic and pepper flakes; spread over roast to within 1 in. of edges. Roll up from a long side; tie with kitchen string at 2-in. intervals. Place in a shallow roasting pan lined with heavy-duty foil.

Combine the glaze ingredients; spoon over roast. Bake, uncovered, at 350° for 1-1/4 to 1-1/2 hours or until a meat thermometer reads 160°, basting occasionally with pan drippings. Let stand for 10-15 minutes before slicing. **YIELD: 12 SERVINGS.**

EDITOR'S NOTE: When cutting hot peppers, disposable gloves are recommended. Avoid touching your face.

Ham and Vegetable Linguine

Pear-Stuffed Pork Loin

Butterflied Pork Chop Dinner

Cover and simmer for 10 minutes; add apple rings and pork chops. Cover and simmer for 13-15 minutes or until apple rings and sweet potatoes are tender and meat is no longer pink.

With a slotted spoon, remove the pork chops, the sweet potatoes and apple to serving plates; keep warm.

Combine cornstarch and remaining apple juice until smooth. Gradually stir into pan juices. Bring to a boil; cook and stir for 1-2 minutes or until thickened. Serve with the pork chops, sweet potatoes and apple. **YIELD: 2 SERVINGS.**

Stuffed Ham with Raisin Sauce

PREP: **30 MIN.** BAKE: **1-3/4 HOURS**

This impressive ham makes a great centerpiece for a holiday dinner, but I've served it most often for brunch. It always draws raves.

Jeanne Miller ✳ Big Sky, Montana

- 1 boneless fully cooked ham (6 to 7 pounds)
- 1 large onion, chopped
- 1/4 cup butter, cubed
- 2 cups corn bread stuffing mix
- 1-1/2 cups chopped pecans, toasted
- 1/2 cup minced fresh parsley
- 1/4 cup egg substitute
- 2 tablespoons prepared mustard
- 1/2 cup honey
- 2 tablespoons orange juice concentrate

RAISIN SAUCE:

- 1/2 cup packed brown sugar
- 2 tablespoons all-purpose flour
- 1/2 teaspoon ground mustard
- 1/2 cup raisins
- 1-1/2 cups water
- 1/4 cup cider vinegar

Using a sharp thin-bladed knife and beginning at one end of the ham, carefully cut a 2-1/2-in. circle about 6 in. deep; remove the cutout. Cut a 1-1/2-in. slice from the end of removed piece; set aside.

Continue cutting a 2-1/2-in. tunnel halfway through ham, using a spoon to remove pieces of ham (save for another use). Repeat from opposite end of the ham, cutting and removing ham until a tunnel has been cut through the entire length of ham.

🍴 Butterflied Pork Chop Dinner

PREP: **10 MIN.** COOK: **35 MIN.**

Sliced apple, sweet potatoes and tender pork chops remind me of a crisp autumn day, but I enjoy this main dish any time of year. I like to serve the chops with salad and dinner rolls.

Angela Leinenbach ✳ Mechanicsville, Virginia

- 2 butterflied pork chops (3/4 inch thick and 3 ounces *each*)
- 1 tablespoon butter
- 1 cup apple juice *or* cider, *divided*
- 1 teaspoon rubbed sage
- 3/4 teaspoon salt
- 1/2 teaspoon pepper
- 2 medium sweet potatoes, peeled and cut into 1/2-inch slices
- 1 green onion, thinly sliced
- 1 medium tart apple, peeled, cored and cut into 1/4-inch rings
- 2 teaspoons cornstarch

In a large skillet, brown pork chops in butter; drain. Remove from skillet and keep warm. In same skillet, combine 3/4 cup apple juice, sage, salt and pepper. Add sweet potatoes and green onion. Bring to a boil. Reduce heat.

In a small skillet, saute onion in butter until tender. In a large bowl, combine the stuffing mix, the pecans, parsley, egg substitute and the mustard. Stir in the onion. Stuff ham; cover end openings with reserved ham slices. Place in a shallow roasting pan.

Bake, uncovered, at 325° for 1-1/4 hours. In a small saucepan, combine honey and orange juice concentrate; cook and stir for 1-2 minutes or until blended. Brush over the ham. Bake 30 minutes longer or until a meat thermometer reads 140°.

For sauce, combine the brown sugar, flour, mustard and raisins in a saucepan. Gradually add water and vinegar. Bring to a boil; cook and stir for 1-2 minutes or until thickened. Serve with the ham. **YIELD: 12-14 SERVINGS.**

EDITOR'S NOTE: Two fully cooked boneless ham halves can be substituted for the whole ham. Simply hollow out each ham; loosely spoon stuffing into each half, then bake as directed.

Stuffed Ham with Raisin Sauce

Bean and Pork Chop Bake

PREP: **15 MIN.** BAKE: **45 MIN.**

This pork chop recipe has an apple-cinnamon flavor with a hint of sweet maple. It's particularly good when fall apples are in season.

LaRita Lang ✳ Lincoln, Nebraska

- 4 boneless pork loin chops (1/2 inch thick and 4 ounces *each*)
- 1 tablespoon canola oil
- 1 large tart apple, peeled and chopped
- 1 small onion, chopped
- 1 can (28 ounces) baked beans
- 1/3 cup raisins
- 1/4 teaspoon ground cinnamon, *divided*
- 1 tablespoon maple pancake syrup
- 1/4 teaspoon salt

In a large skillet, brown pork chops on both sides in oil. Remove and keep warm. In same pan, saute apple and onion until tender. Stir in beans, raisins and 1/8 teaspoon cinnamon.

Spoon into a greased 2-1/2-qt. baking dish; top with pork chops. Cover and bake at 350° for 40 minutes. Brush chops with syrup; sprinkle with the salt and remaining cinnamon. Bake, uncovered for 5-10 minutes longer or until a meat thermometer reads 160°. **YIELD: 4 SERVINGS.**

Bean and Pork Chop Bake

Italian Sausage with Bow Ties

Italian Sausage with Bow Ties

PREP/TOTAL TIME: **25 MIN.**

Here's a family favorite that's requested monthly in our house. The Italian sausage paired with creamy tomato sauce tastes out of this world. Not only is this dish simple to make, it tastes like you slaved over a hot stove for hours!

Janelle Moore ✳ Federal Way, Washington

- 1 package (16 ounces) bow tie pasta
- 1 pound bulk Italian sausage
- 1/2 cup chopped onion
- 1-1/2 teaspoons minced garlic
- 1/2 teaspoon crushed red pepper flakes
- 2 cans (14-1/2 ounces *each*) Italian stewed tomatoes, drained and chopped
- 1-1/2 cups heavy whipping cream
- 1/2 teaspoon salt
- 1/4 teaspoon dried basil

Shredded Parmesan cheese

Cook the pasta according to package directions. Meanwhile, in a Dutch oven, cook the sausage, onion, garlic and pepper flakes over medium heat for 4-5 minutes or until meat is no longer pink; drain.

Stir in the tomatoes, cream, salt and basil. Bring to a boil over medium heat. Reduce heat; simmer, uncovered, for 6-8 minutes or until thickened, stirring occasionally. Drain the pasta; toss with the sausage mixture. Garnish with Parmesan cheese. **YIELD: 5 SERVINGS.**

Waldorf Stuffed Ham

PREP: **35 MIN.** BAKE: **1-1/4 HOURS + STANDING**

I couldn't resist trying something new for the Ham It Up contest, and this entree just popped into my head. I served it to my husband, and he said it's a keeper.

Colleen Vrooman ✳ Waukesha, Wisconsin

- 1-1/2 cups unsweetened apple juice
- 1/4 cup butter, cubed
- 1 package (6 ounces) pork stuffing mix
- 1 medium tart apple, finely chopped
- 1/4 cup chopped sweet onion

1/4 cup chopped celery

1/4 cup chopped walnuts

1 fully cooked spiral-sliced ham (8 pounds)

1 can (21 ounces) apple pie filling

1/4 teaspoon ground cinnamon

In a large saucepan, bring apple juice and the butter to a boil. Remove from heat; stir in the stuffing mix, apple, onion, celery and walnuts.

Place ham on a rack in a shallow roasting pan. Spoon stuffing by tablespoonfuls between ham slices. Spoon pie filling over ham; sprinkle with cinnamon.

Bake, uncovered, at 325° for 1-1/4 to 1-3/4 hours or until a meat thermometer reads 140°. Let stand for 10 minutes before serving. **YIELD: 14-16 SERVINGS.**

Waldorf Stuffed Ham

Ham and Sweet Potato Cups

PREP: **20 MIN.** BAKE: **40 MIN.**

Ham and sweet potatoes is a Southern favorite. This is one of the very best sweet potato recipes I've ever tried. It makes a great light meal all by itself.

Carleen Mullins ✶ Wise, Virginia

2 cups frozen California-blend vegetables

1 egg

2 tablespoons milk, *divided*

3 tablespoons dry bread crumbs

1/8 teaspoon pepper

3/4 pound fully cooked ham, ground

1 can (15 ounces) cut sweet potatoes, drained

1/2 cup condensed cheddar cheese soup, undiluted

Ham and Sweet Potato Cups

Cook the vegetables according to the package directions; drain and set aside. In a large bowl, beat egg and 1 tablespoon milk. Stir in bread crumbs and pepper; add ham.

In another bowl, mash sweet potatoes until smooth; spread onto the bottom and up the sides of four 10-oz. baking cups. Place about 1/3 cup of the ham mixture in each cup. Top with the vegetables. Combine the soup and remaining milk; spoon over vegetables.

Cover and bake at 350° for 40 minutes or until a meat thermometer reads 160°. **YIELD: 4 SERVINGS.**

Asparagus Sausage Crepes

Asparagus Sausage Crepes

PREP: 20 MIN. BAKE: 20 MIN.

This was my favorite recipe when I was growing up in western Michigan, where asparagus is a big spring crop. With its sausage-and-cheese filling, fresh asparagus and rich sour cream topping, these pretty crepes will impress guests.

Lisa Hanson ✳ Glenview, Illinois

- 1 pound bulk pork sausage
- 1 small onion, chopped
- 1 package (3 ounces) cream cheese, cubed
- 1/2 cup shredded Monterey Jack cheese
- 1/4 teaspoon dried marjoram
- 1 cup milk
- 3 eggs
- 1 tablespoon canola oil
- 1 cup all-purpose flour
- 1/2 teaspoon salt
- 32 fresh asparagus spears (about 1 pound), trimmed

TOPPING:
- 1/4 cup butter, softened
- 1/2 cup sour cream

In a large skillet, cook the sausage and onion over medium heat until sausage is no longer pink; drain. Stir in the cream cheese, Monterey Jack cheese and marjoram; set aside.

In a large bowl, combine the milk, eggs and oil. Combine flour and salt; add to milk mixture and mix well. Cover and refrigerate for 1 hour.

Heat a lightly greased 8-in. nonstick skillet over medium heat; pour 2 tablespoons batter into the center of skillet. Lift and tilt pan to coat bottom evenly. Cook until top appears dry; turn and cook 15-20 seconds longer. Remove to a wire rack. Repeat with the remaining batter, greasing skillet as needed. When cool, stack crepes with waxed paper or paper towels in between.

Spoon 2 tablespoons of the sausage mixture onto the center of each crepe. Top with two asparagus spears. Roll up; place in two greased 13-in. x 9-in. baking dishes.

Cover and bake at 375° for 15 minutes. Combine the butter and sour cream; spoon over crepes. Bake 5 minutes longer or until heated through. **YIELD: 8 SERVINGS.**

Pork and Pear Stir-Fry

Pork and Pear Stir-Fry

PREP/TOTAL TIME: **20 MIN.**

I've served this full-flavored stir-fry for years, and I always get rave reviews. Tender pork and ripe pears make a sweet combination, and a spicy sauce adds plenty of zip. This entree is a must for potlucks or fellowship dinners.

Betty Phillips ✳ French Creek, West Virginia

- 2   teaspoons cornstarch
- 3   tablespoons soy sauce
- 2   tablespoons lemon juice
- 1/2 cup plum preserves *or* preserves of your choice
- 1   tablespoon prepared horseradish
- 1/4 teaspoon crushed red pepper flakes
- 1   medium sweet yellow *or* green pepper, julienned
- 1/2 to 1 teaspoon minced fresh gingerroot
- 1   tablespoon canola oil
- 3   medium ripe pears, peeled and sliced
- 1   pound pork tenderloin, cut into 1/4-inch strips
- 1   can (8 ounces) sliced water chestnuts, drained
- 1-1/2 cups fresh *or* frozen snow peas
- 1   tablespoon sliced almonds, toasted

Hot cooked rice

In a small bowl, combine the cornstarch, soy sauce and lemon juice until smooth. Stir in the preserves, horseradish and pepper flakes; set aside. In a skillet or wok, stir-fry yellow pepper and ginger in oil for 2 minutes. Add pears; stir-fry for 1 minute or until pepper is crisp-tender. Remove and keep warm.

Stir-fry half of the pork at a time for 1-2 minutes or until meat is no longer pink. Return pear mixture and all of the pork to the pan. Add water chestnuts and reserved sauce. Bring to a boil; cook and stir for 2 minutes. Add peas; heat through. Sprinkle with almonds. Serve with the rice. **YIELD: 4 SERVINGS.**

Gingered Pork Tenderloin

Gingered Pork Tenderloin

PREP/TOTAL TIME: **30 MIN.**

Ginger, onions and garlic pack a flavorful punch when paired with pork tenderloin. These tasty medallions, smothered in golden caramelized onions, are a simple and satisfying main dish.

Rebecca Evanoff ✳ Holden, Massachusetts

- 2   large onions, thinly sliced
- 4   teaspoons olive oil
- 1/4 cup water
- 4   teaspoons minced fresh gingerroot *or* 1 teaspoon ground ginger
- 2   garlic cloves, minced
- 1/2 cup apple jelly
- 1   pork tenderloin (1 pound)
- 1/4 teaspoon salt

Hot cooked rice pilaf *or* rice

In a large skillet, saute onions in oil and water for 5-6 minutes. Stir in ginger and garlic. Cover and cook for 8-12 minutes or until onions are tender, stirring occasionally. Reduce heat; stir in apple jelly until melted.

Cut tenderloin into eight slices; flatten each to 1/2-in. thickness. Sprinkle with salt. In a large skillet coated with cooking spray, saute pork for 4 minutes on each side or until no longer pink. Top with reserved onions; cover and cook for 5-7 minutes or until the meat juices run clear. Serve with rice pilaf. **YIELD: 2-3 SERVINGS.**

Sage Pork Chops with Cider Pan Gravy

Sage Pork Chops With Cider Pan Gravy

PREP/TOTAL TIME: **30 MIN.**

A creamy sauce flavored with apple cider and sage makes for a quick and tasty weeknight dinner. If you like, serve these lightly seasoned chops with couscous, rice or noodles.

Erica Wilson ✳ Beverly, Massachusetts

- 4 bone-in center-cut pork loin chops
  (6 ounces *each*)

Salt and pepper to taste

- 3 tablespoons dried sage leaves
- 1/4 cup all-purpose flour
- 2 tablespoons butter
- 2 tablespoons canola oil
- 1/2 cup apple cider *or* juice
- 1/2 cup reduced-sodium chicken broth
- 1/4 cup heavy whipping cream

Minced fresh parsley, optional

Sprinkle the pork chops with salt and pepper; rub with sage. Place the flour in a small shallow bowl; coat chops with flour.

In a large skillet over medium heat, brown chops in butter and oil on both sides. Remove and keep warm.

Add the cider, stirring to loosen browned bits from pan. Cook, uncovered, for 3 minutes. Stir in the broth; cook 3 minutes longer. Add cream; cook for 2-3 minutes or until gravy is slightly thickened. Return the chops to the pan; cover and cook for 6-8 minutes or until a meat thermometer reads 160°. Serve chops with sauce. Sprinkle with parsley if desired. **YIELD: 4 SERVINGS.**

Creamy Ham 'n' Macaroni

PREP: **20 MIN.** BAKE: **20 MIN.**

The original comfort food, macaroni and cheese gets a makeover with the addition of cubed ham and grated Parmesan. Kids will love it!

Christy Looper ✳ Colorado Springs, Colorado

- 2 cups uncooked elbow macaroni
- 1/4 cup butter, cubed
- 1/4 cup all-purpose flour
- 2 cups milk
- 4 teaspoons chicken bouillon granules

        1/4 teaspoon pepper
         2   cups (8 ounces) shredded cheddar
             cheese, *divided*
      1-1/2 cups cubed fully cooked ham
        1/4 cup grated Parmesan cheese

Cook macaroni according to package directions;
drain and set aside. In a large saucepan, melt
the butter over low heat; whisk in flour until
smooth. Whisk in the milk, bouillon and pepper.
Bring to a boil; cook and stir for 2 minutes or
until thickened. Remove from the heat. Stir in
1 cup cheddar cheese, ham, Parmesan cheese
and macaroni.

   Transfer to a greased 2-qt. baking dish.
Sprinkle with remaining cheddar cheese. Bake,
uncovered, at 350° for 20-25 minutes or until
bubbly. Let stand for 5 minutes before serving.
YIELD: 6 SERVINGS.

Creamy Ham 'n' Macaroni

Spicy Pork Roast

PREP: 5 MIN. + CHILLING BAKE: 2-1/4 HOURS + STANDING

I work in a kitchen preparing lunch for the students at a
small private school. I enjoy cooking and entertaining
friends and family. This nicely seasoned roast is one of
the entrees I served at these gatherings.

Sandy Birkey ✳ Bloomington, Indiana

         2   teaspoons garlic powder
         2   teaspoons salt
         2   teaspoons pepper
      1-1/2 teaspoons onion powder
      1-1/2 teaspoons ground mustard
      1-1/2 teaspoons paprika
         1   teaspoon rubbed sage
        1/4 to 1/2 teaspoon cayenne pepper
         1   boneless pork loin roast (3 to
             3-1/2 pounds)

Combine the seasonings; rub over entire roast.
Cover and refrigerate overnight.

   Place roast on a greased rack in a roasting
pan. Bake, uncovered, at 350° for 2-1/4 to 2-3/4
hours or until a meat thermometer reads 160°.
Let stand 10 minutes before slicing. **YIELD: 8-10
SERVINGS.**

Spicy Pork Roast

Italian Stuffed Tomatoes

Italian Stuffed Tomatoes

PREP: **35 MIN.** BAKE: **35 MIN.**

Served with crusty French bread, this makes a great summer meal. My husband and our two daughters ask me to fix it for them frequently.

Michele Shank ✳ Gettysburg, Pennsylvania

- 8 medium tomatoes
- 1/2 pound bulk Italian sausage
- 3/4 cup chopped onion
- 2 garlic cloves, minced
- 1 cup chopped zucchini
- 2 tablespoons minced fresh basil
  or 2 teaspoons dried basil
- 1 tablespoon minced fresh oregano
  or 1 teaspoon dried oregano
- 1 tablespoon red wine vinegar
- 1/2 teaspoon salt
- 1/4 teaspoon pepper
- 1-1/2 cups cooked long grain rice
- 3/4 cup shredded provolone *or* part-skim mozzarella cheese
- 6 tablespoons shredded Parmesan cheese, *divided*
- 3 tablespoons chopped fresh parsley

Cut a thin slice off top of each tomato. Leaving a 1/2-in.-thick shell, scoop out the pulp; chop pulp and set aside. Invert the tomatoes onto paper towels to drain.

Meanwhile, cook sausage, onion and garlic in a skillet until sausage is no longer pink; drain. Add the tomato pulp, zucchini, basil, oregano, vinegar, salt and pepper. Simmer, uncovered, for 10 minutes. Remove from the heat. Stir in rice, provolone, 3 tablespoons Parmesan and parsley; spoon about 2/3 cup into each tomato.

Place in an ungreased 13-in. x 9-in. baking dish. Sprinkle the remaining Parmesan on top. Cover and bake at 350° for 20 minutes. Uncover; bake 15 minutes longer or until the tomatoes are heated through. **YIELD: 8 SERVINGS.**

Pork Fajita Kabobs

Pork Fajita Kabobs

PREP/TOTAL TIME: **30 MIN.**

This has become my favorite way to cook pork loin. The grilled vegetable and meat chunks, seasoned with a homemade Southwestern-style spice blend, are appropriately served in a flour tortilla. Just top with salsa and enjoy!

Bea Westphal ✳ Slidell, Louisiana

- 2 teaspoons paprika
- 1-1/2 teaspoons ground cumin
- 1-1/2 teaspoons dried oregano
- 1 teaspoon garlic powder
- 1/8 to 1/4 teaspoon crushed red pepper flakes
- 1-1/2 pounds boneless pork loin chops, cut into 1-inch cubes
- 1 small green pepper, cut into 1-inch pieces
- 1 small onion, cut into eight wedges
- 8 large fresh mushrooms
- 16 grape tomatoes
- 8 flour tortillas (8 inches), warmed
- 3/4 cup chunky salsa

In a large resealable plastic bag, combine the paprika, cumin, oregano, garlic powder and the pepper flakes; add pork. Seal bag and toss to coat. On eight metal or soaked wooden skewers, alternately thread the pork, green pepper, onion, mushrooms and tomatoes.

Grill kabobs, covered, over medium heat for 5-8 minutes on each side or until meat is no longer pink and vegetables are tender. Place each kabob in a tortilla; remove skewers and fold tortillas in half. Serve with the salsa. **YIELD: 4 SERVINGS.**

Apple-Smothered Pork Chops

Apple-Smothered Pork Chops

PREP: **20 MIN.** BAKE: **1 HOUR**

When I serve this entree to my guests, I always get lots of compliments—and requests for the recipe.

Bonnie Riffle ✳ New Lexington, Ohio

- 6 bone-in pork loin chops (3/4 inch thick)
- 3/4 teaspoon salt
- 1/4 teaspoon rubbed sage
- 1 tablespoon canola oil
- 3 medium tart apples, peeled and sliced
- 3 tablespoons molasses
- 3 tablespoons all-purpose flour
- 2 cups water
- 1 tablespoon white vinegar
- 1/3 cup golden raisins

Sprinkle the pork chops with salt and sage. In a large skillet, brown chops on both sides in oil. Transfer to a greased shallow 3-qt. baking dish. Layer the apples over the meat; drizzle with molasses.

Add the flour to pan drippings in skillet; stir until blended. Gradually stir in the water. Bring to a boil; cook and stir for 2 minutes or until thickened. Remove from the heat; stir in the vinegar and raisins. Pour over apples and chops.

Bake, uncovered, at 350° for 1 hour or until a meat thermometer reads 160°. **YIELD: 6 SERVINGS.**

Florentine Spaghetti Bake

Florentine Spaghetti Bake

PREP: **30 MIN.** BAKE: **1 HOUR + STANDING**

This plate-filling sausage dish appeals to most every appetite in my household, from basic meat-and-potatoes fans to gourmets.

Lorraine Martin ✳ Lincoln, California

- 8 ounces uncooked spaghetti
- 1 pound bulk Italian sausage
- 1 cup chopped onion
- 1 garlic clove, minced
- 1 jar (26 ounces) spaghetti sauce
- 1 can (4 ounces) mushroom stems and pieces, drained
- 1 egg, lightly beaten
- 2 cups (16 ounces) 4% cottage cheese
- 1 package (10 ounces) frozen chopped spinach, thawed and squeezed dry
- 1/4 cup grated Parmesan cheese
- 1/2 teaspoon seasoned salt
- 1/4 teaspoon pepper
- 2 cups (8 ounces) shredded part-skim mozzarella cheese

Cook the pasta according to package directions. Meanwhile, in a large skillet, cook the sausage, onion and the garlic over medium heat until sausage is no longer pink; drain. Stir in the spaghetti sauce and mushrooms. Bring to a boil. Reduce heat; cover and cook for 15 minutes or until heated through.

Drain pasta. In a large bowl, combine the egg, cottage cheese, spinach, Parmesan cheese, salt and pepper. Spread 1 cup sausage mixture in a greased 13-in. x 9-in. baking dish; top with spaghetti and remaining sausage mixture. Layer with spinach mixture and mozzarella cheese.

Cover and bake at 375° for 45 minutes. Uncover; bake 15 minutes longer or until lightly browned and heated through. Let stand for 15 minutes before cutting. YIELD: **9 SERVINGS.**

Southwestern Pulled Pork

🕐 Southwestern Pulled Pork

PREP: **5 MIN.** COOK: **8-1/4 HOURS**

The best way to describe this tender pork recipe is yummy! Bottled barbecue sauce, canned green chilies and a few other kitchen staples make preparation fast and easy. We like to wrap the seasoned pork in flour tortillas.

Jill Hartung ✳ Colorado Springs, Colorado

- 2 cans (4 ounces *each*) chopped green chilies
- 1 can (8 ounces) tomato sauce
- 1 cup barbecue sauce
- 1 large sweet onion, thinly sliced
- 1/4 cup chili powder
- 1 teaspoon ground cumin
- 1 teaspoon dried oregano
- 1 boneless pork loin roast (2 to 2-1/2 pounds)

Flour tortillas

TOPPINGS:

Sour cream, shredded lettuce and chopped tomatoes, optional

In a 3-qt. slow cooker, combine chilies, tomato sauce, barbecue sauce, onion, chili powder, cumin and oregano. Cut pork in half; place on top of tomato sauce mixture. Cover and cook on low for 8-9 hours or until meat is tender.

Remove pork. When cool enough to handle, shred meat using two forks. Return to slow cooker and heat through. Spread on tortillas; top with the sour cream, lettuce and tomatoes if desired; roll up. **YIELD: 6-8 SERVINGS.**

Grilled Veggie Pork Bundles

🕐 Grilled Veggie 🍴 Pork Bundles

PREP/TOTAL TIME: **30 MIN.**

During the summer, we enjoy eating dinner on our deck. These colorful bundles are one of our favorite meals, which I serve along with rice and a tall glass of iced tea. For variety, try them with provolone cheese or sweet red peppers...or a substitute chicken breast for the pork chops.

Linda Turner Ludwig ✳ Columbiana, Ohio

- 4 bacon strips
- 2 boneless pork loin chops (4 ounces *each*)
- 1/8 teaspoon salt
- 1/8 teaspoon pepper
- 2 slices onion (1/4 inch thick)
- 2 slices tomato (1/2 inch thick)
- 1/2 medium green pepper, cut in half
- 2 slices Swiss cheese

Cross two bacon strips to form an X; repeat. Sprinkle pork chops with salt and pepper; place over bacon strips. Layer with onion, tomato and green pepper. Wrap bacon strips over vegetables and secure with a toothpick.

Prepare the grill for indirect heat, using a drip pan. Coat grill rack with cooking spray before starting the grill. Place the pork bundles over the drip pan. Grill, covered, over indirect medium heat for 20-25 minutes or until a meat thermometer reads 160°.

Place the cheese slices over bundles; cover and grill 1 minute longer or until cheese is melted. Discard the toothpicks before serving.

YIELD: 2 SERVINGS.

Almond Pork Chops with Honey Mustard

⊘ Almond Pork Chops with Honey Mustard

PREP/TOTAL TIME: **25 MIN.**

I love how crunchy almonds and sweet mustard sauce jazz up this tender pork dish. Usually, I double the recipe. One chop is never enough for my gang of grown children and grandkids.

Lillian Julow ✳ Gainesville, Florida

- 1/2 cup smoked almonds
- 1/2 cup dry bread crumbs
-   2 eggs
- 1/3 cup all-purpose flour
- 1/4 teaspoon salt
- 1/8 teaspoon pepper
-   4 boneless pork loin chops (1 inch thick and 6 ounces *each*)
-   2 tablespoons olive oil
-   2 tablespoons butter
- 1/2 cup reduced-fat mayonnaise
- 1/4 cup honey
-   2 tablespoons Dijon mustard

In a food processor, process the almonds until finely chopped. Transfer to a shallow bowl; add bread crumbs. In another bowl, beat the eggs. In a large resealable plastic bag, combine flour, salt and pepper. Add pork chops, one at a time, and shake to coat. Dip in the eggs, then coat with almond mixture.

In a large skillet over medium heat, cook the chops in oil and butter for 5 minutes on each side or until juices run clear. Meanwhile, in a small bowl, combine the mayonnaise, honey and the mustard. Serve with the pork chops.
YIELD: **4 SERVINGS.**

Cranberry Ham Loaf

Cranberry Ham Loaf

PREP: **20 MIN.** BAKE: **70 MIN.**

A cranberry sauce topping makes this easy-to-prepare ham loaf festive enough for a holiday meal. I find it's a great way to use up leftover ham.

Ronald Heffner ✳ Pawleys Island, South Carolina

-   1 egg, lightly beaten
-   1 cup milk

2 medium onions, chopped
1 medium green pepper, chopped
1 cup soft bread crumbs
1-1/2 pounds ground fully cooked ham
1 pound bulk pork sausage
1 can (16 ounces) whole-berry cranberry sauce
1/4 cup water
1 tablespoon light corn syrup

In a large bowl, combine the egg, milk, onions, green pepper and bread crumbs. Crumble ham and sausage over mixture; mix well.

Pat into an ungreased 9-in. x 5-in. loaf pan (pan will be full). Place on a baking sheet. Bake, uncovered, at 350° for 70-80 minutes or until a meat thermometer reads 160°.

In a small saucepan, combine the cranberry sauce, water and corn syrup. Bring to a boil. Reduce heat; simmer, uncovered, for 5 minutes or until thickened. Remove ham loaf to a serving platter; top with cranberry sauce. **YIELD: 8 SERVINGS.**

Cheese-Stuffed Shells

Cheese-Stuffed Shells

PREP: **35 MIN.** BAKE: **50 MIN.**

When I was living in California, I tasted this rich, cheesy pasta dish at a neighborhood Italian restaurant. I got the recipe and made a few changes to it in my own kitchen.

Lori Mecca ✳ Grants Pass, Oregon

1 pound bulk Italian sausage
1 large onion, chopped
1 package (10 ounces) frozen chopped spinach, thawed and squeezed dry
1 package (8 ounces) cream cheese, cubed
1 egg, lightly beaten
2 cups (8 ounces) shredded part-skim mozzarella cheese, *divided*
2 cups (8 ounces) shredded cheddar cheese
1 cup 4% cottage cheese
1 cup grated Parmesan cheese
1/4 teaspoon salt
1/4 teaspoon pepper
1/8 teaspoon ground cinnamon, optional
24 jumbo pasta shells, cooked and drained

SAUCE:
1 can (29 ounces) tomato sauce
1 tablespoon dried minced onion
1-1/2 teaspoons dried basil
1-1/2 teaspoons dried parsley flakes
2 garlic cloves, minced
1 teaspoon sugar
1 teaspoon dried oregano
1/2 teaspoon salt
1/4 teaspoon pepper

In a large skillet, cook sausage and onion over medium heat until the meat is no longer pink; drain. Transfer to a large bowl. Stir in spinach, cream cheese and egg. Add 1 cup mozzarella, cheddar, cottage cheese, Parmesan, salt, pepper and cinnamon if desired; mix well.

Stuff pasta shells with the sausage mixture. Arrange in two 11-in. x 7-in. baking dishes coated with cooking spray. Combine the sauce ingredients; spoon over shells.

Cover and bake at 350° for 45 minutes. Uncover; sprinkle with remaining mozzarella. Bake 5-10 minutes longer or until bubbly and cheese is melted. Let stand for 5 minutes before serving. **YIELD: 12 SERVINGS.**

Asian Pork Kabobs

Asian Pork Kabobs

PREP: 10 MIN. + MARINATING GRILL: 10 MIN.

Sweet and tangy, these kabobs have a delicious kick, thanks to the hot pepper sauce. This recipe can be adapted to add your favorite vegetables. It's great with rice and a fresh salad.

Trisha Kruse * Eagle, Idaho

- 1/4 cup teriyaki sauce
- 2 tablespoons balsamic vinegar
- 2 tablespoons sesame oil
- 2 tablespoons honey
- 2 teaspoons sriracha Asian hot chili sauce *or* 1 teaspoon hot pepper sauce
- 1 pound pork tenderloin, cut into 1-inch cubes
- 1 medium onion, quartered
- 1 medium sweet red pepper, cut into 2-inch pieces

In a small bowl, combine the teriyaki sauce, vinegar, oil, honey and hot pepper sauce. Pour 1/3 cup marinade into a large resealable plastic bag; add pork. Seal the bag and turn to coat; refrigerate for at least 2 hours. Cover and refrigerate remaining marinade for basting.

Drain and discard marinade from pork. On four metal or soaked wooden skewers, alternately thread the pork, onion and red pepper.

Grill kabobs, covered, over the medium heat for 10-15 minutes or until the vegetables are tender and the meat is no longer pink, turning occasionally and basting frequently with the reserved marinade. **YIELD: 4 SERVINGS.**

Pasta with Chorizo And Spinach

PREP/TOTAL TIME: 20 MIN.

This zippy entree looks and tastes special, but it's a cinch to make. When I get home from work, I like to prepare quick dishes, and this is one of our favorites.

Athena Russell * Florence, South Carolina

- 1-1/4 cups uncooked penne pasta
- 1/3 pound uncooked chorizo *or* bulk spicy pork sausage
- 1 small onion, thinly sliced
- 4 ounces sliced fresh mushrooms
- 1/3 cup water-packed artichoke hearts, rinsed, drained and quartered

1/3 cup chopped oil-packed sun-dried
    tomatoes, drained
  1 garlic clove, minced
1/4 teaspoon dried oregano
1/8 teaspoon salt
1/8 teaspoon pepper
  4 teaspoons olive oil
  3 cups chopped fresh spinach
  2 tablespoons grated Parmesan cheese

Cook the pasta according to package directions.
Meanwhile, in a large skillet, saute the chorizo,
onion, mushrooms, artichokes, tomatoes, garlic,
oregano, salt and pepper in oil until chorizo is
no longer pink and vegetables are tender.

Add spinach; cook and stir for 1-2 minutes
or until wilted. Drain the pasta; top with chorizo
mixture. Sprinkle with Parmesan cheese. **YIELD:**
2 SERVINGS.

Pasta with Chorizo and Spinach

Sunday Boiled Dinner

PREP: **20 MIN.** COOK: **1 HOUR**

This hearty dinner originated with my Pennsylvania
Dutch mother and grandmother. When I first served it
to my husband, he enjoyed it so much that he asked me
to make the entree more frequently.

Arlene Oliver ✳ Bothell, Washington

  1 smoked boneless ham *or* pork shoulder
    (about 2 pounds)
  1 medium onion, quartered
  2 pounds carrots, halved
  2 pounds red potatoes, quartered
  2 pounds rutabagas, peeled and cut into
    1-1/2-inch cubes
  1 teaspoon salt
1/2 teaspoon pepper
  1 medium cabbage, halved
Prepared horseradish, optional

In a large Dutch oven or stockpot, place the ham,
onion, carrots, potatoes, rutabagas, salt and
pepper. Add water just to cover; bring to a boil.

Place cabbage on top of vegetables. Reduce
heat; cover and simmer for 1 hour or until the
vegetables are tender.

Drain. Cut the cabbage into wedges; remove
core. Serve the meat and the vegetables with
horseradish if desired. **YIELD: 8 SERVINGS.**

Sunday Boiled Dinner

Fruit-Pecan Pork Roast

sugar and the remaining butter until butter is melted. Discard bay leaf.

Remove 1/4 cup sauce and stir in preserves; spoon over roast. Set remaining sauce aside. Bake roast 45 minutes longer or until a meat thermometer reads 160°. Let stand 10-15 minutes before slicing. Serve with reserved sauce.
YIELD: 10-12 SERVINGS.

Fruit-Pecan Pork Roast

PREP: **20 MIN.** BAKE: **1-3/4 HOURS + STANDING**

This spectacular roast was a huge hit with members of the cooking club I belong to. The sweet, tangy fruit glaze looks lovely and is a wonderful complement to the juicy pork. It's a family favorite for special occasions and holidays.

Gay Flynn ✳ Bellevue, Nebraska

- 1 boneless rolled pork loin roast (3-1/2 pounds)
- 1/2 cup chopped green onions
- 4 tablespoons butter, *divided*
- 1/4 cup orange juice
- 1 bay leaf
- 1 can (16 ounces) whole-berry cranberry sauce
- 1/2 cup chicken broth
- 1/2 cup chopped pecans
- 1 tablespoon red wine vinegar
- 1/4 teaspoon salt
- 1/8 teaspoon pepper
- 1/8 teaspoon sugar
- 1/4 cup apricot preserves

Place roast on a rack in a shallow roasting pan. Bake, uncovered, at 350° for 1 hour.

Meanwhile, in a skillet, saute the onions in 1 tablespoon butter for 1 minute. Add orange juice and bay leaf; cook and stir over medium-high heat until thickened, about 4 minutes. Add the cranberry sauce, broth, pecans and vinegar; cook and stir until slightly thickened, about 5 minutes. Reduce heat; stir in the salt, pepper,

🖐 Pomegranate Pork Tenderloin

PREP: **20 MIN.** COOK: **20 MIN.**

Tender cubes of pork are paired with a flavorful sweet-tart pomegranate juice sauce. Add a salad or some steamed veggies to complete the meal. If you are making this during the week, try using a long grain and wild rice mix, which cooks more quickly than wild rice.

Elizabeth Dumont ✳ Boulder, Colorado

- 1/4 cup all-purpose flour
- 1/4 cup cornmeal
- 2 teaspoons grated lemon peel
- 1-1/2 teaspoons salt, *divided*
- 1/2 teaspoon pepper
- 1 to 1-1/4 pounds pork tenderloin, cut into 2-inch pieces
- 2 tablespoons olive oil
- 1 cup reduced-sodium chicken broth
- 1 cup pomegranate juice
- 2 tablespoons sugar
- 1 to 2 garlic cloves, minced
- 1/4 teaspoon ground ginger
- 1/8 teaspoon cayenne pepper
- 2 tablespoons cornstarch
- 3 tablespoons cold water
- 2 cups hot cooked wild rice

In a large resealable plastic bag, combine the flour, cornmeal, lemon peel, 1 teaspoon salt and pepper. Add the pork, a few pieces at a time, and shake to coat. In a large skillet, cook the pork in oil for 5-7 minutes on each side or until a meat thermometer reads 160°. Remove and keep warm.

In the same skillet, combine the broth, juice, sugar, garlic, ginger, cayenne and remaining salt.

Bring to a boil. Reduce heat; simmer, uncovered, for 5 minutes. Combine cornstarch and water until smooth; gradually stir into the pan. Bring to a boil; cook and stir for 2 minutes or until thickened. Return pork to the pan and heat through. Serve with rice. **YIELD: 4 SERVINGS.**

NUTRITION FACTS: 4 ounces cooked pork with 1/2 cup sauce and 1/2 cup rice equals 374 calories, 11 g fat (2 g saturated fat), 63 mg cholesterol, 694 mg sodium, 41 g carbohydrate, 2 g fiber, 27 g protein. DIABETIC EXCHANGES: 3 lean meat, 2 starch, 1 fat, 1/2 fruit.

Pomegranate Pork Tenderloin

Roasted Garlic Pork Supper

PREP: **15 MIN.** BAKE: **3-1/2 HOURS + STANDING**

I grow sweet onions and garlic, so they're always on hand when I want to make this roast. I first fixed the recipe for a church retreat, and it was a big hit. Since then, I've prepared it for large groups and family dinners over the years.

Joseph Obbie ✳ Webster, New York

      2 whole garlic bulbs
      2 teaspoons olive oil
    1/2 teaspoon dried basil
    1/2 teaspoon dried oregano
      2 tablespoons lemon juice
      1 boneless pork loin roast (4 to 5 pounds)
      6 medium red potatoes, quartered
      3 cups baby carrots
      1 large sweet onion, thinly sliced
  1-1/2 cups water
      1 teaspoon salt
    1/2 teaspoon pepper

Remove papery outer skin from garlic (do not peel or separate cloves). Cut the top off garlic heads, leaving root end intact. Brush with oil; sprinkle with basil and oregano. Wrap each bulb in heavy-duty foil. Bake at 425° for 30-35 minutes or until softened. Cool for 10-15 minutes. Squeeze softened garlic into a small bowl. Add lemon juice; mix well. Rub over the roast.

Place the roast in a shallow roasting pan. Arrange the potatoes, carrots and onion around roast. Pour water into the pan. Sprinkle meat and vegetables with salt and pepper. Cover and bake at 350° for 1-1/2 hours. Uncover; bake 1-1/2 hours longer or until a meat thermometer reads 160°, basting often. Cover and let stand for 10 minutes before slicing. **YIELD: 10-12 SERVINGS.**

Roasted Garlic Pork Supper

Stuffed Iowa Chops

Stuffed Iowa Chops

PREP: 20 MIN. BAKE: 1 HOUR

Here's a satisfying dish for big appetites. The corn and apples make a tasty stuffing for the chops, while the honey-mustard sauce enhances the flavor.

Judith Smith ✳ Des Moines, Iowa

- 4 bone-in pork loin chops (1-1/2 inches thick and 8 ounces *each*)
- 1 tablespoon canola oil
- 1 cup whole kernel corn
- 1 cup diced peeled apple
- 1 cup dry bread crumbs
- 1 tablespoon minced fresh parsley
- 1 tablespoon finely chopped onion
- 1 tablespoon milk
- 1/4 teaspoon salt
- 1/4 teaspoon rubbed sage
- 1/4 teaspoon pepper

SAUCE:

- 1/4 to 1/2 cup Dijon mustard
- 1/2 cup honey
- 1 teaspoon minced fresh rosemary
- 1/2 teaspoon salt
- 1/4 teaspoon pepper

Cut a pocket in each chop by slicing almost to the bone. In a large skillet, brown the chops in oil over medium heat. Remove from the heat.

In a large bowl, combine the corn, apple, bread crumbs, parsley, onion, milk, salt, sage and pepper. Stuff into pork chops. Place in a greased 13-in. x 9-in. baking dish.

Combine the sauce ingredients; pour half over the chops. Bake, uncovered, at 350° for 1 hour or until a meat thermometer reads 160°, basting occasionally with remaining sauce. **YIELD: 4 SERVINGS.**

Cheesy Sausage Penne

Cheesy Sausage Penne

PREP: **25 MIN.** BAKE: **30 MIN.**

This lasagna-like entree takes me back to my childhood. I got the recipe from a friend's mother, who fixed it for us when we were kids. I made a few changes to it, but it's still quick and delicious.

Dallas McCord ✳ Reno, Nevada

- 1 pound bulk Italian sausage
- 1 garlic clove, minced
- 1 jar (26 ounces) spaghetti sauce
- 1 package (16 ounces) uncooked penne pasta
- 1 package (8 ounces) cream cheese, softened
- 1 cup (8 ounces) sour cream
- 4 green onions, sliced
- 2 cups (8 ounces) shredded cheddar cheese

In a large skillet, cook the sausage and garlic over medium heat until meat is no longer pink; drain. Stir in spaghetti sauce; bring to a boil. Reduce heat; cover and simmer for 20 minutes.

Cook pasta according to package directions; drain. Meanwhile, in a small bowl, combine the cream cheese, sour cream and onions.

In a greased shallow 3-qt. baking dish, layer half of the pasta and sausage mixture. Dollop with half of the cream cheese mixture; sprinkle with half of the cheddar cheese. Repeat layers.

Bake, uncovered, at 350° for 30-35 minutes or until bubbly. **YIELD: 12 SERVINGS.**

Sweet 'n' Sour Cashew Pork

 Sweet 'n' Sour Cashew Pork

PREP/TOTAL TIME: **30 MIN.**

A simple homemade sauce blends the tangy flavors in this stir-fry. Ginger, garlic and pineapple give it a traditional taste, and snow peas, green onions and cashews add a little crunch.

Janet Rodakowski ✳ Wentzville, Missouri

- 2 tablespoons cornstarch, *divided*
- 1 tablespoon sherry *or* chicken broth
- 1 pork tenderloin (1 pound), cut into 1-inch pieces
- 1/4 cup sugar
- 1/3 cup water
- 1/4 cup cider vinegar
- 3 tablespoons reduced-sodium soy sauce
- 3 tablespoons ketchup
- 1 tablespoon canola oil
- 1/3 cup unsalted cashews
- 1/4 cup chopped green onions
- 2 teaspoons minced fresh gingerroot
- 2 garlic cloves, minced
- 1/2 pound fresh snow peas (3 cups)
- 1 can (8 ounces) unsweetened pineapple chunks, drained

Hot cooked rice, optional

In a bowl, combine 1 tablespoon cornstarch and sherry until smooth; add pork and toss to coat. In another bowl, combine sugar and remaining cornstarch. Stir in water, vinegar, soy sauce and ketchup until smooth; set aside.

In a large nonstick skillet or wok, stir-fry the pork in hot oil until no longer pink. Add the cashews, onions, ginger and garlic; stir-fry for 1 minute. Add the peas and pineapple; stir-fry 3 minutes longer or until peas are crisp-tender.

Stir cornstarch mixture and add to the pan. Bring to a boil; cook and stir for 1-2 minutes or until the sauce is thickened. Serve over rice if desired. **YIELD: 4 SERVINGS.**

NUTRITION FACTS: 1 cup pork mixture (calculated without rice) equals 371 calories, 13 g fat (3 g saturated fat), 63 mg cholesterol, 714 mg sodium, 36 g carbohydrate, 3 g fiber, 27 g protein. DIABETIC EXCHANGES: 3 lean meat, 1-1/2 starch, 1 vegetable, 1 fat, 1/2 fruit.

Upper Peninsula Pasties

salt until a very soft dough is formed; cover and refrigerate for 1-1/2 hours.

Quarter and thinly slice the potatoes and rutabagas; place in a large bowl with the onions, beef, pork and seasonings.

Divide dough into 12 equal portions. On a floured surface, roll out one portion at a time into a 10-in. circle. Mound about 2 cups filling on half of each circle; dot with 1 teaspoon butter. Moisten edges with water; fold dough over filling and press edges with a fork to seal.

Place on ungreased baking sheets. Cut several slits in the top of pasties. Brush with cream if desired. Bake at 350° for 1 hour or until golden brown. Cool on wire racks. Serve hot or cold. Store in the refrigerator. **YIELD: 12 SERVINGS.**

Upper Peninsula Pasties

PREP: **35 MIN. + CHILLING** BAKE: **1 HOUR**

I grew up in Michigan's Upper Peninsula, where many people are of English ancestry there. Pasties—traditional meat pies often eaten by hand—are very popular there.

Carole Lynn Derifield ✳ Valdez, Alaska

- 2 cups shortening
- 2 cups boiling water
- 5-1/2 to 6 cups all-purpose flour
- 2 teaspoons salt

FILLING:

- 12 large red potatoes (about 6 pounds), peeled
- 4 medium rutabagas (about 3 pounds), peeled
- 2 medium onions, chopped
- 2 pounds ground beef
- 1 pound ground pork
- 1 tablespoon salt
- 2 teaspoons pepper
- 2 teaspoons garlic powder
- 1/4 cup butter

Half-and-half cream, optional

In a large bowl, stir shortening and water until shortening is melted. Gradually stir in flour and

Pork Chili Verde

PREP: **25 MIN.** COOK: **6-1/2 HOURS**

Pork slowly stews with jalapenos, onion, green enchilada sauce and spices in this flavor-packed Mexican dish. It's great on its own or stuffed in a warm tortilla with sour cream, grated cheese or olives on the side.

Kimberly Burke ✳ Chico, California

- 1 boneless pork sirloin roast (3 pounds), cut into 1-inch cubes
- 4 medium carrots, sliced
- 1 medium onion, thinly sliced
- 1 cup minced fresh cilantro
- 4 garlic cloves, minced
- 3 tablespoons canola oil
- 1 can (28 ounces) green enchilada sauce
- 2 jalapeno peppers, seeded and chopped
- 1 tablespoon cornstarch
- 1/4 cup cold water

Hot cooked rice

Flour tortillas, warmed

In a large skillet, saute the pork, carrots, onion, cilantro and garlic in oil in batches until pork is browned. Transfer to a 5-qt. slow cooker. Add the enchilada sauce and jalapenos.

Cover and cook on low for 6 hours or until the meat is tender.

In a small bowl, combine the cornstarch and water until smooth; stir into the pork mixture. Cover and cook on high for 30 minutes or until thickened. Serve with rice and tortillas. **YIELD: 8 SERVINGS.**

EDITOR'S NOTE: When cutting hot peppers, disposable gloves are recommended. Avoid touching your face.

Pork Chili Verde

Spicy Sausage Spaghetti

PREP: **30 MIN.** COOK: **15 MIN.**

Served with crusty bread and a green salad, this is a good summer supper. It has lots of heat—my husband likes that—and it's colorful on the plate.

Nancy Rollag ✳ Kewaskum, Wisconsin

- 1 pound bulk Italian sausage
- 3 tablespoons olive oil, *divided*
- 3 dried whole red chilies
- 1 can (28 ounces) plum tomatoes, drained and chopped
- 3 garlic cloves, minced
- 2 tablespoons minced fresh oregano *or* 2 teaspoons dried oregano
- 1/2 teaspoon salt
- 1/4 teaspoon pepper
- 3 large sweet red peppers, thinly sliced
- 4 cups hot cooked spaghetti
- 1/2 cup minced fresh parsley
- 1/2 cup shredded Parmesan cheese

In a large skillet, cook the sausage over medium heat, until no longer pink; drain. Set the sausage aside and keep warm.

In another skillet, heat 2 tablespoons of oil; saute red chilies for 5-8 minutes or until they turn black. Discard chilies; cool oil slightly. Add the tomatoes, garlic, oregano, salt and pepper; simmer for 15 minutes. Stir in the red peppers and sausage; heat through.

Toss spaghetti with the remaining oil. Add the tomato sauce; toss to coat. Sprinkle with the parsley and Parmesan cheese. **YIELD: 4 SERVINGS.**

Spicy Sausage Spaghetti

Black-Eyed Pea Sausage Stew

Black-Eyed Pea Sausage Stew

PREP: **15 MIN.** COOK: **30 MIN.**

I've always wanted to try black-eyed peas, and I happened to have smoked sausage on hand one night, so I invented this full-flavored stew. It's the perfect way to heat up a cold night without spending a lot of time in the kitchen. I usually doubled the seasonings because we like our food spicier.

Laura Wimbrow ✳ Bridgeville, Delaware

- 1 package (16 ounces) smoked sausage links, halved lengthwise and sliced
- 1 small onion, chopped
- 2 cans (15 ounces *each*) black-eyed peas, rinsed and drained
- 1 can (14-1/2 ounces) diced tomatoes, drained
- 1 can (8 ounces) tomato sauce
- 1 cup beef broth
- 1/4 teaspoon garlic powder
- 1/4 teaspoon Cajun seasoning
- 1/4 teaspoon pepper
- 1/8 teaspoon salt
- 1/8 teaspoon cayenne pepper
- 1/8 teaspoon hot pepper sauce
- 1-1/2 cups frozen corn, thawed

In a Dutch oven, cook the sausage and onion over medium heat until meat is no longer pink; drain. Stir in the peas, tomatoes, tomato sauce, broth and seasonings.

Cook and stir for 10-12 minutes or until hot and bubbly. Stir in corn; cook 5 minutes longer or until heated through. **YIELD: 6 SERVINGS.**

Spicy Ham 'n' Broccoli Pasta

⏱ Spicy Ham 'n' Broccoli Pasta

PREP/TOTAL TIME: **25 MIN.**

I love pasta but get tired of serving it with tomato sauce all the time. My family really enjoys the different and delicious combination of ham and olives in this easy one-pot meal. It goes together so quickly and makes a great way to use up leftover ham.

Valerie Smith ✳ Aston, Pennsylvania

- 8 ounces uncooked bow tie pasta
- 2-1/2 cups frozen broccoli florets

1 medium onion, halved and thinly sliced
1 teaspoon minced garlic
2 cups cubed deli ham
1 can (2-1/4 ounces) sliced ripe olives, drained
1/4 cup olive oil
1/2 teaspoon salt
1/2 teaspoon Italian seasoning
1/2 teaspoon crushed red pepper flakes
1/2 cup grated Parmesan cheese

In a large saucepan, cook pasta according to package directions, adding the broccoli, onion and garlic during the last 5-7 minutes. Cook until pasta and broccoli are tender; drain. In a large serving bowl, combine the ham, olives and pasta mixture.

In a small bowl, whisk the oil, salt, Italian seasoning and pepper flakes. Pour over pasta mixture. Sprinkle with Parmesan cheese; toss to coat. **YIELD: 4-5 SERVINGS.**

Zippy Raspberry Roast Pork

🌿 Zippy Raspberry Roast Pork

PREP: **20 MIN.** BAKE: **1-1/4 HOURS + STANDING**

Rosemary, sage, thyme and garlic make a great pork rub for this main course. The raspberry sauce gets a slight kick from chipotle peppers, but it goes well with the meat.

Kim Pettipas ✳ Oromocto, New Brunswick

1 boneless whole pork loin roast (3-1/2 pounds)
4 teaspoons olive oil, *divided*
1 tablespoon minced fresh rosemary *or* 1 teaspoon dried rosemary, crushed
1 tablespoon minced fresh sage *or* 1 teaspoon rubbed sage
1 tablespoon minced fresh thyme *or* 1 teaspoon dried thyme
4 garlic cloves, peeled
1 teaspoon salt
1/2 teaspoon pepper
SAUCE:
1/2 cup chopped onion
3 garlic cloves, minced
2 teaspoons olive oil
4 cups fresh raspberries
3/4 cup sugar
1/2 cup raspberry vinegar
2 teaspoons minced chipotle pepper in adobo sauce
1/2 teaspoon salt

In a large nonstick skillet, brown the roast on all sides in 3 teaspoons of oil. Place on a rack in a shallow roasting pan. In a food processor, combine the rosemary, sage, thyme, garlic, salt, pepper and remaining oil; cover and process until smooth. Rub over roast. Bake, uncovered, at 350° for 70 minutes.

Meanwhile, in a large saucepan, saute the onion and garlic in oil until tender. Add the raspberries, sugar, vinegar, chipotle pepper and salt. Bring to a boil. Reduce the heat; simmer, uncovered, for 10 minutes or until the sauce is reduced to 2 cups. Press through a sieve; discard the seeds.

Brush 2 tablespoons sauce over pork. Bake for 5-15 minutes or until a meat thermometer reads 160°. Let stand for 10 minutes before slicing. Serve with the remaining sauce. **YIELD: 12 SERVINGS.**

NUTRITION FACTS: 3 ounces cooked pork with 3-1/2 teaspoons sauce equals 262 calories, 9 g fat (3 g saturated fat), 66 mg cholesterol, 341 mg sodium, 19 g carbohydrate, 3 g fiber, 26 g protein. **DIABETIC EXCHANGES:** 3 lean meat, 1 starch, 1/2 fat.

Potato Pork Pie

and stir for 2 minutes or until thickened. Stir in pork; heat through. Pour over the potato crust.

Pipe or spoon remaining mashed potatoes over top. Bake, uncovered, at 375° for 35-40 minutes or until the potatoes are lightly browned. Sprinkle with remaining parsley.

YIELD: 6 SERVINGS.

Surprise Sausage Bundles

PREP: 45 MIN. + RISING BAKE: 20 MIN.

Kielbasa and sauerkraut star in a tasty filling for these scrumptious stuffed rolls, which make a great dinner with soup or salad. My family also loves leftover bundles right out of the refrigerator for a quick lunch.

Barb Ruis ✳ Grandville, Michigan

- 6 bacon strips, diced
- 1 cup chopped onion
- 1 can (16 ounces) sauerkraut, rinsed and well drained
- 1/2 pound smoked kielbasa *or* Polish sausage, coarsely chopped
- 2 tablespoons brown sugar
- 1/2 teaspoon garlic salt
- 1/4 teaspoon caraway seeds
- 1/8 teaspoon pepper
- 1 package (16 ounces) hot roll mix
- 2 eggs
- 1 cup warm water (120° to 130°)
- 2 tablespoons butter, softened

Poppy seeds

In a large skillet, cook bacon until crisp; remove to paper towels. Reserve 2 tablespoons drippings. Saute onion in drippings until tender. Stir in the sauerkraut, sausage, brown sugar, garlic salt, caraway seeds and pepper. Cook and stir for 5 minutes. Remove from the heat; add bacon. Set aside to cool.

In a large bowl, combine contents of the roll mix and yeast packets. Stir in one egg, water and butter to form a soft dough. Turn onto a floured surface; knead until smooth and elastic, about 5 minutes. Cover dough with a large bowl; let stand for 5 minutes.

Divide dough into 16 pieces. On a floured surface, roll out each piece into a 4-in. circle. Top

Potato Pork Pie

PREP: 55 MIN. BAKE: 35 MIN.

A true comfort food that's impossible to resist, this main dish is hearty and saucy with flavors that blend so nicely together. Many shepherd's pie recipes call for beef, so this pork version is a tasty twist on a classic.

Michelle Ross ✳ Stanwood, Washington

- 2 pounds potatoes, peeled and cubed
- 1/3 cup heavy whipping cream
- 4 tablespoons butter, *divided*
- 3/4 teaspoon salt
- 1/8 teaspoon pepper
- 1 medium onion, chopped
- 1 garlic clove, minced
- 1/4 cup all-purpose flour
- 1 can (14-1/2 ounces) beef broth
- 1 tablespoon Dijon mustard
- 1 teaspoon dried thyme
- 4 tablespoons minced fresh parsley, *divided*
- 2-1/2 cups cubed cooked pork

Place potatoes in a large saucepan and cover with water; bring to a boil. Cover and cook for 20-25 minutes or until very tender. Drain well. Mash potatoes with the cream, 2 tablespoons butter, salt and pepper. Spread 1-1/2 cups of the mashed potatoes into a greased shallow 1-1/2-qt. baking dish.

In a large skillet, saute onion and garlic in remaining butter until tender. Stir in flour until blended. Gradually stir in broth, mustard, thyme and 2 tablespoons parsley. Bring to a boil; cook each with 1/4 cup filling. Fold dough around filling, forming a ball; pinch edges to seal. Place seam side down on greased baking sheets. Cover loosely with plastic wrap that has been coated with cooking spray. Let rise in a warm place for 15 minutes.

Beat the remaining egg; brush over bundles. Sprinkle with poppy seeds. Bake at 350° for 16-17 minutes or until golden brown. Serve warm. **YIELD: 16 SERVINGS.**

Surprise Sausage Bundles

Barbecued Spareribs

PREP: **10 MIN + SIMMERING** BAKE: **10 MIN.**

My husband is a meat cutter at a supermarket and likes to find new ways to smoke or barbecue meat. Several years ago, he discovered this recipe for pork ribs covered in a rich, tangy sauce.

Bette Brotzel ✳ Billings, Montana

- 4 pounds pork spareribs, cut into serving-size pieces
- 1 medium onion, quartered
- 2 teaspoons salt
- 1/4 teaspoon pepper

SAUCE:
- 1/2 cup cider vinegar
- 1/2 cup packed brown sugar
- 1/2 cup ketchup
- 1/4 cup chili sauce
- 1/4 cup Worcestershire sauce
- 2 tablespoons chopped onion
- 1 tablespoon lemon juice
- 1/2 teaspoon ground mustard
- 1 garlic clove, minced

Dash cayenne pepper

In a large Dutch oven or stockpot, place ribs and onion; sprinkle with salt and pepper. Add enough water to cover the ribs; bring to a boil. Reduce heat; cover and simmer for 1-1/2 hours until tender; drain.

In a small saucepan, combine all sauce ingredients. Simmer, uncovered, for 1 hour or until slightly thickened, stirring occasionally.

Arrange ribs on a rack in a broiler pan. Brush with sauce. Broil 5 in. from the heat for 5 minutes on each side, brushing frequently with sauce. **YIELD: 4 SERVINGS.**

Barbecued Spareribs

◔ Smoked Chops with Cherry Sauce

PREP/TOTAL TIME: **20 MIN.**

Grilling out? A sweet-but-spicy sauce is the secret to these moist pork chops.

Betty Kleberger ✳ Florissant, Missouri

- 6 fully cooked smoked boneless pork chops (1 inch thick and 6 ounces *each*)
- 1 can (15 ounces) pitted dark sweet cherries, undrained
- 1 cup mild jalapeno pepper jelly
- 1/2 teaspoon ground coriander, optional

Grill the pork chops, covered, over medium heat for 5-7 minutes on each side or until a meat thermometer reads 160°.

Meanwhile, in a small saucepan, combine the cherries, jelly and coriander if desired. Bring to a boil, stirring constantly. Serve with pork chops. **YIELD: 6 SERVINGS.**

Smoked Chops with Cherry Sauce

Old-Fashioned Glazed Ham

PREP: **15 MIN.** BAKE: **2 HOURS 25 MIN. + STANDING**

The fruit juices combine with the ham liquid to make a sweet gravy my family really enjoys.

Barbara Dalton ✳ Clark, South Dakota

- 1/2 fully cooked bone-in ham (6 to 7 pounds)
- 2 tablespoons whole cloves
- 1 cup packed brown sugar
- 2/3 cup orange juice
- 1/2 cup unsweetened pineapple juice
- 1/3 cup maraschino cherry juice

Old-Fashioned Glazed Ham

Place the ham on a rack in a shallow foil-lined roasting pan. Score the surface of the ham, making diamond shapes 1/2 in. deep; insert a clove into each diamond. Cover and bake at 325° for 2 hours.

Meanwhile, in a small saucepan, bring the brown sugar and juices to a boil. Reduce the heat; simmer, uncovered, for 30 minutes or until glaze is reduced to 1 cup.

Baste ham with 1/3 cup glaze. Bake, uncovered, 25-35 minutes longer or until a meat thermometer reads 140°, basting with the remaining glaze every 10 minutes. Let stand for 15 minutes before slicing. **YIELD: 8-10 SERVINGS.**

Gorgonzola Penne with Chicken, PAGE 244

> *This rich, creamy pasta dish is a snap to throw together for a weeknight meal but special enough for company. You can substitute another cheese for the Gorgonzola if you like.*
>
> **George Schroeder**
> Port Murray, New Jersey

POULTRY

DO YOU HAVE A WINNING RECIPE?

poultry

Pineapple-Stuffed Cornish Hens

PREP: 20 MIN. BAKE: 55 MIN.

My mother brought this recipe back with her from Hawaii about 25 years ago. The tender meat, pineapple-coconut stuffing and sweet-sour sauce made it a favorite of my family and friends. I keep copies of the recipe on hand to share.

Vicki Corners ✳ Rock Island, Illinois

- 2 Cornish game hen (20 ounces *each*)
- 1/2 teaspoon salt, *divided*
- 1 can (8 ounces) crushed pineapple
- 3 cups cubed day-old bread (1/2-inch cubes), crusts removed
- 1 celery rib, chopped
- 1/2 cup flaked coconut
- 2/3 cup butter melted, *divided*
- 1/4 teaspoon poultry seasoning
- 2 tablespoons steak sauce
- 2 tablespoons cornstarch
- 2 tablespoons brown sugar
- 1 cup water
- 1 tablespoon lemon juice

Pineapple-Stuffed Cornish Hens

Sprinkle inside of hens with 1/4 teaspoon salt; set aside. Drain pineapple, reserving juice. In a bowl, combine pineapple, bread cubes, celery and the coconut. Add 6 tablespoons of butter; toss to coat.

Loosely stuff the hens; tie the legs together with kitchen string. Place on a rack in a greased shallow roasting pan. Place remaining stuffing in a greased 1-1/2-cup baking dish; cover and set aside. Add poultry seasoning and remaining salt to remaining butter. Spoon some butter mixture over hens. Bake, uncovered, at 350° for 40 minutes, basting twice with butter mixture.

Stir steak sauce and reserved pineapple juice into remaining butter mixture; baste hens. Bake the reserved stuffing with hens for 30 minutes, basting hens twice.

Uncover stuffing; baste hens with remaining butter mixture. Bake 15-20 minutes longer or until a meat thermometer reads 185° for hens and 165° for stuffing in hens. Remove hens from pan; keep warm.

Pour the drippings into a saucepan; skim fat. Combine cornstarch, brown sugar, water and lemon juice until smooth; add to the drippings. Bring to a boil; cook and stir for 1-2 minutes or until thickened. Serve with hens and stuffing.

YIELD: 2 SERVINGS.

Southwestern Stuffed Turkey Breast

Southwestern Stuffed Turkey Breast

PREP: 40 MIN. BAKE: 1-1/4 HOURS + STANDING

This luscious turkey breast is a sure hit with family and friends around the holidays. The moist stuffing gives it a hint of Southwestern flair.

Bernice Janowski ✳ Stevens Point, Wisconsin

1/3 cup sun-dried tomatoes (not packed in oil)

2/3 cup boiling water

1-1/2 teaspoons dried oregano

1 teaspoon salt

3/4 teaspoon ground cumin

1/2 teaspoon ground coriander

1/4 teaspoon crushed red pepper flakes

1 small onion, chopped

1 small green pepper, diced

1 garlic clove, minced

1 tablespoon olive oil

1 cup frozen corn, thawed

1/2 cup dry bread crumbs

1-1/2 teaspoons grated lime peel

1 boneless skinless turkey breast half (2 pounds)

Place tomatoes in a small bowl; cover with boiling water. Cover and let stand for 5 minutes. Drain, reserving 3 tablespoons liquid; set aside. Meanwhile, combine seasonings in a bowl.

In a large skillet, saute the tomatoes, onion, green pepper and garlic in oil until tender. Stir in the corn and 2 teaspoons seasonings; remove from heat. Stir in bread crumbs and reserved tomato liquid. Add the lime peel to remaining seasonings; set side.

Cover turkey with plastic wrap. Flatten to 1/2-in. thickness; remove the plastic. Sprinkle turkey with half of lime-seasoning mixture; spread vegetable mixture to within 1 in. of edges. Roll up jelly-roll style, starting with a short side; tie with kitchen string. Sprinkle with remaining lime-seasoning mixture. Place on a rack in a shallow roasting pan; cover loosely with foil.

Bake at 350° for 1 hour. Uncover; bake 15-30 minutes longer or until a meat thermometer reads 170°, basting occasionally with the pan drippings. Let stand for 15 minutes before slicing. **YIELD: 8 SERVINGS.**

NUTRITION FACTS: 1 slice equals 200 calories, 3 g fat (1 g saturated fat), 70 mg cholesterol, 458 mg sodium, 12 g carbohydrate, 2 g fiber, 30 g protein. **DIABETIC EXCHANGES:** 4 very lean meat, 1 starch.

Stuffing-Coated Chicken

PREP: 15 MIN. BAKE: 45 MIN.

I found this recipe in an old church cookbook, and it quickly became a favorite. When I reheat the leftovers for lunch, the aroma of garlic and Parmesan cheese grabs the attention of co-workers, and they ask for the recipe.

Patricia Inman * Litchfield, Minnesota

1-1/2 cups stuffing mix, finely crushed
2 tablespoons grated Parmesan cheese
1/4 cup butter, melted
1 garlic clove, minced
5 boneless skinless chicken breast halves (6 ounces *each*)

In a shallow dish, combine the stuffing crumbs and Parmesan cheese. In another shallow dish, combine butter and garlic. Dip chicken in butter mixture, then coat with stuffing mixture. Place in a greased 13-in. x 9-in. baking dish.

Sprinkle with remaining stuffing mixture and drizzle with remaining butter mixture. Bake, uncovered, at 350° for 40-45 minutes or until a meat thermometer reads 170°. **YIELD: 5 SERVINGS.**

Stuffing-Coated Chicken

Pretzel-Crusted Drumsticks

PREP: 10 MIN. BAKE: 50 MIN.

The first time I fixed this main dish for guests, I received plenty of recipe requests. With their pretzel coating, these drumsticks seem to satisfy everyone's appetites.

Joann Frazier Hensley * McGaheysville, Virginia

1/2 cup butter, melted
1 teaspoon cayenne pepper
1/8 teaspoon garlic powder
1 cup finely crushed pretzels
1/4 cup chopped pecans
1/2 teaspoon pepper
1-1/2 to 2 pounds chicken drumsticks

In a shallow bowl, combine the butter, cayenne and garlic powder. In another shallow bowl, combine the pretzels, pecans and the pepper. Dip chicken in butter mixture, then roll in the pretzel mixture.

Place in a greased 13-in. x 9-in. baking dish. Bake, uncovered, at 350° for 50-55 minutes or until a meat thermometer reads 180°, turning once. **YIELD: 5 SERVINGS.**

Pretzel-Crusted Drumsticks

Pepperoni Ziti Casserole

🌿 Pepperoni Ziti Casserole

PREP: 20 MIN. BAKE: 30 MIN.

I took a traditional family recipe and put my own nutritious spin on it to create this casserole. The chopped spinach and turkey pepperoni add color and flair, pleasing both the eyes and the palate.

Andrea Abrahamsen ✳ Brentwood, California

- 1 package (1 pound) uncooked ziti *or* small tube pasta
- 1/2 pound lean ground turkey
- 2 cans (one 29 ounces, one 8 ounces) tomato sauce, *divided*
- 1-1/2 cups (6 ounces) shredded part-skim mozzarella cheese, *divided*
- 1 can (8 ounces) mushroom stems and pieces, drained
- 5 ounces frozen chopped spinach, thawed and squeezed dry
- 1/2 cup reduced-fat ricotta cheese
- 4 teaspoons Italian seasoning
- 2 garlic cloves, minced
- 1/2 teaspoon garlic powder
- 1/2 teaspoon crushed red pepper flakes
- 1/4 teaspoon pepper
- 1/2 cup water
- 1 tablespoon grated Parmesan cheese
- 1-1/2 ounces sliced turkey pepperoni

Cook pasta according to package directions. In a large nonstick skillet, cook the turkey over medium heat until no longer pink; drain. Transfer to a large bowl. Add the 29-oz. can tomato sauce, 1 cup mozzarella cheese, mushrooms, spinach, ricotta cheese, Italian seasoning, garlic, garlic powder, pepper flakes and pepper. Drain pasta; fold into turkey mixture.

Transfer to a 13-in. x 9-in. baking dish coated with cooking spray. Combine water and remaining tomato sauce; pour over the pasta mixture. Sprinkle with Parmesan cheese and remaining mozzarella cheese. Top with pepperoni.

Cover and bake at 350° for 24-30 minutes or until bubbly. Uncover; bake 5 minutes longer or until cheese is melted. **YIELD: 10 SERVINGS.**

NUTRITION FACTS: 1 cup equals 306 calories, 7 g fat (3 g saturated fat), 37 mg cholesterol, 795 mg sodium, 42 g carbohydrate, 4 g fiber, 20 g protein. **DIABETIC EXCHANGES:** 2-1/2 starch, 2 lean meat, 1 vegetable.

Tex-Mex Turkey Tacos

Tex-Mex Turkey Tacos

PREP: **10 MIN.** COOK: **35 MIN.**

I normally don't care for ground turkey, but I love the Southwestern flair of this well-seasoned taco meat mixed with peppers, onions and black beans. It's sure to be a hit at your house, too.

Jodi Fleury ✳ West Gardiner, Maine

- 1 pound lean ground turkey
- 2 medium green peppers, chopped
- 1 medium sweet red pepper, chopped
- 2 medium carrots, halved lengthwise and sliced
- 1 medium onion, chopped
- 2 garlic cloves, minced
- 1 tablespoon olive oil
- 2 cans (15 ounces *each*) black beans, rinsed and drained
- 1 jar (16 ounces) salsa
- 2 tablespoons chili powder
- 1 tablespoon ground cumin
- 24 taco shells
- 3 cups shredded lettuce
- 1-1/2 cups diced fresh tomatoes
- 1/2 cup minced fresh cilantro

In a large nonstick skillet coated with cooking spray, cook turkey over medium heat until no longer pink; remove and set aside. In the same skillet, saute the peppers, carrots, onion and garlic in oil for 8-10 minutes or until vegetables are tender.

Add the turkey, beans, salsa, chili powder and cumin; bring to a boil. Reduce heat; simmer, uncovered, for 10-15 minutes or until thickened. Fill each taco shell with 1/3 cup turkey mixture. Serve with lettuce, tomatoes and cilantro. **YIELD: 12 SERVINGS.**

NUTRITION FACTS: 2 tacos equals 267 calories, 9 g fat (2 g saturated fat), 30 mg cholesterol, 459 mg sodium, 31 g carbohydrate, 8 g fiber, 13 g protein. DIABETIC EXCHANGES: 2 starch, 1-1/2 fat, 1 lean meat, 1 vegetable.

1st place

Smothered Chicken Breasts

Smothered Chicken Breasts

PREP/TOTAL TIME: **30 MIN.**

After trying this chicken dish in a restaurant, I decided to make it at home. Topped with bacon, caramelized onions and zippy shredded cheese, it comes together in no time with ingredients I usually have on hand. Plus, it cooks in one skillet, so it's a cinch to clean up!

Brenda Carpenter ✳ Warrensburg, Missouri

- 4 boneless skinless chicken breast halves (6 ounces *each*)
- 1/4 teaspoon salt
- 1/4 teaspoon lemon-pepper seasoning
- 1 tablespoon canola oil
- 8 bacon strips
- 1 medium onion, sliced
- 1/4 cup packed brown sugar
- 1/2 cup shredded Colby-Monterey Jack cheese

Sprinkle chicken with salt and lemon-pepper. In a large skillet, cook the chicken in the oil for 6-7 minutes on each side or until a meat thermometer reads 170°; remove and keep warm.

In the same skillet, cook bacon over medium heat until crisp. Remove to paper towels; drain, reserving 2 tablespoons drippings.

In the drippings, saute onion and brown sugar until onion is tender and golden brown. Place two bacon strips on each chicken breast half; top with caramelized onions and cheese. **YIELD: 4 SERVINGS.**

Mango Chicken with Plum Sauce

Mango Chicken With Plum Sauce

PREP: 25 MIN. COOK: 15 MIN.

A generous serving of this flavorful chicken, with crunchy fresh veggies and a sweet Asian sauce, will leave you satisfied without bursting at the seams.

Christine Vaught ✳ Salem, Oregon

- 1 tablespoon sugar
- 1 tablespoon cornstarch
- 1/2 teaspoon salt
- 1/2 cup chicken broth
- 1/4 cup teriyaki sauce
- 1/2 pound fresh snow peas, trimmed
- 2 large carrots, sliced diagonally
- 2 medium zucchini, sliced
- 1/2 cup chopped red onion
- 1/2 medium sweet red pepper, sliced
- 1 can (4 ounces) sliced water chestnuts, drained
- 2 tablespoons canola oil
- 1 pound finely chopped cooked chicken breast (about 3 cups)
- 2 medium mangoes, peeled and mashed
- 1/2 cup plum sauce
- 2 cups hot cooked brown rice
- 1/4 cup slivered almonds, toasted

In a small saucepan, combine sugar, cornstarch and salt; stir in the broth and the teriyaki sauce until smooth. Cook and stir until thickened. Set aside.

In a large skillet or wok, stir-fry the snow peas, carrots, zucchini, onion, pepper and water chestnuts in oil until crisp-tender. Add the chicken, mangoes and the broth mixture; heat through. Stir in plum sauce. Serve with rice. Sprinkle with almonds. **YIELD: 6 SERVINGS.**

NUTRITION FACTS: 2 cups stir-fry with 1/3 cup rice equals 413 calories, 10 g fat (1 g saturated fat), 54 mg cholesterol, 888 mg sodium, 54 g carbohydrate, 6 g fiber, 27 g protein.

Feta-Stuffed Chicken

PREP: 10 MIN. BAKE: 40 MIN.

When my husband and I were first married, I only knew how to make a few meals that we'd rotate throughout the week. After some experimenting, I created this great stuffed chicken recipe that's still a favorite today.

Lisa Herbert ✳ Wadsworth, Ohio

- 4 boneless skinless chicken breast halves (6 ounces *each*)
- 1 package (4 ounces) crumbled tomato and basil feta cheese, *divided*
- 1 cup seasoned bread crumbs
- 4 tablespoons balsamic vinegar
- 4 tablespoons olive oil
- 4 plum tomatoes, sliced
- 8 fresh basil leaves

Flatten the chicken to 1/4-in. thickness. Place a tablespoon of feta cheese on each chicken breast half; roll up and secure with toothpicks. Coat with bread crumbs. Place seam side down in a greased 13-in. x 9-in. baking pan. Sprinkle with remaining cheese.

Bake, uncovered, at 350° for 40-45 minutes or until chicken is no longer pink. Immediately drizzle vinegar and oil over chicken. Discard toothpicks. Garnish with tomatoes and basil. **YIELD: 4 SERVINGS.**

Feta-Stuffed Chicken

◐ Apricot Chicken

PREP/TOTAL TIME: **15 MIN.**

This is one of my best ways to fix chicken in a hurry. Everybody just loves it, and leftovers are always just as good the next day. For variation, I've used pork instead of chicken and added additional ingredients like pineapple, mandarin oranges, snow peas and broccoli.

Vicki Ruiz ✳ Twin Falls, Idaho

- 1 **tablespoon cornstarch**
- 2 **tablespoons soy sauce**
- 1 **tablespoon sherry** *or* **chicken broth**
- 1/2 **cup apricot preserves**
- 1 **tablespoon canola oil**
- 1 **teaspoon minced garlic**
- 1/4 **teaspoon ground ginger**
- 1 **pound boneless skinless chicken breasts, cut into strips**
- 1 **medium green pepper, chopped**
- 1/2 **cup salted cashews**

Hot cooked rice

In a large bowl, combine the cornstarch, soy sauce and sherry until smooth. Stir in preserves, oil, garlic and ginger. Add chicken and toss to coat. Transfer to a shallow microwave-safe dish. Cover and microwave on high for 3 minutes, stirring once.

Add the green pepper and cashews. Cover and microwave on high for 2-4 minutes or until the chicken is no longer pink, stirring once. Let stand for 3 minutes. Serve with the rice. **YIELD: 4 SERVINGS.**

EDITOR'S NOTE: This recipe was tested in a 1,100-watt microwave.

1st place

Apricot Chicken

Greek Pasta Bake

🌿 Greek Pasta Bake

PREP: 20 MIN. BAKE: 25 MIN.

I've brought this hot dish to potlucks and people tell me how much they've enjoyed it. There's never a crumb left. Best of all, it's a simple, healthy and hearty supper made with easy-to-find ingredients.

Anne Taglienti ✳ Kennett Square, Pennsylvania

- 1 package (12 ounces) whole wheat penne pasta
- 4 cups cubed cooked chicken breast
- 1 can (29 ounces) tomato sauce
- 1 can (14-1/2 ounces) diced tomatoes, drained
- 1 package (10 ounces) frozen chopped spinach, thawed and squeezed dry
- 2 cans (2-1/4 ounces *each*) sliced ripe olives, drained
- 1/4 cup chopped red onion
- 2 tablespoons chopped green pepper
- 1 teaspoon dried basil
- 1 teaspoon dried oregano
- 1/2 cup shredded part-skim mozzarella cheese
- 1/2 cup crumbled feta cheese

Cook the pasta according to package directions; drain. In a large bowl, combine pasta, chicken, tomato sauce, tomatoes, spinach, olives, onion, green pepper, basil and oregano.

Transfer to a 13-in. x 9-in. baking dish coated with cooking spray. Sprinkle with cheeses. Bake, uncovered, at 400° for 25-30 minutes or until heated through and the cheese is melted. **YIELD: 8 SERVINGS.**

NUTRITION FACTS: 1-1/2 cups equals 366 calories, 7 g fat (2 g saturated fat), 62 mg cholesterol, 847 mg sodium, 43 g carbohydrate, 6 g fiber, 32 g protein. DIABETIC EXCHANGES: 3 very lean meat, 2-1/2 starch, 1 vegetable, 1/2 fat.

Herbed Cranberry Chicken

🌿 Herbed Cranberry Chicken

PREP: 20 MIN. COOK: 15 MIN.

Even though it has no added salt, this dish is full of flavor. The cranberry sauce makes the entree special.

Margee Berry ✳ Trout Lake, Washington

- 6 boneless skinless chicken breast halves (4 ounces *each*)
- 1 tablespoon salt-free herb seasoning blend
- 2 tablespoons olive oil, *divided*

Easy Chicken Potpie

2/3 cup chopped green onions
1/2 cup dried cranberries
1/2 cup reduced-sodium chicken broth
1/3 cup cranberry juice
4-1/2 teaspoons maple syrup
1 tablespoon balsamic vinegar
1/3 cup chopped pecans, toasted

Rub the chicken with seasoning blend. In a large nonstick skillet, cook chicken in 1 tablespoon oil over medium heat for 4-5 minutes on each side or until a meat thermometer reaches 170°. Remove and keep warm.

In the same skillet, saute the onions in remaining oil. Stir in the cranberries, broth, cranberry juice, syrup and vinegar; bring to a boil. Reduce heat; cook and stir for 2 minutes. Return chicken to the pan; cook for 1 minute or until heated through. Sprinkle with the pecans.
YIELD: 6 SERVINGS.

NUTRITION FACTS: 1 chicken breast half with 2 tablespoons cranberry mixture equals 263 calories, 12 g fat (2 g saturated fat), 63 mg cholesterol, 109 mg sodium, 16 g carbohydrate, 1 g fiber, 24 g protein. DIABETIC EXCHANGE: 3 very lean meat, 2 fat, 1/2 starch, 1/2 fruit.

Easy Chicken Potpie

PREP/TOTAL TIME: **30 MIN.**

Why look for potpie in the frozen food aisle when this easy, homemade version tastes much better? Under its golden-brown crust, you'll find the ultimate comfort food for kids and adults.

Amy Briggs ✳ Gove, Kansas

1 medium onion, chopped
2 tablespoons canola oil
1/2 cup all-purpose flour
1 teaspoon poultry seasoning
1 can (14-1/2 ounces) chicken broth
3/4 cup milk
3 cups cubed cooked chicken
2 cups frozen mixed vegetables, thawed
1 sheet refrigerated pie pastry

In a large saucepan, saute the onion in oil until tender. Stir in flour and poultry seasoning until blended; gradually add broth and milk. Bring to a boil; cook and stir for 2 minutes or until thickened. Add chicken and vegetables.

Transfer to a greased 9-in. deep-dish pie plate. Top with the pastry. Trim, seal and flute edges. Cut slits in the pastry. Bake at 450° for 15-20 minutes or until the crust is golden brown and filling is bubbly. **YIELD: 6 SERVINGS.**

Turkey Pepper Kabobs

Turkey Pepper Kabobs

PREP: **15 MIN. + MARINATING** GRILL: **10 MIN.**

This is a summertime favorite at our house. While the turkey is a nice change of pace and goes great with the sweet basting sauce and pineapple, the recipe also works well with chunks of chicken.

Traci Goodman ✳ Paducah, Kentucky

- 1 can (8 ounces) unsweetened pineapple chunks
- 1/4 cup packed brown sugar
- 2 tablespoons canola oil
- 2 tablespoons Worcestershire sauce
- 1 garlic clove, minced
- 1 teaspoon prepared mustard
- 1 pound turkey tenderloin, cut into 1-inch cubes
- 1 large sweet onion, cut into 3/4-inch pieces
- 1 large green pepper, cut into 1-inch pieces
- 1 large sweet red pepper, cut into 1-inch pieces

Drain the pineapple, reserving 1/4 cup juice. In a large bowl, combine the reserved pineapple juice, sugar, oil, Worcestershire sauce, garlic and mustard.

Pour 1/3 cup into a large resealable plastic bag; add the turkey. Seal bag and turn to coat; refrigerate for 2-3 hours. Cover and refrigerate remaining marinade.

If grilling the kabobs, coat the grill rack with cooking spray before starting the grill. Drain and discard marinade from turkey.

On eight metal or soaked wooden skewers, alternately thread the vegetables, turkey and pineapple. Grill, uncovered, over medium heat or broil 4-6 in. from the heat for 4-5 minutes on each side or until the meat is no longer pink, basting frequently with the reserved marinade.
YIELD: 4 servings.

NUTRITION FACTS: 2 kabobs equals 262 calories, 4 g fat (1 g saturated fat), 82 mg cholesterol, 110 mg sodium, 24 g carbohydrate, 3 g fiber, 31 g protein. DIABETIC EXCHANGES: 4 very lean meat, 2 vegetable, 1 fruit.

Italian Sausage And Vegetables

PREP: **20 MIN.** COOK: **5-1/2 HOURS**

This easy and complete meal-in-a-pot is both healthy and delicious. It's wonderful served with a slice of Italian or hot garlic bread.

Ginny Stuby ✳ Altoona, Pennsylvania

- 1-1/4 pounds sweet *or* hot Italian turkey sausage links
- 1 can (28 ounces) diced tomatoes, undrained
- 2 medium potatoes, cut into 1-inch pieces
- 4 small zucchini, cut into 1-inch slices

1 medium onion, cut into wedges
1/2 teaspoon garlic powder
1/4 teaspoon crushed red pepper flakes
1/4 teaspoon dried oregano
1/4 teaspoon dried basil
1 tablespoon dry bread crumbs
3/4 cup shredded pepper Jack cheese

In a nonstick skillet, cook the sausages over medium heat until no longer pink; drain. Place in a 5-qt. slow cooker. Add the vegetables and seasonings. Cover and cook on low for 5-1/2 to 6-1/2 hours or until vegetables are tender.

Remove sausages and cut into 1-in. pieces; return to the slow cooker. Stir in bread crumbs. Serve in bowls; sprinkle with the cheese. **YIELD: 6 SERVINGS.**

Italian Sausage and Vegetables

⏱ Grilled Chicken with Peach Sauce

PREP/TOTAL TIME: **30 MIN.**

I've been cooking since I was a young girl growing up on a farm in Indiana. This recipe was adapted from a pie filling. I've served it many times to family and friends, and folks always seem to like it.

Beverly Minton ✳ Milan, Michigan

1 cup sugar
2 tablespoons cornstarch
1 cup water
2 tablespoons peach *or* orange gelatin
1 medium peach, peeled and finely chopped
4 boneless skinless chicken breast halves
(4 ounces *each*)

In a small saucepan, combine sugar, cornstarch and the water until smooth. Bring to a boil over medium heat; cook and stir for 2 minutes. Remove from the heat. Stir in gelatin powder and peach; mix well until the gelatin powder is dissolved. Set aside 1 cup for serving.

Grill chicken, uncovered, over medium heat for 3 minutes on each side. Baste with some of the remaining peach sauce. Continue grilling for 6-8 minutes or until meat thermometer reads 170°, basting and turning several times. Serve with the reserved peach sauce. **YIELD: 4 SERVINGS.**

Grilled Chicken with Peach Sauce

Chicken Artichoke Pasta

Chicken Artichoke Pasta

PREP/TOTAL TIME: **25 MIN.**

Here's a main course my whole crew likes, including the kids! Similar to a restaurant favorite, it uses canned artichokes and a jar of sun-dried tomatoes.

Beth Washington ✳ Ayer, Massachusetts

- 8 ounces uncooked bow tie pasta
- 1-1/2 pounds boneless skinless chicken breasts, cubed
- 1/2 teaspoon dried oregano
- 1/4 teaspoon salt
- 1/4 teaspoon pepper
- 3 tablespoons olive oil
- 1 to 2 tablespoons minced garlic
- 2 cans (14 ounces *each*) water-packed artichoke hearts, rinsed, drained and quartered
- 1 jar (8-1/2 ounces) oil-packed sun-dried tomatoes, quartered
- 1 can (2-1/4 ounces) sliced ripe olives, drained

Shredded Parmesan cheese

Cook the pasta according to package directions. Meanwhile, sprinkle chicken with the oregano, salt and pepper. In a large skillet, saute chicken in oil until no longer pink. Add garlic; saute 1 minute longer. Stir in the artichokes, tomatoes and olives; heat through. Drain pasta; toss with the chicken mixture. Sprinkle with Parmesan cheese. **YIELD: 6 SERVINGS.**

Baked Chicken and Mushrooms

🌀 Baked Chicken And Mushrooms

PREP: 5 MIN. BAKE: 30 MIN.

I made up this dish years ago, and it still remains a hit with my family. It's a fast and healthy weeknight meal, but the fresh mushrooms and sherry make it special enough for a weekend dinner party.

Lise Prestine ✳ South Bend, Indiana

- 6 boneless skinless chicken breast halves (4 ounces *each*)
- 1/4 teaspoon paprika
- 1/2 pound fresh mushrooms, sliced
- 1 tablespoon butter
- 1/2 cup sherry *or* chicken broth
- 3 green onions, chopped
- 1 garlic clove, minced
- 1/2 teaspoon salt
- 1/8 teaspoon pepper
- 3/4 cup shredded part-skim mozzarella cheese

Arrange the chicken in a 13-in. x 9-in. baking dish coated with cooking spray. Sprinkle with paprika. Bake, uncovered, at 350° for 15 minutes.

Meanwhile, in a large nonstick skillet, saute mushrooms in butter for 5 minutes. Add the sherry, green onions, garlic, salt and pepper. Bring to a boil. Pour over chicken.

Bake 10-15 minutes longer or until a meat thermometer reads 170°. Top with the cheese. Bake for 3-5 minutes or until cheese is melted. **YIELD: 6 SERVINGS.**

NUTRITION FACTS: 1 chicken breast half equals 198 calories, 6 g fat (3 g saturated fat), 79 mg cholesterol, 361 mg sodium, 3 g carbohydrate, 1 g fiber, 31 g protein. **DIABETIC EXCHANGE:** 4 lean meat.

Mexican Chicken Manicotti

PREP: 25 MIN. BAKE: 40 MIN.

Our brood of five enjoys trying different ethnic cuisines. This Italian specialty has a little Mexican zip. Be careful not to overcook the manicotti. If the filled shells happen to break, just place them in the pan seam-side down.

Keely Jankunas ✳ Corvallis, Montana

- 1 package (8 ounces) manicotti shells
- 2 cups cubed cooked chicken

Mexican Chicken Manicotti

- 2 cups (8 ounces) shredded Monterey Jack cheese, *divided*
- 1-1/2 cups (6 ounces) shredded cheddar cheese
- 1 cup (8 ounces) sour cream
- 1 small onion, diced, *divided*
- 1 can (4 ounces) chopped green chilies, *divided*
- 1 can (10-3/4 ounces) condensed cream of chicken soup, undiluted
- 1 cup salsa
- 2/3 cup milk

Cook the manicotti according to the package directions. Meanwhile, in a large bowl, combine the chicken, 1-1/2 cups Monterey Jack cheese, cheddar cheese, sour cream, half of the onion and 6 tablespoons chilies.

In another bowl, combine the soup, salsa, milk and remaining onion and chilies. Spread 1/2 cup in a greased 13-in. x 9-in. baking dish.

Drain the manicotti and rinse in cold water; stuff each with about 1/4 cupful of the chicken mixture. Arrange over the sauce in baking dish. Pour remaining sauce over shells.

Cover and bake at 350° for 30 minutes. Uncover; sprinkle with the remaining Monterey Jack cheese. Bake 10 minutes longer or until cheese is melted. **YIELD: 7 SERVINGS.**

Parmesan Chicken

Parmesan Chicken

PREP: **15 MIN.** BAKE: **50 MIN.**

This oven-fried chicken is the perfect dish to prepare in advance and take on a picnic because it tastes just as good cold as it does warm. It's been a family favorite for years.

Sharon Crider ✳ St. Robert, Missouri

- 1 cup all-purpose flour
- 2 teaspoons salt
- 2 teaspoons paprika
- 1/4 teaspoon pepper
- 2 eggs
- 3 tablespoons milk
- 2/3 cup grated Parmesan cheese
- 1/3 cup dry bread crumbs
- 1 broiler/fryer chicken (3 to 4 pounds), cut up

In a shallow bowl, combine flour, salt, paprika and pepper. In another shallow bowl, beat the eggs and milk. In a third bowl, combine the Parmesan cheese and the bread crumbs. Coat chicken pieces with flour mixture, dip in the egg mixture, then roll in crumb mixture.

Place in a well-greased 15-in. x 10-in. x 1-in. baking pan. Bake at 400° for 50-55 minutes or until chicken juices run clear. **YIELD: 4 SERVINGS.**

🌊 Italian Sausage With Polenta

PREP: **15 MIN.** COOK: **25 MIN.**

This turkey and broccoli mixture over polenta is quick, easy and tastes great. Nutritious and delicious, it makes a comforting meal on a weeknight.

Mary Bilyeu ✳ Ann Arbor, Michigan

- 1 package (20 ounces) Italian turkey sausage links, casings removed
- 1/2 cup chopped red onion
- 4 garlic cloves, minced
- 2-1/2 cups fresh broccoli florets
- 2 cans (15 ounces *each*) crushed tomatoes
- 2 tablespoons prepared pesto
- 1/2 teaspoon crushed red pepper flakes
- 1/4 teaspoon pepper
- 3 cups reduced-sodium chicken broth
- 1 cup cornmeal

Shaved Parmesan cheese, optional

In a large nonstick skillet coated with cooking spray, cook the sausage, onion and garlic over medium heat until meat is no longer pink. Stir in the broccoli. Reduce heat; cover and cook for 5-7 minutes or until broccoli is tender.

Stir in the tomatoes, pesto, pepper flakes and the pepper; bring to a boil. Reduce the heat; simmer, uncovered, for 10 minutes.

Meanwhile, for polenta, bring broth to a boil in a small heavy saucepan. Reduce the heat to a gentle boil; slowly whisk in cornmeal. Continue stirring for 10-12 minutes or until polenta is thickened and has a smooth texture. Spoon onto the plates; top with the sausage mixture. Garnish with the Parmesan cheese if desired. **YIELD: 6 SERVINGS.**

NUTRITION FACTS: 1 cup sausage mixture with 1/2 cup polenta equals 337 calories, 12 g fat (4 g saturated fat), 52 mg cholesterol, 1,131 mg sodium, 35 g carbohydrate, 6 g fiber, 24 g protein.

Two-Cheese Turkey Enchiladas

PREP: **25 MIN.** BAKE: **20 MIN.**

Sour cream and cream cheese create a creamy filling for these yummy turkey enchiladas. The entrée is always a huge hit with my crowd.

Shelly Platten ✳ Amherst, Wisconsin

- 1 pound extra-lean ground turkey
- 1 large onion, chopped
- 1/2 cup chopped green pepper
- 1 teaspoon brown sugar
- 1 teaspoon garlic powder
- 1 teaspoon ground cumin
- 1 teaspoon chili powder
- 1 can (28 ounces) crushed tomatoes, *divided*
- 1 package (8 ounces) reduced-fat cream cheese
- 1/4 cup fat-free sour cream
- 1 can (4 ounces) chopped green chilies
- 1 cup salsa
- 8 fat-free flour tortillas (8 inches), warmed
- 1/2 cup shredded reduced-fat cheddar cheese

Crumble the turkey into a large nonstick skillet; add the onion, green pepper, brown sugar and seasonings. Cook and stir over medium heat until the turkey is no longer pink. Stir in 1 cup crushed tomatoes. Reduce the heat; simmer, uncovered, for 10 minutes, stirring occasionally.

In a small bowl, beat the cream cheese, sour cream and chilies until blended; set aside. Combine salsa and remaining tomatoes; spread 1 cup into a 13-in. x 9-in. baking dish coated with cooking spray.

Spoon about 3 tablespoons cream cheese mixture and 1/3 cup turkey mixture down the center of each tortilla. Roll up and place seam side down in baking dish. Top with remaining salsa mixture; sprinkle with cheddar cheese. Bake, uncovered, at 350° for 20-25 minutes or until bubbly. **YIELD: 8 SERVINGS.**

NUTRITION FACTS: 1 enchilada equals 329 calories, 9 g fat (5 g saturated fat), 49 mg cholesterol, 776 mg sodium, 39 g carbohydrate, 5 g fiber, 24 g protein. DIABETIC EXCHANGES: 2 starch, 2 very lean meat, 2 vegetable, 1-1/2 fat.

Italian Sausage with Polenta

Two-Cheese Turkey Enchiladas

Saucy Chicken Thighs

Saucy Chicken Thighs

PREP: **20 MIN.** COOK: **4 HOURS**

Everyone raves about how sweet the sauce is for these slow-cooked chicken thighs. They're such a breeze because they simmer away while you do other things. Add your favorite side for a nice meal or just serve as is for an appetizer.

Kim Puckett ✻ Reagan, Tennessee

- 9 bone-in chicken thighs (about 3-1/4 pounds)
- 1/2 teaspoon salt
- 1/4 teaspoon pepper
- 1-1/2 cups barbecue sauce
- 1/2 cup honey
- 2 teaspoons prepared mustard
- 2 teaspoons Worcestershire sauce
- 1/8 to 1/2 teaspoon hot pepper sauce

Sprinkle chicken with salt and pepper. Place on a broiler pan. Broil 4-5 in. from the heat for 3-4 minutes on each side or until lightly browned. Transfer to a 5-qt. slow cooker.

In a small bowl, combine barbecue sauce, honey, mustard, Worcestershire sauce and the pepper sauce. Pour over the chicken; stir to coat. Cover and cook on low for 4-5 hours or until heated through. **YIELD: 9 SERVINGS.**

Chicken Italian

PREP: **15 MIN.** BAKE: **1-1/4 HOURS**

This hearty chicken dish is sure to please. A friend gave me the recipe years ago, and I've since added a couple ingredients of my own.

Ann Walsh ✻ Maple Park, Illinois

- 1 can (28 ounces) crushed tomatoes
- 1 can (18 ounces) Italian diced tomatoes
- 1 cup chicken broth
- 1/4 cup red wine vinegar
- 1 can (8 ounces) tomato sauce
- 1 medium green pepper, julienned
- 1 medium sweet red pepper, julienned
- 1 medium onion, chopped
- 6 garlic cloves, minced
- 1 tablespoon brown sugar
- 1 teaspoon dried oregano

Chicken Italian

Peppery Grilled Turkey Breast

1 teaspoon salt

1 teaspoon pepper

2 broiler/fryer chickens (3 to 4 pounds *each*), cut up and skin removed

1 pound Italian sausage links, sliced

Hot cooked spaghetti

In a large roasting pan, combine the tomatoes, broth, vinegar, tomato sauce, peppers, onion, garlic, sugar and seasonings. Place the chicken and sausage over tomato mixture. Bake, uncovered, at 350° for 1-1/4 hours or until chicken is tender and juices run clear, basting occasionally with sauce. Serve with spaghetti. **YIELD: 10 SERVINGS.**

Peppery Grilled Turkey Breast

PREP: **15 MIN.** GRILL: **1-1/4 HOURS + STANDING**

This is a combination of several favorite family recipes. People who try it for the first time are amazed to find that it's not only flavorful but healthy as well.

Mary Elizabeth Relyea ✳ Canastota, New York

2 tablespoons light brown sugar

1 tablespoon salt

2 teaspoons ground cinnamon

1 teaspoon cayenne pepper

1/2 teaspoon ground mustard

1 bone-in turkey breast (5 pounds)

1 cup reduced-sodium chicken broth

1/4 cup white vinegar

1/4 cup jalapeno pepper jelly

2 tablespoons olive oil

In a small bowl, combine the brown sugar, salt, cinnamon, cayenne and mustard. With fingers, carefully loosen the skin from both sides of turkey breast. Spread half of the spice mixture under turkey skin; secure the skin to underside of the breast with wooden toothpicks. Spread remaining spice mixture over the skin.

Coat the grill rack with cooking spray before starting the grill. Prepare grill for indirect heat, using a drip pan. Place the turkey over drip pan. Grill, covered, over indirect medium heat for 30 minutes.

In a small saucepan, combine the broth, vinegar, jelly and oil. Cook and stir over medium heat for 2 minutes or until jelly is melted. Set aside 1/2 cup. Baste turkey with some of the remaining jelly mixture. Grill 45-60 minutes longer or until a meat thermometer reads 170° and juices run clear, basting every 15 minutes.

Cover and let stand for 10 minutes. Remove and discard turkey skin if desired. Brush with the reserved jelly mixture before slicing. **YIELD: 15 SERVINGS.**

NUTRITION FACTS: 4 ounces cooked turkey (with skin removed) equals 167 calories, 3 g fat (trace saturated fat), 78 mg cholesterol, 565 mg sodium, 6 g carbohydrate, trace fiber, 29 g protein. DIABETIC EXCHANGES: 4 very lean meat, 1/2 fat.

Corsican Chicken

⏱ Corsican Chicken

PREP: **20 MIN.** COOK: **4-1/2 HOURS**

Moist and tender chicken thighs make a delicious hot entree for winter months. I like to serve this over polenta slices or rice.

Mary Bergfeld ✳ Eugene, Oregon

- 3 tablespoons butter, softened
- 2 tablespoons herbes de Provence
- 1 teaspoon salt
- 2 garlic cloves, minced
- 1/2 teaspoon coarsely ground pepper
- 2 pounds boneless skinless chicken thighs
- 1 large onion, chopped
- 1/2 cup oil-packed sun-dried tomatoes, julienned
- 1 can (10-1/2 ounces) condensed beef consomme, undiluted
- 1/2 cup dry vermouth *or* orange juice
- 1/2 cup pitted Greek olives, quartered
- 1 teaspoon grated orange peel
- 2 teaspoons cornstarch
- 1 tablespoon cold water
- 2 tablespoons minced fresh basil
- 2 tablespoons diced pimientos
- 2 tablespoons minced fresh parsley

In a bowl, combine the first five ingredients; rub over the chicken. Place in a 5-qt. slow cooker.

Add onion, tomatoes, consomme and vermouth. Cover and cook on low for 4-5 hours or until chicken is no longer pink. Add olives and orange peel. Cover and cook on high for 30 minutes.

Remove the chicken and keep warm. Pour cooking juices into a small saucepan; skim fat. Combine cornstarch and water until smooth; gradually stir into cooking juices. Bring to a boil; cook and stir for 2 minutes or until smooth. Pour over the chicken. Sprinkle with the basil, pimientos and parsley. **YIELD: 6-8 SERVINGS.**

Hearty Chicken Casserole

PREP: **25 MIN.** BAKE: **10 MIN.**

I found this recipe in a cookbook we received as a wedding gift and altered it to fit my family's tastes. Now, I always cook enough extra chicken so we can have this casserole the next day.

Janet Applin ✳ Gladstone, Michigan

- 2-1/2 cups frozen mixed vegetables
- 1/2 cup chopped onion
- 1/2 cup butter, *divided*
- 1/3 cup all-purpose flour
- 1/2 teaspoon dried sage leaves
- 1/2 teaspoon pepper
- 1/4 teaspoon salt
- 2 cups chicken broth
- 3/4 cup milk

- 3 cups cubed cooked chicken
- 1 can (14-1/2 ounces) sliced potatoes, drained and quartered
- 2 cups seasoned stuffing cubes

Cook the vegetables according to the package directions; drain.

In a large saucepan, saute onion in 1/4 cup butter for 2-3 minutes or until tender. Stir in flour, sage, pepper and salt until blended. Gradually add broth and milk. Bring to a boil; cook and stir until thickened. Stir in chicken, potatoes and mixed vegetables; heat through.

Transfer to a greased 13-in. x 9-in. baking dish. Melt remaining butter; toss with stuffing cubes. Sprinkle over the chicken mixture. Bake, uncovered, at 450° for 10-12 minutes or until heated through. **YIELD: 6 SERVINGS.**

Hearty Chicken Casserole

Buffalo Chicken Sandwiches

PREP/TOTAL TIME: 10 MIN.

This is a simple way to dress up breaded chicken patties. We like these sandwiches with additional blue cheese dressing for dipping.

Dawn Onuffer ✳ Crestview, Florida

- 2 refrigerated breaded chicken patties
- 1/4 cup Louisiana-style hot sauce
- 2 teaspoons canola oil
- 2 tablespoons butter, softened
- 2 sandwich buns, split
- 2 slices provolone cheese
- 2 tablespoons blue cheese salad dressing

Lettuce, tomato and red onion slices

Additional hot sauce

Place the chicken patties in a large resealable plastic bag; add hot sauce. Seal bag and turn to coat. In a large skillet, brown patties in oil over medium heat for 1-2 minutes on each side or until heated through. Remove and keep warm.

Spread butter over cut sides of buns. In the same skillet, toast buns, buttered side down, over medium heat for 1-2 minutes or until lightly browned. Serve chicken patties and remaining ingredients on buns. **YIELD: 2 SERVINGS.**

Buffalo Chicken Sandwiches

Turkey Sausage with Root Vegetables

🌿 Turkey Sausage with Root Vegetables

PREP: **10 MIN.** COOK: **30 MIN.**

I had a delicious stew recipe but rarely prepared it because sausage can be high in fat and sodium, so I substituted turkey sausage. Now it not only tastes good, it feels good—both hearty and healthy!

Lisa Zeigler-Day ✳ Forest Park, Illinois

- 1 package (14 ounces) smoked turkey kielbasa, cut into 1/2-inch pieces
- 1 medium onion, chopped
- 1 cup cubed peeled rutabaga
- 1 cup sliced carrots
- 1 teaspoon canola oil
- 4 cups cubed peeled potatoes
- 1 can (14-3/4 ounces) reduced-sodium chicken broth
- 1 teaspoon dried thyme
- 1/4 teaspoon rubbed sage
- 1/4 teaspoon pepper
- 1 bay leaf
- 1/2 medium head cabbage, cut into 6 wedges
- 1 teaspoon all-purpose flour
- 1 tablespoon water
- 1 tablespoon minced fresh parsley
- 2 teaspoons cider vinegar

In a Dutch oven, cook sausage, onion, rutabaga and carrots in oil for 5 minutes or until onion is tender. Add the potatoes, broth, thyme, sage, pepper and bay leaf. Bring to a boil. Place the cabbage wedges on top. Reduce heat; cover and simmer for 20-25 minutes or until potatoes and cabbage are tender.

Using a slotted spoon, carefully remove the cabbage to a shallow serving bowl; keep warm. Discard bay leaf. Combine the flour and water until smooth; stir into sausage mixture. Bring to a boil; cook and stir for 2 minutes or until thickened. Stir in parsley and vinegar. Spoon over cabbage. **YIELD: 6 SERVINGS.**

NUTRITION FACTS: 1-1/2 cups equals 231 calories, 3 g fat (1 g saturated fat), 23 mg cholesterol, 781 mg sodium, 39 g carbohydrate, 6 g fiber, 13 g protein. DIABETIC EXCHANGES: 2 starch, 1 lean meat, 1 vegetable.

1st place

Creamy Chicken Lasagna

Creamy Chicken Lasagna

PREP: 40 MIN. BAKE: 45 + STANDING

I enjoy making recipes like this lasagna, laden with juicy tomatoes and herbs fresh from my own garden.

Janice Christofferson * Eagle River, Wisconsin

- 12 uncooked lasagna noodles
- 2 tablespoons cornstarch
- 1 can (12 ounces) evaporated milk
- 2 cups chicken broth
- 1 can (8 ounces) tomato sauce
- 1/2 cup grated Parmesan cheese
- 2 garlic cloves, minced
- 2 teaspoons Dijon mustard
- 1/2 teaspoon dried basil
- 1/4 teaspoon ground nutmeg
- 1/8 teaspoon cayenne pepper
- 2 cups cooked chicken strips (12 ounces)
- 24 cherry tomatoes, thinly sliced
- 1 cup (4 ounces) shredded cheddar cheese

Paprika and minced fresh parsley

Cook noodles according to package directions. In a large saucepan, combine the cornstarch and milk until smooth. Whisk in broth, tomato sauce, Parmesan cheese, garlic, mustard and seasonings. Bring to a boil over medium heat; cook and stir for 2 minutes or until thickened. Remove from the heat.

Drain the noodles. Spread 1/4 cup sauce in a greased 13-in. x 9-in. baking dish. Set aside 1 cup sauce. Stir chicken and tomatoes into remaining sauce. Layer four noodles and half of chicken mixture in dish. Repeat layers. Top with remaining noodles; spread with reserved sauce. Sprinkle with cheddar cheese and paprika.

Cover and bake at 350° for 45-50 minutes or until bubbly. Let stand for 15 minutes before cutting. Sprinkle with parsley. **YIELD: 9-12 SERVINGS.**

Turkey Primavera

PREP: 25 MIN. COOK: 20 MIN.

This creation has tender turkey and mushrooms, onions and green pepper covered in a zippy tomato sauce. It's become a real favorite for us.

Zita Wilensky * North Miami Beach, Florida

- 1/4 cup all-purpose flour
- 2 teaspoons minced fresh parsley

Turkey Primavera

- 1-1/2 pounds turkey tenderloins, cubed
- 2 tablespoons olive oil
- 1/2 cup chicken broth
- 1 cup sliced fresh mushrooms
- 1 medium onion, chopped
- 4 garlic cloves, minced
- 1/2 medium green pepper, chopped
- 1 can (14-1/2 ounces) beef broth
- 3/4 cup tomato puree
- 1/2 teaspoon dried thyme
- 1/2 teaspoon dried rosemary, crushed
- 1/2 teaspoon dried basil
- 1 bay leaf
- 1/4 teaspoon salt
- 1/8 teaspoon pepper

Hot cooked fettuccine *or* spaghetti

Parmesan cheese, optional

Combine flour and parsley; add turkey and toss to coat. In a skillet, brown the turkey in oil until no longer pink; remove with a slotted spoon and set aside.

In the same skillet, combine chicken broth, mushrooms, onion, garlic and green pepper. Cook and stir for 3-4 minutes. Add beef broth, tomato puree and the seasonings. Cook and stir for 20-25 minutes or until the sauce is desired consistency.

Add the turkey; heat through. Discard the bay leaf. Serve over pasta; sprinkle with Parmesan if desired. **YIELD: 4-6 SERVINGS.**

Creamed Chicken 'n' Biscuits

⏱ Creamed Chicken 'n' Biscuits

PREP/TOTAL TIME: **25 MIN.**

We have a dairy farm and three young children, so I'm always on the lookout for easy, hearty meals like this one. Using leftover or canned chicken, I can whip up this entree in minutes. To save even more time, I sometimes serve the hot chicken mixture on buns.

Shari Zimmerman ✳ Deford, Michigan

BISCUITS:

    2 cups all-purpose flour
    1 tablespoon baking powder
    1 teaspoon salt
  2/3 cup milk
  1/3 cup canola oil

CREAMED CHICKEN:

  1/4 cup finely chopped onion
  1/4 cup butter
  1/4 cup all-purpose flour
  1/4 to 1/2 teaspoon salt
  1/8 teaspoon pepper
    2 cups milk *or* chicken broth
    2 cups chopped cooked chicken

Minced fresh parsley

In a large bowl, combine flour, baking powder and salt; add milk and oil. Stir until the dough forms a ball. On a lightly floured surface, knead 8-10 times or until smooth.

Roll or pat dough into a 6-in. square about 1 in. thick. Cut into six rectangles. Place on a lightly greased baking sheet. Bake at 450° for 10-12 minutes or until golden brown.

Meanwhile, in a large skillet, saute onion in butter until tender. Stir in the flour, salt and pepper until blended. Gradually add milk; bring to a boil. Reduce the heat; cook and stir for 1-2 minutes or until thickened. Stir in chicken and parsley; cook until heated through. Split biscuits; top with creamed chicken. **YIELD: 6 SERVINGS.**

⏱ Chicken with 🖐 Mushroom Sauce

PREP/TOTAL TIME: **25 MIN.**

It looks impressive, but this mouthwatering dish comes together in no time. I think its flavor rivals that of many full-fat entrees found in fancy restaurants.

Jennifer Pemberton ✳ Muncie, Indiana

    2 teaspoons cornstarch
  1/2 cup fat-free milk
    4 boneless skinless chicken breast halves
       (4 ounces *each*)
    1 tablespoon olive oil
  1/2 pound fresh mushrooms, sliced
  1/2 medium onion, sliced and separated
       into rings
    1 tablespoon reduced-fat butter
  1/4 cup sherry *or* chicken broth
  1/2 teaspoon salt
  1/8 teaspoon pepper

In a small bowl, combine cornstarch and milk until smooth; set aside. Flatten the chicken to 1/4-in. thickness. In a large nonstick skillet, cook chicken in oil over medium heat for 5-6 minutes on each side or until meat juices run clear. Remove and keep warm.

In the same skillet, saute mushrooms and onion in butter until tender. Stir in the sherry, salt and pepper; bring to a boil. Stir cornstarch mixture and to the pan. Bring to a boil; cook and stir for 2 minutes or until thickened. Serve with chicken. **YIELD: 4 SERVINGS.**

NUTRITIONAL FACTS: 1 chicken breast half with 1/3 cup sauce equals 212 calories, 8 g fat (2 g saturated fat), 68 mg cholesterol, 387 mg sodium, 7 g carbohydrate, 1 g fiber, 26 g protein. DIABETIC EXCHANGES: 3 very lean meat, 1 vegetable, 1 fat, 1/2 starch.

EDITOR'S NOTE: This recipe was tested with Land O'Lakes light stick butter.

Chicken Potato Bake

PREP: 25 MIN. BAKE: 1 HOUR

When I created this recipe, I was looking for something that didn't require any last-minute fussing. It's great to get compliments on something so simple!

Myrtle Nelson ✳ Wetaskiwin, Alberta

Chicken with Mushroom Sauce

    1 cup dry bread crumbs
  1/2 cup all-purpose flour
    2 teaspoons salt
    2 teaspoons paprika
    1 teaspoon seasoned salt
    1 teaspoon sugar
    1 teaspoon onion powder
    1 teaspoon rubbed sage
    1 teaspoon dried oregano
  1/2 teaspoon pepper
  1/2 teaspoon celery seed
  1/2 teaspoon dried parsley flakes
  1/4 teaspoon garlic powder
    2 tablespoons canola oil
3-1/2 to 4 pounds chicken pieces, skin removed

POTATOES:
    1 teaspoon canola oil
    1 teaspoon seasoned salt
    1 teaspoon dried parsley flakes
  1/2 teaspoon paprika
  1/8 teaspoon garlic powder
  1/8 teaspoon pepper
    4 medium red potatoes, cut into 1-inch cubes

In a shallow bowl, combine the bread crumbs, flour and seasonings. Place the oil in another shallow bowl. Dip the chicken in oil; coat with crumb mixture. Place on greased 15-in. x 10-in. x 1-in. baking pan.

For potatoes, in a large bowl, combine the oil and seasonings. Add the potatoes; toss to coat. Place around the chicken.

Bake, uncovered, at 350° for 1 hour or until chicken juices run clear. **YIELD: 4 SERVINGS.**

Chicken Potato Bake

Chicken Corn Fritters

Place corn in a large bowl; lightly crush with a potato masher. Stir in the chicken, egg, milk, butter, salt and pepper. Combine the flour and baking powder; stir into the corn mixture just until combined.

In a deep-fat fryer or skillet, heat 2 in. of oil to 375°. Drop the batter by 1/4 cupfuls into oil. Fry for 3 minutes on each side or until golden brown. Drain on paper towels; keep warm.

In a large saucepan, melt the butter over medium-low heat. Stir in flour and seasonings until smooth. Add chilies. Gradually stir in milk. Bring to a boil; cook and stir for 2 minutes or until thickened. Serve with the corn fritters; sprinkle with cheese if desired. **YIELD: 1 DOZEN.**

Chicken Corn Fritters

PREP: **20 MIN.** COOK: **15 MIN.**

I've always loved corn fritters, but they weren't satisfying as a main dish. I came up with this recipe and was thrilled when my husband and our three young boys gave it rave reviews. The chicken and zesty sauce make these a wonderful brunch or lunch entree.

Marie Greene ✳ Scottsbluff, Nebraska

- 1   can (15-1/4 ounces) whole kernel corn, drained
- 1   cup finely chopped cooked chicken
- 1   egg, lightly beaten
- 1/2 cup milk
- 2   tablespoons butter, melted
- 1/2 teaspoon salt
- 1/8 teaspoon pepper
- 1-3/4 cups all-purpose flour
- 1   teaspoon baking powder

Oil for deep-fat frying

GREEN CHILI SAUCE:

- 1/3 cup butter, cubed
- 1/4 cup all-purpose flour
- 1/4 teaspoon salt
- 1/8 teaspoon pepper
- 1/8 teaspoon garlic powder
- 1/8 teaspoon ground cumin
- 1   can (4 ounces) chopped green chilies
- 1   cup milk

Shredded cheddar cheese, optional

Gorgonzola Penne With Chicken

PREP/TOTAL TIME: **30 MIN.**

This rich, creamy pasta dish is a snap to throw together for a weeknight meal but special enough for company. You can substitute another cheese for the Gorgonzola if you like.

George Schroeder ✳ Port Murray, New Jersey

- 1   package (16 ounces) penne pasta
- 1   pound boneless skinless chicken breasts, cut into 1/2-inch pieces
- 1   tablespoon olive oil
- 1   large garlic clove, minced
- 1/4 cup white wine
- 1   cup heavy whipping cream
- 1/4 cup chicken broth
- 2   cups (8 ounces) crumbled Gorgonzola cheese
- 6   to 8 fresh sage leaves, thinly sliced

Salt and pepper to taste

Grated Parmigiano-Reggiano cheese and minced fresh parsley

Cook pasta according to package directions.

Meanwhile, in a large skillet over medium heat, brown the chicken in oil on all sides. Add garlic; cook 1 minute longer. Add wine, stirring to loosen browned bits from pan.

Add cream and broth; cook until the sauce is slightly thickened and chicken is no longer pink. Stir in the Gorgonzola cheese, sage, salt and pepper; cook just until cheese is melted.

Drain the pasta; toss with sauce. Sprinkle with Parmigiano-Reggiano cheese and parsley. **YIELD: 8 SERVINGS.**

Gorgonzola Penne with Chicken

Cajun Stir-Fry

PREP/TOTAL TIME: **20 MIN.**

Cubes of chicken and smoked turkey kielbasa, plus plenty of herbs and veggies, make this a hearty stir-fry. I sometimes top off servings with shredded mozzarella cheese and minced basil and parsley.

Sharon Clemens ✳ Groveland, Illinois

- 3/4 **pound boneless skinless chicken breasts, cut into 1-inch cubes**
- 1/2 **pound reduced-fat smoked turkey kielbasa, cut into 1/2-inch slices**
- 1 **medium onion, chopped**
- 3 **garlic cloves, minced**
- 1 **tablespoon olive oil**
- 1 *each* **medium green, sweet red and yellow pepper, coarsely chopped**
- 1 **pound fresh mushrooms, sliced**
- 2 **medium tomatoes, diced**
- 1/4 **cup** *each* **minced fresh basil, oregano and parsley** *or* **4 teaspoons** *each* **dried basil, oregano and parsley flakes**
- 1-1/2 **teaspoons Cajun seasoning**
- 1/2 **teaspoon salt**
- 1/4 **teaspoon pepper**
- 1 **tablespoon cornstarch**
- 2 **tablespoons cold water**

Hot cooked spaghetti

In a large nonstick skillet, stir-fry the chicken, kielbasa, onion and garlic in oil until onion is tender. Add the peppers, mushrooms, tomatoes, herbs, Cajun seasoning, salt and pepper. Cook and stir until the chicken juices run clear and vegetables are crisp-tender.

Combine cornstarch and cold water until smooth; add to the skillet. Bring to a boil; cook and stir for 2 minutes or until thickened. Serve over spaghetti. **YIELD: 8 SERVINGS.**

NUTRITION FACTS: 1 cup stir-fry mixture (calculated without spaghetti) equals 140 calories, 4 g fat (1 g saturated fat), 40 mg cholesterol, 555 mg sodium, 11 g carbohydrate, 2 g fiber, 17 g protein.

Cajun Stir-Fry

Herbed Turkey and Dressing

Herbed Turkey and Dressing

PREP: 55 MIN. + CHILLING BAKE: 5 HOURS

Whenever I serve this succulent golden turkey and delectable dressing, guests fill their plates and I'm buried in compliments.

Marilyn Clay ✳ Palatine, Illinois

BASTING SAUCE:

- 2-1/4 cups chicken broth
- 1/2 cup butter, cubed
- 1/2 teaspoon salt
- 1 teaspoon dried thyme
- 1/4 teaspoon *each* dried marjoram, rubbed sage and dried rosemary, crushed
- 1/4 cup minced fresh parsley
- 2 tablespoons minced chives

DRESSING:

- 1 loaf (1 pound) sliced bread
- 1 pound bulk pork sausage
- 1/2 cup butter, cubed
- 4 cups thinly sliced celery
- 3 cups thinly sliced carrots
- 1/2 pound fresh mushrooms, chopped
- 1/2 pound cubed fully cooked ham
- 2 cups green onions
- 2 cups chopped pecans
- 1 large tart apple, chopped
- 1 cup chopped dried apricots
- 1 tablespoon rubbed sage
- 2 teaspoons dried marjoram
- 1 teaspoon dried rosemary, crushed
- 1 teaspoon salt
- 1/8 teaspoon ground nutmeg
- 1 cup egg substitute
- 1 turkey (16 to 18 pounds)
- 1 cup chicken broth

In a pan, bring the broth, butter and salt to a boil. Add herbs; set aside.

Toast bread; cut into 1/2-in. cubes. Place in a bowl. In a skillet, cook the sausage over medium heat until no longer pink; remove with slotted spoon and add to the bread. Add the butter to the drippings; saute celery, carrots, mushrooms, ham and onions for 15 minutes.

Add to bread mixture; stir in the nuts, fruit and seasonings. Add egg substitute and 3/4 cup basting sauce; mix lightly.

Chicken Wild Rice Casserole

Stuff the turkey with about 8 cups dressing. Skewer openings; tie drumsticks together. Place on rack in roasting pan. Baste with some of remaining basting sauce.

Bake, uncovered, at 325° for 5 to 5-1/2 hours or until a meat thermometer reads 180° for the turkey thigh and 165° for the stuffing, basting every 30 minutes. When turkey begins to brown, cover lightly with foil.

Add the broth to remaining dressing; mix lightly. Place in a greased 2-1/2-qt. baking dish; refrigerate. Remove from the refrigerator 30 minutes before baking. Cover and bake at 325° for 1 hour; uncover and bake 10 minutes. **YIELD: 14-16 SERVINGS (18 CUPS DRESSING).**

Buffalo Chicken Pizza

Chicken Wild Rice Casserole

PREP: **20 MIN.** BAKE: **30 MIN.**

While this special dish is perfect for a company dinner, it's also just too good not to make often for everyday family meals. We think it is very nice served with some crusty rolls or French bread.

Elizabeth Tokariuk ✳ Lethbridge, Alberta

- 1 small onion, chopped
- 1/3 cup butter
- 1/3 cup all-purpose flour
- 1-1/2 teaspoons salt
- 1/2 teaspoon pepper
- 1 can (14-1/2 ounces) chicken broth
- 1 cup half-and-half cream
- 4 cups cubed cooked chicken
- 4 cups cooked wild rice
- 2 jars (4-1/2 ounces *each*) sliced mushrooms, drained
- 1 jar (4 ounces) diced pimientos, drained
- 1 tablespoon minced fresh parsley
- 1/3 cup slivered almonds

In a saucepan, saute onion in butter until tender. Stir in flour, salt and pepper until blended. Gradually stir in broth; bring to a boil. Boil and stir for 2 minutes or until thickened and bubbly. Stir in cream, chicken, rice, mushrooms, pimientos and the parsley; heat through.

Transfer to a greased 2-1/2-qt. baking dish. Sprinkle with the almonds. Bake, uncovered, at 350° for 30-35 minutes or until bubbly. **YIELD: 6-8 SERVINGS.**

Buffalo Chicken Pizza

PREP: **20 MIN.** BAKE: **20 MIN.**

If your family likes spicy chicken wings, they'll love this pizza made with bottled buffalo wing sauce and refrigerated pizza dough.

Shari DiGirolamo ✳ Newton, Pennsylvania

- 1 tube (13.8 ounces) refrigerated pizza crust
- 1 cup buffalo wing sauce, *divided*
- 1-1/2 cups (6 ounces) shredded cheddar cheese
- 1-1/2 cups (6 ounces) part-skim shredded mozzarella cheese
- 2 pounds boneless skinless chicken breasts, cubed
- 1/2 teaspoon *each* garlic salt, pepper and chili powder
- 2 tablespoons butter
- 1/2 teaspoon dried oregano
- Celery sticks and blue cheese salad dressing

Unroll pizza crust into a lightly greased 15-in. x 10-in. x 1-in. baking pan; flatten dough and build up the edges slightly. Bake at 400° for 7 minutes. Brush dough with 3 tablespoons buffalo wing sauce. Combine the cheeses; sprinkle a third over the crust. Set aside.

In a large skillet, cook the chicken, garlic salt, pepper and chili powder in the butter until the chicken is no longer pink. Add the remaining wing sauce; cook and stir over medium heat for about 5 minutes or until the chicken is no longer pink. Spoon over cheese. Sprinkle with oregano and remaining cheese.

Bake for 16-20 minutes or until the crust is golden brown and cheese is melted. Serve with celery and salad dressing. **YIELD: 1 PIZZA (8 SLICES).**

EDITOR'S NOTE: This recipe was tested with Frank's Red Hot Buffalo Wing Sauce.

Italian-Style Cabbage Rolls

In a large bowl, combine the carrot, onion, the egg substitute, 2 tablespoons tomato soup, 2 tablespoons vegetable soup, 1 tablespoon Italian seasoning, cayenne, pepper and rice. Crumble the turkey over mixture and mix well. Place about 1/3 cupful on each cabbage leaf. Overlap cut ends of leaf; fold in sides, beginning from the cut end. Roll up completely to enclose the filling.

Place the rolls seam side down in an 11-in. x 7-in. baking dish coated with cooking spray. Combine remaining soups; pour over cabbage rolls. Sprinkle with remaining Italian seasoning. Cover and bake at 350° for 50-60 minutes or until cabbage is tender and a meat thermometer reads 165°. **YIELD: 5 SERVINGS.**

NUTRITION FACTS: 2 cabbage rolls equals 293 calories, 10 g fat (3 g saturated fat), 74 mg cholesterol, 582 mg sodium, 29 g carbohydrate, 4 g fiber, 22 g protein. **DIABETIC EXCHANGES:** 3 lean meat, 1-1/2 starch, 1 vegetable.

Italian-Style Cabbage Rolls

PREP: **45 MIN.** BAKE: **50 MIN.**

Here's a great way to get your family to eat their vegetables. Not only is this one of my gang's favorite dinners, but my young son loves to help me roll the turkey filling into the cabbage leaves.

Erika Niehoff * Eveleth, Minnesota

- 1/3 cup uncooked brown rice
- 1 medium head cabbage
- 1/2 cup shredded carrot
- 1/4 cup finely chopped onion
- 1/4 cup egg substitute
- 1 can (10-3/4 ounces) reduced-sodium condensed tomato soup, undiluted, *divided*
- 1 can (10-3/4 ounces) reduced-fat reduced-sodium condensed vegetable beef soup, undiluted, *divided*
- 2 tablespoons Italian seasoning, *divided*
- 1/4 teaspoon cayenne pepper
- 1/4 teaspoon pepper
- 1 pound lean ground turkey

Cook the rice according to package directions. Meanwhile, cook cabbage in boiling water just until leaves fall off head. Set aside 10 large leaves for the rolls. (Refrigerate the remaining cabbage for another use.) Cut out the thick vein from the bottom of each reserved leaf, making a V-shaped cut.

Chicken in Potato Baskets

PREP: **20 MIN.** BAKE: **30 MIN.**

These petite pies with their hash brown crusts are so pretty that I like to serve them for special luncheons. Chock-full of meat and vegetables in a creamy sauce, they're a meal-in-one...and a great way to use up leftover chicken or turkey.

Helen Lamison * Carnegie, Pennsylvania

- 4-1/2 cups frozen shredded hash brown potatoes, thawed
- 6 tablespoons butter, melted
- 1-1/2 teaspoons salt
- 1/4 teaspoon pepper

FILLING:

- 1/2 cup chopped onion
- 1/4 cup butter, cubed
- 1/4 cup all-purpose flour
- 2 teaspoons chicken bouillon granules
- 1 teaspoon Worcestershire sauce
- 1/2 teaspoon dried basil
- 2 cups milk
- 3 cups cubed cooked chicken
- 1 cup frozen peas, thawed

In a large bowl, combine the potatoes, butter, salt and pepper. Press into six greased 10-oz. custard cups; set aside.

In a large saucepan, saute onion in butter. Add the flour, bouillon, Worcestershire sauce and basil. Stir in milk. Bring to a boil; cook and stir for 2 minutes or until thickened. Add the chicken and peas. Spoon into prepared crusts.

Bake, uncovered, at 375° for 30-35 minutes or until crust is golden brown. **YIELD: 6 SERVINGS.**

Crescent-Wrapped Drumsticks

PREP: **50 MIN.** BAKE: **15 MIN.**

Looking for a different way to do drumsticks? These drumsticks are simmered in barbecue sauce and then wrapped in crescent roll dough that's sprinkled with Parmesan cheese and Italian seasoning.

Paula Plating * Colorado Springs, Colorado

Chicken in Potato Baskets

- 8 chicken drumsticks
- 1/4 cup butter
- 1/2 cup barbecue sauce
- 1 tube (8 ounces) refrigerated crescent rolls
- 1 egg, lightly beaten
- 2 teaspoons grated Parmesan cheese
- 2 teaspoons Italian seasoning
- 2 teaspoons sesame seeds, toasted

Remove and discard skin from drumsticks. In a large skillet, melt butter over medium heat; stir in the barbecue sauce. Add drumsticks. Bring to a boil. Reduce heat; cover and simmer for 30 minutes or until a meat thermometer reads 170°, turning occasionally. Remove chicken from pan; cool slightly.

Separate crescent dough into eight triangles; place in a lightly greased 15-in. x 10-in. x 1-in. baking pan. Brush dough with some of the beaten egg; sprinkle with Parmesan cheese and Italian seasoning. Place meaty portion of each drumstick at the tip of each triangle, with bony portion extended beyond one long side of triangle. Wrap drumstick in dough; place seam side down. Brush with remaining egg; sprinkle with sesame seeds.

Bake at 375° for 13-15 minutes or until golden brown and a meat thermometer reads 180°. **YIELD: 4 SERVINGS (2 DRUMSTICKS EACH).**

Crescent-Wrapped Drumsticks

Chicken Broccoli Crepes

Chicken Broccoli Crepes

PREP: **40 MIN.** + CHILLING BAKE: **20 MIN.**

When I organized food and nutrition training for our county 4-H group, we had cooking demonstrations representing different countries. We chose crepes for France, and everyone really loved them with this chicken-broccoli filling.

Deanna Naivar ✳ Temple, Texas

- 1 cup plus 2 tablespoons milk
- 2 eggs
- 2 tablespoons butter, melted
- 1 cup all-purpose flour
- 1/4 teaspoon salt

FILLING:

- 1/4 cup butter
- 1/4 cup all-purpose flour
- 2 cups chicken broth
- 2 teaspoons Worcestershire sauce
- 3 cups (12 ounces) shredded cheddar cheese, *divided*
- 2 cups (16 ounces) sour cream
- 2 packages (8 ounces *each*) frozen broccoli spears, cooked and drained
- 2-1/2 cups cubed cooked chicken

In a small bowl, beat the milk, eggs and butter. Combine flour and salt; add to egg mixture and beat until smooth. Cover; refrigerate for 1 hour.

Heat a lightly greased 8-in. nonstick skillet. Stir batter; pour 1/4 cup into the center of skillet. Lift and tilt pan to evenly coat bottom. Cook until top appears dry; turn and cook 15-20 seconds longer. Remove to a wire rack. Repeat with the remaining batter, greasing skillet as needed. When cool, stack crepes with waxed paper or paper towels in between.

In a large saucepan, melt butter. Stir in flour until smooth. Gradually stir in the broth and Worcestershire sauce. Bring to a boil; cook and stir for 2 minutes or until thickened. Reduce heat; stir in 2 cups cheese. Cook and stir for 10 minutes or until cheese is melted. Remove from the heat; stir in sour cream until smooth.

Place four broccoli spears and 1/3 cup chicken down the center of each crepe; top with 1/3 cup cheese sauce. Roll up and place seam side down in a greased 13-in. x 9-in. baking dish. Pour remaining cheese sauce over the crepes; sprinkle with remaining cheese.

Bake, uncovered, at 350° for 20 minutes or until heated through. YIELD: **8 CREPES.**

Ranch Turkey Burgers

Ranch Turkey Burgers

PREP/TOTAL TIME: 30 MIN.

A chopped jalapeno gives this interesting turkey burger a bit of a kick. Every bite is flavorful and cheesy. Top it off with ranch dressing sauce, and it's the best thing under a bun.

Sandy Umber * Springdale, Arkansas

- 5 ounces sharp cheddar cheese, diced
- 1 small sweet onion, diced
- 1 jalapeno pepper, seeded and finely chopped
- 4 teaspoons chili powder
- 2 teaspoons ground cumin
- 2 garlic cloves, minced
- 3/4 teaspoon salt
- 1/4 teaspoon pepper
- 1-1/4 pounds ground turkey
- 3 tablespoons olive oil
- 1/4 cup sour cream
- 4-1/2 teaspoons prepared ranch salad dressing
- 4 hamburger buns, split

In a large bowl, combine cheese, onion, jalapeno and seasonings. Crumble turkey over mixture and mix well. Shape into four patties; brush with the oil.

Grill on a greased indoor grill for 2-3 minutes on each side or until a meat thermometer reads 165° and the juices run clear. Meanwhile, in a small bowl, combine the sour cream and salad dressing. Serve the burgers on buns with sauce. **YIELD: 4 SERVINGS.**

EDITOR'S NOTE: When cutting hot peppers, disposable gloves are recommended. Avoid touching your face.

Spinach Crab Chicken

PREP: 45 MIN. COOK: 40 MIN.

I altered a friend's recipe for crab-stuffed chicken to include one of my favorite vegetables—spinach. Now my husband requests this elegant entree all the time. Served over rice, it's special enough for company.

Vicki Melies * Elkhorn, Nebraska

- 1/2 cup finely chopped onion
- 1/4 cup chopped fresh mushrooms

Spinach Crab Chicken

- 1/4 cup finely chopped celery
- 3 tablespoons butter
- 3 tablespoons all-purpose flour
- 1/2 teaspoon salt, *divided*
- 1 cup chicken broth
- 1/2 cup milk
- 4 boneless skinless chicken breast halves (6 ounces *each*)
- 1/8 teaspoon white pepper
- 1/2 cup dry bread crumbs
- 1 can (6 ounces) crabmeat, drained, flaked and cartilage removed
- 12 fresh spinach leaves, chopped
- 1 tablespoon minced fresh parsley
- 1 cup (4 ounces) shredded Swiss cheese

Hot cooked rice

For sauce, in a large skillet, sauce the onion, mushrooms and celery in butter until tender. Stir in flour and 1/4 teaspoon salt until blended. Gradually add broth and milk. Bring to a boil; cook and stir for 1-2 minutes or until thickened. Remove from the heat.

Flatten chicken to 1/4-in. thickness; sprinkle with pepper and remaining salt. In a large bowl, combine the bread crumbs, crab, spinach and parsley; stir in 1/2 cup sauce. Spoon 1/4 cup down the center of each chicken breast half. Roll up; secure with toothpicks. Place seam side down in a greased 13-in. x 9-in. baking dish. Top with remaining sauce.

Cover and bake at 375° for 35-45 minutes or until chicken is no longer pink. Sprinkle with cheese. Broil 4-6 in. from the heat for 5 minutes or until lightly browned. Discard toothpicks. Serve with rice. **YIELD: 4 SERVINGS.**

Chicken and Asparagus Kabobs

Chicken and Asparagus Kabobs

PREP: **25 MIN.** **+ MARINATING** GRILL: **10 MIN.**

These Asian-flavored kabobs, served with a tasty dipping sauce, are special enough to make for guests at your next backyard get-together. Sometimes I substitute salmon for the chicken.

Kelly Townsend ✳ Syracuse, Nebraska

DIPPING SAUCE:
- 2 cups mayonnaise
- 1/4 cup sugar
- 1/4 cup soy sauce
- 2 tablespoons sesame seeds, toasted
- 1 tablespoon sesame oil
- 1/2 teaspoon white pepper

KABOBS:
- 1/4 cup soy sauce
- 2 tablespoons brown sugar
- 2 tablespoons water
- 1 tablespoon sesame oil
- 1 teaspoon crushed red pepper flakes
- 1 teaspoon minced fresh gingerroot
- 1-1/2 pounds boneless skinless chicken breasts, cut into 1-1/2-inch pieces
- 1 pound fresh asparagus, trimmed and cut into 2-inch pieces
- 2 tablespoons olive oil
- 1/2 teaspoon salt

In a small bowl, combine the sauce ingredients. Cover and refrigerate for 2-4 hours.

In a large resealable plastic bag, combine soy sauce, sugar, water, sesame oil, pepper flakes and ginger. Add chicken; seal bag and turn to coat. Refrigerate for 2 hours, turning occasionally.

Drain and discard marinade. In a bowl, toss asparagus with olive oil and salt. On six metal or soaked wooden skewers, alternately thread one chicken piece and two asparagus pieces.

Grill, covered, over medium heat for 4-5 minutes on each side or until the chicken is no longer pink and asparagus is crisp-tender. Serve with dipping sauce. **YIELD: 6 SERVINGS.**

Honey Orange Chicken

Honey Orange Chicken

PREP: 20 MIN. COOK: 15 MIN.

This dish is elegant enough for company and tastes like you spent all day in the kitchen. With five children to keep up with, I look for recipes that are easy to prepare. They love this chicken and pasta meal, with its honey orange sauce.

Marie Hannah ✳ Hemet, California

- 1 pound boneless skinless chicken breasts, cut into 1/2-inch strips
- 3 tablespoons butter, *divided*
- 1 teaspoon salt
- 1/2 teaspoon paprika
- 1/4 teaspoon pepper
- 1 medium onion, sliced
- 1 tablespoon cornstarch
- 1/2 teaspoon ground ginger
- 1/4 teaspoon ground nutmeg
- 1 cup orange juice
- 1/4 cup honey
- 1/2 cup pitted ripe olives, halved

Hot cooked linguine

In a large skillet, saute chicken in 2 tablespoons butter until chicken is no longer pink. Sprinkle with the salt, paprika and pepper. Remove and keep warm. In the same pan, saute the onion in remaining butter until tender.

In a small bowl, combine cornstarch, ginger, nutmeg, orange juice and honey; gradually pour over onion. Bring to a boil; cook and stir for 2 minutes or until thickened. Add olives and chicken. Simmer, uncovered, for 5 minutes or until chicken is heated through. Serve with linguine. **YIELD: 4 SERVINGS.**

Kung Pao Wings

PREP/TOTAL TIME: 30 MIN.

Served as an entree over hot cooked rice, these delicious drummettes have plenty of personality—with sweet red pepper for color, red pepper flakes for zip and peanuts for crunch.

Kathleen Evans ✳ Lacey, Washington

- 8 whole chicken wings (about 1-1/2 pounds)
- 2 tablespoons sugar
- 2 teaspoons cornstarch

Kung Pao Wings

- 1/4 cup water
- 1/4 cup soy sauce
- 2 tablespoons lemon juice
- 1/4 teaspoon crushed red pepper flakes
- 1 tablespoon canola oil
- 1 small sweet red pepper, diced
- 1/2 cup diced onion
- 1 to 2 garlic cloves, minced
- 1/3 cup peanuts

Hot cooked rice

Cut the chicken wings into three sections; discard wing tip section. Set the wings aside. In a small bowl, combine the sugar, cornstarch, water, soy sauce, lemon juice and pepper flakes until blended; set aside.

In a large skillet, heat oil over medium-high heat. Cook the chicken wings, uncovered, for 10-15 minutes or until the chicken juices run clear, turning occasionally.

Add the red pepper, onion and garlic; cook, uncovered, for 3-5 minutes or until vegetables are crisp-tender. Stir the cornstarch mixture; gradually add to skillet. Bring to a boil; cook and stir for 2 minutes or until sauce is thickened and the vegetables are tender. Sprinkle with peanuts. Serve with rice. **YIELD: 4 SERVINGS.**

EDITOR'S NOTE: Uncooked chicken wing sections (wingettes) may be substituted for whole chicken wings.

Flavorful Chicken Rolls

Flavorful Chicken Rolls

PREP: **25 MIN.** BAKE: **30 MIN.**

This is a great main course for dinner guests...and they never believe how easy it is. The creamy feta-basil filling can be made early and refrigerated until needed. Deli ham and packaged spinach leaves further cut prep time.

Kandi Wysong ✳ Boiling Springs, South Carolina

- 5 boneless skinless chicken breast halves (6 ounces *each*)
- 2 cups fresh baby spinach
- 4 ounces cream cheese, softened
- 4 ounces crumbled feta cheese
- 2 tablespoons chopped fresh basil *or* 2 teaspoons dried basil
- 1/4 teaspoon coarsely ground pepper
- 5 thin slices deli ham
- 1 egg
- 1 tablespoon milk
- 3/4 to 1 cup seasoned bread crumbs

Flatten chicken breasts to 1/4-in. thickness. Place a single layer of spinach over chicken.

In a small bowl, combine the cream cheese, feta cheese, basil and pepper until blended; spread over spinach. Top each chicken breast with a ham slice, trimming if necessary. Roll up and secure with toothpicks.

In a shallow bowl, beat egg and milk. Place bread crumbs in another bowl. Dip chicken rolls in egg mixture, then coat with crumbs.

Place seam side down in a greased 15-in. x 10-in. x 1-in. baking pan. Bake, uncovered, at 375° for 30-35 minutes or until the chicken is no longer pink. Discard toothpicks. **YIELD: 5 SERVINGS.**

Hearty Jambalaya, PAGE 262

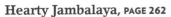

" *I love anything with Cajun spices, so I came up with this slow cooker jambalaya that's just as good as that served in restaurants. If you can't find andouille sausage, chorizo will also work. I like to serve it with warm cornbread and garnished with green onions.* "

Jennifer Fulk
Moreno Valley, California

SEAFOOD

DO YOU HAVE A WINNING RECIPE?

Enter your most prized recipes in the *Taste of Home* recipe contests, and you may win some money and the chance to have your recipe published. Log onto **tasteofhome.com/RecipeContests** for a list of our current contests and submission deadlines. Good luck...we'll be looking for your recipe.

Visit us @
tasteofhome
.com

seafood

Cajun Shrimp Lasagna Roll-Ups

PREP: **30 MIN.** BAKE: **25 MIN. + STANDING**

If you enjoy Creole and Cajun dishes, you'll love this one. The seasoning and andouille sausage give it a nice kick, and seafood fans will appreciate all of the shrimp.

Mary Beth Harris-Murphree ✳ Tyler, Texas

- 1-1/4 pounds uncooked medium shrimp, peeled and deveined
- 1 medium onion, chopped
- 2 tablespoons olive oil
- 4 medium tomatoes, seeded and chopped
- 2 tablespoons Cajun seasoning
- 3 garlic cloves, minced
- 1/4 cup butter, cubed
- 1/4 cup all-purpose flour
- 2 cups milk
- 1-1/2 cups (6 ounces) shredded cheddar cheese
- 1 cup diced fully cooked andouille sausage
- 12 lasagna noodles, cooked and drained
- 4 ounces pepper Jack cheese, shredded
- 1 teaspoon paprika

In a large skillet, saute shrimp and onion in oil until shrimp turn pink. Stir in tomatoes and Cajun seasoning; set aside.

In a large saucepan, saute garlic in butter for 1 minute. Stir in flour until blended. Gradually add milk. Bring to a boil over medium heat; cook and stir for 2 minutes or until thickened. Remove from heat; stir in cheddar cheese until smooth. Add sausage; set aside.

Cajun Shrimp Lasagna Roll-Ups

Spread 1/3 cup shrimp mixture over each noodle. Carefully roll up; place seam side down in a greased 13-in. x 9-in. baking dish. Top with cheese sauce. Sprinkle with pepper Jack cheese and paprika.

Cover and bake at 350° for 15 minutes. Uncover; bake 10-15 minutes longer or until bubbly. Let stand 15 minutes before serving.
YIELD: 6 SERVINGS.

Golden Sea Bass

⏱ Golden Sea Bass

PREP/TOTAL TIME: **25 MIN.**

If you've ever tasted potato-crusted sea bass in a restaurant and wished you could have it at home, this version is for you. Store-bought potato flakes and a salad dressing mix combine for a great coating that's a breeze to whip up.

Judi Markert ✳ Mentor-on-the-Lake, Ohio

- 1 **cup mashed potato flakes**
- 1 **envelope Italian salad dressing mix**
- 1/4 **teaspoon pepper**
- 1 **egg**
- 2 **pounds sea bass fillets** *or* **halibut steaks**
- 2 **tablespoons butter, melted**

Paprika

In a shallow bowl, combine the potato flakes, dressing mix and pepper. In another bowl, beat the egg. Dip the fillets into egg, then coat with potato flake mixture.

Place in a single layer in a 15-in. x 10-in. x 1-in. baking pan coated with cooking spray. Drizzle with butter; sprinkle with paprika.

Bake, uncovered, at 450° for 10-14 minutes or until the fish flakes easily with a fork. **YIELD: 8 SERVINGS.**

🌿 Phyllo-Wrapped Halibut

PREP: **20 MIN.** BAKE: **20 MIN.**

I created this easy entree to convince my husband that seafood doesn't have to taste "fishy." He likes the flaky phyllo wrapping as well as the bright green and red vegetables hidden inside of it.

Carrie Vazzano ✳ Rolling Meadows, Illinois

- 4 **cups fresh baby spinach**
- 3/4 **cup chopped sweet red pepper**
- 3/4 **teaspoon salt-free lemon-pepper seasoning,** *divided*
- 1/2 **teaspoon lemon juice**
- 6 **sheets phyllo dough (14 inches x 9 inches)**
- 2 **tablespoons reduced-fat butter, melted**
- 2 **halibut fillets (4 ounces** *each*)
- 1/4 **teaspoon salt**
- 1/8 **teaspoon pepper**
- 1/4 **cup shredded part-skim mozzarella cheese**

In a large nonstick skillet lightly coated with cooking spray, saute spinach and red pepper until tender. Add 1/2 teaspoon lemon-pepper and lemon juice. Remove from the heat; cool.

Line a baking sheet with foil and coat the foil with cooking spray; set aside. Place one sheet of phyllo dough on a work surface; brush with butter. (Until ready to use, keep the remaining phyllo dough covered with plastic wrap and a damp towel to prevent it from drying out.) Layer the remaining phyllo over the first sheet, brushing each with butter. Cut stack in half widthwise.

Place a halibut fillet in the center of each square; sprinkle with salt and pepper. Top with cheese and spinach mixture. Fold sides and bottom edge over fillet and roll up to enclose it; trim end of phyllo if necessary. Brush with remaining butter; sprinkle with the remaining lemon-pepper.

Place seam side down on prepared baking sheet. Bake at 375° for 20-25 minutes or until golden brown. **YIELD: 2 SERVINGS.**

EDITOR'S NOTE: This recipe was tested with Land O'Lakes light stick butter.

NUTRITION FACTS: 1 serving equals 330 calories, 12 g fat (6 g saturated fat), 64 mg cholesterol, 676 mg sodium, 26 g carbohydrate, 4 g fiber, 33 g protein. DIABETIC EXCHANGES: 4 very lean meat, 2 vegetable, 1-1/2 fat, 1 starch.

Phyllo-Wrapped Halibut

 Tomato Salmon Bake

PREP/TOTAL TIME: **30 MIN.**

I was looking for a healthy alternative to beef and chicken when I found this recipe and decided to personalize it. My husband doesn't usually like fish unless it's fried, but he loves the Italian flavor in this dish. Serve it with a green salad for a great meal.

Lacey Parker ✳ Gainesville, Virginia

- 4 **salmon fillets (6 ounces** *each***)**
- 1 **can (14-1/2 ounces) diced tomatoes, drained**
- 1/2 **cup sun-dried tomato salad dressing**
- 2 **tablespoons shredded Parmesan cheese**

Hot cooked rice

Place salmon in a greased 13-in. x 9-in. baking dish. Combine the tomatoes and salad dressing; pour over salmon. Sprinkle with cheese.

Bake, uncovered, at 375° for 20-25 minutes or until fish flakes easily with a fork. Serve with rice. **YIELD: 4 SERVINGS.**

Tomato Salmon Bake

Easy Crab Cakes

Easy Crab Cakes

PREP/TOTAL TIME: **25 MIN.**

Canned crabmeat makes these delicate patties simple enough for busy weeknight dinners. For a change of pace, try forming the crab mixture into four thick patties instead of eight cakes.

Charlene Spelock * Apollo, Pennsylvania

- 2 cans (6 ounces *each*) crabmeat, drained, flaked and cartilage removed
- 1 cup seasoned bread crumbs, *divided*
- 1 egg, lightly beaten
- 1/4 cup finely chopped green onions
- 1/4 cup finely chopped sweet red pepper
- 1/4 cup reduced-fat mayonnaise
- 1 tablespoon lemon juice
- 1/2 teaspoon garlic powder
- 1/8 teaspoon cayenne pepper
- 1 tablespoon butter

In a large bowl, combine the crab, 1/3 cup bread crumbs, egg, onions, red pepper, mayonnaise, lemon juice, garlic powder and cayenne.

Divide the mixture into eight portions; shape into 2-in. balls. Roll in remaining bread crumbs. Flatten to 1/2-in. thickness. In a large nonstick skillet, cook the crab cakes in butter for 3-4 minutes on each side or until golden brown. **YIELD: 4 SERVINGS.**

NUTRITION FACTS: 2 crab cakes equals 295 calories, 12 g fat (3 g saturated fat), 142 mg cholesterol, 879 mg sodium, 23 g carbohydrate, 1 g fiber, 23 g protein. DIABETIC EXCHANGES: 3 very lean meat, 1-1/2 starch, 1-1/2 fat.

Spicy Salmon Kabobs

Spicy Salmon Kabobs

PREP: **15 MIN. + MARINATING** GRILL: **10 MIN.**

I first made these kabobs for a team of archaeologists excavating a site in the Aleutian Islands. We used fresh sockeye salmon, but other varieties of salmon work well, too.

Terri Mach * Homer, Alaska

- 1-1/2 pounds salmon fillets, cut into 1-1/2-inch cubes
- 1 tablespoon brown sugar

Shrimp 'n' Noodle Bowls

1 teaspoon salt
1 teaspoon garlic powder
1 teaspoon celery seed
1 teaspoon paprika
1 teaspoon pepper
1/2 teaspoon onion powder
1/2 teaspoon cayenne pepper
1/4 teaspoon chili powder
1/8 teaspoon fennel seed, crushed
1/8 teaspoon ground cumin

Place salmon in a large resealable plastic bag. Combine the remaining ingredients; sprinkle over salmon. Seal bag and toss to coat; refrigerate for 30 minutes.

Thread the salmon onto six metal or soaked wooden skewers. Grill, covered, over medium heat for 4-6 minutes on each side or until fish flakes easily with a fork. **YIELD: 6 SERVINGS.**

Shrimp 'n' Noodle Bowls

PREP/TOTAL TIME: **25 MIN.**

This is a great, quick meal that can be made with pick-up ingredients from the grocery store. Cooked shrimp and bagged slaw reduce the time and work required to get it on the table.

Mary Bergfeld ✳ Eugene, Oregon

8 ounces uncooked angel hair pasta
1 pound cooked small shrimp
2 cups broccoli coleslaw mix
6 green onions, thinly sliced
1/2 cup minced fresh cilantro
2/3 cup reduced-fat sesame ginger salad dressing

Cook pasta according to package directions; drain and rinse in cold water. Transfer to a large bowl. Add the shrimp, coleslaw mix, onions and cilantro. Drizzle with dressing; toss to coat. Cover and refrigerate until serving. **YIELD: 6 SERVINGS.**

NUTRITION FACTS: 1-1/3 cups equals 260 calories, 3 g fat (trace saturated fat), 147 mg cholesterol, 523 mg sodium, 36 g carbohydrate, 2 g fiber, 22 g protein. **DIABETIC EXCHANGES:** 2 starch, 2 very lean meat, 1 vegetable.

Seafood Fettuccine Alfredo

Seafood Fettuccine Alfredo

PREP/TOTAL TIME: 30 MIN.

I like to serve this lovely pasta, featuring scallops and shrimp, with crusty Italian bread. Sprinkled with tomato and parsley, it's a pretty dish.

Jimmy Spellings * Oakland, Tennessee

- 4 ounces uncooked fettuccine
- 1/4 pound uncooked medium shrimp, peeled and deveined
- 1/4 pound sea scallops, halved
- 2 tablespoons olive oil, *divided*
- 1 garlic clove, minced
- 1 small shallot, chopped
- 1/4 cup chicken broth
- 1/4 cup white wine *or* additional chicken broth
- 1 cup heavy whipping cream *or* half-and-half cream
- 1/2 cup grated Parmesan cheese
- 1 Roma tomato, diced
- 2 tablespoons minced fresh parsley

Cook the fettuccine according to the package directions. Meanwhile, in a large skillet, saute shrimp and scallops in 1 tablespoon oil for 3-5 minutes or until shrimp turn pink and scallops are opaque. Remove and keep warm.

In the same skillet, saute garlic and shallot in remaining oil until tender. Stir in broth and wine. Bring to a boil. Reduce the heat; simmer, uncovered, for 6-8 minutes or until most of the liquid has evaporated. Stir in the cream; cook, uncovered, over medium heat for 5 minutes or until thickened.

Drain fettuccine; stir into cream sauce. Add the shrimp, scallops and cheese; toss to coat. Sprinkle with the tomato and parsley. YIELD: 2 SERVINGS.

Hearty Jambalaya

PREP: 15 MIN. COOK: 6-1/4 HOURS

I love anything with Cajun spices, so I came up with this slow cooker jambalaya that's just as good as that served in restaurants. If you can't find andouille sausage, chorizo will also work. I like to serve it with warm corn bread and garnished with green onions.

Jennifer Fulk * Moreno Valley, California

- 1 can (28 ounces) diced tomatoes, undrained
- 1 pound fully cooked andouille sausage links, cubed
- 1/2 pound boneless skinless chicken breasts, cut into 1-inch cubes
- 1 can (8 ounces) tomato sauce
- 1 cup diced onion
- 1 small sweet red pepper, diced
- 1 small green pepper, diced
- 1 cup chicken broth
- 1 celery rib with leaves, chopped
- 2 tablespoons tomato paste
- 2 teaspoons dried oregano
- 2 teaspoons Cajun seasoning
- 1-1/2 teaspoons minced garlic
- 2 bay leaves
- 1 teaspoon Louisiana-style hot sauce
- 1/2 teaspoon dried thyme
- 1 pound cooked medium shrimp, peeled and deveined

Hot cooked rice

In a 5-qt. slow cooker, combine the first 16 ingredients. Cover and cook on low for 6-7 hours or until chicken juices run clear. Stir in shrimp. Cover and cook 15 minutes longer or until heated through. Discard bay leaves. Serve with rice. YIELD: 8 SERVINGS.

◗ Lime Shrimp With Asparagus

PREP/TOTAL TIME: **15 MIN.**

For this colorful main dish, I combine shrimp, asparagus and sweet red pepper and flavor them with lime juice, lime peel, garlic and soy sauce. It may look like it takes a long time to prepare, but it goes together fast in the microwave.

Peggy Davies ✳ Canon City, Colorado

- 3/4 pound fresh asparagus, trimmed and cut into 2-inch pieces
- 1 garlic clove, minced
- 2 tablespoons water
- 3/4 pound uncooked medium shrimp, peeled and deveined
- 1 medium sweet red pepper, thinly sliced
- 1 jalapeno pepper, seeded and finely chopped
- 1 teaspoon cornstarch
- 2 tablespoons soy sauce
- 1 tablespoon lime juice
- 1/2 teaspoon grated lime peel

Hot cooked rice

Place asparagus, garlic and water in a 1-1/2-qt. microwave-safe dish. Cover and microwave on high for 3-4 minutes or until the asparagus is crisp-tender. Remove with a slotted spoon; keep warm.

Add the shrimp, red pepper and jalapeno to the dish. Cover and cook on high for 3 minutes or until the shrimp turn pink. Remove with a slotted spoon; keep warm.

In a small bowl, whisk the cornstarch, soy sauce, lime juice and lime peel until blended; stir into cooking juices. Microwave, uncovered, on high for 1 minute or until sauce is thickened and bubbly.

Stir in the shrimp and asparagus mixtures. Cook, uncovered, on high for 30-60 seconds or until heated through. Serve with rice. **YIELD: 4 SERVINGS.**

EDITOR'S NOTE: This recipe was tested in a 1,100-watt microwave.

Hearty Jambalaya

Lime Shrimp with Asparagus

Swordfish with Sauteed Vegetables

Swordfish with Sauteed Vegetables

PREP: **20 MIN. + MARINATING** GRILL: **10 MIN.**

My husband says "wow!" when I prepare swordfish this way. With lots of pretty, fresh vegetables, this dish is all you need for dinner.

Susie Thompson ✳ Dexter, Oregon

- 1/2 cup olive oil
- 2 green onions, sliced
- 2 tablespoons minced fresh rosemary *or* 2 teaspoons dried rosemary, crushed
- 2 tablespoons lime juice
- 2 tablespoons Dijon mustard
- 6 swordfish *or* halibut steaks (6 ounces *each*)

VEGETABLES:

- 2 small zucchini
- 2 small yellow summer squash
- 1/4 cup sliced green onions
- 1 to 2 tablespoons minced fresh rosemary *or* 2 teaspoons dried rosemary, crushed
- 3 tablespoons olive oil
- 1 pound small red potatoes, cooked and cut into 1/2-inch slices
- 2 cups halved cherry tomatoes
- 1/2 to 3/4 teaspoon salt
- 1/4 teaspoon pepper

In a large resealable plastic bag, combine the oil, onions, rosemary, lime juice and mustard; add swordfish. Seal bag and turn to coat; refrigerate for 30-45 minutes.

Drain and discard marinade. If grilling the fish, coat grill rack with cooking spray before starting the grill. Grill swordfish, uncovered, over medium-hot heat or broil 4-6 in. from the heat for 5-7 minutes on each side or until fish flakes easily with a fork.

Cut zucchini and yellow squash lengthwise into 1/4-in. slices, then widthwise into 3-in. pieces. In a large skillet, saute the onions and rosemary in oil for 1-2 minutes or until onions are tender. Add squash; saute for 5-6 minutes or until crisp-tender. Add the potatoes and tomatoes; cook just until heated through. Sprinkle with salt and pepper; toss to coat. Serve with the swordfish. **YIELD: 4 SERVINGS.**

Easy Shrimp Creole

Easy Shrimp Creole

PREP/TOTAL TIME: 25 MIN.

I found this super-quick shrimp recipe in a magazine years ago and have changed it to suit my taste. To speed things along, I cook the rice in the microwave, using chicken broth instead of water. I've only had compliments whenever I've served it.

Jean Gauthier ✷ Rives Junction, Michigan

- 3/4 cup chopped onion
- 3/4 cup chopped celery
- 3/4 cup chopped green pepper
- 2 tablespoons canola oil
- 1 can (10-3/4 ounces) condensed tomato soup, undiluted
- 1 cup tomato juice
- 1/4 cup water
- 1/4 cup salsa
- 2 tablespoons lemon juice
- 1 tablespoon minced fresh parsley
- 2 teaspoons chili powder
- 1-1/4 teaspoons garlic powder
- 1/4 teaspoon pepper
- 1 pound cooked medium shrimp, peeled and deveined

Hot cooked rice

In a large skillet, saute the onion, celery and green pepper in oil for 6-7 minutes or until crisp-tender. Stir in soup, tomato juice, water, salsa, lemon juice, parsley, chili powder, garlic powder and pepper. Bring to a boil. Reduce heat to medium; cover and cook for 6-8 minutes or until heated through.

Add the shrimp; cook, uncovered, for 3-4 minutes or until heated through. Serve with rice. **YIELD: 5 SERVINGS.**

Saucy Orange Roughy

Saucy Orange Roughy

PREP/TOTAL TIME: 15 MIN.

Both the seafood and citrus lovers in your home will request this entree time and again. Not only are the orange roughy fillets tender and the sauce delicious, but the dish is ready in moments.

Bette Hunn ✷ Orosi, California

- 1 tablespoon sugar
- 2 teaspoons cornstarch
- 1/2 teaspoon chicken bouillon granules

Dash pepper

- 1/2 cup orange juice
- 1 teaspoon lemon juice
- 1/4 teaspoon grated orange peel
- 1/8 teaspoon dried tarragon
- 1 pound orange roughy fillets
- 1/2 teaspoon salt

Orange slices and fresh tarragon, optional

In a small microwave-safe dish, combine the sugar, cornstarch, bouillon granules, pepper and juices until smooth. Microwave, uncovered, on high for 45 seconds; stir. Cook 45 seconds longer or until thickened. Stir in the orange peel and tarragon; set aside.

Place fish in an ungreased 11-in. x 7-in. microwave-safe dish, with the thickest side toward the outside of the dish. Sprinkle with salt. Cover and microwave on high for 3 minutes.

Top with the orange sauce. Microwave, uncovered, on high for 30-45 seconds or until fish flakes easily with a fork. Serve with orange slices and fresh tarragon if desired. **YIELD: 4 SERVINGS.**

EDITOR'S NOTE: This recipe was tested in a 1,100-watt microwave.

Spicy Island Shrimp

Spicy Island Shrimp

PREP: 20 MIN. COOK: 20 MIN.

My husband got this recipe while he was living on St. Croix Island. We've served the zippy shrimp dish on several occasions. I'm amazed at how even those who claim not to care for shrimp come out of their shells and devour them when they're prepared this way!

Teresa Methe ✳ Minden, Nebraska

- 1 large green pepper, chopped
- 1 large onion, chopped
- 1/2 cup butter cubed
- 2-1/4 pounds uncooked large shrimp, peeled and deveined
- 2 cans (8 ounces *each*) tomato sauce
- 3 tablespoons chopped green onions
- 1 tablespoon minced fresh parsley
- 1 teaspoon salt
- 1 teaspoon paprika
- 1 teaspoon pepper
- 1/2 teaspoon garlic powder
- 1/2 teaspoon dried oregano
- 1/2 teaspoon dried thyme
- 1/4 to 1/2 teaspoon white pepper
- 1/4 to 1/2 teaspoon cayenne pepper

Hot cooked rice

In a large skillet, saute the green pepper and onion in butter until tender. Reduce heat; add shrimp. Cook for 5 minutes or until the shrimp turn pink.

Stir in the tomato sauce, green onions, parsley and seasonings. Bring to a boil. Reduce the heat; simmer, uncovered, for 20 minutes or until slightly thickened. Serve with rice. **YIELD: 6 SERVINGS.**

Macadamia-Crusted Tilapia

Macadamia-Crusted Tilapia

PREP: **20 MIN.** BAKE: **15 MIN.**

A refreshing pineapple salsa complements these crispy golden fillets. The colorful entree will make an impression with guests. I like to garnish each fillet with a few whole macadamia nuts.

Jennifer Fisher ✷ Austin, Texas

- 2 eggs
- 1/8 teaspoon cayenne pepper
- 1 cup all-purpose flour
- 1-3/4 cups macadamia nuts, finely chopped
- 4 tilapia fillets (6 ounces *each*)
- 1 tablespoon butter, melted

PINEAPPLE SALSA:

- 1 cup cubed fresh pineapple
- 1/4 cup chopped sweet red pepper
- 3 tablespoons thinly sliced green onions
- 2 tablespoons sugar
- 1 jalapeno pepper, seeded and chopped
- 1 tablespoon lime juice
- 1/2 teaspoon minced fresh gingerroot
- 2 tablespoons minced fresh cilantro

In a shallow bowl, whisk eggs and cayenne. Place flour and macadamia nuts in separate shallow bowls. Coat tilapia with flour, then dip in egg mixture and coat with nuts.

Place on a greased baking sheet; drizzle with butter. Bake at 375° for 15-20 minutes or until fish flakes easily with a fork.

Meanwhile, in a small serving bowl, combine the pineapple, red pepper, onions, sugar, jalapeno, lime juice and ginger; sprinkle with cilantro. Serve with fish. YIELD: **4 SERVINGS** (1-1/2 CUPS SALSA).

EDITOR'S NOTE: When cutting hot peppers, disposable gloves are recommended. Avoid touching your face.

Christmas Eve Confetti Pasta

Christmas Eve Confetti Pasta

PREP/TOTAL TIME: **25 MIN.**

This fabulous, easy pasta has become a holiday tradition at my home. All the prep is done before we attend Christmas Eve service. On returning, I just boil water and saute. It's so colorful with a tossed salad and garlic bread—and is always appreciated by my family!

Ellen Fiore ✷ Ridgewood, New Jersey

- 1 package (16 ounces) linguine
- 1 cup chopped sweet red pepper
- 1 cup chopped green pepper
- 1/3 cup chopped onion
- 3 garlic cloves, peeled and thinly sliced
- 1/4 teaspoon salt
- 1/4 teaspoon dried oregano
- 1/8 teaspoon crushed red pepper flakes
- 1/8 teaspoon pepper
- 1/4 cup olive oil
- 1 package (2 pounds) frozen cooked small shrimp, thawed
- 1/2 cup shredded Parmesan cheese

Cook linguine according to package directions. Meanwhile, in a Dutch oven, saute the peppers, onion, garlic and seasonings in oil until the vegetables are tender.

Add the shrimp; cook and stir 2-3 minutes longer or until heated through. Drain linguine; toss with shrimp mixture. Sprinkle with cheese. YIELD: **8 SERVINGS.**

Citrus Grilled Salmon

Citrus Grilled Salmon

PREP: **10 MIN. + MARINATING** GRILL: **15 MIN.**

I grow my own oranges, so I wanted to try a main-dish recipe where the citrus flavor really comes through. It's definitely one of our favorites.

Margaret Pache ✳ Mesa, Arizona

- 1/2 cup orange juice
- 1/2 cup honey
- 2 teaspoons prepared horseradish
- 2 teaspoons teriyaki sauce
- 1 teaspoon grated orange peel
- 1 salmon fillet (about 2-1/2 pounds)

In a small bowl, combine orange juice, honey, horseradish, teriyaki sauce and orange peel; mix well. Pour 2/3 cup into a large resealable plastic bag; add salmon. Seal bag and turn to coat; refrigerate for at least 2 hours. Cover and refrigerate remaining marinade.

Coat grill rack with cooking spray before starting grill. Drain and discard marinade from salmon. Place salmon skin side down on grill rack.

Grill, covered, over medium heat for 5 minutes. Brush with some of the reserved marinade. Grill 10-15 minutes longer or until fish flakes easily with a fork, basting occasionally with remaining marinade. **YIELD: 6-8 SERVINGS.**

Seafood Pizza

PREP: **30 MIN.** BAKE: **15 MIN. + STANDING**

I adapted this rich treat from a friend's seafood enchilada dish. The thick, creamy cheese sauce is an ideal match for the scallops, shrimp and imitation crabmeat.

Sara Watters ✳ Boscobel, Wisconsin

- 1 package (6-1/2 ounces) pizza crust mix
- 3 tablespoons butter, *divided*
- 2 tablespoons all-purpose flour
- 3/4 cup milk
- 1/4 cup chicken broth
- 1/4 cup shredded Monterey Jack cheese
- 1/4 cup shredded Swiss cheese
- 1/4 pound uncooked bay scallops, chopped
- 1/4 pound cooked shrimp, peeled, deveined and chopped
- 1/4 pound imitation crabmeat, chopped
- 2 cups (8 ounces) shredded part-skim mozzarella cheese

Paprika, optional

Prepare the pizza dough according to package directions. Press onto a lightly greased 12-in. pizza pan; build up edges slightly. Prick dough thoroughly with a fork. Bake at 400° for 5-6 minutes or until crust is firm and begins to brown.

Meanwhile, in a large saucepan, melt 2 tablespoons butter over medium heat. Stir in flour until smooth. Gradually stir in milk and broth. Bring to a boil; cook and stir for 2 minutes or until thickened. Reduce the heat. Stir in Monterey Jack and Swiss cheeses until melted. Remove from the heat.

In a large skillet, melt the remaining butter over medium heat. Add scallops; cook and stir for 3-4 minutes or until firm and opaque. Stir in shrimp, crab and 3 tablespoons cheese sauce. Remove from the heat.

Spread remaining cheese sauce over the crust. Top with the seafood mixture, sprinkle with mozzarella cheese and paprika if desired. Bake for 13-16 minutes or until golden brown. Let stand for 5-10 minutes before cutting. **YIELD: 8 SLICES.**

Seafood Pizza

⏱ Curried Shrimp And Apples

PREP/TOTAL TIME: **30 MIN.**

Apples and shrimp, seasoned with curry powder, combine beautifully in this eye-appealing entree. Sometimes I use chicken instead of the shrimp.

Lynda Mack ✳ Neptune Beach, Florida

- 1 medium onion, chopped
- 2 celery ribs, chopped
- 1/4 cup butter, cubed
- 2 medium apples, sliced
- 2 teaspoons all-purpose flour
- 3/4 teaspoon curry powder
- 3/4 cup water
- 1 teaspoon chicken bouillon granules
- 3/4 pound uncooked medium shrimp, peeled and deveined

Hot cooked rice

In a large skillet, saute the onion and celery in butter for 2 minutes. Stir in apples; saute 1-2 minutes longer or until crisp-tender.

Sprinkle with flour and curry powder. Gradually whisk in water and bouillon until smooth. Add shrimp; bring to a boil. Reduce heat; simmer for 2-3 minutes or until shrimp turn pink and sauce is thickened. Serve with rice. **YIELD: 4 SERVINGS.**

Curried Shrimp and Apples

Grilled Salmon Steaks

Grilled Salmon Steaks

PREP: **10 MIN.** + MARINATING GRILL: **15 MIN.**

This is a terrific way to fix salmon...and it's so easy to do. The marinade mellows the fish flavor, and the dill sauce is a wonderful complement. I once served this recipe to 12 people from the Pacific Northwest who declared it was the best salmon they'd ever eaten!

Deb Essen ✳ Victor, Montana

- 2 tablespoons white wine vinegar
- 2 tablespoons sugar
- 1 tablespoon dill weed
- 3/4 teaspoon salt
- 1/8 to 1/4 teaspoon pepper, optional
- 4 salmon steaks (1 inch thick and 6 ounces *each*)

MUSTARD DILL SAUCE:

- 3 tablespoons mayonnaise
- 3 tablespoons Dijon mustard
- 3 tablespoons dill weed
- 1 tablespoon sugar
- 4 teaspoons white wine vinegar
- 1/4 teaspoon pepper, optional

In a large resealable plastic bag, combine the vinegar, sugar, dill, salt and pepper if desired. Add the salmon; seal the bag and turn to coat. Refrigerate for 1 hour, turning occasionally.

In a small bowl, combine sauce ingredients; cover and refrigerate until chilled.

Discard the marinade. Grill salmon, covered, over medium heat for 6-7 minutes on each side or until fish flakes easily with a fork. Serve with mustard dill sauce. **YIELD: 4 SERVINGS.**

Crawfish Fettuccine

PREP: **30 MIN.** COOK: **30 MIN.**

I have lived in this close-knit community all my life and enjoy cooking Cajun dishes, especially those with seafood. Along with a green salad and garlic bread, this dish is great for family gatherings.

Carolyn Lejeune ✳ Welsh, Louisiana

- 1 large onion, chopped
- 1 medium sweet red pepper, chopped
- 2/3 cup sliced green onions

Crawfish Fettuccine

1 celery rib, chopped
1 garlic clove, minced
1-1/4 cups butter, cubed
1/4 cup all-purpose flour
8 ounces process cheese (Velveeta), cubed
1 cup half-and-half cream
1 tablespoon chopped jalapeno pepper
1/2 teaspoon salt
8 ounces uncooked fettuccine
1-1/2 pounds frozen cooked crawfish tails, thawed or cooked medium shrimp, peeled and deveined

In a Dutch oven, saute the onion, red pepper, green onions, celery and garlic in butter for 5 minutes or until vegetables are crisp-tender. Stir in flour until blended; cook and stir for 2 minutes. Add the cheese, cream, jalapeno and salt; cook and stir for 10 minutes or until mixture is thickened and cheese is melted.

Meanwhile, cook fettuccine according to package directions; drain. Stir fettuccine and crawfish into the vegetable mixture. Cook, uncovered, over medium heat for 10 minutes or until heated through, stirring occasionally. **YIELD: 8 SERVINGS.**

EDITOR'S NOTE: When cutting hot peppers, disposable gloves are recommended. Avoid touching your face.

Lemon Shrimp Stir-Fry

🦐 Lemon Shrimp Stir-Fry

PREP: **25 MIN.** COOK: **10 MIN.**

I got this stir-fry about 10 years ago from a friend. The tender shrimp and crisp-tender veggies are coated with a mild, lemony sauce that makes this a colorful keeper.

Caroline Elliott ✻ Grants Pass, Oregon

1 tablespoon cornstarch
1/2 teaspoon sugar
1/2 teaspoon chicken bouillon granules
1/4 teaspoon grated lemon peel
Dash pepper
1/2 cup water
4-1/2 teaspoons lemon juice
1/2 pound uncooked medium shrimp, peeled and deveined
1 tablespoon canola oil
3/4 cup sliced celery
1/2 medium green pepper, cut into strips
1/2 medium sweet red pepper, cut into strips
1 cup sliced fresh mushrooms
3/4 cup fresh sugar snap peas
1 green onion, sliced
1 cup hot cooked long grain rice

In a small bowl, combine first five ingredients. Stir in water and lemon juice until blended; set aside.

In a large skillet or wok, stir-fry shrimp in oil for 1-2 minutes or until no longer pink. Remove with a slotted spoon and keep warm. In the same pan, stir-fry the celery and peppers for 2 minutes. Add mushrooms, peas and onion; stir-fry 3-4 minutes longer or until vegetables are crisp-tender.

Stir cornstarch mixture and add to the pan. Bring to a boil; cook and stir for 2 minutes or until thickened. Add the shrimp; heat through. Serve with rice. **YIELD: 2 SERVINGS.**

Seafood Tortilla Lasagna

Seafood Tortilla Lasagna

PREP: **40 MIN.** BAKE: **30 MIN. + STANDING**

My husband and I enjoy lasagna, seafood and Mexican fare. One evening, I combined all three into this deliciously different entree. It certainly is a tempting, memorable change of pace from traditional Italian-style lasagnas.

Sharon Sawicki * Carol Stream, Illinois

- 1 jar (20 ounces) picante sauce
- 1-1/2 pounds uncooked medium shrimp, peeled and deveined
- 4 to 6 garlic cloves, minced
- 1/8 teaspoon cayenne pepper
- 1 tablespoon olive oil
- 1/3 cup butter
- 1/3 cup all-purpose flour
- 1 can (14-1/2 ounces) chicken broth
- 1/2 cup heavy whipping cream
- 15 corn tortillas (6 inches), warmed
- 1 package (16 ounces) imitation crabmeat, flaked
- 3 cups (12 ounces) shredded Colby-Monterey Jack cheese

Place the picante sauce in a blender; cover and process until smooth. Set side. In a large skillet cook the shrimp, garlic and cayenne in oil for about 3 minutes or until shrimp turn pink; remove and set aside.

In the same skillet, melt the butter. Stir in flour until smooth. Gradually add broth. Bring to a boil; cook and stir for 2 minutes or until thickened. Reduce heat. Stir in cream and picante sauce; heat through.

Spread 1/2 cup of sauce in a greased 13-in. x 9-in. baking dish. Layer with six tortillas, half of the shrimp, crab and white sauce and 1-1/4 cups cheese. Repeat the layers. Tear or cut remaining tortillas; arrange over the cheese. Sprinkle with remaining cheese.

Bake, uncovered, at 375° for 30-35 minutes or until bubbly. Let stand 15 minutes before cutting. YIELD: **12 SERVINGS.**

Shrimp-Stuffed Sole

PREP/TOTAL TIME: **15 MIN.**

If you like stuffed fish, this recipe is the way to go. It's so easy to assemble and cooks in just a few minutes in the microwave. Try it with chicken instead of sole, if you prefer, for a meal that's equally good.

Robert Bishop * Lexington, Kentucky

- 4 sole fillets, halved lengthwise
- 1 tablespoon lemon juice
- 1/8 teaspoon onion salt *or* onion powder
- 1/4 cup butter, melted, *divided*
- 1 can (6 ounces) small shrimp, rinsed and drained
- 1/3 cup milk
- 1/4 cup finely chopped celery
- 2 teaspoons minced fresh parsley
- 1 cup cubed bread, toasted

Dash paprika

Sprinkle the fillets with lemon juice and onion salt; set aside. Pour 2 tablespoons butter into an 8-in. square microwave-safe dish. Add the shrimp, milk, celery and parsley. Cover and microwave on high for 1 to 1-1/2 minutes or until celery is tender. Stir in bread cubes.

Spoon shrimp mixture onto fillets. Starting with a short side, roll up each and secure with toothpicks. Place in a greased shallow microwave-safe dish. Brush with the remaining butter; sprinkle with paprika.

Cover and microwave on high for 4-6 minutes or until fish flakes easily with a fork. Let stand for 5 minutes before serving. Discard toothpicks. YIELD: **4 SERVINGS.**

EDITOR'S NOTE: This recipe was tested in a 1,100-watt microwave.

Swordfish Shrimp Kabobs

PREP: **20 MIN.** + **MARINATING** GRILL: **10 MIN.**

I love beef and lamb kabobs, but my doctor says I need to eat more fish. Since I also love grilling, these kabobs are a healthy alternative. They're great year-round.

Weda Mosellie ✳ Phillipsburg, New Jersey

1/4   cup olive oil

2   tablespoons balsamic vinegar

1/2   teaspoon crushed red pepper flakes

1/2   teaspoon dried oregano

1/4   teaspoon salt

1/8   teaspoon pepper

1/2   pound swordfish steak, skin removed and cut into 1-inch chunks

8   uncooked large shrimp, peeled and deveined

8   cherry tomatoes

1/2   medium red onion, cut into 4 wedges

1/2   medium sweet yellow pepper, cut into 8 chunks

Shrimp-Stuffed Sole

In a small bowl, combine the oil, vinegar and seasonings. Place 3 tablespoons in a large resealable plastic bag; add the swordfish and shrimp. Seal bag and turn to coat; refrigerate for up to 1 hour. Set remaining marinade aside for basting.

On four metal or soaked wooden skewers, thread the swordfish, tomatoes, shrimp, onion and yellow pepper.

Coat grill rack with cooking spray before starting grill. Grill the kabobs, uncovered, over medium heat for 3 minutes, turning once. Baste with some of reserved marinade. Grill 3-4 minutes longer or until fish flakes easily with a fork and shrimp turn pink, turning and basting frequently. **YIELD: 2 SERVINGS.**

Swordfish Shrimp Kabobs

Bacon Shrimp Creole

Bacon Shrimp Creole

PREP: 25 MIN. COOK: 45 MIN.

This dish is a compilation of two Creole recipes that I found in my mother's New Orleans cookbooks. The bacon adds some smoky flavor, and the cayenne gives it a bit of spice.

Jan Tucker ✳ Virginia Beach, Virginia

- 3/4 cup chopped onion
- 2 celery ribs, chopped
- 1/2 cup chopped green pepper
- 2 tablespoons olive oil
- 3 garlic cloves, minced
- 1 can (14-1/2 ounces) diced tomatoes, undrained
- 1 can (8 ounces) tomato sauce
- 3/4 cup cold water, *divided*
- 1/4 cup crumbled cooked bacon
- 1 tablespoon dried parsley flakes
- 1 teaspoon sugar
- 1/2 teaspoon salt
- 1/2 teaspoon dried thyme
- 1/2 teaspoon curry powder
- 1/2 teaspoon pepper
- 1/4 teaspoon cayenne pepper
- 1 tablespoon all-purpose flour
- 1-1/2 pounds uncooked medium shrimp, peeled and deveined
- 3 cups hot cooked long grain rice

In a Dutch oven, saute the onion, celery and green pepper in oil until tender. Add garlic; saute 1 minute longer. Add tomatoes, tomato sauce, 1/2 cup water, bacon, parsley, sugar, salt, thyme, curry powder, pepper and cayenne. Bring to a boil. Reduce heat; cover and simmer for 30 minutes.

Combine flour and remaining water until smooth; gradually stir into tomato mixture. Bring to a boil; cook and stir for 1-2 minutes or until thickened. Reduce heat; add the shrimp. Simmer, uncovered, for 5 minutes or until shrimp turn pink. Serve with rice. **YIELD: 6 SERVINGS.**

NUTRITION FACTS: 3/4 cup shrimp creole with 1/2 cup rice equals 292 calories, 7 g fat (1 g saturated fat), 171 mg cholesterol, 814 mg sodium, 33 g carbohydrate, 3 g fiber, 24 g protein. **DIABETIC EXCHANGES:** 3 very lean meat, 2 vegetable, 1-1/2 starch, 1 fat.

Cheddar Salmon Quiche

Cheddar Salmon Quiche

PREP: **15 MIN.** BAKE: **1 HOUR + STANDING**

My mother-in-law shared this cheesy salmon dish with me. It dresses up convenient canned salmon in a very satisfying way. We enjoy this pretty quiche frequently during Lent.

Jane Horn ✳ Bellevue, Ohio

- 1 cup all-purpose flour
- 1/4 teaspoon salt
- 3 tablespoons cold butter
- 3 tablespoons shortening
- 1/4 cup milk

FILLING:

- 1 can (14-3/4 ounces) salmon, drained, bones and skin removed
- 1 cup (4 ounces) shredded cheddar cheese
- 1/4 cup chopped green pepper
- 1/4 cup chopped onion
- 1 tablespoon all-purpose flour
- 1/2 teaspoon salt
- 1/8 teaspoon pepper
- 3 eggs
- 1-1/4 cups milk

In a large bowl, combine the flour and salt; cut in butter and shortening until crumbly. Stir in milk.

On a floured surface, roll dough into a 10-in. circle. Transfer to an ungreased 9-in. pie plate or quiche dish. Trim and flute edges. Bake at 350° for 10 minutes.

In a large bowl, combine the salmon, cheese, green pepper, onion, flour, salt and pepper; spoon into crust. Combine the eggs and milk; pour over salmon mixture.

Bake for 50-55 minutes or until a knife inserted near the center comes out clean. Let stand for 10 minutes before cutting. **YIELD: 6 SERVINGS.**

Garlic Shrimp Stir-Fry

Garlic Shrimp Stir-Fry

PREP/TOTAL TIME: **15 MIN.**

This entree tastes wonderful and is pretty enough to serve to company. Most of the preparation can be done in advance. Tender shrimp, colorful sweet peppers and crunchy snow peas give it a variety of interesting tastes and textures.

Irene Lalevee ✳ River Vale, New Jersey

- 4 garlic cloves, minced
- 2 tablespoons butter
- 1 pound uncooked medium shrimp, peeled and deveined
- 6 ounces fresh snow peas
- 1/2 cup julienned sweet red pepper
- 1/2 cup julienned sweet yellow pepper
- 3 tablespoons minced fresh basil *or* 1 tablespoon dried basil
- 3 tablespoons minced fresh parsley
- 1/2 teaspoon salt
- 1/4 teaspoon pepper
- 1/4 cup chicken broth

Hot cooked rice

In a large skillet, saute garlic in the butter until tender. Add the shrimp, peas, peppers, basil, parsley, salt and pepper. Stir-fry for 5 minutes or until shrimp turn pink and vegetables are crisp-tender. Add broth. Cook 1 minute longer or until heated through. Serve with the rice. **YIELD: 4 SERVINGS.**

Creole Flounder with Seafood Sauce

Creole Flounder with Seafood Sauce

PREP: **25 MIN.** BROIL: **10 MIN.**

This is one of my family's favorite Creole dishes. The recipe can be made with flounder or sole fillets, but I sometimes use locally caught kingfish bass.

Melinda Sue Daenen ✳ Pineville, Louisiana

- 1 cup diced onion
- 1 cup chopped green pepper
- 2 garlic cloves, minced
- 1/2 cup minced fresh parsley
- 1/2 cup butter, cubed
- 1/4 cup all-purpose flour
- 2 cups half-and-half cream
- 8 ounces Mexican process cheese (Velveeta), cubed
- 2 tablespoons lemon *or* lime juice
- 2 cans (6 ounces *each*) crabmeat, drained, flaked and cartilage removed
- 1/4 cup Creole mustard *or* other spicy mustard
- 2 pounds flounder fillets
- 1-1/2 teaspoons Creole seasoning
- 2 pounds cooked shrimp, peeled and deveined

In a large skillet, saute the onion, green pepper, garlic and parsley in butter until tender. Stir in flour until blended. Gradually add the cream. Bring to a boil; cook and stir for 2 minutes or until thickened. Reduce heat. Stir in cheese and lemon juice; cook and stir until the cheese is melted. Add crab. Cover and keep warm.

Spread mustard on both sides of the fillets. Sprinkle with the Creole seasoning. Place on a greased broiler pan. Broil 4-6 in. from the heat for 3-5 minutes on each side or until fish flakes easily with a fork. Top each fillet with four to five shrimp; serve over the crab sauce. **YIELD: 4-5 SERVINGS.**

EDITOR'S NOTE: The following spices may be substituted for 1 teaspoon Creole seasoning: 1/4 teaspoon *each* salt, garlic powder and paprika; and a pinch *each* of dried thyme, ground cumin and cayenne pepper.

Shrimp with Style

PREP/TOTAL TIME: **25 MIN.**

I created this supper standout one day with just the items in my refrigerator at the time. One taste will leave your mouth watering for more! My family craves this dinner any time of year because it's so delectable and light.

Cyndi McLaughlin ✳ Pinon Pines, California

- 1 package (9 ounces) refrigerated angel hair pasta
- 1/2 pound sliced fresh mushrooms
- 1-1/2 teaspoons minced garlic
- 1 cup butter, cubed
- 1 pound uncooked medium shrimp, peeled and deveined
- 2 packages (3 ounces *each*) julienned sun-dried tomatoes (not packed in oil)
- 1 package (2-1/4 ounces) slivered almonds, toasted
- 1/2 cup crumbled feta cheese
- 1/2 cup minced fresh parsley
- 3 tablespoons white wine *or* chicken broth
- 2 teaspoons lemon juice
- 1/2 teaspoon salt
- 1/2 teaspoon pepper
- 1/2 cup shredded Parmesan cheese

Cook pasta according to the package directions. Meanwhile, in a large skillet, saute mushrooms and garlic in butter for 2 minutes. Add shrimp; cook and stir for 5-7 minutes or until the shrimp turn pink.

Stir in the tomatoes, almonds, feta cheese, parsley, wine, lemon juice, salt and pepper; cook for 3-5 minutes or until heated through. Drain

the pasta and place in a serving bowl; top with the shrimp mixture and the Parmesan cheese.
YIELD: 5 SERVINGS.

Shrimp with Style

Cajun Shrimp Skewers

PREP: **20 MIN. + MARINATING** GRILL: **5 MIN.**

Fresh herbs and Cajun seasoning enhance these delicious shrimp, accompanied by a spicy butter sauce. You can serve them as an entree or as appetizers. You'll love them either way!

Dwayne Veretto ✳ Roswell, New Mexico

- 3/4 cup canola oil
- 1 medium onion, finely chopped
- 2 tablespoons Cajun seasoning
- 6 garlic cloves, minced
- 2 teaspoons ground cumin
- 1 teaspoon minced fresh rosemary
- 1 teaspoon minced fresh thyme
- 2 pounds uncooked large shrimp, peeled and deveined

CAJUN BUTTER:
- 1 cup butter, cubed
- 1 teaspoon minced fresh basil
- 1 teaspoon minced fresh tarragon
- 1 teaspoon Cajun seasoning
- 1/2 teaspoon garlic powder
- 3 drops hot pepper sauce

In a small bowl, combine the oil, onion, Cajun seasoning, garlic, cumin, rosemary and thyme. Place the shrimp in a large resealable plastic bag; add half of the marinade. Seal bag and turn to coat; refrigerate for 1-2 hours. Cover and refrigerate remaining marinade for basting.

In a small saucepan, combine the Cajun butter ingredients; heat until butter is melted. Keep warm.

Drain and discard marinade from shrimp. Thread shrimp onto eight metal or soaked wooden skewers. Grill, uncovered, over medium heat for 2-4 minutes on each side or until shrimp turn pink, basting once with reserved marinade. Serve with Cajun butter. **YIELD: 8 SERVINGS.**

Cajun Shrimp Skewers

Ravioli with Shrimp Tomato Sauce

◐ Ravioli with Shrimp Tomato Sauce

PREP/TOTAL TIME: **30 MIN.**

I came up with this recipe after I sampled a similar dish when my husband and I went out to dinner to celebrate our 25th anniversary. We enjoyed it so much that I now make it at home.

Nettie Smith ✳ Loveland, Colorado

1/2 cup chopped onion
2 tablespoons butter
2 tablespoons all-purpose flour
1 can (14-1/2 ounces) Italian stewed tomatoes
1 tablespoon brown sugar
1 bay leaf
1 whole clove
1/2 teaspoon dried basil
1/2 teaspoon salt
1/8 to 1/4 teaspoon pepper
2 packages (9 ounces *each*) fresh or frozen cheese ravioli
1-1/2 cups heavy whipping cream
1/2 pound cooked medium shrimp, peeled and deveined
1 tablespoon grated Parmesan cheese
1 tablespoon minced chives

In a large skillet, saute the onion in butter until tender. Stir in flour until blended. Bring to a boil; cook and stir until thickened.

Place tomatoes in a blender; cover and process until pureed. Add to onion mixture. Stir in the brown sugar, bay leaf, clove, basil, salt and pepper. Bring to a boil. Reduce heat; cover and simmer for 10 minutes.

Meanwhile, cook the ravioli according to package directions. Remove and discard the bay leaf and clove from the sauce. Reduce the heat; gradually stir in cream. Add the shrimp; heat through. Drain ravioli; top with sauce, Parmesan cheese and chives. YIELD: **5 SERVINGS.**

Mediterranean Vegetable Pasta, PAGE 282

66 *I created this fast-to-fix recipe to use up excess zucchini from our garden, and at the same time, to make a pasta dish that was lower in calories.* 99

Jan Clark
New Florence, Missouri

MEATLESS

meatless

Grilled Chiles Rellenos

PREP: **45 MIN.** GRILL: **10 MIN.**

Here's a healthy version of one of my favorite Mexican dishes. The grilled peppers go great with Spanish rice, gazpacho or a refreshing salad with jicama and citrus.

Lori Nelson ✳ Austin, Texas

- 1 cup (8 ounces) sour cream
- 2 tablespoons lime juice
- 1/2 cup minced fresh cilantro, *divided*
- 1 small onion, finely chopped
- 1 garlic clove, minced
- 1 tablespoon butter
- 1 small yellow summer squash, finely chopped
- 1 small zucchini, finely chopped
- 1 jalapeno pepper, seeded and finely chopped
- 1 large portobello mushroom cap, finely chopped
- 1 can (15 ounces) black beans, rinsed and drained
- 2 cups (8 ounces) shredded Mexican cheese blend, *divided*
- 1 cup frozen corn, thawed
- 1 teaspoon ground cumin
- 1/2 teaspoon salt
- 1/4 teaspoon pepper
- 4 large poblano peppers, halved and seeded

In a small bowl, combine the sour cream, lime juice and 1/4 cup cilantro. Cover and refrigerate until serving.

In a large skillet, saute onion and garlic in butter until onion is tender. Add the yellow squash, zucchini and jalapeno; cook and stir over medium heat for 2 minutes. Add the mushroom; cook and stir for 2 minutes.

Grilled Chiles Rellenos

Stir in the beans, 1-1/2 cups cheese, corn, cumin, salt, pepper and remaining cilantro. Remove from the heat. Spoon into the pepper halves; sprinkle with remaining cheese.

Prepare grill for indirect heat, using a drip pan. Place peppers over pan. Grill, covered, over indirect medium heat for 10-14 minutes or until tender. Serve with the sour cream sauce. **YIELD: 4 SERVINGS.**

EDITOR'S NOTE: When cutting hot peppers, disposable gloves are recommended. Avoid touching your face.

Cheese Enchiladas

Cheese Enchiladas

PREP: **25 MIN.** BAKE: **25 MIN.**

You won't bring home leftovers when you make these easy enchiladas. With a homemade tomato sauce and cheesy filling, they always go fast. You can substitute any type of cheese you wish.

Ashley Schackow ✳ Defiance, Ohio

- 2 cans (15 ounces *each*) tomato sauce
- 1-1/3 cups water
- 2 tablespoons chili powder
- 2 garlic cloves, minced
- 1 teaspoon dried oregano
- 1/2 teaspoon ground cumin
- 16 flour tortillas (8 inches), warmed
- 4 cups (16 ounces) shredded Monterey Jack cheese
- 2-1/2 cups (10 ounces) shredded cheddar cheese, *divided*
- 2 medium onions, finely chopped
- 1 cup (8 ounces) sour cream
- 1/4 cup minced fresh parsley
- 1/2 teaspoon salt
- 1/2 teaspoon pepper

Shredded lettuce, sliced ripe olives and additional sour cream, optional

In a large saucepan, combine the tomato sauce, water, chili powder, garlic, oregano and cumin. Bring to a boil. Reduce heat; simmer, uncovered, for 4-5 minutes or until thickened, stirring occasionally. Spoon 2 tablespoons sauce over each tortilla.

In a large bowl, combine the Monterey Jack, 2 cups cheddar cheese, onions, sour cream, parsley, salt and pepper. Place about 1/3 cup down center of each tortilla. Roll up and place seam side down in two greased 13-in. x 9-in. baking dishes. Pour remaining sauce over top.

Bake, uncovered, at 350° for 20 minutes. Sprinkle with remaining cheddar cheese. Bake 4-5 minutes longer or until cheese is melted. Garnish with lettuce, olives and sour cream if desired. YIELD: **16 ENCHILADAS.**

🕐 Mediterranean 🍴 Vegetable Pasta

PREP/TOTAL TIME: **25 MIN.**

I created this fast-to-fix recipe to use up excess zucchini from our garden, and at the same time, to make a pasta dish that was lower in calories.

Jan Clark ✳ New Florence, Missouri

- 3 ounces uncooked angel hair pasta
- 1 cup chopped zucchini
- 1/2 cup chopped fresh mushrooms
- 1/3 cup chopped green pepper
- 1/4 cup chopped onion
- 1 garlic clove, minced
- 2 teaspoons olive oil
- 1 cup canned Italian diced tomatoes
- 6 pitted ripe olives, halved
- 1/8 teaspoon pepper
- 1/4 cup crumbled reduced-fat feta cheese
- 1 tablespoon shredded Parmesan cheese

Cook pasta according to package directions. Meanwhile, in a large skillet, saute the zucchini, mushrooms, green pepper, onion and garlic in oil until vegetables are crisp-tender. Stir in the tomatoes, olives and pepper; heat through.

Drain the pasta; divide between two plates. Top with vegetable mixture and the cheeses. YIELD: **2 SERVINGS.**

NUTRITION FACTS: 2 cups equals 321 calories, 9 g fat (2 g saturated fat), 7 mg cholesterol, 800 mg sodium, 49 g carbohydrate, 4 g fiber, 12 g protein.

🌸 Roasted Pepper Ravioli Bake

PREP: **25 MIN. + STANDING** BAKE: **30 MIN.**

I serve this dish with a green salad and homemade Italian herb bread. The cheesy casserole always receives compliments and requests for the recipe.

Carol Poindexter ✳ Norridge, Illinois

- 2 *each* medium green, sweet red and yellow peppers
- 1 package (25 ounces) frozen cheese ravioli
- 1 tablespoon olive oil
- 1 teaspoon sugar
- 1/4 teaspoon salt
- 2 cups meatless spaghetti sauce, *divided*
- 4 ounces sliced part-skim mozzarella cheese

Place peppers on a broiler pan. Broil 4 in. from the heat until skins blister, about 6-8 minutes. With tongs, rotate peppers a quarter turn. Broil and rotate until all sides are blistered and blackened. Immediately place the peppers in a bowl; cover and let stand for 15-20 minutes.

Meanwhile, cook the ravioli according to package directions; drain. Peel off and discard charred skin from peppers. Remove stems and seeds. Finely chop peppers; drain. In a large bowl, combine the peppers, oil, sugar and salt.

Spread 1-1/2 cups spaghetti sauce in a 13-in. x 9-in. baking dish coated with cooking spray. Layer with ravioli, pepper mixture and cheese. Top with the remaining spaghetti sauce.

Cover and bake at 350° for 15 minutes. Uncover; bake 15-20 minutes longer or until heated through. YIELD: **8 SERVINGS.**

NUTRITION FACTS: 1 serving equals 335 calories, 11 g fat (5 g saturated fat), 44 mg cholesterol, 415 mg sodium, 44 g carbohydrate, 5 g fiber, 16 g protein. DIABETIC EXCHANGES: 2-1/2 starch, 1-1/2 fat, 1 lean meat, 1 vegetable.

1st place

Mediterranean Vegetable Pasta

Roasted Pepper Ravioli Bake

Vegetarian Linguine

⏱ Vegetarian Linguine

PREP/TOTAL TIME: **30 MIN.**

Looking for a tasty alternative to meat-and-potatoes meals? Try this colorful pasta dish, which is the brainchild of my oldest son. It's a stick-to-the-ribs supper that takes advantage of fresh mushrooms, zucchini and other vegetables as well as basil and provolone cheese.

Jane Bone ✳ Cape Coral, Florida

- 6 ounces uncooked linguine
- 2 medium zucchini, thinly sliced
- 1/2 pound fresh mushrooms, sliced
- 2 green onions, chopped
- 1 garlic clove, minced
- 2 tablespoons butter
- 1 tablespoon olive oil
- 1 large tomato, chopped
- 2 teaspoons minced fresh basil
- 1/2 teaspoon salt
- 1/4 teaspoon pepper
- 4 ounces provolone cheese, shredded
- 3 tablespoons shredded Parmesan cheese

Cook linguine according to package directions. Meanwhile, in a large skillet, saute the zucchini, mushrooms, onions and garlic in butter and oil for 3-5 minutes. Add the tomato, basil, salt and pepper; cover and simmer for 3 minutes. Drain linguine; add to vegetable mixture. Sprinkle with cheeses and toss to coat. **YIELD: 6 SERVINGS.**

⏱ Mushroom Burgers

PREP/TOTAL TIME: **30 MIN.**

Ready to turn over a new burger? I guarantee no one will be missing the beef after they've tasted these vegetarian burgers. They're moist, tender and full of flavor.

Denise Hollebeke ✳ Penhold, Alberta

- 2 eggs, lightly beaten
- 2 cups finely chopped fresh mushrooms
- 1/2 cup dry bread crumbs
- 1/2 cup shredded cheddar cheese
- 1/2 cup finely chopped onion
- 1/4 cup all-purpose flour
- 1/2 teaspoon salt
- 1/4 teaspoon dried thyme
- 1/4 teaspoon pepper
- 1 tablespoon canola oil
- 4 whole wheat hamburger buns, split

In a large bowl, combine the first nine ingredients. Shape into four patties.

In a large skillet, cook patties in oil over medium heat for 3 minutes on each side or until crisp and lightly browned. Serve on buns. **YIELD: 4 SERVINGS.**

Mushroom Burgers

🌿 Black Bean Tortilla Pie

PREP: **50 MIN.** BAKE: **15 MIN.**

I found this Southwestern entree some time ago but decreased the cheese and increased the amount of herbs originally called for.

Wendy Kelly ✳ Voorheesville, New York

- 1 medium onion, chopped
- 1 medium green pepper, chopped
- 3 garlic cloves, minced
- 1 teaspoon ground cumin
- 1/4 teaspoon pepper
- 1 tablespoon olive oil
- 2 cans (15 ounces *each*) black beans, rinsed and drained
- 1 can (14-1/2 ounces) vegetable broth
- 1 package (10 ounces) frozen corn, thawed
- 4 green onions, thinly sliced
- 4 flour tortillas (8 inches)
- 1 cup (4 ounces) shredded reduced-fat cheddar cheese, *divided*

In a large skillet, saute the onion, green pepper, garlic, cumin and pepper in oil. Add beans and broth. Bring to a boil; cook until the liquid is reduced to about 1/3 cup. Stir in corn and green onions; remove from the heat.

Place one tortilla in a 9-in. springform pan coated with cooking spray. Layer with 1-1/2 cups bean mixture and 1/4 cup cheese. Repeat layers twice. Top with remaining tortilla. Place pan on a baking sheet.

Bake, uncovered, at 400° for 15-20 minutes or until heated through. Remove sides of pan. Sprinkle with the remaining cheese. Cut into wedges. **YIELD: 6 SERVINGS.**

NUTRITION FACTS: 1 wedge equals 353 calories, 9 g fat (3 g saturated fat), 14 mg cholesterol, 842 mg sodium, 53 g carbohydrate, 8 g fiber, 17 g protein. DIABETIC EXCHANGES: 3 starch, 1 very lean meat, 1 vegetable, 1 fat.

Black Bean Tortilla Pie

Greek Pizzas

Greek Pizzas

PREP/TOTAL TIME: 30 MIN.

Pita breads make crispy crusts for these individual pizzas. Topped with feta and ricotta cheese as well as spinach, tomatoes and basil, the fast pizzas are a hit with everyone who tries them.

Doris Allers ✴ Portage, Michigan

- 4 pita breads (6 inches)
- 1 cup reduced-fat ricotta cheese
- 1/2 teaspoon garlic powder
- 1 package (10 ounces) frozen chopped spinach, thawed and squeezed dry
- 3 medium tomatoes, sliced
- 3/4 cup crumbled feta cheese
- 3/4 teaspoon dried basil

Place pita breads on a baking sheet. Combine the ricotta cheese and garlic powder; spread over pitas. Top with the spinach, tomatoes, feta cheese and basil.

Bake at 400° for 12-15 minutes or until bread is lightly browned. **YIELD: 4 SERVINGS.**

NUTRITION FACTS: 1 pizza equals 320 calories, 7 g fat (4 g saturated fat), 26 mg cholesterol, 642 mg sodium, 46 g carbohydrate, 6 g fiber, 17 g protein. DIABETIC EXCHANGES: 2 starch, 2 vegetable, 1 lean meat, 1 fat.

Over-the-Top Mac 'n' Cheese

Over-the-Top Mac 'n' Cheese

PREP: **15 MIN.** BAKE: **40 MIN.**

This delicious dish is the ultimate comfort food. With a blend of five cheeses, it makes a beautiful entree or a special side. I served it at our Thanksgiving dinner, and it received rave reviews.

Connie McDowell ✴ Greenwood, Delaware

- 1 package (16 ounces) elbow macaroni
- 2 ounces Muenster cheese, shredded
- 1/2 cup *each* shredded mild cheddar, sharp cheddar and Monterey Jack cheese
- 1/2 cup plus 1 tablespoon butter, *divided*
- 2 cups half-and-half cream
- 2 eggs, lightly beaten
- 1 cup cubed process cheese (Velveeta)
- 1/4 teaspoon seasoned salt
- 1/8 teaspoon pepper

Cook the macaroni according to the package directions. Meanwhile, in a small bowl, combine the Muenster, mild cheddar, sharp cheddar and Monterey Jack cheeses; set aside.

In a large saucepan, melt 1/2 cup butter over medium heat. Stir in the cream, eggs, process cheese, seasoned salt, pepper and 1-1/2 cups of the cheese mixture. Drain the pasta; add to the cheese sauce and stir to coat.

Transfer to a greased 2-1/2-qt. baking dish. Sprinkle with the remaining cheese mixture and dot with remaining butter. Bake, uncovered, at 350° for 40-45 minutes or until a thermometer reads 160°. **YIELD: 7 SERVINGS.**

❈ Vegetable Lentil Stew

PREP: 20 MIN. COOK: 40 MIN.

This delicious stew is nothing but good for you! The chunky mixture, seasoned with chili powder and cumin, is chock-full of hearty beans, lentils and other veggies. Steaming bowls of it make a warm and satisfying supper.

Vi Toews ✳ Bluffton, Alberta

- 4 cups reduced-sodium V8 *or* tomato juice
- 2 cans (14-1/2 ounces *each*) Italian stewed tomatoes
- 1 can (16 ounces) kidney beans, rinsed and drained
- 1 can (15 ounces) garbanzo beans *or* chickpeas, rinsed and drained
- 2 medium carrots, thinly sliced
- 2 medium potatoes, cubed
- 1 large onion, chopped
- 1 green pepper, chopped
- 1 sweet red pepper, chopped
- 1 cup dried lentils, rinsed
- 2 tablespoons minced fresh parsley
- 2 tablespoons chili powder
- 2 teaspoons dried basil
- 1 teaspoon garlic powder
- 1 teaspoon ground cumin
- 1 package (10 ounces) frozen chopped spinach, thawed

Vegetable Lentil Stew

TOPPING:

- 1/2 cup reduced-fat sour cream
- 1/2 cup reduced-fat plain yogurt
- 2 tablespoons minced chives

In a Dutch oven, combine first 15 ingredients. Bring to a boil. Reduce heat; cover and simmer for 35-40 minutes or until lentils and vegetables are tender.

Stir in the spinach; heat through. Combine topping ingredients; dollop about 1 tablespoon on each serving. **YIELD: 13 SERVINGS.**

NUTRITIONAL FACTS: 1 cup equals 216 calories, 2 g fat (0 saturated fat), 4 mg cholesterol, 392 mg sodium, 38 g carbohydrate, 12 g fiber, 12 g protein. DIABETIC EXCHANGES: 2 starch, 1 vegetable, 1/2 meat.

Fresh Tomato Basil Pizza

Fresh Tomato Basil Pizza

PREP: **30 MIN.** BAKE: **15 MIN.**

I crave this bruschetta-like pizza in spring, when I'm planting tomatoes in our garden. Slices make great appetizers when the tomatoes are ripe.

Jennifer Headlee ✳ Baxter, Iowa

  1 tube (8 ounces) refrigerated crescent rolls
  2 garlic cloves, minced
  1 tablespoon olive oil
1/2 cup chopped fresh basil
  8 ounces sliced provolone cheese
  4 medium tomatoes, thinly sliced
1/4 cup grated Parmesan cheese
1/4 teaspoon pepper

Unroll crescent dough into one long rectangle. Press into an ungreased 13-in. x 9-in. baking pan; seal seams and perforations. Bake at 375° for 14-16 minutes or until golden brown.

Meanwhile, in a skillet, saute the garlic in oil for 2 minutes. Reduce heat. Add basil; cook for 2 minutes or until heated through.

Arrange half of the provolone cheese over the crust. Layer with half of the tomatoes, basil mixture, Parmesan cheese and pepper. Repeat layers. Bake for 14-16 minutes or until cheese is melted. **YIELD: 6 SLICES (3 SERVINGS).**

Tortellini Spinach Casserole

PREP: **20 MIN.** BAKE: **20 MIN.**

Spinach gives this popular casserole a fresh taste that will delight even those who say they don't like spinach. Whenever I bring it to a gathering, it doesn't sit around long.

Barbara Kellen ✳ Antioch, Illinois

  2 packages (10 ounces *each*) frozen cheese tortellini
  1 pound sliced fresh mushrooms
  1 teaspoon garlic powder
1/4 teaspoon onion powder
1/4 teaspoon pepper
1/2 cup butter, *divided*
  1 can (12 ounces) evaporated milk
  1 block (8 ounces) brick cheese, cubed
  3 packages (10 ounces *each*) frozen chopped spinach, thawed and squeezed dry
  2 cups (8 ounces) shredded part-skim mozzarella cheese

Tortellini Spinach Casserole

Cook tortellini according to package directions. Meanwhile, in a large skillet, saute the mushrooms, garlic powder, onion powder and pepper in 1/4 cup butter until mushrooms are tender. Remove and keep warm.

In the same skillet, combine the milk and remaining butter. Bring to a gentle boil. Reduce heat; stir in brick cheese. Cook and stir until smooth. Drain the tortellini; place in a large bowl. Stir in the mushroom mixture and spinach. Add cheese sauce and toss to coat.

Transfer to a greased 3-qt. baking dish; sprinkle with the mozzarella cheese. Cover and bake at 350° for 15 minutes. Uncover; bake 5-10 minutes longer or until heated through and the cheese is melted. **YIELD: 12 SERVINGS.**

Veggie Lasagna

Veggie Lasagna

PREP: 70 MIN. BAKE: 1-1/4 HOURS + STANDING

No one will even miss the meat when you serve this vegetable-rich lasagna. It has a fresh, full-bodied flavor. To save time, prepare the carrot and spinach layers in advance.

Mary Jane Jones ✳ Williamstown, West Virginia

- 1 package (16 ounces) frozen sliced carrots
- 1/4 cup finely chopped onion
- 2 tablespoons butter
- 1 cup ricotta cheese
- 1/4 teaspoon *each* salt and pepper

SPINACH LAYER:
- 2 shallots, chopped
- 1 tablespoon olive oil
- 2 packages (10 ounces *each*) frozen chopped spinach, thawed and squeezed dry
- 1 cup ricotta cheese
- 1 egg
- 1/4 teaspoon *each* salt and pepper

EGGPLANT LAYER:
- 1 medium eggplant, peeled and cut into 1/4-inch slices
- 3 garlic cloves, minced
- 6 tablespoons olive oil
- 1/2 teaspoon salt
- 2-1/2 cups marinara sauce
- 12 lasagna noodles, cooked and drained
- 1/4 cup minced fresh basil

- 4 cups (16 ounces) part-skim shredded mozzarella cheese
- 3 cups grated Parmesan cheese

Cook carrots according to package directions; drain and cool. In a small skillet, saute onion in butter until tender. In a food processor, puree the carrots, onion, ricotta, salt and pepper.

In same skillet, saute shallots in oil until tender. In a food processor, puree the shallots, spinach, ricotta, egg, salt and pepper.

In a large skillet, cook eggplant and garlic in oil over medium heat in batches for 7-10 minutes or until tender; drain. Sprinkle with salt.

Spread 1/2 cup marinara sauce in a greased 13-in. x 9-in. baking dish. Layer with the four noodles, the carrot mixture, 1/2 cup sauce, 1 tablespoon basil, 1 cup mozzarella and 3/4 cup Parmesan. Top with four noodles, eggplant, 1/2 cup sauce, 1 tablespoon basil, 1 cup mozzarella and 3/4 cup Parmesan.

Layer with the remaining noodles, spinach mixture, 1/2 cup sauce, 1 tablespoon basil, 1 cup mozzarella and 3/4 cup Parmesan. Top with the remaining sauce, basil, mozzarella and the Parmesan (dish will be full).

Cover and bake at 350° for 1 hour. Uncover; bake 15 minutes longer or until bubbly. Let stand 15 minutes before serving. **YIELD: 12 SERVINGS.**

Thai Tofu Lettuce Wraps

 Thai Tofu Lettuce Wraps

PREP/TOTAL TIME: **25 MIN.**

I couldn't keep this yummy, light lunch under wraps. The original recipe featured chicken, but I modified it for my vegetarian husband. Now both of us prefer the Thai-style tofu version.

Laureen Pittman ✳ Riverside, California

- 1/4 cup rice vinegar
- 1/4 cup canola oil
- 2 tablespoons lime juice
- 2 tablespoons mayonnaise
- 2 tablespoons creamy peanut butter
- 1 tablespoon brown sugar
- 1 tablespoon soy sauce
- 2 teaspoons minced fresh gingerroot
- 1 teaspoon sesame oil
- 1 teaspoon Thai chili sauce
- 1 garlic clove, peeled
- 1/2 cup minced fresh cilantro, *divided*
- 1 package (14 ounces) firm tofu, drained and cut into 1/2-inch cubes
- 1/2 cup chopped green onions
- 1/2 cup shredded carrots
- 1 small sweet red pepper, diced
- 3/4 cup dry roasted peanuts, chopped, *divided*
- 8 Bibb *or* Boston lettuce leaves

For dressing, in a blender, combine the first 11 ingredients; cover and process until smooth. Stir in 1/4 cup cilantro.

In a large bowl, combine the tofu, onions, carrots, red pepper, 1/2 cup peanuts and remaining cilantro. Add dressing and toss to coat. Divide among lettuce leaves; sprinkle with remaining peanuts. Fold lettuce over filling. **YIELD: 4 SERVINGS.**

Creamy Succotash, PAGE 300

" *This is a creation from my sister, Jenny. When I saw her make it, I didn't think the combination would be very tasty, but I changed my mind immediately once I ate it.* "

Shannon Koene
Blacksburg, Virginia

SIDES

sides

Just Delish Veggie Kabobs

PREP: **30 MIN. + MARINATING** GRILL: **10 MIN.**

I first tried these kabobs at my son's cottage a few years ago; they were a real hit. Invite your neighbors over for a grilling get-together and serve these wonderful skewers.

Agnes Ward ✳ Stratford, Ontario

8	small red potatoes, halved
3	tablespoons unsweetened apple juice
3	tablespoons red wine vinegar
2	tablespoons minced fresh basil
1	tablespoon Dijon mustard
1	tablespoon honey
1	tablespoon reduced-sodium soy sauce
2	teaspoons olive oil
2	garlic cloves, minced
1/4	teaspoon pepper
12	medium fresh mushrooms
1	large sweet red pepper, cut into 1-inch pieces
1	medium zucchini, cut into 1/2-inch slices

Place the potatoes in a steamer basket; place in a large saucepan over 1 in. of water. Bring to a boil; cover and steam for 7-9 minutes or just until tender. Cool.

In a large resealable plastic bag, combine the apple juice, vinegar, basil, Dijon mustard, honey, soy sauce, oil, garlic and pepper. Add the mushrooms, red pepper, zucchini and cooked potatoes. Seal bag and turn to coat; refrigerate for 2 hours.

Coat the grill rack with cooking spray before starting the grill. Drain and reserve marinade; thread vegetables onto four metal or soaked wooden skewers. Grill, covered, over medium heat for 10-15 minutes, turning and basting occasionally with the reserved marinade. **YIELD: 4 SERVINGS.**

NUTRITION FACTS: 1 kabob equals 168 calories, 3 g fat (trace saturated fat), 0 cholesterol, 258 mg sodium, 32 g carbohydrate, 4 g fiber, 5 g protein. DIABETIC EXCHANGES: 1-1/2 starch, 1 vegetable, 1/2 fat.

Just Delish Veggie Kabobs

Vegetable Brown Rice

🌀 Vegetable Brown Rice

PREP: **25 MIN.** COOK: **30 MIN.**

Loaded with carrots, onions and peas, this rice makes a terrific side dish, but it can even stand on its own as a light main course. Raisins offer a slight sweetness, and pecans add a little crunch.

Denith Hull ✳ Bethany, Oklahoma

2 cups water
1 cup uncooked brown rice
1/2 teaspoon dried basil
2 medium carrots, cut into thin 1-inch strips
1 cup chopped onion
9 green onions, cut into 1-inch strips
1/2 cup raisins
2 tablespoons olive oil
1 package (10 ounces) frozen peas, thawed
1 teaspoon salt
1 cup pecan halves, toasted

In a small saucepan, bring the water to a boil. Stir in rice and basil. Reduce heat to medium-low; cover and simmer for 30-35 minutes or until rice is tender and water is absorbed. Fluff with a fork.

In a large nonstick skillet, stir-fry the carrots, onion, green onions and raisins in oil for 5-7 minutes or until vegetables are lightly browned. Add the peas and salt. Cook for 1 minute or until vegetables are tender. Stir in pecans and rice; heat through. **YIELD: 9 SERVINGS.**

NUTRITION FACTS: 3/4 cup equals 242 calories, 11 g fat (1 g saturated fat), 0 cholesterol, 313 mg sodium, 32 g carbohydrate, 5 g fiber, 5 g protein. DIABETIC EXCHANGES: 2 fat, 1-1/2 starch, 1 vegetable, 1/2 fruit.

◑ Tomatoes with Horseradish Sauce

PREP/TOTAL TIME: **15 MIN.**

Lightly sauteed tomatoes and a tangy sauce make this a very tasty recipe. I occasionally use both red and green tomatoes to add even more color.

Phyllis Shaughnessy
Livonia, New York

Refrigerated butter-flavored spray

- 4 large tomatoes, sliced
- 3 tablespoons mayonnaise
- 2 tablespoons half-and-half cream
- 1 tablespoon prepared horseradish

Minced fresh parsley

Coat a large skillet with refrigerated butter-flavored spray. Heat skillet over medium heat. Add tomato slices; cook for 2-3 minutes on each side or until edges begin to brown.

In a small bowl, whisk the mayonnaise, cream and horseradish. Spoon over tomatoes. Sprinkle with parsley. **YIELD: 4 SERVINGS.**

1st place

Tomatoes with Horseradish Sauce

◑ Spicy Asparagus Spears

PREP/TOTAL TIME: **20 MIN.**

This no-fuss side gets its zippy taste from Cajun seasoning and crushed red pepper flakes. Even those who don't like asparagus will enjoy these buttery spears.

Marlies Kinnell ✳ Barrie, Ontario

- 2 tablespoons butter
- 1/2 teaspoon onion powder
- 1/2 teaspoon seasoned salt
- 1/2 teaspoon Cajun seasoning

Crushed red pepper flakes to taste

1-3/4 pounds fresh asparagus, trimmed

In a large skillet, melt butter. Stir in the onion powder, seasoned salt, Cajun seasoning and red pepper flakes. Add asparagus spears; stir gently to coat. Cover and cook for 5-7 minutes or until vegetables are crisp-tender, stirring occasionally. **YIELD: 6 SERVINGS.**

Spicy Asparagus Spears

Herbed Veggie Platter

🌙 Herbed Veggie Platter

PREP/TOTAL TIME: **25 MIN.**

This eye-appealing combination is an interesting twist on mixed vegetables. Topped with herb butter and Parmesan cheese, the crowd-pleaser is an ideal addition to buffets.

Patricia Vandiver ✳ Tucson, Arizona

- 1 small head cauliflower, broken into florets
- 1 medium bunch broccoli, cut into florets
- 2 medium zucchini, cut into 1/4-inch slices
- 1/2 cup butter, cubed
- 3/4 teaspoon dried thyme
- 3/4 teaspoon dried parsley flakes
- 1/2 teaspoon onion salt
- 2 medium tomatoes, cut into wedges
- 1/3 cup grated Parmesan cheese

On a large round microwave-safe platter, arrange the cauliflower, broccoli and zucchini. Cover and microwave on high for 5-1/2 minutes or until crisp-tender, stirring occasionally; drain.

In a small microwave-safe bowl, combine the butter, thyme, parsley and onion salt. Cover and microwave on high for 45 seconds or until the butter is melted.

Arrange tomatoes on platter. Drizzle butter mixture over vegetables; sprinkle with cheese. Cook, uncovered, on high for 1-2 minutes or until heated through. **YIELD: 8-10 SERVINGS.**

EDITOR'S NOTE: This recipe was tested in a 1,100-watt microwave.

Curried Corn on the Cob

🌵 Curried Corn on the Cob

PREP: **15 MIN. + SOAKING** GRILL: **25 MIN.**

Here's a deliciously different way to enjoy corn on the cob. If goat cheese is not to your liking, try queso fresco or any other crumbly cheese such as feta.

Laura Fall-Sutton ✳ Buhl, Idaho

- 6 medium ears sweet corn in husks
- 1/2 cup goat cheese
- 1 tablespoon sugar
- 2 teaspoons salt-free seasoning blend
- 1/2 teaspoon curry powder
- 1/4 teaspoon salt
- 1/4 teaspoon pepper

Two-Season Squash Medley

Peel back corn husks to within 1 in. of bottoms; remove silk. Rewrap corn in husks and secure with kitchen string. Place in a stockpot; cover with cold water. Soak for 20 minutes; drain.

Grill the corn, covered, over medium heat for 25-30 minutes or until tender, turning often. In a small bowl, combine the remaining ingredients; spread over the warm corn. Serve immediately. **YIELD: 6 SERVINGS.**

NUTRITION FACTS: 1 ear of corn with 4 teaspoons cheese mixture equals 203 calories, 7 g fat (4 g saturated fat), 15 mg cholesterol, 214 mg sodium, 33 g carbohydrate, 4 g fiber, 8 g protein. **DIABETIC EXCHANGES:** 2 starch, 1 fat.

◐ Two-Season Squash Medley

PREP/TOTAL TIME: **30 MIN.**

Both winter and summer squash star in this fun, colorful vegetable stir-fry. I've cooked in several restaurants and for many guests in my home, and this dish has been well-received for years.

Mary Beth LaFlamme ✳ Eagle Bridge, New York

2 **tablespoons butter**
2 **tablespoons olive oil**

1 **medium yellow summer squash, sliced**
1 **medium zucchini, sliced**
3/4 **pound butternut squash, peeled, seeded and julienned**
1 **medium onion, sliced**
1 **medium green pepper, julienned**
1 **medium sweet red pepper, julienned**
3 to 4 **garlic cloves, minced**
1 **tablespoon minced fresh thyme or 1 teaspoon dried thyme**
1/4 **teaspoon garlic salt**
1/4 **teaspoon pepper**

In a large skillet, heat the butter and oil over medium heat. Add the vegetables, garlic and thyme. Cook and stir until tender, about 15 minutes. Season with garlic salt and pepper. **YIELD: 6-8 SERVINGS.**

Stir-Fried Veggies with Pasta

Cook pasta according to package directions. Meanwhile, in a large nonstick skillet or wok, stir-fry the carrots, leek, zucchini, peppers and beans in hot olive oil for 3-4 minutes or until crisp-tender.

Drain pasta; add to the vegetable mixture. Drizzle with sesame oil. Stir-fry for 2 minutes. In a small bowl, combine the vinegar, honey, salt, chili powder and ginger. Pour over pasta mixture; toss to coat. **YIELD: 6 SERVINGS.**

NUTRITION FACTS: 1-1/2 cups equals 210 calories, 5 g fat (1 g saturated fat), 0 cholesterol, 218 mg sodium, 37 g carbohydrate, 4 g fiber, 5 g protein. DIABETIC EXCHANGES: 2 vegetable, 1-1/2 starch, 1 fat.

Stir-Fried Veggies With Pasta

PREP/TOTAL TIME: **30 MIN.**

This delightful dish has lots of vitamin-packed veggies. Not only is it a quick recipe to whip up, but it is one that my husband requests frequently.

Tracy Holaday ✳ Muncie, Indiana

- 2 cups uncooked spiral pasta
- 2 medium carrots, julienned
- 1 medium leek (white portion only), julienned
- 2 small zucchini, julienned
- 1 *each* medium sweet red, yellow and green pepper, cut into thin strips
- 1 cup fresh green beans, cut into 1-inch pieces
- 1 tablespoon olive oil
- 1 tablespoon sesame oil
- 2 tablespoons rice vinegar
- 2 tablespoons honey
- 1/2 teaspoon salt
- 1/4 teaspoon chili powder
- 1/4 teaspoon ground ginger

Sweet Potatoes and Apples au Gratin

PREP: **25 MIN.** BAKE: **45 MIN.**

This is a favorite of ours that we make regularly...and people on both sides of our family just love it! My mother-in-law drove over to my house to tell me to enter the Slimmed-Down Thanksgiving Sides Contest when she read about it. I'm glad she did!

Erica Vickerman ✳ Hopkins, Minnesota

- 3 cups thinly sliced tart apples (about 3 large)
- 1 teaspoon lemon juice
- 3 pounds sweet potatoes (about 5 medium), peeled and thinly sliced
- 1/4 cup maple syrup
- 1 tablespoon butter, melted
- 1/2 teaspoon salt
- 1/4 teaspoon pepper
- 1 cup soft bread crumbs
- 2 teaspoons olive oil
- 1/4 teaspoon ground cinnamon
- 1/4 teaspoon ground nutmeg
- 1/4 teaspoon cider vinegar

Place the apples in a large bowl; sprinkle with lemon juice. Add the sweet potatoes, syrup, butter, salt and pepper; toss to coat.

Transfer to a 3-qt. baking dish coated with cooking spray. Bake, uncovered, at 400° for 35-40 minutes or until apples and sweet potatoes are tender, stirring once.

In a small bowl, combine the bread crumbs, oil, cinnamon, nutmeg and vinegar; sprinkle over potato mixture. Bake for 10-15 minutes or until topping is golden brown. **YIELD: 12 SERVINGS.**

NUTRITION FACTS: 1 serving equals 130 calories, 2 g fat (1 g saturated fat), 3 mg cholesterol, 136 mg sodium, 27 g carbohydrate, 3 g fiber, 2 g protein. DIABETIC EXCHANGE: 2 starch.

Sweet Potatoes and Apples au Gratin

Thai-Style Green Beans

PREP/TOTAL TIME: **20 MIN.**

Two for Thai, anyone? Peanut butter, soy and hoisin sauce flavor this fast and fabulous bean dish.

Candy McMenamin
Lexington, South Carolina

- 1 tablespoon reduced-sodium soy sauce
- 1 tablespoon hoisin sauce
- 1 tablespoon creamy peanut butter
- 1/8 teaspoon crushed red pepper flakes
- 1 tablespoon chopped shallot
- 1 teaspoon minced fresh gingerroot
- 1 tablespoon canola oil
- 1/2 pound fresh green beans, trimmed

Minced fresh cilantro and chopped dry roasted peanuts, optional

In a bowl, combine the soy sauce, hoisin sauce, peanut butter and red pepper flakes; set aside.

In a small skillet, saute shallot and ginger in oil over medium heat for 2 minutes or until crisp-tender. Add green beans; cook and stir for 3 minutes or until crisp-tender. Add reserved sauce; toss to coat. Sprinkle with cilantro and peanuts if desired. **YIELD: 2 SERVINGS.**

Thai-Style Green Beans

Colorful Vegetable Saute

Colorful Vegetable Saute

PREP/TOTAL TIME: **20 MIN.**

This pretty mixture is delicious...and a great way to enjoy your garden's bounty. A sprinkling of toasted sesame seeds adds a pleasant crunch to the savory saute.

Regena Hofer ✳ Meadows, Manitoba

- 2 medium sweet red peppers, julienned
- 2 medium green peppers, julienned
- 2 medium zucchini, julienned
- 4 medium carrots, julienned
- 1 teaspoon olive oil
- 4 cups thinly sliced red cabbage
- 1/4 teaspoon salt
- 1/4 teaspoon pepper
- 4 teaspoons cider vinegar
- 1/4 cup water
- 1 tablespoon sesame seeds, toasted

In a large skillet, saute peppers, zucchini and carrots in oil for 5 minutes. Add cabbage, salt and pepper; saute 1 minute longer.

In a small bowl, combine vinegar and water; pour over the vegetables. Cook and stir for 2-3 minutes or until heated through. Sprinkle with sesame seeds; cook and stir 1 minute longer.
YIELD: **8-10 SERVINGS.**

Creamy Succotash

Creamy Succotash

PREP: **10 MIN.** COOK: **20 MIN. + COOLING**

This is a creation from my sister, Jenny. When I saw her make it, I didn't think the combination would be very tasty, but I changed my mind once I ate it.

Shannon Koene ✳ Blacksburg, Virginia

- 4 cups frozen lima beans
- 1 cup water
- 4 cups frozen corn
- 2/3 cup reduced-fat mayonnaise
- 2 teaspoons Dijon mustard
- 1/2 teaspoon onion powder
- 1/2 teaspoon garlic powder
- 1/4 teaspoon salt
- 1/4 teaspoon pepper
- 2 medium tomatoes, finely chopped
- 1 small onion, finely chopped

Spaghetti Squash with Red Sauce

In large saucepan, bring lima beans and water to a boil. Reduce heat; cover and simmer for 10 minutes. Add corn; return to a boil. Reduce heat; cover and simmer 5-6 minutes longer or until the vegetables are tender. Drain; cool for 10-15 minutes.

Meanwhile, in a large bowl, combine the mayonnaise, mustard, onion powder, garlic powder, salt and pepper. Stir in bean mixture, tomatoes and onion. Serve immediately or refrigerate. **YIELD: 10 SERVINGS.**

NUTRITION FACTS: 3/4 cup equals 198 calories, 6 g fat (1 g saturated fat), 6 mg cholesterol, 238 mg sodium, 31 g carbohydrate, 6 g fiber, 7 g protein. DIABETIC EXCHANGES: 2 starch, 1 fat.

Spaghetti Squash with Red Sauce

PREP: 25 MIN. COOK: 15 MIN.

This fabulous meatless main dish is a great way to get the kids to eat lots of vegetables...and a great way for you to use some of the fresh harvest from your garden.

Kathryn Pehl ✳ Prescott, Arizona

- 1 medium spaghetti squash (about 4 pounds)
- 2 cups chopped fresh tomatoes
- 1 cup sliced fresh mushrooms
- 1 cup diced green pepper
- 1/2 cup shredded carrot
- 1/4 cup diced red onion
- 2 garlic cloves, minced
- 2 teaspoons Italian seasoning
- 1/8 teaspoon pepper
- 1 tablespoon olive oil
- 1 can (15 ounces) tomato sauce

Grated Parmesan cheese, optional

Cut squash in half lengthwise; discard seeds. Place squash cut side down on a microwave-safe plate. Microwave, uncovered, on high for 14-16 minutes or until tender.

Meanwhile, in a large skillet, saute the tomatoes, mushrooms, green pepper, carrot, onion, garlic, Italian seasoning and pepper in oil for 6-8 minutes or until tender. Add tomato sauce; heat through.

When squash is cool enough to handle, use a fork to separate strands. Place squash on a serving platter; top with sauce. Sprinkle with cheese if desired. **YIELD: 6 SERVINGS.**

EDITOR'S NOTE: This recipe was tested in a 1,100-watt microwave.

Ginger Garlic Linguine

Ginger Garlic Linguine

PREP/TOTAL TIME: 25 MIN.

While this recipe's ginger sauce was designed for pasta, it's also good over green beans, pierogies or salmon. I've often tripled the sauce, then froze the extra so I could whip this dish up even faster on busy nights.

Julie Miske * Acworth, Georgia

- 12 ounces uncooked linguine
- 4 green onions, finely chopped
- 2 tablespoons minced fresh gingerroot
- 2 teaspoons minced garlic
- 1 teaspoon dried basil
- 1/4 teaspoon cayenne pepper
- 1/2 cup butter
- 1/4 cup grated Parmesan cheese

Cook linguine according to package directions. Meanwhile, in a large skillet, saute the onions, ginger, garlic, basil and cayenne in butter for 3-4 minutes or until onions are tender. Drain the linguine; add to skillet and toss to coat. Sprinkle with cheese. YIELD: 6 SERVINGS.

Shoepeg Corn Casserole

PREP: 15 MIN. BAKE: 20 MIN.

This comforting bake makes a creamy side to most any entree. Not only can you double it for larger crowds, but you can use reduced-fat or low-sodium ingredients.

Lori Talamao * Baton Rouge, Louisiana

- 2 cans (11 ounces *each*) shoepeg or white corn, drained
- 1 can (10-3/4 ounces) condensed cream of celery soup, undiluted
- 1 cup (8 ounces) sour cream
- 1 cup (4 ounces) shredded cheddar cheese
- 1/2 cup chopped onion
- 1/2 cup chopped celery
- 1/4 cup chopped green pepper
- 3/4 cup crushed butter-flavored crackers (about 18 crackers)
- 2 tablespoons butter, melted

In a large bowl, combine the corn, soup, sour cream, cheddar cheese, onion, celery and pepper.

Shoepeg Corn Casserole

Almond Vegetable Stir-Fry

Transfer to a greased 2-qt. baking dish. Sprinkle with the cracker crumbs; drizzle with butter. Bake, uncovered, at 350° for 20-25 minutes or until bubbly. **YIELD: 6 SERVINGS.**

Almond Vegetable Stir-Fry

PREP/TOTAL TIME: **20 MIN.**

While broccoli florets and chunks of red pepper give this medley plenty of color, it's the fresh ginger, garlic, soy sauce and sesame oil that round out the flavor.

Mary Relyea ✳ Canastota, New York

1 teaspoon cornstarch
1 teaspoon sugar
3 tablespoons cold water
2 tablespoons reduced-sodium soy sauce
1 teaspoon sesame oil
4 cups fresh broccoli florets
2 tablespoons canola oil
1 large sweet red pepper, cut into
   1-inch chunks
1 small onion, cut into thin wedges
2 garlic cloves, minced
1 tablespoon minced fresh gingerroot
1/4 cup slivered almonds, toasted

In a small bowl, combine the cornstarch and sugar. Stir in the water, soy sauce and sesame oil until smooth; set aside.

In a large nonstick wok or skillet, stir-fry broccoli in hot oil for 3 minutes. Add the pepper, onion, garlic and ginger; stir-fry for 2 minutes. Reduce heat; stir the soy sauce mixture. Stir into vegetables along with nuts. Cook and stir for 2 minutes or until thickened. **YIELD: 5 SERVINGS.**

NUTRITION FACTS: 3/4 cup equals 143 calories, 10 g fat (1 g saturated fat), 0 cholesterol, 260 mg sodium, 11 g carbohydrate, 3 g fiber, 4 g protein. **DIABETIC EXCHANGES:** 2 vegetable, 2 fat.

Sweet Potato Fries

In a shallow bowl, whisk egg and water. In a resealable plastic bag, combine bread crumbs, cheese, cayenne and pepper. Cut sweet potato into 1/4-in. strips. Add to egg mixture, a few at a time; toss to coat. Add to the crumb mixture, a few at a time; seal bag and shake to coat.

Arrange potato strips in a single layer on a baking sheet coated with cooking spray; drizzle with oil. Bake at 450° for 25-30 minutes or until golden brown and crisp, turning occasionally.

In a small bowl, combine the mayonnaise, chutney, curry powder and salt. If desired, sprinkle parsley over fries. Serve with mango chutney mayonnaise. **YIELD: 2 SERVINGS.**

Cherry Tomato Mozzarella Saute

PREP/TOTAL TIME: **25 MIN.**

Fast to fix and full of zest, this warm, refreshing side dish makes the most of cherry tomatoes, pairing them with fresh mozzarella cubes and seasoning the combination with thyme.

Summer Jones ✳ Pleasant Grove, Utah

- 1/4 cup chopped shallots
- 1 garlic clove, minced
- 1 teaspoon minced fresh thyme
- 2 teaspoons olive oil
- 2-1/2 cups cherry tomatoes, halved
- 1/4 teaspoon salt
- 1/4 teaspoon pepper
- 4 ounces fresh mozzarella cheese, cut into 1/2-inch cubes

In a large skillet, saute the shallots, garlic and thyme in oil until tender. Add the tomatoes, salt and pepper; heat through. Remove from the heat; stir in cheese. **YIELD: 4 SERVINGS.**

Sweet Potato Fries

PREP: **15 MIN.** BAKE: **25 MIN.**

Sweet potatoes add subtle flavor to these extra-crunchy fries. With the tasty mayo-chutney dip, this super side could double as a party appetizer!

Kelly McWherter ✳ Houston, Texas

- 2 tablespoons beaten egg
- 1 tablespoon water
- 1/3 cup dry bread crumbs
- 2 tablespoons grated Parmesan cheese
- 1/4 teaspoon cayenne pepper
- 1/4 teaspoon pepper
- 1 large sweet potato (14 ounces), peeled
- 2 teaspoons olive oil

MANGO CHUTNEY MAYONNAISE:
- 1/4 cup mayonnaise
- 2 tablespoons mango chutney
- 1/4 teaspoon curry powder

Dash salt
- 2 teaspoons minced fresh parsley, optional

Wholesome Apple-Hazelnut Stuffing

PREP: **20 MIN.** BAKE: **30 MIN.**

Try this whole grain, fruit and nut stuffing for a delicious new slant on a holiday staple. Herbs balance the sweetness of the apples and make this dish absolutely scrumptious!

Donna Noel ✳ Gray, Maine

- 2 celery ribs, chopped
- 1 large onion, chopped
- 1 tablespoon olive oil
- 1 small carrot, shredded
- 2 garlic cloves, minced
- 3 tablespoons minced fresh parsley *or* 1 tablespoon dried parsley flakes
- 1 tablespoon minced fresh rosemary *or* 1 teaspoon dried rosemary, crushed
- 4 cups cubed day-old whole wheat bread
- 1-1/2 cups shredded peeled tart apples (about 2 medium)
- 1/2 cup chopped hazelnuts, toasted
- 1 egg, lightly beaten
- 3/4 cup apple cider *or* unsweetened apple juice
- 1/2 teaspoon coarsely ground pepper
- 1/4 teaspoon salt

In a large nonstick skillet, saute celery and onion in oil for 4 minutes. Add the carrot, garlic, parsley and rosemary; saute 2-4 minutes longer or until vegetables are tender.

In a large bowl, combine the vegetable mixture, bread cubes, apples and hazelnuts. In a small bowl, combine the egg, cider, pepper and salt. Add to stuffing mixture and mix well.

Transfer to an 8-in. square baking dish coated with cooking spray. Cover and bake at 350° for 20 minutes. Uncover; bake 10-15 minutes longer or until a thermometer reads 160°. **YIELD: 6 CUPS.**

NUTRITION FACTS: 3/4 cup equals 159 calories, 8 g fat (1 g saturated fat), 27 mg cholesterol, 195 mg sodium, 20 g carbohydrate, 4 g fiber, 4 g protein. **DIABETIC EXCHANGES:** 1-1/2 fat, 1 starch.

Cherry Tomato Mozzarella Saute

Wholesome Apple-Hazelnut Stuffing

Rhubarb Corn Bread Stuffing

Rhubarb Corn Bread Stuffing

PREP: **20 MIN.** BAKE: **40 MIN.**

This distinctive stuffing is awesome alongside ham, chicken or turkey. I've been a rhubarb fan since I was a girl, so when a friend suggested this recipe, I had to try it. Now when I serve this bake, my guests are usually curious about my special ingredient...and they love it!

Kathy Petrullo ✳ Long Island City, New York

> 5 cups chopped fresh *or* frozen rhubarb (1/2-inch pieces), thawed
> 1/2 cup sugar
> 1 medium onion, chopped
> 1/2 cup butter, *divided*
> 3 cups crushed corn bread stuffing
> 1/2 cup chopped walnuts

In a large bowl, toss rhubarb and sugar; set aside. In a large skillet, saute the onion in 2 tablespoons butter until tender; add to rhubarb mixture. Stir in stuffing and walnuts.

In a small skillet, melt the remaining butter over medium heat; pour over stuffing mixture and toss lightly.

Spoon into a greased 2-qt. shallow baking dish. Bake, uncovered, at 325° for 40-45 minutes or until stuffing is heated through and top is lightly browned. Serve warm. **YIELD: 6-8 SERVINGS.**

EDITOR'S NOTE: If using frozen rhubarb, measure rhubarb while still frozen, then thaw completely. Drain in a colander, but do not press liquid out.

Root Vegetable Medley

Root Vegetable Medley

PREP: **25 MIN.** COOK: **20 MIN.**

Equally good with pork or beef roast—or even with a turkey—this side is one my husband requests at least once a month.

Marilyn Smudzinski * Peru, Illinois

- 6 small red potatoes, quartered
- 1 medium rutabaga, peeled and cut into 1-inch cubes
- 1/2 teaspoon salt
- 3 medium carrots, cut into 1/2-inch slices
- 1 medium turnip, peeled and cut into 1-inch cubes
- 1 to 2 medium parsnips, peeled and cut into 1/2-inch slices
- 1 medium onion, cut into eighths

GLAZE:

- 1 tablespoon butter
- 3 tablespoons brown sugar
- 1 teaspoon cornstarch
- 1/4 cup water
- 3 tablespoons lemon juice
- 1/2 teaspoon dill weed
- 1/8 teaspoon pepper
- 1/2 teaspoon salt

Place the potatoes and rutabaga in a saucepan; cover with water. Add the salt. Bring to a boil. Reduce heat; cover and simmer for 8 minutes.

Add remaining vegetables; return to a boil. Reduce heat; cover and simmer for 10 minutes or until vegetables are tender; drain.

For glaze, melt butter in a small saucepan; stir in brown sugar and cornstarch. Stir in the water, lemon juice, dill, pepper and salt. Bring to a boil; cook and stir for 2 minutes or until thickened. Pour over vegetables and toss to coat.
YIELD: **8 SERVINGS.**

Cranberry-Walnut Sweet Potatoes

Cranberry-Walnut Sweet Potatoes

PREP: **25 MIN.** BAKE: **1 HOUR**

For me, the best part of Thanksgiving dinner is the sweet potatoes! You can make the sauce for these up to a day ahead, just omit the walnuts until you're ready to serve.

Mary Wilhelm * Sparta, Wisconsin

- 4 large sweet potatoes
- 1/4 cup finely chopped onion
- 1 tablespoon butter
- 1 cup fresh *or* frozen cranberries
- 1/3 cup maple syrup
- 1/4 cup water
- 1/4 cup cranberry juice
- 1/4 teaspoon salt, *divided*
- 1/2 cup chopped walnuts, toasted
- 1 teaspoon Dijon mustard
- 1/4 teaspoon pepper
- 2 tablespoons minced chives

Scrub and pierce sweet potatoes. Bake at 400° for 1 hour or until tender.

In a saucepan, saute onion in butter until tender. Add cranberries, syrup, water, cranberry juice and 1/8 teaspoon salt. Bring to a boil. Reduce heat; cover and simmer for 10-15 minutes or until berries pop, stirring occasionally. Stir in walnuts and mustard; heat through.

Cut potatoes in half lengthwise; sprinkle with pepper and remaining salt. Top each with 2 tablespoons cranberry mixture; sprinkle with chives. YIELD: **8 SERVINGS.**

NUTRITION FACTS: 1/2 potato equals 249 calories, 6 g fat (1 g saturated fat), 4 mg cholesterol, 120 mg sodium, 46 g carbohydrate, 6 g fiber, 5 g protein.

Golden Diced Potatoes

Golden Diced Potatoes

PREP: **15 MIN.** COOK: **30 MIN.**

My aunt once made potatoes like these. When I couldn't remember her exact recipe, I created this version. The lightly seasoned coating on the potatoes cooks to a pretty golden brown.

Angela Tiffany Wegerer ✳ Colwich, Kansas

- 3/4 cup all-purpose flour
- 1 teaspoon seasoned salt
- 1/2 teaspoon onion powder
- 1/4 teaspoon garlic powder
- 1/4 teaspoon pepper
- 4 medium potatoes, peeled and cut into 1/2-inch pieces
- 1/2 cup butter

In a large resealable plastic bag, combine the flour, salt, onion powder, garlic powder and pepper. Add 1/2 cup potatoes at a time; shake well to coat.

In two large skillets, melt the butter. Add the potatoes; cook and stir over medium heat for 25-30 minutes or until the potatoes are tender. **YIELD: 6 SERVINGS.**

Herbed Baked Spinach

PREP: **10 MIN.** BAKE: **40 MIN.**

Parmesan cheese and garlic liven up the spinach, which goes well with meat entrees and main-dish casseroles. Sometimes, I use broccoli as a spinach substitute. It's equally delicious.

Verna Hart ✳ Seattle, Washington

- 1/2 cup chopped onion
- 1 garlic clove, minced
- 2 tablespoons butter
- 2 packages (10 ounces *each*) frozen chopped spinach, thawed and squeezed dry
- 1/2 cup heavy whipping cream
- 1/3 cup milk
- 5 tablespoons shredded Parmesan cheese, *divided*
- 1/4 cup dry bread crumbs
- 1/2 teaspoon salt
- 1/4 teaspoon dried marjoram
- 1/8 teaspoon pepper

In a skillet, saute onion and garlic in butter until onion is tender. Stir in spinach, cream and milk.

Remove from heat; stir in 4 tablespoons cheese, bread crumbs, salt, marjoram and pepper.

Spoon into the greased 1-qt. baking dish. Sprinkle with the remaining cheese. Bake, uncovered, at 350° for 40-45 minutes or until cheese is lightly browned. **YIELD: 6 SERVINGS.**

Country Corn

PREP/TOTAL TIME: 20 MIN.

I cook church dinners for 120 people, so I'm always looking for fast, inexpensive menu items. After watching a chef put this corn bake together, I prepared it at church several times. There was never any left over.

Kathleen Mancuso ✳ Niskayuna, New York

- 6 green onions, chopped
- 3 tablespoons butter
- 1 package (16 ounces) frozen corn, thawed
- 2 teaspoons cornstarch
- 1/2 cup half-and-half cream
- 1/4 cup water
- 1/2 teaspoon salt
- 1/4 to 1/2 teaspoon pepper
- 1 cup grape tomatoes, halved

In a skillet, saute the onions in butter for 2-3 minutes or until tender. Stir in corn; cover and cook for 4-5 minutes or until heated through.

Meanwhile, in a small bowl, combine the cornstarch, cream, water, salt and pepper until smooth. Gradually stir into corn mixture. Bring to a boil. Cook, uncovered, for 2 minutes or until thickened. Stir in tomatoes. **YIELD: 6 SERVINGS.**

Herbed Baked Spinach

Country Corn

Golden Mashed Potato Bake

Golden Mashed Potato Bake

PREP: 30 MIN. BAKE: 50 MIN.

My husband and his brother are partners in a dairy farm, so I use lots of dairy products in cooking. These comforting, creamy potatoes complement many main dishes.

Cathy Hanehan ✳ Saratoga Springs, New York

- 8 medium potatoes, peeled and cubed
- 1 package (8 ounces) cream cheese, cubed
- 2 eggs
- 2 tablespoons all-purpose flour
- 2 tablespoons minced fresh parsley
  or 2 teaspoons dried parsley flakes
- 2 tablespoons minced chives
- 2 teaspoons salt
- 1/4 teaspoon pepper
- 1 can (2.8 ounces) french-fried onions

Place potatoes in a saucepan and cover with water. Bring to a boil. Reduce heat; cover and simmer for 15-20 minutes or until tender. Drain.

In a large bowl, beat potatoes and cream cheese until smooth. Beat in the eggs, flour, parsley, chives, salt and pepper and mix well.

Transfer to a greased 3-qt. baking dish. Bake, uncovered, at 350° for 45 minutes or until a thermometer reads 160°. Sprinkle with onions; bake 5-10 minutes longer or until golden brown. **YIELD: 12 SERVINGS.**

Asparagus Cheese Bundles

◖Asparagus Cheese Bundles

PREP/TOTAL TIME: 30 MIN.

Here's an interesting side dish that will have folks asking for seconds. It's the perfect vegetable for Easter dinner.

Pat Habiger ✳ Spearville, Kansas

- 1 cup water
- 1/2 pound fresh asparagus, trimmed and cut into 2-inch pieces
- 2 medium carrots, julienned
- 1 package (8 ounces) cream cheese, softened

Chunky Roasted Tomatoes

1 egg

2 tablespoons minced fresh basil *or*
2 teaspoons dried basil

1/2 cup crumbled feta cheese

8 flour tortillas (8 inches), warrmed

2 tablespoons milk

2 teaspoons sesame seeds

In a large saucepan, bring water to a boil. Add asparagus and carrots. Cook, uncovered, for 5 minutes; drain.

In a small bowl, beat the cream cheese, egg and basil; stir in feta cheese.

Place a mound of vegetables in the center of each tortilla. Top with 2 rounded tablespoonfuls of cheese mixture. Fold the ends and sides over filling and roll up.

Place seam side down on an ungreased baking sheet. Brush with milk; sprinkle with sesame seeds. Bake at 425° for 10-14 minutes until heated through and golden brown. **YIELD: 8 SERVINGS.**

Chunky Roasted Tomatoes

PREP: 15 MIN. BAKE: 50 MIN.

Vine-ripened tomatoes roast up into a versatile sauce that's excellent over pasta, grilled chicken and fish or on toasted French bread for bruschetta. I often double or triple the recipe, and my husband still can't get enough.

Amanda Cerza ✳ Wilmington, Illinois

2 pounds plum tomatoes

2 tablespoons olive oil

1 small onion, chopped

1 garlic clove, minced

1 teaspoon salt

1 teaspoon sugar

1/2 teaspoon dried basil

1/2 teaspoon dried oregano

1/4 teaspoon pepper

Hot cooked pasta

Shredded Parmesan cheese

Cut tomatoes into wedges; discard seeds. Place tomatoes in a greased 13-in. x 9-in. baking dish. Drizzle with oil. Sprinkle with onion, garlic and seasonings; toss to coat. Spread in a single layer.

Bake, uncovered, at 350° for 50-60 minutes or until heated through, stirring twice. Toss with pasta; sprinkle with the Parmesan cheese. **YIELD: 3-4 SERVINGS.**

Creamy Zucchini

◔ Creamy Zucchini

PREP/TOTAL TIME: **20 MIN.**

Here's a different treatment for zucchini that's a favorite in our home. Even though the creamy Parmesan sauce is homemade, the recipe's cooking time is short.

Marguerite Shaeffer ✳ Sewell, New Jersey

- 4 medium zucchini, julienned
- 1-1/2 teaspoons minced garlic
- 2 tablespoons olive oil
- 2 packages (3 ounces *each*) cream cheese, cubed
- 1 cup half-and-half cream
- 1/2 cup shredded Parmesan cheese
- 1/4 teaspoon salt
- 1/8 teaspoon coarsely ground pepper
- Dash ground nutmeg
- Shredded Swiss cheese

In a large skillet, saute the zucchini and garlic in oil for 3-5 minutes or until tender. Drain; remove the zucchini mixture with a slotted spoon and keep warm.

In the same skillet, combine cream cheese and cream; cook and stir over low heat until smooth. Stir in the Parmesan cheese. Return the zucchini mixture to the pan. Cook and stir 1-2 minutes longer or until heated through. Sprinkle with the salt, pepper, nutmeg and Swiss cheese. **YIELD: 6 SERVINGS.**

◔ Can't-Be-Beet Roasted Potato Salad

PREP: **20 MIN.** BAKE: **35 MIN.**

You'll love the combination of beets and balsamic dressing in this tasty addition to a holiday meal!

Jennifer Fisher ✳ Austin, Texas

- 1-1/2 pounds small red potatoes, halved
- 2 medium red onions, cut into wedges
- 1/2 teaspoon salt, *divided*
- 2 tablespoons olive oil
- 1-1/2 pounds fresh beets, peeled and cut into wedges
- 2/3 cup reduced-sodium chicken broth *or* vegetable broth
- 1/3 cup balsamic vinegar
- 2 teaspoons brown sugar
- 2 teaspoons minced fresh thyme *or* 1/2 teaspoon dried thyme
- 1/2 teaspoon pepper
- 2 tablespoons minced fresh parsley

Place potatoes and onions in two 15-in. x 10-in. x 1-in. baking pans coated with cooking spray. Sprinkle with 1/4 teaspoon salt; drizzle with oil and toss to coat.

Place the beets in pans (do not stir). Bake, uncovered, at 425° for 35-40 minutes or until vegetables are tender.

For dressing, in a small saucepan, combine the broth, vinegar, brown sugar, thyme, pepper and remaining salt. Bring to a boil. Reduce heat; simmer, uncovered, until reduced to 1/3 cup. Transfer vegetables to a large bowl. Drizzle with dressing and toss to coat. Sprinkle with parsley. **YIELD: 9 SERVINGS.**

NUTRITION FACTS: 3/4 cup equals 135 calories, 3 g fat (trace saturated fat), 0 cholesterol, 244 mg sodium, 24 g carbohydrate, 3 g fiber, 3 g protein. **DIABETIC EXCHANGES:** 1 starch, 1 vegetable, 1/2 fat.

◑ Never-Fail Egg Noodles

PREP/TOTAL TIME: **20 MIN.**

Some years ago, the small church I attended held a chicken and noodles fund-raiser supper. I was put in charge of noodles for 200 people! A dear lady shared this recipe and said it had been tried and tested by countless cooks. These noodles are just plain good eating!

Kathryn Roach ✳ Edgemont, Arkansas

2 cups all-purpose flour
1 teaspoon salt
1 egg plus 3 egg yolks
3 tablespoons cold water
Minced fresh parsley, optional

In a bowl, combine flour and salt. Make a well in the center. Beat egg, egg yolks and water; pour into well. Stir together, forming a dough. Turn dough onto a floured surface; knead 8-10 times.

Divide into thirds. Roll out each portion to 1/8-in. thickness. Cut into 1/2-in. strips; cut the strips into 2-in. pieces. Place in boiling salted water or chicken broth; cover and cook for 7-9 minutes or until tender. Drain; sprinkle with parsley if desired. **YIELD: ABOUT 5-1/2 CUPS.**

Can't-Be-Beet Roasted Potato Salad

Never-Fail Egg Noodles

Duo Tater Bake

Duo Tater Bake

PREP: **40 MIN.** BAKE: **20 MIN. + CHILLING**

I made this creamy and comforting potato dish for Thanksgiving, and it was a winner with my family. They said to be sure to include it at every holiday dinner!

Joan McCulloch ✳ Abbotsford, British Columbia

- 4 pounds russet *or* Yukon Gold potatoes, peeled and cubed
- 3 pounds sweet potatoes, peeled and cubed
- 2 cartons (8 ounces *each*) spreadable chive and onion cream cheese, *divided*
- 1 cup (8 ounces) sour cream, *divided*
- 1/4 cup shredded Colby-Monterey Jack cheese
- 1/3 cup milk
- 1/4 cup shredded Parmesan cheese
- 1/2 teaspoon salt
- 1/2 teaspoon pepper

TOPPING:
- 1 cup (4 ounces) shredded Colby-Monterey Jack cheese
- 1/2 cup chopped green onions
- 1/4 cup shredded Parmesan cheese

Place russet potatoes in a Dutch oven and cover with water. Bring to a boil. Reduce heat; cover and cook for 15-20 minutes or until tender.

Meanwhile, place sweet potatoes in a large saucepan; cover with water. Bring to a boil. Reduce heat; cover and cook for 15-20 minutes or until tender. Drain; mash with half of cream cheese and sour cream and all of Colby cheese.

Drain the russet potatoes; mash with the remaining cream cheese and sour cream. Stir in the milk, Parmesan cheese, salt and pepper.

Spread 2-2/3 cups of the russet potato mixture into each of two greased 11-in. x 7-in. baking dishes. Layer with 4 cups sweet potato mixture. Repeat layers. Spread with remaining russet potato mixture.

Bake, uncovered, at 350° for 15 minutes or until potatoes are heated through. Combine topping ingredients; sprinkle over casseroles. Bake 2-3 minutes longer or until cheese is melted. YIELD: **2 CASSEROLES (10 SERVINGS EACH).**

Blueberry Quick Bread, PAGE 334

66 This sweet bread recipe has won a blue ribbon at our state fair, perhaps because the crushed pineapple and coconut give it a mild but delicious twist. It makes two loaves, so you can freeze one for a future treat. 99

Lois Everest
Goshen, Indiana

QUICK BREADS

DO YOU HAVE A WINNING RECIPE?
Enter your most prized recipes in the *Taste of Home* recipe contests, and you may win some money and the chance to have your recipe published. Log onto **tasteofhome.com/RecipeContests** for a list of our current contests and submission deadlines. Good luck...we'll be looking for your recipe.

quick breads

Rhubarb-Ribbon Brunch Cake

Rhubarb-Ribbon Brunch Cake

PREP: **30 MIN.** BAKE: **1 HOUR + COOLING**

My dad has always had a flourishing rhubarb patch. So when I read about a rhubarb contest, I knew I should try to create a recipe with his endless supply. This cake can be served as a coffee cake at breakfast or an elegant finish to a special meal.

Mary Blenk ✳ Cumberland, Maine

- 3/4 **cup sugar**
- 3 **tablespoons cornstarch**
- 1/4 **teaspoon ground cinnamon**
- 1/8 **teaspoon ground nutmeg**
- 1/3 **cup cold water**
- 2-1/2 **cups sliced fresh *or* frozen rhubarb**
- 3 **to 4 drops food coloring, optional**

BATTER:

- 2-1/4 **cups all-purpose flour**
- 3/4 **cup sugar**
- 3/4 **cup cold butter, cubed**
- 1/2 **teaspoon baking powder**
- 1/2 **teaspoon baking soda**
- 1/2 **teaspoon salt**
- 1 **egg, lightly beaten**
- 1 **carton (6 ounces) vanilla yogurt**
- 1 **teaspoon vanilla extract**

TOPPING:

- 1 **egg, beaten**
- 8 **ounces Mascarpone cheese**
- 1/4 **cup sugar**
- 1/2 **cup chopped pecans**
- 1/4 **cup flaked coconut**

In a saucepan, combine the sugar, cornstarch, cinnamon, nutmeg and water until smooth. Add rhubarb. Bring to a boil; cook and stir for 2 minutes or until thickened. Add food coloring if desired. Set aside.

In a large bowl, combine flour and sugar; cut in the butter until mixture resembles coarse crumbs. Set aside 1 cup for topping. Add the baking powder, baking soda and salt to the remaining crumb mixture. In a small bowl, combine the egg, yogurt and vanilla; stir into batter until smooth. Spread into a greased 9-in. springform pan.

Combine the egg, Mascarpone cheese and sugar; spoon over the batter. Top with rhubarb mixture. Add pecans and coconut to reserved crumb mixture; sprinkle over top.

Bake at 350° for 60-65 minutes or until a toothpick inserted near the center comes out clean. Cool on a wire rack for 20 minutes; remove sides of pan. Cool completely. **YIELD: 12 SERVINGS.**

EDITOR'S NOTE: If using frozen rhubarb, measure rhubarb while still frozen, then thaw completely. Drain in a colander, but do not press liquid out.

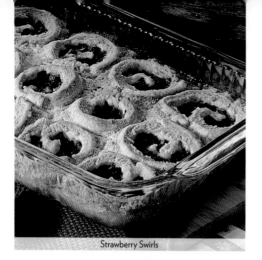
Strawberry Swirls

Bake at 350° for 40-45 minutes or until golden brown and edges are bubbly. Serve warm with whipped cream if desired. **YIELD: 12 SERVINGS.**

EDITOR'S NOTE: As a substitute for 1-1/2 cups self-rising flour, place 2-1/4 teaspoons baking powder and 3/4 teaspoon salt in a measuring cup. Add all-purpose flour to measure 1 cup. Combine with an additional 1/2 cup all-purpose flour.

Strawberry Swirls

PREP: **20 MIN.** BAKE: **40 MIN.**

My mother-in-law's apple cobbler was the inspiration for my swirls. We—my husband, grown son and I—consider it our special spring treat. And it is amazing how many family members and friends "pop over" during strawberry season! Actually, though, about any time is the right time to enjoy it.

Paula Steele ✳ Obion, Tennessee

> 2 cups sugar
> 2 cups water
> 1/2 cup butter, melted
> 1/2 cup shortening
> 1-1/2 cups self-rising flour
> 1/2 cup milk
> 2 cups finely chopped fresh strawberries, drained

Whipped cream, optional

In a large saucepan, combine sugar and water; cook and stir over medium heat until sugar is dissolved. Remove from the heat; allow to cool. Pour butter into a 13-in. x 9-in. baking dish and set aside.

In a small bowl, cut shortening into flour until mixture resembles coarse crumbs. Stir in milk until moistened.

Turn onto a lightly floured surface; knead until smooth, about 8-10 times. Roll the dough into a 12-in. x 8-in. rectangle; sprinkle with the strawberries. Roll up jelly-roll style, starting with a long side; seal the seam. Cut into 12 slices. Place with the cut side down over butter. Carefully pour syrup around rolls.

Gingerbread Muffins

PREP: **45 MIN.** BAKE: **15 MIN.**

Growing up, I adored my mom's gingerbread cake with lemon sauce, so I re-created the combination for my family. The spice- and molasses-flavored muffins spread with homemade lemon curd are a favorite with my kids.

Kelly Trupkiewicz ✳ Fort Collins, Colorado

LEMON CURD:

> 2/3 cup sugar
> 3/4 teaspoon cornstarch
> 1/3 cup lemon juice
> 5 egg yolks, lightly beaten
> 1/4 cup butter, cubed
> 2 teaspoons grated lemon peel

MUFFINS:

> 2 cups all-purpose flour
> 1/4 cup sugar
> 2-1/2 teaspoons baking powder
> 2 teaspoons ground ginger
> 1 teaspoon ground cinnamon
> 1/4 teaspoon salt
> 1/4 teaspoon ground cloves
> 1 egg
> 3/4 cup milk
> 1/4 cup canola oil
> 1/4 cup molasses

In a large heavy saucepan, combine the sugar, cornstarch and lemon juice until smooth. Cook and stir over medium-high heat until thickened and bubbly. Reduce heat to low; cook and stir for 2 minutes longer. Remove from the heat. Stir a small amount of hot filling into egg yolks; return all to the pan, stirring constantly. Bring to a gentle boil; cook and stir for 2 minutes. Remove from the heat; gently stir in butter and lemon peel until blended. Pour into a large bowl; cover the surface with plastic wrap. Cover and refrigerate until serving.

In a large bowl, combine the flour, sugar, baking powder, ginger, cinnamon, salt and cloves. In another bowl, whisk the egg, milk, oil and molasses until smooth; stir into dry ingredients just until moistened.

Fill paper-lined muffin cups half full. Bake at 375° for 15-20 minutes or until a toothpick comes out clean. Cool for 5 minutes before removing from pan to a wire rack. Serve warm with lemon curd. **YIELD: 1 DOZEN (1 CUP LEMON CURD).**

Gingerbread Muffins

Marmalade Monkey Bread

PREP: **15 MIN.** BAKE: **30 MIN.**

We love this pretty pull-apart bread, and drop-in company just raves about it. Because it uses refrigerated biscuits, it's so easy and quick to fix. You can try whatever jam you have on hand in place of the marmalade.

Delia Kennedy ✳ Deer Park, Washington

- 2/3 cup orange marmalade
- 1/2 cup chopped pecans *or* walnuts
- 1/4 cup honey
- 2 tablespoons butter, melted
- 2 tubes (7-1/2 ounces *each*) refrigerated buttermilk biscuits

In a bowl, combine the marmalade, pecans, honey and butter. Cut each biscuit into four pieces. Layer half of the pieces in a greased 10-in. tube pan; top with half of the marmalade mixture. Repeat.

Bake at 375° for 27-30 minutes or until golden brown. Cool in pan for 5 minutes before inverting onto a serving plate. Serve warm. **YIELD: 8 SERVINGS.**

Marmalade Monkey Bread

Sweet Potato Bread

Sweet Potato Bread

PREP: 20 MIN. BAKE: 65 MIN. + COOLING

I enjoy making this bread because it lets me use sweet potatoes in something besides pie. I found the recipe in an old Southern cookbook, but changed a few things. The orange juice in the glaze adds a nice citrus taste to the loaf.

Ann Jovanovi ✳ Chicago, Illinois

3-1/2 cups all-purpose flour
   2 teaspoons baking soda
   1 teaspoon baking powder
1/2 teaspoon salt
   1 teaspoon ground cinnamon
   1 teaspoon ground nutmeg
1/2 teaspoon ground cloves
   2 cups mashed sweet potatoes
   3 eggs
   1 cup canola oil
   3 cups sugar
   1 cup chopped walnuts
   1 cup raisins

GLAZE:

1-1/2 cups confectioners' sugar
   4 to 5 teaspoons orange juice
   1 teaspoon grated orange peel
1/3 cup chopped walnuts

In a large bowl, combine the flour, baking soda, baking powder, salt and spices. Whisk together the sweet potatoes, eggs and oil. Add sugar; whisk until smooth. Stir into dry ingredients just until combined. Fold in walnuts and raisins (batter will be thick). Transfer to two greased 9-in. x 5-in. loaf pans.

Bake at 350° for 65-70 minutes or until a toothpick inserted near the center comes out clean. Cool in the pans for 10 minutes before removing to wire racks.

For glaze, combine the confectioners' sugar, orange juice and peel until blended. Spread over the loaves; sprinkle with walnuts. **YIELD: 2 LOAVES (16 SLICES EACH).**

Creamy Cranberry Coffee Cake

Creamy Cranberry Coffee Cake

PREP: **15 MIN.** BAKE: **70 MIN. + COOLING**

Chopped cranberries and orange peel give this coffee cake bursts of tart flavor, but a cream cheese layer on top sweetens it nicely. It's so lovely, you'll want to serve it when company comes.

Nancy Roper ✳ Etobicoke, Ontario

- 2 cups all-purpose flour
- 1 cup sugar
- 1-1/2 teaspoons baking powder
- 1/2 teaspoon baking soda
- 1 egg
- 3/4 cup orange juice
- 1/4 cup butter, melted
- 1 teaspoon vanilla extract
- 2 cups coarsely chopped fresh *or* frozen cranberries
- 1 tablespoon grated orange peel

CREAM CHEESE LAYER:

- 1 package (8 ounces) cream cheese, softened
- 1/3 cup sugar
- 1 egg
- 1 teaspoon vanilla extract

TOPPING:

- 3/4 cup all-purpose flour
- 1/2 cup sugar, cubed
- 1/2 cup cold butter

In a large bowl, combine the flour, sugar, baking powder and baking soda. Combine the egg, orange juice, butter and vanilla; stir into dry ingredients until well combined. Fold in the cranberries and orange peel. Pour into a greased 9-in. springform pan.

In a small bowl, beat cream cheese and sugar until smooth. Beat in egg and vanilla. Spread over batter. Combine flour and sugar; cut in butter until the mixture resembles coarse crumbs. Sprinkle over top.

Place pan on a baking sheet. Bake at 350° for 70-75 minutes or until golden brown. Cool on a wire rack for 15 minutes before removing sides of pan. **YIELD: 12 SERVINGS.**

Chili Corn Muffins

Chili Corn Muffins

PREP: **15 MIN.** BAKE: **20 MIN.**

Hot corn bread was one of my childhood favorites. This muffin version with a kick from chili powder and green chilies is now my and my husband's favorite.

Sarah Hovley ✳ Santa Cruz, California

- 2-1/2 cups all-purpose flour
- 1 cup yellow cornmeal
- 1/4 cup sugar
- 5 teaspoons baking powder
- 1-1/2 teaspoons salt
- 1 teaspoon chili powder
- 2 eggs
- 1-1/2 cups milk
- 2/3 cup canola oil
- 1/2 cup finely chopped onion
- 1 can (4 ounces) chopped green chilies, drained

In a large bowl, combine the flour, cornmeal, sugar, baking powder, salt and chili powder. In a small bowl, beat the eggs; add milk, oil, onion and chilies. Stir into the dry ingredients just until moistened.

Fill greased or paper-lined muffin cups two-thirds full. Bake at 400° for 20-25 minutes or until a toothpick inserted near the center comes out clean. Cool for 5 minutes before removing from the pans to wire racks. Serve warm. **YIELD: ABOUT 1-1/2 DOZEN.**

⏱ PB&J Spirals

PREP/TOTAL TIME: **30 MIN.**

Kids young and old love these PB&J treats. Using refrigerated crescent roll dough, they're a fun snack for hungry youngsters to assemble. Parents just have to help with the baking. Plus, they're easy to vary using different jelly flavors and nuts to suit each child's taste.

Lisa Renshaw ✳ Kansas City, Missouri

- 1 tube (8 ounces) refrigerated crescent rolls
- 8 teaspoons creamy peanut butter
- 8 teaspoons grape jelly
- 1/4 cup chopped unsalted peanuts
- 2 tablespoons confectioners' sugar

Unroll crescent dough; separate into triangles. Spread 1 teaspoon each of peanut butter and jelly on the wide end of each triangle; sprinkle with the peanuts. Roll up from the wide end and place point side down 2 in. apart on an ungreased baking sheet. Curve ends to form a crescent shape.

Bake at 375° for 11-13 minutes or until lightly browned. Dust with confectioners' sugar. Serve warm. **YIELD: 8 SERVINGS.**

Cinnamon-Swirl Coffee Ring

PREP: **10 MIN.** BAKE: **55 MIN. + COOLING**

I first sampled this coffee cake at an inn that serves a marvelous breakfast for its guests. The ring has a pretty cinnamon swirl and a hint of cardamom flavor. I like to make it for my Thursday morning quilt group.

Stell Pierce ✳ Franklin, Virginia

- 3 cups all-purpose flour
- 2 cups sugar
- 1 teaspoon baking powder
- 1 teaspoon baking soda
- 1/2 teaspoon salt
- 1/2 teaspoon ground cardamom
- 1 package (8 ounces) cream cheese, softened
- 3 eggs
- 1 cup milk
- 1/2 cup butter, melted
- 1 teaspoon vanilla extract

FILLING:

- 1/2 cup 4% cottage cheese
- 2/3 cup sugar
- 2 teaspoons ground cinnamon

Confectioners' sugar, optional

In a large bowl, combine the flour, sugar, baking powder, baking soda, salt and cardamom. In another bowl, beat cream cheese until smooth. Beat in the eggs, milk, butter and vanilla. Gradually add to the dry ingredients, beating until combined.

For filling, combine cottage cheese, sugar and cinnamon in a small bowl. Beat on medium speed for 2 minutes.

Spoon half of the batter into a greased 10-in. fluted tube pan; top with filling and remaining batter. Bake at 350° for 55-65 minutes or until a toothpick inserted near the center comes out clean. Cool for 10 minutes before removing from pan to a wire rack. Dust with confectioners' sugar if desired. **YIELD: 12-14 SERVINGS.**

Cinnamon-Swirl Coffee Ring

Feta 'n' Chive Muffins

PREP: **15 MIN.** BAKE: **20 MIN.**

This is a "spring" variation on a savory muffin my husband has made for years. It has a light texture almost like a popover and tastes best eaten hot right from the oven.

Angela Buchanan ✳ Boulder, Colorado

1-1/2 cups all-purpose flour
   3 teaspoons baking powder
 1/4 teaspoon salt
   2 eggs
   1 cup milk
   2 tablespoons butter, melted
 1/2 cup crumbled feta cheese
   3 tablespoons snipped chives

In a large bowl, combine flour, baking powder and salt. In another bowl, whisk the eggs, milk and butter; stir into dry ingredients just until moistened. Fold in the feta cheese and chives.

Fill greased or paper-lined muffin cups two-thirds full. Bake at 400° for 18-22 minutes or until a toothpick inserted near the center comes out clean. Cool for 5 minutes before removing from pan to a wire rack. Serve warm. Refrigerate leftovers. **YIELD: 1 DOZEN.**

Feta 'n' Chive Muffins

Berry Cheesecake Muffins

Berry Cheesecake Muffins

PREP: 30 MIN. BAKE: 25 MIN./BATCH

I adapted this recipe over the years for my family, and they think it's wonderful. Not only are the muffins delicious, but they're bursting with fantastic color, too.

Jeanne Bilhimer ✳ Midland, Michigan

- 1/3 cup butter, softened
- 3/4 cup sugar
- 2 eggs
- 1-1/2 cups all-purpose flour
- 1-1/2 teaspoons baking powder
- 1 teaspoon ground cinnamon
- 1/3 cup milk

CREAM CHEESE FILLING:
- 2 packages (3 ounces *each*) cream cheese, softened
- 1/3 cup sugar
- 1 egg
- 3/4 cup fresh raspberries
- 3/4 cup fresh blueberries

STREUSEL TOPPING:
- 1/4 cup all-purpose flour
- 2 tablespoons brown sugar
- 1/2 teaspoon ground cinnamon
- 1 tablespoon cold butter

In a large bowl, cream the butter and sugar until light and fluffy. Add the eggs, one at a time, beating well after each addition. Combine the flour, baking powder and cinnamon; gradually add to creamed mixture alternately with the milk. Fill greased or paper-lined muffin cups one-third full.

For filling, in a small bowl, beat the cream cheese, sugar and egg until smooth. Fold in the berries. Drop a rounded tablespoonful into the center of each muffin.

For topping, combine the flour, brown sugar and cinnamon in a small bowl; cut in butter until crumbly. Sprinkle over batter. (Muffin cups will be full.)

Bake at 375° for 25-30 minutes or until a toothpick inserted near the center comes out clean. Cool for 5 minutes before removing from pans to wire racks. Serve warm. Refrigerate leftovers. **YIELD: 21 MUFFINS.**

Orange-Rhubarb Breakfast Bread

Orange-Rhubarb Breakfast Bread

PREP: **20 MIN.** BAKE: **55 MIN. + COOLING**

Nothing is better than starting my day with a slice of this fabulous sweet bread alongside eggs, sausage and orange juice. It's full of tangy flavor and crunchy almonds.

Sonya Goergen ✳ Moorhead, Minnesota

- 1/3 cup butter, softened
- 1 cup sugar
- 2 eggs
- 1 teaspoon vanilla extract
- 2 cups all-purpose flour
- 1-1/2 teaspoons baking powder
- 1/2 teaspoon baking soda
- 1/2 teaspoon salt
- 1/4 teaspoon ground ginger
- 1/4 teaspoon ground nutmeg
- 1/2 cup orange juice
- 1 cup chopped fresh *or* frozen rhubarb
- 1/2 cup slivered almonds
- 2 teaspoons grated orange peel

In a large bowl, cream butter and sugar until light and fluffy. Add eggs, one at a time, beating well after each addition. Beat in vanilla.

Combine the flour, baking powder, baking soda, salt, ginger and nutmeg; add to creamed mixture alternately with orange juice. Fold in the rhubarb, almonds and orange peel.

Transfer to a greased 9-in. x 5-in. loaf pan. Bake at 350° for 55-65 minutes or until a toothpick inserted near the center comes out clean. Cool for 10 minutes before removing from pan to a wire rack. **YIELD: 1 LOAF (16 SLICES).**

EDITOR'S NOTE: If using frozen rhubarb, measure rhubarb while still frozen, then thaw completely. Drain in a colander, but do not press liquid out.

Mini Italian Biscuits

Mini Italian Biscuits

PREP/TOTAL TIME: **20 MIN.**

A seafood restaurant by me serves these delightful biscuits. I experimented in my kitchen until I was able to get the same great taste in these fast little bites.

Elaine Whiting ✳ Salt Lake City, Utah

- 2 cups biscuit/baking mix
- 1/2 cup finely shredded cheddar cheese
- 1/2 teaspoon garlic powder
- 1/2 teaspoon dried oregano
- 1/2 teaspoon dried basil
- 2/3 cup milk

In a large bowl, combine the biscuit mix, cheese, garlic powder, oregano and basil. With a fork, stir in milk just until moistened.

Drop by rounded teaspoonfuls onto a lightly greased baking sheet. Bake at 450° for 7-8 minutes or until golden brown. Serve warm. **YIELD: ABOUT 3 DOZEN.**

Sticky Bun Coffee Ring

Pumpkin Chip Muffins

PREP: **10 MIN.** BAKE: **20 MIN. + COOLING**

I started cooking and baking at a young age—just like my sisters and brothers. Our mother was a very good teacher, and she told us all we would learn our way around the kitchen. Now, I've let our children know the same thing!

Cindy Middleton ✳ Champion, Alberta

- 4 eggs
- 2 cups sugar
- 1 can (15 ounces) solid-pack pumpkin
- 1-1/2 cups canola oil
- 3 cups all-purpose flour
- 2 teaspoons baking soda
- 1 teaspoon baking powder
- 1 teaspoon ground cinnamon
- 1 teaspoon salt
- 2 cups (12 ounces) semisweet chocolate chips

In a large bowl, beat the eggs, sugar, pumpkin and oil until smooth. Combine the flour, baking soda, baking powder, cinnamon and salt; gradually add to pumpkin mixture and mix well. Fold in chocolate chips. Fill greased or paper-lined muffin cups three-fourths full.

Bake at 400° for 16-20 minutes or until a toothpick inserted near the center comes out clean. Cool in pan 10 minutes before removing to a wire rack to cool. **YIELD: ABOUT 2 DOZEN MUFFINS.**

Sticky Bun Coffee Ring

PREP/TOTAL TIME: **30 MIN.**

Everyone thinks I went to a lot of trouble when I bring out this pretty nut-topped ring of caramel rolls. In fact, these tasty treats are easy to put together using refrigerated biscuits.

Viola Shepard ✳ Bay City, Michigan

- 3 tablespoons butter, melted, *divided*
- 3 tablespoons maple syrup
- 1/4 cup packed brown sugar
- 1/4 cup chopped pecans
- 1/4 cup chopped almonds
- 1/2 teaspoon ground cinnamon
- 1 tube (12 ounces) refrigerated buttermilk biscuits

Brush a 10-in. fluted tube pan with 1 tablespoon butter. In a small bowl, combine syrup and remaining butter. Drizzle 2 tablespoons into the pan. Combine brown sugar, nuts and cinnamon; sprinkle 1/3 cupful over syrup mixture.

Separate biscuits; place in prepared pan with edges overlapping. Top with remaining syrup and nut mixtures. Bake at 375° for 15 minutes or until golden brown. Cool for 1-2 minutes; invert onto a serving platter. Serve warm. **YIELD: 10 SERVINGS.**

Cranberry Orange Scones

PREP: **20 MIN.** BAKE: **15 MIN.**

Serve these cranberry-dotted goodies with the delicate orange butter. Your gang will appreciate the special scones.

Karen McBride ✳ Indianapolis, Indiana

- 2 cups all-purpose flour
- 10 teaspoons sugar, *divided*
- 1 tablespoon grated orange peel
- 2 teaspoons baking powder
- 1/2 teaspoon salt
- 1/4 teaspoon baking soda
- 1/3 cup cold butter
- 1 cup dried cranberries
- 1/4 cup orange juice
- 1/4 cup half-and-half cream
- 1 egg
- 1 tablespoon milk

GLAZE (optional):

- 1/2 cup confectioners' sugar
- 1 tablespoon orange juice

ORANGE BUTTER:

- 1/2 cup butter, softened
- 2 to 3 tablespoons orange marmalade

In a large bowl, combine the flour, 7 teaspoons sugar, orange peel, baking powder, salt and baking soda. Cut in the butter until the mixture resembles coarse crumbs; set aside. In a small bowl, combine the cranberries, orange juice, cream and egg. Add to dry ingredients and stir until a soft dough forms.

On a floured surface, gently knead 6-8 times. Pat the dough into an 8-in. circle. Cut into 10 wedges. Separate the wedges and place on an ungreased baking sheet. Brush with the milk; sprinkle with the remaining sugar.

Bake at 400° for 12-15 minutes or until lightly browned. Remove to a wire rack.

Combine glaze ingredients if desired; drizzle over scones. Combine orange butter ingredients; serve with warm scones. **YIELD: 10 SCONES.**

Pumpkin Chip Muffins

Cranberry Orange Scones

Appalachian Corn Bread

Appalachian Corn Bread

PREP: **15 MIN.** BAKE: **20 MIN.**

On this westernmost ridge of the Appalachians, we get abundant rain and sunshine, which allows our children to grow a super-sweet corn crop. This corn bread is just one way we use some of the bounty!

Anne Wiehler * Farmington, Pennsylvania

- 2 tablespoons chopped onion
- 4 tablespoons canola oil, *divided*
- 1 cup all-purpose flour
- 1 cup cornmeal
- 2 tablespoons sugar
- 4 teaspoons baking powder
- 1/2 teaspoon salt
- 2 eggs
- 1 cup milk
- 1/2 cup fresh *or* frozen corn, thawed
- 1/3 cup shredded cheddar cheese
- 1/4 cup salsa
- 2 tablespoons minced chives

In a saucepan, saute the onion in 1 tablespoon oil until tender; set aside.

In a large bowl, combine the flour, cornmeal, sugar, baking powder and salt. In another bowl, whisk the eggs, milk and remaining oil. Stir in corn, cheese, salsa, chives and reserved onion. Stir into dry ingredients just until moistened.

Transfer to a greased 9-in. square baking pan. Bake at 425° for 20-25 minutes or until a toothpick inserted near the center comes out clean and top is lightly browned. Cut into squares; serve warm. **YIELD: 9 SERVINGS.**

Parmesan Herb Loaf

Parmesan Herb Loaf

PREP: **15 MIN.** BAKE: **30 MIN.**

This moist loaf is one of my very best quick breads. I like to serve slices accompanied by individual ramekins filled with extra-virgin olive oil, infused with herbs for dipping.

Dianne Culley * Nesbit, Mississippi

1-1/4 cups all-purpose flour
   3 tablespoons plus 1 teaspoon grated Parmesan cheese, *divided*

1st place

1-1/2 teaspoons sugar

1-1/2 teaspoons dried minced onion

1-1/4 teaspoons Italian seasoning, *divided*

1/2 teaspoon baking soda

1/4 teaspoon salt

1/2 cup sour cream

2 tablespoons plus 2 teaspoons 2% milk

4-1/2 teaspoons butter, melted

1 egg white, lightly beaten

In a small bowl, combine flour, 3 tablespoons Parmesan cheese, sugar, onion, 1 teaspoon Italian seasoning, baking soda and salt. In another bowl, combine the sour cream, milk and butter. Stir into the dry ingredients just until moistened.

Turn onto a floured surface; knead for 1 minute. Shape into a round loaf; place on a baking sheet coated with cooking spray. With scissors, cut a 1/4-in.-deep cross in top of loaf.

Brush with the egg white. Sprinkle with the remaining cheese and Italian seasoning. Bake at 350° for 30-35 minutes or until golden brown. Serve warm. **YIELD: 1 LOAF (4 WEDGES).**

Spiced Walnut Bread

PREP: **15 MIN.** BAKE: **1 HOUR + COOLING**

I received this delicious bread recipe from a co-worker years ago. Many friends have asked for it since then. People especially like the topping that's slightly crunchy with brown sugar, cinnamon and walnuts.

Kristine Skinner ✳ Marion, New York

2 cups all-purpose flour

1 teaspoon baking soda

1/2 teaspoon baking powder

1/4 teaspoon salt

1/2 teaspoon ground cinnamon

1/4 teaspoon ground allspice

1/4 teaspoon ground nutmeg

2 eggs, lightly beaten

1-1/4 cups unsweetened applesauce

1 cup sugar

Spiced Walnut Bread

1/2 cup canola oil

3 tablespoons milk

1/2 cup chopped walnuts

TOPPING:

1/4 cup chopped walnuts

1/4 cup packed brown sugar

1/2 teaspoon ground cinnamon

In a large bowl, combine the flour, baking soda, baking powder, salt and spices. In a small bowl, combine the eggs, applesauce, sugar, oil and milk; add to the dry ingredients just until moistened. Fold in the walnuts. Transfer to a greased and floured 9-in. x 5-in. loaf pan.

Combine the topping ingredients; sprinkle over the batter. Bake at 350° for 1 hour or until a toothpick inserted near the center comes out clean. Cool for 10 minutes before removing to a wire rack. **YIELD: 1 LOAF (12 SLICES).**

Nutcracker Bread

✿ Nutcracker Bread

PREP: 20 MIN. BAKE: 35 MIN. + COOLING

This tender loaf has a wonderful sugar and spice taste. Holiday turkey, ham or velvety cream cheese and jelly sandwiches always taste better on slices of this bread.

Jacqueline McComas ✳ Paoli, Pennsylvania

- 1 cup chopped walnuts, toasted and cooled
- 3/4 cup packed brown sugar
- 2 cups all-purpose flour
- 1-1/4 teaspoons baking powder
- 1/2 teaspoon salt
- 1/4 teaspoon baking soda
- 3 eggs
- 1/2 cup reduced-fat sour cream
- 1/2 cup fat-free milk
- 1 tablespoon cider vinegar

In a food processor, combine the walnuts and brown sugar; cover and pulse until finely chopped. Transfer to a large bowl. Stir in the flour, baking powder, salt and baking soda.

In a small bowl, beat the eggs, sour cream, milk and vinegar. Stir into dry ingredients just until moistened.

Transfer to an 8-in. springform pan coated with cooking spray. Bake at 350° for 35-40 minutes or until a toothpick inserted near the center comes out clean.

Cool on a wire rack for 10 minutes. Remove sides and bottom of pan; cool completely on a wire rack. **YIELD: 1 LOAF (16 SLICES).**

NUTRITION FACTS: 1 slice equals 170 calories, 6 g fat (1 g saturated fat), 42 mg cholesterol, 150 mg sodium, 24 g carbohydrate, 1 g fiber, 5 g protein. **DIABETIC EXCHANGES:** 1-1/2 starch, 1 fat.

Jumbo Onion Cheese Muffins

PREP: 15 MIN. BAKE: 20 MIN.

Chopped green onions and three types of cheese perk up these suppertime specialties. The large, light-textured muffins have a golden look and savory flavor that's ideal with any entree.

Valerie Collier ✳ Charleston, South Carolina

- 2 cups all-purpose flour
- 3 teaspoons baking powder
- 1/4 teaspoon pepper
- Dash ground nutmeg
- 1-1/4 cups milk
- 1/4 cup butter, melted
- 1 egg
- 1/4 cup chopped green onions
- 1/4 cup shredded part-skim mozzarella cheese
- 1/4 cup grated Romano cheese
- 1/4 cup shredded Parmesan cheese

In a bowl, combine the flour, baking powder, pepper and nutmeg. In another bowl, combine milk, butter and egg; stir into dry ingredients just until moistened. Fold in onions and cheeses.

Fill greased jumbo muffin cups two-thirds full. Bake at 400° for 20-25 minutes or until a toothpick inserted near the center comes out clean. Cool for 5 minutes before removing from pan to a wire rack. Serve warm. **YIELD: 6 MUFFINS.**

EDITOR'S NOTE: Muffins may be baked in regular-size muffin cups for 16-18 minutes; recipe makes 1 dozen.

🌾 Apricot Nut Bread

PREP: 25 MIN. BAKE: 55 MIN. + COOLING

My family likes bread, apricots and nuts, so I put the three together to create this recipe. It's fairly easy to make, and everyone loves it. It never lasts long in our house.

Robert Logan ✳ Clayton, California

1 cup boiling water
1-1/4 cups chopped dried apricots
2 cups all-purpose flour
2/3 cup sugar
1-1/2 teaspoons baking powder
1 teaspoon salt
1/4 teaspoon baking soda
1 egg
3/4 cup apricot nectar
2 tablespoons butter, melted
1/4 cup chopped pecans
1 tablespoon grated orange peel

GLAZE:
2 tablespoons brown sugar
1 tablespoon butter
1-1/2 teaspoons fat-free milk
2 tablespoons finely chopped pecans

Jumbo Onion Cheese Muffins

In a small bowl, pour boiling water over the apricots; set aside. In a large bowl, combine the flour, sugar, baking powder, salt and baking soda. Whisk the egg, apricot nectar and butter; stir into dry ingredients just until moistened. Drain apricots; fold into batter with pecans and orange peel.

Transfer to an 8-in. x 4-in. loaf pan coated with cooking spray. Bake at 350° for 55-65 minutes or until a toothpick inserted near the center comes out clean. Cool for 10 minutes before removing from pan to a wire rack.

For glaze, combine the brown sugar, butter and milk in a small saucepan. Cook and stir over medium heat until butter is melted and mixture is smooth. Cool to room temperature; drizzle over bread. Sprinkle with pecans. **YIELD: 1 LOAF (12 SLICES).**

NUTRITION FACTS: 1 slice equals 233 calories, 6 g fat (2 g saturated fat), 25 mg cholesterol, 320 mg sodium, 42 g carbohydrate, 2 g fiber, 3 g protein. **DIABETIC EXCHANGES:** 2 starch, 1 fruit, 1 fat.

Apricot Nut Bread

Coconut Chip Coffee Cake

Coconut Chip Coffee Cake

PREP: **15 MIN.** BAKE: **45 MIN. + COOLING**

I combined coconut, chocolate chips and walnuts to make the yummy filling in this coffee cake. My husband and two of my sons don't like coconut, but they still enjoy this treat.

Char Fricke ✳ St. Charles, Illinois

- 1/2 cup butter, softened
-   1 cup sugar
-   2 eggs
-   1 teaspoon vanilla extract
-   2 cups all-purpose flour
-   1 teaspoon baking powder
-   1 teaspoon baking soda
- 1/4 teaspoon salt
-   1 cup (8 ounces) sour cream

FILLING/TOPPING:

- 1/2 cup sugar
- 1/2 cup flaked coconut
- 1/2 cup semisweet chocolate chips
- 1/2 cup chopped walnuts

In a large bowl, cream butter and sugar until light and fluffy. Add the eggs, one at a time, beating well after each addition. Beat in vanilla. Combine the flour, baking powder, baking soda and salt; gradually add to the creamed mixture alternately with sour cream.

Spoon half of the batter into a greased 10-in. tube pan. Combine the filling ingredients; sprinkle half over the batter. Repeat layers.

Bake at 350° for 45-50 minutes or until a toothpick inserted near the center comes out clean. Cool for 10 minutes before removing from pan to a wire rack. YIELD: **12-16 SERVINGS.**

Apple Streusel Muffins

Apple Streusel Muffins

PREP: **20 MIN.** BAKE: **15 MIN. + COOLING**

My family loves these tender coffee cake-like muffins as a quick breakfast or snack on the run. The drizzle of glaze makes them pretty enough for company.

Dulcy Grace ✳ Roaring Spring, Pennsylvania

-   2 cups all-purpose flour
-   1 cup sugar

1 teaspoon baking powder

1/2 teaspoon baking soda

1/2 teaspoon salt

2 eggs

1/2 cup butter, melted

1-1/4 teaspoons vanilla extract

1-1/2 cups chopped peeled tart apples

STREUSEL TOPPING:

1/3 cup packed brown sugar

1 tablespoon all-purpose flour

1/8 teaspoon ground cinnamon

1 tablespoon cold butter

GLAZE:

1-1/2 cups confectioners' sugar

1 to 2 tablespoons milk

1 teaspoon butter, melted

1/4 teaspoon vanilla extract

1/8 teaspoon salt

In a large bowl, combine the flour, sugar, baking powder, baking soda and salt. In another bowl, whisk the eggs, butter and vanilla; stir into dry ingredients just until moistened (batter will be stiff). Fold in apples.

Fill greased or paper-lined muffin cups three-fourths full. In a small bowl, combine the brown sugar, flour and cinnamon; cut in butter until crumbly. Sprinkle over batter.

Bake at 375° for 15-20 minutes or until a toothpick inserted near the center comes out clean. Cool for 5 minutes before removing from pan to a wire rack to cool completely. Combine glaze ingredients; drizzle over the muffins. YIELD: 1 DOZEN.

Berry Bread with Spread

PREP: **20 MIN.** BAKE: **50 MIN. + COOLING**

The recipe for these two loaves and the strawberry spread came from my mother's collection. I added macadamia nuts to give the fruit bread a fun crunch and tropical flair.

Pat Stewart ✳ Lees Summit, Missouri

1 package (8 ounces) cream cheese, softened

2 packages (10 ounces *each*) frozen sweetened sliced strawberries, thawed

Berry Bread with Spread

3 cups all-purpose flour

2 cups sugar

1 teaspoon salt

1 teaspoon baking soda

4 eggs

1 cup canola oil

1 jar (3 ounces) macadamia nuts, chopped

For strawberry spread, in a small bowl, beat the cream cheese until smooth. Drain strawberries, reserving 1/4 cup juice for bread batter. Beat 6 tablespoons berries into the cream cheese. Set the remaining berries aside. Chill spread until serving.

In a large bowl, combine the flour, sugar, salt and baking soda. Combine the eggs, oil, reserved berries and juice. Stir into the dry ingredients just until moistened. Fold in the nuts (batter will be stiff). Transfer to two greased 8-in. x 4-in. loaf pans.

Bake at 350° for 50-55 minutes or until a toothpick inserted near the center comes out clean. Cool for 10 minutes before removing from pans to wire racks to cool completely. Serve with spread. YIELD: 2 LOAVES (10 SLICES EACH) AND ABOUT 1 CUP SPREAD.

Blueberry Quick Bread

🌼 Blueberry Quick Bread

PREP: **25 MIN.** BAKE: **50 MIN. + COOLING**

This sweet bread recipe has won a blue ribbon at our state fair, perhaps because the crushed pineapple and coconut give it a mild but delicious twist. It makes two loaves, so you can freeze one for a future treat.

Lois Everest ✳ Goshen, Indiana

- 2/3 cup butter, softened
- 1-1/4 cups sugar blend
- 2 eggs
- 4 egg whites
- 1-1/2 teaspoons lemon juice
- 3 cups all-purpose flour
- 3-3/4 teaspoons baking powder
- 1/2 teaspoon salt
- 1/2 cup fat-free milk
- 2 cups fresh *or* frozen blueberries
- 1 cup canned unsweetened crushed pineapple, drained
- 1/2 cup chopped pecans *or* walnuts
- 1/2 cup flaked coconut

In a large bowl, cream butter and sugar blend. Add the eggs, egg whites and lemon juice; mix well. Combine the flour, baking powder and salt; add to creamed mixture alternately with milk. Fold in the blueberries, pineapple, pecans and coconut.

Transfer to two 8-in. x 4-in. loaf pans coated with the cooking spray. Bake at 350° for 50-60 minutes or until a toothpick inserted near the center comes out clean. Cool for 10 minutes before removing from pans to wire racks. YIELD: **2 LOAVES (12 SLICES EACH).**

EDITOR'S NOTE: This recipe was tested with Splenda sugar blend. If using frozen blueberries, do not thaw before adding to batter.

NUTRITION FACTS: 1 slice equals 193 calories, 8 g fat (4 g saturated fat), 31 mg cholesterol, 186 mg sodium, 27 g carbohydrate, 1 g fiber, 3 g protein. DIABETIC EXCHANGES: 1-1/2 starch, 1-1/2 fat.

Almond-Filled Butterhorns, PAGE 357

"" *I add potato flakes to make my butterhorns moist and tender. The rolls complement any meal wonderfully and have just the right sweetness to make them a coffee-hour favorite. Remember to hide a few for yourself!* ""

Loraine Meyer
Bend, Oregon

YEAST BREADS

DO YOU HAVE A WINNING RECIPE?
Enter your most prized recipes in the *Taste of Home* recipe contests, and you may win some money and the chance to have your recipe published. Log onto **tasteofhome.com/RecipeContests** for a list of our current contests and submission deadlines. Good luck...we'll be looking for your recipe.

yeast breads

Sunshine Sweet Rolls

PREP: **30 MIN.** + RISING BAKE: **25 MIN.**

This bread-machine recipe is my new favorite. The cream cheese filling and drizzled icing make these golden brown rolls a special treat for breakfast or snacking.

Alice Shepherd ✳ Maryville, Tennessee

- 1-1/2 cups warm water (110° to 115°)
- 1/4 cup canola oil
- 1/4 cup shredded carrot
- 4-1/2 cups all-purpose flour
- 1/4 cup sugar
- 1-1/2 teaspoons salt
- 2 teaspoons active dry yeast

FILLING:
- 1 package (8 ounces) cream cheese, softened
- 1/4 cup sugar
- 1 teaspoon vanilla extract
- 1 package (3 ounces) cook-and-serve vanilla pudding mix
- 1 jar (6 ounces) carrot baby food
- 1 teaspoon ground cinnamon

GLAZE:
- 1/2 cup confectioners' sugar
- 2 to 3 teaspoons orange juice
- 1/2 teaspoon grated orange peel
- 1/4 teaspoon vanilla extract

In a bread machine pan, place the first seven ingredients in order suggested by manufacturer. Select the dough setting (check the dough after 5 minutes of mixing; add 1 to 2 tablespoons of water or flour if needed).

Meanwhile, in a small bowl, beat the cream cheese, sugar and vanilla until smooth; set aside. In a microwave-safe bowl, combine the pudding mix, baby food and cinnamon until smooth. Cover and microwave on high for 2 minutes; stir.

Sunshine Sweet Rolls

When cycle is completed, turn dough onto a lightly floured surface. Divide in half; shape each portion into a ball. Roll each into a 9-in. x 8-in. rectangle. Spread cream cheese mixture to within 1/2 in. of edges; top with carrot mixture. Roll up jelly-roll style, starting with a long side; pinch seam to seal.

Cut each into six rolls. Place cut side up in two greased 9-in. square baking pans. Cover and let rise in a warm place until doubled, about 30 minutes.

Bake at 350° for 25-30 minutes or until golden brown. Cool on wire racks for 5 minutes. Combine glaze ingredients; drizzle over warm rolls. Refrigerate leftovers. **YIELD: 1 DOZEN.**

EDITOR'S NOTE: This recipe was tested in a 1,100-watt microwave.

Herbed Dinner Rolls

Herbed Dinner Rolls

PREP: **20 MIN. + RISING** BAKE: **15 MIN.**

After I had my sixth child, a friend dropped off dinner. Included in the meal were these rolls, which start in a bread machine. They were so delicious that I quickly bought my own machine so I could make them myself.

Dana Lowry ✳ Hickory, North Carolina

- 1 cup water (70° to 80°)
- 2 tablespoons butter, softened
- 1 egg
- 1/4 cup sugar
- 1 teaspoon salt
- 1/2 teaspoon *each* dried basil, oregano, thyme and rosemary, crushed
- 3-1/4 cups bread flour
- 2-1/4 teaspoons active dry yeast
- Additional butter, melted
- Coarse salt, optional

In a bread machine pan, place the water, butter, egg, sugar, salt, herbs, flour and yeast in order suggested by the manufacturer. Select the dough setting (check dough after 5 minutes of mixing; add 1 to 2 tablespoons of water or flour if needed).

When cycle is completed, turn dough onto a lightly floured surface. Divide dough into 16 portions; shape each into a ball. Place 2 in. apart on greased baking sheets. Cover and let rise in a warm place until doubled, about 30 minutes.

Bake at 375° for 12-15 minutes or until golden brown. If desired, brush with butter and sprinkle with coarse salt. Remove from pans to wire racks. **YIELD: 16 ROLLS.**

EDITOR'S NOTE: We recommend you do not use a bread machine's time-delay feature for this recipe.

Soft Bread Twists

PREP: **30 MIN. + RISING** BAKE: **10 MIN.**

My family loves eating these zesty bread twists with a spaghetti supper. Soft and light as a feather, they have a perfect balance of garlic and oregano. Be sure to snatch one before passing them around the table.

Kathy Ksyniuk ✳ MacDowall, Saskatchewan

- 1 package (1/4 ounce) active dry yeast
- 2 teaspoons sugar
- 1 cup warm water (110° to 115°)
- 1 cup warm milk (110° to 115°)
- 1 egg, lightly beaten
- 1/2 cup canola oil
- 1-1/4 teaspoons salt, *divided*
- 5-1/2 to 6 cups all-purpose flour
- 1/4 cup cornmeal
- 1/2 teaspoon dried oregano
- 1/2 teaspoon garlic powder
- 1/4 cup butter, melted
- Pizza sauce *or* salsa, optional

In a large bowl, dissolve the yeast and sugar in warm water; let stand for 5 minutes. Add the milk, egg, oil, 1 teaspoon salt and 4 cups flour; beat on low speed until smooth. Beat 3 minutes longer. Stir in enough remaining flour to form a soft dough.

Turn onto a lightly floured surface; knead until smooth and elastic, about 8-10 minutes (dough will be sticky). Place in a greased bowl, turning once to grease top. Cover and let rise in a warm place until doubled, about 1 hour.

Do not punch down. Divide the dough into eight pieces. Combine cornmeal and oregano; sprinkle over work surface. Roll each piece of dough in cornmeal mixture and shape into a 15-in.-long rope. Cut each rope into three pieces. Twist each piece and place on greased baking sheets.

Bake at 400° for 8-12 minutes. Combine the garlic powder and remaining salt. Immediately brush twists with melted butter, then sprinkle with garlic powder mixture. Serve with pizza sauce if desired. **YIELD: 2 DOZEN.**

Muenster Bread

PREP: **20 MIN. + RISING** BAKE: **45 MIN. + COOLING**

This recipe makes a beautiful, round loaf. With a layer of cheese peeking out of every slice, it's definitely worth the effort.

Melanie Mero ✳ Ida, Michigan

- 2 packages (1/4 ounce *each*) active dry yeast
- 1 cup warm milk (110° to 115°)
- 1/2 cup butter, softened
- 2 tablespoons sugar
- 1 teaspoon salt
- 3-1/4 to 3-3/4 cups all-purpose flour
- 1 egg plus 1 egg yolk
- 4 cups (1 pound) shredded Muenster cheese
- 1 egg white, beaten

In a large bowl, dissolve yeast in milk. Add the butter, sugar, salt and 2 cups flour; beat until smooth. Stir in enough remaining flour to form a soft dough.

Turn onto a floured surface; knead until smooth and elastic, about 6-8 minutes. Place in a greased bowl, turning once to grease top. Cover and let rise in a warm place until doubled, about 1 hour.

In a large bowl, beat the egg and yolk; stir in cheese. Punch the down dough; roll into a 16-in. circle.

Place in a greased 9-in. round baking pan, letting dough drape over the edges. Spoon the cheese mixture into center of dough. Gather dough up over filling in 1-1/2-in. pleats. Gently squeeze pleats together at top and twist to make a top knot. Allow to rise 10-15 minutes.

Brush the loaf with egg white. Bake at 375° for 40-45 minutes. Cool on a wire rack for 20 minutes. Serve warm. Refrigerate leftovers. **YIELD:** 1 LOAF (**16 SLICES**).

Soft Bread Twists

Muenster Bread

Soft Pumpkin Yeast Bread

⬤ Soft Pumpkin Yeast Bread

PREP: 15 MIN. BAKE: 3-4 HOURS

This large hearty loaf, with its pumpkin flavor, is a perfect way to round out fall meals.

Sybil Brown ✳ Highland, California

- 1/2 cup canned pumpkin
- 1 cup warm evaporated milk (70° to 80°)
- 2 tablespoons butter, softened
- 2 tablespoons brown sugar
- 1/2 teaspoon salt
- 1/4 cup whole wheat flour
- 3 cups bread flour
- 2 to 3 teaspoons pumpkin pie spice
- 1/2 cup ground walnuts
- 2-1/4 teaspoons active dry yeast

In a bread machine pan, place all ingredients in order suggested by manufacturer. Select basic bread setting. Choose crust color and loaf size if available.

Bake according to bread machine directions (check dough after 5 minutes of mixing; add 1 to 2 tablespoons of water or flour if needed). **YIELD: 1 LOAF (16 SLICES).**

EDITOR'S NOTE: We recommend you do not use a bread machine's time-delay feature for this recipe.

Cardamom Braids

PREP: 25 MIN. + RISING BAKE: 25 MIN.

This is an old recipe that I like to make for breakfast. The bread is great for dunking in a cup of coffee.

Walter Dust ✳ Rapid City, Michigan

- 1 package (1/4 ounce) active dry yeast
- 1-1/2 cups warm milk (110° to 115°), *divided*
- 1 cup sugar, *divided*
- 3 eggs yolks, lightly beaten
- 1/2 cup butter, softened
- 1 tablespoon ground cardamom
- 1/2 teaspoon salt
- 5 to 6 cups all-purpose flour
- 2 tablespoons milk

In a bowl, dissolve yeast in 1/2 cup warm milk. Add 3/4 cup sugar, egg yolks, butter, cardamom, salt, 3 cups of flour and the remaining warm milk; beat until smooth. Stir in enough of the remaining flour to form a soft dough.

Turn onto a floured surface; knead until smooth and elastic, about 6-8 minutes. Place in a greased bowl, turning once to grease top. Cover and let rise in a warm place until doubled, about 1-1/4 hours.

Punch the dough down; divide into six pieces. Shape each piece into a 16-in. rope. Place three ropes on a greased baking sheet; braid. Pinch ends firmly and tuck under. Repeat with remaining three ropes on another baking sheet. Cover and let rise until doubled, about 45 minutes.

Brush braids with milk and sprinkle with remaining sugar. Bake at 350° for 25-30 minutes or until golden brown. Remove to wire racks to cool. **YIELD: 2 LOAVES (16 SLICES EACH).**

Cardamom Braids

Basil Garlic Bread

PREP: **15 MIN.** BAKE: **3-4 HOURS**

My family members have always been big on bread. And when I created this simple loaf, they asked for it time and again.

Christine Burger ✳ Grafton, Wisconsin

- 2/3 cup warm milk (70° to 80°)
- 1/4 cup warm water (70° to 80°)
- 1/4 cup warm sour cream (70° to 80°)
- 1-1/2 teaspoons sugar
- 1 tablespoon butter, softened
- 1 tablespoon grated Parmesan cheese
- 1 teaspoon salt
- 1/2 teaspoon minced garlic
- 1/2 teaspoon dried basil
- 1/2 teaspoon garlic powder
- 3 cups bread flour
- 2-1/4 teaspoons active dry yeast

In bread machine pan, place all ingredients in order suggested by manufacturer. Select basic bread setting. Choose crust color and loaf size if available.

Bake according to bread machine directions (check dough after 5 minutes of mixing; add 1 to 2 tablespoons of water or flour if needed). **YIELD: 1 LOAF (16 SLICES).**

EDITOR'S NOTE: We recommend you do not use a bread machine's time-delay feature for this recipe.

Basil Garlic Bread

Herbed Peasant Bread

Herbed Peasant Bread

PREP: 30 MIN. + RISING BAKE: 25 MIN.

The recipe for this beautiful, flavorful loaf came from our daughter-in-law, Karen. We all thoroughly enjoy this bread.

Ardath Effa ✳ Villa Park, Illinois

- 1/2 cup chopped onion
- 3 tablespoons butter
- 1 cup plus 2 tablespoons warm milk (120° to 130°)
- 1 tablespoon sugar
- 1-1/2 teaspoons salt
- 1/2 teaspoon dill weed
- 1/2 teaspoon dried basil
- 1/2 teaspoon dried rosemary, crushed
- 1 package (1/4 ounce) active dry yeast
- 3 to 3-1/2 cups all-purpose flour

Melted butter

In a skillet, cook onion in butter over low heat until tender, about 8 minutes. Cool for 10 minutes.

Place in a large bowl. Add the milk, sugar, salt, herbs, yeast and 3 cups flour; beat until smooth. Stir in enough remaining flour to form a soft dough.

Turn onto a floured board; knead until smooth and elastic, about 6 to 8 minutes. Place in a greased bowl, turning once to grease top. Cover and let rise in a warm place until doubled, about 45 minutes.

Punch the dough down. Shape into a ball and place on a greased baking sheet. Cover and let rise until doubled, about 45 minutes.

Bake at 375° for 25 to 30 minutes. Remove to a wire rack; brush with melted butter. Cool.

YIELD: 1 LOAF.

Bacon-Onion Crescent Buns

Bacon-Onion Crescent Buns

PREP: **40 MIN.** + RISING BAKE: **15 MIN.**

These savory crescents are a hit with everyone. They're very tasty served alongside many main dishes.

Helen Wilson ✳ San Benito, Texas

4-3/4 to 5-1/4 cups all-purpose flour
  1/2 cup sugar
    1 package (1/4 ounce) active dry yeast
  1/2 teaspoon salt
    1 cup milk
  1/2 cup butter, cubed
  1/2 teaspoon caraway seeds
    3 eggs
    1 pound sliced bacon, diced
    1 small onion, finely chopped
  1/8 teaspoon white pepper
    2 tablespoons water

In a bowl, combine 2 cups flour, sugar, yeast and salt. In a small saucepan, heat milk and butter to 120°-130°. Add to dry ingredients; beat on medium speed for 2 minutes. Add caraway seeds and 2 eggs; beat until smooth. Stir in enough remaining flour to form a stiff dough.

Turn onto a floured surface; knead until smooth and elastic, about 6-8 minutes. Place in a greased bowl, turning once to grease top. Cover and let rise in a warm place until doubled, about 1 hour.

Meanwhile, in a skillet, cook the bacon over medium heat until crisp. Using a slotted spoon, remove to paper towels; drain, reserving the drippings. Saute onion in the drippings; remove onion with a slotted spoon and set aside. When cool, combine bacon, onion and pepper; set aside.

Punch the dough down. Turn onto a lightly floured surface; divided into four portions. Roll each into a 12-in. circle; cut into 12 wedges. Sprinkle a heaping teaspoonful of bacon mixture over each wedge. Roll up from the wide end. Place point end down 2 in. part on greased baking sheets. Cover and let rise, about 30 minutes.

In a small bowl, beat water and remaining egg; brush over rolls. Bake at 350° for 12-14 minutes or until golden brown. Remove to wire racks. Refrigerate leftovers. **YIELD: 4 DOZEN.**

Yummy Yeast Rolls

Yummy Yeast Rolls

PREP: **30 MIN.** + RISING BAKE: **20 MIN.**

I've won prizes in several baking contests with these rolls. My granddaughters like them so much that I send some home with them after each visit.

Chris Litsey ✳ Elwood, Indiana

    2 packages (1/4 ounce *each*) active dry yeast
  3/4 cup warm milk (110° to 115°)
  3/4 cup lemon-lime soda
  1/2 cup butter, cubed
    4 eggs
  3/4 cup sugar
    1 teaspoon salt
5-3/4 to 6-1/2 cups all-purpose flour

In a large bowl, dissolve yeast in warm milk. In a saucepan, heat soda and butter to 110°-115°. Add the warm soda mixture, eggs, sugar, salt and 2 cups flour to yeast mixture; beat until smooth. Stir in enough remaining flour to form a soft dough.

Turn onto a floured surface; knead until smooth and elastic, about 6-8 minutes. Place in a greased bowl, turning once to grease top. Cover and let rise in a warm place until doubled, about 1 hour.

Punch the dough down. Turn onto a lightly floured surface; divide into four portions. Divide each portion into nine pieces. Shape each into a ball. Place on greased baking sheets. Cover and let rise until doubled, about 45 minutes.

Bake at 350° for 18-20 minutes or until golden brown. Remove to wire racks to cool. **YIELD: 3 DOZEN.**

Cream Cheese Coils

2 minutes. Add egg and 1/2 cup flour; beat on high for 2 minutes. Stir in enough remaining flour to form a stiff dough. Cover and refrigerate for 2 hours.

Turn dough onto a lightly floured surface; divide into 18 pieces. Shape each piece into a ball; roll each into a 15-in. rope. Holding one end of rope, loosely wrap dough around, forming a coil. Tuck end under; pinch to seal.

Place coils 2 in. apart on greased baking sheets. Cover and let rise until doubled, about 1 hour.

In a small bowl, beat the cream cheese, egg yolk, vanilla and remaining sugar until smooth. Using the back of a spoon, make a 1-in.-wide indentation in the center of each coil; spoon a round tablespoon of cream cheese mixture into each indentation.

Bake at 400° for 10-12 minutes or until lightly browned. Remove from pans to wire racks to cool.

In a small bowl, combine the confectioners' sugar, vanilla and enough water to achieve drizzling consistency. Drizzle over cooled rolls. Store in the refrigerator. **YIELD: 1-1/2 DOZEN.**

Cream Cheese Coils

PREP: **30 MIN. + CHILLING** BAKE: **10 MIN.**

These fantastic sweet rolls are easy to make but look like you spent a lot of time on them.

Susan Peck ✳ Republic, Missouri

3-3/4 to 4-1/4 cups all-purpose flour
 3/4 cup sugar, *divided*
 2 packages (1/4 ounce *each*) active dry yeast
1-1/2 teaspoons salt
 3/4 cup milk
 1/2 cup water
 1/2 cup butter, cubed
 1 egg
 1 package (8 ounces) cream cheese, softened
 1 egg yolk
 1/2 teaspoon vanilla extract
GLAZE:
 1 cup confectioners' sugar
 1/2 teaspoon vanilla extract
 3 to 4 teaspoons water

In a large bowl, combine 1 cup flour, 1/2 cup sugar, yeast and salt. In a small saucepan, heat the milk, water and butter to 120°-130°. Add to the dry ingredients; beat on medium speed for

Sunflower Wheat Bread

PREP: **10 MIN.** BAKE: **3 HOURS**

The bread machine does almost all the work for this unusual wheat bread. The orange juice-honey flavor combination is delightful.

Karen Ann Bland ✳ Gove, Kansas

 1 cup warm milk (70° to 80°)
 3/4 cup water
 2 tablespoons salted sunflower kernels
 2 tablespoons honey
 1 tablespoon orange juice
4-1/2 teaspoons butter, softened
 1 teaspoon salt
 1/2 teaspoon grated orange peel
 3 cups bread flour
 1/2 cup whole wheat flour
 1/3 cup old-fashioned oats
 2 teaspoons active dry yeast

In bread machine pan, place all ingredients in order suggested by manufacturer. Select basic bread setting. Choose crust color and loaf size if available.

Bake according to bread machine directions (check the dough after 5 minutes of mixing; add 1 to 2 tablespoons of water or flour if needed). **YIELD: 1 LOAF (8 SLICES).**

EDITOR'S NOTE: We recommend you do not use a bread machine's time-delay feature for this recipe.

Sunflower Wheat Bread

Italian Cheese Bread

PREP: 15 MIN. + RISING BAKE: 15 MIN.

People are astounded to learn I make this savory Italian bread from scratch in less that an hour. With this recipe from my brother-in-law, warm slices are a delicious and easy alternative to garlic toast. I'll sometimes use it as a snack or appetizer.

Sandra Wingert ✳ Star City, Saskatchewan

2-1/2 cups all-purpose flour
  1 teaspoon salt
  1 teaspoon sugar
  1 tablespoon quick-rise yeast
  1 cup warm water (120° to 130°)
  1 tablespoon canola oil

TOPPING:
  1/4 to 1/3 cup prepared Italian salad dressing
  1/4 teaspoon salt
  1/4 teaspoon garlic powder
  1/4 teaspoon dried oregano
  1/4 teaspoon dried thyme
Dash pepper
  1 tablespoon grated Parmesan cheese
  1/2 cup shredded part-skim mozzarella cheese

In a bowl, combine the flour, salt, sugar and yeast. Combine the water and oil; add to flour mixture. Add additional flour if needed to form a soft dough.

Turn onto a floured surface; knead for 1-2 minutes or until smooth and elastic. Place in a greased bowl, turning once to grease top. Cover and let rise in a warm place for 20 minutes.

Punch the dough down; place on a greased 12-in. pizza pan and pat into a 12-in. circle. Brush with the salad dressing. Combine the seasonings; sprinkle over the top. Sprinkle with the cheeses.

Bake at 450° for 15 minutes or until golden brown. Serve warm. **YIELD: 1 LOAF (16 SLICES).**

Italian Cheese Bread

Jalapeno Bread

Jalapeno Bread

PREP: **30 MIN.** + STANDING BAKE: **35 MIN.** + COOLING

This bread is a big hit at our house. Its unusual texture makes it a conversation piece, so almost everybody tries it.

Mary Alice Watt * Upton, Wyoming

- 2 loaves (1 pound *each*) frozen bread dough, thawed
- 1 can (8-3/4 ounces) whole kernel corn, drained
- 1 egg, lightly beaten
- 1 can (3-1/2 ounces) whole jalapenos, chopped
- 2 tablespoons taco seasoning
- 1 jar (2 ounces) sliced pimientos, drained
- 1-1/2 teaspoons vinegar

Cut bread dough into 1-in. pieces. Place all ingredients in a large bowl and toss to mix well. Spoon into two greased 8-in. x 4-in. loaf pans. Cover and let stand for 15 minutes.

Bake at 350° for 35-40 minutes. Cool in pan 10 minutes before removing to a wire rack. Serve warm if desired. YIELD: **2 LOAVES (16 SLICES EACH).**

EDITOR'S NOTE: Remove seeds from the jalapenos before chopping for a milder bread. When cutting hot peppers, disposable gloves are recommended. Avoid touching your face.

Three-Cheese Twists

PREP: **20 MIN.** + RISING BAKE: **15 MIN.**

Although these twists look like you fussed, convenient frozen dinner rolls hurry along the preparation.

June Poepping * Quincy, Illinois

- 1/2 cup butter, melted
- 1/4 teaspoon garlic salt
- 1-1/2 cups (6 ounces) finely shredded cheddar cheese
- 1-1/2 cups (6 ounces) finely shredded part-skim mozzarella cheese
- 3/4 cup grated Parmesan cheese
- 1 tablespoon dried parsley flakes
- 24 frozen bread dough dinner rolls, thawed

In a shallow bowl, combine butter and garlic salt. In bowl, combine cheeses and parsley. On a lightly floured surface, roll each dinner roll into a 10-in. rope. Dip in butter mixture, then in cheese mixture.

Three-Cheese Twists

Great-Grandma's Prune Roll

Fold each rope in half and twist twice; pinch ends together to seal. Place 2 in. apart on greased baking sheets. Cover and let rise in a warm place until almost doubled, about 30 minutes. Bake at 350° for 15 minutes or until golden brown. **YIELD: 2 DOZEN.**

Great-Grandma's Prune Roll

PREP: 30 MIN. + RISING BAKE: 25 MIN.
Here's an old-fashioned favorite that's sure to bring back memories of home cooking.

Marci Kulla ✳ Brush Prairie, Washington

- 1 package (1/4 ounce) active dry yeast
- 1 cup warm milk (110° to 115°)
- 1/2 cup butter, softened
- 1/2 cup shortening
- 3 egg yolks
- 3 tablespoons sugar
- 1 teaspoon salt
- 4 cups all-purpose flour

FILLING:

- 2 cups pitted dried plums
- 1/2 cup water
- 1/2 cup sugar
- 2 tablespoons lemon juice
- 1/4 cup butter
- 1/2 teaspoon ground cinnamon

GLAZE:

- 1 cup confectioners' sugar
- 1/4 teaspoon vanilla extract
- 2 to 3 tablespoons water

In a large bowl, dissolve yeast in warm milk. Add the butter, shortening, egg yolks, sugar and salt and 3 cups flour. Beat until smooth. Stir in enough remaining flour to form a soft dough. Cover and refrigerate overnight.

In a saucepan, cook plums in water 12-15 minutes or until liquid is absorbed. Mash; add sugar and lemon juice. Cook for 8-10 minutes over low heat until thickened. Cool and refrigerate.

Turn dough onto a lightly floured surface; divide in half. Roll each portion into a 3-in. x 9-in. rectangle. Dot with butter; sprinkle with cinnamon. Spread about 1/3 cup plum filling down the center of each.

Fold a third of the dough lengthwise over filling. Fold remaining dough over top; pinch seams to seal and tuck ends under. Place seam side down in two greased 15-in. x 10-in. x 1-in. baking pans. Cover and let rise in a warm place for 2 hours or until doubled.

Bake at 350° for 25-30 minutes or until golden brown. Remove from pans to wire racks to cool. Combine the glaze ingredients; drizzle over loaves. **YIELD: 2 LOAVES (12 SLICES EACH).**

Cranberry Kolaches

Turn dough onto a floured surface; roll to 1/2-in. thickness. Cut with a floured 2-1/2-in. biscuit cutter. Place 2 in. apart on lightly greased baking sheets. Cover and let rise in a warm place until doubled, about 1 hour.

Using the back of a spoon, make a 1-1/2-in.-wide well in the center of each roll. Combine filling ingredients; spoon into each well. Bake at 350° for 15-20 minutes or until golden brown. Remove from pans to wire racks to cool.

If glaze is desired, combine confectioners' sugar, extract and enough milk to achieve drizzling consistency. Drizzle over rolls. Store in the refrigerator. **YIELD: 1-1/2 DOZEN.**

Cinnamon-Swirl Pear Bread

PREP: **50 MIN. + RISING** BAKE: **35 MIN.**

Pears add moisture to this delightful bread. I've been making it for many years, and it's become a favorite of my family and friends.

Joan Anderson ✳ Winnipeg, Manitoba

- 3 cups chopped peeled ripe pears (about 3 medium)
- 1/2 cup water
- 1-1/4 cups plus 1 teaspoon sugar, *divided*
- 3 packages (1/4 ounce *each*) active dry yeast
- 1/2 cup warm water (110° to 115°)
- 4 eggs, lightly beaten
- 1/2 cup butter, softened
- 1/2 cup honey
- 2 teaspoons salt
- 1 teaspoon almond extract
- 10 to 11 cups all-purpose flour
- 1 tablespoon ground cinnamon

In a large saucepan, combine pears, water and 1/2 cup sugar. Simmer, uncovered, for 10-12 minutes or until tender. Drain well, reserving syrup. If necessary, add cold water to syrup to measure 1 cup; set aside.

In a bowl, dissolve yeast in warm water. Add 1 teaspoon sugar; let stand for 10 minutes. Add eggs, butter, honey, salt, extract, 4 cups flour and reserved pears and syrup. Beat until smooth. Add enough remaining flour to form a soft dough.

Turn onto a floured surface; knead until smooth and elastic, about 6-8 minutes. Place in a greased bowl; turn once to grease top. Cover and let rise in a warm place until doubled, about 1-1/4 hours.

Cranberry Kolaches

PREP: **20 MIN. + RISING** BAKE: **15 MIN.**

Besides cranberry, I've filled these with cooked pitted prunes, apricots, pie filling and even jam or jelly.

Shirley Dehler ✳ Columbus, Wisconsin

- 4 to 4-1/2 cups all-purpose flour
- 1/4 cup sugar
- 1 package (1/4 ounce) active dry yeast
- 1 teaspoon salt
- 3/4 cup milk
- 1/2 cup water
- 1/4 cup butter, cubed
- 1 egg

FILLING:
- 1 cup whole-berry cranberry sauce
- 1 cup grated peeled tart apple
- 1/2 teaspoon ground cinnamon

GLAZE (optional):
- 1 cup confectioners' sugar
- 1/4 teaspoon vanilla *or* orange extract
- 1 to 2 tablespoons milk

In a bowl, combine 2 cups flour, sugar, yeast and salt. In a saucepan, heat the milk, water and butter to 120°-130°. Add to the dry ingredients; beat just until moistened. Add the egg; beat until smooth. Stir in enough remaining flour to form a soft dough (dough will be sticky). Do not knead. Cover and let rest for 20 minutes.

Punch dough down; divide into thirds. Roll each portion into a 16-in. x 8-in. rectangle. Combine cinnamon and remaining 3/4 cup sugar; sprinkle over dough to within 1/2 in. of edges.

Roll up, jelly-roll style, starting with a short side; pinch seams to seal. Place, seam side down, in three greased 9-in. x 5-in. loaf pans. Cover and let rise until doubled, about 45 minutes.

Bake at 375° for 20 minutes. Cover loosely with foil. Bake 15-20 minutes longer or until bread tests done. Remove from pans to wire rack to cool. **YIELD: 3 LOAVES (16 SLICES EACH).**

Cinnamon-Swirl Pear Bread

Banana Yeast Bread

PREP: **25 MIN. + RISING** BAKE: **30 MIN.**

Though our two children dislike bananas, they've always enjoyed this. It's been a standby since my grandmother shared the recipe before I was married.

Maralee Meyer ✳ Milford, Nebraska

- 3/4 cup milk
- 1/2 cup butter
- 1/2 cup sugar
- 5-1/4 to 6 cups all-purpose flour
-   2 packages (1/4 ounce *each*) active dry yeast
-   1 teaspoon salt
-   3 eggs
-   3 medium ripe bananas, mashed
-   1 teaspoon water

In a large saucepan, cook and stir the milk, butter and sugar over medium heat until butter is melted; cool to 120°-130°. In a large bowl, combine 2 cups of flour, yeast, salt, 2 eggs, bananas and milk mixture; beat on low speed until combined. Beat on medium for 3 minutes. Stir in enough remaining flour to form a firm dough.

Turn onto a floured surface; knead until smooth and elastic, about 4-6 minutes. Place in a greased bowl, turning once to grease top. Cover and let rise in a warm place until doubled, about 45 minutes.

Divide dough in half; shape each into a round loaf. Place on a greased baking sheet; cut slits in tops. Cover and let rise until doubled, about 45 minutes.

Beat remaining egg with water; brush over the loaves. Bake at 375° for 30-35 minutes or until golden brown. Remove from pans to wire racks. **YIELD: 2 LOAVES (14 SLICES EACH).**

Banana Yeast Bread

Maple Sticky Buns

Maple Sticky Buns

PREP: **30 MIN.** + RISING BAKE: **25 MIN.**

My family has a small sugaring operation in our backyard. These buns make good use of the maple syrup we make. It's a family tradition to serve this treat on Thanksgiving every year.

Priscilla Rossi ✳ East Barre, Vermont

- 2 packages (1/4 ounce *each*) active dry yeast
- 2 cups warm water (110° to 115°)
- 1/4 cup shortening
- 1/2 cup sugar
- 1 egg
- 2 teaspoons salt
- 6 to 6-1/2 cups all-purpose flour
- 6 tablespoons butter, softened
- 3/4 cup packed brown sugar
- 1 tablespoon ground cinnamon
- 3/4 cup chopped walnuts
- 1-1/2 cup maple syrup
- Additional brown sugar

In a large bowl, dissolve yeast in water. Add the shortening, sugar, egg, salt and 5 cups flour. Beat until smooth. Add enough remaining flour to form a soft dough. Cover and refrigerate for 24 hours.

Punch dough down. Turn onto a floured surface; knead until smooth and elastic, about 6-8 minutes, adding more flour if needed. Divide into thirds. Roll each portion into a 16-in. x 10-in. rectangle.

On each rectangle, spread 2 tablespoons butter and sprinkle with 1/4 cup brown sugar, 1 teaspoon cinnamon and 1/4 cup walnuts. Pour syrup into three greased 9-in. round baking pans. Sprinkle with brown sugar.

Tightly roll up each rectangle, jelly-roll style, starting with the short side. Slice each roll into 10 pieces; place over syrup. Cover and let rise until doubled, about 30 minutes.

Bake at 350° for 25-30 minutes or until golden brown. Cool in pans for 5 minutes; invert onto a wire rack. YIELD: **2-1/2 DOZEN**.

EDITOR'S NOTE: 11-in. x 7-in. baking pans may be substituted for the 9-in. round pans.

Sausage Cheese Braid

Sausage Cheese Braid

PREP: **35 MIN. + RISING** BAKE: **20 MIN.**

This braided bread looks so pretty on a buffet table. A yummy filling of pork sausage and cheese is tucked into each slice!

Christena Weed ✳ Levant, Kansas

      2 packages (1/4 ounce *each*) active dry yeast
1-1/4 cups warm water (110° to 115°)
      2 tablespoons sugar
1-1/2 teaspoons salt
      1 teaspoon Italian seasoning
      2 eggs
   1/4 cup butter, softened
      4 to 4-1/2 cups all-purpose flour
      1 pound bulk hot pork sausage
      1 cup (4 ounces) shredded part-skim
         mozzarella *or* cheddar cheese

In a large bowl, dissolve yeast in water. Add the sugar, salt, Italian seasoning, 1 egg, butter and 2 cups flour; beat until smooth. Add enough remaining flour to form a soft dough.

Turn onto a floured surface; knead until smooth and elastic, about 6-8 minutes. Place in a greased bowl, turning once to grease top. Cover and let rise in a warm place until doubled, about 1 hour.

Meanwhile, in a large skillet, cook sausage until no longer pink; drain and set aside to cool.

Punch the dough down; divide in half. On a floured surface, roll each half into a 14-in. x 12-in. rectangle. Cut each one into three 14-in. x 4-in. strips. Combine cheese and sausage; spoon 1/2 cup down the center of each strip. Bring long edges together over filling; pinch to seal.

Place three strips with seam side down on greased baking sheets. Braid strips together; secure ends. Cover and let rise until doubled, about 45 minutes.

Beat remaining egg and brush over loaves. Bake at 400° for 20-25 minutes or until golden. Immediately remove from baking sheets to wire racks. Serve warm. Refrigerate leftovers.

YIELD: 2 LOAVES (10 SLICES EACH).

Finnish Bread

Finnish Bread

PREP: **20 MIN. + RISING** BAKE: **40 MIN.**

This recipe was brought over from Finland by pioneers who settled the area. We make this bread for a local festival that features foods from different countries.

Arthur Luama ✳ Red Lodge, Montana

      1 package (1/4 ounce) active dry yeast
      2 cups warm water (110° to 115°)
      1 cup whole wheat flour
   1/4 cup butter, melted, *divided*
      1 tablespoon brown sugar
      2 teaspoons salt
4-1/2 to 5 cups all-purpose flour

In a large bowl, dissolve yeast in water. Add whole wheat flour, 2 tablespoons of butter, brown sugar, salt and 2 cups of all-purpose flour; beat until smooth. Add enough remaining all-purpose flour to form a soft dough.

Turn onto a floured surface; knead until smooth and elastic, about 6-8 minutes. Place in a greased bowl, turning once to grease top. Cover and let rise in a warm place until doubled, about 1 hour.

Punch the dough down. Shape into two 6-in. rounds; place on a greased baking sheet. Cut slashes in top with a knife. Cover and let rise in warm place until doubled, about 40 minutes.

Bake at 400° for 40-45 minutes or until golden brown. Brush with the remaining butter.

YIELD: 2 LOAVES (12 SLICES EACH).

Almond Streusel Rolls

In a large bowl, dissolve yeast in warm water. Add the milk, butter, sugar, eggs and salt and 2 cups flour. Beat until smooth. Stir in enough remaining flour to form a soft dough.

Turn onto a floured surface; knead until smooth and elastic, about 6-8 minutes. Place in a greased bowl, turning once to grease top. Cover and let rise in a warm place until doubled, about 1 hour.

Punch dough down; roll out to a 15-in. x 10-in. rectangle. In a large bowl, beat filling ingredients until smooth. Spread over dough.

Roll up jelly-roll style, starting with a short side; seal seams. Cut into 12 slices. Place in a greased 13-in. x 9-in. baking pan. Cover and let rise in a warm place until doubled, about 30 minutes.

Combine topping ingredients; sprinkle over rolls. Bake at 350° for 35-40 minutes or until golden brown. Cool on a wire rack.

In a small bowl, combine confectioners' sugar, extract and enough milk to achieve drizzling consistency; drizzle over rolls. **YIELD: 1 DOZEN.**

Almond Streusel Rolls

PREP: 40 MIN. + RISING BAKE: 35 MIN. + COOLING

These are just wonderful sweet rolls. I've used them as a deliciously different dessert also. Often, they don't even get to cool before the pan is empty!

Perlene Hoekema ✳ Lynden, Washington

2 packages (1/4 ounce *each*) active dry yeast
3/4 cup warm water (110° to 115°)
3/4 cup warm milk (110° to 115°)
1/4 cup butter, softened
1/2 cup sugar
2 eggs
1 teaspoon salt
5-1/4 to 5-1/2 cups all-purpose flour
FILLING:
1/2 cup almond paste
1/4 cup butter, softened
1/2 cup packed brown sugar
1/4 teaspoon almond extract
TOPPING:
3 tablespoons sugar
1 tablespoon all-purpose flour
1 tablespoon butter
ICING:
1-1/2 cups confectioners' sugar
1/4 teaspoon almond extract
1 to 2 tablespoons milk

Whole Wheat Bread

PREP: 20 MIN. + RISING BAKE: 40 MIN.

I make this bread with my mother, who got the recipe from her mother. I usually make the dough, and my mom bakes it.

Freida Stutman ✳ Fillmore, New York

1 package (1/4 ounce) active dry yeast
3 cups warm water (110° to 115°), *divided*
3/4 cup canola oil
1/4 cup sugar
1/4 cup molasses
1 tablespoon salt
5 to 5-1/2 cups all-purpose flour
3 cups whole wheat flour

In a large bowl, dissolve yeast in 3/4 cup warm water. Add the oil, sugar, molasses, salt and remaining water. Combine flours; add 3 cups flour to mixture. Beat until smooth. Add enough remaining flour to form a firm dough.

Turn onto a floured surface; knead until smooth and elastic, about 6-8 minutes. Place in a greased bowl, turning once to grease top. Cover and let rise in a warm place until doubled, about 1 hour.

Punch the dough down. Turn onto a lightly floured surface; divide in half. Shape each portion into a loaf. Place in two greased 9-in. x 5-in. loaf pans. Cover and let rise until doubled, about 30 minutes.

Bake at 350° for 40-45 minutes or until golden brown. Remove from pans to cool on wire racks. **YIELD: 2 LOAVES (16 SLICES).**

Whole Wheat Bread

◐ Mexican Bread

PREP: **15 MIN.** BAKE: **3-4 HOURS**

Chopped green chilies and flakes of red pepper provide flecks of color in every slice of this large loaf. Slightly spicy with ground cumin, it's great for sandwiches or as an accompaniment to mild soups.

Loni McCoy ✳ Blaine, Minnesota

- 1 cup plus 2 tablespoons water (70° to 80°)
- 1/2 cup shredded Monterey Jack cheese
- 1 can (4 ounces) chopped green chilies
- 1 tablespoon butter, softened
- 2 tablespoons sugar
- 1 to 2 tablespoons crushed red pepper flakes
- 1 tablespoon nonfat dry milk powder
- 1 tablespoon ground cumin
- 1-1/2 teaspoons salt
- 3-1/4 cups bread flour
- 2-1/2 teaspoons active dry yeast

In a bread machine pan, place all ingredients in order suggested by manufacturer. Select basic bread setting. Choose crust color and loaf size if available.

Bake according to bread machine directions; (check dough after 5 minutes of mixing; add 1 to 2 tablespoons of water or flour if needed). **YIELD: 1 LOAF (16 SLICES).**

EDITOR'S NOTE: We recommend you do not use a bread machine's time-delay feature for this recipe.

Mexican Bread

Molasses Oat Bread

Molasses Oat Bread

PREP: **20 MIN.** + **RISING** BAKE: **45 MIN.**

This recipe has been passed down through my family from my Swedish great-grandmother. One Christmas, my mom made and distributed 25 of these loaves.

Patricia Finch Kelly ✳ Rindge, New Hampshire

- 4 cups boiling water
- 2 cups old-fashioned oats
- 1 cup molasses
- 1/4 cup sugar
- 3 tablespoons canola oil
- 3 teaspoons salt
- 1 package (1/4 ounce) active dry yeast
- 9 to 10 cups all-purpose flour

In a large bowl, pour boiling water over cereal. Add the molasses, sugar, oil and salt. Let stand until the mixture cools to 110°-115°, stirring occasionally. Stir in yeast. Add 8 cups flour. Beat until smooth. Add enough remaining flour to form a soft dough.

Turn onto a floured surface; knead until smooth and elastic, about 6-8 minutes. Place in a greased bowl, turning once to grease top. Cover and let rise in a warm place until doubled, about 1-1/2 hours.

Punch dough down and divide into thirds; shape into loaves. Place in three greased 9-in. x 5-in. loaf pans. Cover and let rise until doubled, about 1 hour.

Bake at 350° for 45-50 minutes or until golden brown. Remove from pans to wire racks to cool. YIELD: **3 LOAVES (12 SLICES EACH).**

Potato Pan Rolls

PREP: **55 MIN.** + **RISING** BAKE: **20 MIN.**

Beautiful color and light-as-a-feather texture make these rolls our family's favorite for holiday meals. I won the Reserve Champion award at a 4-H yeast bread competition with this recipe.

LeAnne Hofferichter ✳ Floresville, Texas

- 2 medium potatoes, peeled and quartered
- 1-1/2 cups water

Potato Pan Rolls

2 packages (1/4 ounce *each*) active dry yeast
1 teaspoon sugar
1/2 cup butter, melted
1/2 cup honey
1/4 cup canola oil
2 eggs
2 teaspoons salt
6 to 7 cups all-purpose flour

In a large saucepan, bring potatoes and water to a boil. Reduce heat; cover and simmer for 15-20 minutes or until tender. Drain, reserving 1 cup cooking liquid; cool liquid to 110°-115°. Mash potatoes; set aside 1 cup to cool to 110°-115° (save remaining potatoes for another use).

In a large bowl, dissolve yeast and sugar in reserved potato liquid; let stand for 5 minutes. Add reserved mashed potatoes, butter, honey, oil, eggs, salt and 1-1/2 cups flour; beat until smooth. Stir in enough remaining flour to form a soft dough.

Turn onto a floured surface; knead until smooth and elastic, about 6-8 minutes. Place in a greased bowl, turning once to grease top. Cover and let rise in a warm place until doubled, about 1 hour.

Punch dough down and turn onto a floured surface; divide into 30 pieces. Shape each piece into a ball. Place 10 balls each in three greased 9-in. round baking pans. Cover and let rise until doubled, about 30 minutes.

Bake at 400° for 20-25 minutes or until golden brown. Remove from pans to wire racks to cool. **YIELD: 2-1/2 DOZEN.**

Golden Raisin Wheat Bread

PREP: 35 MIN. + RISING BAKE: 35 MIN.

Since I'm single, I freeze extra loaves in freezer bags when I bake this tasty bread. Then the night before I'm about to run out of bread, I take a loaf out and thaw it at room temperature. It was only after I retired that I became interested in cooking and baking. Now, when relatives and I get together at Christmastime, I'm the one who's asked to bring the bread.
Nilah Schenck ✴ Beloit, Wisconsin

3/4 cup golden raisins
1/2 cup boiling water

Golden Raisin Wheat Bread

3 cups whole wheat flour
2 packages (1/4 ounce *each*) active dry yeast
1 tablespoon salt
1 teaspoon baking soda
1 carton (16 ounces) plain yogurt
1 cup water
1/3 cup honey
5 tablespoons butter
4-1/2 to 5 cups all-purpose flour

In a small bowl, combine raisins and water; let stand for 10 minutes. Drain well; set aside. In a large bowl, combine whole wheat flour, yeast, salt and baking soda. In a saucepan, heat the yogurt, water, honey and butter to 120°-130°. Add to dry ingredients. Add raisins and enough all-purpose flour to form a soft dough.

Turn onto a floured surface; knead until smooth and elastic, about 6-8 minutes. Place in a greased bowl, turning once to grease top. Cover and let rise in a warm place until doubled, about 1 hour.

Punch dough down; divide into thirds. Shape into loaves. Place in three greased 9-in. x 5-in. loaf pans. Cover and let rise until doubled, about 30 minutes.

Bake at 350° for 35-40 minutes or until golden brown. Remove from pans to cool on wire racks. **YIELD: 3 LOAVES (16 SLICES EACH).**

Cheddar English Muffins

Cheddar English Muffins

PREP: **20 MIN.** + RISING COOK: **20 MIN./BATCH**

These chewy English muffins have a scrumptious mild cheese flavor that intensifies when they're split and toasted. My family really enjoys them at breakfast or brunch.

Marge Goral ✳ Ridgefield, Connecticut

- 3 to 3-1/4 cups bread flour
- 1 tablespoon sugar
- 1 package (1/4 ounce) active dry yeast
- 1 teaspoon salt
- 3/4 cup warm water (120° to 130°)
- 2 tablespoons canola oil
- 1 egg
- 1 tablespoon cider vinegar
- 1/2 cup shredded cheddar cheese
- 4 tablespoons cornmeal, *divided*

In a large bowl, combine 2 cups flour, sugar, yeast and salt. Add the water and oil; beat on medium speed for 2 minutes. Add egg and vinegar; beat on high for 2 minutes. Stir in cheese and enough remaining flour to form a stiff dough.

Turn onto a floured surface; knead until the dough is smooth and no longer sticky, about 2 minutes.

Roll dough to about 1/2-in. thickness. Cut with a 3-in. round cutter. Roll scraps if desired. Coat baking sheets with cooking spray and sprinkle with 2 tablespoons cornmeal. Cover and let rise until doubled, about 1 hour.

Heat an ungreased griddle or electric skillet to 325°. Cook muffins for 20-25 minutes or until golden brown, turning every 5 minutes. Remove to wire racks to cool. Split with a fork and toast if desired. YIELD: **ABOUT 16 MUFFINS.**

Italian Snack Bread

PREP: **30 MIN.** + RISING BAKE: **25 MIN.**

This snack bread's very versatile—I've served it with spaghetti, as an appetizer and as a main dish. Because it stays so moist, I often bake it the day before I serve it.

Joan Nowacki ✳ Pewaukee, Wisconsin

- 1 package (1/4 ounce) active dry yeast
- 1 cup warm water (120° to 130°)
- 1 egg, lightly beaten
- 2 tablespoons olive oil
- 2-1/2 teaspoons dried oregano
- 1/2 teaspoon salt
- 2-1/2 cups all-purpose flour

TOPPING:

- 1-1/2 cups thinly sliced onion
- 1/4 cup olive oil
- 1 teaspoon dried rosemary, crushed
- 1 teaspoon coarse salt, optional

In a large bowl, dissolve yeast in warm water. Add egg, oil, oregano, salt and 1-1/2 cups flour. Beat until smooth. Stir in enough remaining flour to form a soft dough. Cover and let rest 10 minutes. Pat into a greased 13-in. x 9-in. baking pan; set aside.

In a large skillet, saute onion in oil until tender. Spoon evenly over dough. Sprinkle with rosemary and salt if desired. Cover and let rise in warm place until doubled, about 30 minutes.

Bake at 400° for 25-30 minutes or until lightly browned. Cut into small squares. Serve warm or at room temperature. YIELD: **ABOUT 8 SERVINGS.**

Almond-Filled Butterhorns

PREP: 30 MIN. + RISING BAKE: 10 MIN./BATCH

I add potato flakes to make my butterhorns tender. The rolls complement any meal wonderfully and have just the right sweetness to make them a coffee-hour favorite. Remember to hide a few for yourself!

Loraine Meyer ✳ Bend, Oregon

3-1/4 teaspoons active dry yeast
   2 cups warm milk (110° to 115°)
   4 eggs
   1 cup mashed potato flakes
   1 cup butter, softened
1/2 cup sugar
1-1/8 teaspoons salt
   7 to 8 cups all-purpose flour
   1 can (12-1/2 ounces) almond cake and pastry filling

Italian Snack Bread

In a large bowl, dissolve yeast in milk. Add the eggs, potato flakes, butter, sugar, salt and 4 cups flour. Beat on medium speed for 3 minutes. Beat until smooth. Stir in enough remaining flour to form a soft dough (dough will be sticky).

Turn onto a floured surface; knead until smooth and elastic, about 6-8 minutes. Place in a greased bowl, turning once to grease top. Cover and let rise in a warm place until doubled, about 1 hour.

Punch the dough down. Turn onto a lightly floured surface; divide into thirds. Roll each portion into a 12-in. circle; spread each with filling. Cut each circle into 12 wedges.

Roll up wedges from the wide end and place point side down 2 in. apart on greased baking sheets. Curve ends to form a crescent. Cover and let rise until doubled, about 30 minutes.

Bake at 375° for 10-12 minutes or until lightly browned. Remove from pans to wire racks. Serve warm. **YIELD: 3 DOZEN.**

EDITOR'S NOTE: This recipe was tested with Solo brand cake and pastry filling. Look for it in the baking aisle.

Almond-Filled Butterhorns

1st place

Bacon-Cheese Pinwheel Rolls

Bacon-Cheese Pinwheel Rolls

PREP: 30 MIN. + RISING BAKE: 25 MIN.

It's no wonder my husband adores these pinwheels. I got the original recipe from his mother. They taste great warm or cold and freeze well in plastic bags.

Wendy Mallard ✳ Stony Plain, Alberta

- 2 packages (1/4 ounce *each*) active dry yeast
- 2 teaspoons plus 1/2 cup sugar, *divided*
- 2 cups warm water (110° to 115°), *divided*
- 1 cup warm milk (110° to 115°)
- 2/3 cup butter, melted
- 2 eggs, lightly beaten
- 2 teaspoons salt
- 8-3/4 to 9-1/4 cups all-purpose flour
- 1 pound sliced bacon, diced
- 1/2 cup finely chopped onion
- 4 cups (16 ounces) shredded cheddar cheese

In a large bowl, dissolve yeast and 2 teaspoons of sugar in 1 cup warm water; let stand for 5 minutes. Add milk, butter, eggs, salt, 7 cups flour and remaining water and sugar. Beat until smooth. Stir in enough remaining flour to form a soft dough.

Turn onto a floured surface; knead until smooth and elastic, about 6-8 minutes. Place in a greased bowl, turning once to grease top. Cover and let rise in a warm place until doubled, about 1 hour.

Meanwhile, in a skillet, cook the bacon over medium heat until crisp. Using a slotted spoon, remove to paper towels; drain, reserving 1 tablespoon drippings. Cook onion in drippings until tender; set aside.

Punch the dough down. Turn onto a lightly floured surface; divide into fourths. Roll each portion into a 15-in. x 10-in. rectangle. Sprinkle each with a fourth of the cheese, about 1/3 cup bacon and about 2 tablespoons onion.

Roll up jelly-roll style, starting with a long side; pinch seam to seal. Cut each into 12 slices. Place cut side down 2 in. apart on ungreased baking sheets. Cover and let rise until doubled, about 30 minutes.

Bake at 350° for 25-30 minutes or until golden brown. Remove from pans to wire racks. Store in the refrigerator. **YIELD: 4 DOZEN.**

Spiced Raisin Bread

Spiced Raisin Bread

PREP: **15 MIN.** BAKE: **3-4 HOURS**

I have two bread machines, and one is often busy baking this soft, chewy loaf. The bread's nutmeg, cloves and orange peel fill my home with a wonderful aroma. Slices of this wonderful bread are great for peanut butter sandwiches.

Margaret Otley ✳ Waverly, Nebraska

1	cup plus 2 tablespoons water (70° to 80°)
3/4	cup raisins
2	tablespoons butter, softened
2	tablespoons brown sugar
2	teaspoons ground cinnamon
1	teaspoon salt
1/4	teaspoon ground nutmeg
1/4	teaspoon ground cloves
1/4	teaspoon grated orange peel
3	cups bread flour
2-1/4	teaspoons active dry yeast

In a bread machine pan, place all ingredients in order suggested by manufacturer. Select basic bread setting. Choose crust color and loaf size if available.

Bake according to bread machine directions (check dough after 5 minutes of mixing; add 1 to 2 tablespoons water or flour if needed). **YIELD: 1 LOAF (1-1/2 POUNDS, 24 SLICES).**

EDITOR'S NOTE: We recommend you do not use a bread machine's time-delay feature for this recipe.

Granola Raisin Bread

Granola Raisin Bread

PREP: **10 MIN.** BAKE: **3-4 HOURS**

Made with granola, oats, raisins and honey, this bread has a subtle sweetness. It's so delightful that friends often request the recipe. Slices of the crusty loaf are especially good toasted. If you prefer a softer crust, rub margarine or butter on the loaf while it's warm.

Patricia Nelson ✳ Kenosha, Wisconsin

1-2/3	cups water (70° to 80°)
1/3	cup honey
2	tablespoons butter
1-1/2	teaspoons salt
3-1/2	cups bread flour
1	cup quick-cooking oats
1	tablespoon active dry yeast
1	cup granola
3/4	cup golden raisins

In a bread machine pan, place the first seven ingredients in order suggested by manufacturer. Select basic bread setting. Choose crust color and loaf size if available.

Bake according to bread machine directions (check dough after 5 minutes of mixing; add 1 to 2 tablespoons of water or flour if needed). Just before the final kneading (your machine may audibly signal this), add the granola and raisins. **YIELD: 1 LOAF (2 POUNDS, 16 SLICES).**

Herbed Cheese Ring

Herbed Cheese Ring

PREP: **35 MIN. + RISING** BAKE: **20 MIN. + CHILLING**

This savory cheese loaf is great sliced in thin wedges to go with soup, salads or casseroles. I've served it to large crowds and received many compliments. One year, I gave it to our neighbor for Christmas.

Evelyn Bear ✳ Kingston, Idaho

- 1 package (1/4 ounce) active dry yeast
- 1/4 cup warm water (110° to 115°)
- 1 cup warm milk (110° to 115°)
- 1/4 cup canola oil
- 2 tablespoons honey
- 1 egg
- 1 teaspoon salt
- 1 cup whole wheat flour
- 2-1/2 cups all-purpose flour
- 1 teaspoon *each* dried oregano, basil and rosemary, crushed

FILLING:

- 1-1/2 cups (6 ounces) shredded cheddar cheese
- 1/2 teaspoon dried parsley flakes
- 1/4 teaspoon garlic powder
- 1/4 teaspoon paprika

TOPPING:

- 1 egg, lightly beaten
- 2 teaspoons sesame seeds
- 4 teaspoons grated Parmesan cheese

In a large bowl, dissolve yeast in warm water. Add the milk, oil, honey, egg, salt, whole wheat flour, 1 cup all-purpose flour and herbs. Beat until blended. Stir in enough remaining all-purpose flour to form a soft dough. Cover and refrigerate overnight.

Punch dough down and turn onto a floured surface; divide in half. Roll one portion into a 15-in. x 10-in. rectangle. Combine the filling ingredients; sprinkle half over dough. Roll up jelly-roll style, starting with a long side; pinch seams to seal.

Place seam side down on a greased baking sheet; pinch the ends together to form a ring. With a sharp knife, cut 1/2-in. slashes at 2-in. intervals. Repeat with remaining dough and filling. Cover and let rise in a warm place until doubled, about 30 minutes.

Brush each ring with egg; sprinkle with the sesame seeds and cheese. Bake at 350° for 20-25 minutes or until golden brown. Remove from pans to wire racks. **YIELD: 2 LOAVES (12 SLICES EACH).**

Frosted Rhubarb Cookies, PAGE 365

❝ *We have two prolific rhubarb plants, so I'm always looking for new ways to use the harvest. The recipe for these soft, delectable cookies, flavored with coconut, was given to me by a friend.* ❞

Shauna Schneyder
Idaho Falls, Idaho

COOKIES & CANDIES

DO YOU HAVE A WINNING RECIPE?

Enter your most prized recipes in the *Taste of Home* recipe contests, and you may win some money and the chance to have your recipe published. Log onto **tasteofhome.com/RecipeContests** for a list of our current contests and submission deadlines. Good luck...we'll be looking for your recipe.

Visit us @
tasteofhome
.com

cookies & candies

⏱ Peanut Butter Popcorn Bars

PREP/TOTAL TIME: **30 MIN.**

If you're looking for a fun snack for kids, try these chewy popcorn bars that have a mild peanut butter taste. They're easy to stir up and can be pressed into a pan to form bars or shaped into balls.

Kathy Oswald ✳ Wauzeka, Wisconsin

- 10 cups popped popcorn
- 1/2 cup sugar
- 1/2 cup light corn syrup
- 1/2 cup creamy peanut butter
- 1/2 teaspoon vanilla extract

Place popcorn in a large bowl; set aside. In a saucepan over medium heat, bring sugar and corn syrup to a boil, stirring constantly. Boil for 1 minute. Remove from the heat.

Stir in peanut butter and vanilla; mix well. Pour over popcorn and mix until well coated. Press into a buttered 13-in. x 9-in. pan. Cool slightly before cutting. YIELD: **2 DOZEN.**

Peanut Butter Popcorn Bars

⏱ Quick Elephant Ears

PREP/TOTAL TIME: **15 MIN.**

Our eight children love helping make these sweet crunchy treats. We fry flour tortillas for a few seconds in oil, then sprinkle with cinnamon and sugar. I usually do the frying, then have one of the older kids add the coating.

Terry Lynn Ayers ✳ Anderson, Indiana

- 1-1/2 cups sugar
- 2 teaspoons ground cinnamon
- Oil for frying
- 10 flour tortillas (6 inches)

In a large resealable plastic bag, combine sugar and cinnamon; set aside. In a small skillet, heat 1/2 in of oil. Place one tortilla at a time in skillet, cook for 5 seconds; turn and cook 10 seconds longer or until browned. Place in the sugar mixture; toss to coat. Serve immediately. YIELD: **10 SERVINGS.**

Quick Elephant Ears

Blond Brownies a la Mode

1st place

Blond Brownies a la Mode

PREP: 25 MIN. BAKE: 25 MIN. + COOLING

We attend a lot of church socials, and I'm always looking for something new and different to prepare. These brownies, drizzled with a sweet maple sauce, are a sure hit...with or without the ice cream.

Pat Parker ✳ Chester, South Carolina

    3/4 cup butter, softened
      2 cups packed brown sugar
      4 eggs
      2 teaspoons vanilla extract
      2 cups all-purpose flour
      2 teaspoons baking powder
      1 teaspoon salt
  1-1/2 cups chopped pecans
MAPLE CREAM SAUCE:
      1 cup maple syrup
      2 tablespoons butter
    1/4 cup evaporated milk
Vanilla ice cream and chopped pecans

In a large bowl, cream butter and brown sugar until light and fluffy. Add eggs, one at a time, beating well after each addition. Beat in vanilla. Combine the flour, baking powder and salt; gradually add to creamed mixture. Stir in pecans.

Spread into a greased 13-in. x 9-in. baking pan. Bake at 350° for 25-30 minutes or until a toothpick inserted near the center comes out clean. Cool on a wire rack.

For the sauce, combine syrup and butter in a saucepan. Bring to a boil; cook and stir for 3 minutes. Remove from the heat; stir in milk. Cut brownies into squares; cut in half if desired.

Place on dessert plates with a scoop of ice cream. Top with sauce; sprinkle with pecans. YIELD: 20 SERVINGS.

Hazelnut Toffee

PREP: 30 MIN. + STANDING

I always make plenty of this delicious toffee to serve at Christmas and give as gifts.

Earlene Ertelt ✳ Woodburn, Oregon

  1-3/4 cups finely chopped hazelnuts
  1-1/2 cups sugar
    1/2 cup water
    1/3 cup light corn syrup
      1 cup butter
    1/4 teaspoon salt
    1/4 teaspoon baking soda
    1/4 teaspoon orange extract
      1 cup (6 ounces) semisweet chocolate chips

Place the hazelnuts in a greased 15-in. x 10-in. x 1-in. baking pan. Bake at 300° for 15 minutes or until toasted; set aside.

In a heavy saucepan, combine sugar, water and corn syrup; bring to a boil over medium heat. Cover and boil for 2 minutes. Stir in butter; cook over medium heat, stirring occasionally, until mixture reaches 300° (hard-crack stage) on a candy thermometer. Remove from the heat; quickly stir in salt, baking soda, orange extract and 1-1/4 cups toasted hazelnuts.

Pour into a greased baking sheet and spread to 1/4-in. thickness. Let stand at room temperature until cool, about 1 hour.

In a microwave, melt chocolate chips; stir until smooth. Spread over toffee. Sprinkle with the remaining hazelnuts. Let stand for 1 hour. Break into bite-size pieces. YIELD: 2 POUNDS.

Frosted Rhubarb Cookies

PREP: **30 MIN.** BAKE: **10 MIN./BATCH + COOLING**

We have two prolific rhubarb plants, so I'm always eager to find new ways to use the harvest. The recipe for these soft, delectable cookies, flavored with coconut, was given to me by a friend.

Shauna Schneyder ✳ Idaho Falls, Idaho

1	cup shortening
1-1/2	cups packed brown sugar
2	eggs
3	cups all-purpose flour
1	teaspoon baking soda
1/2	teaspoon salt
1-1/2	cups diced fresh *or* frozen rhubarb
3/4	cup flaked coconut

FROSTING:

1	package (3 ounces) cream cheese, softened
1	tablespoon butter, softened
1-1/2	cups confectioners' sugar
3	teaspoons vanilla extract

In a bowl, cream shortening and brown sugar until light and fluffy. Beat in eggs. Combine the flour, baking soda and salt; gradually add to creamed mixture and mix well. Fold in the rhubarb and coconut.

Drop by rounded tablespoonfuls 2 in. apart onto greased baking sheets. Bake at 350° for 10-14 minutes or until cookies are golden brown. Cool for 1 minute before removing to wire racks to cool completely.

For frosting, in a small bowl, beat cream cheese and butter until fluffy. Beat in the confectioners' sugar and vanilla. Spread over cookies. **YIELD: 4 DOZEN.**

EDITOR'S NOTE: If using frozen rhubarb, measure rhubarb while still frozen, then thaw completely. Drain in a colander, but do not press liquid out.

Hazelnut Toffee

Frosted Rhubarb Cookies

Pistachio Cranberry Biscotti

🌙 Pistachio Cranberry Biscotti

PREP: **30 MIN.** BAKE: **35 MIN. + COOLING**

These biscotti taste great with a cup of coffee or even with a glass of sweet white wine for dessert. The lemon drizzle makes them seem indulgent.

Marta Perez-Stable ✴ Westlake, Ohio

1-1/2   cups dried cranberries

  2   tablespoons orange juice

1/3   cup butter, softened

2/3   cup sugar

  2   eggs

  1   teaspoon vanilla extract

  2   cups all-purpose flour

  2   teaspoons baking powder

1/2   teaspoon salt

  1   cup shelled pistachios

  4   teaspoons grated lemon peel

ICING:

  1   cup confectioners' sugar

  1   teaspoon grated lemon peel

  1   to 2 tablespoons fat-free milk

Place cranberries in a small bowl; sprinkle with orange juice. In a large bowl, cream butter and sugar. Add eggs, one at a time, beating well after each addition. Beat in the vanilla. Combine the flour, baking powder and salt; gradually add to creamed mixture. Stir in pistachios and lemon peel. Drain cranberries; stir into dough.

On a lightly floured surface, divide the dough into thirds. On a baking sheet coated with cooking spray, shape each portion into a 12-in. x 2-in. rectangle. Bake at 350° for 20-25 minutes or until golden brown. Cool for 5 minutes.

Transfer to a cutting board; with a serrated knife, cut each loaf into 20 slices. Place cut side down on baking sheets coated with cooking spray. Bake for 12-15 minutes or until firm, turning once. Remove to wire racks to cool.

For icing, combine confectioners' sugar and lemon peel; stir in enough milk to achieve the desired drizzling consistency. Drizzle over biscotti. Store in an airtight container. **YIELD: 5 DOZEN.**

NUTRITION FACTS: 2 cookies equals 129 calories, 4 g fat (2 g saturated fat), 20 mg cholesterol, 109 mg sodium, 21 g carbohydrate, 1 g fiber, 2 g protein. **DIABETIC EXCHANGES:** 1-1/2 starch, 1/2 fat.

Coffee Shop Fudge

PREP: **15 MIN. + CHILLING**

This smooth, creamy fudge has an irresistible crunch from pecans. The coffee and cinnamon blend nicely to provide subtle flavor.

Beth Osborne Skinner ✴ Bristol, Tennessee

  1   cup chopped pecans

  3   cups (18 ounces) semisweet chocolate chips

  1   can (14 ounces) sweetened condensed milk

2 tablespoons strong brewed coffee, room temperature

1 teaspoon ground cinnamon

1/8 teaspoon salt

1 teaspoon vanilla extract

Line an 8-in. square pan with foil and butter the foil; set aside. Place pecans in a microwave-safe pie plate. Microwave, uncovered, on high for 3 minutes, stirring after each minute; set aside.

In a 2-qt. microwave-safe bowl, combine the chocolate chips, milk, coffee, cinnamon and salt. Microwave, uncovered, on high for 1 minute. Stir until smooth. Stir in vanilla and pecans. Immediately spread into the prepared pan.

Cover and refrigerate until firm, about 2 hours. Remove from pan; cut into 1-in. squares. Store, covered, at room temperature. **YIELD: 2 POUNDS.**

EDITOR'S NOTE: This recipe was tested in a 1,100-watt microwave.

1st place

Coffee Shop Fudge

White Candy Bark

PREP: 20 MIN. + CHILLING

Here's a speedy candy recipe that can be varied depending on the type of fruit or nuts you have on hand. Since we have a walnut tree, I use walnuts, but pecans could also be substituted as well as dried cherries for the cranberries.

Marcia Snyder ✳ Grand Junction, Colorado

1 tablespoon butter, melted

2 packages (10 to 12 ounces *each*) vanilla *or* white chips

1-1/2 cups walnut halves

1 cup dried cranberries

1/4 teaspoon ground nutmeg

Line a 15-in. x 10-in. x 1-in. pan with foil. Brush with butter; set aside. Place the chips in a microwave-safe bowl. Microwave, uncovered, at 70% power for 1 minute; stir. Microwave at additional 10- to 20-second intervals, stirring until smooth. Stir in the walnuts, cranberries and nutmeg. Spread into prepared pan. Chill until firm. Break into pieces. **YIELD: 2 POUNDS.**

EDITOR'S NOTE: This recipe was tested in a 1,100-watt microwave.

White Candy Bark

Raspberry Coconut Bars

Raspberry Coconut Bars

PREP: 20 MIN. BAKE: 20 MIN. + CHILLING

I've been whipping up these delicious bars for over 10 years, most recently with help from my young daughter. I bake them every Christmas and have received many compliments and recipe requests. The chocolate drizzle makes such a pretty, lacy effect.

Barb Bovberg * Fort Collins, Colorado

1-2/3 cups graham cracker crumbs
  1/2 cup butter, melted
2-2/3 cups flaked coconut
    1 can (14 ounces) sweetened condensed milk
    1 cup seedless raspberry preserves
  1/3 cup chopped walnuts, toasted
  1/2 cup semisweet chocolate chips
  1/4 cup vanilla *or* white chips

In a bowl, combine graham cracker crumbs and butter. Press into a 13-in. x 9-in. baking dish coated with cooking spray. Sprinkle with the coconut; drizzle with milk. Bake at 350° for 20-25 minutes or until lightly browned. Cool completely on a wire rack.

   Spread preserves over the crust. Sprinkle with walnuts. In a microwave-safe bowl, melt the chocolate chips; stir until smooth. Drizzle over walnuts. Repeat with vanilla chips. Cut into bars. Refrigerate for 30 minutes or until chocolate is set. **YIELD: 3 DOZEN.**

Fudgy Oat Brownies

PREP: 30 MIN. BAKE: 35 MIN. + COOLING

These cake-like brownies have a rich, crunchy oat crust and are topped with a smooth homemade chocolate frosting. A packaged brownie mix makes the recipe easy to prepare. Make it even easier by using canned frosting.

Diana Otterson * Canandaigua, New York

1-1/2 cups quick-cooking oats
  3/4 cup all-purpose flour
  3/4 cup packed brown sugar
  1/4 teaspoon baking soda

Fudgy Oat Brownies

1/4 teaspoon salt

3/4 cup butter, melted

1 package fudge brownie mix
(13-inch x 9-inch pan size)

FROSTING:

3 tablespoons butter

1-1/2 squares (1-1/2 ounces *each*)
unsweetened chocolate

2-1/4 cups confectioners' sugar

3 to 4 tablespoons hot water, *divided*

1-1/2 teaspoons vanilla extract

In a large bowl, combine the oats, flour, brown sugar, baking soda and salt. Stir in butter until combined. Press into an ungreased 13-in. x 9-in. baking pan. Bake at 350° for 10-11 minutes or until puffed and edges are lightly browned.

Meanwhile, prepare brownie mix according to package directions for cake-like brownies. Spread batter over crust. Bake 25-30 minutes longer or until a toothpick inserted near the center comes out clean.

For frosting, in a small saucepan, melt butter and chocolate over low heat; stir until smooth. Remove from the heat; immediately stir in confectioners' sugar, 2 tablespoons water and vanilla until smooth. Add remaining water; stir until smooth. Immediately spread over the brownies. Cool on a wire rack until firm. Cut into bars. **YIELD: 3 DOZEN.**

Holiday Pecan Logs

PREP: **25 MIN. + CHILLING** COOK: **10 MIN. + COOLING**

For 50 years, I've turned to this beloved recipe to make candy to give away at the holidays. Of the many types I've tried, these pecan logs continue to be the most popular.

Maxine Ruhl ✳ Fort Scott, Kansas

2 teaspoons plus 1/2 cup butter,
softened, *divided*

3-3/4 cups confectioners' sugar

1/2 cup nonfat dry milk powder

1/2 cup sugar

1/2 cup light corn syrup

Holiday Pecan Logs

1 teaspoon vanilla extract

1 package (14 ounces) caramels

1 tablespoon milk *or* half-and-half cream

2 cups chopped pecans

Butter an 8-in. square pan with 2 teaspoons butter; set aside. Combine the confectioners' sugar and milk powder; set aside. In a heavy saucepan, combine 1/2 cup butter, sugar and corn syrup; cook and stir until sugar is dissolved and the mixture comes to a boil. Stir in the confectioners' sugar mixture, about a third at a time, until blended.

Remove from heat; stir in vanilla. Continue stirring until the mixture mounds slightly when dropped from a spoon. Spread into prepared pan. Cool.

Cut candy into four strips; cut each strip in half. Shape each into a log; wrap in waxed paper and twist ends. Freeze or refrigerate until firm.

In a microwave, melt caramels with milk, stirring often. Roll logs in caramel mixture, then in pecans. Wrap in waxed paper. Store at room temperature in airtight containers. Cut into slices with a serrated knife. **YIELD: ABOUT 3-1/4 POUNDS.**

Cookie Dough Truffles

1st place

Cookie Dough Truffles

PREP: **1 HOUR + CHILLING**

The flavorful filling at the center of these yummy candies tastes like genuine chocolate chip cookie dough...without the worry of uncooked eggs. That's what makes them so appealing. Plus, they're easy to make.

Lanita Dedon * Slaughter, Louisiana

- 1/2 cup butter, softened
- 3/4 cup packed brown sugar
- 1 teaspoon vanilla extract
- 2 cups all-purpose flour
- 1 can (14 ounces) sweetened condensed milk
- 1/2 cup miniature semisweet chocolate chips
- 1/2 cup chopped walnuts
- 1-1/2 pounds semisweet candy coating, chopped

In a large bowl, cream the butter and brown sugar until light and fluffy. Beat in the vanilla. Gradually add the flour, alternately with the milk, beating well after each addition. Stir in the chocolate chips and walnuts. Shape into 1-in. balls; place on waxed paper-lined baking sheets. Loosely cover and refrigerate for 1-2 hours or until firm.

In a microwave-safe bowl, melt candy coating; stir until smooth. Dip balls in coating, allowing excess to drip off; place on waxed paper-lined baking sheets. Refrigerate until firm, about 15 minutes. If desired, remelt the remaining candy coating and drizzle over candies. Store in refrigerator. YIELD: **5-1/2 DOZEN**

Meringue Candy Canes

PREP: **20 MIN. BAKE: 50 MIN. + STANDING**

These red-and-white striped cookies get lots of compliments for their cute looks and minty taste. The seasonal confections are easy to make and so light that they melt in your mouth!

Anne Lindway * Indianapolis, Indiana

- 3 egg whites
- 1/2 teaspoon cream of tartar
- 3/4 cup sugar
- 1/4 teaspoon peppermint extract
- Red paste food coloring

In a large bowl, beat the egg whites until foamy. Add cream of tartar; beat on medium speed until soft peaks form. Gradually add the sugar, 1 tablespoon at a time, beating on high until stiff peaks form and sugar is dissolved, about 6 minutes. Beat in peppermint extract.

Cut a small hole in the corner of a pastry bag; insert star tip #21. On the inside of the bag, brush three evenly spaced 1/4-in. strips of red food coloring from the tip to three-fourths of the way to the top of the bag. Carefully fill bag with meringue.

Pipe 3-in. candy canes onto parchment-lined baking sheets. Bake at 225° for 25 minutes; rotate baking sheets to a different oven rack. Bake 25 minutes longer or until firm to the touch. Turn the oven off; leave cookies in oven with door ajar for at least 1 hour or until cool. YIELD: **4 DOZEN**.

NUTRITION FACTS: 1 cookie equals 13 calories, 0 fat (0 saturated fat), 0 cholesterol, 3 mg sodium, 3 g carbohydrate, 0 fiber, trace protein. DIABETIC EXCHANGE: Free food.

Chocolate Cheese Layered Bars

PREP: **20 MIN. BAKE: 25 MIN.**

You can't beat the many layers of goodness in these tempting bars when you're looking for a satisfying treat. With a chocolaty crust, a creamy layer with chocolate chips and marshmallows and a luscious topping, these bars are popular for any event or gathering.

Sharon Schaa * Murray, Iowa

- 1/2 cup butter, softened
- 1 cup sugar

2 eggs

1 square (1 ounce) unsweetened
   chocolate, melted

1 teaspoon vanilla extract

1 cup all-purpose flour

1 teaspoon baking powder

1/2 cup chopped pecans

CHEESE LAYER:

6 ounces cream cheese, softened

1/4 cup butter, softened

1/2 cup sugar

1 egg

2 tablespoons all-purpose flour

1/2 teaspoon vanilla extract

1/4 cup chopped pecans

1 cup (6 ounces) semisweet chocolate chips

3 cups miniature marshmallows

TOPPING:

1/4 cup butter

2 ounces cream cheese, softened

1 square (1 ounces) unsweetened chocolate

2 tablespoons milk

3 cup confectioners' sugar

1 teaspoon vanilla extract

Meringue Candy Canes

In a large bowl, cream butter and sugar until light and fluffy. Beat in eggs. Beat in chocolate and vanilla until well blended. Combine flour and baking powder; stir into chocolate mixture. Fold in pecans. Pour into a greased 13-in. x 9-in. baking pan.

In another bowl, combine cream cheese and butter. Beat in the sugar, egg, flour and vanilla until well combined. Fold in pecans. Spread over the chocolate layer; sprinkle with chips.

Bake at 350° for 20-25 minutes or until edges pull away from the sides of the pan. Sprinkle with marshmallows; bake 2 minutes longer or until puffed. Spread evenly over cream cheese layer. Cool on a wire rack.

In a saucepan, combine first four topping ingredients. Cook and stir over low heat until smooth. Transfer to a large bowl. Add the confectioners' sugar and the vanilla; beat until smooth. Spread over cooled bars. Store in the refrigerator. YIELD: 2 DOZEN.

Chocolate Cheese Layered Bars

Almond Sugar Cookies

⊘ Almond Sugar Cookies

PREP/TOTAL TIME: **30 MIN.**

It's a tradition in our house to start baking Christmas cookies early in the season and try some new types every year. This nutty, glazed, melt-in-your-mouth cookie is one of the best.

Lisa Hummell ✳ Phillipsburg, New Jersey

  1 **cup butter, softened**
3/4 **cup sugar**
  1 **teaspoon almond extract**
  2 **cups all-purpose flour**
1/2 **teaspoon baking powder**
1/4 **teaspoon salt**
Additional sugar
GLAZE:
  1 **cup confectioners' sugar**
1-1/2 **teaspoons almond extract**
  2 **to 3 teaspoons water**
Green food coloring, optional
Sliced almonds, toasted

In a large bowl, cream butter and sugar until light and fluffy. Beat in the almond extract. Combine the flour, baking powder and salt; gradually add to creamed mixture and mix well. Roll into 1-in. balls.

Place 2 in. apart on ungreased baking sheets. Coat bottom of a glass with cooking spray; dip in sugar. Flatten cookies with prepared glass, dipping glass in sugar again as needed.

Bake at 400° for 7-9 minutes or until edges are lightly browned. Cool for 1 minute before removing to wire racks.

In a bowl, whisk together the confectioners' sugar, almond extract and enough water to achieve glaze consistency. Tint glaze with food coloring if desired; drizzle over cookies. Sprinkle with almonds. **YIELD: ABOUT 4-1/2 DOZEN.**

Brownie Ice Cream Cones

PREP: **20 MIN.** BAKE: **20 MIN. + COOLING**

Often, I'll find a recipe that sounds interesting, copy it down and put my own twist on it. That's just what I did with these. I make them for our children when they have friends over.

Marlene Rhodes ✳ Panama City, Florida

  1 **package (4 ounces) German sweet chocolate**
1/4 **cup butter, cubed**
3/4 **cup sugar**
  2 **eggs**

1/2 cup all-purpose flour
1/2 cup chopped walnuts, optional
1 teaspoon vanilla extract
24 ice cream cake cones (about 3 inches tall)
24 scoops ice cream
Colored sprinkles

In a microwave, melt chocolate and butter; stir until smooth. Cool slightly; pour into a large bowl. Add sugar and eggs until well blended. Stir in the flour, walnuts if desired and vanilla.

Place ice cream cones in muffin cups; fill half full with batter. Bake at 350° for 20-22 minutes or until brownies are set on top and a toothpick inserted near the center comes out with moist crumbs (do not overbake). Cool completely.

Before serving, top each with a scoop of ice cream and garnish with sprinkles. **YIELD: 2 DOZEN.**

Brownie Ice Cream Cones

Triple Peanut Pizza

PREP: 20 MIN. BAKE: 15 MIN. + CHILLING

The classic combination of chocolate and peanut butter has been a longtime favorite of mine, and now our son, Blake, enjoys it, too. Since most kids love pizza, I created this fun, fuss-free treat for his birthday.

Tracy Houdeshell ✳ Marion, Iowa

1 tube (18 ounces) refrigerated peanut butter cookie dough
1 cup (6 ounces) semisweet chocolate chips
1 package (8 ounces) cream cheese, softened
1/3 cup creamy peanut butter
1/4 cup packed brown sugar
1 teaspoon vanilla extract
2 cups chopped peanut butter cups (about 15 large)

Press cookie dough onto a greased 14-in. pizza pan. Bake at 350° for 12-15 minutes or until golden brown. Sprinkle with chocolate chips; let stand for 4-5 minutes. Spread melted chips over crust. Freeze for 10 minutes or until set.

Meanwhile, in a small bowl, beat the cream cheese, peanut butter, brown sugar and vanilla until creamy. Spread over the the chocolate. Sprinkle with the peanut butter cups. Chill until serving. Refrigerate leftovers. **YIELD: 12-14 SLICES.**

Triple Peanut Pizza

Cookie Dough Brownies

Cookie Dough Brownies

PREP: 20 MIN. + CHILLING BAKE: 30 MIN. + COOLING

When I take these rich brownies to any get-together, I carry the recipe, too, because it always gets requested. Children of all ages love the tempting cookie dough filling. This special treat is typically the first to disappear from the buffet table—even before the entrees!

Wendy Bailey * Elida, Ohio

4	eggs
1	cup canola oil
2	cups sugar
2	teaspoons vanilla extract
1-1/2	cups all-purpose flour
1/2	cup baking cocoa
1/2	teaspoon salt
1/2	cup chopped walnuts, optional

FILLING:

1/2	cup butter, softened
1/2	cup packed brown sugar
1/4	cup sugar
2	tablespoons milk
1	teaspoon vanilla extract
1	cup all-purpose flour

GLAZE:

1	cup (6 ounces) semisweet chocolate chips
1	tablespoon shortening
3/4	cup chopped walnuts

In a bowl, beat eggs, oil and sugar. Stir in vanilla. Combine the flour, cocoa and salt; gradually add to egg mixture. Stir in walnuts if desired.

Pour into a greased 13-in. x 9-in. baking pan. Bake at 350° for 30 minutes or until brownies test done. Cool completely.

For filling, in a large bowl, cream butter and sugars until light and fluffy. Beat in milk and vanilla. Gradually beat in flour. Spread over the brownies; chill until firm.

For glaze, in a microwave, melt the chocolate chips and shortening; stir until smooth. Spread over filling. Immediately sprinkle with nuts, pressing down slightly. **YIELD: 3 DOZEN.**

Peppermint Taffy

Peppermint Taffy

PREP: 1-3/4 HOURS + COOLING

For a fun afternoon, get the kids or a friend involved in an old-fashioned taffy pull. The soft, chewy taffy has a mild, minty taste, and it won't stick to the wrapper. You can change the color and flavor, too.

Elaine Chichura * Kingsley, Pennsylvania

2-1/2 cups sugar
1-1/2 cups light corn syrup
     4 teaspoons white vinegar
   1/4 teaspoon salt
   1/2 cup evaporated milk
   1/4 teaspoon peppermint oil
Red food coloring

Butter a 15-in. x 10-in. x 1-in. pan; set aside. In a heavy large saucepan, combine the sugar, corn syrup, vinegar and salt. Cook and stir over low heat until sugar is dissolved. Bring to a boil over medium heat. Slowly add the milk; cook and stir until a candy thermometer reads 248° (firm-ball stage).

Remove from the heat; stir in peppermint oil and food coloring, keeping face away from the mixture, as odor is very strong. Pour into prepared pan. Let stand for 8 minutes or until cool enough to handle.

With well-buttered fingers, quickly pull candy until firm but pliable (color will become light pink). Pull into a 1/2-in. rope; cut into 1-in. pieces. Wrap each in waxed paper. **YIELD: 1-3/4 POUNDS.**

EDITOR'S NOTE: We recommend that you test your candy thermometer before each use by bringing water to a boil; the thermometer should read 212°. Adjust your recipe temperature up or down based on your test.

Anise Hard Candy

PREP: 25 MIN. COOK: 10 MIN.

Making this classic hard candy has become an annual Christmas tradition for me since I first prepared it at a friend's house. To vary the recipe a little, you can substitute peppermint extract for the anise and green food coloring for red.

Jobyna Carpenter * Poulsbo, Washington

1-1/2 teaspoons butter, softened
   3/4 cup water

Anise Hard Candy

   2/3 cup light corn syrup
     2 cups sugar
     1 teaspoon anise extract
Red food coloring
     2 to 3 tablespoons confectioners' sugar

Butter an 8-in. square dish with 1-1/2 teaspoons butter; set aside. In a heavy saucepan, combine the water, corn syrup and sugar. Bring to a boil over medium heat, stirring occasionally. Cover and cook for 3 minutes to dissolve any sugar crystals. Uncover; cook over medium-high heat, without stirring, until a candy thermometer reads 300° (hard-crack stage). Remove from the heat; stir in extract and food coloring (keep face away from mixture as odor is very strong).

Pour into prepared dish. Using a sharp knife, score into 3/4-in. squares. Cool. Separate into squares, using a sharp knife if necessary. Place confectioners' sugar in a pan; add candy and roll until coated. Brush off excess sugar with a pastry brush. Store at room temperature in an airtight container. **YIELD: ABOUT 1 POUND (ABOUT 8 DOZEN).**

EDITOR'S NOTE: We recommend that you test your candy thermometer before each use by bringing water to a boil; the thermometer should read 212°. Adjust your recipe temperature up or down based on your test.

Caramel Truffles

Caramel Truffles

PREP: **1 HOUR + CHILLING**

These candies disappear as fast as I can make them. The five-ingredient microwave recipe is easy and fun to do. When drizzled with white almond bark, they make a lovely gift.

Charlotte Midthun ✳ Granite Falls, Minnesota

- 26 caramels
- 1 cup milk chocolate chips
- 1/4 cup heavy whipping cream
- 1-1/3 cups semisweet chocolate chips
- 1 tablespoon shortening

Line an 8-in. square dish with plastic wrap; set aside. In a microwave-safe bowl, combine the caramels, milk chocolate chips and cream. Microwave, uncovered, on high for 1 minute; stir. Microwave 1 minute longer, stirring every 15 seconds or until caramels are melted and mixture is smooth. Spread into prepared dish; refrigerate for 1 hour or until firm.

Using plastic wrap, lift candy out of pan. Cut into 30 pieces; roll each piece into a 1-in. ball. Cover and refrigerate for 1 hour or until firm.

In a microwave-safe bowl, melt semisweet chips and shortening; stir until smooth. Dip the caramels in chocolate; allow excess to drip off. Place on waxed paper; let stand until set. Refrigerate until firm. **YIELD: 2-1/2 DOZEN.**

EDITOR'S NOTE: This recipe was tested in a 1,100-watt microwave.

Berry-Cream Cookie Snaps

PREP: **40 MIN. + CHILLING** BAKE: **5 MIN./BATCH + COOLING**

My mom and I made up this recipe by combining two others. These cute cookies are crispy on the outside and light and fluffy inside. You could also bake the cookies flat and serve the filling as a cookie dip.

Crystal Briddick ✳ Colfax, Illinois

- 4 ounces cream cheese, softened
- 1/4 cup sugar
- 2 tablespoons seedless strawberry jam
- 1/4 cup heavy whipping cream, whipped
- 1 to 3 drops red food coloring, optional

BATTER:
- 1/2 cup sugar
- 1/3 cup all-purpose flour
- 2 egg whites
- 1/4 teaspoon vanilla extract
- 1/8 teaspoon salt
- 1/4 cup butter, melted and cooled
- 1/2 cup chopped fresh strawberries

Additional sugar

For filling, in a bowl, combine cream cheese, sugar and jam until blended. Fold in whipped cream and food coloring if desired. Chill.

In a small bowl, whisk the sugar, flour, egg whites, vanilla and salt until smooth. Whisk in butter until blended. Line baking sheets with parchment paper. Preparing four cookies at a time, drop batter by 1-1/2 teaspoonfuls 4 in. apart onto prepared pan. Bake at 400° for 5-8 minutes or until edges are lightly browned.

Immediately remove one cookie at a time from parchment and form into a tube around a greased clean round wooden clothespin. Press lightly to seal; hold until set, about 20 seconds.

Remove cookie from clothespin; place on waxed paper to cool. Continue with remaining cookies. If the cookies become too cool to shape, return to oven for 1 minute to soften. Repeat with remaining batter.

Just before serving, pipe or spoon filling into the cookie shells. Dip the end of cookie into strawberries and additional sugar. Refrigerate leftovers. **YIELD: ABOUT 2 DOZEN.**

Chocolate Caramel Thumbprints

PREP: 25 MIN. + CHILLING BAKE: 10 MIN./BATCH + COOLING

Covered in chopped nuts and sprinkled with chocolate, these cookies are delicious and pretty, too. Everybody looks forward to munching on them during the holidays.

Elizabeth Marino ✳ San Juan Capistrano, California

- 1/2 cup butter, softened
- 2/3 cup sugar
- 1 egg, *separated*
- 2 tablespoons milk
- 1 teaspoon vanilla extract
- 1 cup all-purpose flour
- 1/3 cup baking cocoa
- 1/4 teaspoon salt
- 1 cup finely chopped pecans

FILLING:

- 12 to 14 caramels
- 3 tablespoons heavy whipping cream
- 1/2 cup semisweet chocolate chips
- 1 teaspoon shortening

In a bowl, cream butter and sugar until light and fluffy. Beat in the egg yolk, milk and vanilla. Combine the flour, cocoa and salt; gradually add to creamed mixture and mix well. Cover and refrigerate for 1 hour or until easy to handle.

Roll into 1-in. balls. Beat egg white. Place egg whites in a shallow bowl. Place nuts in another shallow bowl. Dip balls into egg white and coat with nuts.

Place 2 in. apart on greased baking sheets. Using the end of a wooden spoon handle, make a 3/8-to 1/2-in. indentation in the center of each ball. Bake at 350° for 10-12 minutes or until set. Remove to wire racks to cool.

Meanwhile, in a large heavy saucepan, melt caramels with cream over low heat; stir until smooth. Using about 1/2 teaspoon caramel mixture, fill each cookie. In a microwave, melt the chocolate chips and shortening; stir until smooth. Drizzle over the cookies. **YIELD: ABOUT 2-1/2 DOZEN.**

Berry-Cream Cookie Snaps

Chocolate Caramel Thumbprints

Butter Pecan Fudge

Butter Pecan Fudge

PREP: **20 MIN. + COOLING**

Toasted pecans add a nutty crunch to this creamy, buttery fudge. I have given this candy with its wonderful caramel flavor as gifts at Christmastime, and people always rave about this delicious sweet!

Pam Smith ✳ Alta Loma, California

- 1/2 cup butter
- 1/2 cup sugar
- 1/2 cup packed brown sugar
- 1/2 cup heavy whipping cream
- 1/8 teaspoon salt
- 1 teaspoon vanilla extract
- 2 cups confectioners' sugar
- 1 cup pecan halves, toasted and coarsely chopped

In a large heavy saucepan, combine the butter, sugars, cream and salt. Bring to a boil over medium heat, stirring occasionally. Boil for 5 minutes, stirring constantly. Remove from the heat; stir in vanilla. Stir in confectioners' sugar until smooth. Fold in pecans.

Spread into a buttered 8-in. square dish. Cool to room temperature. Cut into 1-in. squares. Store in an airtight container in the refrigerator. **YIELD: 1-1/4 POUNDS.**

Double Chip Cheesecake Bars

Double Chip Cheesecake Bars

PREP: **15 MIN.** BAKE: **40 MIN. + COOLING**

I love to cook and sometimes create my own recipes. I got creative one afternoon, and this bar was the result.

Beth Allard ✳ Belmont, New Hampshire

- 2 cups all-purpose flour
- 1/2 cup confectioners' sugar
- 1 cup cold butter, cubed

FILLING:
- 2 packages (8 ounces *each*) cream cheese, softened
- 1/2 cup packed brown sugar
- 2 eggs

- 1 teaspoon almond extract
- 1 cup (6 ounces) semisweet chocolate chips, *divided*
- 1/2 cup butterscotch chips
- 1/2 cup chopped walnuts

In a bowl, combine the flour and confectioners' sugar. Cut in butter until mixture resembles coarse crumbs. Press into an ungreased 13-in. x 9-in. baking pan. Bake at 350° for 18-22 minutes or until lightly browned.

Meanwhile, in a bowl, beat cream cheese and brown sugar until smooth. Add eggs and extract; beat on low speed just until combined. Stir in 1/2 cup chocolate chips, butterscotch chips and walnuts. Spread over crust. Sprinkle with the remaining chocolate chips.

Bake at 350° for 20-25 minutes or until the center is almost set. Cool completely on a wire rack before cutting. Refrigerate leftovers. **YIELD: 3 DOZEN.**

Chunky Peanut Brittle

Chunky Peanut Brittle

PREP: **10 MIN.** COOK: **20 MIN. + COOLING**

As a farm girl, I often made holiday goodies with my mother for our family of eight candy-loving kids. Now, my own children and grandkids say the season wouldn't by the same without a tray filled with this chocolaty peanut brittle.

Janet Gonola ✳ East McKeesport, Pennsylvania

- 1-1/2 teaspoons plus 1-1/2 cups butter, *divided*
- 2 cups peanut butter chips, *divided*
- 1-3/4 cups sugar
- 3 tablespoons light corn syrup
- 3 tablespoons water
- 1-1/2 cups salted peanuts, coarsely chopped
- 1/2 cup semisweet chocolate chips

Butter the bottom and sides of a 15-in. x 10-in. x 1-in. pan with 1-1/2 teaspoons of butter. Sprinkle with 1 cup peanut butter chips; set aside.

In a heavy saucepan, bring sugar, corn syrup, water and the remaining butter to a boil over medium heat, stirring constantly. Cook and stir until butter is melted. Cook, without stirring, until a candy thermometer reads 300° (hard-cracked stage).

Remove from the heat; stir in the peanuts. Quickly pour onto prepared pan; sprinkle with chocolate chips and the remaining peanut butter chips. With a knife, gently swirl softened chips over top of brittle. Cool before breaking into pieces. Store in an airtight container. **YIELD: 2-1/2 POUNDS.**

EDITOR'S NOTE: We recommend that you test your candy thermometer before each use by bringing water to a boil; the thermometer should read 212°. Adjust your recipe temperature up or down based on your test.

Peanut Lover's Brownies

until set. Cool on a wire rack. Sprinkle peanuts over crust.

In a microwave, melt butter and chocolate; stir until smooth. In a bowl, combine the eggs, sugar, vanilla and chocolate mixture. Gradually add flour. Spread over crust. Bake for 30-40 minutes or until a toothpick inserted near the center comes out clean. Cool on a wire rack.

For topping, warm the peanut butter for 30 seconds in a microwave. Gradually fold in the whipped topping; spread over brownies. Refrigerate for 1 hour. Sprinkle with chopped peanut butter cups. Using foil, lift brownies out of pan; remove foil. Cut into bars. Store in the refrigerator. **YIELD: 2 DOZEN.**

Peanut Lover's Brownies

PREP: **30 MIN.** + COOLING BAKE: **30 MIN.** + CHILLING

Peanut butter lovers won't be able to eat just one of these delectable squares. These chocolaty brownies are sandwiched between a graham cracker crust and peanut butter mousse. They're irresistible!

April Phillips ✶ Lafayette, Indiana

- 1/2 cup butter, softened
- 3/4 cup all-purpose flour
- 1/2 cup graham cracker crumbs
- 1/4 cup sugar
- 1/2 cup salted peanuts, chopped

BROWNIE LAYER:

- 3/4 cup butter, cubed
- 4 squares (1 ounce *each*) unsweetened chocolate, chopped
- 4 eggs
- 2 cups sugar
- 2 teaspoons vanilla extract
- 1 cup all-purpose flour

PEANUT CREAM TOPPING:

- 1 cup creamy peanut butter
- 1 carton (12 ounces) frozen whipped topping, thawed
- 12 miniature peanut butter cups, coarsely chopped

Line a 13-in. x 9-in. baking pan with foil; grease the foil. In a small bowl, combine the butter, flour, cracker crumbs and sugar; press into prepared pan. Bake at 350° for 10-12 minutes or

Lemon-Lime Bars

PREP: **20 MIN.** BAKE: **20 MIN.** + COOLING

I baked these bars for a luncheon on a hot summer day. A gentleman made his way to the kitchen to compliment the cook who made them.

Holly Wilkins ✶ Lake Elmore, Vermont

- 1 cup butter, softened
- 1/2 cup confectioners' sugar
- 2 teaspoons grated lime peel
- 1-3/4 cups all-purpose flour
- 1/4 teaspoon salt

FILLING:

- 4 eggs
- 1-1/2 cups sugar
- 1/4 cup all-purpose flour
- 1/2 teaspoon baking powder
- 1/3 cup lemon juice
- 2 teaspoons grated lemon peel

Confectioners' sugar

In a large bowl, cream butter and confectioners' sugar until light and fluffy. Beat in lime peel. Combine the flour and salt; gradually add to creamed mixture and mix well.

Press into a greased 13-in. x 9-in. baking dish. Bake at 350° for 13-15 minutes or just until edges are lightly browned.

Meanwhile, in another large bowl, beat the eggs and sugar. Combine the flour and baking powder. Gradually add to egg mixture. Stir in the lemon juice and peel; beat until frothy. Pour over hot crust.

Bake for 20-25 minutes or until light golden brown. Cool on a wire rack. Dust with the confectioners' sugar. Cut into squares. Store in the refrigerator. **YIELD: 4 DOZEN.**

Lemon-Lime Bars

Pecan Clusters

PREP: 1-1/4 HOURS + CHILLING

I made these "turtle-like" concoctions one Christmas for a sweets exchange. My dad saw them on the counter waiting to be boxed up and couldn't believe I made them. He said they looked like they came from a candy shop.

Carrie Burke ✳ Conway, Massachusetts

- 1 teaspoon plus 1 cup butter, *divided*
- 1 cup light corn syrup
- 2-1/4 cups packed brown sugar
- 1/8 teaspoon salt
- 1 can (14 ounces) sweetened condensed milk
- 1 teaspoon vanilla extract
- 1-1/2 pounds pecan halves, toasted
- 3/4 cup milk chocolate chips
- 3/4 cup semisweet chocolate chips
- 4 teaspoons shortening

Line baking sheets with waxed paper; lightly coat with cooking spray and set aside. Butter the sides of a heavy saucepan with 1 teaspoon butter. Cube remaining butter; place in pan. Add corn syrup, brown sugar and salt. Cook and stir until sugar is melted.

Gradually stir in milk. Cook and stir over medium heat until mixture comes to a boil. Cook and stir until a candy thermometer reads 248° (firm-ball stage), about 16 minutes. Remove from the heat; stir in vanilla. Gently stir in pecans. Drop by rounded teaspoonfuls onto prepared baking sheets. Refrigerate until firm, about 12 minutes.

In a microwave-safe bowl, melt the chips and shortening; stir until smooth. Drizzle over the clusters. Chill clusters until firm. Store in the refrigerator. **YIELD: ABOUT 6 DOZEN.**

EDITOR'S NOTE: We recommend that you test your candy thermometer before each use by bringing water to a boil; the thermometer should read 212°. Adjust your recipe temperature up or down based on your test.

Pecan Clusters

Frosted Brownie Pizza

Frosted Brownie Pizza

PREP: **10 MIN.** BAKE: **15 MIN. + COOLING**

It's impossible to eat just one piece of this dessert pizza featuring a chewy, chocolaty crust, creamy peanut butter frosting and mouthwatering sweet and crunchy toppings.

Paula Riehl ✳ Boise, Idaho

- 1/2 cup butter, cubed
- 2 squares (1 ounce *each*) unsweetened chocolate
- 1 cup sugar
- 3/4 cup all-purpose flour
- 2 eggs, lightly beaten

FROSTING:
- 1 cup confectioners' sugar
- 1/3 cup creamy peanut butter
- 1-1/2 teaspoons vanilla extract
- 2 to 4 tablespoons milk

TOPPINGS:
- 3/4 cup plain M&M's
- 1/2 cup flaked coconut, toasted
- 1/2 cup chopped pecans, toasted

In a small saucepan over low heat, melt the butter, chocolate and sugar. Remove from the heat; stir in flour until smooth. Add eggs and beat until smooth. Spread onto a greased 12-in. pizza pan.

Bake at 350° for 15 minutes or until a toothpick inserted near the center comes out clean. Cool completely.

For frosting, in a bowl, beat the sugar, peanut butter, vanilla and enough milk to achieve the desired spreading consistency. Spread over the brownie crust. Top with M&M's, coconut and pecans. YIELD: **8-10 SERVINGS.**

Raisin Pumpkin Bars

Raisin Pumpkin Bars

PREP: **20 MIN.** BAKE: **25 MIN. + COOLING**

These moist bars will keep well—if your family doesn't eat them all right away! They're nice to take to a potluck supper or for a snack or dessert anytime.

Mrs. J. B. Hendrix ✳ Ganado, Texas

- 2 cups sugar
- 1 can (15 ounces) solid-pack pumpkin

1 cup canola oil

4 eggs

2 cups all-purpose flour

2 teaspoons baking powder

1 teaspoon baking soda

1 teaspoon ground cinnamon

1 teaspoon ground nutmeg

1/2 teaspoon salt

1/8 teaspoon ground cloves

1/2 cup raisins

1/3 cup chopped pecans *or* walnuts

FROSTING:

1/3 cup butter, softened

1 package (3 ounces) cream cheese, softened

1 tablespoon milk

1 teaspoon vanilla extract

2 cups confectioners' sugar

In a large bowl, beat the sugar, pumpkin, oil and eggs. Combine the flour, baking powder, baking soda, cinnamon, nutmeg, salt and the cloves; gradually add to pumpkin mixture and mix well. Stir in raisins and nuts.

Pour into a greased 15-in. x 10-in. x 1-in. baking pan. Bake at 350° for 25-30 minutes or until a toothpick is inserted near the center comes out clean. Cool on a wire rack.

For frosting, combine butter, cream cheese, milk and vanilla in a bowl; beat until smooth. Gradually beat in confectioners' sugar. Spread over bars. Store in the refrigerator. **YIELD: ABOUT 2 DOZEN.**

Cranberry Walnut White Fudge

PREP: 25 MIN. + COOLING

A visit to several Oregon cranberry farms inspired my fruit-flavored white fudge. I make it for family and friends at holidays and for special occasions. I was thrilled when the recipe earned first place at our county fair.

Wanda Green ✳ Woodland, California

1 teaspoon plus 1/2 cup butter, *divided*

2 cups sugar

Cranberry Walnut White Fudge

3/4 cup sour cream

1 package (10 to 12 ounces) vanilla *or* white chips

1 jar (7 ounces) marshmallow creme

1 teaspoon vanilla extract

3 cups coarsely chopped walnuts

1 cup dried cranberries, coarsely chopped

Line an 8-in. square pan with foil and butter the foil with 1 teaspoon butter; set aside. In a heavy saucepan, bring the sugar, sour cream and remaining butter to a boil over medium heat. Cook and stir until a candy thermometer reads 234° (soft-ball stage), about 15 minutes.

Remove from the heat. Stir in the chips, marshmallow creme and vanilla until smooth. Fold in walnuts and cranberries. Pour into prepared pan. Let stand at room temperature until cool.

Using foil, lift fudge out of pan. Discard foil; cut fudge into 1-in. squares. Store in an airtight container in the refrigerator. **YIELD: 3 POUNDS.**

EDITOR'S NOTE: We recommend that you test your candy thermometer before each use by bringing water to a boil; the thermometer should read 212°. Adjust your recipe temperature up or down based on your test.

Chocolate Pecan Bars

Spread evenly over hot crust. Bake for 25-30 minutes or until firm around the edges. Cool on a wire rack.

In a microwave, melt the chocolate and shortening; stir until smooth. Drizzle over bars.
YIELD: 4 DOZEN.

Chocolate Peanut Squares

PREP: 20 MIN. + COOLING

If you're a fan of peanut butter cups, you'll enjoy these two-layer treats. A slightly crunchy graham cracker and peanut butter layer is topped with a smooth coating of melted chocolate chips and peanut butter. Yum!

Nicole Trudell ✳ Fort Langley, British Columbia

    2 cups confectioners' sugar
  3/4 cup creamy peanut butter
  2/3 cup graham cracker crumbs
  1/2 cup butter, melted
TOPPING:
  2/3 cup semisweet chocolate chips
4-1/2 teaspoons creamy peanut butter
  1/2 teaspoon butter

Line a 9-in. square pan with foil and butter the foil; set aside. In a bowl, combine confectioners' sugar, peanut butter, graham cracker crumbs and butter. Spread into prepared pan.

Combine topping ingredients in a microwave-safe bowl; heat until melted. Spread over the peanut butter layer. Refrigerate until cool. Using the foil, left out of pan. Cut into 1-in. squares. Store in an airtight container in the refrigerator.
YIELD: 1-1/2 POUNDS.

Chocolate Pecan Bars

PREP: 25 MIN. BAKE: 25 MIN. + COOLING

These chewy, chocolaty bars are great for Thanksgiving or Christmas...and always a big hit with everyone. They're easy to prepare and make a big batch. We find them simply irresistible!

Carole Fraser ✳ North York, Ontario

  2/3 cup butter, softened
  1/3 cup sugar
    2 cups all-purpose flour
FILLING:
    6 squares (1 ounce *each*) semisweet
       chocolate
1-1/4 cups light corn syrup
1-1/4 cups sugar
    4 eggs, lightly beaten
1-1/4 teaspoons vanilla extract
2-1/4 cups chopped pecans
GLAZE:
    4 squares (1 ounce *each*) semisweet
       chocolate
1-1/4 teaspoons shortening

In a small bowl, cream butter and sugar until light and fluffy. Beat in the flour. Press into a greased 15-in. x 10-in. x 1-in. baking pan. Bake at 350° for 12-15 minutes or until golden brown.

Meanwhile, in a saucepan, melt chocolate with corn syrup over low heat; stir until smooth. Remove from the heat. Stir in the sugar, eggs and vanilla. Add pecans.

Butter Fudge Fingers

PREP: **40 MIN.** BAKE: **20 MIN.** + COOLING

These scrumptious brownies get dressed up with a delicious browned butter frosting. The combination is delightfully different and assures that these yummy treats vanish fast around the house or at a party.

Peggy Mangus * Worland, Wyoming

- 2/3 cup butter, cubed
- 4 squares (1 ounce *each*) unsweetened chocolate
- 4 eggs
- 1 teaspoon salt
- 2 cups sugar
- 1-1/2 cups all-purpose flour
- 1 teaspoon baking powder
- 1 cup chopped pecans

BROWNED BUTTER FROSTING:
- 1/2 cup butter, cubed
- 4 cups confectioners' sugar
- 1/3 cup heavy whipping cream
- 2 teaspoons vanilla extract

GLAZE:
- 1 square (1 ounce) unsweetened chocolate
- 1 tablespoon butter

In a microwave, melt butter and chocolate; stir until smooth. Cool for 10 minutes.

In a bowl, beat eggs and salt until foamy. Gradually add sugar until well blended. Stir in chocolate mixture. Combine flour and baking powder; gradually add to batter. Stir in pecans.

Pour into a greased 15-in. x 10-in. x 1-in. baking pan. Bake at 350° for 20-25 minutes or until a toothpick inserted near the center comes out clean. Cool in pan on a wire rack.

For frosting, in a large heavy saucepan, cook butter over medium heat for 5-7 minutes or until golden brown. Pour into a large bowl; beat in the confectioners' sugar, cream and vanilla until smooth. Frost bars.

For glaze, in a microwave, melt the chocolate and the butter; stir until smooth. Cool slightly. Drizzle over bars. **YIELD: ABOUT 5 DOZEN.**

Chocolate Peanut Squares

Butter Fudge Fingers

Five Star Brownies

Five Star Brownies

PREP: **15 MIN.** BAKE: **30 MIN. + COOLING**

There's a bit of my state's history behind these brownies' name and shape. When I entered them at our state fair in 1990, Kansas was celebrating the 100th birthday of a famous native son...Dwight Eisenhower. In fact, that occasion was the theme of the fair. So I renamed my brownies, in honor of the rank he'd achieved as a general, and cut them out with a star cookie cutter. They ended up winning a blue ribbon!

Pam Buerki Rogers * Victoria, Kansas

>   3 eggs
>   2 cups sugar
> 1-1/2 teaspoons vanilla extract
>   1/2 cup butter, melted
>   1/4 cup shortening, melted
> 1-1/2 cups all-purpose flour
>   3/4 cup baking cocoa
> 1-1/4 teaspoons salt
>   1 cup chopped nuts, optional

In a large bowl, beat the eggs, sugar and vanilla until blended. Beat in butter and shortening until smooth. Combine the flour, cocoa and salt; gradually add to egg mixture. Stir in the nuts if desired.

Line a 13-in. x 9-in. baking pan with foil and grease the foil; pour batter into pan. Bake at 350° for 30 minutes or until a toothpick inserted near the center comes out clean. Cool in pan on a wire rack.

Using foil, lift brownies out of pan. Discard the foil. Cut with a star cutter or cut into bars.
YIELD: ABOUT 3 DOZEN.

Oat Pecan Cookie Mix

Oat Pecan Cookie Mix

PREP: **15** MIN. BAKE: **10** MIN./BATCH **+ COOLING**

This present will be welcomed by anyone who enjoys homemade cookies. The mix is simple to prepare, and the results are yummy.

Bev Woodcock ✳ Kingston, Ontario

- 1 cup all-purpose flour
- 1/2 cup sugar
- 1/2 teaspoon baking soda
- 1/2 teaspoon baking powder
- 1/2 cup packed brown sugar
- 3/4 cup old-fashioned oats
- 1/2 cup chopped pecans
- 1 cup crisp rice cereal

ADDITIONAL INGREDIENTS:

- 1/2 cup butter, softened
- 1 egg
- 1 teaspoon vanilla extract

In a small bowl, combine the flour, sugar, baking soda and baking powder. In a 1-qt. glass jar, layer the flour mixture, brown sugar, oats, pecans and rice cereal, packing well between each layer. Cover and store in a cool dry place for up to 6 months. YIELD: **1 BATCH (ABOUT 4 CUPS TOTAL).**

TO MAKE COOKIES: In a bowl, cream the butter until light and fluffy. Beat in the egg and vanilla. Gradually add cookie mix. Drop by rounded teaspoonfuls 2 in. apart onto greased baking sheets. Bake at 350° for 8-10 minutes or until cookies are golden brown. Cool for 2 minutes before removing from pans to wire racks. YIELD: **ABOUT 3 DOZEN.**

Chocolate-Covered Cherries

Chocolate-Covered Cherries

PREP: **30** MIN. **+ CHILLING**

For these cute candies, maraschino cherries are dressed in a chocolate coating. Kids will have fun helping make the sweets, but they will have to wait a week or two for the filling to set before enjoying the fruits of their labors.

Janice Pehrson ✳ Omaha, Nebraska

- 60 maraschino cherries with stems
- 2 cups confectioners' sugar
- 3 tablespoons butter, softened
- 3 tablespoons light corn syrup
- 1/4 teaspoon salt
- 2 cups (12 ounces) semisweet chocolate chips
- 2 tablespoons shortening

Pat cherries dry with paper towels; set aside. In a small bowl, combine the sugar, butter, corn syrup and salt; mix well. Knead until smooth. Cover and refrigerate for 1 hour.

Roll into 1/2-in. balls; flatten each into a 2-in. circle. Wrap each circle around a cherry and lightly roll in hands. Place the cherries with stems up on waxed paper-lined baking sheets. Cover loosely and refrigerate for 1 hour.

In a microwave or saucepan, melt chocolate chips and shortening; stir until smooth. Holding onto the stem, dip each cherry into chocolate; allow excess to drip off. Place on waxed paper; let stand until set. Refrigerate until hardened. Store in a covered container. Refrigerate for 1-2 weeks before serving. YIELD: **5 DOZEN.**

Mocha Truffle Cookies

🐾 Mocha Truffle Cookies

PREP: 15 MIN. BAKE: 10 MIN. + COOLING

Crisp on the outside, gooey on the inside, these mocha-flavored treats are perfect for chasing away winter doldrums. Why not invite a friend over some snowy afternoon to share a plateful and a cup of coffee?

Pamela Jessen ✳ Calgary, Alberta

- 1/4 cup butter
- 1/4 cup semisweet chocolate chips
- 1-1/2 teaspoons instant coffee granules
- 1/3 cup sugar
- 1/3 cup packed brown sugar
- 1 egg, lightly beaten
- 1 teaspoon vanilla extract
- 1 cup all-purpose flour
- 2 tablespoons plus 2 teaspoons baking cocoa
- 1/4 teaspoon baking powder
- 1/8 teaspoon salt
- 1/3 cup English toffee bits *or* almond brickle chips
- 1 square (1 ounce) milk chocolate, melted

In a microwave-safe bowl, melt the butter and chocolate; stir until smooth. Stir in the coffee granules until dissolved; cool for 5 minutes. Transfer to a small bowl. Add the sugars, egg and vanilla.

Combine the flour, cocoa, baking powder and salt; add to chocolate mixture and mix well. Stir in toffee bits.

Drop dough by rounded tablespoonfuls 2 in. apart onto a baking sheet lightly coated with cooking spray.

Bake at 350° for 8-10 minutes or until set. Cool for 1 minute before removing to a wire rack to cool completely. Drizzle with melted milk chocolate. **YIELD: 15 COOKIES.**

Noel Cookie Gems

PREP: 35 MIN. BAKE: 10 MIN./BATCH + COOLING

I found these cookies when my husband and I were dating. Since our last name is Noel, I whip up a batch every Christmas. They're a cinch to assemble and freeze, saving time during the holiday rush, and can be filled with other jams for a change of pace.

Patsy Noel ✳ Exeter, California

- 1/4 cup butter, softened
- 1/4 cup shortening
- 3/4 cup sugar
- 1 egg
- 1 teaspoon vanilla extract
- 2-2/3 cups all-purpose flour
- 1/2 teaspoon salt
- 1/4 teaspoon baking powder
- 1/4 teaspoon baking soda
- 1/2 cup sour cream
- 3/4 cup finely chopped nuts
- 1/3 cup seedless strawberry jam

In a large bowl, cream the butter, shortening and sugar until light and fluffy. Beat in egg and vanilla. Combine the flour, salt, baking powder and baking soda; gradually add to the creamed mixture alternately with sour cream, beating well after each addition. Shape into 1-1/4-in. balls; roll in nuts.

Place 2 in. apart on greased baking sheets. Using the end of a wooden spoon handle, make a 3/8- to 1/2-in.-deep indentation in the center of each ball. Fill with jam.

Bake at 350° for 10-12 minutes or until lightly browned. Remove to wire racks to cool. **YIELD: 3 DOZEN.**

Chocolate Chip Graham Bars

PREP: **15 MIN.** BAKE: **25 MIN. + COOLING**

These moist, chewy bars are a satisfying snack any time of day. Packed with oats, chocolate chips, crunchy peanuts and graham cereal, they have something for everyone.

Sandi Michalski ✳ Macy, Indiana

- 3/4 cup butter, softened
- 3/4 cup sugar
- 3/4 cup packed brown sugar
- 2 eggs
- 1 teaspoon vanilla extract
- 1-1/2 cups all-purpose flour
- 1-1/2 cups Golden Grahams, crushed
- 3/4 cup plus 2 tablespoons quick-cooking oats, *divided*
- 1 teaspoon baking soda
- 1/2 teaspoon baking powder
- 1/2 teaspoon salt
- 1 cup salted peanuts, *divided*
- 1 cup (6 ounces) semisweet chocolate chips, *divided*

In a large bowl, cream butter and sugars until light and fluffy. Add eggs, one at a time, beating well after each addition. Beat in the vanilla. Combine the flour, cereal, 3/4 cup oats, baking soda, baking powder and salt; gradually add to creamed mixture and beat well. Stir in 3/4 cup peanuts and 2/3 cup chocolate chips.

Spread into a greased 13-in. x 9-in. baking pan. Coarsely chop remaining peanuts; sprinkle over the top with remaining oats and chips.

Bake at 350° for 25-30 minutes or until golden brown. Cool on a wire rack. Cut into bars.

YIELD: 2 DOZEN.

Noel Cookie Gems

Chocolate Chip Graham Bars

Giant Peanut Butter Ice Cream Sandwich

Giant Peanut Butter Ice Cream Sandwich

PREP: **30 MIN.** BAKE: **20 MIN. + FREEZING**

I created this treat for my husband, adding light and low-fat products to the cookie dough. It was so fantastic that I fixed it with conventional ingredients for guests. They actually shrieked in ecstasy! Since it can be made ahead of time and frozen, it cuts stress for busy hostesses.

JoAnn Belack ✳ Bradenton, Florida

- 2 packages (16 ounces *each*) ready-to-bake refrigerated peanut butter cup cookie dough
- 6 whole chocolate graham crackers, crushed
- 1 cup cold milk
- 1 cup heavy whipping cream
- 1 package (3.4 ounces) instant vanilla pudding mix
- 1 package (8 ounces) cream cheese, softened
- 1-1/3 cups creamy peanut butter
- 3 cups vanilla ice cream, softened
- 1/4 cup chocolate hazelnut spread

Let dough stand at room temperature for 5-10 minutes to soften. Press into two ungreased 9-in. springform pans; sprinkle with graham cracker crumbs. Bake at 350° for 20-25 minutes or until set. Cool completely.

In a large bowl, whisk the milk, cream and the pudding mix for 2 minutes. Let stand for 2 minutes or until soft-set. In another bowl, beat cream cheese and peanut butter until smooth. Add pudding and ice cream; beat until smooth.

Spread over one cookie crust. Remove sides of second pan; place the crust, crumb side down, over filling. Cover and freeze for 4 hours or until firm.

Remove from the freezer 15 minutes before serving. Place the hazelnut spread in a small microwave-safe bowl; cover and microwave at 50% power for 1-2 minutes or until smooth, stirring twice. Remove sides of pan; cut dessert into slices. Drizzle with hazelnut spread. **YIELD: 12 SERVINGS.**

Magnolia Dream Cheesecake, PAGE 393

" *Your guests will be amazed when they learn that this gorgeous cheesecake was made by you. This Italian-style dessert is flavored with a delightful combination of hazelnut and peach.* "

Charlene Chambers
Ormond Beach, Florida

CAKES & CHEESECAKES

DO YOU HAVE A WINNING RECIPE?

Enter your most prized recipes in the *Taste of Home* recipe contests, and you may win some money and the chance to have your recipe published. Log onto **tasteofhome.com/RecipeContests** for a list of our current contests and submission deadlines. Good luck...we'll be looking for your recipe.

cakes &
cheesecakes

Magnolia Dream Cheesecake

PREP: **50 MIN.**
BAKE: **1-1/2 HOURS + CHILLING**

Your guests will be amazed when they learn that this gorgeous cheesecake was made by you. This Italian-style dessert is flavored with a delightful combination of hazelnuts and peaches.

Charlene Chambers ✴ Ormond Beach, Florida

- 1 cup hazelnuts, toasted, *divided*
- 12 whole graham crackers
- 1/4 cup sugar
- 6 tablespoons unsalted butter, melted

FILLING:
- 1-1/2 pounds ricotta cheese
- 2 packages (8 ounces *each*) cream cheese, softened
- 2 cups (16 ounces) sour cream
- 1-1/2 cups sugar
- 6 tablespoons all-purpose flour
- 4 tablespoons hazelnut liqueur, *divided*
- 6 eggs, lightly beaten
- 3 medium peaches

Magnolia Dream Cheesecake

Place a greased 10-in. springform pan on a double thickness of heavy-duty foil (about 18 in. square). Securely wrap foil around pan.

Place hazelnuts in a food processor; cover and pulse until coarsely chopped. Set aside 1/4 cup for garnish. Add graham crackers and sugar to food processor; cover and process until finely chopped. Add butter; process until blended. Press onto the bottom and 1 in. up the sides of prepared pan. Place pan on a baking sheet. Bake at 325° for 10 minutes. Cool on a wire rack.

In a large bowl, beat the ricotta, cream cheese, sour cream and sugar until well blended. Beat in flour and 2 tablespoons liqueur. Add the eggs; beat on low speed just until combined. Pour into crust. Place springform pan in a large baking pan; add 1 in. of hot water to larger pan.

Bake at 325° for 1-1/2 hours or until center is just set and top appears dull. Remove pan from water bath. Cool on a wire rack for 10 minutes. Carefully run a knife around edge of pan to loosen; cool 1 hour longer. Chill overnight.

Peel peaches if desired. Cut into thin slices. Toss peaches with remaining liqueur; arrange over top of the cheesecake. Sprinkle reserved hazelnuts in the center. **YIELD: 16 SERVINGS.**

Chocolate Cream Cheese Cupcakes

another bowl, whisk the water, oil and vinegar; stir into dry ingredients just until moistened.

Fill paper-lined muffin cups half full with batter. Drop filling by heaping tablespoonfuls into the center of each.

Bake at 350° for 24-26 minutes or until a toothpick inserted in cake comes out clean. Cool for 10 minutes before removing from pans to wire racks to cool completely.

For frosting, in a large bowl, combine the confectioners' sugar, cocoa, butter, milk and vanilla; beat until blended. Frost cupcakes; sprinkle with pecans. Store in the refrigerator.
YIELD: 20 CUPCAKES.

Chocolate Cream Cheese Cupcakes

PREP: **30 MIN.** BAKE: **25 MIN. + COOLING**

I got the directions for these moist, filled cupcakes from a dear friend years ago. I have made them many times for my family and for church functions. They're irresistible.

Vivian Morris ✳ Cleburne, Texas

- 1 package (8 ounces) cream cheese, softened
- 1-1/2 cups sugar, *divided*
- 1 egg
- 1 teaspoon salt, *divided*
- 1 cup (6 ounces) semisweet chocolate chips
- 1-1/2 cups all-purpose flour
- 1/4 cup baking cocoa
- 1 teaspoon baking soda
- 1 cup water
- 1/3 cup canola oil
- 1 tablespoon white vinegar

FROSTING:

- 3-3/4 cups confectioners' sugar
- 3 tablespoons baking cocoa
- 1/2 cup butter, melted
- 6 tablespoons milk
- 1 teaspoon vanilla extract
- 1/3 cup chopped pecans

For filling, in a small bowl, beat cream cheese and 1/2 cup sugar until smooth. Beat in egg and 1/2 teaspoon salt until combined. Fold in chocolate chips; set aside.

In a large bowl, combine the flour, cocoa, baking soda, and remaining sugar and salt. In

Spring Breeze Cheesecake Pie

PREP: **30 MIN. + CHILLING** COOK: **15 MIN. + COOLING**

I combined two of my favorites (cheesecake and rhubarb) to come up with this mouthwatering dessert. It's so creamy and colorful. Everyone who tries it likes it.

Deanna Taylor ✳ Ainsworth, Nebraska

- 1 package (8 ounces) cream cheese, softened
- 1/3 cup sugar
- 1 cup (8 ounces) sour cream
- 2 teaspoons vanilla extract
- 1 carton (8 ounces) frozen whipped topping, thawed
- 1 graham cracker crust (9 inches)

TOPPING:

- 3 cups chopped fresh *or* frozen rhubarb
- 1/3 cup sugar
- 1/8 teaspoon ground cinnamon
- 1 tablespoon cornstarch
- 2 tablespoons cold water

In a small bowl, beat cream cheese until smooth. Gradually beat in sugar. Beat in sour cream and vanilla. Set aside 1/2 cup whipped topping for garnish; cover and refrigerate. Beat 1/2 cup whipped topping into cream cheese mixture; fold in remaining whipped topping. Spoon into the crust. Cover and refrigerate for at least 2 hours.

For topping, in a large saucepan, bring the rhubarb, sugar and cinnamon to a boil. Reduce heat; simmer, uncovered, for 5-8 minutes or until rhubarb is tender. In a small bowl, combine the cornstarch and cold water until smooth. Gradually stir into rhubarb mixture. Return to a boil; cook and stir for 1-2 minutes or until thickened. Cool to room temperature.

Cut pie into slices. Top each slice with rhubarb sauce and reserved whipped topping.
YIELD: 6-8 SERVINGS.

Walnut Banana Cupcakes

PREP: **25 MIN.** BAKE: **20 MIN. + COOLING**

What makes these tender banana cupcakes extra special is the nutmeg, but make sure it's fresh.

Rachel Krupp ✳ Perkiomenville, Pennsylvania

- 1/4 cup butter, softened
- 3/4 cup sugar
- 2 eggs
- 1/2 cup mashed ripe banana
- 1 teaspoon vanilla extract
- 1 cup all-purpose flour
- 1/2 teaspoon baking soda
- 1/2 teaspoon ground nutmeg
- 1/4 teaspoon salt
- 1/4 cup sour cream

CREAM CHEESE FROSTING:
- 4 ounces cream cheese, softened
- 1/2 teaspoon vanilla extract
- 1-3/4 cups confectioners' sugar
- 3 tablespoons chopped walnuts

In a large bowl, cream butter and sugar until light and fluffy. Add eggs, one at a time, beating well after each addition. Beat in banana and vanilla. Combine the flour, baking soda, nutmeg and salt; gradually add to creamed mixture alternately with sour cream, mixing well after each addition.

Fill paper-lined muffin cups half full. Bake at 350° for 18-22 minutes or until a toothpick inserted near the center comes out clean. Cool for 10 minutes before removing from pan to a wire rack to cool completely.

For frosting, in a bowl, beat the cream cheese and vanilla until smooth. Gradually beat in confectioners' sugar. Frost cupcakes; sprinkle with walnuts. Store in the refrigerator.
YIELD: 1 DOZEN.

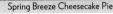
Spring Breeze Cheesecake Pie

Walnut Banana Cupcakes

Chocolate-Caramel Topped Cheesecake

Chocolate-Caramel Topped Cheesecake

PREP: **30 MIN.** BAKE: **45 MIN. + CHILLING**

We serve this confection at our house on special occasions. The topping on the cheesecake tastes like Turtle candy.

Amy Masson ✳ Cypress, California

- 1-1/3 cups shortbread cookie crumbs
- 1/4 cup butter, melted

FILLING:

- 3 packages (8 ounces *each*) cream cheese, softened
- 3/4 cup sugar
- 1/4 cup packed brown sugar
- 1 tablespoon vanilla extract
- 1/4 cup milk
- 2 tablespoons all-purpose flour
- 2 eggs, lightly beaten
- 1 egg yolk, lightly beaten

TOPPING:

- 1/2 cup semisweet chocolate chips
- 1-1/2 teaspoons shortening
- 1/2 cup coarsely chopped pecans, toasted
- 2 tablespoons caramel ice cream topping

In a small bowl, combine cookie crumbs and butter. Press onto the bottom of a greased 9-in. springform pan; set aside.

In a large bowl, beat the cream cheese, sugars and vanilla until smooth. Beat in milk and flour. Add eggs and egg yolk, beating on low speed just until combined. Pour into crust. Place on a baking sheet.

Bake at 325° for 45-50 minutes or until center is almost set. Cool on wire rack for 10 minutes. Carefully run a knife around edge of pan to loosen; cool 1 hour longer. Cover and refrigerate for at least 6 hours or overnight.

Remove side of pan. In a microwave, melt the chocolate chips and shortening; stir until smooth. Top cheesecake with pecans; drizzle with chocolate mixture and caramel topping. Refrigerate leftovers. YIELD: **12-14 SERVINGS.**

Oatmeal Cake with Broiled Frosting

🌾 Oatmeal Cake with Broiled Frosting

PREP: **30 MIN.** BAKE: **30 MIN.**

The broiled coconut frosting makes this tender snack cake terrific. It's great for a dessert after a special meal...or even as a morning treat.

Pat Van Cleve
Winston-Salem, North Carolina

- 1 cup quick-cooking oats
- 1-1/2 cups boiling water
- 1 cup sugar
- 1 cup packed brown sugar
- 1/2 cup unsweetened applesauce
- 2 eggs, lightly beaten
- 1-1/2 cups all-purpose flour
- 2 teaspoons baking powder
- 2 teaspoons ground cinnamon
- 1 teaspoon salt
- 1/2 teaspoon baking soda
- 1/4 teaspoon ground nutmeg

FROSTING:
- 1 cup flaked coconut
- 1/2 cup packed brown sugar
- 1/2 cup chopped walnuts
- 1/4 cup fat-free half-and-half
- 2 tablespoons butter, melted
- 1/2 teaspoon vanilla extract

In a small bowl, combine oats and water; let stand for 20 minutes. In a large bowl, combine sugars, applesauce and eggs. Add oat mixture; mix well. Combine the flour, baking powder, cinnamon, salt, baking soda and nutmeg; gradually add to batter and mix well.

Pour into a 13-in. x 9-in. baking pan coated with cooking spray. Bake at 350° for 25-30 minutes or until a toothpick inserted near the center comes out clean.

Combine frosting ingredients; spread over hot cake. Broil 6 in. from the heat for 1-2 minutes or until lightly browned and bubbly.
YIELD: 15 SERVINGS.

NUTRITION FACTS: 1 piece equals 288 calories, 7 g fat (3 g saturated fat), 32 mg cholesterol, 305 mg sodium, 53 g carbohydrate, 2 g fiber, 4 g protein.

Brownie Kiss Cupcakes

Brownie Kiss Cupcakes

PREP: **10 MIN.** BAKE: **20 MIN. + COOLING**

It's fun to prepare individual brownie cupcakes with a chocolaty surprise inside. My goddaughter, Cara, asks me to make them for her birthday to share at school. This year, she requested 32. I later found out she only needed 27 for her class...wonder where the other five went!

Pamela Lute ✳ Mercersburg, Pennsylvania

- 1/3 cup butter, softened
- 1 cup sugar
- 2 eggs
- 1 teaspoon vanilla extract
- 3/4 cup all-purpose flour
- 1/2 cup baking cocoa
- 1/4 teaspoon baking powder
- 1/4 teaspoon salt
- 9 milk chocolate kisses

In a large bowl, beat butter and sugar. Beat in eggs and vanilla. Combine the flour, cocoa, baking powder and salt; gradually add to the creamed mixture and mix well.

Fill paper, or foil-lined muffin cups two-thirds full. Place a chocolate kiss, tip end down, in the center of each.

Bake at 350° for 20-25 minutes or until top of brownies spring back when lightly touched. Cool for 10 minutes; remove from pans to wire racks to cool completely. **YIELD: 9 CUPCAKES.**

Rhubarb Upside-Down Cake

In a small bowl, beat egg whites and cream of tartar on medium speed until stiff peaks form. Gradually fold into creamed mixture, about 1/2 cup at a time. Gently spoon over rhubarb (pan will be full, about 1/4 in. from the top of pan).

Bake at 325° for 50-60 minutes or until cake springs back when lightly touched. Cool for 10 minutes before inverting onto a serving plate. Serve warm with whipped cream if desired. **YIELD: 10-12 SERVINGS.**

EDITOR'S NOTE: If using frozen rhubarb, measure rhubarb while still frozen, then thaw completely. Drain in a colander, but do not press liquid out.

Rhubarb Upside-Down Cake

PREP: **30 MIN.** BAKE: **40 MIN. + COOLING**
This tender and airy yellow cake is moist but not too sweet, and the caramelized rhubarb topping adds tangy taste and eye appeal. We like it served with strawberry ice cream.

Joyce Rowe ✶ Stratham, New Hampshire

    2/3 cup packed brown sugar
      3 tablespoons butter, melted
  2-1/4 cups diced fresh or frozen rhubarb
  4-1/2 teaspoons sugar
BATTER:
      6 tablespoons butter, softened
    3/4 cup sugar
      2 eggs, separated
      1 teaspoon vanilla extract
      1 cup plus 2 tablespoons all-purpose flour
  1-1/2 teaspoons baking powder
    1/2 teaspoon salt
    1/4 cup milk
    1/4 teaspoon cream of tartar
Whipped cream, optional

In a small bowl, combine brown sugar and butter. Spread into a greased 9-in. round baking pan. Layer with rhubarb; sprinkle with sugar. Set aside.

In a large bowl, cream butter and sugar until light and fluffy. Beat in egg yolks and vanilla. Combine the flour, baking powder and salt; add to creamed mixture alternately with milk, beating well after each addition.

Cupid's Chocolate Cake

PREP: **20 MIN.** BAKE: **25 MIN. + COOLING**
I'm pleased to share the recipe for the very best chocolate cake I have ever had. I prepare this treat every year on Valentine's Day. It's rich, delectable and absolutely irresistible.

Shelaine Duncan ✶ North Powder, Oregon

      1 cup butter, softened
  2-1/2 cups sugar
      4 eggs
  2-1/2 teaspoons vanilla extract, divided
  2-3/4 cups all-purpose flour
      1 cup baking cocoa
      2 teaspoons baking soda
    1/2 teaspoon baking powder
    1/2 teaspoon salt
      2 cups water
      1 cup heavy whipping cream
    1/4 cup confectioners' sugar
      4 cups buttercream frosting of your choice

In a large bowl, cream butter and sugar until light and fluffy. Add the eggs, one at a time, beating well after each addition. Beat in 1-1/2 teaspoons vanilla. Combine dry ingredients; gradually add to creamed mixture alternately with water, beating well after each addition.

Pour into three greased and floured 9-in. round baking pans. Bake at 350° for 25-30 minutes or until a toothpick inserted near center comes out clean. Cool for 10 minutes; remove from pans to wire racks to cool completely.

For filling, in a large bowl, beat cream until soft peaks form. Beat in confectioners' sugar and remaining vanilla until stiff.

Place bottom cake layer on a serving plate; spread with half of the filling. Repeat. Place top layer on cake; frost top and sides of cake with buttercream frosting. Store in the refrigerator. **YIELD: 12-14 SERVINGS.**

Cranberry Crumb Cake

PREP: **20 MIN.** BAKE: **35 MIN.**

This cranberry cake is easy to prepare and goes great with a cup of coffee. The flavor of cranberry comes through in every sweet-tart bite...and the streusel topping looks so pretty.

Sue Ellen Smith ✳ Philadelphia, Mississippi

- 1 cup all-purpose flour
- 1/2 cup plus 1/3 cup sugar, *divided*
- 2 teaspoons baking powder
- 1/2 teaspoon salt
- 1 egg, lightly beaten
- 1/2 cup fat-free milk
- 1 tablespoon orange juice
- 1 tablespoon canola oil
- 1/4 teaspoon almond extract
- 2 cups fresh *or* frozen cranberries, chopped

TOPPING:
- 1/4 cup all-purpose flour
- 3 tablespoons sugar
- 2 tablespoons cold butter

Cupid's Chocolate Cake

In a bowl, combine flour, 1/2 cup sugar, baking powder and salt. Combine the egg, milk, orange juice, oil and extract; stir into dry ingredients. Spoon into an 8-in. square baking dish coated with cooking spray. Combine cranberries and remaining sugar; spoon over batter.

For topping, combine flour and sugar in a small bowl; cut in the butter until crumbly. Sprinkle over cranberries. Bake at 375° for 35-45 minutes or until edges begin to pull away from the sides of pan. Refrigerate leftovers. **YIELD: 9 SERVINGS.**

NUTRITION FACTS: 1 piece equal 212 calories, 5 g fat (2 g saturated fat), 31 mg cholesterol, 203 mg sodium, 40 g carbohydrate, 1 g fiber, 3 g protein. DIABETIC EXCHANGES: 2 starch, 1 fat, 1/2 fruit.

Cranberry Crumb Cake

Moist Chocolate Cake

Moist Chocolate Cake

PREP: **15 MIN.** BAKE: **45 MIN. + COOLING**

You don't have to spend a lot of time to serve an elegant and delicious dessert. You can quickly mix up the batter in one bowl, bake your cake and serve a crowd.

Christa Hageman ✳ Telford, Pennsylvania

- 2 cups sugar
- 1-3/4 cups all-purpose flour
- 3/4 cup baking cocoa
- 2 teaspoons baking soda
- 1 teaspoon baking powder
- 1 teaspoon salt
- 2 eggs
- 1 cup strong brewed coffee
- 1 cup buttermilk
- 1/2 cup canola oil
- 1 teaspoon vanilla extract
- 1 tablespoon confectioners' sugar

In a large bowl, combine the sugar, flour, cocoa, baking soda, baking powder and salt. Add the eggs, coffee, buttermilk, oil and vanilla; beat on medium speed for 2 minutes (batter will be thin). Pour into a greased and floured 10-in. fluted tube pan.

Bake at 350° for 45-50 minutes or until a toothpick inserted near the center comes out clean. Cool for 10 minutes before removing from pan to a wire rack to cool completely. Dust with confectioners' sugar. YIELD: **12 SERVINGS.**

Grandma's Apple Carrot Cake

PREP: **25 MIN.** BAKE: **25 MIN.**

Rich, tender and cinnamony, this old-fashioned cake was handed down from our beloved Grandma Kelly. It's a perfect way to use up a few carrots and an apple...and it's ideal for smaller families.

Jackie Kohn ✳ Duluth, Minnesota

- 2 eggs
- 1/2 cup canola oil
- 1/2 cup sugar
- 1/2 cup packed brown sugar
- 1 cup all-purpose flour

Grandma's Apple Carrot Cake

    2 teaspoons ground cinnamon
  1/2 teaspoon baking powder
  1/4 teaspoon baking soda
  1/4 teaspoon salt
1-1/2 cups finely shredded carrots
    1 cup finely shredded apple

CREAM CHEESE FROSTING:
    1 package (3 ounces) cream cheese,
      softened
    1 tablespoon butter, softened
    1 teaspoon lemon juice
  1/4 teaspoon vanilla extract
1-1/4 cups confectioners' sugar

In a large bowl, beat the eggs, oil and sugars until smooth. Combine the flour, cinnamon, baking powder, baking soda and salt; gradually add to egg mixture just until combined. Stir in carrots and apple.

Spoon into a greased 9-in. square baking pan. Bake at 350° for 25-30 minutes or until a toothpick inserted near the center comes out clean. Cool on a wire rack.

In a small bowl, combine the frosting ingredients; beat until smooth. Spread over cake. Store in the refrigerator. **YIELD: 9 SERVINGS.**

Peanut Butter Layer Cake

PREP: **25 MIN.** BAKE: **30 MIN. + COOLING**

My husband loves peanut butter, so this dessert is his favorite. Sometimes I switch frosting recipes and use a chocolate frosting garnished with peanuts.

Carolyn Hylton ✳ Covington, Virginia

  1/2 cup butter, softened
1-1/4 cups sugar
  1/2 cup peanut butter chips, melted
    2 eggs
    1 teaspoon vanilla extract
    2 cups all-purpose flour
    1 teaspoon baking soda
  1/2 teaspoon baking powder
  1/4 teaspoon salt
1-1/2 cups milk

Peanut Butter Layer Cake

PEANUT BUTTER FROSTING:
    1 cup peanut butter chips, melted
    1 package (8 ounces) cream cheese,
      softened
    1 teaspoon vanilla extract
  1/8 teaspoon salt
    3 cups confectioners' sugar
    2 to 3 tablespoons milk

In a large bowl, cream butter and sugar until light and fluffy. Beat in melted peanut butter chips. Add eggs, one at a time, beating well after each addition. Beat in vanilla. Combine the flour, baking soda, baking powder and salt; gradually add to creamed mixture alternately with milk, beating well after each addition.

Pour into two greased and floured 9-in. round baking pans. Bake at 350° for 30-35 minutes or until a toothpick inserted near the center comes out clean. Cool for 10 minutes; remove from pans to wire racks to cool completely.

For frosting, in a small bowl, beat the melted chips, cream cheese, vanilla and salt until light and fluffy. Add confectioners' sugar alternately with enough of the milk to achieve spreading consistency. Spread frosting between layers and over top and sides of cake. **YIELD: 12-14 SERVINGS.**

Harvest Snack Cake

In a large bowl, combine the flour, brown sugar, baking soda, cinnamon, nutmeg and ginger. Combine the eggs, applesauce and vanilla; stir into dry ingredients just until moistened. Fold in the carrots and raisins (batter will be thick).

Spread evenly in a 13-in. x 9-in. baking pan coated with cooking spray. Bake at 350° for 30-35 minutes or until a toothpick inserted near the center comes out clean. Cool on a wire rack.
YIELD: 15 SERVINGS.

NUTRITION FACTS: 1 piece equals 170 calories, 1 g fat (trace saturated fat), 28 mg cholesterol, 191 mg sodium, 39 g carbohydrate, 3 g fiber, 3 g protein. DIABETIC EXCHANGES: 1-1/2 starch, 1 fruit.

Harvest Snack Cake

PREP: **15 MIN.** BAKE: **30 MIN. + COOLING**

This tasty treat was my first successful attempt at baking light. The ginger, cinnamon and nutmeg give it a familiar spice cake flavor, and raisins and shredded carrots help keep it moist.

Hilary Carroll ✳ Dearborn, Michigan

      2   cups whole wheat flour
1-1/4   cups packed brown sugar
      2   teaspoons baking soda
   3/4   teaspoon ground cinnamon
   1/2   teaspoon ground nutmeg
   1/8   to 1/4 teaspoon ground ginger
      2   eggs
   1/2   cup unsweetened applesauce
      1   teaspoon vanilla extract
1-1/2   cups shredded carrots
      1   cup raisins

Cranberry Pear Cake

PREP: **40 MIN.** BAKE: **45 MIN. + COOLING**

If you want a change-of-pace cake that's full of fall flavors, try this pairing of cranberries and pears. The nutty filling and glaze topping elevate it to a special dessert.

Jeanne Holt ✳ Mendota Heights, Minnesota

      1   cup packed brown sugar
   3/4   cup chopped pecans
   1/3   cup chopped dried cranberries
      1   teaspoon apple pie spice
BATTER:
   1/2   cup butter, softened
      1   cup sugar
      3   eggs
      1   teaspoon vanilla extract
      2   cups all-purpose flour
      2   teaspoons baking powder
      1   teaspoon baking soda
   1/2   teaspoon salt
      1   cup (8 ounces) sour cream
      2   cups chopped peeled ripe pears
GLAZE:
      1   cup confectioners' sugar
      5   teaspoons milk
4-1/2   teaspoons butter, melted
   1/4   teaspoon apple pie spice
   1/4   teaspoon vanilla extract

In a small bowl, combine the brown sugar, pecans, cranberries and apple pie spice; set aside. In a large bowl, cream butter and sugar until fluffy. Add eggs, one at a time, beating after each addition. Beat in vanilla. Combine the flour, baking powder, baking soda and salt; add to creamed mixture alternately with sour cream. Beat just until combined. Fold in pears.

Pour half of the batter into a greased and floured 10-in. fluted tube pan. Sprinkle with half of the pecan mixture; top with remaining batter and pecan mixture.

Bake at 350° for 45-50 minutes or until a toothpick inserted near the center comes out clean. Cool for 10 minutes before removing from pan to a wire rack to cool completely. In a bowl, whisk the glaze ingredients until smooth; drizzle over cake. **YIELD: 12-14 SERVINGS.**

Cranberry Pear Cake

No-Bake Cheesecake Pie

PREP: 15 MIN. + CHILLING

I came up with this creamy white chocolate cheesecake after remembering one evening that I needed to bring a treat to the office the next day. It was a tremendous hit.

Geneva Mayer ✳ Olney, Illinois

- 1 cup vanilla *or* white chips
- 2 packages (8 ounces *each*) cream cheese, cubed
- 1 carton (8 ounces) frozen whipped topping, thawed
- 1 graham cracker crust (9 inches)
- 1/3 cup English toffee bits *or* almond brickle chips

In a heavy saucepan, melt chips over medium-low heat; stir until smooth. Remove from the heat; stir in cream cheese until smooth. Fold in whipped topping. Pour into the crust.

Cover and refrigerate overnight or until set. Just before serving, sprinkle with toffee bits. **YIELD: 6-8 SERVINGS.**

No-Bake Cheesecake Pie

Coconut Cream Dream Cake

Almond Praline Cake

🍴 Coconut Cream Dream Cake

PREP: **30 MIN.** BAKE: **20 MIN. + COOLING**

This pretty four-layer cake is easy to make with an instant pudding filling and a seven-minute frosting. It tastes like coconut cream pie, so it's like getting the best of two desserts in one.

Pamela Shank ✳ Parkersburg, West Virginia

- 3/4 cup sugar
- 2 tablespoons shortening
- 2 tablespoons butter, softened
- 1 egg
- 1 egg yolk
- 3/4 teaspoon vanilla extract
- 1 cup all-purpose flour
- 1 teaspoon baking powder
- 1/2 teaspoon salt
- 1/2 cup 2% milk

FROSTING/FILLING:

- 1/2 cup sugar
- 4 teaspoons water
- 2 teaspoons light corn syrup
- 1 egg white
- 1/4 teaspoon cream of tartar
- 1/4 teaspoon vanilla extract
- 1 cup cold 2% milk
- 1/2 teaspoon coconut extract
- 1/2 cup instant vanilla pudding mix
- 6 tablespoons flaked coconut, *divided*

In a small bowl, cream the sugar, shortening and butter until light and fluffy. Beat in egg and yolk. Add vanilla. Combine the flour, baking powder and salt; add to the creamed mixture alternately with milk. Beat just until combined.

Pour into two 6-in. round baking pans coated with cooking spray. Bake at 350° for 20-25 minutes or until a toothpick comes out clean. Cool for 10 minutes; remove from pans to wire racks. Cool completely.

In a double boiler over simmering water, combine the sugar, water, corn syrup, egg white and cream of tartar. With a portable mixer, beat on low speed for 1 minute. Continue beating on low over low heat until frosting reaches 160°, about 5 minutes. Pour into a small bowl; add vanilla. Beat on high until stiff peaks form, about 7 minutes.

In a bowl, whisk the milk, extract and pudding mix for 2 minutes. Let stand for 2 minutes or until soft-set. Finely chop 1/4 cup coconut; fold into pudding mix.

Split each cake into two horizontal layers. Spread a third of the pudding over one cake layer; repeat layers twice. Top with remaining cake. Frost the top and sides. Toast remaining coconut; sprinkle over the top. Store in the refrigerator. **YIELD: 6 SERVINGS.**

Apple Bundt Cake

Almond Praline Cakes

PREP: 20 MIN. BAKE: 20 MIN.

Cute and chocolaty, these mini cakes are moist and rich with a crunchy almond crust. The original recipe was so good that I just had to pare it down, and the new recipe is still delicious without a lot of leftovers.

Kendra Doss ✳ Smithville, Missouri

- 2 tablespoons butter
- 1/3 cup packed brown sugar
- 2 tablespoons 2% milk
- 1/4 cup chopped almonds

BATTER:
- 2 tablespoons butter, softened
- 1/2 cup sugar
- 1 egg
- 1/4 teaspoon vanilla extract
- 1/2 cup all-purpose flour
- 2 tablespoons baking cocoa
- 1/2 teaspoon baking powder
- 1/4 teaspoon baking soda
- 1/3 cup 2% milk

In a saucepan, melt butter over medium heat. Stir in brown sugar and milk. Cook and stir until sugar is dissolved, about 1 minute. Pour into four 8-oz. ramekins or custard cups coated with cooking spray. Sprinkle with almonds; set aside.

In a small bowl, cream butter and sugar until light and fluffy. Beat in egg and vanilla. Combine the flour, cocoa, baking powder and baking soda; gradually add to the creamed mixture alternately with milk. Spoon over almonds.

Bake at 350° for 20-25 minutes or until a toothpick comes out clean. Cool on a wire rack for 5 minutes. Carefully run a knife around the edge of ramekins to loosen. Invert cakes onto dessert plates. Serve cakes warm or at room temperature. **YIELD: 4 SERVINGS.**

Apple Bundt Cake

PREP: 20 MIN. BAKE: 1-1/4 HOURS + COOLING

I'm just wild about the thin, crunchy crust and soft, delectable inside of this cake. With the butter cream sauce, it's almost like eating candy.

Virginia Horst ✳ Mesa, Washington

- 2 eggs
- 2 cups sugar
- 1-1/2 cups canola oil
- 3 cups all-purpose flour
- 1 teaspoon baking soda
- 1 teaspoon ground cinnamon
- 1/2 teaspoon salt
- 3 cups diced peeled apples
- 1 cup chopped pecans

BUTTER CREAM SAUCE:
- 1/2 cup butter, cubed
- 1 cup sugar
- 1/2 cup heavy whipping cream
- 1 teaspoon vanilla extract

In a large bowl, beat the eggs, sugar and oil. Combine the flour, baking soda, cinnamon and salt; gradually add to batter (batter will be very stiff). Fold in apples and pecans.

Pour into a greased 10-in. fluted tube pan. Bake at 325° for 1-1/4 to 1-1/2 hours or until a toothpick inserted near the center comes out clean. Cool for 10 minutes before removing from pan to a wire rack.

For sauce, melt butter in a small saucepan. Add the sugar, cream and vanilla. Cook and stir over low heat until sugar is dissolved and sauce is heated through. Slice the cake; serve with warm sauce. Refrigerate leftover sauce. **YIELD: 12-16 SERVINGS.**

Berry Pinwheel Cake

Bake at 375° for 10-12 minutes or until cake springs back when lightly touched. Cool for 5 minutes. Turn cake onto a kitchen towel dusted with confectioners' sugar. Peel off waxed paper. Roll up cake in towel jelly-roll style, starting with a short side. Cool on a wire rack.

In a large bowl, beat cream until soft peaks form; gradually add sugar, beating until stiff peaks form. Fold in lemon curd; gradually fold in strawberries.

Unroll cake; spread filling evenly to within 1/2 in. of edges. Roll up again; dust with the confectioners' sugar. Cover and refrigerate for 1 hour before serving. Refrigerate leftovers. **YIELD: 8 SERVINGS.**

Berry Pinwheel Cake

PREP: **30 MIN.** BAKE: **10 MIN. + CHILLING**

Perfect for special meals, this lovely chiffon cake is a nice change from strawberry pie or shortcake. Don't be afraid to try this jelly-roll-style dessert...it's easy to make. Plus, the waxed paper-lined pan helps make cleanup a breeze!

Becky Ruff ✳ Monona, Iowa

- 4 egg yolks
- 2 eggs
- 1/2 cup sugar
- 4-1/2 teaspoons water
- 2 teaspoons canola oil
- 1 teaspoon vanilla extract
- 1 cup cake flour
- 1 teaspoon baking powder
- 1/2 teaspoon salt

Confectioners' sugar

FILLING:

- 1 cup heavy whipping cream
- 1 tablespoon sugar
- 3 tablespoons lemon curd
- 2 cups chopped fresh strawberries

In a large bowl, beat the egg yolks, eggs and sugar until thick and lemon-colored. Beat in the water, oil and vanilla. Combine flour, baking powder and salt; gradually add to egg mixture. Grease a 15-in. x 10-in. x 1-in. baking pan and line with waxed paper; grease and flour the paper. Spread batter into pan.

Chocolate Potato Cake

PREP: **40 MIN.** BAKE: **25 MIN. + COOLING**

I won grand champion honors in a potato festival baking contest with this moist chocolate cake. The icing recipe can be doubled for real sweet tooths.

Catherine Hahn ✳ Winamac, Indiana

- 1 cup butter, softened
- 2 cups sugar
- 2 eggs
- 1 cup cold mashed potatoes (without added milk and butter)
- 1 teaspoon vanilla extract
- 2 cups all-purpose flour
- 1/2 cup baking cocoa
- 1 teaspoon baking soda
- 1 cup milk
- 1 cup chopped walnuts or pecans

CARAMEL ICING:

- 1/2 cup butter, cubed
- 1 cup packed brown sugar
- 1/4 cup evaporated milk
- 2 cups confectioners' sugar
- 1/2 teaspoon vanilla extract

In a large bowl, cream butter and sugar until light and fluffy. Add eggs, one at a time, beating well after each addition. Add potatoes and vanilla. Combine the flour, cocoa and baking soda; gradually add to the creamed mixture alternately with milk, beating well after each addition. Stir in nuts.

Pour into two greased and floured 9-in. round baking pans. Bake at 350° for 25-30 minutes or until a toothpick inserted near the center comes out clean. Cool for 10 minutes before removing from pans to wire racks to cool completely.

For icing, in a saucepan over low heat, cook butter and brown sugar until butter is melted and mixture is smooth. Stir in evaporated milk; bring to a boil, stirring constantly. Remove from the heat; cool to room temperature. Stir in confectioners' sugar and vanilla until smooth. Spread between layers and over top of cake. **YIELD: 10-12 SERVINGS.**

Chocolate Potato Cake

Rhubarb Dessert Cake

PREP: 10 MIN. BAKE: 30 MIN. + COOLING

A relative of mine shared this delightful cake with me. I freeze rhubarb when it's in season so I can make it year-round.

Loraine Meyer ✳ Bend, Oregon

- 2 tablespoons butter, melted
- 1 cup packed brown sugar
- 4 cups sliced fresh *or* frozen rhubarb
- 1-1/2 cups sugar
- 1-1/2 cups all-purpose flour
- 1-1/2 teaspoons baking powder
- 1/8 teaspoon salt
- 3 eggs
- 1/2 cup water
- 1 teaspoon vanilla extract

Whipped cream *or* vanilla ice cream

In a greased 13-in. x 9-in. baking dish, combine butter and brown sugar. Top with the rhubarb.

In a bowl, combine the sugar, flour, baking powder and salt. In another bowl, whisk the eggs, water and vanilla; stir into dry ingredients just until moistened. Pour over rhubarb.

Bake at 350° for 30-35 minutes or until cake springs back when lightly touched. Cool for 10 minutes on a wire rack. Serve warm or at room temperature with the whipped cream or ice cream. **YIELD: 12 SERVINGS.**

EDITOR'S NOTE: If using frozen rhubarb, measure rhubarb while still frozen, then thaw completely. Drain in a colander, but do not press liquid out.

Rhubarb Dessert Cake

Apple Harvest Cake

Apple Harvest Cake

PREP: **20 MIN.** BAKE: **40 MIN. + COOLING**

Tender apple slices and subtle flavors make this old-fashioned cake one of our all-time favorites.

E. Bartuschat ✳ Abington, Massachusetts

- 2-1/4 cups sugar, *divided*
- 1 cup canola oil
- 4 eggs
- 1/4 cup orange juice
- 2-1/2 teaspoons vanilla extract
- 3 cups all-purpose flour
- 3 teaspoons baking powder
- 1/2 teaspoon salt
- 4 medium tart apples, peeled and cubed
- 2 teaspoons ground cinnamon

Whipped cream and additional cinnamon, optional

In a large bowl, beat 2 cups sugar, oil, eggs, orange juice and vanilla until blended. Combine flour, baking powder and salt; gradually beat into sugar mixture until blended. Stir in apples.

Spread half of batter into a greased 13-in. x 9-in. baking dish. Combine the cinnamon and remaining sugar; sprinkle over batter. Carefully spread remaining batter over the top.

Bake at 350° for 40-50 minutes or until a toothpick inserted near the center comes out clean. Cool on a wire rack. Garnish with the whipped cream and additional cinnamon if desired. YIELD: **12-15 SERVINGS.**

Light Lemon Cheesecake

PREP: **20 MIN.** BAKE: **70 MIN. + CHILLING**

We love cheesecake, but we don't care for the fat that usually comes with it. This alternative offers a creamy texture and full flavor without the guilt!

Deborah Lobe ✳ Olympia, Washington

- 3/4 cup reduced-fat cinnamon graham cracker crumbs (about 4 whole crackers)
- 3 packages (8 ounces *each*) fat-free cream cheese
- 2 packages (8 ounces *each*) reduced-fat cream cheese
- 1-2/3 cups sugar

Light Lemon Cheesecake

1/8 teaspoon salt

9 egg whites

1/4 cup lemon juice

1-1/2 teaspoons vanilla extract

1 teaspoon grated lemon peel

8 strawberries, sliced

2 medium kiwifruit, peeled and sliced

Rhubarb Swirl Cheesecake

Sprinkle graham cracker crumbs on the bottom and up the sides of a 9-in. springform pan well coated with cooking spray; set aside.

In a large bowl, beat cream cheese, sugar and salt until smooth. Add egg whites; beat on low speed just until combined, about 2 minutes. Stir in the lemon juice, vanilla and lemon peel.

Pour into prepared pan. Bake at 325° for 70-80 minutes or until center is almost set. Turn oven off; leave cheesecake in oven with door ajar for 30 minutes.

Remove from oven. Carefully run a knife around edge of pan to loosen. Cool 1 hour longer. Refrigerate overnight. Remove sides of pan. Top with strawberries and kiwi. Refrigerate leftovers. **YIELD: 12 SERVINGS.**

NUTRITION FACTS: 1 piece equals 300 calories, 8 g fat (5 g saturated fat), 26 mg cholesterol, 522 mg sodium, 42 g carbohydrate, 1 g fiber, 15 g protein. **DIABETIC EXCHANGES:** 2 fat-free milk, 1 fruit, 1 fat.

Rhubarb Swirl Cheesecake

PREP: 40 MIN. BAKE: 1 HOUR + CHILLING

I love cheesecake and my husband loves chocolate, so this is a favorite dessert of ours. The rhubarb adds a tartness that complements the sweet flavors so well.

Carol Witczak ✳ Tinley Park, Illinois

2-1/2 cups thinly sliced fresh *or* frozen rhubarb

1/3 cup plus 1/2 cup sugar, *divided*

2 tablespoons orange juice

1-1/4 cups graham cracker crumbs

1/4 cup butter, melted

3 packages (8 ounces *each*) cream cheese, softened

2 cups (16 ounces) sour cream

1 tablespoon cornstarch

2 teaspoons vanilla extract

1/2 teaspoon salt

3 eggs, lightly beaten

8 squares (1 ounce *each*) white baking chocolate, melted

In a large saucepan, bring rhubarb, 1/3 cup sugar and orange juice to a boil. Reduce heat; cook and stir until thickened and rhubarb is tender. Set aside.

In a small bowl, combine cracker crumbs and butter. Press onto the bottom of a greased 9-in. springform pan. Place on a baking sheet. Bake at 350° for 7-9 minutes or until lightly browned. Cool on a wire rack.

In a large bowl, beat the cream cheese, sour cream, cornstarch, vanilla, salt and remaining sugar until smooth. Add eggs; beat just until combined. Fold in white chocolate.

Pour half of the filling into crust. Top with half of the rhubarb sauce; cut through batter with a knife to gently swirl rhubarb. Layer with the remaining filling and rhubarb sauce; cut through the top layers with a knife to gently swirl rhubarb.

Place pan on a double thickness of heavy-duty foil (about 16 in. square). Securely wrap foil around pan. Place in a large baking pan; add 1 in. of hot water to larger pan. Bake at 350° for 60-70 minutes or until center is almost set.

Cool on a wire rack for 10 minutes. Remove foil. Carefully run a knife around edge of pan to loosen; cool 1 hour longer. Cover and chill overnight. Remove sides of pan. Refrigerate leftovers. **YIELD: 12-14 SERVINGS.**

EDITOR'S NOTE: If using frozen rhubarb, measure rhubarb while still frozen, then thaw completely. Drain in a colander, but do not press liquid out.

Caramel Nut Torte

🧈 Caramel Nut Torte

PREP: 30 MIN. BAKE: **20 MIN.** + **COOLING**

The full-size version of this recipe caught my eye many years ago because it uses apple cider. My father has a small orchard and makes cider. We all love this scrumptious cake.

Karla Stichter ✷ New Paris, Indiana

- 3 eggs, *separated*
- 1/4 cup apple cider *or* juice
- 1 teaspoon vanilla extract
- 1/2 teaspoon baking powder
- 1/4 teaspoon ground cinnamon
- 2/3 cup sugar, *divided*
- 1 cup graham cracker crumbs
- 1/2 cup ground almonds

CARAMEL SAUCE:

- 1/4 cup packed brown sugar
- 1-1/2 teaspoons cornstarch
- 3 tablespoons butter
- 2 tablespoons plus 2 teaspoons apple cider *or* juice, *divided*
- 4 ounces cream cheese, softened

FROSTING:

  1/2 cup heavy whipping cream
    1 tablespoon sugar
  1/4 teaspoon vanilla extract

Line two 6-in. round baking pans with parchment paper; coat with cooking spray. In a small bowl, lightly beat egg yolks. Set aside 1 tablespoon. Add cider, vanilla, baking powder, cinnamon and 1/2 cup sugar to remaining yolks.

In another bowl, beat egg whites on medium until soft peaks form. Beat in remaining sugar, about 1 tablespoon at a time, on high until stiff peaks form and sugar is dissolved. Fold a fourth of the whites into batter; then fold in remaining whites. Fold in crumbs and almonds.

Gently spoon into prepared pans. Bake at 325° for 20-25 minutes or until cake springs back when lightly touched. Cool for 10 minutes; remove from pans to wire racks. Cool completely.

In a saucepan, combine the brown sugar, cornstarch, butter and 2 tablespoons cider. Bring to a boil over medium heat, stirring constantly. Cook and stir for 2 minutes or until thickened. Stir a small amount into reserved yolk; return all to pan. Bring to a gentle boil, stirring constantly. Cool.

In a small bowl, beat cream cheese until fluffy. Beat in 2 tablespoons caramel sauce until smooth. Spread over one cake; top with the remaining cake. Add the remaining cider to the remaining caramel sauce to achieve a drizzling consistency.

Beat cream until it begins to thicken. Add sugar and vanilla; beat until soft peaks form. Frost top and sides of cake. Drizzle with caramel sauce. **YIELD: 6 SERVINGS.**

Sweet Cherry Cheese Dessert

PREP: 30 MIN. + CHILLING

I like the combination of this sweet treat's soft, creamy filling and crunchy crust with a wonderfully nutty flavor. The layer of cherries on top makes for a beautiful presentation. It's not difficult—and is simply delicious.

Diane Lombardo ✳ New Castle, Pennsylvania

  1/2 cup cold butter, cubed
  2-1/2 cups crushed pecan shortbread cookies

Sweet Cherry Cheese Dessert

    2 cans (21 ounces *each*) cherry pie filling
    1 teaspoon almond extract
    1 teaspoon vanilla extract
    1 package (8 ounces) cream cheese, softened
    2 cups confectioners' sugar
    1 carton (12 ounces) frozen whipped topping, thawed

In a large bowl, cut butter into crushed cookies until mixture resembles coarse crumbs. Press into an ungreased 13-in. x 9-in. baking pan. Bake at 350° for 15-18 minutes or until crust is lightly browned. Cool on a wire rack.

In a large bowl, combine the pie filling and extracts; set aside. In a large bowl, beat cream cheese and confectioners' sugar until fluffy. Fold in whipped topping. Spread over crust. Top with filling. Cover and refrigerate for 1-2 hours or until set. **YIELD: 15 SERVINGS.**

Walnut Glory Cake

Walnut Glory Cake

PREP: **15 MIN.** BAKE: **45 MIN.**

I've served this sponge cake at church dinners, reunions and other occasions for 40 years. It's always on the table when any of our children and their families visit our log home in the Georgia mountains.

Marjorie Yoder * Epworth, Georgia

      9 eggs, *separated*
1-1/2 cups sugar, *divided*
      2 teaspoons vanilla extract
   3/4 cup all-purpose flour
      2 teaspoons ground cinnamon
      1 teaspoon salt
      2 cups finely chopped walnuts
      2 cups confectioners' sugar
      2 to 3 tablespoons milk

In a large bowl, beat egg yolks until slightly thickened. Gradually add 3/4 cup sugar, beating until thick and lemon-colored. Beat in vanilla. Combine flour, cinnamon and salt; gradually add to batter and beat until smooth.

In a bowl, beat egg whites on medium speed until soft peaks form. Add remaining sugar, 1 tablespoon at a time, beating on high until stiff peaks form. Fold a fourth of egg whites into batter; fold in remaining egg whites. Fold in walnuts.

Spoon into an ungreased 10-in. tube pan (pan will be full). Bake at 350° for 45-50 minutes or until cake springs back when lightly touched.

Immediately invert pan; cool completely. Run a knife around the side of the cake and remove from the pan. In a small bowl, combine the confectioners' sugar and enough milk to achieve drizzling consistency; drizzle over the cake. **YIELD: 10-12 SERVINGS.**

Breakfast Upside-Down Cake

Breakfast Upside-Down Cake

PREP: **20 MIN. + RESTING** BAKE: **40 MIN.**

This moist, golden morning treat quickly became my husband's favorite. And because it calls for a boxed blueberry muffin mix and canned pineapple, I never have a problem finding the time to make it for him.

Stacy Walker * Winsor Heights, Iowa

   1 package (18-1/4 ounces) blueberry muffin mix
   1 package (1/4 ounce) quick-rise yeast

1 can (8 ounces) pineapple slices
1 egg, lightly beaten
1/3 cup packed brown sugar
1/4 cup butter, melted
4 maraschino cherries, halved
Fresh blueberries, optional

Rinse and drain blueberries from muffin mix; set aside. Place muffin mix and yeast in a large bowl; set aside.

Drain the pineapple, reserving the juice in a measuring cup. Set the pineapple aside. Add enough water to juice to measure 2/3 cup.

Pour into saucepan; heat to 120°-130°. Add to muffin mix; stir just until moistened. Beat in the egg. Cover and let rest for 10 minutes.

Combine brown sugar and butter; pour into a greased 9-in. round baking pan. Cut each pineapple slice in half; arrange over brown sugar mixture. Tuck cherries into pineapple.

Spoon half of batter over pineapple. Sprinkle with the reserved blueberries. Spread with the remaining batter.

Bake at 350° for 40-45 minutes or until a toothpick inserted into cake comes out clean. Immediately invert onto a serving plate. Cool completely. Garnish with fresh blueberries if desired. **YIELD: 8 SERVINGS.**

Berry Nectarine Buckle

🌼 Berry Nectarine Buckle

PREP: **25 MIN.** BAKE: **35 MIN.**

I found this tasty recipe in a magazine a long time ago, but modified it over the years. We enjoy its combination of blueberries, raspberries, blackberries and nectarines, particularly when the cake is served warm with low-fat frozen yogurt.

Lisa Sjursen-Darling ✳ Scottsville, New York

1/3 cup all-purpose flour
1/3 cup packed brown sugar
1 teaspoon ground cinnamon
3 tablespoons cold butter
BATTER:
6 tablespoons butter, softened
3/4 cup plus 1 tablespoon sugar, *divided*
2 eggs
1-1/2 teaspoons vanilla extract
2-1/4 cups all-purpose flour
2-1/2 teaspoons baking powder
1/2 teaspoon salt
1/2 cup fat-free milk
1 cup fresh blueberries
1 pound medium nectarines, peeled, sliced and patted dry *or* 1 package (16 ounces) frozen unsweetened sliced peaches, thawed and patted dry
1/2 cup fresh raspberries
1/2 cup fresh blackberries

For topping, in a small bowl, combine the flour, brown sugar and cinnamon; cut in butter until crumbly. Set aside.

In a bowl, cream butter and 3/4 cup sugar until light and fluffy. Add eggs, one at a time, beating well after each addition. Beat in vanilla. Combine flour, baking powder and salt; add to creamed mixture alternately with milk, beating well after each addition. Set aside 3/4 cup batter. Fold blueberries into remaining batter.

Spoon into a 13-in. x 9-in. baking dish coated with cooking spray. Arrange nectarines on top; sprinkle with remaining sugar. Drop reserved batter by teaspoonfuls over nectarines. Sprinkle with the raspberries, blackberries and the reserved topping.

Bake at 350° for 35-40 minutes or until a toothpick inserted near the center comes out clean. Serve warm. **YIELD: 20 SERVINGS.**

NUTRITION FACTS: 1 piece equals 177 calories, 6 g fat (3 g saturated fat), 35 mg cholesterol, 172 mg sodium, 28 g carbohydrate, 1 g fiber, 3 g protein. DIABETIC EXCHANGES: 2 starch, 1 fat.

Raspberry Peach Cupcakes

Raspberry Peach Cupcakes

PREP: **25 MIN.** BAKE: **15 MIN. + COOLING**

These easy cupcakes, which start with a cake mix, have an appealing combination of fresh fruit and white chocolate. The luscious lemon buttercream frosting adds a citrus tang to the sweet treats. My family loves them!

Arlene Kay Butler * Ogden, Utah

    1 cup vanilla or white chips
    6 tablespoons butter, cubed
    1 package (18-1/4 ounces) white cake mix
    1 cup milk
    3 eggs
    1 teaspoon vanilla extract
    1 cup fresh raspberries
  1/2 cup chopped peeled fresh peaches or
       frozen unsweetened peach slices, thawed
       and chopped

LEMON FROSTING:

  1/2 cup butter, softened
    3 cups confectioners' sugar
    2 tablespoons lemon juice

Fresh raspberries and peach pieces, optional

In a microwave, melt the chips and butter at 70% power for 1 minute; stir. Microwave at additional 10- to 20-second intervals, stirring until smooth.

In a large bowl, combine the cake mix, milk, eggs, vanilla and melted chips; beat on low speed for 30 seconds. Beat on medium for 2 minutes. Fold in raspberries and peaches.

Fill paper-lined muffin cups three-fourths full. Bake at 350° for 15-20 minutes or until a toothpick inserted near the center comes out clean. Cool for 10 minutes before removing from pans to wire racks to cool completely.

For frosting, in a small bowl, beat the butter, confectioners' sugar and lemon juice until smooth. Frost the cupcakes. Top with the fruit if desired. YIELD: **2 DOZEN.**

EDITOR'S NOTE: This recipe was tested with Betty Crocker cake mix.

Cinnamon Apple Cheesecake

PREP: **40 MIN.** BAKE: **40 MIN. + CHILLING**

An attractive topping of cinnamon-spiced apple slices and a homemade oat-and-walnut crust make this creamy dessert a definite showstopper.

Emily Ann Young * Edmond, Oklahoma

  1/2 cup butter, softened
  1/4 cup packed brown sugar
    1 cup all-purpose flour
  1/4 cup quick-cooking oats
  1/4 cup finely chopped walnuts
  1/2 teaspoon ground cinnamon

FILLING:

    2 packages (8 ounces each) cream cheese,
       softened
    1 can (14 ounces) sweetened condensed milk
  1/2 cup thawed apple juice concentrate
    3 eggs, lightly beaten

TOPPING:

    2 medium tart apples, peeled and sliced
    1 tablespoon butter
    1 teaspoon cornstarch
  1/4 teaspoon ground cinnamon
  1/4 cup thawed apple juice concentrate

In a small bowl, cream butter and brown sugar until light and fluffy. Gradually add flour, oats, walnuts and cinnamon until well blended. Press onto the bottom and 1-1/2 in. up the sides of a greased 9-in. springform pan.

Place on a baking sheet. Bake at 325° for 10 minutes or until set. Cool on a wire rack.

In a large bowl, beat cream cheese until fluffy. Beat in milk and juice concentrate until smooth. Add eggs; beat on low speed just until combined (batter will be thin). Pour into crust.

Return pan to baking sheet. Bake at 325° for 40-45 minutes or until center is almost set. Cool on a wire rack for 10 minutes. Carefully run a knife around edge of pan to loosen; cool 1 hour longer. Refrigerate overnight.

In a large skillet, cook and stir apples in butter over medium heat until crisp-tender, about 5 minutes. Cool to room temperature. Arrange over cheesecake.

In a saucepan, combine the cornstarch, cinnamon and juice concentrate until smooth. Bring to a boil. Reduce heat; cook and stir for 1 minute or until the mixture is thickened. Immediately brush over apples. Chill for 1 hour. Remove sides of pan. Refrigerate leftovers. **YIELD: 12 SERVINGS.**

Cinnamon Apple Cheesecake

Pecan Angel Food Cake

PREP: 30 MIN. BAKE: 40 MIN.

Chopped pecans add a deliciously nutty flavor and texture to angel food cake. It's a unique variation from plain angel food.

Margaret Wampler ✳ Butler, Pennsylvania

1-1/2 cups egg whites (about 10)
    1 cup all-purpose flour
    1 teaspoon cream of tartar
    2 teaspoons vanilla extract
1-1/2 cups sugar
1-1/2 cups finely chopped pecans
Whipped cream, optional

Place egg whites in a large bowl; let stand at room temperature for 30 minutes. Sift flour twice; set aside. Add cream of tartar and vanilla to egg whites; beat on medium speed until soft peaks form. Gradually beat in sugar, about 2 tablespoons at a time, on high until stiff glossy peaks form. Gradually fold in flour, about 1/4 cup at a time. Fold in pecans.

Gently spoon into an ungreased 10-in. tube pan. Cut through batter with a knife to remove air pockets. Bake on the lowest oven rack at 350° for 35-40 minutes or until lightly browned and entire top appears dry.

Immediately invert pan; cool completely, about 1 hour. Run a knife around side and center tube of pan; remove cake. Serve with whipped cream if desired. **YIELD: 12-16 SERVINGS.**

Pecan Angel Food Cake

Cranberry-Carrot Layer Cake

Cranberry-Carrot Layer Cake

PREP: **20 MIN.** BAKE: **25 MIN. + COOLING**

This moist cake smothered with rich cream cheese frosting makes any dinner festive. Every autumn, I go to a cranberry festival in Wisconsin and load up on fresh cranberries to freeze for year-round cooking.

Nellie Runne ✳ Rockford, Illinois

- 4 eggs
- 1-1/2 cups packed brown sugar
- 1-1/4 cups canola oil
- 1 teaspoon grated orange peel
- 2 cups all-purpose flour
- 1 teaspoon baking soda
- 1 teaspoon ground cinnamon
- 3/4 teaspoon baking powder
- 1/2 teaspoon salt
- 1/4 teaspoon ground cloves
- 2 cups shredded carrots
- 1 cup dried cranberries

CREAM CHEESE FROSTING:

- 2 packages (8 ounces *each*) cream cheese, softened
- 3/4 cup butter, softened
- 4 cups confectioners' sugar
- 1 tablespoon milk
- 1/2 teaspoon ground ginger
- 1/2 teaspoon grated orange peel, optional

In a large bowl, combine the eggs, brown sugar, oil and orange peel. Combine the flour, baking soda, cinnamon, baking powder, salt and cloves; gradually add to egg mixture and mix well. Stir in carrots and cranberries.

Pour into two greased and floured 9-in. round baking pans. Bake at 350° for 25-30 minutes or until a toothpick inserted near the center comes out clean. Cool for 10 minutes; remove from pans to wire racks to cool completely.

For frosting, in a large bowl, beat cream cheese and butter until fluffy. Gradually beat in confectioners' sugar, milk, ginger and orange peel if desired.

Cut each cake horizontally into two layers. Place bottom layer on a serving plate; spread frosting between layers and over top and sides of cake. YIELD: **12-14 SERVINGS.**

Cinnamon-Sugar Rhubarb Cake

Cinnamon-Sugar Rhubarb Cake

PREP: 30 MIN. BAKE: 40 MIN.

A real crowd-pleaser, this tender snack-like cake is chock-full of diced rhubarb and sprinkled with a sweet cinnamon-sugar topping. Everyone will be asking for the recipe... or seconds!

Maryls Haber ✳ White, South Dakota

- 1/2 cup shortening
- 1 cup packed brown sugar
- 1 cup sugar, *divided*
- 1 egg
- 1 teaspoon vanilla extract
- 2 cups all-purpose flour
- 1 teaspoon baking soda
- 1/2 teaspoon salt
- 1 cup buttermilk
- 2 cups diced fresh *or* frozen rhubarb
- 1 teaspoon ground cinnamon

In a large bowl, cream the shortening, brown sugar and 1/2 cup sugar until light and fluffy. Add the egg and vanilla; beat for 2 minutes. Combine the flour, baking soda and salt; add to creamed mixture alternately with buttermilk, beating well after each addition. Stir in rhubarb.

Pour into a greased 13-in. x 9-in. baking dish. Combine the cinnamon and remaining sugar; sprinkle over the batter. Bake at 350° for 40-45 minutes or until a toothpick inserted near the center comes out clean. Serve cake warm. **YIELD: 12-16 SERVINGS.**

EDITOR'S NOTE: If using frozen rhubarb, measure rhubarb while still frozen, then thaw completely. Drain in a colander, but do not press liquid out.

Pumpkin Angel Cake

PREP: 45 MIN. BAKE: 40 MIN. + COOLING

I created this recipe one fall when I had a bumper crop of pumpkins. Since there's no fat in this cake, it's a healthier choice for dessert.

Judiann McNulty ✳ Newberg, Oregon

- 1-1/2 cups egg whites (about 10)
- 1 cup cake flour

Pumpkin Angel Cake

- 1-1/4 cups sugar, *divided*
- 1 teaspoon ground cinnamon
- 1/2 teaspoon ground nutmeg
- 1-1/2 teaspoons cream of tartar
- 1 teaspoon vanilla extract
- 1/2 teaspoon salt
- 1/2 cup canned pumpkin
- Confectioners' sugar

Place egg whites in a large bowl; let stand at room temperature for 30 minutes. Sift the flour, 1 cup sugar, cinnamon and nutmeg together twice; set aside.

Add the cream of tartar, vanilla and salt to egg whites; beat on medium speed until soft peaks form. Gradually beat in remaining sugar, about 1 tablespoon at a time, on high until stiff glossy peaks form and sugar is dissolved. Gradually fold in flour mixture, about 1/2 cup at a time. Fold in pumpkin.

Gently spoon into an ungreased 10-in. tube pan. Cut through batter with a knife to remove air pockets. Bake on the lowest oven rack at 350° for 40-45 minutes or until lightly browned and entire top appears dry. Immediately invert pan; cool completely, about 1 hour.

Run a knife around sides and center tube of pan. Remove to a serving plate. Sprinkle cake with confectioners' sugar. **YIELD: 12 SERVINGS.**

Cranberry Cheesecake

Cranberry Cheesecake

PREP: **40 MIN.** BAKE: **65 MIN. + CHILLING**

The cranberry topping on this cheesecake is so good that I serve it separately as a Thanksgiving side dish.

Mary Simonson ✳ Kelso, Washington

- 9 whole cinnamon graham crackers, crushed
- 1 tablespoon plus 1 cup sugar, *divided*
- 1/4 cup butter, melted
- 2 packages (8 ounces *each*) reduced-fat cream cheese, cubed
- 1 package (8 ounces) fat-free cream cheese, cubed
- 3/4 cup fat-free sour cream
- 3 egg whites, lightly beaten
- 1 tablespoon lemon juice
- 2 teaspoons vanilla extract
- 1 teaspoon rum extract

TOPPING:

- 3/4 cup sugar
- 1/4 cup orange juice
- 2 tablespoons water
- 1-1/2 teaspoons grated orange peel
- 1/4 teaspoon minced fresh gingerroot
- 2 cups fresh *or* frozen cranberries
- 1/4 cup chopped pecans

Combine cracker crumbs, 1 tablespoon sugar and butter. Press onto the bottom and 1 in. up the sides of a 9-in. springform pan coated with cooking spray. Place on a baking sheet. Bake at 350° for 10 minutes. Cool on a wire rack.

In a large bowl, beat the cream cheese, sour cream and remaining sugar until smooth. Add egg whites; beat on low just until combined. Stir in lemon juice and extracts. Pour into crust.

Place pan on a double thickness of heavy-duty foil (about 16 in. square). Securely wrap foil around pan. Place in a larger baking pan. Add 1 in. of hot water to larger pan.

Bake at 350° or 55-60 minutes or until center is just set. Remove pan from water bath. Cool on a wire rack for 10 minutes. Remove foil. Carefully run a knife around edge of pan to loosen; cool 1 hour longer. Remove foil. Chill overnight.

In a small saucepan, combine the first five topping ingredients; bring to a boil. Add the cranberries. Cook over medium heat until berries pop, about 10 minutes. Stir in pecans; cool. Cover and chill for at least 1 hour.

Remove sides of springform pan. Spoon topping over cheesecake to within 1 in. of edges. Refrigerate leftovers. **YIELD: 16 SERVINGS.**

NUTRITION FACTS: 1 slice equals 269 calories, 11 g fat (6 g saturated fat), 31 mg cholesterol, 294 mg sodium, 35 g carbohydrate, 1 g fiber, 7 g protein. DIABETIC EXCHANGES: 2 starch, 2 fat.

White Chocolate Banana Cake

PREP: **30 MIN.** BAKE: **25 MIN. + COOLING**

Packed with ripe bananas and white chocolate in the batter, this cake tastes wonderful even without frosting.

Yvonne Artz ✳ Greenville, Ohio

- 1/2 cup shortening
- 2 cups sugar
- 2 eggs
- 1-1/2 cups mashed ripe bananas (about 3 medium)
- 3 teaspoons vanilla extract
- 3 cups all-purpose flour
- 1 teaspoon baking powder
- 1/2 teaspoon baking soda
- 1/2 teaspoon salt
- 1 cup buttermilk
- 4 squares (1 ounce *each*) white baking chocolate, melted and cooled

CREAM CHEESE FROSTING:

- 1 package (8 ounces) cream cheese, softened
- 3/4 cup butter, softened
- 1 teaspoon vanilla extract
- 5 cups confectioners' sugar
- 1/2 cup finely chopped pecans, toasted

In a large bowl, cream shortening and sugar until light and fluffy. Add eggs, one at a time, beating well after each addition. Beat in bananas and vanilla. Combine the flour, baking powder, baking soda and salt; add to creamed mixture alternately with buttermilk, beating well after each addition. Fold in chocolate.

Pour into three greased and floured 9-in. round baking pans. Bake at 350° for 25-30 minutes or until a toothpick inserted near the center comes out clean. Cool for 10 minutes before removing cake from pans to wire racks to cool completely.

For frosting, in a large bowl, beat the cream cheese, butter and vanilla until smooth. Gradually beat in confectioners' sugar. Spread between layers and over top and sides of cake. Sprinkle with pecans. Store in refrigerator. **YIELD: 12-16 SERVINGS.**

White Chocolate Banana Cake

Tastes Like Eggnog Cake

PREP: **30 MIN.** BAKE: **25 MIN. + COOLING**

My holiday eggnog cake uses a convenient boxed mix and comes out perfect every time. It always gets compliments, and most people think that I spend hours in the kitchen working on it! My husband's colleagues at work ask for it every Christmas.

Lisa Barrett ✳ Durango, Colorado

    1 **package (18-1/4 ounces) yellow cake mix**
    1 **teaspoon ground nutmeg**
 1/4 **teaspoon ground ginger**
FROSTING:
1-1/2 **cups heavy whipping cream**
    3 **tablespoons confectioners' sugar**
    1 **teaspoon rum extract**

Prepare cake batter according to the package directions, adding nutmeg and ginger to dry ingredients. Pour into a greased 13-in. x 9-in. baking pan.

Bake at 350° for 25-30 minutes or until a toothpick inserted near the center comes out clean. Cool on a wire rack.

For frosting, in a small bowl, beat cream and confectioners' sugar until stiff peaks form. Fold in extract. Spread over the cake. Store in the refrigerator. **YIELD: 12-15 SERVINGS.**

Tastes Like Eggnog Cake

Family-Favorite Cheesecake

Family-Favorite Cheesecake

PREP: 20 MIN. + COOLING BAKE: 1 HOUR + CHILLING

This fluffy, delicate cheesecake has been our preferred choice for years. I've shared it at many gatherings over the years and have even started baking it for our friends instead of Christmas cookies.

Esther Wappner ✳ Mansfield, Ohio

2-1/2 cups graham cracker crumbs (about 40 squares)
1/3 cup sugar
1/2 teaspoon ground cinnamon
1/2 cup butter, melted
FILLING:
3 packages (8 ounces *each*) cream cheese, softened
1-1/2 cups sugar
1 teaspoon vanilla extract
4 eggs, *separated*
TOPPING:
1/2 cup sour cream
2 tablespoons sugar
1/2 teaspoon vanilla extract
1/2 cup heavy whipping cream, whipped

In a small bowl, combine the cracker crumbs, sugar and cinnamon; stir in butter. Press onto the bottom and 2 in. up the sides of a greased 9-in. springform pan. Bake at 350° for 5 minutes. Cool on a wire rack. Reduce heat to 325°.

In a large bowl, beat the cream cheese, sugar and vanilla until smooth. Add egg yolks; beat on low just until combined.

In a small bowl, beat egg whites until soft peaks form; fold into cream cheese mixture. Pour over crust.

Bake for 1 hour or until center is almost set. Cool on a wire rack for 10 minutes. Carefully run a knife around edge of pan to loosen; cool 1 hour longer. Refrigerate until completely cooled.

Combine the sour cream, sugar and vanilla; fold in whipped cream. Spread over cheesecake. Refrigerate overnight. Remove the sides of the pan. **YIELD: 12 SERVINGS.**

Bat Cupcake

Bat Cupcakes

PREP: **25 MIN.** BAKE: **20 MIN. + COOLING**

Even my adult children love these Halloween cupcakes! We serve them every year at our pumpkin-carving party.

Joyce Moynihan ✳ Lakeville, Minnesota

- 1 package (18-1/4 ounces) chocolate cake mix
- 1 can (16 ounces) chocolate frosting
- 24 fudge-striped cookies
- 24 milk chocolate kisses

Red decorating icing

Prepare and bake the cake batter according to the package directions for cupcakes, using paper liners. Cool completely.

Set aside the 2 tablespoons chocolate frosting. Frost cupcakes with remaining frosting. For bat wings, cut cookies in half and add scalloped edges if desired. Insert two cookie halves into each cupcake. Gently press chocolate kisses into frosting for heads. Pipe the ears with reserved frosting; add eyes with decorating icing. **YIELD: 2 DOZEN.**

Fudgy Pecan Cake

PREP: **45 MIN.** BAKE: **35 MIN. + CHILLING**

This fudgy cake looked so stunning at our New Year's Day supper, I almost wished it wouldn't have been eaten!

Joyce Price ✳ Whitefish, Ontario

- 1-1/4 cups pecans, toasted
- 1 cup (6 ounces) semisweet chocolate chips
- 3/4 cup butter
- 4 eggs, *separated*
- 3/4 cup sugar, *divided*
- 2 tablespoons all-purpose flour
- 1/4 teaspoon cream of tartar

GLAZE:
- 1 cup (6 ounces) semisweet chocolate chips
- 1/2 cup heavy whipping cream

Place the pecans in a blender; cover and process until ground. Set aside 1 cup for cake (save any remaining ground nuts for another use). In a microwave, melt chocolate chips and butter; stir until smooth. Cool to room temperature.

Fudgy Pecan Cake

In a large bowl, beat egg yolks and 1/2 cup sugar until slightly thickened; stir in cooled chocolate mixture. Combine flour and reserved ground nuts; stir into egg yolk mixture. Set aside.

In another large bowl, beat egg whites and cream of tartar on medium speed until soft peaks form. Gradually beat in remaining sugar, 1 tablespoon at a time, on high until stiff glossy peaks form and sugar is dissolved. Fold a third of the egg whites into batter, then fold in remaining whites.

Spoon into a greased and waxed paper-lined 9-in. springform pan. Bake at 350° for 35-40 minutes or until a toothpick inserted near the center comes out with moist crumbs. Cool on a wire rack. (Cake top will puff, then fall during cooling.) Gently push down top and sides of cake to even surface. Run a knife around edge of cake to loosen. Remove sides of pan; invert cake onto a plate and gently peel off waxed paper.

For glaze, heat chocolate chips and cream in a microwave until melted; stir until smooth. Cool until slightly thickened. Spread a thin layer of glaze over top and sides of cake. Pour remaining glaze over cake; spread over top and sides, allowing glaze to drip down sides. Chill until glaze is set, about 30 minutes. Cut into wedges. **YIELD: 12 SERVINGS.**

EDITOR'S NOTE: This cake uses only 2 tablespoons of flour, so the texture is very dense.

Sweet Potato Mini Cake

Sweet Potato Mini Cakes

PREP: **40 MIN.** BAKE: **25 MIN. + COOLING**

Whenever I make these cute desserts, I think of my grandmother. She always used extra sweet potatoes from her garden in pies, breads and cakes and added black walnuts from her trees for good measure.

Joyce Larson * New Market, Iowa

- 2 cups all-purpose flour
- 1 cup sugar
- 1 cup packed brown sugar
- 1 teaspoon baking powder
- 1 teaspoon baking soda
- 1 teaspoon salt
- 1 teaspoon ground cinnamon
- 1 teaspoon pumpkin pie spice
- 4 eggs
- 1-1/4 cups canola oil
- 3 cups shredded peeled sweet potatoes
- 1 teaspoon rum extract
- 1 can (8 ounces) crushed pineapple, drained
- 1 cup golden raisins
- 1 cup chopped walnuts

FROSTING:

- 1 package (8 ounces) cream cheese, softened
- 1 cup butter, softened
- 5 cups confectioners' sugar
- 4 teaspoons brown sugar
- 1 teaspoon vanilla extract
- 1/2 teaspoon rum extract
- 1-1/2 cups ground walnuts

In a large bowl, combine the flour, sugars, baking powder, baking soda, salt, cinnamon and pie spice. Add eggs, oil, potatoes and extract; beat until combined. Stir in pineapple, raisins and walnuts.

Fill 12 greased or paper-lined jumbo muffin cups three-fourths full. Bake at 350° for 25-30 minutes or until a toothpick inserted in center comes out clean. Cool for 10 minutes; remove from pans to wire racks to cool completely.

For frosting, in a large bowl, beat the cream cheese and butter until fluffy. Beat in the sugars and extracts until smooth. Frost sides of cakes; roll in walnuts. Place the cakes upside down and frost tops with the remaining frosting. **YIELD: 1 DOZEN.**

Apple Praline Pie, PAGE 438

" You can make this pie without the nuts if you prefer, and it is still very delicious. It's even better topped with a scoop of vanilla ice cream. "

Noelle Myers
Grand Forks, North Dakota

PIES

DO YOU HAVE A WINNING RECIPE?
Enter your most prized recipes in the *Taste of Home* recipe contests, and you may win some money and the chance to have your recipe published. Log onto **tasteofhome.com/RecipeContests** for a list of our current contests and submission deadlines. Good luck...we'll be looking for your recipe.

pies

Upside-Down Apple Pie

Upside-Down Apple Pie

PREP: **30 MIN.** + CHILLING BAKE: **50 MIN.** + COOLING

This pie has won eight ribbons at area fairs. People say it looks and tastes like a giant apple-cinnamon bun. I take time off from work around the holidays to fill pie requests from family and friends. This recipe is everyone's favorite.

Susan Frisch ✳ Germansville, Pennsylvania

- 2 cups all-purpose flour
- 1/2 teaspoon salt
- 6 tablespoons shortening
- 2 tablespoons cold butter
- 5 to 7 tablespoons orange juice

FILLING:

- 6 tablespoons butter, melted, *divided*
- 1/2 cup packed brown sugar
- 1/2 cup chopped pecans
- 1 cup sugar
- 1/3 cup all-purpose flour
- 3/4 teaspoon ground cinnamon
- 1/4 teaspoon ground nutmeg
- 8 cups thinly sliced peeled Golden Delicious apples (about 1/8 inch thick)

GLAZE:

- 1/2 cup confectioners' sugar
- 2 to 3 teaspoons orange juice

In a large bowl, combine the flour and salt; cut in the shortening and butter until crumbly. Gradually add orange juice, tossing with a fork until dough forms a ball. Divide dough into two balls. Wrap in plastic wrap; refrigerate for at least 30 minutes.

Line a 9-in. deep-dish pie plate with heavy-duty foil, leaving 1-1/2 in. beyond edge; coat the foil with cooking spray. Combine 4 tablespoons butter, brown sugar and the pecans; spoon into prepared pie plate.

In a large bowl, combine the sugar, flour, cinnamon, nutmeg, apples and the remaining butter; toss gently.

On waxed paper, roll out one ball of pastry to fit pie plate. Place pastry over nut mixture, pressing firmly against mixture and sides of the plate; trim to 1 in. beyond plate edge. Fill with the apple mixture.

Roll out the remaining pastry to fit top of pie; place over filling. Trim to 1/4 in. beyond plate edge. Fold bottom pastry over top pastry; seal and flute edges. Cut four 1-in. slits in top pastry.

Bake at 375° for 20 minutes. Cover the edges loosely with foil. Bake 30 minutes longer or until apples are tender and crust is golden brown.

Cool for 15 minutes on a wire rack. Invert onto a serving platter; carefully remove the foil. Combine glaze ingredients; drizzle over the pie.

YIELD: **8 SERVINGS.**

Raspberry-Lemon Pie

Hawaiian Cream Pie

PREP: **20 MIN.** BAKE: **15 MIN.**

When it comes to pie, coconut cream is my favorite, while my husband is a banana cream fan. I decided to make us both happy and combine them in this dessert. Pineapple naturally accents the tropical flavor.

Jane Wilsdorf * Holliday, Missouri

- 2/3 cup sugar
- 1/4 cup cornstarch
- 1/2 teaspoon salt
- 2 cups milk
- 3 egg yolks, lightly beaten
- 2 tablespoons butter
- 1 teaspoon vanilla extract
- 1/2 cup crushed pineapple, drained
- 1/4 cup flaked coconut
- 1 to 2 large firm bananas, sliced
- 1 pastry shell (9 inches), baked

MERINGUE:

- 3 egg whites
- 1/4 teaspoon cream of tartar
- 6 tablespoons sugar
- 1/4 cup flaked coconut

In a saucepan, combine the sugar, cornstarch and salt. Stir in milk until smooth. Cook and stir over medium-high heat for 2 minutes or until thickened and bubbly. Reduce the heat; cook and stir 2 minutes longer. Remove from heat. Stir a small amount of hot filling into egg yolks; return all to pan, stirring constantly. Bring to a gentle boil; cook and stir 2 minutes more. Remove from the heat; stir in butter and vanilla. Fold in the pineapple and coconut. Place sliced bananas into pastry shell; set aside.

In a large bowl, beat egg whites and cream of tartar on medium speed until soft peaks form. Gradually beat in sugar, 1 tablespoon at a time, on high until stiff glossy peaks form and sugar is dissolved. Pour hot filling over bananas. Spread meringue evenly over hot filling, sealing edges to crust. Sprinkle with coconut.

Bake at 350° for 15 minutes or until the meringue is golden. Cool on a wire rack for 1 hour. Refrigerate for at least 3 hours before serving. YIELD: **8 SERVINGS.**

Raspberry-Lemon Pie

PREP: **25 MIN. + CHILLING**

This pretty, refreshing pie is easy to prepare and can be made in advance, so it's perfect for a party; we really enjoy it during the summer months.

Jan Louden * Branson, Missouri

- 24 chocolate wafers, *divided*
- 1/4 cup butter, melted
- 2 tablespoons sugar
- 1 package (3 ounces) raspberry gelatin
- 1 cup boiling water
- 1 carton (6 ounces) reduced-fat lemon yogurt
- 1 cup heavy whipping cream
- 3 tablespoons confectioners' sugar
- 1 cup fresh *or* frozen raspberries, thawed

Grated lemon peel and additional fresh raspberries, optional

Cut a thin slice from a wafer so that wafer will stand flat against wall of pie plate; repeat nine times. Set aside. Crush the remaining wafers and trimmed portions.

Combine wafer crumbs, butter and sugar; press onto the bottom of an ungreased 9-in. pie plate. Arrange trimmed wafers around the edge of pie plate, lightly pressing into crust. Cover and refrigerate.

In a large bowl, dissolve the gelatin in boiling water. Cover and refrigerate for 45 minutes or until partially set. Beat on medium speed for 5 minutes or until fluffy. Fold in yogurt.

In another bowl, beat cream until it begins to thicken. Add confectioners' sugar; beat until stiff peaks form. Fold whipped cream and raspberries into gelatin mixture. Spread into crust.

Cover and refrigerate for at least 4 hours. Garnish with the lemon peel and additional raspberries if desired. YIELD: **10 SERVINGS.**

Pumpkin Cheesecake Pie

PREP: 30 MIN. BAKE: 45 MIN. + CHILLING

If you're looking for a classic autumn dessert, try this pumpkin cheesecake pie. It's a winner at potlucks and on the Thanksgiving table. The gingersnap crust forms a spicy, sweet foundation.

Sharon Crockett ✳ La Palma, California

- 1-1/2 cups crushed gingersnap cookies
- 1 tablespoon sugar
- 1/4 cup butter, melted

FILLING:
- 2 packages (8 ounces *each*) cream cheese, softened
- 3/4 cup sugar
- 2 eggs, lightly beaten
- 1 can (15 ounces) solid-pack pumpkin
- 1 teaspoon ground cinnamon
- 1/4 teaspoon ground ginger
- 1/4 teaspoon ground nutmeg
- 1/8 teaspoon salt

TOPPING:
- 1 cup (8 ounces) sour cream
- 1/4 cup sugar
- 1 teaspoon vanilla extract

Ground cinnamon, optional

In a bowl, combine the gingersnap crumbs and sugar. Stir in the butter. Press onto the bottom and up the sides of a greased 9-in. deep-dish pie plate. Bake at 350° for 8-10 minutes or until lightly browned.

In a large bowl, beat cream cheese and sugar until smooth. Add eggs; beat on low speed just until combined. Stir in the pumpkin, cinnamon, ginger, nutmeg and salt.

Pour into the crust. Bake for 35-40 minutes or until center is almost set.

In a bowl, combine the sour cream, sugar and vanilla. Spread over pie. Bake 8-12 minutes longer or until set. Cool on a wire rack. Cover and chill for at least 4 hours. Sprinkle with the cinnamon if desired. **YIELD: 10 SERVINGS.**

Hawaiian Cream Pie

Pumpkin Cheesecake Pie

Dreamy Creamy Peanut Butter Pie

Dreamy Creamy Peanut Butter Pie

PREP: **30 MIN.** BAKE: **10 MIN.** + CHILLING

Peanut butter fans love both the crust and creamy filling of this popular dessert. With two young children in the house, a lot of my baking happens after bedtime!

Dawn Moore ✳ Warren, Pennsylvania

- 24 peanut butter cream-filled sandwich cookies, crushed
- 1/3 cup butter, melted
- 1 cup cold milk
- 1 package (3.4 ounces) instant vanilla pudding mix
- 1 cup creamy peanut butter
- 4 ounces cream cheese, softened
- 1/2 cup sweetened condensed milk
- 1/4 cup hot fudge ice cream topping, warmed
- 1 cup heavy whipping cream
- 2 tablespoons sugar

Chocolate curls

Combine cookie crumbs and butter; press onto the bottom and up the sides of an ungreased 9-in. pie plate. Bake at 350° for 6-8 minutes or until crust is lightly browned. Cool on a wire rack.

In a small bowl, whisk milk and pudding mix for 2 minutes. Let stand for 2 minutes or until soft-set. Meanwhile, in a large bowl, beat the peanut butter, cream cheese and condensed milk until smooth; stir in pudding. Set aside.

Gently spread ice cream topping into crust. In a large bowl, beat the cream until it begins to thicken. Add sugar; beat until stiff peaks form. Fold 1-1/2 cups into pudding mixture; pour into crust. Spread remaining whipped cream over top; garnish with chocolate curls. Refrigerate until serving. **YIELD: 8 SERVINGS.**

Spiced Peach Pie

PREP: **20 MIN.** + CHILLING

Chilled peach pie is a delectable change of pace from the traditional baked one. With its peachy gelatin filling sandwiched between layers of fluffy cream, it always draws compliments.

Lois Dunlop ✳ Venice, Florida

- 1 can (15 ounces) sliced peaches
- 2 tablespoons brown sugar
- 1/4 teaspoon ground ginger
- 1 cinnamon stick (3 inches)

1 package (3 ounces) peach *or* orange gelatin

4 ounces cream cheese, softened

2 tablespoons butter, softened

1/8 teaspoon ground nutmeg

1 pastry shell (9 inches), baked

1 carton (8 ounces) frozen whipped topping, thawed

Fresh mint, optional

Drain the syrup from the peaches into a 2-cup measuring cup. Add enough water to measure 1-1/3 cups. Chop peaches and set aside.

In a saucepan, combine the syrup, brown sugar, ginger and cinnamon stick. Bring to a boil. Reduce heat; cook and stir for 5 minutes. Remove from the heat.

Discard cinnamon stick. Stir the gelatin into syrup mixture until dissolved. Add reserved peaches. Refrigerate until partially set, about 40 minutes.

In a bowl, beat the cream cheese, butter and nutmeg until smooth. Spread over the bottom and up the sides of the crust. Pour the gelatin mixture over cream cheese layer.

Chill until serving. Spread with the whipped topping. Serve with the mint if desired. **YIELD: 8 SERVINGS.**

Spiced Peach Pie

Cherry-Nut Chocolate Pie

PREP: 10 MIN. + FREEZING

I love chocolate and cherries, but couldn't find the flavor combination in any ice cream. So I came up with this rich confection that has a nice crunch from nuts. This treat is handy to keep in the freezer for unexpected company.

Diana Wilson Wing ✳ Centerville, Utah

2 pints dark chocolate ice cream, softened

1 jar (10 ounces) maraschino cherries, drained and coarsely chopped

3/4 cup slivered almonds

1 chocolate crumb crust (8 inches)

Whipped topping

In a large bowl, combine the ice cream, cherries and almonds. Spoon into the crust. Cover and freeze overnight. Remove from the freezer 10 minutes before cutting. Garnish with whipped topping. **YIELD: 8 SERVINGS.**

Cherry-Nut Chocolate Pie

Cranberry Pear Pie

Cranberry Pear Pie

PREP: 20 MIN. BAKE: 50 MIN. + COOLING

When we are invited to holiday gatherings, this pie usually comes with us. You can make it with a double crust and replace the pears with baking apples. Serve it with ice cream or whipped topping.

Helen Toulantis ✳ Wantagh, New York

Pastry for single-crust pie (9 inches)
- 2 tablespoons all-purpose flour
- 1/2 cup maple syrup
- 2 tablespoons butter, melted
- 5 cups sliced peeled fresh pears
- 1 cup fresh or frozen cranberries

TOPPING:
- 1/2 cup all-purpose flour
- 1/4 cup packed brown sugar
- 1 teaspoon ground cinnamon
- 1/3 cup cold butter, cubed
- 1/2 cup chopped walnuts

Line a 9-in. pie plate with pastry; trim and flute edges. Set aside. In a large bowl, combine the flour, syrup and butter until smooth. Add the pears and cranberries; toss to coat. Spoon into crust. For topping, combine flour, brown sugar and cinnamon; cut in butter until crumbly. Stir in walnuts. Sprinkle over filling.

Cover the edges of crust loosely with foil to prevent overbrowning. Bake at 400° for 15 minutes. Reduce heat to 350°. Remove foil; bake 35-40 minutes longer or until crust is golden brown and filling is bubbly. Cool on a wire rack.
YIELD: 8 SERVINGS.

Strawberry Banana Pie

Strawberry Banana Pie

PREP: 45 MIN. + FREEZING

With its sugar-cone crust and layers of bananas and strawberry ice cream, this pretty pie never seems to last long. It's a favorite year-round, but we really enjoy it in summer, when fresh strawberries are plentiful.

Bernice Janowski ✳ Stevens Point, Wisconsin

- 1 package (5-1/4 ounces) ice cream sugar cones, crushed
- 1/4 cup ground pecans

1/3 cup butter, melted
   2 cups vanilla ice cream, softened
   2 medium ripe bananas, mashed
   2 large firm bananas, cut into 1/4-inch slices
   2 cups strawberry ice cream, softened
   1 pint fresh strawberries
   1 carton (8 ounces) frozen whipped topping, thawed

In a large bowl, combine the crushed ice cream cones, pecans and butter. Press onto the bottom and up the sides of a greased 10-in. pie plate. Refrigerate for at least 30 minutes.

In another large bowl, combine vanilla ice cream and mashed bananas. Spread over the crust; cover and freeze for 30 minutes.

Arrange sliced bananas over the ice cream; cover and freeze for 30 minutes. Top with the strawberry ice cream; cover and freeze for about 45 minutes.

Hull and halve strawberries; place around edge of pie. Mound or pipe whipped topping in the center of pie. Cover and freeze for up to 1 month. Remove from the freezer about 30 minutes before serving. **YIELD: 10 SERVINGS.**

Greek Honey Nut Pie

Greek Honey Nut Pie

PREP: **30 MIN.** BAKE: **40 MIN. + COOLING**

I love Greek pastry, so I thought, "Why not use phyllo, honey and nuts to make a pie?" This allows me to have a bigger piece.

Rosalind Jackson ✳ Stuart, Florida

   4 cups chopped walnuts
1/4 cup packed brown sugar
   1 teaspoon ground cinnamon
   1 package (16 ounces, 14-inch x 9-inch sheet size) frozen phyllo dough, thawed
   1 cup butter, melted
SYRUP:
3/4 cup sugar
1/2 cup water
1/2 cup honey
   1 teaspoon vanilla extract
Confectioners' sugar, lemon peel strips and additional honey

In a large bowl, combine the walnuts, brown sugar and cinnamon; set aside.

Place a sheet of phyllo dough in a greased 9-in. pie plate; brush with the butter. (Keep remaining phyllo covered with plastic wrap and a damp towel to prevent it from drying out.) Repeat seven times. Sprinkle 1-1/3 cups nut mixture into crust.

Place a sheet of phyllo over the nut mixture; brush with butter. Repeat three times. Sprinkle with 1-1/3 cups nut mixture. Layer with another sheet of phyllo; brush with butter. Repeat three times. Sprinkle with remaining nut mixture.

Top with a sheet of phyllo; brush with butter. Repeat seven times. Fold ends up onto top of pie; brush with butter.

Using a sharp knife, score the pie into eight pieces. Cut a remaining phyllo sheet into thin strips and roll into rose shapes; arrange on top. Save remaining phyllo dough for another use.

Bake at 350° for 40-45 minutes or until golden brown. Meanwhile, in a small saucepan, combine the sugar, water and honey; bring to a boil. Reduce heat; simmer, uncovered, for 10 minutes. Remove from heat. Stir in vanilla. Pour over the warm pie. Cool on a wire rack. Garnish with the confectioners' sugar, lemon peel and additional honey. Refrigerate leftovers. **YIELD: 8 SERVINGS.**

Sour Cream Peach Pecan Pie

Bake at 425° for 30 minutes. Meanwhile, in a small bowl, combine the flour, sugars, pecans and cinnamon. Cut in butter until crumbly; sprinkle over pie. Cover the edges of crust to prevent overbrowning.

Bake for 15-20 minutes or until a knife inserted in the center comes out clean and topping is golden brown. Cool on a wire rack for 1 hour. Store in the refrigerator. **YIELD: 8 SERVINGS.**

Mixed Nut 'n' Fig Pie

PREP: 30 MIN. BAKE: 1 HOUR + COOLING

A hint of orange flavor complements the figs in this festive confection. It's a lovely treat for Thanksgiving, Christmas or any occasion.

Barbara Estabrook ✳ Rhinelander, Wisconsin

Pastry for single-crust pie (9 inches)
- 1/2 cup chopped dried Calimyrna figs
- 3 tablespoons water
- 2 tablespoons orange marmalade
- 3/4 cup packed brown sugar
- 1 tablespoon cornstarch
- 3 eggs
- 1 cup corn syrup
- 6 tablespoons unsalted butter, melted
- 2 teaspoons vanilla extract
- 1-1/2 cups deluxe mixed nuts

TOPPING:
- 1 cup heavy whipping cream
- 2 tablespoons sugar
- 1 tablespoon orange marmalade

Line a 9-in. pie plate with pastry; trim and flute edges. Line pastry with a double thickness of heavy-duty foil. Bake at 450° for 8 minutes. Remove the foil; bake 5 minutes longer. Cool on a wire rack.

In a saucepan, combine figs and water. Cook and stir over low heat until water is absorbed. Remove from the heat; stir in marmalade. In a large bowl, whisk brown sugar and cornstarch. Add the eggs, corn syrup, butter, vanilla and fig mixture; stir in nuts. Pour into pastry.

Bake at 300° for 1 to 1-1/4 hours or until set. Cover edges with foil during the last 30 minutes

Sour Cream Peach Pecan Pie

PREP: 30 MIN. BAKE: 45 MIN. + COOLING

Fresh peaches, good Southern pecans and real vanilla make this pie a special summertime treat.

Sherrell Dikes ✳ Holiday Island, Arkansas

Pastry for single-crust pie (9 inches)
- 4 cups sliced peeled peaches
- 2 tablespoons peach preserves
- 1 cup sugar
- 1 cup (8 ounces) sour cream
- 3 egg yolks
- 1/4 cup all-purpose flour
- 1 teaspoon vanilla extract

TOPPING:
- 1/2 cup all-purpose flour
- 1/2 cup packed brown sugar
- 1/4 cup sugar
- 3 tablespoons chopped pecans
- 1 teaspoon ground cinnamon
- 1/4 cup cold butter

Line a 9-in. pie plate with pastry; trim and flute the edges.

In a bowl, combine peaches and preserves. Transfer to pastry. In a small bowl, whisk the sugar, sour cream, egg yolks, flour and vanilla. Pour over the peaches.

to prevent overbrowning if necessary. Cool on a wire rack.

In a small bowl, beat cream until it begins to thicken. Add sugar and marmalade; beat until stiff peaks form. Serve with the pie. Refrigerate leftovers. **YIELD: 8 SERVINGS.**

Mixed Nut 'n' Fig Pie

Lemon Pie in Meringue Shell

PREP: **25 MIN. + STANDING** BAKE: **25 MIN. + COOLING**

A delicious and different dessert, this lemon pie is a part of all our family's special times. Typically, I prepare it the day before and refrigerate it overnight.

Carol Mumford ✳ Casstown, Ohio

      3 egg whites
    1/4 teaspoon cream of tartar
  1-1/2 cups sugar, *divided*
      4 egg yolks
      3 tablespoons lemon juice
      1 tablespoon grated lemon peel
    1/8 teaspoon salt
      2 cups heavy whipping cream, whipped

Place the egg whites in a small bowl; let stand at room temperature for 30 minutes. Add cream of tartar; beat until soft peaks form. Gradually add 1 cup of sugar, 1 tablespoon at a time, beating until stiff peaks form. Spread onto the bottom and up the sides of a greased 9-in. pie plate. Bake at 350° for 25-30 minutes. Cool on a wire rack.

In a large saucepan, combine the egg yolks, lemon juice and peel, salt and remaining sugar. Cook and stir over medium heat until mixture reaches 160° or is thick enough to coat the back of a metal spoon. Reduce the heat; cook and stir 2 minutes longer. Remove from the heat. Cool to room temperature without stirring.

Fold half of the whipped cream into lemon filling; spread into meringue shell. Top with the remaining whipped cream. Refrigerate leftovers. **YIELD: 8 SERVINGS.**

Lemon Pie in Meringue Shell

Vermont Maple Oatmeal Pie

Vermont Maple Oatmeal Pie

PREP: 20 MIN. BAKE: 50 MIN. + COOLING

This yummy pie has an old-fashioned feeling, but it's so easy to prepare. Serve it with ice cream, drizzled with maple syrup or top it with maple- or cinnamon-flavored whipped cream.

Barbie Miller ✳ Oakdale, Minnesota

- 1 sheet refrigerated pie pastry
- 4 eggs
- 1 cup sugar
- 3 tablespoons all-purpose flour
- 1 teaspoon ground cinnamon
- 1/2 teaspoon salt
- 1 cup quick-cooking oats
- 3/4 cup corn syrup
- 1/2 cup maple syrup
- 1/4 cup butter, melted
- 3 teaspoons vanilla extract
- 1 cup flaked coconut

Vanilla ice cream, optional

Unroll pastry into a 9-in. pie plate; flute edges.

In a bowl, combine the eggs, sugar, flour, cinnamon and salt. Stir in oats, syrups, butter and vanilla; pour into the crust. Sprinkle with the coconut.

Bake at 350° for 50-60 minutes or until set. Cover the edges with foil during the last 15 minutes to prevent overbrowning if necessary. Cool on a wire rack. Serve with ice cream if desired. Refrigerate leftovers. **YIELD: 8 SERVINGS.**

Peach Plum Pie

Peach Plum Pie

PREP: 15 MIN. + STANDING BAKE: 45 MIN.

When I want to impress guests, this is the pie I prepare. Peaches, plums and a bit of lemon peel are a refreshing trio. It's a family favorite that's requested often.

Susan Osborne ✳ Hatfield Point, New Brunswick

- 2 cups sliced peeled fresh *or* frozen peaches, thawed and drained
- 2 cups sliced peeled fresh purple plums

Mayan Chocolate Pecan Pie

1 tablespoon lemon juice

1/4 teaspoon almond extract

1-1/2 cups sugar

1/4 cup quick-cooking tapioca

1/2 to 1 teaspoon grated lemon peel

1/4 teaspoon salt

Pastry for double-crust pie (9 inches)

2 tablespoons butter

In a bowl, combine the peaches, plums, lemon juice and extract. In another bowl, combine the sugar, tapioca, lemon peel and salt. Add to fruit mixture and stir gently; let stand for 15 minutes. Line a 9-in. pie plate with bottom crust; add the filling. Dot with butter.

Roll out remaining pastry to fit top of pie; cut slits in pastry. Place over filling. Trim, seal and flute edges. Cover the edges loosely with foil.

Bake at 450° for 10 minutes. Reduce heat to 350°. Remove the foil; bake 35 minutes longer or until crust is golden brown and filling is bubbly. **YIELD: 8 SERVINGS.**

EDITOR'S NOTE: This recipe was tested with a Keebler extra-servings-size graham cracker crust. This pie crust size is needed for the large amount of filling.

Mayan Chocolate Pecan Pie

PREP: **20 MIN.** BAKE: **55 MIN. + COOLING**

This started off as a regular pecan pie for Thanksgiving Day, and it's evolved into something extra special.

Chris Michalowski ✳ Dallas, Texas

1/2 cup chopped pecans

1/2 cup dark chocolate chips

1 unbaked deep-dish pastry shell (9 inches)

3 eggs

1 cup sugar

1 cup dark corn syrup

2 tablespoons butter, melted

1 tablespoon coffee liqueur

1 teaspoon ground ancho chili pepper

1 teaspoon vanilla extract

1 cup pecan halves

Sprinkle chopped pecans and chocolate chips into pastry shell. In a small bowl, whisk the eggs, sugar, corn syrup, butter, liqueur, pepper and vanilla. Pour into pastry; arrange pecan halves over filling.

Bake at 350° for 55-60 minutes or until set. Cool on a wire rack. Refrigerate leftovers. **YIELD: 8 SERVINGS.**

EDITOR'S NOTE: Ground ancho chili pepper is available from Penzeys Spices. Call 1-800/741-7787 or visit www.penzeys.com.

Caramel Apple Cream Pie

In a skillet over medium heat, melt butter and brown sugar. Stir in apples and 1 teaspoon pumpkin pie spice; simmer for 12-15 minutes, stirring frequently, or until tender.

Stir in the flour; cook and stir for 1 minute. Drizzle the caramel topping over pastry shell; sprinkle with pecans. Spoon apple mixture over pecans; set aside.

In a bowl, beat the cream cheese, sugar, egg, lemon juice and vanilla until smooth. Pour over apples. Bake at 350° for 35-45 minutes or until a knife inserted into the cream cheese layer comes out clean.

Cool on a wire rack. Chill thoroughly. To serve, top with dollops of whipped topping; sprinkle with the remaining pumpkin pie spice.
YIELD: 8 SERVINGS.

Caramel Apple Cream Pie

PREP: **30 MIN. + CHILLING** BAKE: **35 MIN. + COOLING**

When I first made this pie for my family, the reactions weren't real words—they were more "Ooh!" and "Mmm!" I created it to enter in a local fair. My goal was an apple pie like no other, and it ended up winning third prize.

Lisa DiNuccio ✳ Boxford, Massachusetts

- 1 pastry shell (9 inches)
- 1/4 cup butter, cubed
- 1/2 cup packed brown sugar
- 4 medium tart apples, peeled and cut into 1/2-inch chunks
- 1-1/2 teaspoons pumpkin pie spice, *divided*
- 1 to 2 tablespoons all-purpose flour
- 1/2 cup caramel ice cream topping
- 1/2 cup chopped pecans
- 1 package (8 ounces) cream cheese, softened
- 1/4 cup sugar
- 1 egg
- 1 tablespoon lemon juice
- 1 teaspoon vanilla extract

Whipped topping

Let pastry shell stand at room temperature for 10 minutes. Line unpricked pastry shell with a double thickness of heavy-duty foil. Bake at 450° for 8 minutes. Remove the foil; bake 5 minutes longer. Cool on a wire rack.

Butternut Cream Pie

PREP: **35 MIN. + CHILLING**

I enjoy making up recipes and began experimenting with squash a couple years ago. Last fall, my garden was loaded with squash, so I came up with this creamy pie. It really went over well at Thanksgiving dinner.

Sandra Kreuter ✳ Burney, California

- 1 medium butternut squash (about 2 pounds)
- 1/4 cup hot water
- 1 package (8 ounces) cream cheese, softened
- 1/4 cup sugar
- 2 tablespoons caramel ice cream topping
- 1 teaspoon ground cinnamon
- 1/2 teaspoon salt
- 1/2 teaspoon ground ginger
- 1/4 teaspoon ground cloves
- 3/4 cup plus 2 tablespoons cold milk
- 1 package (5.1 ounces) instant vanilla pudding mix
- 1 pastry shell (9 inches), baked

Whipped cream and toasted flaked coconut

Cut squash in half; discard seeds. Place squash cut side down in a microwave-safe dish; add hot water. Cover and microwave for 13-15 minutes or until tender. When cool enough to handle, scoop out pulp and mash. Set aside 1-1/2 cups squash (save remaining squash for another use).

In a bowl, beat cream cheese until smooth. Stir in the squash until blended. Beat in the sugar, caramel topping, cinnamon, salt, ginger and cloves until blended.

In a bowl, whisk cold milk and pudding mix for two minutes. Let stand for 2 minutes or until soft set. Stir into squash mixture.

Spoon into pastry shell. Refrigerate for at least 3 hours. Garnish with whipped cream and coconut. **YIELD: 8 SERVINGS.**

Butternut Cream Pie

Mud Pie

PREP: 15 MIN. + CHILLING

Coming from the South, we fell in love with this rich chocolate pie that's filled with pecans. It could take all day to put together, but my version takes just 15 minutes of preparation before it's stored in the refrigerator until you're ready to serve.

Deboraha Woolard ✳ Las Vegas, Nevada

- 3 squares (1 ounce *each*) semisweet chocolate
- 1/4 cup sweetened condensed milk
- 1 chocolate crumb crust (8 inches)
- 1/2 cup chopped pecans
- 2 cups cold milk
- 2 packages (3.9 ounces *each*) instant chocolate pudding mix
- 1 carton (8 ounces) frozen whipped topping, thawed, *divided*

In a microwave, melt the chocolate; stir in the condensed milk until smooth. Pour into crust; sprinkle with pecans.

In a small bowl, whisk milk and pudding mixes for 2 minutes. Let stand for 2 minutes or until soft-set. Carefully spread 1-1/2 cups of pudding mixture over pecans.

Fold in a 1/2 cup whipped topping into the remaining pudding mixture; spoon over pudding layer. Top with the remaining whipped topping. Refrigerate until set. **YIELD: 8 SERVINGS.**

Mud Pie

Apple Praline Pie

Apple Praline Pie

PREP: **30 MIN.** BAKE: **1 HOUR + COOLING**

You can make this pie without the nuts if you prefer, and it is still very delicious. It's even better topped with a scoop of vanilla ice cream.

Noelle Myers ✳ Grand Forks, North Dakota

1-3/4 cups all-purpose flour
1 teaspoon sugar
1/2 teaspoon salt
1 cup cold butter
1 teaspoon cider vinegar
4 to 6 tablespoons cold water

FILLING:

6 cups thinly sliced peeled tart apples
1 tablespoon ginger ale
1 teaspoon lemon juice
1 teaspoon vanilla extract
3/4 cup sugar
1/4 cup all-purpose flour
3 teaspoons ground cinnamon
1/4 teaspoon ground nutmeg
2 tablespoons butter, cubed

TOPPING:

1/4 cup butter, cubed
1/2 cup packed brown sugar
2/3 cup pecan halves
2 tablespoons heavy whipping cream
1/2 teaspoon vanilla extract

In a large bowl, combine the flour, sugar and salt; cut in butter until crumbly. Sprinkle with vinegar. Gradually add water, tossing with a fork until dough forms a ball.

Divide dough in half so that one portion is slightly larger than the other. Roll out larger portion to fit a 9-in. pie plate. Transfer pastry to pie plate. Trim pastry even with edge.

In a large bowl, toss apples with ginger ale, lemon juice and vanilla. Combine sugar, flour, cinnamon and nutmeg; add to apple mixture and toss to coat. Spoon into crust; dot with butter.

Roll out remaining pastry to fit top of pie. Place over filling. Trim, seal and flute edges. Cut slits in pastry. Bake at 400° for 55-65 minutes or until crust is golden brown and filling is bubbly. Cover edges with foil during the last 30 minutes to prevent overbrowning if necessary.

Butter Pecan Pumpkin Pie

1st place

Meanwhile, in a saucepan over medium heat, melt the butter. Stir in brown sugar; cook and stir until mixture comes to a boil and sugar is dissolved. Stir in the pecans; cook 1 minute longer. Remove from the heat; stir in cream and vanilla. Immediately pour over pie. Bake 3-5 minutes longer or until topping is bubbly. Cool on a wire rack. **YIELD: 8 SERVINGS.**

Butter Pecan Pumpkin Pie

PREP: 20 MIN. + FREEZING

This treat was always a family favorite at holidays. Everyone thought I'd worked all day to make it, but it's actually so easy to assemble.

Arletta Slocum ✳ Venice, Florida

- 1 quart butter pecan ice cream, softened
- 1 pastry shell (9 inches), baked
- 1 cup canned pumpkin
- 1/2 cup sugar
- 1/4 teaspoon *each* ground cinnamon, ginger and nutmeg
- 1 cup heavy whipping cream, whipped
- 1/2 cup caramel ice cream topping
- 1/2 cup chocolate ice cream topping, optional

Additional whipped cream

Spread the ice cream into the crust; freeze for 2 hours or until firm. In a bowl, combine the pumpkin, sugar, cinnamon, ginger and nutmeg; fold in whipped cream. Spread over ice cream. Cover and freeze for 2 hours or until firm. May be frozen for up to 2 months.

Remove from the freezer 15 minutes before slicing. Drizzle with caramel ice cream topping. Drizzle with the chocolate ice cream topping if desired. Dollop with whipped cream. **YIELD: 8 SERVINGS.**

Frosty Coffee Pie

Frosty Coffee Pie

PREP: 15 MIN. + FREEZING

This pie was inspired by my husband, who loves coffee ice cream, and his mom, who makes a cool, creamy dessert using pudding mix.

April Timboe ✳ Siloam Springs, Arkansas

- 1/4 cup hot fudge ice cream topping, warmed
- 1 chocolate crumb crust (9 inches)
- 3 cups coffee ice cream, softened
- 1 package (5.9 ounces) instant chocolate pudding mix
- 1/2 cup cold strong brewed coffee
- 1/4 cup cold milk
- 1-3/4 cups whipped topping
- 1 cup marshmallow creme
- 1/4 cup miniature semisweet chocolate chips

Spread ice cream topping into crust. In a large bowl, beat the ice cream, pudding mix, coffee and milk until blended; spoon into crust.

In another small bowl, combine the whipped topping and marshmallow creme; spread over top. Sprinkle with chocolate chips. Cover and freeze until firm. **YIELD: 8 SERVINGS.**

Chocolate-Caramel Supreme Pie

Chocolate-Caramel Supreme Pie

PREP: 20 MIN. + STANDNG COOK: **5 MIN.**

At a church fund-raiser, I purchased a pie-a-month package furnished by a local family. From among all the varieties they made, this one was the best, with its chocolate crust, creamy caramel filling and fluffy topping.

Diana Stewart ✳ Oelwein, Iowa

- 30 caramels
- 3 tablespoons butter, melted
- 2 tablespoons water
- 1 chocolate crumb crust (9 inches)
- 1/2 cup chopped pecans, toasted
- 1 package (3 ounces) cream cheese, softened
- 1/3 cup confectioners' sugar
- 3/4 cup milk chocolate chips
- 3 tablespoons hot water
- 1 carton (8 ounces) frozen whipped topping, thawed

Chocolate hearts *or* curls, optional

In a saucepan, add caramels, butter and water. Cook and stir over medium heat until caramels are melted. Spread over the crust; sprinkle with pecans. Refrigerate for 1 hour.

In a bowl, beat cream cheese and sugar until smooth; spread over caramel layer. Refrigerate.

In a large saucepan, melt chocolate chips with hot water over low heat; stir until smooth. Cool slightly.

Fold in the whipped topping. Spread over the cream cheese layer. Garnish with the chocolate hearts or curls if desired. Chill until serving. **YIELD: 8 SERVINGS.**

Frosted Orange Pie

PREP: 30 MIN. + CHILLING COOK: 10 MIN. + COOLING

I discovered the recipe for this distinctive pie in a very old church cookbook. With its fresh-tasting filling and light frosting, it's truly an elegant final course. I'm happy to make it all year-round.

Delores Edgecomb ✳ Atlanta, New York

- 3/4 cup sugar
- 1/2 cup all-purpose flour
- 1/4 teaspoon salt
- 1-1/4 cups water
- 2 egg yolks, lightly beaten
- 1/2 cup orange juice
- 2 tablespoons lemon juice
- 2 to 3 tablespoons grated orange peel
- 1/2 teaspoon grated lemon peel
- 1 pastry shell (9 inches), baked

FROSTING:
- 1/2 cup sugar
- 2 egg whites
- 2 tablespoons water
- 1/8 teaspoon cream of tartar
- 1/8 teaspoon salt
- 1/2 cup flaked coconut, toasted, optional

In a large saucepan, combine the sugar, flour and salt. Stir in water until smooth. Cook and stir over medium-high heat until thickened and bubbly. Reduce heat; cook and stir 2 minutes longer. Remove from heat. Stir a small amount of hot filling into egg yolks; return all to pan, stirring constantly. Bring to a gentle boil; cook and stir 2 minutes longer. Remove from heat. Gently stir in the juices and orange and lemon peel. Cool to room temperature without stirring.

Pour into pastry shell. Cool on a wire rack for 1 hour. Chill at least 3 hours.

In a heavy saucepan, combine the sugar, egg whites, water, cream of tartar and salt over low heat. With a hand mixer, beat on low speed for

1 minute. Continue beating on low over low heat until frosting reaches 160°, about 8-10 minutes. Pour into the bowl of a heavy-duty stand mixer. Beat on high until frosting forms stiff peaks, about 7 minutes.

Spread over chilled pie. Just before serving, sprinkle with coconut. **YIELD: 8 SERVINGS.**

Frosted Orange Pie

Grasshopper Pie

PREP: 45 MIN. + CHILLING

After a hearty meal, this delicate, refreshing pie hits the spot. Chocolate and mint are definitely meant for each other. I make this festive treat at Christmas and whenever my son comes to visit. He loves it with sweet cherries on top.

Sally Vandermus ✳ Rochester, Minnesota

- 2/3 cup semisweet chocolate chips
- 2 tablespoons heavy whipping cream
- 2 teaspoons shortening
- 1 cup finely chopped walnuts

FILLING:

- 35 large marshmallows
- 1/4 cup milk
- 1/4 teaspoon salt
- 3 tablespoons green creme de menthe
- 3 tablespoons clear creme de cacao
- 1-1/2 cups heavy whipping cream, whipped

Chocolate curls, optional

Line a 9-in. pie plate with foil; set aside. In a heavy saucepan, combine the chocolate chips, cream and shortening; cook over low heat until chips are melted. Stir in the walnuts. Pour into prepared pie plate; spread evenly over bottom and sides of plate. Chill for 1 hour or until set.

In a large heavy saucepan, combine the marshmallows, milk and salt; cook over low heat until marshmallows are melted, stirring occasionally. Remove from heat; stir in creme de menthe and creme de cacao. Refrigerate for 1 hour or until slightly thickened.

Carefully remove foil from chocolate crust and return crust to pie plate. Fold the whipped cream into filling; pour into crust. Refrigerate overnight. Garnish with the chocolate curls if desired. **YIELD: 8 SERVINGS.**

Grasshopper Pie

Blueberry Pie with Lemon Crust

plate. Transfer pastry to pie plate; trim to 1 in. beyond edge of plate.

In a bowl, combine the blueberries, sugar, flour, lemon peel and salt; spoon into the crust. Drizzle with lemon juice; dot with butter. Roll out remaining pastry; place over filling. Seal and flute edges. Cut slits in top crust.

Bake at 400° for 40-45 minutes or until crust is golden brown and filling is bubbly. Cool on a wire rack. Store in refrigerator. **YIELD: 8 SERVINGS.**

Maple Apple Cream Pie

PREP: 30 MIN. + CHILLING COOK: 15 MIN. + COOLING

We think this deliciously different dessert is a nice change from a traditional apple pie. Who can resist its tender apples smothered in a silky maple-flavored cream? This treat is definitely worth a try.

Christi Paulton * Phelps, Wisconsin

    1 unbaked pastry shell (9 inches)
    2 tablespoons butter
    6 medium Golden Delicious apples
       (about 2 pounds), peeled and cut
       into eighths
  1/2 cup packed brown sugar
    2 tablespoons cornstarch
  1/3 cup maple syrup
    1 can (12 ounces) evaporated milk
    1 egg yolk, lightly beaten
    1 teaspoon vanilla extract
  1/2 cup heavy whipping cream
    1 tablespoon sugar
  1/4 teaspoon ground cinnamon

Let pastry shell stand at room temperature for 10 minutes. Line unpricked pastry shell with a double thickness of heavy-duty foil. Bake at 450° for 8 minutes. Remove foil; bake 5 minutes longer. Cool on a wire rack.

In a skillet, melt the butter. Add apples and brown sugar; cook and stir until apples are tender and coated, 15-20 minutes. Cool to room temperature. Spread evenly into shell.

In a small saucepan, combine the cornstarch and syrup until smooth; gradually add the milk. Cook and stir over medium-high heat until thickened and bubbly. Reduce the heat; cook

Blueberry Pie with Lemon Crust

PREP: 30 MIN. + CHILLING BAKE: 40 MIN.

Mom and I have had loads of enjoyment making this pie together, and I hope one day to be a great baker like she is.

Sara West * Broken Arrow, Oklahoma

    2 cups all-purpose flour
    1 teaspoon salt
  1/2 teaspoon grated lemon peel
  2/3 cup shortening
    1 tablespoon lemon juice
    4 to 6 tablespoons cold water
FILLING:
    4 cups fresh blueberries
  3/4 cup sugar
    3 tablespoons all-purpose flour
  1/2 teaspoon grated lemon peel
Dash salt
    1 to 2 teaspoons lemon juice
    1 tablespoon butter

In a bowl, combine the flour, salt and lemon peel. Cut in the shortening until crumbly. Add lemon juice. Gradually add water, tossing with a fork until a ball forms. Cover and refrigerate for 1 hour.

Divide the dough in half. On a lightly floured surface, roll out one portion to fit a 9-in. pie and stir 2 minutes longer. Remove from the heat. Stir a small amount of hot filling into egg yolk; return all to pan, stirring constantly. Bring to a gentle boil; cook and stir 2 minutes longer. Remove from heat; add vanilla. Cool to room temperature without stirring. Pour over apples. Chill until set, about 2 hours.

In a small bowl, beat cream until it begins to thicken. Gradually add sugar and cinnamon; beat until stiff peaks form. Serve with pie or pipe around edge of pie. **YIELD: 8 SERVINGS.**

Maple Apple Cream Pie

Ricotta Nut Pie

PREP: 20 MIN. + CHILLING BAKE: 10 MIN. + COOLING

I'm proud to serve this pie at special dinners for family and guests. Similar to a traditional Italian ricotta pie but with a few fun twists, it's a satisfying dessert that's not overly sweet. I can't resist the yummy combination of almonds, ricotta cheese, apricots and chocolate.

Renee Bennett ✳ Manlius, New York

- 1-1/2 cups crushed vanilla wafers (about 45 wafers)
- 1/2 cup butter, softened
- 1/4 cup apricot preserves
- 1 carton (15 ounces) ricotta cheese
- 1/2 cup sugar
- 1 teaspoon vanilla extract
- 3 squares (1 ounce *each*) semisweet chocolate, chopped
- 1/2 cup finely chopped toasted almonds
- 1/4 cup chopped dried apricots
- 1 cup heavy whipping cream, whipped
- 1/4 cup slivered almonds, toasted

In a small bowl, combine the wafer crumbs and butter; press onto the bottom and up the sides of an ungreased 9-in. pie plate.

Bake at 375° for 6-8 minutes or until crust is lightly browned; cool on a wire rack. Spread preserves over crust.

In a bowl, beat the ricotta cheese, sugar and vanilla until smooth. Stir in chocolate, chopped almonds and apricots. Fold in whipped cream. Spoon into the crust. Sprinkle with the slivered almonds. Cover and refrigerate overnight. **YIELD: 8 SERVINGS.**

Ricotta Nut Pie

Chocolate Chip Banana Cream Pie

Glazed Pineapple Pie

Chocolate Chip Banana Cream Pie

PREP: **25 MIN.** BAKE: **10 MIN. + CHILLING**

This rich treat is a hit every time I serve it. The chilled filling, brimming with bananas, is refreshing, and the cookie crust provides a chocolaty crunch. Even a small slice will satisfy the biggest sweet tooth.

Taylor Carroll ✳ Parkesburg, Pennsylvania

> 1 tube (16-1/2 ounces) refrigerated chocolate chip cookie dough
> 1/3 cup sugar
> 1/4 cup cornstarch
> 1/8 teaspoon salt
> 2-1/3 cups milk
> 5 egg yolks, lightly beaten
> 2 tablespoons butter
> 2 teaspoons vanilla extract, *divided*
> 3 medium firm bananas
> 1-1/2 cups heavy whipping cream
> 3 tablespoons confectioners' sugar

Cut the cookie dough in half widthwise. Let one portion stand at room temperature for 5-10 minutes to soften (return the other half to the refrigerator for another use).

Press the dough onto the bottom and up the sides of an ungreased 9-in. pie plate. Bake at 375° for 11-12 minutes or until lightly browned. Cool on a wire rack.

In a saucepan, combine sugar, cornstarch and salt. Stir in the milk until smooth. Cook and stir over medium-high heat until thickened and bubbly. Reduce the heat; cook and stir 2 minutes longer. Remove from heat. Stir a small amount of hot filling into egg yolks; return all to the pan, stirring constantly. Bring to a gentle boil; cook and stir 2 minutes longer. Remove from heat; stir in butter and 1 teaspoon vanilla.

Spread 1 cup filling into prepared crust. Slice bananas; arrange over filling. Pour remaining filling over bananas. Refrigerate for 2 hours or until set.

In a chilled large bowl, beat cream until it begins to thicken. Add confectioners' sugar and remaining vanilla; beat until stiff peaks form. Spread over pie. Refrigerate for 1 hour or until chilled. **YIELD: 8 SERVINGS.**

Glazed Pineapple Pie

PREP: **15 MIN.** BAKE: **35 MIN.**

I enter my favorite pies in area contests and fairs. This one is a guaranteed winner. It's so pretty with a golden crust and drizzles of glaze. Plus, the coconut adds a tropical accent to the pineapple filling.

Joyce Dubois ✳ Wolsey, South Dakota

- 1 can (20 ounces) crushed pineapple
- Pastry for double-crust pie (9 inches)
- 3/4 cup flaked coconut
- 1 cup sugar
- 1/4 cup all-purpose flour
- 1/4 teaspoon salt
- 1 tablespoon lemon juice
- 1 tablespoon butter, melted

GLAZE:
- 1/2 cup confectioners' sugar
- 1/4 teaspoon rum or vanilla extract

Drain pineapple, reserving 2 tablespoons juice; set pineapple aside. Line a 9-in. pie plate with bottom pastry; trim the pastry even with edge of plate. Sprinkle with coconut.

In a small bowl, combine the sugar, flour, salt, lemon juice, butter and reserved pineapple. Spread over coconut. Roll out remaining pastry to fit top of pie; place over filling. Trim, seal and flute edges. Cut slits in the pastry. Add decorative cutouts if desired.

Cover edges loosely with foil. Bake at 400° for 30 minutes. Remove foil; bake 5-10 minutes longer or until crust is golden brown and filling is bubbly.

In a small bowl, combine the confectioners' sugar, extract and enough of the reserved pineapple juice to achieve glaze consistency. Drizzle over warm pie. Cool on a wire rack. Store in the refrigerator. **YIELD: 8 SERVINGS.**

Peach Melba Ice Cream Pie

Peach Melba Ice Cream Pie

PREP: **20 MIN. + FREEZING** BAKE: **15 MIN. + COOLING**

On a hot night, this pie makes a very delightful dessert. Like most wonderful recipes, it came from a friend. As the third oldest among nine children, I've been cooking for a crowd as long as I can remember!

Judy Vaske ✳ Bancroft, Iowa

- 1-1/2 cups flaked coconut
- 1/3 cup chopped pecans
- 3 tablespoons butter, melted
- 1 quart frozen peach yogurt, softened
- 1 pint vanilla ice cream, softened
- 1 tablespoon cornstarch
- 1 tablespoon sugar
- 1 package (10 ounces) frozen raspberries in syrup, thawed
- 1 cup sliced fresh or frozen peaches, thawed

Combine the coconut, pecans and butter; press onto bottom and up the sides of an ungreased 9-in. pie plate. Bake at 350° for 12 minutes or until crust begins to brown around the edges. Cool completely.

Spoon frozen yogurt into crust; smooth the top. Spread ice cream over yogurt. Cover and freeze for 2 hours or until firm.

In a small saucepan, combine the cornstarch and sugar; drain raspberry juice into pan. Bring to a boil; cook and stir for 2 minutes. Remove from the heat; add raspberries. Cover and chill.

Remove from the freezer 10 minutes before serving. Arrange peaches on top of pie; drizzle with a little of the sauce. Pass the remaining sauce. **YIELD: 8 SERVINGS.**

Coconut Peach Pie

Coconut Peach Pie

PREP: **20 MIN. + CHILLING** BAKE: **30 MIN. + COOLING**

A relative shared this recipe with me. I love peaches, and the wonderful meringue crust is tender and crispy. It's one of my best summertime desserts.

Beatrice Crutchfield ✳ Norcross, Georgia

> 3 egg whites
Dash salt
> 3/4 cup plus 2 tablespoons sugar, *divided*
> 1-1/4 cups flaked coconut, toasted, *divided*
> 1/3 cup chopped almonds, toasted
> 3-1/2 cups sliced peeled peaches
> (about 6 medium)
> 1 cup heavy whipping cream

In a bowl, beat egg whites and salt on medium speed until foamy. Gradually add 3/4 cup sugar, 1 tablespoon at a time, beating on high until stiff peaks form. Fold in 1 cup coconut and the almonds. Spread onto the bottom and up the sides of a greased 9-in. pie plate.

Bake at 350° for 30 minutes or until light golden brown. Cool completely on a wire rack.

Arrange peaches in the crust. In a large bowl, beat the whipping cream with remaining sugar until stiff peaks form. Spread over the peaches; sprinkle with remaining coconut. Refrigerate for 1 hour before slicing. **YIELD: 8 SERVINGS.**

Chocolate Raspberry Pie

PREP: **30 MIN. + CHILLING** BAKE: **15 MIN. + COOLING**

After tasting this pie at my sister-in-law's house, I had to have the recipe. I love the chocolate and raspberry layers separated by a dreamy cream layer. It's a joy to serve this standout treat!

Ruth Bartel ✳ Morris, Manitoba

> 1 unbaked pastry shell (9 inches)
> 3 tablespoons sugar
> 1 tablespoon cornstarch
> 2 cups fresh *or* frozen unsweetened
> raspberries, thawed
FILLING:
> 1 package (8 ounces) cream
> cheese, softened
> 1/3 cup sugar
> 1/2 teaspoon vanilla extract
> 1/2 cup heavy whipping cream, whipped
TOPPING:
> 2 squares (1 ounce *each*) semisweet
> chocolate
> 3 tablespoons butter

Let pastry shell stand at room temperature for 10 minutes. Line unpricked pastry shell with a double thickness of heavy-duty foil. Bake at 450° for 8 minutes. Remove foil; bake 5 minutes longer. Cool on a wire rack.

In a large saucepan, combine the sugar and cornstarch. Stir in the raspberries; bring to a boil over medium heat. Boil and stir for 2 minutes. Remove from heat; cool for 15 minutes. Spread into shell; refrigerate.

In a large bowl, beat the cream cheese, sugar and vanilla until fluffy. Fold in whipped cream. Carefully spread over raspberry layer. Cover and refrigerate for at least 1 hour.

In a microwave, melt chocolate and butter; stir until smooth. Cool for 4-5 minutes. Pour over the top. Cover and chill for at least 2 hours. **YIELD: 8 SERVINGS.**

Vanilla Custard Pie

PREP: 30 MIN. BAKE: 15 MIN. + CHILLING

The directions for this great pie have been passed down through many generations. With a graham cracker crust, custard filling and meringue topping, it was one of my favorites when I was growing up and it still is today.

Mrs. Bernard Parys ✳ Ixonia, Wisconsin

- 1-1/4 cups graham cracker crumbs
- 3 tablespoons brown sugar
- 1/3 cup butter, melted

FILLING:
- 1/2 cup sugar
- 1/4 cup all-purpose flour
- 1/2 teaspoon salt
- 2 cups milk
- 2 egg yolks, lightly beaten
- 2 teaspoons vanilla extract

MERINGUE:
- 2 egg whites
- 1/4 teaspoon vanilla extract
- 1/8 teaspoon cream of tartar
- 1/4 cup sugar
- 1/4 cup graham cracker crumbs

Chocolate Raspberry Pie

Combine the graham cracker crumbs, brown sugar and butter; press onto the bottom and up the sides of an ungreased 9-in. pie plate. Bake at 350° for 8-10 minutes or until crust is lightly browned. Cool on a wire rack.

In a small saucepan, combine the sugar, flour and salt. Stir in milk until smooth. Cook and stir over medium-high heat until thickened and bubbly. Reduce the heat; cook and stir 2 minutes longer. Remove from the heat. Stir a small amount of hot filling into the egg yolks; return all to the pan. Bring to a gentle boil, stirring constantly; cook and stir 2 minutes longer. Remove from the heat. Gently stir in the vanilla. Pour into crust.

In a small bowl, beat the egg whites, vanilla and cream of tartar on medium speed until soft peaks form. Gradually beat in the sugar, 1 tablespoon at a time, on high until stiff peaks form. Spread over hot filling, sealing edges to crust. Sprinkle with graham cracker crumbs.

Bake at 350° for 15 minutes or until golden. Cool on a wire rack for 1 hour. Chill for at least 3 hours before serving. **YIELD: 8 SERVINGS.**

Vanilla Custard Pie

German Chocolate Pie

German Chocolate Pie

PREP: 45 MIN. + CHILLING

Thanksgiving dinner at our house includes an average of 25 guests and a dozen different pies. This one has all the luscious flavor of German chocolate cake.

Debbie Clay ✳ Farmington, New Mexico

- 1 package (4 ounces) German sweet chocolate
- 1 tablespoon butter
- 1 teaspoon vanilla extract
- 1/3 cup sugar
- 3 tablespoons cornstarch
- 1-1/2 cups milk
- 2 egg yolks, lightly beaten
- 1 pastry shell (9 inches), baked

TOPPING:

- 2/3 cup evaporated milk
- 1/2 cup sugar
- 1/4 cup butter, cubed
- 1 egg, lightly beaten
- 1-1/3 cups flaked coconut, toasted
- 1/2 cup chopped pecans, toasted

In a microwave, melt chocolate and butter; stir until smooth. Stir in vanilla; set aside.

In a saucepan, combine sugar, cornstarch and the milk until smooth. Cook and stir over medium-high heat until thickened and bubbly. Reduce the heat; cook and stir 2 minutes longer. Remove from the heat. Stir a small amount of hot filling into egg yolks; return all to the pan, stirring constantly. Bring to a gentle boil; cook and stir 2 minutes longer. Remove from the heat. Gently stir in chocolate mixture. Spoon into pastry shell.

In a saucepan, combine the evaporated milk, sugar and butter. Cook and stir until butter is melted and the mixture just comes to a boil. Remove from the heat. Stir a small amount of hot liquid into egg; return all to the pan, stirring constantly. Bring to a gentle boil; cook and stir 2 minutes longer.

Remove from the heat. Stir in coconut and pecans. Pour over the filling. Cool on a wire rack. Cover and refrigerate for at least 3 hours. **YIELD: 8 SERVINGS.**

Blueberries 'n' Cream Pie

Blueberries 'n' Cream Pie

PREP: 15 MIN. BAKE: 30 MIN.

After taking one bite of this appealing dessert, friends always ask for the recipe. It's especially good served warm. You can substitute peaches for the berries with equally fantastic results.

Roger Meyers ✴ Chambersburg, Pennsylvania

- 1/2 cup plus 1 tablespoon fat-free milk, *divided*
- 3 tablespoons butter
- 1 egg
- 3/4 cup all-purpose flour
- 1 package (.8 ounces) sugar-free cook-and-serve vanilla pudding mix
- 1 teaspoon baking powder
- 1/8 teaspoon salt
- 2 cups fresh *or* frozen blueberries, thawed
- 1 package (8 ounces) reduced-fat cream cheese
- 1/2 cup sugar

TOPPING:

- 2 teaspoons sugar
- 1/8 teaspoon ground cinnamon

In a bowl, beat 1/2 cup milk, butter and egg. Combine the flour, pudding mix, baking powder and salt; stir into the egg mixture just until moistened. Pour into a 9-in. pie plate coated with cooking spray. Arrange blueberries over batter to within 1/2 in. of edge of plate.

In a large bowl, beat the cream cheese, sugar and remaining milk until smooth. Spread over blueberries to within 1 in. of berry edge.

For topping, combine sugar and cinnamon; sprinkle over the cream cheese mixture. Bake at 350° for 30-35 minutes or until set. Serve warm. Refrigerate leftovers. **YIELD: 8 SERVINGS.**

NUTRITION FACTS: 1 piece equals 249 calories, 12 g fat (7 g saturated fat), 60 mg cholesterol, 302 mg sodium, 31 g carbohydrate, 1 g fiber, 6 g protein. DIABETIC EXCHANGES: 2 fat, 1-1/2 starch, 1/2 fruit.

Frozen Strawberry Pie

Frozen Strawberry Pie

PREP: 25 MIN. + FREEZING

This recipe makes two attractive pies using store-bought chocolate crumb crusts. I serve each slice with a dollop of whipped cream, a strawberry and chocolate curls.

Awynne Thurstenson ✴ Siloam Springs, Arkansas

- 1 package (8 ounces) cream cheese, softened
- 1 cup sugar
- 1 teaspoon vanilla extract
- 4 cups chopped fresh strawberries
- 1 carton (12 ounces) frozen whipped topping, thawed
- 1/2 cup chopped pecans, toasted
- 2 chocolate crumb crusts (9 inches)

In a bowl, beat cream cheese, sugar and vanilla until smooth. Beat in the strawberries. Fold in the whipped topping and pecans. Pour into the crusts. Cover and freeze for 3-4 hours or until firm. Remove from the freezer 15-20 minutes before serving. **YIELD: 2 PIES (6 SERVINGS EACH).**

Frozen Chocolate Mint Pie

Frozen Chocolate Mint Pie

PREP: **40 MIN.** BAKE: **1 HOUR + FREEZING**

This refreshing pie was featured at a small resort my family visited regularly as I was growing up. When I make it now, I relish compliments from tasters along with fond memories of sunny days at the beach and good home cooking.

Jenny Falk * Sauk Rapids, Minnesota

- 3 egg whites
- 1/4 teaspoon cream of tartar
- 1 cup sugar

CHOCOLATE SAUCE:

- 1/4 cup butter, cubed
- 1 square (1 ounce) unsweetened chocolate
- 1 cup sugar
- 3/4 cup evaporated milk
- 1/2 teaspoon vanilla extract
- 1/8 teaspoon peppermint extract

Dash salt

- 2 cups vanilla ice cream, softened
- 1-1/3 cups heavy whipping cream, whipped

Place the egg whites in a small bowl; let stand at room temperature for 30 minutes. Add cream of tartar; beat until soft peaks form. Gradually add sugar, 1 tablespoon at a time, beating until stiff peaks form.

Spread onto the bottom and up the sides of a greased and floured 9-in. deep-dish pie plate. Bake at 275° for 1 hour. Turn off oven and do not open door; let meringue cool completely inside the oven.

For chocolate sauce, in heavy saucepan, melt butter and chocolate; stir until smooth. Stir in sugar and evaporated milk. Cook over low heat for 45-60 minutes or until thickened, stirring occasionally. Remove from the heat; stir in extracts and salt. Cool to room temperature.

Spread ice cream into meringue crust. Fold whipped cream into cooled chocolate sauce. Spread over ice cream layer; cover and freeze until firm. **YIELD: 8 SERVINGS.**

Chocolate-Cherry Ice Cream Pie, PAGE 462

" *No one would ever dream that the fancy taste and look of this luscious freezer pie could come from only five simple ingredients! This makes an unbelievably easy dessert—whether for an elegant dinner party or as a cool, high-energy kids' treat on a sweltering day.* "

Kimberly West
Prairieville, Louisiana

DESSERTS

DO YOU HAVE A WINNING RECIPE?
Enter your most prized recipes in the *Taste of Home* recipe contests, and you may win some money and the chance to have your recipe published. Log onto **tasteofhome.com/RecipeContests** for a list of our current contests and submission deadlines. Good luck...we'll be looking for your recipe.

desserts

Ultimate Caramel Apples

PREP: **45 MIN.** COOK: **25 MIN. + CHILLING**

I have such a sweet tooth that I've been known to make a dessert just to satisfy my craving. One day when I was in the mood for caramel, I came up with these fun treats.

Clarissa Loyd ✳ Mineral Wells, Texas

- 6 medium Red Delicious apples
- 6 Popsicle sticks
- 1 cup sugar
- 1 cup light corn syrup
- 1/4 cup water
- Pinch baking soda
- 1/4 cup butter, cubed
- 1/4 cup heavy whipping cream
- 1/2 cup shelled pistachios, chopped, *divided*
- 3 squares (1 ounce *each*) white baking chocolate, chopped
- 3 squares (1 ounce *each*) semisweet chocolate, chopped

Ultimate Caramel Apples

Line a baking sheet with waxed paper and grease the paper; set aside. Wash and thoroughly dry apples. Insert a Popsicle stick into each; place on prepared pan. Chill.

In a large saucepan, combine the sugar, corn syrup and water; bring to a boil over medium heat, stirring occasionally. Stir in baking soda. Stir in butter until melted; gradually add cream, stirring constantly. Cook and stir until a candy thermometer reads 242° (firm-ball stage). Remove from heat and cool to 200°.

Place 1/4 cup pistachios in a shallow dish. Dip the apples into the caramel mixture until completely coated, then dip the bottom of each in pistachios. Return to baking sheet; chill.

In a small microwave-safe bowl, microwave white chocolate at 50% power for 1-2 minutes or until melted; stir until smooth. Transfer to a small heavy-duty resealable plastic bag; cut a small hole in a corner of the bag. Drizzle over apples. Repeat with the semisweet chocolate. Sprinkle the tops with the remaining pistachios if desired. Chill until set. **YIELD: 6 SERVINGS.**

EDITOR'S NOTE: We recommend that you test your candy thermometer before each use by bringing water to a boil; the thermometer should read 212°. Adjust your recipe temperature up or down based on your test.

Almond Fruit Crisp

In a large bowl, combine the flour, sugar, baking powder and salt. Cut in the butter and almond paste until crumbly. Combine the egg and extract; stir into crumb mixture just until blended. Sprinkle over fruit. Top with almonds.

Place on a baking sheet coated with the cooking spray. Bake, uncovered, at 400° for 20-25 minutes or until the fruit is bubbly and topping is golden brown. Cool for 15-20 minutes before serving. **YIELD: 10 SERVINGS.**

Almond Fruit Crisp

PREP: **35 MIN.** + **STANDING** BAKE: **20 MIN.** + **COOLING**

Sliced almonds give extra crunch to these yummy individual crisps made with plums and nectarines. We love this dessert. I usually serve it with ice cream.

Elizabeth Sicard * Summerfield, Florida

1-1/2   **pounds nectarines or peaches, cubed**

1-1/2   **pounds red plums, cubed**

1/4   **cup lemon juice**

1   **cup sugar**

2   **tablespoons quick-cooking tapioca**

Dash salt

ALMOND TOPPING:

1   **cup all-purpose flour**

1/2   **cup sugar**

1/2   **teaspoon baking powder**

Dash salt

1/4   **cup cold butter**

3   **tablespoons almond paste**

1   **egg, lightly beaten**

1/4   **teaspoon almond extract**

1/3   **cup sliced almonds**

In a large bowl, combine nectarines and plums. Drizzle with lemon juice; toss to coat. Combine the sugar, tapioca and salt; sprinkle over fruit and toss to coat evenly. Let stand for 15 minutes. Spoon into 10 greased 6-oz. custard cups.

Strawberry Popovers

PREP: **20 MIN.** BAKE: **30 MIN.**

These tender popovers "pop up" nicely in the oven and hold a delicate cream filling dotted with fresh chopped strawberries. If you don't have a popover pan on hand, you might try muffin cups.

Sandy Holton-Vanthoff * San Diego, California

1   **cup heavy whipping cream**

1/3   **cup sugar**

1   **teaspoon vanilla extract**

2   **cups chopped fresh strawberries**

4-1/2   **teaspoons shortening**

POPOVERS:

4   **eggs**

2   **cups milk**

2   **cups all-purpose flour**

1   **tablespoon sugar**

1   **teaspoon salt**

In a large bowl, beat the cream until it begins to thicken. Gradually add the sugar and vanilla; beat until stiff peaks form. Fold in strawberries. Cover and refrigerate until serving.

Using 1/2 teaspoon shortening for each cup, grease the bottom and sides of nine popover cups. In a small bowl, beat eggs; beat in milk. Add the flour, sugar and salt; beat until smooth (do not overbeat). Fill prepared cups half full.

Bake at 450° for 15 minutes. Reduce heat to 350°; bake 15 minutes longer or until very firm.

Immediately cut a slit in the top of each popover to allow the steam to escape. Spoon the strawberry filling into the popovers. Serve immediately. **YIELD: 9 SERVINGS.**

Cherry Nut Ice Cream

PREP: **15 MIN. + CHILLING** PROCESS: **30 MIN. + FREEZING**

Since my husband is a cherry grower, I had our grandsons help me develop an ice cream recipe that used the fruit. This is what we came up with. Loaded with nuts, coconut, chocolate and cherries, this ice cream has become our family's all-time favorite.

Mary Lou Patrick ✳ East Wenatchee, Washington

- 6 cups heavy whipping cream
- 1 cup sugar
- 1/8 teaspoon salt
- 3 egg yolks
- 3 teaspoons almond extract
- 2 cups fresh *or* frozen pitted dark sweet cherries, thawed and cut into quarters
- 1 cup flaked coconut, toasted
- 1 cup sliced almonds, toasted
- 1 milk chocolate candy bar (7 ounces), chopped

Strawberry Popovers

In a large saucepan, heat cream over medium heat until bubbles form around the sides of the saucepan; stir in sugar and salt until dissolved. Whisk a small amount of the cream into the eggs. Return all to the pan, whisking constantly. Cook and stir over low heat until the mixture reaches at least 160° and coats the back of a metal spoon. Remove from heat. Stir in extract. Cool quickly by placing the pan in a bowl of ice water; stir for 2 minutes. Press waxed paper onto surface of custard. Refrigerate for several hours or overnight.

Fill cylinder of ice cream freezer two-thirds full; freeze according to the manufacturer's directions. Refrigerate remaining mixture until ready to freeze.

Stir the cherries, coconut, almonds and chocolate into ice cream just until combined. Transfer to a freezer container; freeze for 2-4 hours before serving. YIELD: **1-1/2 QUARTS.**

Cherry Nut Ice Cream

Chocolate Velvet Dessert

Chocolate Velvet Dessert

PREP: 20 MIN. + CHILLING BAKE: 45 MIN. + COOLING

This creamy concoction is the result of several attempts to duplicate a dessert I enjoyed on vacation. It looks so beautiful on a buffet table that many folks are tempted to forgo the main course in favor of this chocolaty treat.

Molly Seidel ✳ Edgewood, New Mexico

1-1/2 cups chocolate wafer crumbs
   2 tablespoons sugar
  1/4 cup butter, melted
   2 cups (12 ounces) semisweet chocolate chips
   6 egg yolks
1-3/4 cups heavy whipping cream
   1 teaspoon vanilla extract

CHOCOLATE BUTTERCREAM FROSTING:

  1/2 cup butter, softened
   3 cups confectioners' sugar
   3 tablespoons baking cocoa
   3 to 4 tablespoons milk

In a small bowl, combine the wafer crumbs and sugar; stir in the butter. Press onto the bottom and 1-1/2 in. up the sides of a greased 9-in. springform pan. Place on a baking sheet. Bake at 350° for 10 minutes. Cool on a wire rack.

In a microwave, melt the chocolate chips; stir until smooth. Cool. In a small bowl, combine the egg yolks, cream and vanilla. Gradually stir a third of the cream mixture into the melted chocolate until blended. Fold in remaining cream mixture just until blended. Pour into crust.

Place pan on a baking sheet. Bake at 350° for 45-50 minutes or until center is almost set. Cool on a wire rack for 10 minutes. Carefully run a knife around edge of pan to loosen; cool 1 hour longer. Refrigerate overnight.

In a bowl, combine the butter, confectioners' sugar, the cocoa and enough milk to achieve a piping consistency. Using a large star tip, pipe frosting on dessert. **YIELD: 12-16 SERVINGS.**

Chocolate-Cherry Cream Crepes

Chocolate-Cherry Cream Crepes

PREP: **30 MIN. + CHILLING** COOK: **15 MIN.**

My son calls me a gourmet cook whenever I make his favorite crepes. Sometimes, for a change, I substitute apple pie filling for the cherries and top the golden crepes with warm caramel sauce.

Kimberly Witt ✳ Minot, North Dakota

- 1-1/4 cups milk
- 3 eggs
- 2 tablespoons butter, melted
- 3/4 cup all-purpose flour
- 1 tablespoon sugar
- 1/4 teaspoon salt
- 1 package (8 ounces) cream cheese, softened
- 1/2 cup confectioners' sugar
- 1 teaspoon vanilla extract
- 1 can (21 ounces) cherry pie filling

Chocolate fudge ice cream topping and whipped topping

In a bowl, combine the milk, eggs and butter. Combine the flour, sugar and salt; add to egg mixture and mix well. Cover and refrigerate for 1 hour. For filling, in a small bowl, beat cream cheese until fluffy. Beat in confectioners' sugar and vanilla until smooth; set aside.

Heat a lightly greased 8-in. nonstick skillet; pour 2 tablespoons batter into the center of skillet. Lift and tilt pan to evenly coat bottom. Cook until top appears dry; turn and cook 15-20 seconds longer.

Remove to a wire rack. Repeat with the remaining batter, greasing skillet as needed. Stack crepes with waxed paper between. Cover and freeze 10 crepes for another use. Crepes may be frozen for up to 3 months.

Pipe the filling onto the center of each remaining crepe. Top with 2 tablespoons pie filling. Fold the side edges of crepe to the center. Drizzle with the fudge topping and garnish with the whipped topping. Serve immediately. **YIELD: 8 SERVINGS.**

Apple Pie in a Goblet

Apple Pie in a Goblet

PREP: **10 MIN.** COOK: **25 MIN.**

This dish is not only easy but very elegant. I got the recipe from a church cooking class and now fix it often, with rave reviews. You can serve it in bowls, but I always get more oohs and aahs when I put it in lovely goblets.

Renee Zimmer ✳ Gig Harbor, Washington

- 3 large tart apples, peeled and coarsely chopped
- 1/4 cup sugar
- 1/4 cup water
- 3/4 teaspoon ground cinnamon
- 1/4 teaspoon ground nutmeg
- 12 shortbread cookies, crushed
- 2 cups vanilla ice cream

Whipped cream

In a large saucepan, combine the apples, sugar, water, cinnamon and nutmeg. Bring to a boil. Reduce heat; cover and simmer for 10 minutes or until apples are tender. Uncover; cook 9-11 minutes longer or until most of the liquid has evaporated. Remove from the heat.

In each of four goblets or parfait glasses, layer 1 tablespoon cookie crumbs, 1/2 cup ice cream and a fourth of the apple mixture. Top with remaining cookie crumbs and whipped cream. Serve immediately. **YIELD: 4 SERVINGS.**

Hazelnut Cheesecake Parfaits

In a small saucepan, melt chocolate chips with cream over low heat; stir until smooth. Remove from heat; cool to room temperature. In a small bowl, beat cream cheese and brown sugar until blended. Beat in yogurt and vanilla; fold in whipped topping.

In two parfait glasses, layer graham crackers, yogurt mixture, chocolate mixture and hazelnuts. Chill. Garnish with chocolate curls and whipped topping if desired. **YIELD: 2 SERVINGS.**

Jeweled Gelatin Torte

PREP: **25 MIN. + CHILLING**

My mother made this special torte for all our holiday dinners when I was young. I love the colorful stained-glass look of the gelatin cubes and the dainty ladyfingers in this elegant dessert.

Kimberly Adams ✳ Falmouth, Kentucky

 1 package (3 ounces) cherry gelatin
 3 cups boiling water, *divided*
 2 cups cold water, *divided*
 1 package (3 ounces) lime gelatin
 1 package (3 ounces) orange gelatin
 1 cup pineapple juice
 1 package (3 ounces) lemon gelatin
 1/4 cup sugar
 36 ladyfingers
 1 carton (8 ounces) frozen whipped topping, thawed
Citrus slices and fresh mint, optional

In a small bowl, dissolve cherry gelatin in 1 cup boiling water; stir in 1/2 cup cold water. Pour into a 9-in. x 5-in. loaf pan coated with cooking spray. Repeat with the lime and orange gelatin, using two more loaf pans. Refrigerate until firm, about 1-1/2 hours.

In a small saucepan, bring pineapple juice to a boil. Stir in the lemon gelatin and sugar until dissolved. Stir in the remaining cold water. Refrigerate until syrupy, about 45 minutes. Meanwhile, line the sides and bottom of a 9-in. springform pan with ladyfingers; set aside.

Cut the cherry, lime and orange gelatins into 1/2-in. cubes. Pour lemon gelatin mixture into a large bowl; fold in whipped topping. Gently fold

🍴 Hazelnut Cheesecake Parfaits

PREP: **25 MIN. + CHILLING**

These parfaits are rich and impressive-looking, but light and not too sweet—the perfect finale for a romantic dinner. The sugar-toasted hazelnuts add gourmet flavor.

Shelly Platten ✳ Amherst, Wisconsin

 1/4 cup chopped hazelnuts
 1/2 teaspoon sugar
 1/3 cup semisweet chocolate chips
 2 tablespoons half-and-half cream
 2 tablespoons whipped cream cheese
 2 teaspoons brown sugar
 1/2 cup reduced-fat coffee-flavored yogurt
 1/4 teaspoon vanilla extract
 2/3 cup whipped topping
 2 whole chocolate graham crackers, crushed
Chocolate curls and additional whipped topping, optional

In a heavy skillet, cook and stir the hazelnuts over medium heat until toasted, about 4 minutes. Sprinkle with the sugar; cook and stir for 2-4 minutes or until sugar is melted. Spread on foil to cool.

in the gelatin cubes. Pour into prepared pan. Refrigerate until set. Garnish with the citrus and mint if desired. **YIELD: 10-12 SERVINGS.**

Peanut Butter Banana Pudding

PREP/TOTAL TIME: **20 MIN.**

If there's anything I like better than bananas, it's bananas paired with peanut butter. That's how I came up with this pudding. Graham cracker crumbs add a pleasant crunch. It's a satisfying conclusion to any meal.

Laura McGinnis ✳ Colorado Springs, Colorado

- 4 cups milk
- 1 package (3 ounces) vanilla cook-and-serve pudding mix
- 1 package (3-1/2 ounces) butterscotch cook-and-serve pudding mix
- 1-1/2 cups peanut butter, *divided*
- 1 cup graham cracker crumbs
- 1 cup confectioners' sugar
- 4 medium firm bananas, sliced

In a large saucepan, combine the milk and pudding mixes until blended. Bring to a boil over medium heat, stirring constantly. Remove from the heat; stir in 1/2 cup peanut butter until blended. Cover and refrigerate until chilled.

Meanwhile, in a small bowl, combine the cracker crumbs and confectioners' sugar; cut in remaining peanut butter until crumbly.

In individual dessert bowls, layer half of the pudding, half of the crumb mixture and half of the bananas. Repeat layers. **YIELD: 12 SERVINGS.**

EDITOR'S NOTE: This dessert may also be prepared in one large serving bowl.

Jeweled Gelatin Torte

Peanut Butter Banana Pudding

Strawberry Cheesecake Ice Cream

Strawberry Cheesecake Ice Cream

PREP: **20 MIN.** + COOLING PROCESS: **20 MIN.** + FREEZING

The custard-like ice cream is so rich and creamy that it tastes like you fussed for hours. But it's easy to make...and pretty, too. I like to serve it with chocolate fudge sauce.

Irene Yoder ✳ Fillmore, New York

    3   cups sugar
    3   tablespoons all-purpose flour
Dash salt
    8   cups milk
    4   eggs, lightly beaten
    1   package (8 ounces) cream cheese, cubed
    1   teaspoon vanilla extract
    3   cups fresh or frozen unsweetened
        strawberries, thawed
    2   cups heavy whipping cream

In a heavy saucepan, combine the sugar, flour and salt. Gradually add milk until smooth. Bring to a boil over medium heat; cook and stir for 2 minutes or until thickened. Remove from the heat; cool slightly.

Whisk a small amount of hot milk mixture into the eggs; return all to the pan, whisking constantly. Cook and stir over low heat until the mixture reaches at least 160° and coats the back of a metal spoon. Stir in cream cheese until melted.

Remove from heat. Cool quickly by placing pan in a bowl of ice water; stir for 2 minutes. Stir in the vanilla. Press plastic wrap onto surface of custard. Refrigerate for several hours or overnight.

Stir the strawberries and cream into custard. Fill cylinder of ice cream freezer two-thirds full; freeze according to the manufacturer's directions. Refrigerate remaining mixture until ready to freeze. When the ice cream is frozen, transfer to a freezer container; freeze for 2-4 hours before serving. **YIELD: 1 GALLON.**

Roasted Pears in Pecan Sauce

PREP: **20 MIN.** BAKE: **30 MIN.**

Whenever I bring home pears from the store, my family begs me to make this recipe. They love the tender roasted fruit smothered in creamy pecan sauce. It's luscious over cake.

Darlene King ✳ Estevan, Saskatchewan

    4   medium pears, peeled and cut into wedges
    3   tablespoons brown sugar

3 tablespoons unsweetened apple juice

3 tablespoons butter, melted

1/4 cup chopped pecans

3 tablespoons heavy whipping cream

Vanilla ice cream, optional

Place the pears in an ungreased 13-in. x 9-in. baking dish. In a small bowl, combine the brown sugar, the apple juice and butter; pour over the pears. Bake, uncovered, at 400° for 20 minutes, basting occasionally.

Sprinkle with the pecans. Bake 10-15 minutes longer or until pears are tender. Transfer pears to serving dishes. Pour cooking juices into a small bowl; whisk in the cream until blended. Drizzle over the pears. Serve with ice cream if desired. **YIELD: 4 SERVINGS.**

Roasted Pears in Pecan Sauce

Chocolate 'n' Toffee Rice Pudding

PREP: **10 MIN.** COOK: **15 MIN. + CHILLING**

I can't think of a more comforting dessert than this pudding. The toffee bits add a fun, unexpected crunch. It looks especially pretty layered in a parfait glass.

Joann Vess Hilliard ✳ East Liverpool, Ohio

3 cups milk

3 cups cooked rice

1/2 cup packed brown sugar

3 tablespoons butter

1/4 teaspoon salt

1 teaspoon vanilla extract

1/4 cup flaked coconut, toasted

1/4 cup English toffee bits *or* almond brickle chips

1/4 cup miniature semisweet chocolate chips

1/2 cup whipped topping

7 maraschino cherries

Chocolate 'n' Toffee Rice Pudding

In a large saucepan, combine the milk, rice, brown sugar, butter and salt; bring to a boil over medium heat. Cook for 15 minutes or until thick and creamy, stirring occasionally. Remove from the heat; stir in vanilla. Cool.

Spoon half of pudding into dessert dishes. Combine the coconut, toffee bits and chocolate chips; sprinkle half over pudding. Repeat layers. Refrigerate until serving. Top with the whipped topping and cherries. **YIELD: 7 SERVINGS.**

Chocolate-Cherry Ice Cream Pie

Chocolate-Cherry Ice Cream Pie

PREP: **15 MIN. + FREEZING**

No one would ever dream that the fancy taste and look of this luscious freezer pie could come from only five simple ingredients! This makes an unbelievably easy dessert—whether for an elegant dinner party or as a cool, high-energy kids' treat on a sweltering day.

Kimberly West ✳ Prairieville, Louisiana

- 1 bottle (7-1/4 ounces) chocolate hard-shell ice cream topping, *divided*
- 1 graham cracker crust (9 inches)
- 1 jar (10 ounces) maraschino cherries, drained
- 1 quart vanilla ice cream, softened
- 2 packages (1-1/2 ounces *each*) peanut butter cups, chopped

Following package directions, drizzle half of the ice cream topping over the crust; gently spread to coat bottom and sides. Freeze until firm.

Meanwhile, set aside six cherries for garnish; chop remaining cherries. In a bowl, combine ice cream and chopped cherries. Spread into prepared crust. Sprinkle with peanut butter cups; drizzle with remaining ice cream topping.

Garnish with the reserved cherries. Cover and freeze for 2 hours or until firm. Remove from freezer 15 minutes before serving. **YIELD: 6 SERVINGS.**

Blueberry Cornmeal Cobbler

Blueberry Cornmeal Cobbler

PREP: **20 MIN. + STANDING** BAKE: **35 MIN.**

Cornbread, blueberries and maple syrup butter give this confection a taste that's different from any cobbler you've had before. I came across the recipe many years ago.

Judy Watson ✳ Tipton, Indiana

- 4 cups fresh blueberries
- 1 cup plus 2 tablespoons sugar
- 1 tablespoon quick-cooking tapioca

2 teaspoons grated lemon peel

1 teaspoon ground cinnamon

1/4 to 1/2 teaspoon ground nutmeg

TOPPING:

1/2 cup butter, softened, *divided*

1 cup confectioners' sugar

1 egg

1 cup all-purpose flour

1/2 cup cornmeal

2 teaspoons baking powder

1/2 teaspoon baking soda

1/2 teaspoon salt

3/4 cup buttermilk

2 tablespoons maple syrup

In a large bowl, combine the blueberries, sugar, tapioca, lemon peel, cinnamon and nutmeg. Let stand for 15 minutes. Pour into a greased 11-in. x 7-in. baking dish.

In a small bowl, beat 1/4 cup butter and the confectioners' sugar. Add the egg; beat well. Combine the flour, cornmeal, baking powder, baking soda and salt; add to creamed mixture alternately with buttermilk, beating just until combined. Pour over berry mixture. Bake at 375° for 35-40 minutes or until a toothpick inserted near the center comes out clean.

In a small saucepan, melt remaining butter over low heat. Remove from the heat; stir in the syrup. Brush over corn bread. Broil 4-6 in. from the heat for 1-2 minutes or until bubbly. Serve warm. **YIELD: 12 SERVINGS.**

Angel Berry Trifle

PREP/TOTAL TIME: 15 MIN.

I usually serve this in summer when fresh berries are bountiful, but I recently prepared it with frozen cherries and light cherry pie filling instead. It was a delicious glimpse of summer-to-come!

Brenda Paine ✳ Clinton Township, Michigan

1-1/2 cups cold fat-free milk

1 package (1 ounce) sugar-free instant vanilla pudding mix

Angel Berry Trifle

1 cup (8 ounces) fat-free vanilla yogurt

6 ounces reduced-fat cream cheese, cubed

1/2 cup reduced-fat sour cream

2 teaspoons vanilla extract

1 carton (12 ounces) frozen reduced-fat whipped topping, thawed, *divided*

1 prepared angel food cake (18 inches), cut into 1-inch cubes

1 pint *each* blackberries, raspberries and blueberries

In a bowl, whisk the milk and pudding mix for 2 minutes or until soft-set. In a bowl, beat the yogurt, cream cheese, sour cream and vanilla until smooth. Fold in the pudding mixture and 1 cup whipped topping.

Place a third of the cake cubes in a 4-qt. trifle bowl. Top with a third of the pudding mixture, a third of the berries and half of the remaining whipped topping. Repeat layers once. Top with remaining cake, pudding and berries. Serve immediately or refrigerate. **YIELD: 14 SERVINGS.**

NUTRITION FACTS: 3/4 cup equals 209 calories, 6 g fat (5 g saturated fat), 10 mg cholesterol, 330 mg sodium, 32 g carbohydrate, 3 g fiber, 5 g protein. **DIABETIC EXCHANGES:** 1 starch, 1 fat, 1/2 fruit, 1/2 reduced-fat milk.

Creamy Banana Crepes

Creamy Banana Crepes

PREP: **10 MIN.** + CHILLING COOK: **10 MIN.**

My husband and I enjoy taking turns fixing weekend breakfasts. These crepes are frequently on our menus. The sweet-and-sour banana filling is delicious. You'll want to serve them for lunch, dinner and dessert!

Parrish Smith ✳ Lincoln, Nebraska

- 3/4 cup water
- 3/4 cup milk
- 2 eggs
- 2 tablespoons butter, melted
- 1/2 teaspoon vanilla extract
- 1 cup all-purpose flour
- 1 tablespoon sugar
- 1/2 teaspoon salt

BANANA FILLING:

- 3 tablespoons butter
- 3 tablespoons brown sugar
- 3 medium firm bananas, cut into 1/4-inch slices

SOUR CREAM FILLING:

- 1 cup (8 ounces) sour cream
- 2 tablespoons confectioners' sugar
- 1/2 cup slivered almonds, toasted

Additional confectioners' sugar and toasted almonds

In a small bowl, combine the water, milk, eggs, butter and vanilla. Combine the flour, sugar and salt; add to milk mixture and mix well. Cover and refrigerate for 1 hour.

Heat a lightly greased 8-in. nonstick skillet; pour 3 tablespoons batter into the center of skillet. Lift and tilt pan to evenly coat bottom. Cook for 1-2 minutes until top appears dry; turn and cook 15-20 seconds longer. Remove to a wire rack. Repeat with remaining batter. When cool, stack crepes with waxed paper or paper towels in between.

In a small skillet, heat the butter and brown sugar over medium heat until the sugar is dissolved. Add bananas; toss to coat. Remove from the heat; keep warm.

In a small bowl, combine sour cream and confectioners' sugar. Spread over each crepe. Spoon banana filling over sour cream filling; sprinkle with almonds. Roll up crepes; sprinkle with the additional confectioners' sugar and toasted almonds. **YIELD: 1 DOZEN.**

Peanut Butter Chocolate Dessert

PREP: **20 MIN.** + CHILLING

For me, the ideal treat combines the flavors of chocolate and peanut butter. So when I came up with this rich sweet, it quickly became my all-time favorite. It's a cinch to whip together because it doesn't require any baking.

Debbie Price ✳ LaRue, Ohio

- 20 chocolate cream-filled chocolate sandwich cookies, *divided*
- 2 tablespoons butter, softened
- 1 package (8 ounces) cream cheese, softened
- 1/2 cup peanut butter
- 1-1/2 cups confectioners' sugar, *divided*
- 1 carton (16 ounces) frozen whipped topping, thawed, *divided*
- 15 miniature peanut butter cups, chopped
- 1 cup cold milk
- 1 package (3.9 ounces) instant chocolate fudge pudding mix

Crush 16 cookies; toss with the butter. Press into an ungreased 9-in. square dish; set aside.

In a large bowl, beat cream cheese, peanut butter and 1 cup confectioners' sugar until smooth. Fold in half of the whipped topping.

Spread over the crust. Sprinkle with the peanut butter cups.

In a large bowl, beat the milk, pudding mix and the remaining confectioners' sugar on low speed for 2 minutes Let stand for 2 minutes or until soft-set. Fold in remaining whipped topping.

Spread over the peanut butter cups. Crush the remaining cookies; sprinkle over the top. Cover and refrigerate for at least 3 hours. **YIELD: 12-16 SERVINGS.**

Peanut Butter Chocolate Dessert

🌾 Watermelon Berry Sorbet

PREP: 30 MIN. + FREEZING

Strawberries, watermelon and three other items are all you need for this icy sensation that's virtually free of fat. A friend gave me the recipe, promising it was the ultimate in refreshing, summer delight. I couldn't agree more.

Jill Swavely ✳ Green Lane, Pennsylvania

- 1 **cup water**
- 1/2 **cup sugar**
- 2 **cups cubed seedless watermelon**
- 2 **cups fresh strawberries, hulled**
- 1 **tablespoon minced fresh mint**

In a small heavy saucepan, bring the water and sugar to a boil. Cook and stir until sugar is dissolved. Remove from the heat; cool slightly.

Place the watermelon and strawberries in a blender; add sugar syrup. Cover and process for 2-3 minutes or until smooth. Strain and discard the seeds and pulp. Transfer puree to a 13-in. x 9-in. dish. Freeze for 1 hour or until edges begin to firm.

Stir in mint. Freeze 2 hours longer or until firm. Just before serving, transfer to a blender; cover and process for 2-3 minutes or until smooth. **YIELD: 6 SERVINGS.**

NUTRITION FACTS: 1/2 cup equals 95 calories, trace fat (trace saturated fat), 0 cholesterol, 3 mg sodium, 25 g carbohydrate, 2 g fiber, 1 g protein. DIABETIC EXCHANGES: 1 starch, 1/2 fruit.

Watermelon Berry Sorbet

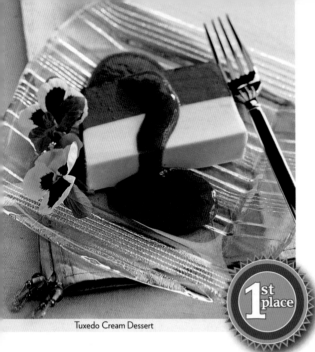

Tuxedo Cream Dessert

Tuxedo Cream Dessert

PREP: **40 MIN. + CHILLING**

My adaptation of my grandmother's signature dessert always garners lots of compliments. It's pretty and deliciously rich and creamy. Gran and I have both considered it a favorite for entertaining because it can be made up a day ahead.

Camilla Saulsbury ✴ Nacogdoches, Texas

- 1-3/4 teaspoons unflavored gelatin
- 2 tablespoons cold water
- 1-1/2 cups heavy whipping cream, *divided*
- 3/4 cup semisweet chocolate chips

VANILLA LAYER:

- 1-3/4 teaspoons unflavored gelatin
- 2 tablespoons cold water
- 1-2/3 cups heavy whipping cream, *divided*
- 1/4 cup sugar
- 2 teaspoons vanilla extract

STRAWBERRY SAUCE:

- 2 cups sliced fresh strawberries
- 2 to 3 tablespoons sugar

In a small bowl, sprinkle gelatin over cold water; let stand for 1 minute. In a small saucepan, bring 1 cup cream to a simmer. Stir 1/2 cup into the gelatin mixture until gelatin is completely dissolved. Stir chocolate chips into remaining warm cream until melted. Stir in gelatin mixture and remaining cream.

Transfer to an 8-in. x 4-in. loaf pan coated with cooking spray. Cover and refrigerate for 30 minutes or until firm.

For vanilla layer, in a small bowl, sprinkle gelatin over cold water; let stand for 1 minute. In a small saucepan, bring 1 cup cream and sugar to a simmer. Stir in gelatin mixture until gelatin is completely dissolved. Stir in vanilla and remaining cream. Carefully spoon over chocolate layer. Cover and refrigerate for at least 2 hours or until firm.

For sauce, in a blender, puree strawberries and the sugar. Transfer to a bowl; cover and refrigerate until serving.

Just before serving, unmold the dessert and cut into slices. Serve with the strawberry sauce.

YIELD: **6-8 SERVINGS.**

Coconut Angel Squares

Coconut Angel Squares

PREP: 15 MIN. + CHILLING

I have so many speedy dessert recipes, but this one is truly special. A friend shared it with me, and it immediately became the one I prefer because it tastes like a coconut cream pie with only a fraction of the work.

Betty Claycomb * Alverton, Pennsylvania

- 1 prepared angel food cake (8 inches), cut into 1/2-inch cubes
- 1-1/2 cups cold milk
- 1 teaspoon coconut extract
- 2 packages (3.4 ounces *each*) instant vanilla pudding mix
- 1 quart vanilla ice cream, softened
- 1 cup flaked coconut, *divided*
- 1 carton (8 ounces) frozen whipped topping, thawed

Place cake cubes in a greased 13-in. x 9-in. dish. In a bowl, whisk the milk, extract and pudding mixes for 2 minutes. Let stand for 2 minutes or until soft-set. Add the ice cream and 3/4 cup coconut; beat on low just until combined.

Spoon over the cake cubes. Spread with whipped topping. Toast the remaining coconut; sprinkle over top. Cover and chill for at least 1 hour. Refrigerate leftovers. **YIELD: 12-15 SERVINGS.**

Raspberry-Filled Meringue Torte

PREP: 30 MIN. + STANDING BAKE: 30 MIN. + CHILLING

My family always asks for this impressive sweet during the holidays. I've relied on this light meringue recipe for as long as I can remember—it's a surefire success each and every time I serve it.

Rosemarie Cook * Haliburton, Ontario

- 6 egg whites
- 1/4 teaspoon cream of tartar
- 1-1/2 cups sugar
- 1 cup flaked coconut
- 1/2 cup cornstarch

FILLING:

- 2 packages (10 ounces *each*) frozen sweetened raspberries

Raspberry-Filled Meringue Torte

- 3 tablespoons cornstarch
- 2 tablespoons sugar
- 1 carton (8 ounces) frozen reduced-fat whipped topping, thawed
- 10 fresh raspberries

Line baking sheets with parchment paper and trace five 7-1/2-in. circles on paper; set aside.

Place egg whites in a large bowl; let stand for 30 minutes at room temperature. Add cream of tartar; beat on medium speed until soft peaks form. Gradually beat in sugar, 1 tablespoon at a time, on high until stiff glossy peaks form and sugar is dissolved. Combine the coconut and cornstarch; fold into meringue.

Spread meringue evenly over each circle on prepared pans. Bake at 300° for 30 minutes or until firm and lightly golden. Cool for 5 minutes. Gently remove meringues from baking sheets to wire racks to cool completely.

Meanwhile, drain the raspberries, reserving juice. Set the berries aside. Add enough water to juice to measure 2 cups. In a small saucepan, combine the cornstarch and sugar; stir in the raspberry liquid until smooth. Bring to a boil; cook and stir for 2 minutes or until thickened. Cool completely. Fold in sweetened raspberries.

To assemble, place one meringue on a serving plate; top with 2/3 cup whipped topping and 3/4 cup raspberry filling. Repeat three times. Top with remaining meringue layer and whipped topping. Refrigerate for 1 hour before serving. Garnish with fresh berries. Cut with a serrated knife. **YIELD: 10 SERVINGS.**

NUTRITION FACTS: 1 piece equals 332 calories, 6 g fat (6 g saturated fat), 0 cholesterol, 59 mg sodium, 66 g carbohydrate, 3 g fiber, 3 g protein.

Tart Cherry Meringue Dessert

Drain cherries, reserving juice; set cherries aside. Add enough water to juice to measure 1 cup. In a saucepan, combine egg yolks, 3/4 cup sugar, tapioca and the cherry juice mixture. Let stand for 5 minutes. Bring to a boil over medium heat, stirring constantly; cook and stir for 2 minutes or until thickened. Stir in the cherries, lemon juice and food coloring if desired. Pour into crust.

In a small bowl, beat the egg whites, vanilla and cream of tartar on medium speed until soft peaks form. Gradually add the remaining sugar, beating on high until stiff peaks form. Fold in nuts. Spread evenly over the hot filling, sealing edges to crust. Bake at 350° for 22-25 minutes or until meringue is golden brown. Cool on a wire rack for 1 hour; chill for at least 3 hours before serving. Store in the refrigerator. **YIELD: 9 SERVINGS.**

Tart Cherry Meringue Dessert

PREP: 25 MIN. BAKE: 25 MIN. + CHILLING

I've made this cherry dessert for years to serve at baby showers, birthday parties and other special occasions. People really enjoy the tender crust, cherry filling and melt-in-your-mouth meringue. Every time I serve it, someone asks for it.

Kathryn Dawley ✳ Gray, Maine

- 2 cups all-purpose flour
- 1 teaspoon salt
- 1 cup shortening
- 1 egg

FILLING:

- 1 can (14-1/2 ounces) pitted tart cherries
- 3 eggs, *separated*
- 1-1/2 cups sugar, *divided*
- 3 tablespoons quick-cooking tapioca
- 2 teaspoons lemon juice
- 6 to 8 drops red food coloring, optional
- 1 teaspoon vanilla extract
- 1/4 teaspoon cream of tartar
- 3/4 cup finely chopped almonds

In a small bowl, combine the flour and salt. Cut in shortening until mixture resembles coarse crumbs. Add the egg; mix well. Press onto the bottom and up the sides of a greased 11-in. x 7-in. baking dish. Bake at 375° for 20-22 minutes or until lightly browned.

Ultimate Fruit Pizza

PREP: 30 MIN. BAKE: 15 MIN. + CHILLING

Here's a classic recipe that makes a refreshing snack any time of year. We made smaller individual pizzas at school with our junior-high students. All of them enjoyed choosing their favorite fruits to make the pizzas and then eating them. They're a quick, fun idea for all ages!

Peggy Galyen ✳ Tilden, Nebraska

- 1 tube (16-1/2 ounces) refrigerated sugar cookie dough
- 1 package (8 ounces) cream cheese, softened
- 1/2 cup confectioners' sugar
- 1 teaspoon lemon juice
- 1 can (21 ounces) cherry pie filling
- 1-1/2 cups pineapple tidbits, drained
- 3/4 cup mandarin oranges, drained
- 3/4 cup green grapes, halved
- 3/4 cup fresh strawberries, halved

GLAZE:

- 1 tablespoon sugar
- 2 teaspoons cornstarch
- 1 can (5-1/2 ounces) unsweetened apple juice

Let the dough stand at room temperature for 5-10 minutes to soften. Press onto an ungreased

12-in. pizza pan. Bake at 350° for 12-14 minutes or until set and lightly browned. Cool on a wire rack.

In a small bowl, beat the cream cheese, confectioners' sugar and lemon juice. Spread over the crust. Top with the pie filling; arrange the pineapple, oranges, grapes and strawberries over the filling.

In a small saucepan, combine the sugar and cornstarch. Gradually stir in the apple juice. Bring to a boil; cook and stir for 1-2 minutes or until thickened. Cool; brush over the fruit. Refrigerate for at least 1 hour before serving. **YIELD: 10-12 SERVINGS.**

Ultimate Fruit Pizza

⏱ Toffee-Crunch Coffee Sundaes

PREP/TOTAL TIME: **15 MIN.**

This fast, flavorful, foolproof fudge sauce made in the microwave has a secret ingredient: coffee ice cream. I created it one day when I was out of heavy cream and wanted to make hot fudge sauce for company. It was a huge success with my guests.

Beth Royals ✳ Richmond, Virginia

- 1 cup (6 ounces) semisweet chocolate chips
- 1 quart coffee ice cream, *divided*
- 1 tablespoon light corn syrup
- 1/2 cup chopped Heath candy bars (about 1-1/2 bars)

Whipped cream

Additional Heath candy bars, cut into triangles, optional

In a microwave-safe bowl, combine chocolate chips, 1/2 cup ice cream and corn syrup. Microwave on high for 45 seconds or until smooth.

Spoon 1/3 cup of ice cream into four parfait glasses. Top with 2 tablespoons chocolate sauce and 1 tablespoon chopped candy bars. Repeat layers. Top with remaining ice cream. Garnish with whipped cream and additional candy bars if desired. **YIELD: 4 SERVINGS.**

EDITOR'S NOTE: This recipe was tested in a 1,100-watt microwave.

Toffee-Crunch Coffee Sundaes

Old-Fashioned Pear Dessert

Old-Fashioned Pear Dessert

PREP: **20 MIN.** BAKE: **35 MIN. + COOLING**

This never-fails pear recipe turns out moist, firm and fruity every time. Some members of our family request these rich squares instead of cake for their birthdays.

Eileen Ueberroth ✳ Toledo, Ohio

2-1/4 cups all-purpose flour
    5 tablespoons sugar, *divided*
  3/4 teaspoon salt
  3/4 cup cold butter
    3 egg yolks
4-1/2 teaspoons lemon juice

FILLING:

  1/2 cup sugar
    4 tablespoons cornstarch, *divided*
  1/2 teaspoon salt
  1/2 teaspoon ground cinnamon
  3/4 cup water
    2 tablespoons plus 1-1/2 teaspoons lemon juice
    2 tablespoons butter
    1 teaspoon vanilla extract
    5 cups chopped peeled ripe pears

In a large bowl, combine the flour, 3 tablespoons sugar and salt; cut in the butter until crumbly. In a small bowl, whisk the egg yolks and lemon juice; stir into the dry ingredients with a fork. Remove 1 cup to another bowl; stir in the remaining sugar and set aside for the topping.

Press the remaining crumb mixture onto the bottom and up the sides of a greased 8-in. square baking dish. Bake at 375° for 10-12 minutes or until edges are lightly browned.

Meanwhile, for filling, combine the sugar, 2 tablespoons cornstarch, salt and cinnamon in a small saucepan. Slowly stir in the water and lemon juice until smooth. Bring to a boil over medium heat; cook and stir for 1 minute or until thickened. Remove from the heat; stir in butter and vanilla.

Toss the pears with remaining cornstarch; spoon over crust. Top with filling. Sprinkle with reserved topping. Bake for 35-40 minutes or until the filling is bubbly and topping is lightly browned. Cool on a wire rack. YIELD: **9 SERVINGS.**

Blueberries 'n' Dumplings

Blueberries 'n' Dumplings

PREP: 25 MIN. COOK: 40 MIN.

Here's a versatile dumpling that's excellent as a sweet breakfast sprinkled with whole grain cereal or for dessert. Blueberries are one of my favorite fruits, and this dish is a fantastic way to enjoy them.

Melissa Radulovich * Littleton, Colorado

- 3 cups apple cider *or* juice
- 1/4 cup quick-cooking tapioca
- 4 cups fresh blueberries
- 1/3 cup packed brown sugar
- 1/2 teaspoon almond extract

DUMPLINGS:
- 1 cup all-purpose flour
- 1 tablespoon sugar
- 1-1/2 teaspoons baking powder
- 1/2 teaspoon salt
- 1/4 teaspoon ground nutmeg
- 1 egg
- 6 tablespoons milk
- 1 tablespoon canola oil
- 3/4 cup cold heavy whipping cream
- 1 tablespoon maple syrup

In a Dutch oven, combine cider and tapioca; let stand for 5 minutes. Add blueberries and brown sugar. Bring to a boil. Reduce heat to medium-low; simmer, uncovered; stir occasionally. Stir in almond extract; continue simmering.

For dumplings, in a large bowl, combine the flour, sugar, baking powder, salt and nutmeg. In a small bowl, beat the egg, milk and oil; stir into dry ingredients just until moistened (batter will be stiff).

Drop batter by 1/4 cupfuls onto simmering blueberry mixture. Cover and simmer for 25 minutes or until a toothpick inserted in the dumplings comes out clean (do not lift the lid while simmering).

In a small bowl, beat cream and syrup until soft peaks form. Spoon blueberry mixture into serving bowls; top with dumplings. Serve with maple cream. **YIELD: 4 SERVINGS.**

Banana Cream Brownie Dessert

Banana Cream Brownie Dessert

PREP: 20 MIN. BAKE: 30 MIN. + COOLING

I always keep the ingredients for this extremely delicious treat on hand because I make it quite often for potlucks and family gatherings. I'm always asked for the directions. After one bite, you'll understand why.

Julie Nowakowski * LaSalle, Illinois

- 1 package fudge brownie mix (13-inch x 9-inch pan size)
- 1 cup (6 ounces) semisweet chocolate chips, *divided*
- 3/4 cup dry roasted peanuts, chopped, *divided*
- 3 medium firm bananas
- 1-2/3 cups cold milk
- 2 packages (5.1 ounces *each*) instant vanilla pudding mix
- 1 carton (8 ounces) frozen whipped topping, thawed

Prepare the brownie batter according to the package directions for fudge-like brownies. Stir in 1/2 cup chocolate chips and 1/4 cup peanuts. Spread into a greased 13-in. x 9-in. baking pan. Bake at 350° for 28-30 minutes or until a toothpick inserted near the center comes out clean. Cool on a wire rack.

Slice the bananas; arrange in a single layer over brownies. Sprinkle with 1/4 cup chips and 1/4 cup peanuts.

In a large bowl, beat milk and pudding mixes on low speed for 2 minutes. Fold in whipped topping. Spread over the top. Sprinkle with the remaining chips and peanuts. Refrigerate until serving. **YIELD: 12-15 SERVINGS.**

Magic Pumpkin Buckle

Magic Pumpkin Buckle

PREP: **15 MIN.** BAKE: **55 MIN.**

This is my family's favorite pumpkin dessert that I've been making since my two daughters were small. The crust mixture, which is actually poured in first, rises to the top during baking to form a rich layer. So you don't get a soggy bottom crust like you do with a pie.

Darlene Brenden ✴ Salem, Oregon

- 1/2 cup butter, melted
- 1 cup all-purpose flour
- 1 cup sugar
- 4 teaspoons baking powder
- 1/2 teaspoon salt
- 1 cup milk
- 1 teaspoon vanilla extract

FILLING:

- 3 cups cooked *or* canned pumpkin
- 1 cup evaporated milk
- 2 eggs
- 1 cup sugar
- 1/2 cup packed brown sugar
- 1 tablespoon all-purpose flour
- 1 teaspoon ground cinnamon
- 1/2 teaspoon salt
- 1/4 teaspoon *each* ground ginger, cloves and nutmeg

TOPPING:

- 1 tablespoon butter
- 2 tablespoons sugar

Pour butter into a 13-in. x 9-in. baking dish; set aside. In a large bowl, combine the flour, sugar, baking powder and salt. Stir in milk and vanilla until smooth. Pour into prepared pan.

In a large bowl, beat the pumpkin, milk and eggs. Combine the remaining filling ingredients; add to pumpkin mixture. Pour over the crust mixture (do not stir). Dot with the butter and sprinkle with sugar.

Bake at 350° for 55-60 minutes or until a knife inserted near the center comes out clean and the top is golden brown. YIELD: **12 SERVINGS.**

Cran-Apple Crisp

PREP: **30 MIN.** BAKE: **35 MIN. + COOLING**

An eggnog sauce gives this crunchy oat-topped crisp a distinctive flavor. The apples and cranberries make it a natural for autumn celebrations and holiday meals.

Mary Lou Timpson ✴ Centennial Park, Arizona

- 2 snack-size cups (4 ounces *each*) vanilla pudding
- 1 cup eggnog
- 3/4 cup sugar
- 2 tablespoons all-purpose flour
- 5 cups thinly sliced peeled tart apples
- 2 cups fresh *or* frozen cranberries, thawed

TOPPING:

- 1 cup quick-cooking oats
- 3/4 cup packed brown sugar
- 2/3 cup all-purpose flour
- 1/2 teaspoon ground cinnamon
- 1/2 cup cold butter, cubed

In a bowl, combine pudding and eggnog until blended; cover and refrigerate until serving. In a large bowl, combine sugar and flour. Add the apples and cranberries; toss to coat. Transfer to an ungreased 13-in. x 9-in. baking dish.

In a bowl, combine the oats, brown sugar, flour and cinnamon; cut in butter until crumbly. Sprinkle over fruit mixture.

Bake at 375° for 35-40 minutes or until filling is bubbly and the topping is golden brown. Cool for 10 minutes. Serve with eggnog sauce. YIELD: **12-14 SERVINGS.**

EDITOR'S NOTE: This recipe was tested with commercially prepared eggnog.

Chocolate Crunch Ice Cream

PREP: 30 MIN. + CHILLING PROCESS: 2 HOURS + FREEZING

Making ice cream goes smoothly when you do prep work in advance. I make the custard ahead and refrigerate it overnight. Plus, I toast the almonds beforehand and separate my add-ins into labeled containers.

Rosalie Peters ✳ Caldwell, Texas

- 1-1/2 cups milk
- 3/4 cup sugar, *divided*
- 4 egg yolks
- 2-1/2 teaspoons instant coffee granules
- 2 cups 60% cocoa bittersweet chocolate baking chips, melted and cooled
- 1-1/2 cups heavy whipping cream
- 1 teaspoon vanilla extract
- 3/4 cup semisweet chocolate chips, melted
- 3/4 cup slivered almonds, toasted
- 1/3 cup milk chocolate toffee bits

In a large saucepan, heat milk to 175°; stir in 1/2 cup sugar until dissolved. In a small bowl, whisk egg yolks and remaining sugar. Stir in the coffee granules and the bittersweet chocolate. Whisk in a small amount of hot milk mixture. Return all to the pan, whisking constantly.

Cook and stir over low heat until mixture reaches at least 160° and coats the back of a metal spoon. Remove from heat. Cool quickly by placing pan in a bowl of ice water; let stand for 30 minutes, stirring frequently.

Transfer to a bowl; stir in cream and vanilla. Press the plastic wrap onto surface of custard. Refrigerate for several hours or overnight.

Line a baking sheet with waxed paper; spread melted semisweet chocolate to 1/8-in. thickness. Chill for 20 minutes; chop coarsely.

Fill cylinder of ice cream freezer two-thirds full with custard; freeze according to manu-facturer's directions. Stir in some of the chopped chocolate, almonds and toffee bits. Refrigerate remaining custard until ready to freeze. Stir in remaining chocolate, almonds and toffee bits. Transfer to a freezer container; freeze ice cream for 2-4 hours before serving.

YIELD: 1-1/2 QUARTS.

Cran-Apple Crisp

1st place

Chocolate Crunch Ice Cream

White Chocolate Cherry Parfaits

White Chocolate Cherry Parfaits

PREP: **40 MIN. + CHILLING**

Layers of silky white chocolate mousse and sweet cherry sauce with a hint of orange make up this delectable treat. I use a pastry bag to pipe the mousse into pretty dishes handed down from my husband's grandmother.

Rita Sherman ✳ Coleville, California

      1/2 cup sugar
        2 tablespoons cornstarch
      1/2 cup water
        2 cups fresh *or* frozen pitted tart cherries
      1/2 teaspoon orange extract

WHITE CHOCOLATE MOUSSE:

        3 tablespoons sugar
        1 teaspoon cornstarch
      1/2 cup milk
        2 egg yolks, lightly beaten
        4 squares (1 ounce *each*) white baking chocolate, chopped
      1/2 teaspoon vanilla extract
    1-1/2 cups heavy whipping cream, whipped

In a saucepan, combine sugar and cornstarch; stir in water until smooth. Add cherries. Bring to a boil over medium heat; cook and stir for 2 minutes or until thickened. Remove from the heat; stir in extract. Refrigerate until chilled.

In another saucepan, combine the sugar and cornstarch; stir in milk until smooth. Bring to a boil over medium heat. Reduce heat; cook and stir for 2 minutes. Remove from heat. Whisk a small amount of the hot filling into egg yolks; return all to the pan, whisking constantly. Bring to a gentle boil; cook and stir for 2 minutes. Remove from heat. Stir in chocolate and vanilla until the chocolate is melted. Cool to room temperature. Fold in whipped cream

Spoon 1/4 cup mousse into each parfait glass. Top with a rounded 1/4 cup of the cherry mixture. Repeat layers. Refrigerate until chilled. YIELD: 6 SERVINGS.

1st place

Blackberry Cobbler

Blackberry Cobbler

PREP: 15 MIN. + STANDING BAKE: 45 MIN.

This tasty treat has helped my family stay healthy, lose weight and still be able to enjoy dessert! Other kinds of berries or even fresh peaches are just as delicious in this cobbler.

Leslie Browning ✳ Lebanon, Kentucky

- 1/2 cup sugar
- 4-1/2 teaspoons quick-cooking tapioca
- 1/4 teaspoon ground allspice
- 5 cups fresh *or* frozen blackberries, thawed
- 2 tablespoons orange juice

DOUGH:
- 1 cup all-purpose flour
- 1/3 cup plus 1 tablespoon sugar, *divided*
- 1/4 teaspoon baking soda
- 1/4 teaspoon salt
- 1/3 cup reduced-fat vanilla yogurt
- 1/3 cup fat-free milk
- 3 tablespoons butter, melted

In a large bowl, combine the sugar, tapioca and allspice. Add blackberries and orange juice; toss to coat. Let stand for 15 minutes. Spoon into a 2-qt. baking dish coated with cooking spray.

In a large bowl, combine the flour, 1/3 cup sugar, baking soda and salt. Combine yogurt, milk and butter; stir into dry ingredients until smooth. Spread over the berry mixture.

Bake at 350° for 20 minutes. Sprinkle with the remaining sugar. Bake 25-30 minutes longer or until golden brown. Serve cobbler warm.
YIELD: 10 SERVINGS.

NUTRITION FACTS: 1 serving equals 199 calories, 4 g fat (2 g saturated fat), 10 mg cholesterol, 135 mg sodium, 40 g carbohydrate, 4 g fiber, 3 g protein. DIABETIC EXCHANGES: 1-1/2 starch, 1 fruit, 1/2 fat.

Rich Hot Fudge Sauce

Rich Hot Fudge Sauce

PREP/TOTAL TIME: 30 MIN.

I've made this scrumptious topping, and it always turns out smooth and yummy. The dark chocolate flavor, with a hint of rum extract, is not overly sweet but will still satisfy a chocoholic's craving.

Carol Hanihan ✳ Ann Arbor, Michigan

- 1 cup heavy whipping cream
- 3/4 cup butter, cubed
- 1-1/3 cups packed brown sugar
- 1/4 cup sugar

Dash salt
- 1 cup baking cocoa
- 1/2 cup plus 2 tablespoons light corn syrup
- 2 squares (1 ounce *each*) unsweetened chocolate
- 3 teaspoons vanilla extract
- 1 to 2 teaspoons rum extract

In a saucepan, combine cream and butter. Cook and stir over medium-low heat until butter is melted. Add the sugars and salt; cook and stir until sugar is dissolved, about 4 minutes. Stir in the cocoa and corn syrup; cook and stir for 3 minutes or until cocoa is blended.

Add chocolate; cook and stir 3-4 minutes longer or until chocolate is melted. Reduce heat to low. Simmer for 12-16 minutes or until desired thickness is reached, stirring constantly. Remove from the heat; stir in the extracts. Cool slightly. Serve warm over ice cream. Refrigerate leftovers. **YIELD: ABOUT 3-1/2 CUPS.**

Cheesecake Squares

Cheesecake Squares

PREP: **10 MIN.** BAKE: **1 HOUR + CHILLING**

I lived on a dairy farm when I was young, and my mom always had a lot of sour cream to use. She never wasted any, and this treat was one of my family's favorites. It's great topped with blackberry sauce.

Shirley Forest ✳ Eau Claire, Wisconsin

> 2 packages (8 ounces *each*) cream cheese, softened
> 1 cup ricotta cheese
> 1-1/2 cups sugar
> 4 eggs
> 1/4 cup butter, melted and cooled
> 3 tablespoons cornstarch
> 3 tablespoons all-purpose flour
> 1 tablespoon vanilla extract
> 2 cups (16 ounces) sour cream

Seasonal fresh fruit, optional

In a large bowl, beat cream cheese, ricotta and sugar until smooth. Add the eggs, one at a time, mixing well after each addition. Beat in butter, cornstarch, flour and vanilla until smooth. Fold in the sour cream.

Pour into a greased 13-in. x 9-in. baking pan. Bake, uncovered, at 325° for 1 hour or until almost set. Cool on a wire rack for 10 minutes. Carefully run a knife around the edge of pan to loosen; cool 1 hour longer.

Chill for several hours or overnight. Top each serving with fruit if desired. **YIELD: 20 SERVINGS.**

Strawberry Crepes

PREP: **25 MIN. + CHILLING** COOK: **1 HOUR**

I always feel like a French chef when I serve these pretty crepes. Although they take a little time to prepare, they're well worth the effort. My guests are always impressed.

Debra Latta ✳ Port Matilda, Pennsylvania

> 1-1/2 cups milk
> 3 eggs
> 2 tablespoons butter, melted
> 1/2 teaspoon lemon extract
> 1-1/4 cups all-purpose flour
> 2 tablespoons sugar

Dash salt

TOPPING:

> 1/2 cup sugar
> 2 tablespoons cornstarch
> 3/4 cup water
> 1 tablespoon lemon juice
> 1 teaspoon strawberry extract
> 1/4 teaspoon red food coloring, optional
> 4 cups sliced fresh strawberries

FILLING:

> 1 cup heavy whipping cream
> 1 package (8 ounces) cream cheese, softened
> 2 cups confectioners' sugar
> 1 teaspoon vanilla extract

In a large bowl, combine milk, eggs, butter and extract. Combine flour, sugar and salt; add to the milk mixture and beat until smooth. Cover and refrigerate for 1 hour.

Heat a lightly greased 8-in. nonstick skillet. Stir the batter; pour 2 tablespoons into center of skillet. Lift and tilt pan to evenly coat bottom. Cook until top appears dry; turn and cook 15-20 seconds longer. Remove to a wire rack. Repeat with the remaining batter, greasing skillet as needed. When cool, stack crepes with waxed paper or paper towels in between.

In a small saucepan, combine the sugar and cornstarch; stir in the water and lemon juice until smooth. Bring to a boil over medium heat; cook and stir for 1 minute or until thickened. Stir in extract and food coloring if desired. Cool. Add the strawberries.

In a small bowl, beat cream until stiff peaks form; set aside. In a large bowl, beat the cream cheese, confectioners' sugar and vanilla until smooth; fold in the whipped cream. Spoon 2 rounded tablespoons of filling down the center of each crepe; roll up. Top with the strawberry topping. **YIELD: 22 CREPES.**

Chocolate Ice Cream Sandwiches

PREP: **20 MIN.** BAKE: **10 MIN. + COOLING**

These cute, chewy cookies made with two kinds of chocolate form a perfect sandwich for vanilla ice cream...or any flavor ice cream you prefer. I really enjoy making desserts for my family, and this one hits the spot on hot Texas days.

Michelle Wolford ✳ San Antonio, Texas

- 1/3 cup butter, softened
- 1/3 cup sugar
- 1/3 cup packed brown sugar
- 1 egg
- 1/2 teaspoon vanilla extract
- 3/4 cup plus 2 tablespoons all-purpose flour
- 1/4 cup baking cocoa
- 1/2 teaspoon baking powder
- 1/4 teaspoon baking soda
- 1/4 teaspoon salt
- 1/2 cup semisweet chocolate chips
- 1 pint vanilla ice cream

In a large bowl, cream butter and sugars until light and fluffy. Beat in egg and vanilla. Combine the flour, cocoa, baking powder, baking soda and salt; add to creamed mixture and mix well.

Drop by rounded tablespoonfuls 2 in. apart onto greased baking sheets, forming 16 cookies. Flatten slightly with a glass. Sprinkle with the chocolate chips. Bake at 375° for 8-10 minutes or until set. Remove to wire racks to cool.

To assemble the sandwiches, place 1/4 cup ice cream on the bottom of half the cookies. Top with the remaining cookies. Wrap each in the plastic wrap. Freeze overnight. **YIELD: 8 ICE CREAM SANDWICHES.**

Strawberry Crepes

Chocolate Ice Cream Sandwiches

Mocha Fondue

Mocha Fondue

PREP/TOTAL TIME: **20 MIN.**

At our friends' 25th anniversary celebration, several couples had fun concocting this chocolate fondue. With the fresh fruit, marshmallows, pretzels and vanilla wafers as dippers, everyone will want to dive into dessert!

Karen Boehner ✳ Glen Elder, Kansas

- 2 cups (12 ounces) semisweet chocolate chips
- 1/4 cup butter
- 1 cup heavy whipping cream
- 3 tablespoons strong brewed coffee
- 1/8 teaspoon salt
- 2 egg yolks, lightly beaten

Cubed pound cake, sliced bananas and fresh strawberries and pineapple chunks

In a heavy saucepan, melt the chocolate chips, butter, cream, coffee and salt. Stir 1/2 cup into egg yolks; return all to the pan. Cook and stir until mixture reaches 160°. Transfer to a fondue pot and keep warm. Serve with cake and fruit. **YIELD: 10 SERVINGS.**

Chocolate Meringue Cups

PREP: **30 MIN. + CHILLING** BAKE: **45 MIN. + STANDING**

Looking for something low in cholesterol that will satisfy your sweet tooth? Give this airy cloud of cocoa meringue and chocolate mousse a try! It's a bit fussy, but it's well worth the effort.

Ellen Govertsen ✳ Wheaton, Illinois

- 4 egg whites
- 1 teaspoon vanilla extract
- 1/2 teaspoon salt
- 1/2 teaspoon white vinegar
- 1 cup sugar
- 2 tablespoons baking cocoa

CHOCOLATE MOUSSE:

- 1 cup fat-free milk
- 1 egg
- 1/4 cup plus 2 teaspoons corn syrup, *divided*
- 1/4 cup baking cocoa

Chocolate Meringue Cups

- 3 squares (1 ounce *each*) semisweet chocolate, coarsely chopped
- 4 ounces reduced-fat cream cheese, cubed
- 2 teaspoons unflavored gelatin
- 1/4 cup plus 1 tablespoon cold water, *divided*
- 1 teaspoon vanilla extract
- 4 egg whites
- 3/4 cup sugar
- 1/4 teaspoon cream of tartar
- 15 peppermint candies, crushed

Place the egg whites in a large bowl; let stand at room temperature for 30 minutes. Beat the egg whites until foamy. Beat in the vanilla, salt and vinegar; beat on medium speed until soft peaks form. Gradually add the sugar, 1 tablespoon at a time, beating on high until stiff peaks form. Sift cocoa over egg whites; fold into egg whites.

Drop 15 heaping tablespoonfuls onto parchment-lined baking sheets. Shape into 3-in. cups with the back of a spoon. Bake at 275° for 45 minutes or until golden brown. Turn the oven off; leave meringues in oven for 1-1/2 hours.

In a large saucepan, combine the milk, egg, 1/4 cup corn syrup and cocoa. Cook and stir over medium heat until the mixture reaches 160° and coats a metal spoon. Remove from the heat. Add the chocolate and cream cheese; stir until melted.

In a small saucepan, sprinkle gelatin over 1/4 cup water; let stand for 1 minute. Cook and stir over low heat until gelatin is dissolved. Stir gelatin and vanilla into chocolate mixture. Cool.

In a saucepan, combine egg whites, sugar, cream of tartar, and remaining corn syrup and water. Cook over low heat and beat with a hand mixer on low until mixture reaches 160°.

Pour into a large bowl; beat on high until soft peaks form. Fold into chocolate mixture. Chill for 1-2 hours or until mixture mounds.

Just before serving, spoon the mousse into meringue cups; sprinkle with the peppermint candy pieces. **YIELD: 15 SERVINGS.**

NUTRITION FACTS: 1 filled cup equals 201 calories, 4 g fat (2 g saturated fat), 19 mg cholesterol, 153 mg sodium, 40 g carbohydrate, 2 g fiber, 5 g protein. DIABETIC EXCHANGES: 2-1/2 starch.

Three-Fruit Frozen Yogurt

Three-Fruit Frozen Yogurt

PREP: **15 MIN. + FREEZING**

I received this super-easy recipe from a friend. It takes just minutes to combine the bananas, strawberries and pineapple with a few other ingredients before popping everything in the freezer. I've been told the luscious mixture tastes even better than ice cream.

Wendy Hilton ✴ Laurel, Mississippi

- 2 medium ripe bananas
- 1 package (10 ounces) frozen sweetened sliced strawberries, thawed and drained
- 1 can (8 ounces) crushed pineapple, drained
- 1 carton (6 ounces) strawberry yogurt
- 1/2 cup sugar
- 1 carton (8 ounces) frozen whipped topping, thawed

In a bowl, mash the bananas and strawberries. Stir in the pineapple, yogurt and sugar. Fold in the whipped topping. Cover and freezer until firm. May be frozen for up to 1 month. **YIELD: 1-1/2 QUARTS.**

Rhubarb Fritters

Rhubarb Fritters

PREP/TOTAL TIME: **30 MIN.**

I got this recipe from my niece's son. Since we live in apple country, we have enjoyed apple fritters for many years. This rhubarb treat is a nice change for spring when apples are few and rhubarb is plentiful.

Helen Budinock ✳ Wolcott, New York

- 1 cup all-purpose flour
- 1 cup plus 1 tablespoon sugar, *divided*
- 1/2 teaspoon salt
- 2 eggs, *separated*
- 1/2 cup milk
- 1 tablespoon butter, melted
- 2 cups finely chopped fresh *or* frozen rhubarb, thawed and drained

Oil for deep-fat frying

Confectioners' sugar

In a large bowl, combine flour, 1 cup sugar and salt. In a small bowl, whisk the egg yolks, milk and butter. Gradually add to the dry ingredients, stirring until smooth.

Toss rhubarb with remaining sugar; gently stir into batter. In a small bowl, beat egg whites until stiff. Fold into batter.

In an electric skillet or deep-fat fryer, heat the oil to 375°. Drop batter by tablespoonfuls into the oil. Fry a few at a time, turning with a slotted spoon until golden brown. Drain on paper towels. Dust with confectioners' sugar. Serve warm. **YIELD: ABOUT 3 DOZEN.**

EDITOR'S NOTE: If using frozen rhubarb, measure rhubarb while still frozen, then thaw completely. Drain in a colander, but do not press liquid out.

Chocolate Pecan Ice Cream Torte

PREP: **20 MIN. + FREEZING**

This delectable concoction layers my favorite ice cream (chocolate) and my husband's favorite (butter pecan) on a shortbread crust, along with chocolate candy pieces, toasted pecans and caramel topping. It never fails to impress our guests.

Kelly Arvay ✳ Barberton, Ohio

- 1 jar (12-1/4 ounces) caramel ice cream topping
- 2 milk chocolate candy bars (1.55 ounces *each*), chopped
- 12 pecan shortbread cookies, crushed
- 3 tablespoons butter, melted
- 1 cup pecan halves, toasted, *divided*
- 1/2 gallon butter pecan ice cream, slightly softened
- 1/2 gallon chocolate ice cream, slightly softened

In a microwave-safe bowl, combine the caramel topping and candy bars. Microwave, uncovered, on high for 1-1/2 minutes or until candy bars are melted, stirring every 30 seconds. Cool.

In a small bowl, combine the cookie crumbs and butter. Press onto the bottom of a greased 10-in. springform pan. Chop 1/2 cup pecans; set aside. Spoon half of the butter pecan ice cream over crust. Drizzle with 2 tablespoons caramel sauce; sprinkle with 1/4 cup chopped pecans.

Spread half of the chocolate ice cream over top. Drizzle with 2 tablespoons caramel sauce; sprinkle with remaining chopped pecans.

Spoon the remaining butter pecan ice cream around the edge of pan; spread the remaining chocolate ice cream in center of pan. Cover and freeze overnight.

Carefully run a knife around the edge of pan to loosen; remove the sides of pan. Garnish with the remaining pecan halves; drizzle with 2 tablespoons of the caramel sauce. Serve with remaining caramel sauce. **YIELD: 16-20 SERVINGS.**

EDITOR'S NOTE: This recipe was tested in a 1,100-watt microwave.

Strawberry Pretzel Dessert

PREP: **15 MIN. + CHILLING**

I love the sweet-salty flavor of this pretty layered dish. Sliced strawberries and gelatin top a smooth cream cheese filling and crispy pretzel crust. I think it's best when eaten within a day of being made.

Wendy Weaver ∗ Leetonia, Ohio

- 1/3 cup crushed pretzels
- 2 tablespoons butter, softened
- 2 ounces cream cheese, softened
- 1/4 cup sugar
- 3/4 cup whipped topping
- 2 tablespoons plus 1-1/2 teaspoons strawberry gelatin powder
- 1/2 cup boiling water
- 1 cup sliced fresh strawberries

In a large bowl, combine the pretzels and butter. Press onto the bottom of two 10-oz. greased custard cups. Bake at 375° for 6-8 minutes or until set. Cool on a wire rack.

In a small bowl, combine cream cheese and sugar until smooth. Fold in whipped topping. Spoon over crust. Refrigerate for 30 minutes.

Meanwhile, in a small bowl, dissolve gelatin in the boiling water. Cover and refrigerate for 20 minutes or until slightly thickened. Fold in the strawberries. Carefully spoon over the filling. Cover and refrigerate for at least 3 hours.

YIELD: **2 SERVINGS.**

Chocolate Pecan Ice Cream Torte

Strawberry Pretzel Dessert

Glazed Apricot Sorbet

Glazed Apricot Sorbet

PREP: **10 MIN. + FREEZING**

This fruity dessert is refreshingly cool and light with a hint of richness. It's just right for a company meal or a pleasant afternoon treat. I like to serve it in sherbet glasses with mint sprigs for an elegant look.

Nina Rohlfs ✳ Unadilla, Nebraska

     1 can (20 ounces) apricot halves, drained
     1 jar (10 ounces) apricot preserves
1-1/2 teaspoons grated orange peel
     2 tablespoons lemon juice
     5 tablespoons heavy whipping cream

In a food processor, combine the apricots, preserves, orange peel and lemon juice; cover and process until smooth. Pour into a freezer container; cover and freeze for at least 3 hours. May be frozen for up to 3 months.

Remove from the freezer at least 15 minutes before serving. Scoop into the dessert dishes; drizzle with the cream. YIELD: **5 SERVINGS.**

Rocky Road Freeze

PREP: **15 MIN. + FREEZING**

Vary my recipe if you like. In place of peanuts, try using walnuts, pecans or cashews, or substitute peanut putter chips for the chocolate chips. For a luscious dessert-on-the-go, put a double dip into a cone. You can also serve this for fancy occasions in a clear-glass sauce dish.

Sheila Berry ✳ Carrying Place, Ontario

     1 can (14 ounces) sweetened condensed milk
   1/2 cup chocolate syrup
     2 cups heavy whipping cream
     1 cup miniature marshmallows
   1/2 cup miniature chocolate chips
   1/2 cup chopped salted peanuts

In a bowl, combine milk and chocolate syrup; set aside. In a large bowl, beat the cream until stiff peaks form. Fold in the chocolate mixture, marshmallows, chocolate chips and peanuts.

Transfer to a freezer-proof container; cover and freeze for 5 hours or until firm. Remove from freezer 10 minutes before serving. YIELD: **ABOUT 1-1/2 QUARTS.**

Rocky Road Freeze

1st place

Chocolate Velvet Dessert, PAGE 456

❝ *This creamy concoction is the result of several attempts to duplicate a dessert I enjoyed on vacation. It looks so beautiful on a buffet table that many folks are tempted to forgo the main course in favor of this chocolaty treat.* ❞

Molly Seidel
Edgewood, New Mexico

INDEXES

alphabetical index

This handy index lists every recipe in alphabetical order, so you can easily find your favorite recipe.

Fiery Chicken Spinach Salad

Curried Chicken Salad Sandwiches

1st place

general
recipe index

This handy index lists the recipes by food category, major ingredient and/or by icon, so you can easily locate recipes that suit your needs.

Gorgonzola Penne with Chicken

Chicken and Asparagus Kabobs
1st place

Mushroom Burgers, 284
Pineapple-Stuffed Burgers, 130
Pizza Burgers, 182
Ranch Turkey Burgers, 251
Southwestern Burgers, 132
Stuffed Burgers on
　Portobellos, 174
Zesty Onion Burgers, 170
Zesty Turkey Burgers, 120

CABBAGE

Beef Cabbage Roll-Ups, 156
Bratwurst Potato Soup, 111
Colorful Coleslaw, 71
Colorful Vegetable Saute, 300
Italian-Style Cabbage Rolls, 248
Kielbasa Cabbage Soup, 89
Minestrone with Italian
　Sausage, 89
Peanut Chicken Salad, 49
Sunday Boiled Dinner, 207
Surprise Sausage Bundles, 216
Turkey Sausage with Root
　Vegetables, 240
Wontons with Sweet-Sour
　Sauce, 28

CAKES
(also see Cheesecakes; Coffee Cakes; Cupcakes)
Almond Praline Cakes, 405
Apple Bundt Cake, 405
Apple Harvest Cake, 408
Berry Nectarine Buckle, 413
Berry Pinwheel Cake, 406
Breakfast Upside-Down
　Cake, 412
Caramel Nut Torte, 410
Chocolate Potato Cake, 406
Cinnamon-Sugar Rhubarb
　Cake, 417
Coconut Cream Dream
　Cake, 404
Cranberry-Carrot Layer
　Cake, 416
Cranberry Crumb Cake, 399
Cranberry Pear Cake, 402
Cupid's Chocolate Cake, 398
Fudgy Pecan Cake, 421

Grandma's Apple Carrot
　Cake, 400
Harvest Snack Cake, 402
Moist Chocolate Cake, 400
Oatmeal Cake with Broiled
　Frosting, 396
Peanut Butter Layer Cake, 401
Pecan Angel Food Cake, 415
Pumpkin Angel Cake, 417
Rhubarb Dessert Cake, 407
Rhubarb Upside-Down
　Cake, 398
Sweet Potato Mini Cakes, 422
Tastes Like Eggnog Cake, 419
Walnut Glory Cake, 412
White Chocolate Banana
　Cake, 418

CANDIES

Anise Hard Candy, 375
Butter Pecan Fudge, 378
Caramel Truffles, 376
Chocolate-Covered Cherries, 387
Chunky Peanut Brittle, 379
Coffee Shop Fudge, 366
Cookie Dough Truffles, 370
Cranberry Walnut White
　Fudge, 383
Hazelnut Toffee, 364
Holiday Pecan Logs, 369
Pecan Clusters, 381
Peppermint Taffy, 375
White Candy Bark, 367

CARROTS

Asian Pot Roast, 179
Asparagus Cheese Bundles, 310
Beefy Vegetable Soup, 182
Black-Eyed Pea Salad, 74
Chicken Lettuce Wraps, 19
Colorful Coleslaw, 71
Colorful Vegetable Saute, 300
Cranberry-Carrot Layer Cake, 416
Garlic Butternut Bisque, 87
Ginger Chicken Burgers with
　Sesame Slaw 116
Golden Seafood Chowder, 96
Grandma's Apple Carrot
　Cake, 400

Mediterranean Vegetable Pasta

Harvest Snack Cake, 402
Hearty Beef Barley Soup, 100
Hearty Beef Vegetable Soup, 83
Herbed Pot Roast, 160
Kielbasa Cabbage Soup, 89
Kielbasa Split Pea Soup, 95
Mango Chicken with Plum
　Sauce, 226
Mushroom Potato Soup, 93
Oven Beef Stew, 171
Roasted Carrot Dip, 11
Roasted Garlic Pork Supper, 209
Root Vegetable Medley, 307
Stir-Fried Veggies with
　Pasta, 298
Sunday Boiled Dinner, 207
Sweet 'n' Sour Meatballs, 152
Tex-Mex Turkey Tacos, 225
Thai Beef Stir-Fry, 169
Turkey Sausage with Root
　Vegetables, 240
Vegetable Beef Potpie, 160
Vegetable Brown Rice, 294
Vegetable Lentil Stew, 287
Veggie Lasagna, 289

CASSEROLES

Bean and Pork Chop Bake, 193
Cheese-Stuffed Shells, 205
Cheesy Sausage Penne, 211
Chicken Wild Rice
　Casserole, 247
Creamy Chicken Lasagna, 241

Parmesan Herb Loaf

1st place

Beefy Vegetable Soup, 182
Black Bean Tortilla Pie, 285
Black-Eyed Pea Sausage
    Stew, 214
Cheese-Topped Vegetable
    Soup, 98
Chicken Corn Fritters, 244
Chicken Tortilla Soup, 110
Chipotle Butternut Squash
    Soup, 93
Chunky Taco Soup, 107
Corn Medley Salad, 64
Country Corn, 309
Creamy Corn Crab Soup, 104
Creamy Succotash, 300
Curried Corn on the Cob, 296
Fiery Chicken Spinach
    Salad, 56
Ham and Corn Chowder, 111
Jalapeno Bread, 346
Land of Enchantment
    Posole, 105
Refried Bean Soup, 86
Rocky Ford Chili, 84
Shoepeg Corn Casserole, 302
Southwest Beef Stew, 184
Southwestern Chicken Black
    Bean Soup, 91
Southwestern Stuffed Turkey
    Breast, 222
Stuffed Iowa Chops, 210

CORNMEAL

Appalachian Corn Bread, 328
Blueberry Cornmeal
    Cobbler, 462
Chili Corn Muffins, 321
Cornmeal Onion Rings, 36
Italian Sausage with
    Polenta, 234

CREAM CHEESE

Appetizers
    Beef 'n' Cheese Dip, 18
    Chocolate Chip
        Cheese Ball, 35
    Chocolate Fruit Dip, 12
    Chunky Blue Cheese Dip, 24
    Horseradish Crab Dip, 43

Party Cheese Balls, 13
Rosemary Cheese Patties, 26
Savory Ham Cheesecake, 9
Swiss Walnut Cracker
    Snack, 40
Warm Bacon Cheese
    Spread, 10
Beverages
    Rhubarb Cheesecake
        Smoothies, 29
Breads
    Berry Cheesecake
        Muffins, 324
    Cream Cheese Coils, 344
Desserts (also see Cheesecakes)
    Berry-Cream Cookie
        Snaps, 376
    Blueberries 'n' Cream Pie, 449
    Butternut Cream Pie, 436
    Chocolate Cheese Layered
        Bars, 370
    Chocolate Cream Cheese
        Cupcakes, 394
    Double Chip Cheesecake
        Bars, 378
    Hazelnut Cheesecake
        Parfaits, 458
    Strawberry Cheesecake
        Ice Cream, 460
    Ultimate Fruit Pizza, 468

CUPCAKES

Bat Cupcakes, 421
Brownie Kiss Cupcakes, 397
Chocolate Cream Cheese
    Cupcakes, 394
Raspberry Peach Cupcakes, 414
Walnut Banana Cupcakes, 395

DEEP-FAT
FRYER RECIPES

Chicken Corn Fritters, 244
Cornmeal Onion Rings, 36
Deep-Fried Chicken Wings, 32
Jelly Doughnuts, 143
Rhubarb Fritters, 480
Wontons with Sweet-Sour
    Sauce, 28

Almond-Filled Butterhorns

DESSERTS
(also see Bars; Brownies;
Cakes; Candies; Cheesecakes;
Cookies; Cupcakes; Pies)

Almond Fruit Crisp, 454
Angel Berry Trifle, 463
Apple Pie in a Goblet, 457
Banana Cream Brownie
    Dessert, 471
Blackberry Cobbler, 475
Blueberries 'n' Dumplings, 471
Blueberry Cornmeal
    Cobbler, 462
Cherry Nut Ice Cream, 455
Chocolate 'n' Toffee Rice
    Pudding, 461
Chocolate-Cherry Cream
    Crepes, 457
Chocolate Crunch Ice
    Cream, 473
Chocolate Ice Cream
    Sandwiches, 477
Chocolate Meringue Cups, 478
Chocolate Pecan Ice Cream
    Torte, 480
Chocolate Velvet Dessert, 456
Coconut Angel Squares, 467
Cran-Apple Crisp, 472
Creamy Banana Crepes, 464
Glazed Apricot Sorbet, 482
Hazelnut Cheesecake
    Parfaits, 458
Jeweled Gelatin Torte, 458
Magic Pumpkin Buckle, 472
Mocha Fondue, 478
Old-Fashioned Pear Dessert, 470

Smothered Chicken Breasts

1st place

Coconut Cream Dream Cake

Caramel Nut Torte

1st place

Lemon Shrimp Stir-Fry, 271
Mandarin Couscous Salad, 60
Mango Chicken with Plum
    Sauce, 226
Pork and Pear Stir-Fry, 197
Sweet 'n' Sour Cashew Pork, 211
Vegetable Brown Rice, 294

PEPPERONI & SALAMI

Genoa Sandwich Loaf, 124
Hearty Muffuletta, 115
Macaroni 'n' Cheese Pizza, 183
Mini Bagelizzas, 7
Pepperoni Ziti Casserole, 224
Pizza Burgers, 182
Pizza Loaf, 128
Spiral Pepperoni Pizza Bake, 177
Whole Wheat Pepperoni
    Pizzas, 14

PEPPERS

Almond Vegetable Stir-Fry, 303
Apricot Chicken, 227
Asian Pork Kabobs, 206
Barley Corn Salad, 67
Beef Fajita Salad, 71
Beef Stir-Fry on a Stick, 157
Black Bean Bow Tie Salad, 54
Black-Eyed Pea Salad, 74
Buffalo Wing Poppers, 15
Cajun Stir-Fry, 245
Cheese-Topped Vegetable
    Soup, 98
Chicken Italian, 236
Christmas Eve Confetti
    Pasta, 267
Colorful Coleslaw, 71
Colorful Vegetable Saute, 300
Confetti Broccoli Slaw, 67
Corn Medley Salad, 64
Garlic Shrimp Stir-Fry, 275
Goat Cheese 'n' Veggie
    Quesadillas, 8
Grilled Chiles Rellenos, 281
Grilled Veggie Pork Bundles, 203
Hearty Beef Vegetable Soup, 83
Honey-Dijon Potato Salad, 73
Jalapeno Bread, 346

Just Delish Veggie Kabobs, 293
Lemon Shrimp Stir-Fry, 271
Lime Chicken Chili, 94
Pork 'n' Pepper Tacos, 90
Pork Fajitas Kabobs, 201
Roasted Pepper Ravioli Bake, 283
Roasted Yellow Pepper Soup, 99
Sausage Chicken Soup, 95
Spicy Sausage Spaghetti, 213
Stir-Fried Veggies with
    Pasta, 298
Summer Avocado Salad, 76
Sweet 'n' Sour Meatballs, 152
Tex-Mex Turkey Tacos, 225
Turkey Pepper Kabobs, 230
Two-Season Squash Medley, 297
Vegetable Lentil Stew, 287
Wontons with Sweet-Sour
    Sauce, 28

PIES

Fruit Pies

Apple Praline Pie, 438
Blueberries 'n' Cream Pie, 449
Blueberry Pie with Lemon
    Crust, 442
Cranberry Pear Pie, 430
Glazed Pineapple Pie, 445
Peach Plum Pie, 434
Sour Cream Peach Pecan
    Pie, 432
Upside-Down Apple Pie, 425

Other Pies

Greek Honey Nut Pie, 431
Mayan Chocolate Pecan
    Pie, 435
Mixed Nut 'n' Fig Pie, 432
Vermont Maple Oatmeal
    Pie, 434
Refrigerator and Freezer Pies
Butternut Cream Pie, 436
Butter Pecan Pumpkin Pie, 439
Caramel Apple Cream Pie, 436
Cherry-Nut Chocolate Pie, 429
Chocolate-Caramel Supreme
    Pie, 440
Chocolate-Cherry Ice Cream
    Pie, 462

Berry Nectarine Buckle

Chocolate Chip Banana
    Cream Pie, 444
Chocolate Raspberry Pie, 446
Coconut Peach Pie, 446
Dreamy Creamy Peanut
    Butter Pie, 428
Frosted Orange Pie, 440
Frosty Coffee Pie, 439
Frozen Chocolate Mint
    Pie, 450
Frozen Strawberry Pie, 449
German Chocolate Pie, 448
Grasshopper Pie, 441
Hawaiian Cream Pie, 426
Lemon Pie in Meringue
    Shell, 433
Maple Apple Cream Pie, 442
Mud Pie, 437
No-Bake Cheesecake Pie, 403
Peach Melba Ice Cream
    Pie, 445
Pumpkin Cheesecake Pie, 427
Raspberry-Lemon Pie, 426
Ricotta Nut Pie, 443
Spiced Peach Pie, 428
Spring Breeze Cheesecake
    Pie, 394
Strawberry Banana Pie, 430
Vanilla Custard Pie, 447

PINEAPPLE

Albacore Tuna Salad, 69
Asian Pot Roast, 179
Blueberry Quick Bread, 334
Breakfast Upside-Down
    Cake, 412

Rhubarb Swirl Cheesecake

1st place

1st place

Cranberry Pear Pie

Sour Cream Peach Pecan Pie

Butter Pecan Pumpkin Pie
1st place

my favorite recipes

Use this handy chart to jot down your family's favorite dishes from this book. As you fill in these pages, you'll create a handy reference of your most memorable recipes. Then use this guide as a tool when you are planning special meals.

RECIPE TITLE	PAGE	COMMENTS/NOTES
main courses		
sides		
desserts		

my favorite recipes

Use this handy chart to jot down your family's favorite dishes from this book. As you fill in these pages, you'll create a handy reference of your most memorable recipes. Then use this guide as a tool when you are planning special meals.

RECIPE TITLE	PAGE	COMMENTS/NOTES
snacks		
breakfast		
lunch		

FOOD EQUIVALENTS

FOOD	EQUIVALENT
Apples	1 pound (3 medium) = 2-3/4 cups sliced
Apricots	1 pound (8 to 12 medium) = 2-1/2 cups sliced
Bananas	1 pound (3 medium) = 1-1/3 cups mashed or 1-1/2 to 2 cups sliced
Berries	1 pint = 1-1/2 to 2 cups
Bread	1 loaf = 16 to 20 slices
Bread Crumbs	1 slice = 1/2 cup soft crumbs or 1/4 cup dry crumbs
Butter or Margarine	1 pound = 2 cups or 4 sticks 1 stick = 8 tablespoons
Cheese	
Cottage	1 pound = 2 cups
Shredded	4 ounces = 1 cup
Cherries	1 pound = 3 cups whole or 3-1/2 cups halved
Chocolate Chips	6 ounces = 1 cup
Cocoa, Baking	1 pound = 4 cups
Coconut, Flaked	14 ounces = 5-1/2 cups
Cornmeal	1 pound = 3 cups uncooked
Corn Syrup	16 ounces = 2 cups
Cranberries	12 ounces = 3 cups whole or 2-1/2 cups finely chopped
Cream Cheese	8 ounces = 16 tablespoons
Cream, Whipping	1 cup = 2 cups whipped
Dates, Dried	1 pound = 2-3/4 cups pitted and chopped
Dates, Dried and Chopped	10 ounces = 1-3/4 cups
Egg Whites	1 cup = 8 to 10 whites
Flour	
All-Purpose	1 pound = about 3-1/2 cups
Cake	1 pound = about 4-1/2 cups
Whole Wheat	1 pound = about 3-3/4 cups
Frozen Whipped Topping	8 ounces = 3-1/2 cups
Gelatin, Unflavored	1 envelope = 1 tablespoon
Graham Crackers	16 crackers = 1 cup crumbs
Grapefruit	1 medium = 3/4 cup juice or 1-1/2 cups segments

FOOD	EQUIVALENT
Grapes	1 pound = 3 cups
Honey	1 pound = 1-1/3 cups
Lemons	1 medium = 3 tablespoons juice or 2 teaspoons grated peel
Limes	1 medium = 2 tablespoons juice or 1-1/2 teaspoons grated peel
Marshmallows	
Large	1 cup = 7 to 9 marshmallows
Miniature	1 cup = about 100 marshmallows
Nectarines	1 pound (3 medium) = 3 cups sliced
Nuts	
Almonds	1 pound = 3 cups halves or 4 cups slivered
Ground	3-3/4 ounces = 1 cup
Hazelnuts	1 pound = 3-1/2 cups whole
Pecans	1 pound = 4-1/2 cups chopped
Walnuts	1 pound = 3-3/4 cups chopped
Oats	
Old-Fashioned	1 pound = 5 cups
Quick-Cooking	1 pound = 5-1/2 cups
Oranges	1 medium = 1/3 to 1/2 cup juice or 4 teaspoons grated peel
Peaches	1 pound (4 medium) = 2-3/4 cups sliced
Pears	1 pound (3 medium) = 3 cups sliced
Pineapples	1 medium = 3 cups chunks
Popcorn	1/3 to 1/2 cup unpopped = 8 cups popped
Raisins	15 ounces = 2-1/2 cups
Rhubarb	1 pound = 3 cups chopped (raw) or 2 cups (cooked)
Shortening	1 pound = 2 cups
Strawberries	1 pint = 2 cups hulled and sliced
Sugar	
Brown Sugar	1 pound = 2-1/4 cups
Confectioners' Sugar	1 pound = 4 cups
Granulated	1 pound = 2-1/4 to 2-1/2 cups
Yeast, Active Dry	1 envelope = 2-1/4 teaspoons

INGREDIENT SUBSTITUTIONS

WHEN YOU NEED:	IN THIS AMOUNT:	SUBSTITUTE:
Baking Powder	1 teaspoon	1/2 teaspoon cream of tartar plus 1/4 teaspoon baking soda
Broth	1 cup	1 cup hot water plus 1 teaspoon bouillon granules or 1 bouillon cube
Buttermilk	1 cup	1 tablespoon lemon juice or white vinegar plus enough milk to measure 1 cup; let stand 5 minutes. Or 1 cup plain yogurt
Cajun Seasoning	1 teaspoon	1/4 teaspoon cayenne pepper, 1/2 teaspoon dried thyme, 1/4 teaspoon dried basil and 1 minced garlic clove
Chocolate, Semisweet	1 square (1 ounce)	1 square (1 ounce) unsweetened chocolate plus 1 tablespoon sugar or 3 tablespoons semisweet chocolate chips
Chocolate	1 square (1 ounce)	3 tablespoons baking cocoa plus 1 tablespoon shortening or canola oil
Cornstarch (for thickening)	1 tablespoon	2 tablespoons all-purpose flour
Corn Syrup, Dark	1 cup	3/4 cup light corn syrup plus 1/4 cup molasses
Corn Syrup, Light	1 cup	1 cup sugar plus 1/4 cup water
Cracker Crumbs	1 cup	1 cup dry bread crumbs
Cream, Half-and-Half	1 cup	1 tablespoon melted butter plus enough whole milk to measure 1 cup
Egg	1 whole	2 egg whites or 2 egg yolks or 1/4 cup egg substitute
Flour, Cake	1 cup	1 cup minus 2 tablespoons (7/8 cup) all-purpose flour
Flour, Self-Rising	1 cup	1-1/2 teaspoons baking powder, 1/2 teaspoon salt and enough all-purpose flour to measure 1 cup
Garlic, Fresh	1 clove	1/8 teaspoon garlic powder
Gingerroot, Fresh	1 teaspoon	1/4 teaspoon ground ginger
Honey	1 cup	1-1/4 cups sugar plus 1/4 cup water
Lemon Juice	1 teaspoon	1/4 teaspoon cider vinegar
Lemon Peel	1 teaspoon	1/2 teaspoon lemon extract
Milk, Whole	1 cup	1/2 cup evaporated milk plus 1/2 cup water or 1 cup water plus 1/3 cup nonfat dry milk powder
Molasses	1 cup	1 cup honey
Mustard, Prepared	1 tablespoon	1/2 teaspoon ground mustard plus 2 teaspoons cider or white vinegar
Onion	1 small (1/3 cup chopped)	1 teaspoon onion powder or 1 tablespoon dried minced onion
Poultry Seasoning	1 teaspoon	3/4 teaspoon rubbed sage plus 1/4 teaspoon dried thyme
Sour Cream	1 cup	1 cup plain yogurt
Sugar	1 cup	1 cup packed brown sugar or 2 cups sifted confectioners' sugar
Tomato Juice	1 cup	1/2 cup tomato sauce plus 1/2 cup water
Tomato Sauce	2 cups	3/4 cup tomato paste plus 1 cup water
Yeast	1 package (1/4 ounce) active dry	1 cake (5/8 ounce) compressed yeast